A TEXT BOOK OF STRUCTURAL ANALYSIS - II

For

T.E. SEMESTER – I

THIRD YEAR DEGREE COURSES IN CIVIL ENGINEERING

As Per New Revised Syllabus of UoP, 2014

Dr SR PAREKAR

M. E. (Structures)
Associate Professor & Head,
Civil Engineering Department,
Sinhgad Academy of Engineering,
Kondhawa (BK), PUNE.

HM SOMAYYA

M. E. (Structures)
Former, Assistant Professor,
Applied Mechanics Department,
Maharashtra Institue of Technology,
PUNE.

STRUCTURAL ANALYSIS - II

First Edition : Jullly 2014

ISBN 978-93-5164-125-4

© : **Authors**

The text of this publication, or any part thereof, should not be transmitted or reproduced in any form or stored in any computer storage system or device for distribution including photocopy, recording, taping or information retrieval system or reproduced on any disc, tape, perforated media or other information storage device etc., without the written permission of Authors with whom the rights are reserved. Breach of this condition is liable for legal action.

Every effort has been made to avoid errors or omissions in this publication. In spite of this, errors may have crept in. Any mistake, error or discrepancy so noted and shall be brought to our notice shall be taken care of in the next edition. It is notified that neither the publisher nor the authors or seller shall be responsible for any damage or loss of action to any one, of any kind, in any manner, therefrom.

Published By :
NIRALI PRAKASHAN
Abhyudaya Pragati, 1312, Shivaji Nagar,
Off J.M. Road, PUNE – 411005
Tel – (020) 25512336/37/39, Fax – (020) 25511379
Email : niralipune@pragationline.com

Printed By :
RACHANA OFFSETS
REPRO INDIA LTD.
Mumbai.

DISTRIBUTION CENTRES

PUNE

Nirali Prakashan
119, Budhwar Peth, Jogeshwari Mandir Lane
Pune 411002, Maharashtra
Tel : (020) 2445 2044, 66022708, Fax : (020) 2445 1538
Email : bookorder@pragationline.com

Nirali Prakashan
S. No. 28/25, Dhyari,
Near Pari Company, Pune 411041
Tel : (022) 24690204 Fax : (020) 24690316
Email : dhyari@pragationline.com
bookorder@pragationline.com

MUMBAI
Nirali Prakashan
385, S.V.P. Road, Rasdhara Co-op. Hsg. Society Ltd.,
Girgaum, Mumbai 400004, Maharashtra
Tel : (022) 2385 6339 / 2386 9976, Fax : (022) 2386 9976
Email : niralimumbai@pragationline.com

DISTRIBUTION BRANCHES

NAGPUR
Pratibha Book Distributors
Above Maratha Mandir, Shop No. 3, First Floor,
Rani Jhanshi Square, Sitabuldi, Nagpur 440012,
Maharashtra, Tel : (0712) 254 7129

BENGALURU
Pragati Book House
House No. 1, Sanjeevappa Lane, Avenue Road Cross,
Opp. Rice Church, Bengaluru – 560002.
Tel : (080) 64513344, 64513355,
Mob : 9880582331, 9845021552
Email:bharatsavla@yahoo.com

JALGAON
Nirali Prakashan
34, V. V. Golani Market, Navi Peth, Jalgaon 425001,
Maharashtra, Tel : (0257) 222 0395
Mob : 94234 91860

KOLHAPUR
Nirali Prakashan
New Mahadvar Road,
Kedar Plaza, 1st Floor Opp. IDBI Bank
Kolhapur 416 012, Maharashtra. Mob : 9855046155

CHENNAI
Pragati Books
9/1, Montieth Road, Behind Taas Mahal, Egmore,
Chennai 600008 Tamil Nadu, Tel : (044) 6518 3535,
Mob : 94440 01782 / 98450 21552 / 98805 82331, Email : bharatsavla@yahoo.com

RETAIL OUTLETS

PUNE

Pragati Book Centre
157, Budhwar Peth, Opp. Ratan Talkies,
Pune 411002, Maharashtra
Tel : (020) 2445 8887 / 6602 2707, Fax : (020) 2445 8887

Pragati Book Centre
Amber Chamber, 28/A, Budhwar Peth,
Appa Balwant Chowk, Pune : 411002, Maharashtra,
Tel : (020) 20240335 / 66281669
Email : pbcpune@pragationline.com

Pragati Book Centre
676/B, Budhwar Peth, Opp. Jogeshwari Mandir,
Pune 411002, Maharashtra
Tel : (020) 6601 7784 / 6602 0855

PBC Book Sellers & Stationers
152, Budhwar Peth, Pune 411002, Maharashtra
Tel : (020) 2445 2254 / 6609 2463

MUMBAI
Pragati Book Corner
Indira Niwas, 111 – A, Bhavani Shankar Road, Dadar (W), Mumbai 400028, Maharashtra
Tel : (022) 2422 3526 / 6662 5254, Email : pbcmumbai@pragationline.com

PREFACE ......

The book titled **"Structural Analysis - II"** is written according to the New revised syllabus of Pune University. This book serves as a text book for the students of third year degree course in civil engineering 2014 Pattern.

It consists of 6 units covering all six units of new revised syllabus. Each topic gives fundamental and simple treatment to the subject with a clear and distinct presentation of theoretical concepts and well-graded examples.

We express our sincere thanks, to Prof. Wakchaure and Prof. Sable (Amrutvahini, COE, Sangamner), Prof. Awari (AISSPMS COE), Prof. Deulkar, Dr. Lad AISSMS COE, Prof. Bajare SAE, Kondhwa, Pune.

We will be missing if we don't thank our family and wives Mrs. Chhaya Somayya and Mrs. Smita Parekar whose moral support and wishes have gone a long way in the making of this book.

We express our sincere thanks to Shri. Dineshbhai Furia, Jignesh Furia and M. P. Munde for publishing this book. We are also thankful to Mrs. Deepali Lachake, Mrs. Roshan Khan for their kind help.

Suggestions for improvement and constructive criticism of this book are warmly welcomed and will be incorporated in next edition.

Pune   **Authors**

SYLLABUS ......

Unit I   (08 hours)
(a) Slope-deflection method of analysis: Slope-deflection equations, equilibrium equation of slope-deflection method, application to beams with and without joint translation and rotation, yielding of support, application to non-sway rigid jointed rectangular portal frames, shear force and bending moment diagram.

(b) Sway analysis of rigid jointed rectangular portal frames using slope-deflection method (Involving not more than three unknowns)

Unit II   (08 hours)
(a) Moment distribution method of analysis: Stiffness factor, carry over factor, distribution factor, application to beams with and without joint translation and yielding of support, application to non-sway rigid jointed rectangular portal frames, shear force and bending moment diagram.

b) Sway analysis of rigid jointed rectangular single bay single storey portal frames using moment distribution method (Involving not more than three unknowns).

Unit III   (08 hours)
(a) Fundamental concepts of flexibility method of analysis, formulation of flexibility matrix, application to pin jointed plane trusses (Involving not more than three unknowns).

(b) Application of flexibility method to beams and rigid jointed rectangular portal frames (Involving not more than three unknowns).

Unit IV   (08 hours)
(a) Fundamental concepts of stiffness method of analysis, formulation of stiffness matrix, application to trusses by member approach. Application to beams by structure approach only, (Involving not more than three unknowns).

(b) Application to rigid jointed rectangular portal frames by structure approach only (Involving not more than three unknowns).

Unit V   (08 hours)
(a) Finite Difference Method – Introduction, application to deflection problems of determinate beams by central difference method

(b) Approximate methods of analysis of multi-storied multi-bay 2 - D rigid jointed fames by substitute frame method, cantilever method and portal method.

Unit VI   (08 hours)
(a) Finite element method : Introduction, discretization, types of elements-1D, 2D, 3D, isoparametric and axisymmetric, convergence criteria, Pascals triangle, direct stiffness method, principal of minimum potential energy. (No numerical)

(b) Shape functions: CST, LST elements by using polynomials, 1D, 2D elements by using Lagrange's method, concept of local and global stiffness matrix

CONTENTS ......

Unit - I

1. Slope-deflection Method   1.1-1.118
    1.1   Preliminaries   1.1
    1.2   Introduction of Slope-Deflection Method   1.3
    1.3   Reference System and Sign Conventions   1.4
    1.4   SD Equations   1.6
    1.5   Fem   1.13
    1.6   Equilibrium Equations of SD Method   1.13
    1.7   Procedure of SD Method   1.17
    1.8   SD Method Applied to Beams   1.18
        1.8.1   Beams Without Joint Translations   1.19
        1.8.2   Application of SD Method to Beams Without Joint Translations   1.19
        1.8.3   Beams with Unknown Joint Translations   1.43
        1.8.4   Application of SD Method to Beams with Unknown Joint Translations   1.44
    1.9   SD Method Applied to Rectangular Frames   1.50
        1.9.1   Frames Without Sway or Non-Sway Frames   1.50
        1.9.2   Application of SD Method to Non-Sway Frames   1.50
        1.9.3   Sway Frames   1.63
        1.9.4   Application of SD Method to Frames With Side Sway   1.64
        1.9.5   Frames Having Known Yielding of Supports   1.86
        1.9.6   Application of SD Method to Frames Having Known Yielding of Supports   1.86
    1.10 Introduction   1.100
        1.10.1   Structure with the Overhanging Part   1.100
        1.10.2   Symmetrical Structure   1.100
        1.10.3   Structure Without Joint Translation and With Hinge or Roller Support At Ends   1.105
               1.10.3.1   Unloaded Hinge or Roller Support   1.105
               1.10.3.2   Application of modified SD equations to structures without joint translations and with unloaded hinged or roller support at the end   1.107
               1.10.3.3   Loaded Hinged or Roller Support   1.111
               1.10.3.4   Application of modified SD equations to structures without joint translation and with loaded hinged or roller support at the ends   1.111
        1.10.4   Structure with Joint Translation and with Hinged or Roller Support at the End   1.114
        1.10.5   Application of Modified SD Equations to Structures with Joint Translations and with Hinged or Roller Support at the Ends   1.115

Unit - II

2. Moment Distribution Method   2.1-2.118

    2.1   Stiffness and Carryover Factor   2.1
    2.2   Distribution Factor   2.4
    2.3   Introduction to MD Method   2.10
         2.3.1   Sign Conventions for Member-End Moments   2.11
    2.4   Procedure of MD Method   2.11
    2.5   Application of MD Method to Beams with Unknown Joint Translations   2.31
    2.6   Application of MD Method to Frames without Joint Translations   2.39
    2.7   Application of MD Method to Frames with Joint Translations   2.57
    2.8   Application of MD Method to Frames with Yielding of Supports   2.86

Unit - III

3. Flexibility Method   3.1-3.106

    3.1   Force Method or Flexibility Method   3.1
         3.1.1   General   3.1
         3.1.2   Procedure of Force Method   3.2
         3.1.3   Flexibility Matrix   3.3
         3.1.4   Procedure of Flexibility Matrix Method   3.5
    3.2   Indeterminate Trusees   3.7
         3.2.1   General   3.7
         3.2.2   Force Method for Analysis of Indeterminate Trusses   3.8
         3.2.3   Basic Formulation of Force Method for Trusses   3.10
         3.2.4   Externally Indeterminate Trusses   3.14
         3.2.5   Internally Indeterminate Trusses   3.25
         3.2.6   Indeterminate Trusses with Lack of Fit   3.36
         3.2.7   Temperature Effects in Indeterminate Trusses   3.42
         3.2.8   Effects of Yielding of Support in Indeterminate Trusses   3.48
    3.3   Flexibility Method Applied to Beams and Frames   3.54

Unit - IV

4. Stiffness Method   4.1-4.88

    4.1   Displacement Method or Stiffness Method   4.1
         4.1.1   General   4.1
         4.1.2   Procedure of Displacement Method   4.2
         4.1.3   Simple Problem of Displacement Method   4.3

4.2	Stiffness Matrix	4.6
4.3	Procedure of Stiffness Matrix Method	4.3
4.4	Stiffness Coefficients of Member	4.10
	4.4.1 A Beam Member or Frame Member	4.10
4.5	Stiffness Method Applied to Beams and Frames	4.13
4.6	Comparison of Flexibility and Stiffness Methods	4.69
	Exercise	4.70

Unit - V

5. Finite Difference Method & Approximate Analysis of Multistoried Frames — 5.1-5.62

5.1	Introduction	5.1
5.2	Finite Differences	5.1
5.3	Introduction	5.25
5.4	Substitute Frame Method	5.26
5.5	Portal Method	5.35
5.6	Cantilever Method	5.43

Unit - IV

6. Finite Element Method — 6.1-6.88

6.1	Introduction	6.1
6.2	Discretization	6.2
6.3	Truss Element	6.2
	6.3.1 Nodes	6.4
	6.3.1.1 External Nodes	6.4
	6.3.1.2 Internal Nodes	6.5
6.4	Co-Ordinate Systems	6.5
	6.4.1 Natural Co-Ordinates in One Dimension	6.6
	6.4.2 Natural Co-Ordinates for Triangular Elements	6.8
6.5	Element Shapes	6.10
	6.5.1 One-Dimensional Elements	6.10
	6.5.2 2D Elements	6.10
	6.5.3 Constant Strain/Stress Triangle (CST)	6.10
	6.5.4 Linear Strain Triangle (LST)	6.10
	6.5.5 Quadratic Strain Triangle (QST)	6.11
	6.5.6 3D Stress-Strain Relation	6.12
6.6	Isoparametric Elements	6.14
6.7	Axisymmetric Stress Analysis	6.15

6.8	Strain Displacement Matrix	6.20
	6.8.1 Strain Displacement Matrix for Bar Element	6.20
	6.8.2 Strain Displacement Matrix for CST Element	6.21
6.9	Principle of Minimum Potential Energy	6.25
6.10	Shape-Functions	6.27
	6.10.1 Properties of Shape Functions	6.27
	6.10.2 Criteria for Choice of Displacement Model	6.27
	6.10.3 Pascal Triangle	6.28
	6.10.4 Derivation of Shape Functions Using Polynomials	6.29
6.11	Determine the Shape Functions for the Constant Strain Triangle (CST)	6.34
6.12	Shape Functions in Terms of Natural Co-Ordinate Systems	6.36
6.13	Determine the Shape Function for LST Element, Use Natural Co-Ordinate System	6.40
6.14	Determine the Shape Functions for Four Noded Rectangular Elements	6.42
6.15	Determine the Shape Function for Quadratic Rectangular Element	6.44
6.16	Shape Functions Using Lagrange Polynomials	6.46
6.17	Stiffness Matrix for a Two Dimensional Beam	6.50
6.18	Assemblage of Stiffness Matrix	6.53
	6.18.1 Alternative method for assemblage of matrix	6.56
	Exercise	6.84

Chapter 1
SLOPE-DEFLECTION METHOD

1.1 PRELIMINARIES

Indeterminate rigid jointed plane framed structures are analysed by the slope-deflection method, denoted hereafter by SD method. Beams and plane frames or portals are considered as rigid jointed plane framed structures. Members, joints, supports, forces, deformations and displacements of the structure are in one plane i.e. the plane of structure which contains the axes of symmetry of cross-sections of all members of the structure. Such structures are diagrammatically represented by lines, as the axes of members, as in Figs. 1.1 and 1.2 showing (a) geometrical arrangement of members, joints and supports; called structural configuration; including dimensions, member properties and (b) applied loads including magnitude, direction and position.

Members are prismatic i.e. straight and of uniform cross-section. Members are mainly flexural members.

Joints are the (a) points of intersection of the prismatic members, (b) points of supports and (c) free ends of the members. The joints are mainly rigid. A rigid joint of a structure rotates as a whole and resists a moment as shown in Figs. 1.1 and 1.2.

At a rigid joint, the angles between the tangents to the elastic curves of the members meeting at the joint remain the same as those in the original undeformed members. In short, at a rigid joint, the angle between the members meeting the joint does not change. In general, joint of prismatic members in beams is considered as 180° rigid joint and a joint of prismatic members in rectangular frames is considered as 90° rigid joint as shown in Figs. 1.1 and 1.2.

Supports may be (a) roller support, (b) hinged support, and (c) fixed support.

Forces including moments are in the plane of structure. Moments have their vectors normal to the plane of a structure. Forces to be considered are as follows :

(1) Applied Loads :
   (a) Member loads may be concentrated forces or moments and distributed loads, acting directly or indirectly through arrangements like brackets, pulleys, cables etc. as shown in Figs. 1.1 and 1.2.
   (b) Joint loads are concentrated forces and moments acting at the point of joint directly or indirectly as shown in Figs. 1.1 and 1.2.

(2) Reactive Forces :

Actions of supports on a structure are the reactive forces or reactions and may be force and/or moment acting at the point of support according to the type of constraint as shown in Figs. 1.1 and 1.2.

(3) Internal Forces :

Forces at a cut-section are the internal forces, considered as either stress resultants or actions of the cut-part of a structure. Member-end forces are the internal forces as the actions of the joints. Member-end forces may be (a) axial force, (b) shear force, and (c) bending moment as shown in Figs. 1.1 and 1.2. It may be noted that there is no twisting moment because of special characteristics of rigid-jointed plane structure and loading condition. The internal forces at a point in a structure are self-equilibrated forces as actions and reactions.

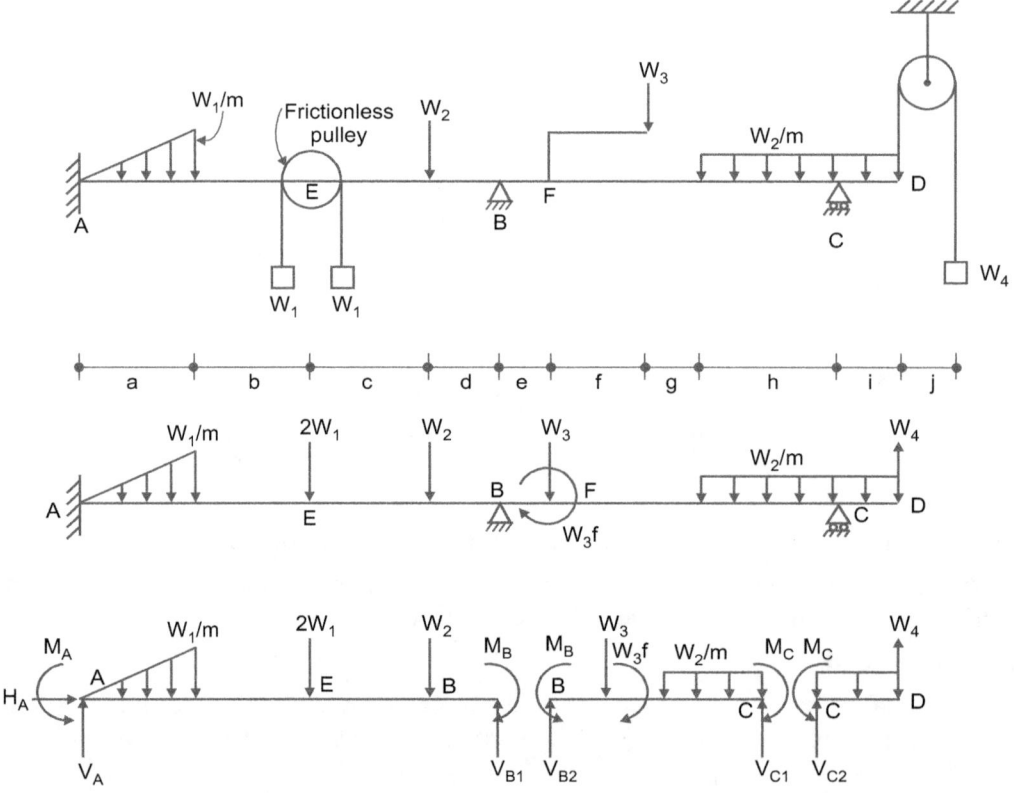

Fig. 1.1 : Beam showing members, joints, supports, structural configuration, loads, and internal forces

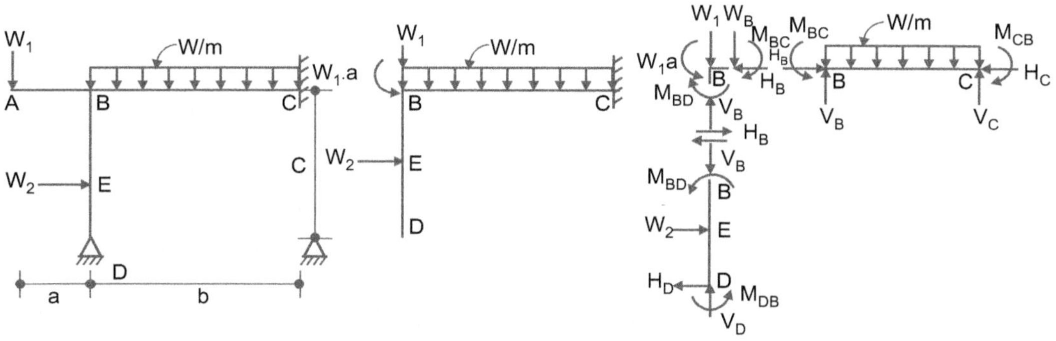

STRUCTURAL ANALYSIS – II   SLOPE-DEFLECTION METHOD

Fig. 1.2 : Frame showing types of members, joints, supports, loads, and internal forces

Structural deformations are due to the stresses and strains developed in the structure when it is subjected to the forces or other disturbances. Deformations are compatible with respect to the joints and the supports of a structure. Only flexural deformation is considered. Axial deformation and shear deformation are neglected. The deformed shape of a member/structure is called as the elastic curve as shown in Figs. 1.1 and 1.2.

Displacements are the cumulative effects of deformations. Displacement at a point in the plane structure may be (a) translation i.e. linear displacement in horizontal and vertical directions and (b) rotation i.e. angle between the tangent to the elastic curve at the point and the line of original member. Displacements are as shown in Figs. 1.1 and 1.2 in the plane of a structure. Rotations have their vectors normal to the plane of a structure.

Rotation of a joint is called slope. Deflection is the translation perpendicular to the axis of member. The translation along the axis of member is not considered in SD method. It may be noted that there can not be rigid body displacements in a stable structure. Slope and deflections are important in SD method of structural analysis.

In general sense, a force means a force or a moment at a point and displacement means a translation or a rotation at a point. A force at a point is associated with the translation at the same point and in the same direction of the force, and a moment at a point is associated with the rotation at the same point and in the same direction of the moment. This is called one to one correspondence between force and displacement and plays important role in structural analysis.

1.2 INTRODUCTION OF SLOPE-DEFLECTION METHOD

SD method is basically a displacement method i.e. stiffness method (i.e. equilibrium method). Unlike other methods, SD method is based on (a) compatibility of joint displacements including support points, (b) moment - equilibrium of joints and force -

equilibrium of a structure also called shear-equilibrium and (c) relations between member-end moments and member-end displacements. The method mainly involves slopes and deflections of the member at its joints and hence it is named as SD method.

SD method begins with the compatible joint displacements and it ends with the equilibrium equations called simultaneous equations. Therefore, SD method is the method of simultaneous solution of equations. The basic unknowns in SD method are the non-zero joint displacements of a structure. The number of such non-zero joint displacements is the degree of kinematic indeterminacy of a structure or degree of freedom. Therefore, kinematically indeterminate structures are analysed by SD method. Rigidity of a joint implies one single rotation at the joint. Selecting the appropriate unknown joint displacements, the compatibility is indirectly satisfied.

Member end displacements are the same as its joint displacements and called as slope and deflection. For every member of a structure, member-end moments are related to (a) member-end slopes and deflections, and (b) loading on the member by slope-deflection equations of the member, to be denoted hereafter by SD equations.

Using SD equations of all members of a structure, moment-equilibrium equations for the joints and shear-equilibrium equations for the structure are formulated in terms of unknown joint displacements. It should be noted that number of equilibrium equations must be same as the number of unknown joint displacements. The equilibrium equations are solved to obtain unknown joint displacements.

Knowing the joint displacements, member-end moments are found from SD equations of the members and rest of the analysis is completed by laws of statics.

Thus the SD method is pivoted on the SD equations and it is the member approach.

1.3 REFERENCE SYSTEM AND SIGN CONVENTIONS

Member and its two end joints are the basic components of SD method. To represent a member with its two ends, following reference system is suitable. One of the ends is taken as the origin. Member axis is considered as the x-axis. The y-axis, perpendicular to the member, is so chosen that the right hand system of Cartesian coordinates is formed as shown in Fig. 1.3. Accordingly for horizontal member, left end of the member as the origin, x-axis along the member and y-axis normal to the member will be the reference system. For vertical member, bottom end of the member as the origin x-axis along the member and y-axis normal to the member become the reference system.

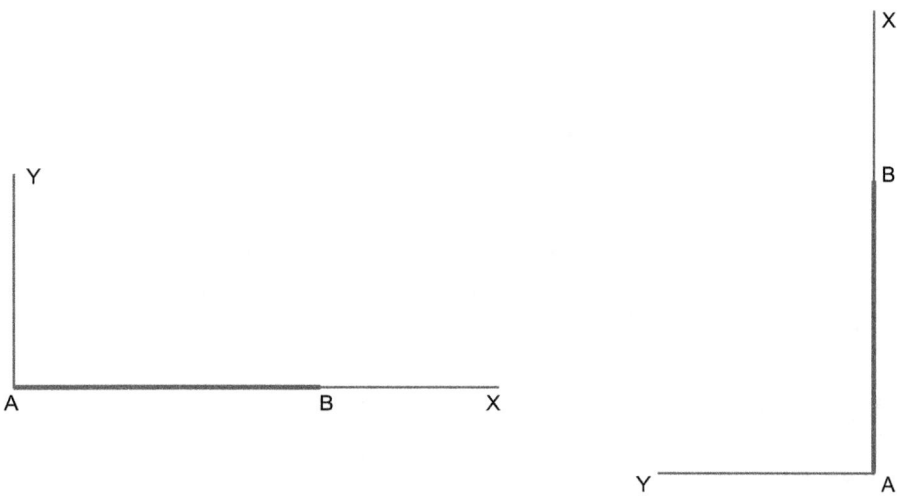

Fig. 1.3 : Frame of reference

Basic quantities of SD method are (a) member-end moment, (b) member-end slope or joint rotation, (c) member-end deflection or joint translation. Consistent with the reference system, following sign conventions are adopted for the basic quantities as shown in Fig. 1.4.

A member-end moment in anticlockwise direction is considered as positive. It is negative if clockwise.

A member end slope or a joint rotation in anticlockwise direction is considered as positive. It is taken negative if clockwise. A member-end deflection or a joint translation is considered positive if it is in positive y direction. It is taken negative in negative y direction.

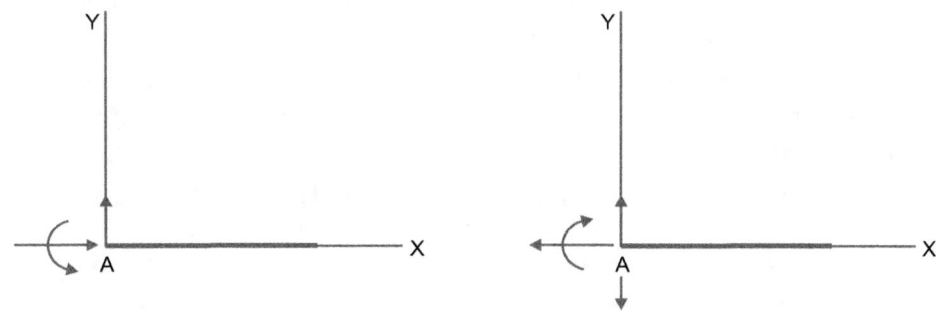

+ve member-end forces and displacements   −ve member-end forces and displacements

Fig. 1.4 : Sign convention for member-end moments and forces

Other member-end forces i.e. axial force and shear force are considered positive if they are in positive direction of x and y axes and negative in negative direction of axes.

Sign conventions for bending moment (BM), shear force (SF) and axial force (AF) at a section of a member of a structure are different and should not be mixed with that of member-end moments and forces.

Sagging bending moment is considered as positive and hogging bending moment is negative. When member-end moment is considered as a bending moment, the sign convention of bending moment is applicable. Shear force to the left of the section, in positive y-axis of a member is considered as positive. Shear force to the left of the section, in negative axis of a member is taken as negative.

Pull i.e. tensile axial force is treated as positive and push or thrust i.e. compressive axial force is taken as negative.

1.4 SD Equations

A member of a structure is bounded by two rigid joints at its ends. When a structure is loaded, member deforms, joints are displaced and internal forces are developed. The member-end moments can be expressed in terms of (a) the fixed-end moments of the member due to transverse loads on the member, (b) the member end-slopes or the joint rotations and (c) the member-end deflections or the joint translations. These expressions are called SD equations of the member.

There are two SD equations for a member of a structure, corresponding to the member-end moment at two ends i.e. joints. SD equations are the primary requirements of SD method. SD equations for a rigid jointed prismatic member are derived systematically from the superposition of the member-end moments caused by the following sequential operations.

(i) Restraining the member-end displacements i.e. locking the member-end joints and considering the fixed member-end moments due to the applied transverse loading on the member.

(ii) Releasing the restrained member for its end joint displacements one at a time and obtaining the member-end moments due to the released displacement, such a operation is carried out sequentially for all the four displacements, two at each end i.e. slope and deflection.

During these operations, to obtain member-end moment separately due to each cause, the following fundamental principles of analysis are applied.

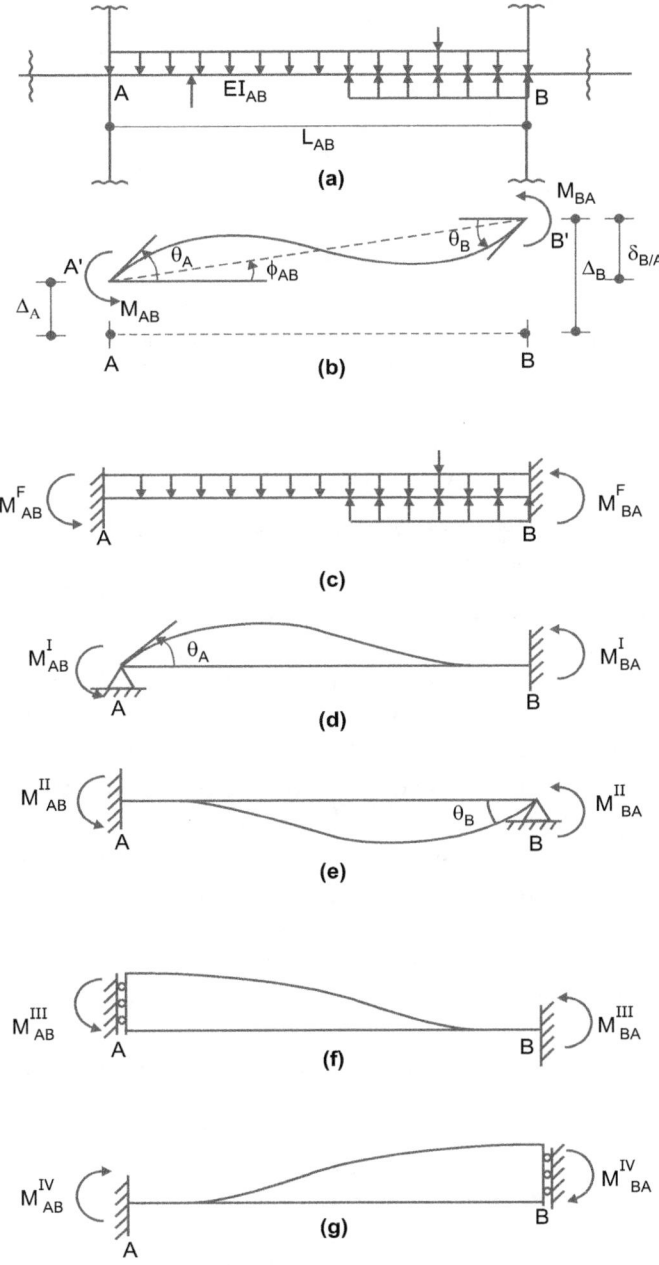

Fig. 1.5 : Development of SD equations by superposition

(i) Compatibility of member-end displacements.
(ii) Equilibrium of member loads and / or member-end forces.
(iii) Force-displacement relations in terms of flexural rotational and translational stiffnesses of the member.

This superposition technique is illustrated in Fig. 1.5 and SD equations are developed using some standard results of the member-end moments due to its joint displacements. These results are already derived earlier.

Before recapitulation of the results for the superposition, following points are worth to be noted with reference to Fig. 1.5.

- All primary quantities of SD equations are treated positive as per sign conventions, although the resisting forces are opposite to the deformations.
- As SD equations involve only member-end moments, only member-end moments are shown in Fig. 1.5, although other member-end forces exist for the equilibrium.
- Fig. 1.5 (a) shows a prismatic member AB of a structure, connected to the rigid joints A and B. The length of the member is L_{AB} and its flexural rigidity is denoted by EI_{AB}. The applied loads on the member AB, whatever may be, are also shown symbolically in Fig. 1.5 (a).
- The general deformed shape of the member AB, due to the loads on the structure, is sketched in Fig. 1.5 (b). Basic displacements of joints A and B are shown in Fig. 1.5 (b); and considered to establish general SD equations of the member. The translation along the member is of no interest and hence not shown.

The joint displacements are represented by following symbols :

θ_A = Member-end slope at A or the rotation of the joint A
θ_B = Member-end slope at B or the rotation of the joint B
Δ_A = Member-end deflection at A or the translation of joint A
Δ_B = Member-end deflection at B or the translation of joint B
$\Delta_{B/A}$ = Relative translation of joint B with respect to joint A
ϕ_{AB} = Angle between the undeformed member and the line joining the deflected joints. Relative rotation as a rigid body.

$$\phi_{AB} \cong \tan \phi_{AB} = \frac{\Delta_{B/A}}{L_{AB}}$$

Δ_B is assumed to be more than Δ_A, so that $\Delta_{B/A}$ is positive and consequently ϕ_{AB} is anticlockwise i.e. positive.

- The member-end moments developed due to the loads on the structure are shown in Fig. 1.5 (b) and are termed as,

M_{AB} = Moment at A for the member AB
M_{BA} = Moment at B for the member AB.

- Fig. 1.5 (c) shows the restrained member AB with the applied loads on the member. This is the fixed beam action. Fixed member-end moments to be denoted hereafter by FEM, due to the transverse loads on AB are shown in the figure and expressed as :

M_{AB}^F = Fixed-end moment at A for the member AB

M_{BA}^F = Fixed-end moment at B for the member AB

- The unloaded restrained beam AB is released for θ_A only as shown in Fig. 1.5 (d). According to the flexural rotational stiffness of the member, the member-end moment required at the end A and the member-end moment developed at the end B to cause θ_A are given by,

$$M_{AB}^I = \left(\frac{4\,EI_{AB}}{L_{AB}}\right) \times \theta_A$$

$$M_{BA}^I = \left(\frac{2\,EI_{AB}}{L_{AB}}\right) \times \theta_A$$

These member-end moments are shown in Fig. 1.5 (d).

- The restrained beam AB is then released for θ_B only and member-end moments, as shown in Fig. 1.5 (e) are obtained by similar concepts of stiffnesses. They are written as

$$M_{AB}^{II} = \left(\frac{2\,EI_{AB}}{L_{AB}}\right) \times \theta_B$$

$$M_{BA}^{II} = \left(\frac{4\,EI_{AB}}{L_{AB}}\right) \times \theta_B$$

- The restrained beam AB is now released for Δ_A only.

This is the case of flexural translational stiffness. The member-end moments are of interest as shown in Fig. 1.5 (f). Using standard results, these moments are taken as

$$M_{AB}^{III} = \left(\frac{6\,EI_{AB}}{L_{AB}^2}\right) \times \Delta_A$$

$$M_{BA}^{III} = \left(\frac{6\,EI_{AB}}{L_{AB}^2}\right) \times \Delta_A$$

- Similarly, when the restrained beam AB is released for Δ_B only, member-end moments, as shown in Fig. 1.5 (g), are given by

$$M_{AB}^{IV} = -\left(\frac{6\,EI_{AB}}{L_{AB}^2}\right) \times \Delta_B$$

$$M_{BA}^{IV} = -\left(\frac{6\,EI_{AB}}{L_{AB}^2}\right) \times \Delta_B$$

It may be noted that M_{AB}^{IV} and M_{BA}^{IV} are negative for the positive Δ_B.

- Joint displacements along the member do not cause any member end moments.

Superposing the moments obtained due to all causes, the equations for the resulting member-end moments are simplified as follows :

$$M_{AB} = M_{AB}^F + M_{AB}^I + M_{AB}^{II} + M_{AB}^{III} + M_{AB}^{IV}$$

STRUCTURAL ANALYSIS – II   SLOPE-DEFLECTION METHOD

$$= M_{AB}^F + \frac{4\,EI_{AB}}{L_{AB}}(\theta_A) + \frac{2\,EI_{AB}}{L_{AB}}(\theta_B) + \frac{6\,EI_{AB}}{L_{AB}^2}(\Delta_A) - \frac{6\,EI_{AB}}{L_{AB}^2}(\Delta_B)$$

$$= M_{AB}^F + \frac{4\,EI_{AB}}{L_{AB}}(\theta_A) + \frac{2\,EI_{AB}}{L_{AB}}(\theta_B) - \frac{6\,EI_{AB}}{L^2}(\Delta_{B/A}) \qquad \ldots (1.1\text{ a})$$

If $\Delta_{B/A}$ is known to be negative as in the case of sinking of support or assumed to be negative as in the case of sway frames; the SD equation of M_{AB} will be,

$$M_{AB} = M_{AB}^F + \frac{4\,EI_{AB}}{L_{AB}}(\theta_A) + \frac{2\,EI_{AB}}{L_{AB}}(\theta_B) + \frac{6\,EI_{AB}}{L_{AB}^2}(\Delta_{B/A})$$

and

$$M_{BA} = M_{BA}^F + \overset{I}{M_{BA}} + \overset{II}{M_{BA}} + \overset{III}{M_{BA}} + \overset{IV}{M_{BA}}$$

$$= M_{BA}^F + 2\frac{EI_{AB}}{L_{AB}}(\theta_A) + \frac{4\,EI_{AB}}{L_{AB}}(\theta_B) + \frac{6\,EI_{AB}}{L_{AB}^2}(\Delta_A) - \frac{6\,EI_{AB}}{L_{AB}^2}(\Delta_B)$$

$$= M_{BA}^F + \frac{2\,EI_{AB}}{L_{AB}}(\theta_A) + \frac{4\,EI_{AB}}{L_{AB}}(\theta_B) - \frac{6\,EI_{AB}}{L_{AB}^2}(\Delta_{B/A}) \qquad \ldots (1.1\text{ b})$$

If $\Delta_{B/A}$ is known to be negative as in the case of sinking of supports, or assumed to be negative as in the case of sway frames, the SD equation of M_{BA} will be

$$M_{BA} = M_{BA}^F + \frac{2\,EI_{AB}}{L_{AB}}(\theta_A) + \frac{4\,EI_{AB}}{L_{AB}}(\theta_B) + \frac{6\,EI_{AB}}{L_{AB}^2}(\Delta_{B/A})$$

The member end moment equations 1.1 (a) and 1.1 (b) expressed in terms of joint displacements and the applied loading are termed as the general SD equations for a member. The SD equations are applicable irrespective of the orientation of the member.

It is interesting to note the different terms in SD equation of a member and its interpretation. Each term in SD equation represents the moment contribution due to the different causes. The member end of interest is called the near-end and other end is termed as the far-end. Accordingly, in the expression of M_{AB}, the moments at the end A are of interest, therefore A is the near-end and B is the far-end and different moment-contributions are as follows :

- M_{AB}^F is FEM contribution due to the applied loads on AB, at A.
- $\left[\dfrac{4\,EI_{AB}}{L_{AB}}(\theta_A)\right]$ is the near-end rotation contribution at A.
- $\left[\dfrac{2\,EI_{AB}}{L_{AB}}(\theta_B)\right]$ is the far-end rotation contribution at A.
- $\left[\dfrac{6\,EI_{AB}}{L_{aB}^2}(\Delta_{B/A})\right]$ is the relative translation contribution at A.

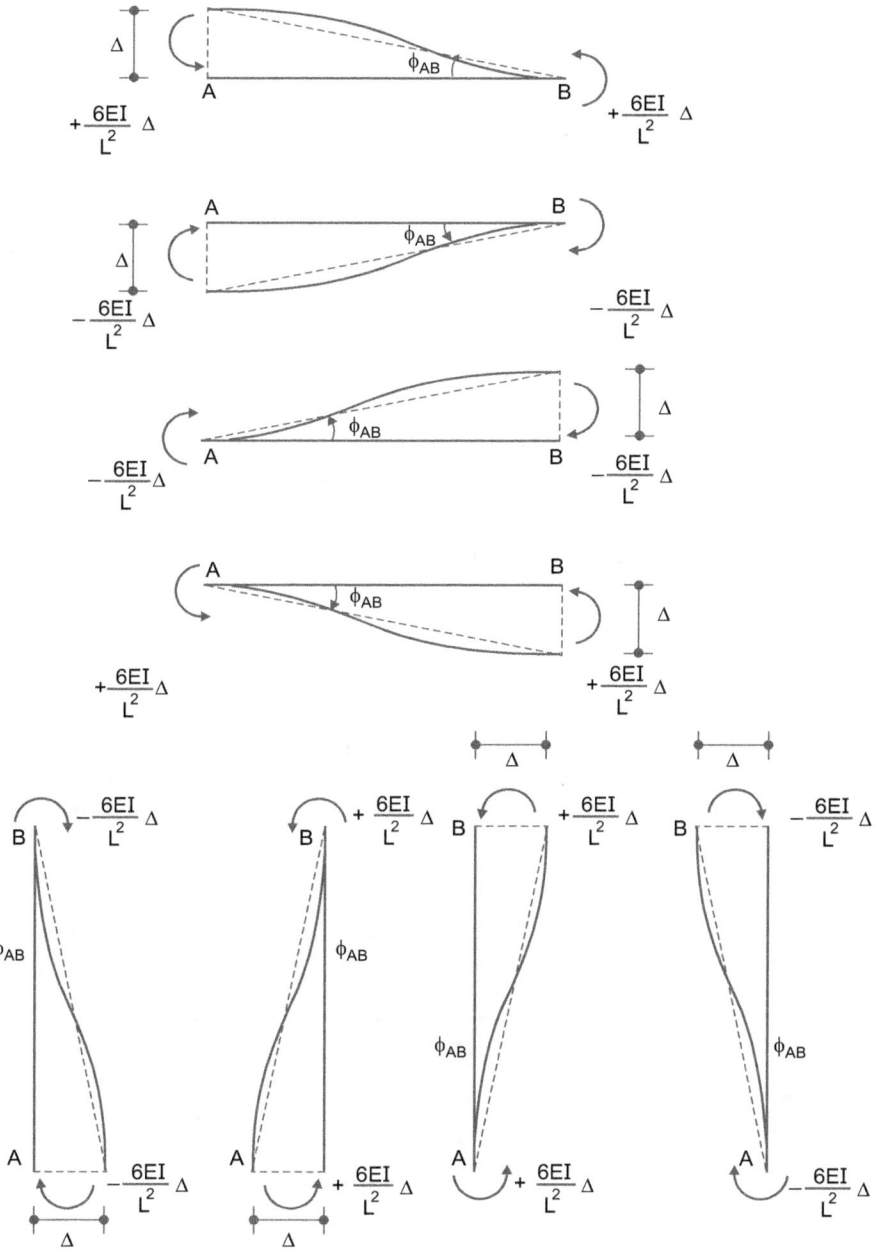

Fig. 1.6 : Relative translation contribution

Similarly for the end B, the contributions in the expression of M_{BA} can be stated.

In general, it can be remembered that :

- The near-end rotation contribution is always $\left[\dfrac{4EI}{L}\theta\right]$.

- The far-end rotation contribution is always $\left[\dfrac{2EI}{L}\theta\right]$.

- The relative translation contribution is always $\left[\dfrac{6EI}{L^2}\Delta\right]$.

Again it is emphasised to take care of the direction of the relative translation contribution in SD equations.

For the solution of problems of analysis of structures, the SD equations for any K^{th} member having joints i and j, are written in the following generalized form :

$$\left.\begin{array}{l} M_{ij} = M_{ij}^F + \dfrac{4EI_{ij}}{L_{ij}}(\theta_i) + \dfrac{2EI_{ij}}{L_{ij}}(\theta_j) \pm \dfrac{6EI_{ij}}{L_{ij}^2}(\Delta_{j/i}) \\[2ex] M_{ji} = M_{ji}^F + \dfrac{2EI_{ij}}{L_{ij}}(\theta_i) + \dfrac{4EI_{ij}}{L_{ij}}(\theta_j) \pm \dfrac{6EI_{ij}}{L_{ij}^2}(\Delta_{j/i}) \end{array}\right\} \quad \ldots (1.2)$$

It may be noted that for positive $\Delta_{j/i}$, the angle between the undeformed i.e. original member and the line joining the deflected joints, ϕ_{ij} is anticlockwise as shown in Fig. 1.6 and the quantity $\dfrac{6EI_{ij}}{L_{ij}^2}\Delta_{j/i}$ is negative. And for negative $\Delta_{j/i}$, the angle between the undeformed member and the line joining the deflected joints, ϕ_{ij} is clockwise as shown in figure and the quantity $\dfrac{6EI_{ij}}{L_{ij}^2}(\Delta_{j/i})$ is positive. Therefore, it is suggested that as per the direction of ϕ_{ij}, decide the sign for $\dfrac{6EI_{ij}}{L_{ij}^2}(\Delta_{j/i})$ and do not give sign to $\Delta_{j/i}$ i.e. use absolute value of $\Delta_{j/i}$. The general rule is, if ϕ_{ij} is anticlockwise take $\dfrac{6EI_{ij}}{L_{ij}^2}(\Delta_{j/i})$ as negative and if ϕ_{ij} is clockwise take $\dfrac{6EI_{ij}}{L_{ij}^2}(\Delta_{j/i})$ as positive.

If there are no joint translations, i.e. member end deflections, the SD equations are reduced to the following simple form :

$$\left.\begin{array}{l} M_{ij} = M_{ij}^F + \dfrac{4\,EI_{ij}}{L_{ij}}(\theta_i) + \dfrac{2\,EI_{ij}}{L_{ij}}(\theta_j) \\[2mm] M_{ji} = M_{ji}^F + \dfrac{2\,EI_{ij}}{L_{ij}}(\theta_i) + \dfrac{4\,EI_{ij}}{L_{ij}}(\theta_j) \end{array}\right\} \qquad \ldots (1.3)$$

The joint translations are absent in the following special situations :
- Beams consisting of prismatic members in between the supports which are non-yielding.
- Non-sway rectangular frames i.e. symmetrical rectangular frames.

1.5 FEM

Fixed end moments (FEM) are the pre-requisites of the SD method. FEM at two ends of a fixed beam, prismatic along its length, due to standard transverse loads on the beam are listed in Table 1.5. These results of FEM can be directly used in SD equations without its derivation from the first principles. If a member of a structure carries the combination of the standard loads, the FEM are computed by the superposition technique. For a member supporting distributed loads partly on the span, FEM are obtained by integrating the effects of infinitesimal elements and special tricks of compensations. The directions of FEM should be carefully accounted for considering as member end moment and not as BM. Generally for horizontal member ij with vertical downward transverse loads, the FEM are hogging bending moments, but with respect to sign conventions of member end moments, M_{ij}^F is positive as it is anticlockwise and M_{ji}^F is negative being clockwise. Special attention should be given to the direction of FEM due to the couple as a member load.

1.6 EQUILIBRIUM EQUATIONS OF SD METHOD

Equilibrium equations of SD method are expressed initially in terms of the member end moments of the structure. When a structure is in equilibrium, its part and parcel must be in equilibrium i.e. every member, each joint, every point, any part of the structure should be in equilibrium. FBD is the best tool for equilibrium. The forces in FBD, in a plane must satisfy three equations of equilibrium,

(i) $\sum F_x = 0,$ (ii) $\sum F_y = 0,$ (iii) $\sum M = 0.$

Moment equilibrium of a joint and shear equilibrium of a structure are the key considerations of SD method.

(A) Moment Equilibrium of a Joint :

Member-end moments act on the connecting joints in the reversed direction as a action of a member on the joint. Moment equilibrium of a rigid joint therefore involves (a) the member-end moments in reversed direction of the members connected to the joint, and (b) the applied joint moment if any. Moment equilibrium of a joint requires that sum of all moments must be zero. To illustrate this, consider a rigid jointed structure loaded with the moment, M_A at A as shown in Fig. 1.7 (a). The FBD of the joint A is shown in Fig. 1.7 (b), indicating only moments for convenience.

Assuming member-end moments, M_{AB} and M_{AC} as anticlockwise and also applied moment M_A as anticlockwise, the moment equilibrium for the joint A leads to

$$\sum M_A = 0$$

i.e. $\quad M_A - M_{AB} - M_{AC} = 0$

i.e. $\quad M_A - [M_{AB} + M_{AC}] = 0$

i.e. $\quad M_A = M_{AB} + M_{AC}$

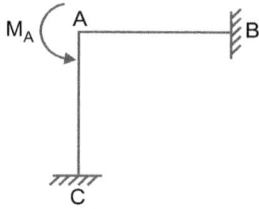

(a) Frame with moment at joint A

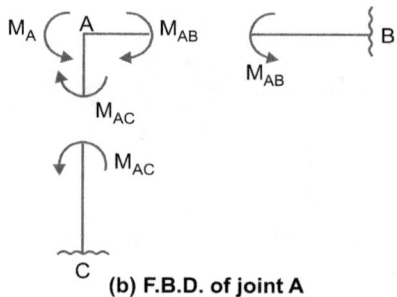

(b) F.B.D. of joint A

Fig. 1.7 : Moment equilibrium of joint

i.e. Applied moment at joint A = Sum of the member-end moments for the members meeting at the joint. As the applied joint moment and member-end moment are written on opposite side of the equation, it is concluded that the same sign conventions can be used for the applied joint moment and the member-end moment. This may be noted for further treatment of SD method. Therefore, general rule of moment equilibrium of joint is to equate the sum of the member end moments, meeting at the joint to the applied moment at the joint. This can be expressed, in general, at i^{th} joint as

$$\sum M_{ij} = M_i \quad \quad \ldots (1.4 \text{ a})$$

It is also interesting to note that if there is no applied moment at a joint, the sum of the end moments of the members meeting at the joint must be zero to satisfy the condition of equilibrium.

i.e.
$$\sum M_{ij} = 0 \quad \quad \ldots (1.4 \text{ b})$$

This is the common situation as the joints are seldom loaded with the moment.

Joint equilibrium conditions are adequate if unknowns are only joint rotations and joint translations are zero. This also indicates association of rotation with moment and one to one correspondence of force and displacement.

(B) Shear Equilibrium of Structure :

Joint equilibrium equations are inadequate if the unknown joint displacements are translations in addition to rotations.

According to one to one correspondence of force and displacement, the unknown translations need force equilibrium conditions of the structure in addition to moment equilibrium of joints.

Force equilibrium condition is called shear equilibrium with reference to SD method.

The shear equilibrium involves the members connected to the supports of the structure. Considering FBD of member, the end shear force at the support joint of the member is related to the member end moments and the applied member loads. This relationship is established by taking moments about the joint other than support joint. The end shears of the members connected to the supports also correspond to the reaction components of the supports of the structure. For equilibrium of the structure, the algebraic sum of (a) the end shears of the members at the support points of the structure and (b) the applied forces on the structure in the direction of shears, must be zero.

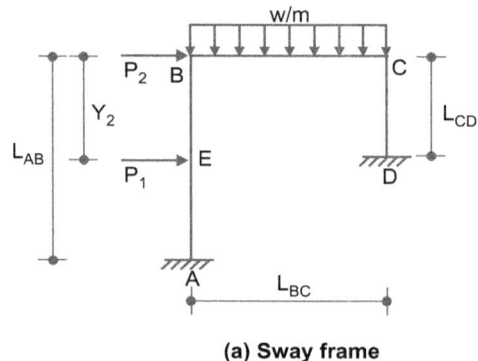

(a) Sway frame

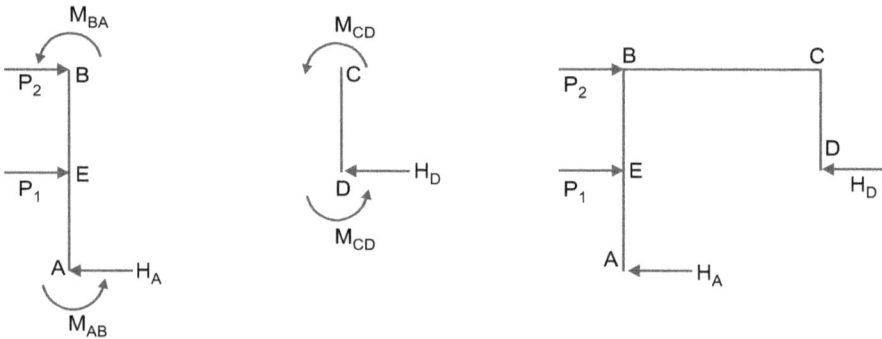

(b) F.B.D. of columns (c) Shear equilibrium

Fig. 1.8 : Shear Equilibrium of frame

The concept of shear equilibrium is illustrated with the rectangular frame as shown in Fig. 1.8 (a). The FBD of the members AB and DC connected to the supports are shown in Fig. 1.8 (b). It may be noted that only member end moments, member end shears at the supports and applied member loads are shown in FBD. Member-end moments are considered positive for formulation of shear equilibrium. From FBD of the member AB and taking moments about B, the equilibrium equation $\sum M_B = 0$ is written as

$$H_A \times L_{AB} - M_{AB} - M_{BA} - P_1 \times Y_1 = 0$$

From this, the shear of AB at A is given by,

$$\therefore \quad H_A = \frac{(M_{AB} + M_{BA} + P_1 Y_1)}{L_{AB}}$$

Similarly from FBD of the member DC and taking moments about C, the equilibrium equation $\sum M_C = 0$ gives end shear H_D of DC, as

$$H_D = \frac{(M_{DC} + M_{CD})}{L_{CD}}$$

Fig. 1.8 (c) shows the structure consisting of only forces in the direction of shears. The force equilibrium, $\sum F_x = 0$, establishes the necessary shear equilibrium as :

$$P_1 + P_2 - H_A - H_D = 0$$

i.e. $\quad H_A + H_D = P_1 + P_2$

In general, shear equilibrium can be stated as :

Sum of the end shears of the members connected to the supports = Sum of the applied forces on the structure, in the direction of shears with due care of signs.

1.7 Procedure of SD Method

The SD method is very systematic. The important steps of procedure of SD method to analyse rigid jointed structure are given below :

(A) Data :
1. Configuration of the structure - line diagram showing the arrangement of joints and members and support conditions including dimensions.
2. Applied loads on members and joints of the structure showing position, direction and magnitude.
3. Sectional properties of members moment of inertia (relative values).
4. Properties of materials - modulus of elasticity.
5. Yielding of supports (translational and rotational) stiffness of elastic supports, if any.

(B) Objectives :
1. Joint displacements - translations and rotations (i.e. slopes and deflections).
2. Member-end moments.
3. Member-end forces - axial force and shear force - FBD of members.
4. FBD of joints.
5. Reactions at supports - FBD of structure.
6. Variation of shear force and bending moment along the length of members SFD and BMD.
7. Elastic curve

(C) Equations and Concepts :
1. SD equations.
2. Moment-equilibrium equations of joints.
3. Shear-equilibrium equations for structure.

4. Equilibrium of member - FBD.
5. Equilibrium of structure - FBD.

(D) Procedure :
1. Unknown joint displacement - Degree of kinematic indeterminacy.
2. FEM of members.
3. SD equations of members.
4. Formulation of equilibrium equations in terms of member-end moments.
   (a) Moment equilibrium of joint
   (b) Shear equilibrium of structure.
5. Verification of number of unknown displacements is equal to number of equilibrium equations.
6. Formulation of a problem by substituting SD equations in equilibrium equations.
7. Formation of simultaneous equations for unknown joint displacements.
8. Verification of diagonal symmetry of the simultaneous equations.
9. Solution of simultaneous equations to obtain unknown joint displacements.
10. Member-end moments by substituting joint displacements in SD equations of members.
11. Member-end forces-axial and shear from equilibrium of FBD of members.
12. FBD of members.
13. FBD of joints.
14. FBD of structure-reactions of supports.
15. SFD
16. BMD
17. Elastic curve (qualitative).

1.8 SD Method Applied to Beams

Statically indeterminate beams having more than two supports of any type i.e. continuous beams are analysed by SD method by hand calculations if unknown displacements are few, say three. If unknowns are more, the method becomes tedious as it involves large number of simultaneous equations which demand the use of computer. The general procedure given in the previous article is applied to analyse the continuous beams with the necessary simplifications wherever possible. Following situations are common in the analysis of beams.

1.8.1 Beams Without Joint Translations

The necessary and sufficient conditions for no joint translations in a continuous beam are as follows :

1. The members of the beam in between the supports are prismatic i.e. of uniform section. This means that the joints are only at support points.
2. All joints in the beam must remain in their original locations. This means that the supports are non-sinking and axial deformation is neglected.

The analysis of the beams without joint translations by SD method involves only (a) joint rotations and (b) moment equilibrium of joints.

1.8.2 Application of SD Method to Beams Without Joint Translations

Example 1.1 : A beam BCD fixed at B and D and continuous over C. BC = 3 m and CD = 4m. BC is loaded with UDL of intensity 40 kN/m and CD is loaded with UDL of intensity 50 kN/m.

Solution : (1) Data : The beam is supported and loaded as shown in Fig. 1.9.

(2) All supports are at same level.

Object : Structural analysis.

Equations : S. D. Equations.

Procedure : Step I : Degree of kinematic indeterminary.

Unknown displacement : $\theta_C = D_{KP} = 1$

Known displacmenet : $\theta_B = \theta_D = 0$

Step II : Fixed end moments :

$$\overline{M}_{BC} = -\overline{M}_{CB} = -\frac{wl^2}{12} = \frac{-40 \times 3 \times 3}{12} = -30 \text{ kN-m}$$

$$\overline{M}_{CD} = -\overline{M}_{DC} = -\frac{wl^2}{12}$$

$$= -\frac{50 \times 4 \times 4}{12} = -66.67 \text{ kN-m}$$

Step III : Slope deflection equations :

$$\therefore \quad M_{BC} = -\overline{M}_{BC} + \frac{2EI}{l}\left(2\theta_B + \theta_C - \frac{3\delta}{l}\right)$$

$\delta = 0, \quad \theta_B = 0$

$$\therefore \quad M_{BC} = -30 + \frac{2EI}{3}(\theta_C)$$

$$M_{CB} = \overline{M}_{CB} + \frac{2EI}{l}\left(2\theta_c + \theta_b - \frac{3\delta}{l}\right)$$

$$\therefore \quad M_{CB} = 30 + \frac{2EI}{3}(2\theta_C)$$

$$M_{CD} = -66.67 + \frac{2EI}{4}(2\theta_C)$$

$$M_{DC} = 66.67 + \frac{2EI}{4}(\theta_C)$$

Step IV : Equilibrium equations :

$$\therefore \quad M_{CB} + M_{CD} = 0$$

Step V : Formulation of equilibrium equations :

$$-36.67 + 4\,EI\theta_c\left(\frac{1}{3} + \frac{1}{4}\right) = 0$$

Step VI : Solution of equations for joint displacements :

$$\theta_c = \left(\frac{15.71}{EI}\right)$$

Step VII : Member end moments :

$$M_{BC} = -30 + \frac{2EI}{3}(\theta_c)$$

$$= -30 + \frac{2EI}{3}\left(\frac{15.71}{EI}\right)$$

$$= -19.52 \text{ kN-m}$$

$$M_{CB} = 30 + \frac{2EI}{3}(2\theta_c)$$

$$= 30 + \frac{2EI}{3}\left(2 \times \frac{15.71}{EI}\right)$$

$$= 50.95 \text{ kN-m}$$

$$M_{CD} = -66.67 + \frac{2EI}{4}(2\theta_c)$$

$$= -66.67 + \frac{2EI}{4}\left(\frac{2 \times 15.71}{EI}\right)$$

$$= -50.95 \text{ kN-m}$$

$$M_{DC} = 66.67 + \frac{2EI}{4}(\theta_c)$$

$$= 66.67 + \frac{2EI}{4}\left(\frac{15.71}{EI}\right) = 74.525 \text{ kN-m}$$

Reaction at A = 60 − 10.48 = 49.52 kN

Reaction at B = 60 + 100 + 10.48 − 5.9 = 164.58 kN

Reaction at C = 100 + 5.9 − 105.9 kN

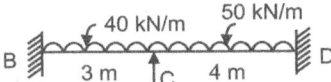
(a) Given structure

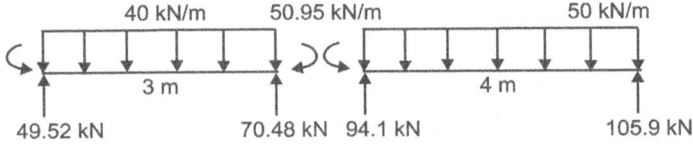
(b) FBD of members

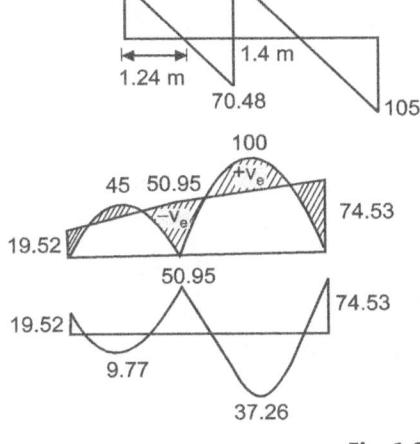
(c) S.F.D.

(d) BMD by superposition

(e) BMD on tension side

Fig. 1.9

Example 1.2 : A two span continuous beam is fixed at A and simply supported at B and C. Given AB = BC = 6 m with $I_{AB} = 3I$ and $I_{BC} = 2I$.

The span AB carries a UDL of 40 kN/m, while a concentrated load of 100 kN acts at the centre of span BC. Using slope deflection method, analyze the beam and compute the support moments at A, B and C. Draw S. F. D and B.M.D. **(P.U. Oct. 97)**

Solution : (1) Data : The beam is supported and loaded as shown in Fig. 1.10.

(2) All supports are at same level.

Object : Structural analysis.

Equations : S. D. Equations.

Procedure : Step I : Degree of kinematic indeterminacy

$$= D_{ki} = 2$$

Unknown displacement : θ_B, θ_C

Known displacment : $\theta_A = 0$

Step II : Fixed end moments :

$$\overline{M}_{AB} = -\frac{wl^2}{2} = -\frac{40 \times 6 \times 6}{12} = -120 \text{ kN-m}$$

$$\overline{M}_{BA} = \frac{wl^2}{12} = 120 \text{ kN-m}$$

$$\overline{M}_{BC} = -\frac{wl}{8} = -\frac{100 \times 6}{8} = -75 \text{ kN-m}$$

$$\overline{M}_{CB} = \frac{wl}{8} = 75 \text{ kN-m}$$

Step III : Slope deflection equations :

$$M_{AB} = \overline{M}_{AB} + \frac{2EI}{l}(2\theta_A + \theta_B) \qquad \theta_A = 0 \text{ as end A is fixed}$$

$$\therefore \quad M_{AB} = -120 + \frac{2E(3I)}{6}(\theta_B)$$

$$= -120 + EI\theta_B$$

$$M_{BA} = \overline{M}_{BA} + \frac{2EI}{l}(2\theta_B + \theta_A)$$

$$= 120 + \frac{2E(3I)}{6}(2\theta_B)$$

$$= 120 + 2\,EI\theta_B$$

$$M_{BC} = \overline{M}_{BC} + \frac{2EI}{l}(2\theta_B + \theta_C)$$

$$= -75 + 0.67\,EI\,(2\theta_B + \theta_C)$$

$$M_{CB} = \overline{M}_{CB} + \frac{2EI}{l}(2\theta_C + \theta_B)$$

$$= 75 + 0.67\,EI\,(2\theta_C + \theta_B)$$

Step IV : Equilibrium equations :

1. $\quad M_{BA} + M_{BC} = 0$
2. $\quad M_{CB} = 0$

Step V : Formulation of equilibrium equations :

1. $\quad M_{BA} + M_{BC} = 0$

$$120 + 2\,EI\theta_B - 75 + 1.34\,EI\theta_B + 0.67\,EI\theta_C = 0$$

$$3.34\,EI\theta_B + 0.67\,EI\theta_C = -45$$

2. $\quad M_{CB} = 0$

$$75 + 0.67\,EI\theta_B + 1.34\,EI\theta_C = 0$$

$$0.67\,EI\theta_B + 1.34\,EI\theta_C = -75$$

Step VI : Solution of equations of joint displacements :

$$EI\,\theta_B = -2.5$$
$$EI\,\theta_C = -54.7$$

Step VII : Member end moments :

$$M_{AB} = -120 + EI\,\theta_B = -120 + (-2.5) = -122.5 \text{ kN-m}$$

$$M_{BA} = 120 + 2\,EI\,\theta_B = 120 + 2 \times (-2.5) = 115 \text{ kN-m}$$

$$M_{BC} = -75 + 0.67\,EI\,(2\theta_B + \theta_C)$$

$$= -75 + 0.67\,EI\,(2 \times -2.5 - 54.7)$$

$$= -115 \text{ kN-m}$$

$$M_{CB} = 75 + 0.67\,EI\,(2\theta_C + \theta_B)$$

$$= 75 + 0.67\,EI\,(2 \times -54.7 - 2.5) = 0$$

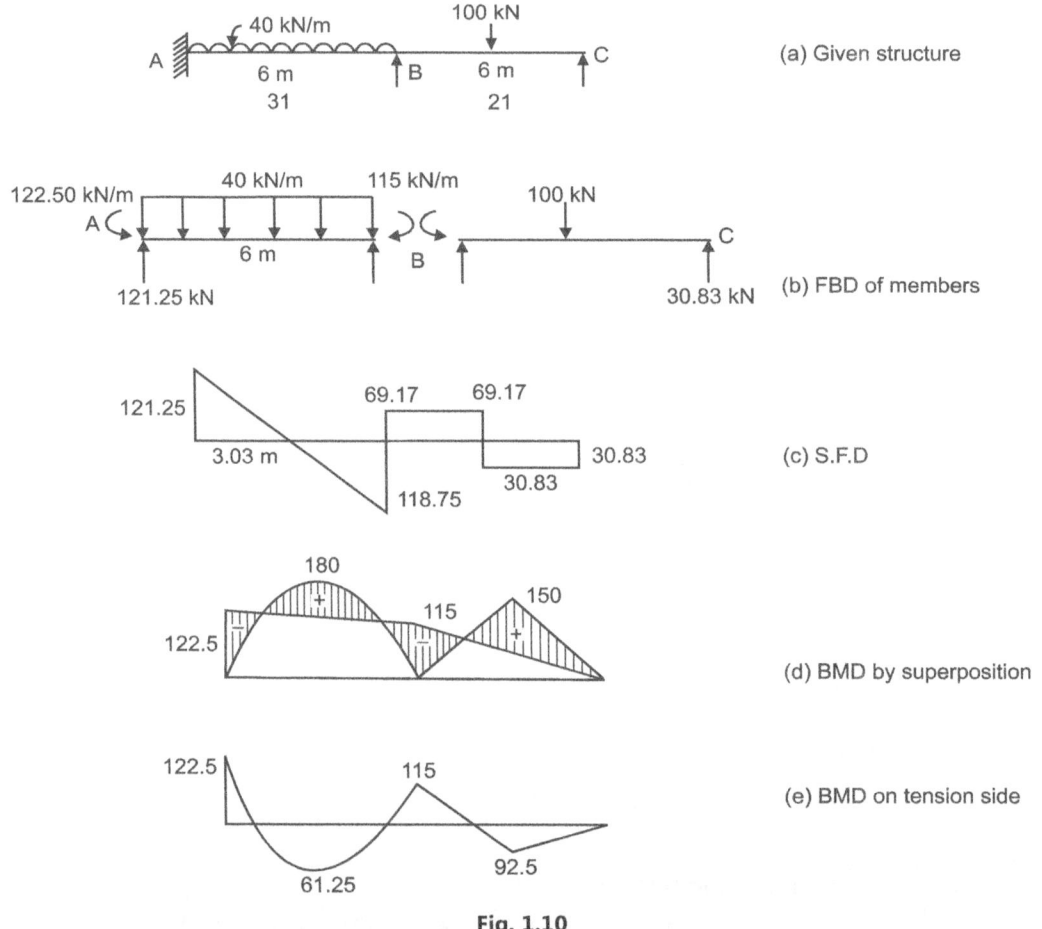

Fig. 1.10

Example 1.3 : Analyze the continuous beam by slope deflection method. Also draw shear force and bending moment diagrams. **(IES 95)**

Solution : (1) Data : The beam is supported and loaded as shown in Fig. 1.11.

(2) All supports are at same level.

Object : Structural analysis.

Equations : S. D. Equations.

Procedure : Step I : Degree of kinematic indeterminancy

$$= D_{ki} = 2$$

Unknown displacements : θ_A, θ_B

Known displacement : $\theta_C = 0$

Step II : Fixed end moments :

$$\overline{M}_{AB} = -\overline{M}_{BA} = -\frac{wl}{8} = \frac{-24 \times 3}{8} = -9 \text{ kN-m}$$

$$\overline{M}_{BC} = \overline{M}_{CB} = \frac{M}{4} = -\frac{40}{4} = -10 \text{ kN-m}$$

Step III : Slope deflection equations :

$$M_{AB} = \overline{M}_{AB} + \frac{2EI}{L}(2\theta_A + \theta_B)$$

$$= -9 + \frac{2EI}{3}(2\theta_A + \theta_B)$$

$$M_{BA} = 9 + \frac{2EI}{3}(2\theta_B + \theta_A)$$

$$M_{BC} = -10 + \frac{2EI}{3}(2\theta_B + \theta_C)$$

$$= -10 + \frac{2EI}{3}(2\theta_B)$$

Step IV : Equilibrium equations :

$$M_{BA} + M_{BC} = 0, \quad M_{AB} = 0$$

Step V : Formulation of equilibrium equations :

$$9 + \frac{2E(1.5)}{3}(2\theta_B + \theta_A) - 10 + \frac{2EI}{3}(2\theta_B) = 0$$

$$2EI\,\theta_B + EI\,\theta_A + \frac{4EI\theta_B}{3} = 1$$

$$\frac{10\,EI}{3}\theta_B + EI\,\theta_A = 1 \qquad \ldots(1)$$

$$M_{AB} = 0$$

$$-9 + \frac{2E}{3}(1.5\,I)(2\theta_A + \theta_B) = 0$$

$$2EI\theta_A + EI\theta_B = 9 \qquad \ldots(2)$$

Step VI : Solution of equations for joint displacements :

$$\theta_B = \frac{-1.23}{EI} \text{ and } \theta_A = \frac{5.11}{EI}$$

STRUCTURAL ANALYSIS – II   SLOPE-DEFLECTION METHOD

Step VII : Member end moments :

$$M_{BA} = \overline{M}_{AB} + \frac{2EI}{l}(2\theta_B + \theta_A)$$

$$= 9 + \frac{2E(1.5\,I)}{3}(2 \times 5.11 - 1.234)$$

$$= 11.642 \text{ kN-m}$$

$$M_{BC} = -10 + \frac{2EI}{3}(2 \times -1.23) = -11.642 \text{ kN-m}$$

$$M_{CB} = -10 + \frac{2EI}{3}(-1.23) = -10.826 \text{ kN-m}$$

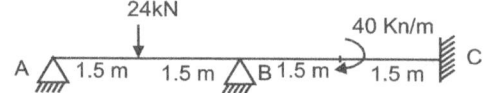

(a) Given structure

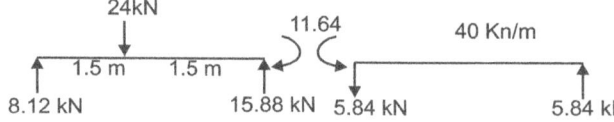

(b) F.B.D of members

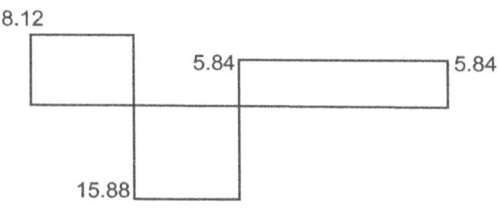

(c) S.F.D

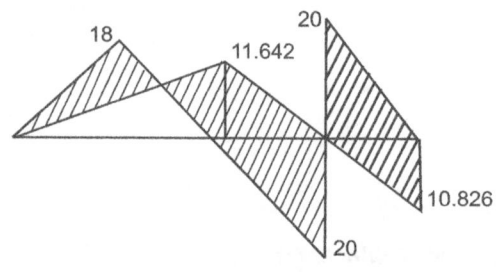

(d) BMD by superposition

Fig. 1.11

Example 1.4 : *Find the moments at continuous support for beam ABC. AB = 5 m, BC = 6 m. A point load of 20 kN is acting on AB at 3 m from B and BC is loaded with UDL of 10 kN/m. EI is constant for the beam. Supports A and C are simple supports.*

Solution : (1) Data : The beam is supported and loaded as shown in Fig. 1.12.

(2) All supports are at same level.

Object : Structural analysis.

Equations : S. D. Equation.

Procedure : Step I : Degree of kinematic indeterminacy = D_{ki} = 3

Unknown displacements : $\theta_A, \theta_B, \theta_C$

Step II : Fixed end moments :

$$\overline{M}_{AB} = -\frac{wab^2}{l^2} = -\frac{20 \times 2 \times 3^2}{5^2} = -14.4 \text{ kN-m}$$

$$\overline{M}_{BA} = \frac{wa^2b}{l} = \frac{20 \times 2^2 \times 3}{5^2} = 9.6 \text{ kN-m}$$

$$\overline{M}_{BC} = -\overline{M}_{CB} = -\frac{wl^2}{12} = -\frac{10 \times 6^2}{12} = -30 \text{ kN-m}$$

Step III : Slope deflection equations :

Span AB :

$$M_{AB} = \overline{M}_{AB} + \frac{2EI}{l}\left(2\theta_A + \theta_B - \frac{3\delta}{l}\right)$$

$$\delta = 0$$

$$M_{AB} = -14.4 + \frac{2EI}{5}(2\theta_A + \theta_B)$$

$$M_{BA} = \overline{M}_{BA} + \frac{2EI}{l}(\theta_A + 2\theta_B)$$

$$= 9.6 + \frac{2EI}{5}(\theta_A + 2\theta_B)$$

Span BC :

$$M_{BC} = -30 + \frac{2EI}{6}(2\theta_B + \theta_C)$$

$$M_{CB} = 30 + \frac{2EI}{6}(\theta_B + 2\theta_C)$$

Ends A and C are simply supported.

Step IV : Equilibrium equations:

$$M_{AB} = 0 \quad \text{(As simple support)}$$
$$M_{CB} = 0 \quad \text{(As simple support)}$$
$$M_{BA} + M_{BC} = 0$$

Step V : Formulation of equilibrium equations in terms of joint displacements:

$$\therefore \quad M_{AB} = 0 = -14.4 + \frac{2EI}{5}(2\theta_A + \theta_B)$$

$$\therefore \quad 2\theta_A + \theta_B = \frac{36}{EI} \quad \ldots(1)$$

$$M_{CB} = 0 = 30 + \frac{2EI}{6}(2\theta_C + \theta_B)$$

$$\therefore \quad 2\theta_C + \theta_B = -\frac{90}{EI} \quad \ldots(2)$$

$$M_{BA} + M_{BC} = 0$$

$$9.6 + \frac{2EI}{5}(\theta_A + 2\theta_B) - 30 + \frac{2EI}{6}(2\theta_B + \theta_C) = 0$$

$$-20.4 + 0.4\theta_A + 0.8\theta_B + 0.667\theta_B + 0.33\theta_C = 0$$

$$-20.4 + 0.5\theta_A + 1.467\theta_B + 0.44\theta_C = 0 \quad \ldots(3)$$

Step VI : Solution of equations for joint displacements :

Solving equations (1), (2) and (3),

$$\theta_A = 5.28/EI$$
$$\theta_B = 25.45/EI$$
$$\theta_C = -57.72/EI$$

Step VII : Member end moments :

$$\therefore \quad M_{AB} = -14.4 + \frac{2EI}{5}(2\theta_A + \theta_B)$$

$$= -14.4 + \frac{2EI}{5}(2 \times 5.28 + 25.45)$$

$$= 0$$

$$M_{BA} = 9.6 + \frac{2EI}{5}(\theta_A + 2\theta_B) = 9.6\frac{2EI}{5}(5.17 + 2 \times 25.67)$$

$$= 32.28$$

$$M_{BC} = -30 + \frac{2EI}{6}(2\theta_B + \theta_C) = -30 + \frac{2EI}{6}(2 \times 25.67 - 57.84)$$

$$= -32.28$$

$$M_{CB} = 30 + \frac{2EI}{l}(2\theta_C + \theta_B) = 30 + \frac{2EI}{6}(2 \times -57.84 + 25.67)$$

$$= 0.0$$

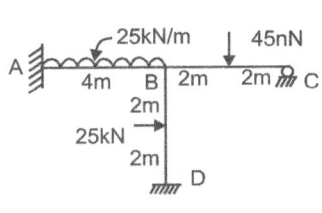

(a) Given structure

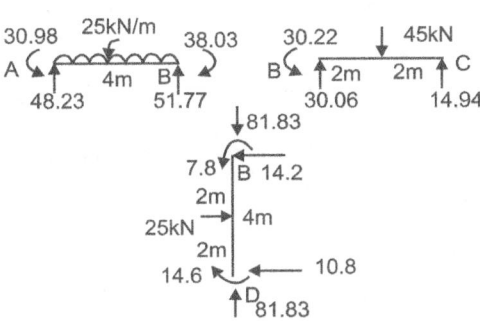

(b) FBD of members

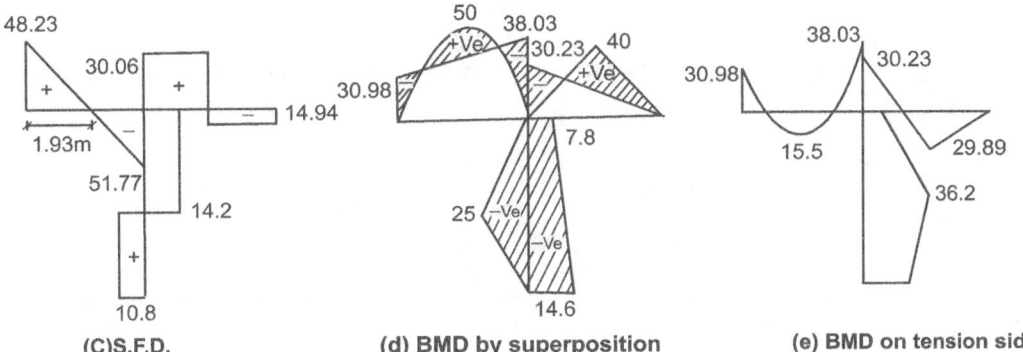

(C) S.F.D. (d) BMD by superposition (e) BMD on tension side

Fig. 1.12

STRUCTURAL ANALYSIS – II   SLOPE-DEFLECTION METHOD

Example 1.5 : Analyse the beam as shown in Fig. 1.9 (a) by slope-deflection method.

(a) Given structure

(b) F.B.D. of members

(c) S.F.D.

(d) B.M.D. by superposition

(e) B.M.D. on tension side

(f) F.B.D. of structure

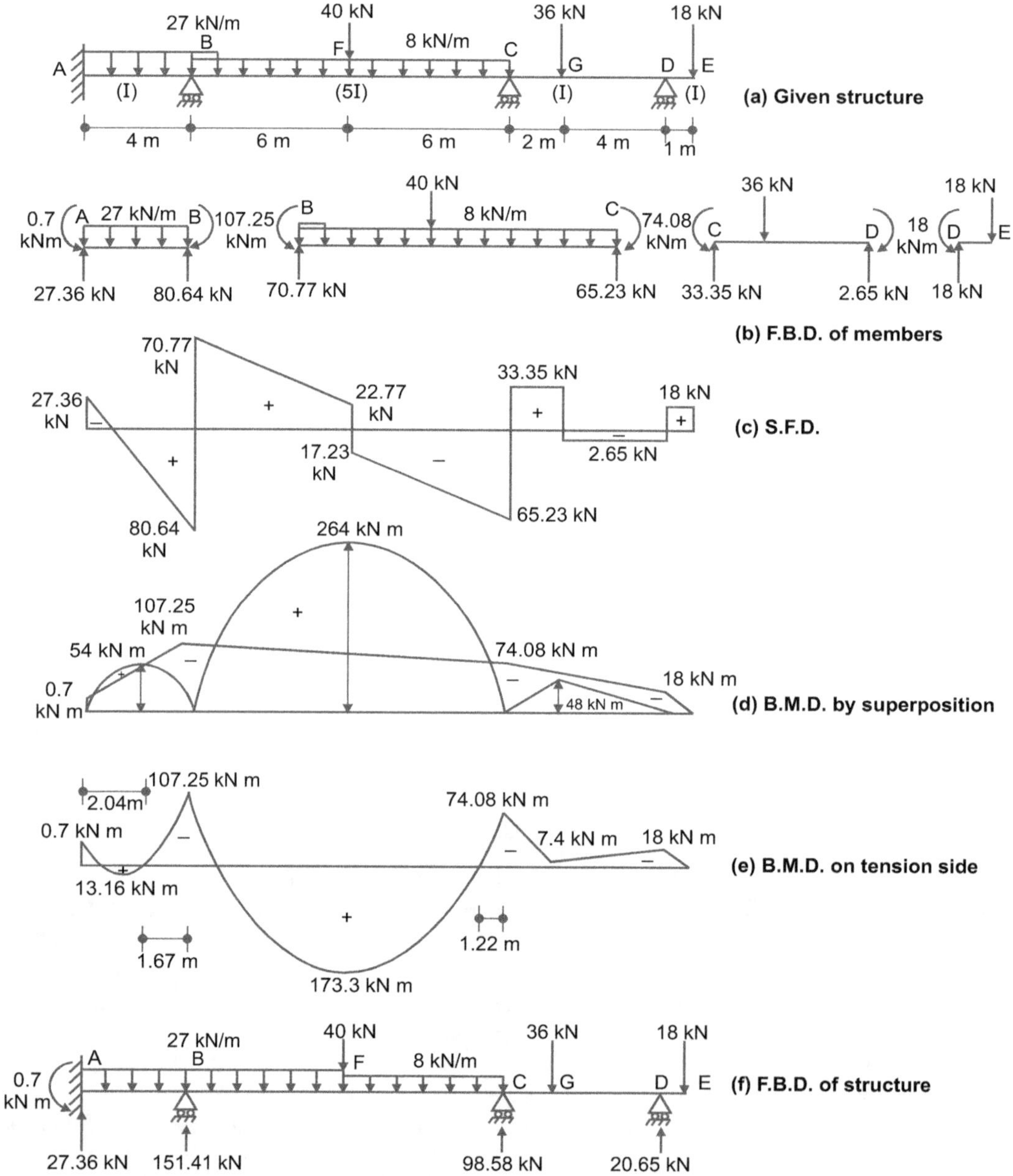

Fig. 1.13 : For Illustrative Example 1.5

Solution : (1) Data : The beam is supported and loaded as shown in Fig. 1.13 (b).

(2) All supports are at same levels.

Object : Structural analysis which includes;
1. Joint displacement;
2. Member-end moments;
3. Member-end forces – FBD of members;
4. Reactions at supports for structure – FBD of structure;
5. Variation of shear force and bending moment along the length of member – plotting SFD and BMD; and
6. Elastic curve – Deflected shape of structure.

Equations :

$$M_{ij} = \frac{4EI}{L}(\theta_i) + \frac{2EI}{L}(\theta_j) \pm \frac{6EI}{L^2}(\Delta) + M_{ij}^F$$

$$M_{ji} = \frac{4EI}{L}(\theta_j) + \frac{2EI}{L}(\theta_i) \pm \frac{6EI}{L}(\Delta) + M_{ji}^F$$

Procedure :

Step I : Degree of kinematic indeterminacy = D_{ki} = 5 ($\theta_B, \theta_C, \theta_D, \theta_E, \Delta_{VE}$) for given structure.

Degree of kinematic indeterminacy = D_{ki} = 3 ($\theta_B, \theta_C, \theta_D$) for modified structure.

Unknown displacements = $\theta_B, \theta_C, \theta_D$

Known displacement = θ_A = 0

Step II : Fixed moments :

$$M_{AB}^F = -M_{BA}^F = \frac{wl^2}{12} = \frac{27 \times 4^2}{12} = 36 \text{ kNm}$$

$$M_{BC}^F = -M_{CB}^F = \frac{wl^2}{12} + \frac{WL}{8} = \frac{8 \times 12^2}{12} + \frac{40 \times 12}{8} = 156 \text{ kNm}$$

$$M_{CD}^F = \frac{Wab^2}{L^2} = \frac{36 \times 2 \times (4)^2}{(6)^2} = 32 \text{ kNm}$$

$$M_{DC}^F = \frac{-Wa^2b}{L^2} = \frac{-36 \times (2)^2 \times 4}{(6)^2} = -16 \text{ kNm}$$

Step III : Slope-deflection equations :

Member AB :
$$M_{AB} = \frac{4EI}{L}(\theta_A) + \frac{2EI}{L}(\theta_B) \pm \frac{6EI}{L^2}(\Delta) + M_{AB}^F$$
$$= 0.5\,EI\,(\theta_B) + 36 \quad \ldots\text{(i)}$$

$$M_{BA} = \frac{4EI}{L}(\theta_B) + \frac{2EI}{L}(\theta_A) \pm \frac{6EI}{L^2}(\Delta) + M_{BA}^F$$
$$= EI\,(\theta_B) - 36 \quad \ldots\text{(ii)}$$

Member BC :
$$M_{BC} = \frac{4EI}{L}(\theta_B) + \frac{2EI}{L}(\theta_C) \pm \frac{6EI}{L^2}(\Delta) + M_{BC}^F$$
$$= \frac{4(5EI)}{12}(\theta_B) + \frac{2(5EI)}{12}(\theta_C) + 156$$
$$= 1.67\,EI\,(\theta_B) + 0.83\,EI\,(\theta_C) + 156 \quad \ldots\text{(iii)}$$

$$M_{CB} = \frac{4EI}{L}(\theta_C) + \frac{2EI}{L}(\theta_B) \pm \frac{6EI}{L^2}(\Delta) + M_{CB}^F$$
$$= \frac{4(5EI)}{12}(\theta_C) + \frac{2(5EI)}{12}(\theta_B) - 156$$
$$= 1.67\,EI\,(\theta_C) + 0.83\,EI\,(\theta_B) - 156 \quad \ldots\text{(iv)}$$

Member CD :
$$M_{CD} = \frac{4EI}{L}(\theta_C) + \frac{2EI}{L}(\theta_D) \pm \frac{6EI}{L^2}(\Delta) + M_{CD}^F$$
$$= \frac{4EI}{6}(\theta_C) + \frac{2EI}{6}(\theta_D) + 32$$
$$= 0.67\,EI\,(\theta_C) + 0.34\,EI\,(\theta_D) + 32 \quad \ldots\text{(v)}$$

$$M_{DC} = \frac{4EI}{L}(\theta_D) + \frac{2EI}{L}(\theta_C) \pm \frac{6EI}{L^2}(\Delta) + M_{DC}^F$$
$$= \frac{4EI}{6}(\theta_D) + \frac{2EI}{6}(\theta_C) - 16$$
$$= 0.67\,EI\,(\theta_D) + 0.34\,EI\,(\theta_C) - 16 \quad \ldots\text{(vi)}$$

Step IV : Moment equilibrium condition for joints :

At joint B ; $\quad M_{BA} + M_{BC} = 0 \quad \ldots$(A)

At joint C ; $\quad M_{CB} + M_{CD} = 0 \quad \ldots$(B)

At joint D ; $\quad M_{DC} = -18$ kNm $\quad \ldots$(C)

Step V : Formulation of equilibrium equations in terms of joint displacement :

Substituting equations (ii) and (iii) in equation (A), we get

$$(EI\ \theta_B - 36) + (1.67\ EI\ \theta_B + 0.83\ EI\ \theta_C + 156) = 0$$
$$2.67\ EI\ \theta_B + 0.83\ EI\ \theta_C + 120 = 0 \qquad \ldots (A)$$

Substituting equations (iv) and (v) in equation (B), we get
$$(1.67\ EI\ \theta_C + 0.83\ EI\ \theta_B - 156) + (0.67\ EI\ \theta_C + 0.33\ EI\ \theta_D + 32) = 0$$
$$0.83\ EI\ \theta_B + 2.34\ EI\ \theta_C + 0.33\ EI\ \theta_D - 124 = 0 \qquad \ldots (B)$$

Substituting equation (vi) in equation (C), we get
$$0.67\ EI\ \theta_D + 0.33\ EI\ \theta_C - 16 = -18$$
$$0.67\ EI\ \theta_D + 0.33\ EI\ \theta_C + 2 = 0 \qquad \ldots (C)$$

Step VI : Solution of equations for joint displacement :
$$\theta_B = \frac{-71.25}{EI},\quad \theta_C = \frac{84.62}{EI},\quad \theta_D = \frac{-44.66}{EI}$$

Step VII : Member-end moments :

Substituting values of above displacements in slope-deflection equations, member-end moments are obtained as under :

$$M_{AB} = 0.5\ EI\left(-\frac{71.25}{EI}\right) + 36 = 0.7\ kNm$$

$$M_{BA} = EI\left(-\frac{71.25}{EI}\right) - 36 = -107.25\ kNm$$

$$M_{BC} = 1.67\ EI\left(-\frac{71.25}{EI}\right) + 0.83\ EI\left(\frac{84.62}{EI}\right) + 156 = 107.25\ kNm$$

$$M_{CB} = 1.67\ EI\left(\frac{84.62}{EI}\right) + 0.83\ EI\left(-\frac{71.25}{EI}\right) - 156 = 14.08\ kNm$$

$$M_{CD} = 0.67\ EI\left(\frac{84.62}{EI}\right) + 0.33\ EI\left(-\frac{44.66}{EI}\right) + 32 = 74.08\ kNm$$

$$M_{DC} = 0.67\ EI\left(-\frac{44.66}{EI}\right) + 0.33\ EI\left(\frac{84.62}{EI}\right) - 16 = -18\ kNm$$

$$M_{DE} = 18\ kNm$$

Step VIII : FED of members : as shown in Fig. 1.13 (b).
Step IX : Shear force diagram : as shown in Fig. 1.13 (c).
Step X : Bending moment diagram :
BMD by superposition is shown in Fig. 1.13 (d).
BMD on tension side is shown in Fig. 1.13 (e).
Step XI : FBD of structure : as shown in Fig. 1.13 (f).

Example 1.6 : *A beam is fixed at A and D and continuous over supports B and C, AB = 9 m, BC = 6 m and CD = 8 m. The span AB carries UDL 20 kN/m, a concentrated load of 80 kN acts at the centre of BC and the span CD carries UDL of 15 kN/m. Analyse the beam using slope- deflection method. EI is given in Fig. 1.14 (a).*

Solution : (1) The beam is supported and loaded as shown in Fig. 1.14 (a).

(2) All supports are at same level.

Object : Structural analysis.

Equations : SD equations.

Procedure : Step I : Degree of kinematic indeterminacy = D_{ki} = 2.

Unknown displacements : θ_B, θ_C.

Known displacements : $\theta_A = \theta_D = 0$.

Step II : Fixed-end moments :

$$M_{AB}^F = -M_{AB}^F = \frac{WL^2}{12} = \frac{20 \times 9^2}{12} = 135 \text{ kN-m}$$

$$M_{BC}^F = -M_{CB}^F = \frac{WL}{8} = \frac{80 \times 6}{8} = 60 \text{ kN-m}$$

$$M_{CD}^F = -M_{DC}^F = \frac{WL^2}{12} = \frac{15 \times 8^2}{12} = 80 \text{ kN-m}$$

Step III : Slope-deflection equations :

Member AB :
$$M_{AB} = \frac{4EI}{L}(\theta_A) + \frac{2EI}{L}(\theta_B) \pm \frac{6EI\Delta}{L^2} + M_{AB}^F = \frac{2E}{9}\left(\frac{4}{3}I\right)\theta_B + 135$$

$$= 0.29EI\,\theta_B + 135 \qquad \ldots \text{(i)}$$

$$M_{BA} = \frac{4EI}{L}(\theta_B) + \frac{2EI}{L}(\theta_A) \pm \frac{6EI\Delta}{L^2} + M_{BA}^F = \frac{4E}{9}\left(\frac{4}{3}I\right)\theta_B - 135$$

$$= 0.59EI\,\theta_B - 135 \qquad \ldots \text{(ii)}$$

Member BC :
$$M_{BC} = \frac{4EI}{L}(\theta_B) + \frac{2EI}{L}(\theta_C) \pm \frac{6EI\Delta}{L^2} + M_{BC}^F$$

$$= \frac{4E}{6}\left(\frac{2}{3}I\right)\theta_B + \frac{2E}{6}\left(\frac{2}{3}I\right)\theta_C + 60$$

$$= 0.44EI\,\theta_B + 0.22EI\,\theta_C + 60 \qquad \ldots \text{(iii)}$$

$$M_{CB} = \frac{4EI}{L}(\theta_C) + \frac{2EI}{L}(\theta_B) \pm \frac{6EI\Delta}{L^2} + M_{CB}^F$$

$$= \frac{4E}{6}\left(\frac{2}{3}I\right)\theta_C + \frac{2E}{6}\left(\frac{2}{3}I\right)\theta_B - 60$$

STRUCTURAL ANALYSIS – II   SLOPE-DEFLECTION METHOD

$$= 0.44EI\,\theta_C + 0.22EI\,\theta_B - 60 \qquad \ldots \text{(iv)}$$

Member CD : $\quad M_{CD} = \dfrac{4EI}{L}(\theta_C) + \dfrac{2EI}{L}(\theta_D) + \dfrac{6EI\Delta}{L^2} + M_{CD}^F = \dfrac{4EI}{8}\theta_C + 80$

$$= 0.5EI\,\theta_C + 80 \qquad \ldots \text{(v)}$$

$$M_{DC} = \dfrac{4EI}{L}(\theta_D) + \dfrac{2EI}{L}(\theta_C) \pm \dfrac{6EI\Delta}{L^2} + M_{DC}^F = \dfrac{2EI}{8}(\theta_C) - 80$$

$$= 0.25EI\,\theta_C - 80 \qquad \ldots \text{(vi)}$$

Step IV : Moment equilibrium condition for joint :

At joint B : $\quad M_{BA} + M_{BC} = 09 \qquad \ldots \text{(A)}$

At joint C : $\quad M_{CB} + M_{CD} = 0 \qquad \ldots \text{(B)}$

Step V : Formulation of equilibrium equations in terms of joint displacement.

Substituting equations (ii) and (iii) in equation (A),

$$0.593EI\,\theta_B - 135 + 0.444EI\,\theta_B + 0.222EI\,\theta_C + 60 = 0$$

$$1.037EI\,\theta_B + 0.222EI\,\theta_C - 75 = 0 \qquad \ldots \text{(A)}$$

Substituting equations (iv) and (v) in equation (B),

$$0.444EI\,\theta_C + 0.222EI\,\theta_B - 60 + 0.5EI\,\theta_C + 80 = 0$$

$$0.222EI\,\theta_B + 0.944EI\,\theta_C + 20 = 0 \qquad \ldots \text{(B)}$$

Step VI : Solution of equations for joint displacement :

$$\theta_B = \dfrac{80.93}{EI},\quad \theta_C = -\dfrac{40.22}{EI}$$

Step VII : Member-end moments :

$$M_{AB} = 0.296EI\left(\dfrac{80.93}{EI}\right) + 135 = 159.95\ \text{kN-m}$$

$$M_{BA} = 0.593EI\left(\dfrac{80.93}{EI}\right) - 135 = 87.01\ \text{kN-m}$$

$$M_{BC} = 0.444EI\left(\dfrac{81.43}{EI}\right) + 0.222EI\left(-\dfrac{40.33}{EI}\right) + 60 = 87.01\ \text{kN-m}$$

$$M_{CB} = 0.444EI\left(-\dfrac{40.22}{EI}\right) + 0.222EI\left(\dfrac{80.93}{EI}\right) - 60 = -59.89\ \text{kN-m}$$

$$M_{CD} = 0.5EI\left(-\dfrac{40.22}{EI}\right) + 80 = 59.89\ \text{kN-m}$$

$$M_{DC} = 0.25EI\left(-\dfrac{40.22}{EI}\right) - 80 = -90.06\ \text{kN-m}$$

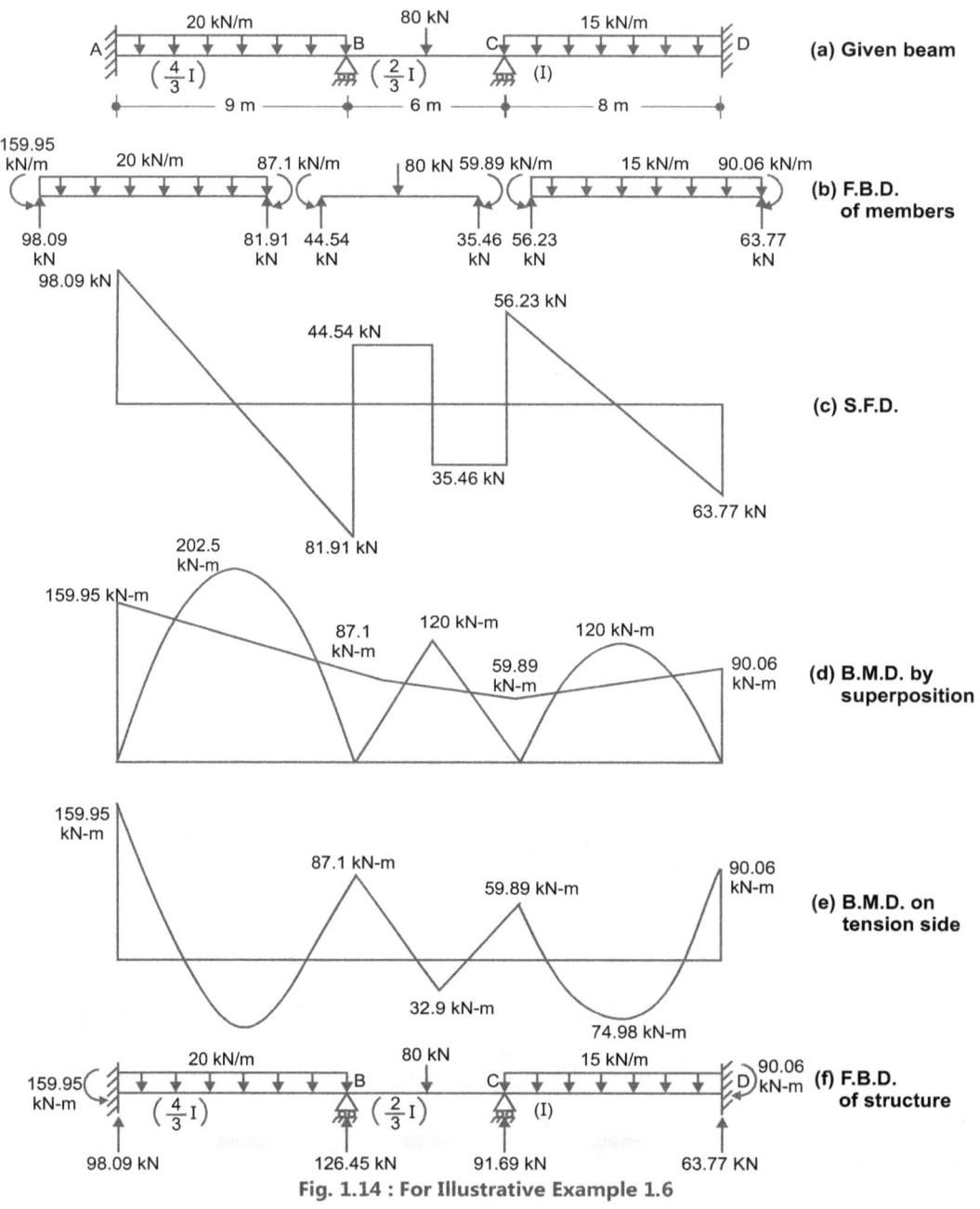

Fig. 1.14 : For Illustrative Example 1.6

Step VIII : FBD of members is as shown in Fig. 1.14 (b).

Step IX : Shear force diagram is as shown in Fig. 1.14 (c).

Step X : Bending moment diagram.

BMD by superposition is as shown in Fig. 1.14 (d).

BMD on tension side is as shown in Fig. 1.14 (e).

Step XI : FBD of structure is as shown in Fig. 1.14 (f).

Example 1.7 : *A continuous beam ABCD is fixed at D and continuous over supports B and C and portion AB is overhanged. The beam is loaded as shown in Fig. 1.15 (a). Analyse the beam using slope-deflection deflection method. The support D sinks by 2 mm. Draw SFD and BMD. $E = 2 \times 10^5$ N/mm^2, $I = 10,000$ cm^4.*

Solution : (1) Data : The beam is loaded and supported as shown in Fig. 1.15 (a).

(2) Supports B and C are at same level and support D sinks by 2 mm.

Object : Structural analysis.

Equations : SD equations.

Procedure : Step I : Degree of kinematic indeterminacy = D_{ki} = 2.

Unknown displacements : θ_B, θ_C, θ_D.

Step II : Fixed-end moments.

$$M_{BA}^F = -10 \times 2 = -20 \text{ kN-m}$$

$$M_{BC}^F = -M_{CB}^F = \frac{WL^2}{12} = \frac{16 \times 6^2}{12} = 48 \text{ kN-m}$$

$$M_{CD}^F = -M_{DC}^F = \frac{WL}{8} = \frac{8 \times 4}{8} = 4 \text{ kN-m}$$

Step III : Slope-deflection equations.

$$EI = 2 \times 10^5 \times 10000 \times 10^4 = 2 \times 10^{13} \text{ N-mm}^2 = 2 \times 10^4 \text{ kN-m}^2$$

Member AB : $M_{BA} = M_{BA}^F = -20$ kN-m ... (i)

Memebr BC :
$$M_{BC} = \frac{4 EI}{L}(\theta_B) + \frac{2 EI}{L}(\theta_C) + \frac{6 EI\Delta}{L^2} + M_{BC}^F$$

$$= \frac{4 EI}{6}(\theta_B) + \frac{2 EI}{6}(\theta_C) + 48$$

$$= 0.67 \, EI \, \theta_B + 0.33 \, EI \, \theta_C + 48 \quad ... (ii)$$

$$M_{CB} = \frac{4 EI}{L}(\theta_C) + \frac{2 EI}{L}(\theta_B) \pm \frac{6 EI\Delta}{L^2} - 48$$

$$= \frac{4\,EI}{6}(\theta_C) + \frac{2\,EI}{6}(\theta_B) - 48$$

$$= 0.67\,EI\,\theta_C + 0.33\,EI\,\theta_B - 48 \quad \ldots \text{(iii)}$$

Member CD :
$$M_{CD} = \frac{4\,EI}{L}(\theta_C) + \frac{2\,EI}{L}(\theta_D) \pm \frac{6\,EI\Delta}{L^2} + M^F_{CD}$$

$$= \frac{4EI}{4}\left(\theta_C + \frac{2EI}{4}\theta_D\right) + \frac{6 \times 2 \times 10^4 \times 2 \times 10^{-3}}{4^2} + 4$$

$$= EI\,\theta_C + 0.5\,EI\,\theta_D + 15 + 4$$

$$= EI\,\theta_C + 0.5\,EI\,\theta_D + 19 \quad \ldots \text{(iv)}$$

$$M_{DC} = \frac{4\,EI}{L}(\theta_D) + \frac{2\,EI}{L}(\theta_C) + \frac{6\,EI\Delta}{L^2} + M^F_{DC}$$

$$= \frac{4\,EI}{4}(\theta_D) + \frac{2\,EI}{4}(\theta_C) + \frac{6 \times 2 \times 10^4 \times 2 \times 10^{-3}}{4^2} - 4$$

$$= EI\,\theta_D + 0.5\,EI\,\theta_C + 15 - 4$$

$$= EI\,\theta_D + 0.5\,EI\,\theta_C + 11 \quad \ldots \text{(v)}$$

Step IV : Moment equilibrium conditions for joint.

At joint B : $M_{BA} + M_{BC} = 0$ ... (A)

At joint C : $M_{CB} + M_{CD} = 0$ ... (B)

At joint D : $M_{DC} = 0$ ... (C)

Step V : Formulation of equilibrium equations in terms of joint displacement.

Substituting equations (i) and (ii) equation (A),

$- 20 + 0.667\,EI\,\theta_B + 0.333\,EI\,\theta_C + 48 = 0$

$0.667\,EI\,\theta_B + 0.333\,EI\,\theta_C + 28 = 0$ ... (I)

Substituting equations (iii) and (iv) in equation (B),

$0.667\,EI\,\theta_C + 0.33\,EI\,\theta_B - 48 + EI\,\theta_C + 0.5\,EI\,\theta_D + 19 = 0$

$1.667\,EI\,\theta_C + 0.33\,EI\,\theta_B + 0.5\,EI\,\theta_D - 29 = 0$ ... (II)

Substituting equation (v) in equation (C),

$EI\,\theta_D + 0.5\,EI\,\theta_C + 11 = 0$ ... (III)

Step VI : Solution of equation for joint displacement.

$$\theta_B = -\frac{61.33}{EI}, \quad \theta_C = \frac{38.76}{EI}, \quad \theta_D = -\frac{30.38}{EI}$$

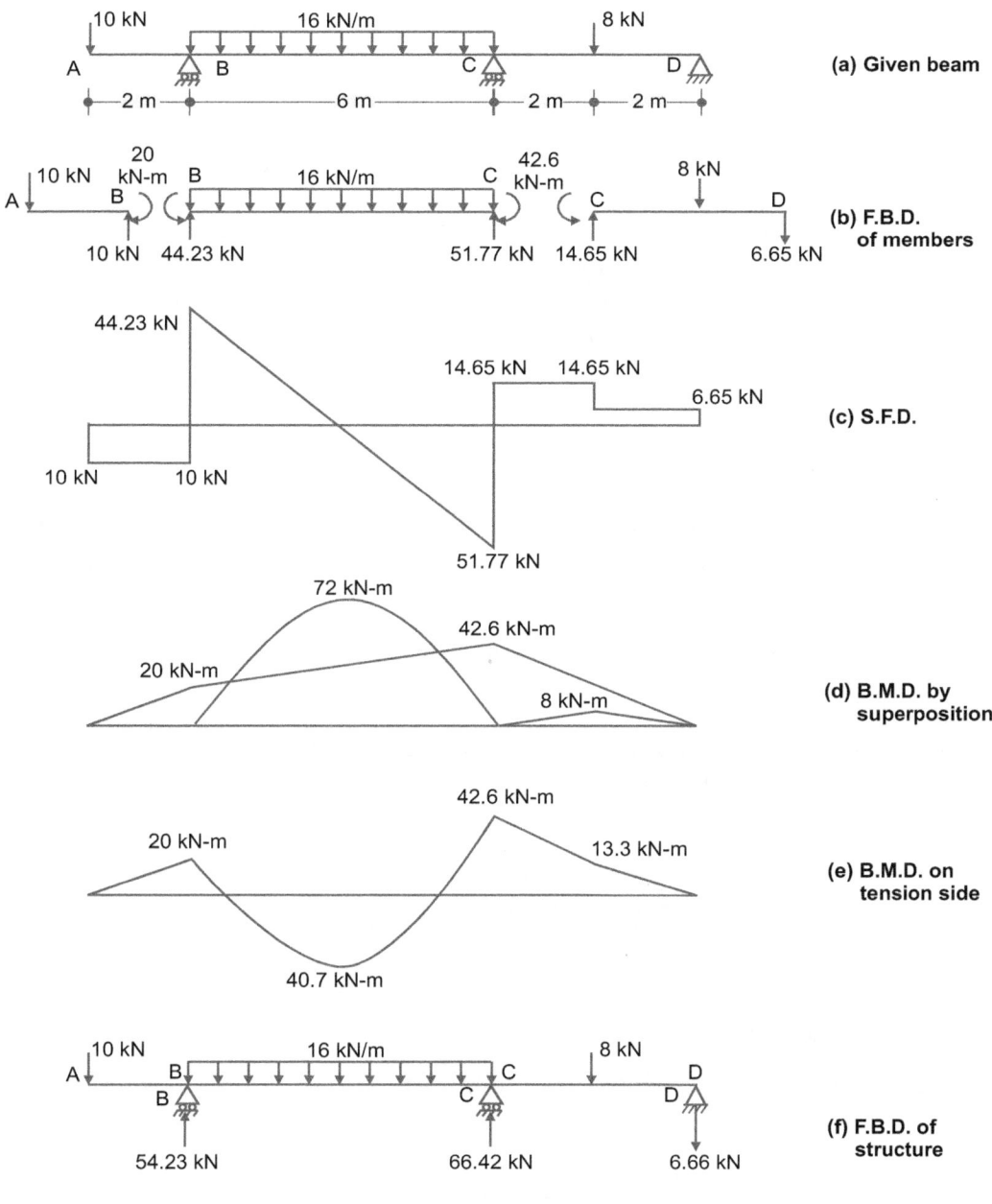

Fig. 1.15 : For Illustrative Example 1.7

Step VII : Member-end moments :

$$M_{BA} = -20 \text{ kN-m}$$

$$M_{BC} = 0.67 \text{ EI}\left(-\frac{61.33}{EI}\right) + 0.333 \text{ EI}\left(\frac{38.76}{EI}\right) + 48 = 20 \text{ kN-m}$$

$$M_{CB} = 0.67 \text{ EI}\left(\frac{38.76}{EI}\right) + 0.33 \text{ EI}\left(-\frac{61.33}{EI}\right) - 48 = -42.6 \text{ kN-m}$$

$$M_{CD} = \text{EI}\left(\frac{38.76}{EI}\right) + 0.5 \text{ EI}\left(-\frac{30.38}{EI}\right) + 19 = 42.6 \text{ kN-m}$$

$$M_{DC} = \text{EI}\left(\frac{-30.38}{EI}\right) + 0.5 \text{ EI}\left(\frac{38.76}{EI}\right) + 11 = 0$$

Step VIII : FBD of members is as shown in Fig. 1.15 (b).
Step IX : Shear force diagram is as shown in Fig. 1.15 (c).
Step X : Bending moment diagram.
BMD by superposition is as shown in Fig. 1.15 (d).
BMD on tension side is as shown in Fig. 1.15 (e).
Step XI : FBD of structure is as shown in Fig. 1.15 (f).

Example 1.8 : *A beam is supported and loaded as shown in Fig. 1.16 (a). The support B sinks by 25 mm. EI of the beam is 3800 kN-m². Using slope-deflection method, analyse the beam and draw SFD and BMD.*

Solution : (1) Data : The beam is supported and loaded as shown in Fig. 1.16 (b).
(2) Supports A and C are at same level and B sinks by 25 mm.
Object : Structural analysis.
Equations : SD equations.
Procedure : Step I : Degree of kinematic indeterminacy = D_{ki} = 2.
Unknown displacements : θ_B, θ_C.
Step II : Fixed-end moments :

$$M^F_{AB} = -M^F_{BA} = \frac{Wl^2}{12} = \frac{10 \times 6^2}{12} = 30 \text{ kN-m}$$

$$M^F_{BC} = \frac{Wab^2}{L^2} = \frac{30 \times 2 \times 4^2}{6^2} = 26.67 \text{ kN-m}$$

$$M^F_{CB} = -\frac{Wa^2b}{L^2} = -\frac{30 \times 2^2 \times 4}{6^2} = -13.33 \text{ kN-m}$$

Step III : Slope-deflection equations :

Member AB : $M_{AB} = \frac{4 \text{ EI}}{L}(\theta_A) + \frac{2 \text{ EI}}{L}(\theta_B) \pm \frac{6 \text{ EI}\Delta}{L^2} + M^F_{AB}$

$$= \frac{4 \text{ EI}}{6}(\theta_A) + \frac{2 \text{ EI}}{6}(\theta_B) + \frac{6 \text{ EI}(\Delta)}{6^2} + 30$$

$$= 0.33 \text{EI } \theta_B + \frac{6 \times 3500 \times 25 \times 10^{-3}}{6^2} + 30$$

$$= 0.33\, EI\, \theta_B + 15.83 + 30 = 0.33\, EI\, \theta_B + 45.83 \qquad \ldots (i)$$

$$M_{BA} = \frac{4\,EI}{L}(\theta_B) + \frac{2\,EI}{L}(\theta_A) + \frac{6\,EI\Delta}{L^2} + M^F_{BA}$$

$$= \frac{4\,EI}{6}(\theta_B) + \frac{2\,EI}{6}(\theta_A) + \frac{6 \times 3800 \times 25 \times 10^{-3}}{6^2} - 30$$

$$= 0.67\, EI\, \theta_B - 14.17 \qquad \ldots (ii)$$

Member BC :

$$M_{BC} = \frac{4\,EI}{L}(\theta_B) + \frac{2\,EI}{L}(\theta_C) - \frac{6\,EI\Delta}{L^2} + M^F_{BC}$$

$$= \frac{4\,EI}{6}(\theta_B) + \frac{2\,EI}{6}(\theta_C) - \frac{6 \times 3800 \times 25 \times 10^{-3}}{6^2} + 26.67$$

$$= 0.67\, EI\, \theta_B + 0.33\, EI\, \theta_C - 15.83 + 26.67$$

$$= 0.67\, EI\, \theta_B + 0.33\, EI\, \theta_C + 10.84 \qquad \ldots (iii)$$

$$M_{CB} = \frac{4\,EI}{L}(\theta_C) + \frac{2\,EI}{L}(\theta_B) - \frac{6\,EI\Delta}{L^2} + M^F_{CB}$$

$$= \frac{4\,EI}{6}(\theta_C) + \frac{2\,EI}{6}(\theta_B) - \frac{6 \times 3800 \times 25 \times 10^{-3}}{6^2} - 13.33$$

$$= 0.67\, EI\, \theta_C + 0.33\, EI\, \theta_B - 29.16 \qquad \ldots (iv)$$

Step IV : Moment equilibrium condition for joint.
At joint B : $M_{BA} + M_{BC} = 0$ $\qquad \ldots$ (A)
At joint C : $\qquad M_{CB} = 0$ $\qquad \ldots$ (B)

Step V : Formulation of equilibrium equations in terms of joint displacement.
Substituting equations (ii) and (iii) in equation (A),
$\quad 0.667\, EI\, \theta_B - 14.17 + 0.667\, EI\, \theta_B + 0.33\, EI\, \theta_C + 10.84 = 0$
$\quad 1.334\, EI\, \theta_B + 0.333\, EI\, \theta_C - 3.33 = 0$ $\qquad \ldots$ (I)
Substituting equation (iv) in equation (B),
$\quad 0.667\, EI\, \theta_C + 0.333\, EI\, \theta_B - 29.16 = 0$ $\qquad \ldots$ (II)

Step VI : Solution of equations for joint displacement.

$$\theta_B = \frac{-9.64}{EI}, \quad \theta_C = \frac{48.55}{EI}$$

Step VII : Member-end moments.

$$M_{AB} = 0.333\, EI \left(\frac{-9.64}{EI}\right) + 45.83 = 42.62 \text{ kN-m}$$

$$M_{BA} = 0.667\, EI \left(\frac{-9.64}{EI}\right) - 14.17 = -20.58 \text{ kN-m}$$

$$M_{BC} = 0.667\, EI \left(\frac{-9.64}{EI}\right) + 0.333\, EI \left(\frac{48.55}{EI}\right) + 10.84 = 20.58 \text{ kN-m}$$

$$M_{CB} = 0.67\, EI \left(\frac{48.14}{EI}\right) + 0.333\, EI \left(\frac{-9.37}{EI}\right) - 29.16 = 0$$

STRUCTURAL ANALYSIS – II SLOPE-DEFLECTION METHOD

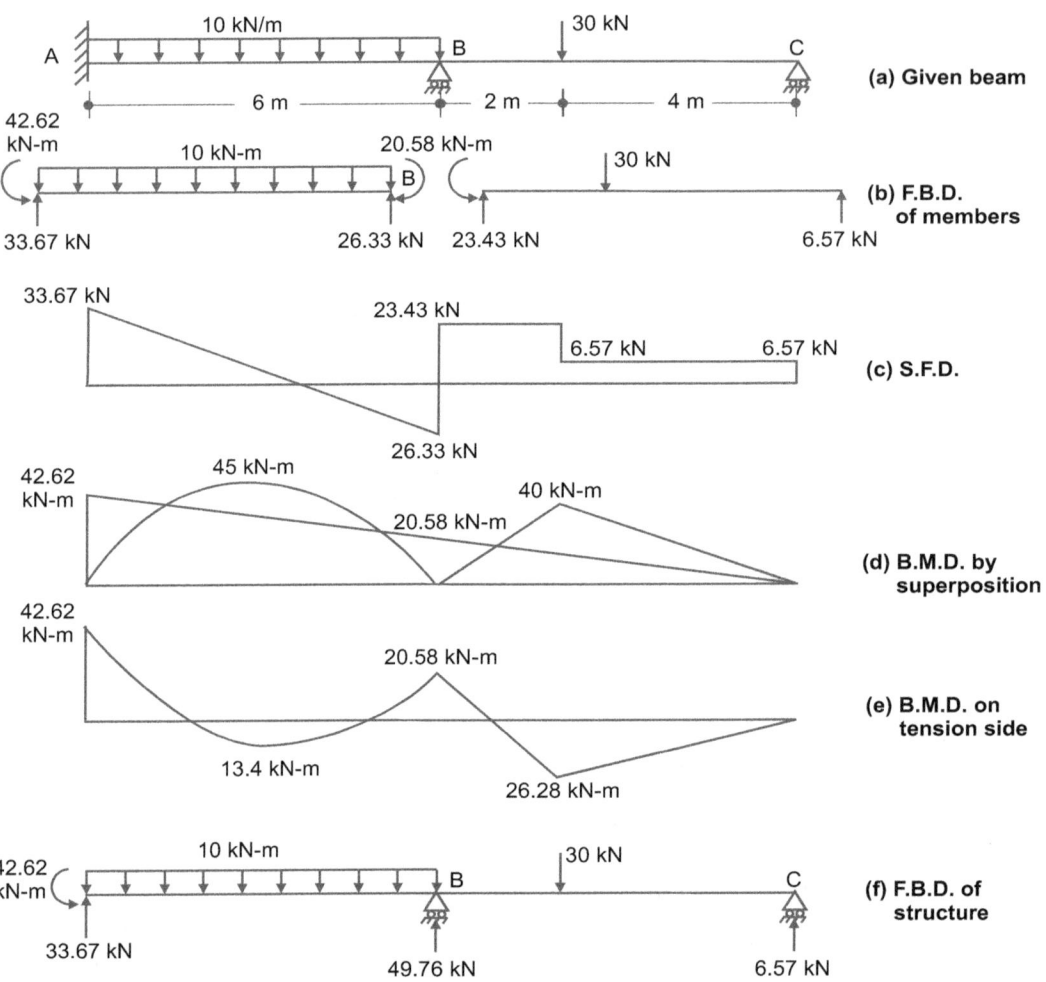

Fig. 1.16 : For Illustrative Example 1.8

Step VIII : FBD of members is as shown in Fig. 1.16 (b).

Step IX : Shear force diagram is as shown in Fig. 1.16 (c).

Step X : Bending moment diagram.

   BMD by superposition is as shown in Fig. 1.16 (d).

   BMD on tension side is as shown in Fig. 1.16 (e).

Step XI : FBD of structure is as shown in Fig. 1.16 (f).

1.8.3 Beams with Unknown Joint Translations

When a beam consists of non-prismatic member between the supports, additional joint is considered at the point where moment of inertia changes. At this point, both translation and rotation exist. Therefore, shear equilibrium exists and the general procedure of SD method is used.

The shear equilibrium for such a case is illustrated in Fig. 1.17 and developed as follows :

In FBD of the members connected to supports, only positive member-end moments and member-end shears at supports are shown in Fig. 1.17 (b). For FBD of AB and applying $\sum M_B = 0$, V_A is obtained as follows :

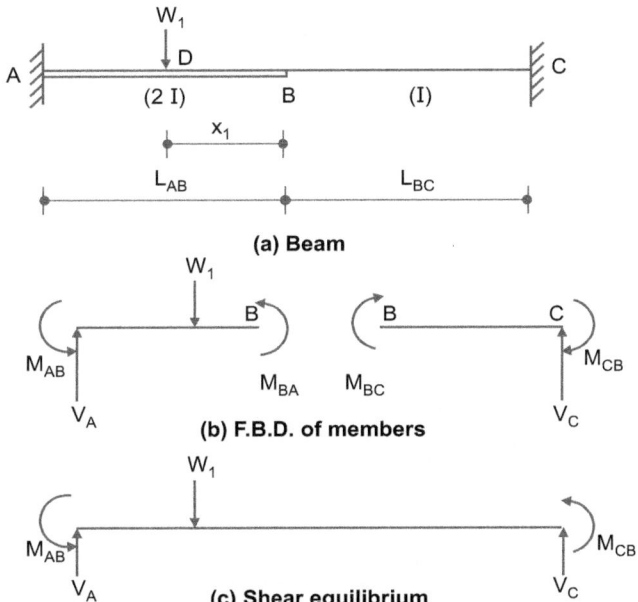

Fig. 1.17 : Shear equilibrium of beam

$$V_A \times L_{AB} - W_1 \times x_1 - M_{AB} - M_{BA} = 0$$

i.e. $$V_A = \frac{M_{AB} + M_{BA} + W_1 x_1}{L_{AB}}$$

For FBD of BC, $\sum M_B = 0$ will lead to

$$V_C \times L_{BC} - M_{BC} - M_{CB} = 0$$

i.e. $$V_C = \frac{M_{BC} + M_{CB}}{L_{BC}}$$

Considering only forces shown in FBD of structure, shear equilibrium equation is given by,

$$V_A - V_C = W_1$$

i.e. $\left(\dfrac{M_{AB} + M_{BA} + W_1 x_1}{L_{AB}}\right) - \left(\dfrac{M_{BC} + M_{CB}}{L_{BC}}\right) = W_1$ ... (1.5)

1.8.4 Application of SD Method to Beams with Unknown Joint Translations

Example 1.9 *: Analyse the beam shown in Fig. 1.18 (a) by slope-defection method. Draw SFD, BMD and elastic curve.*

Solution : (1) Data : The beam is supported and loaded as shown in Fig. 1.18 (a).

(2) All supports are at same level.

(3) **Object :** Structural analysis.

Equations : SD equations.

Procedure :

Step I : Degree of kinematic indeterminacy D_{ki} = 2. (Considering point B as node).

Unknown displacements = θ_B; Δ_B

Known displacements = $\theta_A = \theta_C = 0$

Step II : Fixed-end moments :

$$M_{AB}^F = -M_{BA}^F = \dfrac{WL}{8} = \dfrac{100 \times 2}{8} = 25 \text{ kNm}$$

$$M_{BC}^F = M_{CB}^F = 0$$

Step III : SD equations : (Assuming Δ_B upwards i.e. positive).

Member AB :

$$M_{AB} = \dfrac{4EI}{L}(\theta_A) + \dfrac{2EI}{L}(\theta_B) \pm \dfrac{6EI}{L^2}(\Delta_B) + M_{AB}^F$$

$$= \dfrac{2(2EI)}{2}(\theta_B) - \dfrac{6(2EI)}{2^2}(\Delta_B) + 25$$

$$= 2EI(\theta_B) - 3EI(\Delta_B) + 25 \qquad ... (i)$$

$$M_{BA} = \dfrac{4EI}{L}(\theta_B) + \dfrac{2EI}{L}(\theta_A) + \dfrac{6EI}{L^2}(\Delta_B) + M_{BA}^F$$

$$= \dfrac{4(2EI)}{2}(\theta_B) - \dfrac{6(2EI)}{2^2}(\Delta_B) - 25$$

$$= 4EI(\theta_B) - 3EI(\Delta_B) - 25 \qquad ... (ii)$$

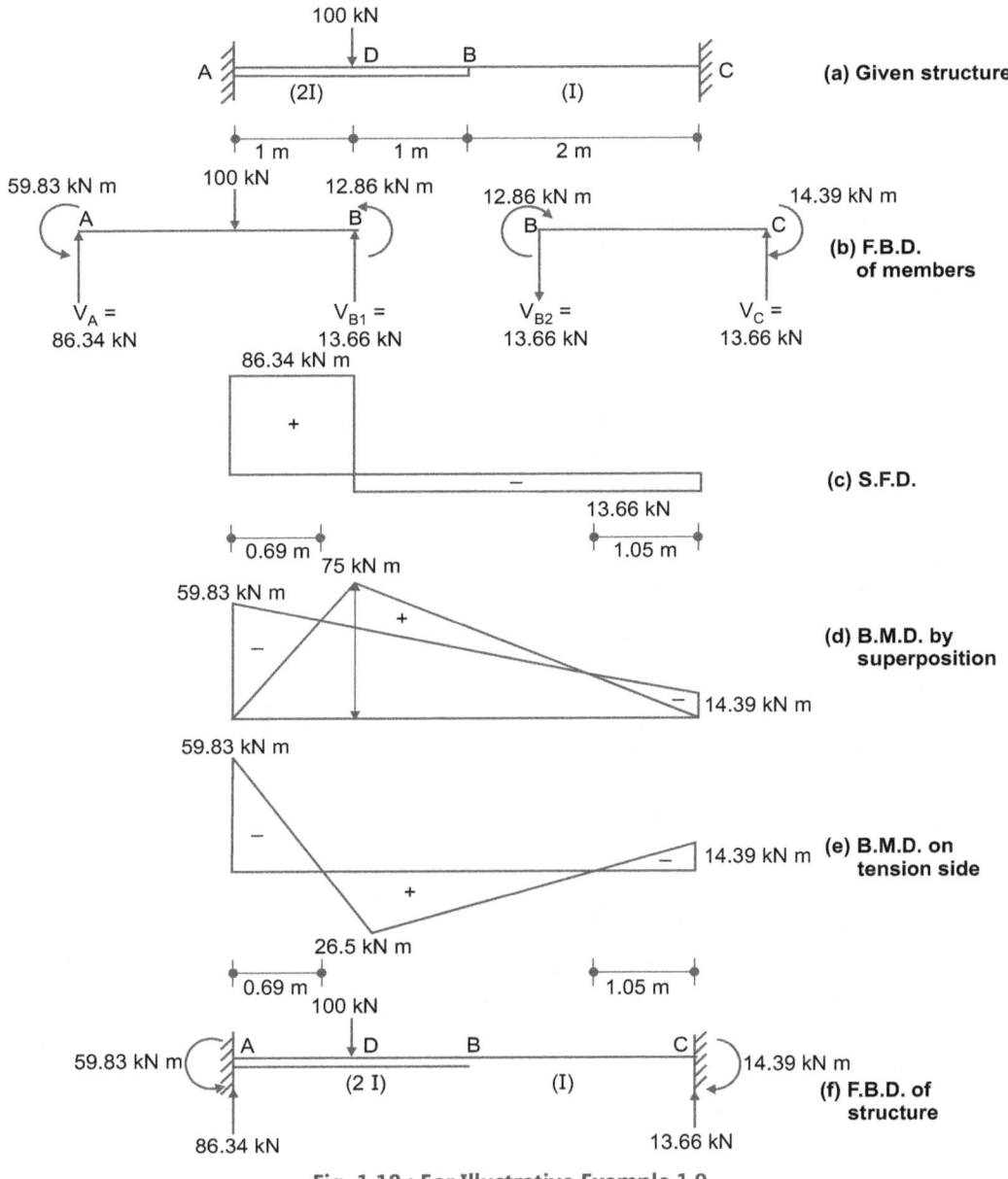

Fig. 1.18 : For Illustrative Example 1.9

Member BC : $\quad M_{BC} = \dfrac{4\,EI}{L}(\theta_B) + \dfrac{2\,EI}{L}(\theta_C) \pm \dfrac{6\,EI}{L^2}(\Delta_B) + M_{BC}^F$

$$= \frac{4EI}{2}(\theta_B) + \frac{6EI}{2^2}(\Delta_B) = 2EI(\theta_B) + 1.5EI(\Delta_B) \quad \ldots \text{(iii)}$$

$$M_{CB} = \frac{4EI}{L}(\theta_C) + \frac{2EI}{L}(\theta_B) \pm \frac{6EI}{L^2}(\Delta_B) + M_{CB}^F$$

$$= \frac{2EI}{2}(\theta_B) + \frac{6EI}{2^2}(\Delta_B) = EI(\theta_B) + 1.5EI(\Delta_B) \quad \ldots \text{(iv)}$$

Step IV : Equilibrium conditions for joints :

Moment equilibrium at joint B; $\quad M_{AB} + M_{BC} = 0 \quad \ldots \text{(A)}$

Shear equilibrium for structure, $\quad V_A - V_C - 100 = 0 \quad \ldots \text{(B)}$

where, $V_A = \dfrac{M_{AB} + M_{BA}}{2} + 50$ and $V_C = \dfrac{M_{BC} + M_{CB}}{2}$

equation (B) becomes,

$$\left(\frac{M_{AB} + M_{BA}}{2} + 50\right) - \left(\frac{M_{BC} + M_{CB}}{2}\right) - 100 = 0$$

$$M_{AB} + M_{BA} + 100 - M_{BC} - M_{CB} - 200 = 0$$

i.e. $\quad M_{AB} + M_{BA} - M_{BC} - M_{CB} = 100 \quad \ldots \text{(B)}$

Step V : Formulation of equilibrium equations in terms of joint displacements.

Substituting equations (ii) and (iii) in equation (A), we get

$[4EI(\theta_B) - 3EI(\Delta_B) - 25] + [2EI(\theta_B) + 1.5EI(\Delta_B)] = 0$

$$6EI(\theta_B) - 1.5EI(\Delta_B) - 25] \quad \ldots \text{(A)}$$

Substituting equations (i), (ii), (iii) and (iv) in equation (B), we get

$[2EI(\theta_B) - 3EI(\Delta_B) + 25] + [4EI(\theta_B) - 3EI(\Delta_B) - 25] -$
$\quad [2EI(\theta_B) + 1.5EI(\Delta_B)] - [EI(\theta_B) + 1.5EI(\Delta_B)] = 100$

$$3EI(\theta_B) - 9EI(\Delta_B) = 100 \quad \ldots \text{(B)}$$

Step VI : Solution of equations for joint displacements : Solving equations (A) and (B), we get,

$$\boxed{\theta_B = \frac{1.515}{EI} \text{ and } \Delta_B = -\frac{10.60}{EI}}$$

Step VII : Member-end moments : Substituting the values of above displacements in SD equations, member-end moments are obtained as under :

$$M_{AB} = 2EI\left(\frac{1.515}{EI}\right) - 3EI\left(-\frac{10.60}{EI}\right) + 25 = 59.83 \text{ kNm}$$

$$M_{BA} = 4EI\left(\frac{1.515}{EI}\right) - 3EI\left(\frac{-10.60}{EI}\right) - 25 = 12.86 \text{ kNm}$$

$$M_{BC} = 2EI\left(\frac{1.515}{EI}\right) + 1.5EI\left(-\frac{10.60}{EI}\right) = -12.86 \text{ kNm}$$

$$M_{CB} = EI\left(\frac{1.515}{EI}\right) + 1.5EI\left(-\frac{10.60}{EI}\right) = -14.385 \text{ kNm}$$

Step VIII : FBD of members is as shown in Fig. 1.14 (b). Support reactions :
$\sum M_B = 0_{(AB)}$, $59.83 + 12.86 + 100 \times 1 - V_A \times 2 = 0 \Rightarrow V_A = 86.345$ kN (↑)
$\sum F_y = 0$; $V_A + V_C = 100$ $V_C = 13.655$ (↑)

Step IX : Shear force diagram is as shown in Fig. 1.18 (c).

Step X : Bending moment diagram :
BMD by superposition is shown in Fig. 1.18 (d).
BMD on tension side is shown in Fig. 1.18 (e).

Step XI : FBD of structure is as shown in Fig. 1.18 (f).

Example 1.10 : *Analyse the beam shown in Fig. 1.19 (a) by slope-deflection method. Draw SFD and BMD.*

Solution : (1) Data : The beam is supported and loaded as shown in Fig. 1.19 (a).
(2) All supports are at same level.

Object : Structural analysis.

Equations : SD equations.

Procedure :

Step I : Degree of kinematic indeterminacy = $D_{ki} = 3$.
Unknown displacements : $\theta_{BA}, \theta_{BC}, \Delta_B$.
Known displacements : $\theta_A = \theta_C = 0$.

Step II : Fixed-end moments :

$$M^F_{AB} = -M^F_{BA} = \frac{wl^2}{12} = \frac{60 \times 1^2}{12} = 5 \text{ kNm}$$

$$M^F_{BC} = -M^F_{CB} = \frac{wl^2}{12} = \frac{60 \times 2^2}{12} = 20 \text{ kNm}$$

Step III : SD equations : (Assuming Δ_B upwards i.e. positive).

Member AB : $M_{AB} = \frac{4EI}{L}(\theta_A) + \frac{2EI}{L}(\theta_{BA}) \pm \frac{6EI}{L^2}(\Delta) + M^F_{AB}$

$= 2EI(\theta_{BA}) - 6EI(\Delta) + 5$ ... (i)

$M_{BA} = \frac{4EI}{L}(\theta_{BA}) + \frac{2EI}{L}(\theta_A) \pm \frac{6EI}{L^2}(\Delta) + M^F_{BA}$

$= 4EI(\theta_{BA}) - 6EI(\Delta) - 5$ ... (ii)

Member BC : $M_{BC} = \frac{4EI}{L}(\theta_{BC}) + \frac{2EI}{L}(\theta_C) \pm \frac{6EI}{L^2}(\Delta) + M^F_{BC}$

$= \frac{4EI}{2}(\theta_{BC}) + \frac{6EI}{2^2}(\Delta) + 20$

$= 2EI(\theta_{BC}) + 1.5EI(\Delta) + 20$ ... (iii)

$M_{CB} = \frac{4EI}{L}(\theta_C) + \frac{2EI}{L}(\theta_{BC}) \pm \frac{6EI}{L^2}(\Delta) + M^F_{CB}$

STRUCTURAL ANALYSIS – II SLOPE-DEFLECTION METHOD

$$= \frac{2\,EI}{2}(\theta_{BC}) + \frac{6\,EI}{2^2}(\Delta) - 20$$

$$= EI(\theta_{BC}) + 1.5\,EI(\Delta) - 20 \qquad \ldots \text{(iv)}$$

Step IV : Equilibrium conditions for joint. Moment equilibrium at joint B,

$$M_{BA} = 0 \qquad \ldots \text{(A)}$$

and

$$M_{BC} = 0 \qquad \ldots \text{(B)}$$

Shear equilibrium of structure,

$$V_A - V_C - 60 \times 3 = 0 \qquad \ldots \text{(C)}$$

where,

$$V_A = M_{AB} + M_{BA} + 60 \times 1 \times \frac{1}{2} = M_{AB} + M_{BA} + 30$$

$$V_C = \frac{M_{CB} + M_{BC}}{2} - 60$$

Equation (C) becomes,

$$[M_{AB} + M_{BA} + 30] - \left[\frac{M_{CB} + M_{BC}}{2} - 60\right] - 180 = 0$$

$$M_{AB} + M_{BA} - \left[\frac{M_{CB} + M_{BC}}{2}\right] - 90 = 0 \qquad \ldots \text{(C)}$$

Step V : Formulation of equilibrium equations in terms of displacements :

Substituting equation (ii) in equation (A), we get

$$4\,EI(\theta_{BA}) - 6\,EI(\Delta) - 5 = 0 \qquad \ldots \text{(I)}$$

Substituting equation (iii) in equation (A), we get

$$2\,EI(\theta_{BC}) + 1.5\,EI(\Delta) + 20 = 0 \qquad \ldots \text{(II)}$$

Substituting equations (i), (ii), (iii) and (iv) in equation (C), we get

$$[2\,EI(\theta_{BA}) - 6\,EI(\Delta) + 5 + 4\,EI(\theta_{BA}) - 6\,EI(\Delta) - 5]$$

$$-\frac{1}{2}[2\,EI(\theta_{BC}) + 1.5\,EI(\Delta) + 20 + EI(\theta_{BC}) + 1.5\,EI(\Delta) - 20] - 90 = 0$$

$$6\,EI(\theta_{BA}) - 1.5\,EI(\theta_{BC}) - 13.5\,EI(\Delta) - 90 = 0 \qquad \ldots \text{(III)}$$

Step VI : Solution of equations for joint displacements :

Solving equations (I), (II) and (III), we get

$$\boxed{\theta_{BA} = -\frac{28.75}{EI};\ \theta_{BC} = \frac{5}{EI};\ \Delta = \frac{-20}{EI}}$$

Step VII : Member-end moments : Substituting the values of above joint displacements in
SD equations, member-end moments are obtained as under :

$$M_{AB} = 2\,EI\left(-\frac{28.75}{EI}\right) - 6\,EI\left(-\frac{20}{EI}\right) + 5 = 67.5 \text{ kNm}$$

$$M_{BA} = 4\,EI\left(-\frac{28.75}{EI}\right) - 6\,EI\left(-\frac{20}{EI}\right) - 5 = 0$$

STRUCTURAL ANALYSIS – II SLOPE-DEFLECTION METHOD

$$M_{BC} = 2EI\left(\frac{5}{EI}\right) + 1.5 EI\left(-\frac{20}{EI}\right) + 20 = 0$$

$$M_{CB} = EI\left(\frac{5}{EI}\right) + 1.5 EI\left(-\frac{20}{EI}\right) - 20 = -45 \text{ kNm}$$

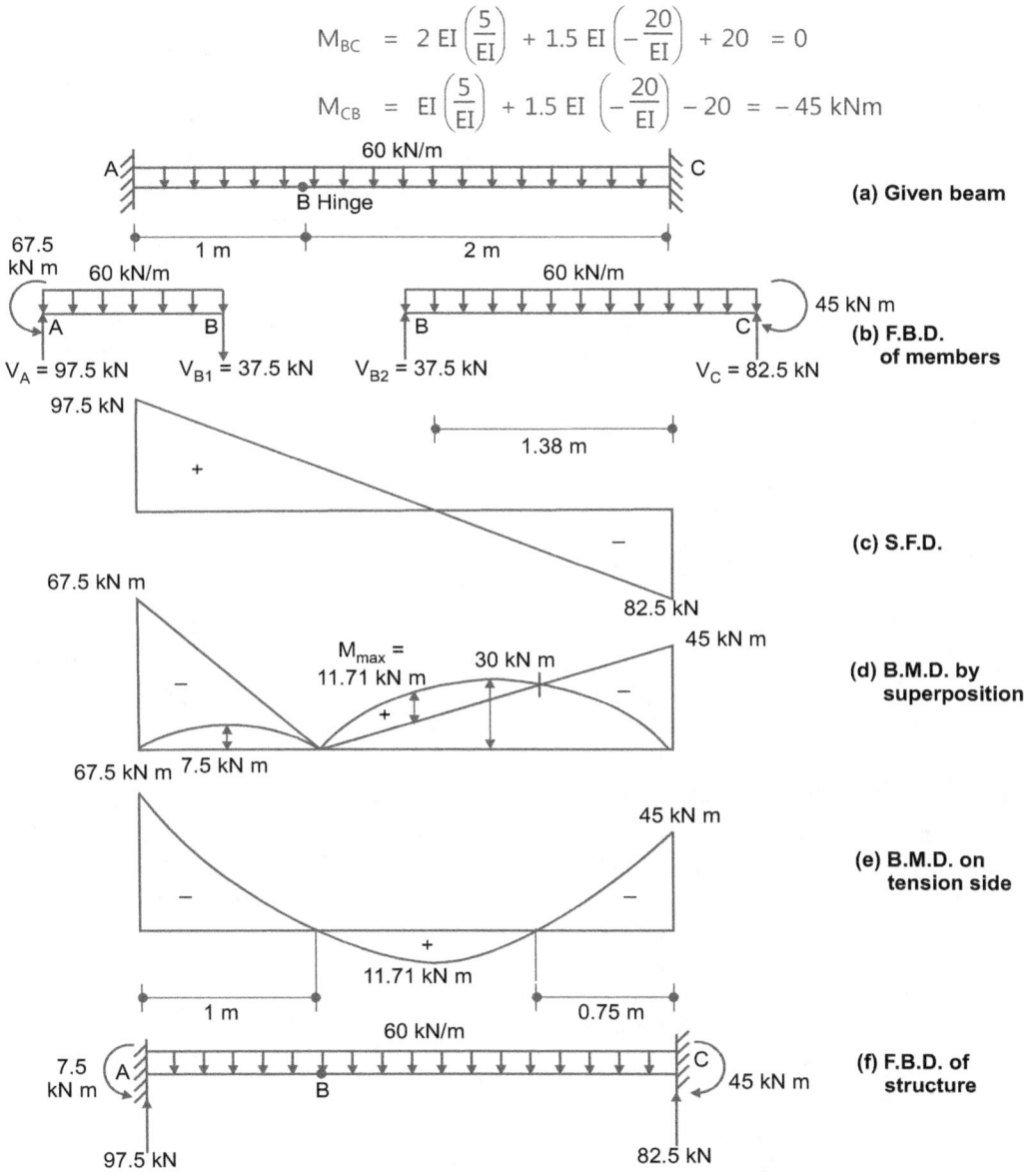

Fig. 1.19 : For Illustrative Example 1.10

Step VIII : FBD of members is as shown in Fig. 1.19 (b). Considering equilibrium of each member and of complete structure, all support reaction components are found out as shown in figure.

Step IX : Shear force diagram is as shown in Fig. 1.19 (c).
Step X : Bending moment diagram is BMD by superposition is shown in Fig. 1.19 (d). BMD on tension side is shown in Fig. 1.19 (e).
Step XI : FBD of structure is as shown in Fig. 1.19 (f).

1.9 SD Method Applied to Rectangular Frames

A structure, consisting of horizontal and vertical members connected by rigid joints is called a *rectangular frame*. Though the members are basically flexural members, the vertical members are called columns and horizontal members are beams. A large multibay, multi-storeyed frames are difficult to analyse by hand calculations of SD method because of large number of unknown displacements. Therefore, small frames like bent, single bay single storey frame, etc. are considered for analysis by SD method. The axial deformation is neglected. Therefore vertical translation is not possible if there is no uneven settlements of supports. The horizontal translation at a joint is called side sway or only sway. Axial forces are present as the shear of one member has effect of axial force on orthogonal member. Following cases of frames are involved in analysis by SD method.

1.9.1 Frames Without Sway or Non-Sway Frames

The basic requirement in such a frame is that all joints should not change the position during deformation. This may be possible because of constraints or configuration and loading condition. Symmetrical frames are non-sway frames. There should be symmetry in all respects i.e. configuration, supports, sectional properties, loads etc. Only joint rotations are unknown in a non- sway frame. A rigid joint implies one rotation. Moment equilibrium of joints formulates the analysis completely by SD method.

1.9.2 Application of SD Method to Non-Sway Frames

Example 1.11 : *Analyse the portal frame shown in Fig. 1.20 (a) by slope-deflection method. Draw SFD and BMD.*

Solution : (1) Data : The frame is supported and loaded as shown in Fig. 1.20 (a).
(2) Frame type : Non-sway frame.
(3) Structural analysis.

Equations : SD equations.

Procedure : Step I : Degree of kinematic indeterminacy = D_{ki} = 2

Unknown displacements : θ_B; θ_C.

Known displacements : $\theta_A = \theta_D = \theta_E = 0$. And horizontal sway = $\Delta = 0$.

Step II : Fixed-end moments :

$$M^F_{AB} = -M^F_{BA} = \frac{wl^2}{12} = \frac{40 \times 4^2}{12} = 53.33 \text{ kNm}$$

$$M^F_{BC} = -M^F_{CB} = \left[\frac{50 \times 1 \times 2^2}{3^2} + \frac{50 \times 2 \times 1^2}{3^2}\right] = 33.33 \text{ kNm}$$

STRUCTURAL ANALYSIS – II SLOPE-DEFLECTION METHOD

$$M_{DB}^F = M_{BD}^F = M_{EC}^F = M_{CE}^F = 0$$

Step III : SD equations :

Member AB :

$$M_{AB} = \frac{4EI}{L}(\theta_A) + \frac{2EI}{L}(\theta_B) \pm \frac{6EI}{L^2}(\Delta) + M_{AB}^F$$

$$= \frac{2(3EI)}{4}(\theta_B) + 53.33 = 1.5\,EI\,(\theta_B) + 53.33 \qquad \ldots (i)$$

$$M_{BA} = \frac{4EI}{L}(\theta_B) + \frac{2EI}{L}(\theta_A) \pm \frac{6EI}{L^2} + M_{BA}^F$$

$$= \frac{4(3EI)}{4}(\theta_B) - 53.33 = 3\,EI\,(\theta_B) - 53.33 \qquad \ldots (ii)$$

Member BC :

$$M_{BC} = \frac{4EI}{L}(\theta_B) + \frac{2EI}{L}(\theta_C) \pm \frac{6EI}{L^2}(\Delta) + M_{BC}^F$$

$$= \frac{4(2EI)}{3}(\theta_B) + \frac{2(2EI)}{3}(\theta_C) + 33.33$$

$$= 2.67\,EI\,(\theta_B) + 1.33\,EI\,(\theta_C) + 33.33 \qquad \ldots (iii)$$

$$M_{CB} = \frac{4EI}{L}(\theta_C) + \frac{2EI}{L}(\theta_B) \pm \frac{6EI}{L^2}(\theta_B) + M_{CB}^F$$

$$= \frac{4(2EI)}{3}(\theta_C) + \frac{2(2EI)}{3}(\theta_B) - 33.33$$

$$= 2.67\,EI\,(\theta_C) + 1.33\,EI\,(\theta_B) - 33.33 \qquad \ldots (iv)$$

Member DB :

$$M_{DB} = \frac{4EI}{L}(\theta_D) + \frac{2EI}{L}(\theta_B) \pm \frac{6EI}{L^2}(\Delta) + M_{DB}^F$$

$$= \frac{2EI}{3}(\theta_B) \qquad \ldots (v)$$

$$M_{BD} = \frac{4EI}{L}(\theta_B) + \frac{2EI}{L}(\theta_D) \pm \frac{6EI}{L^2}(\Delta) + M_{BD}^F$$

$$= \frac{4EI}{3}(\theta_B) \qquad \ldots (vi)$$

Member EC :

$$M_{EC} = \frac{4EI}{L}(\theta_E) + \frac{2EI}{L}(\theta_C) \pm \frac{6EI}{L^2}(\Delta) + M_{EC}^F$$

$$= \frac{2EI}{3}(\theta_C) \qquad \ldots (vii)$$

$$M_{CE} = \frac{4EI}{L}(\theta_C) + \frac{2EI}{L}(\theta_E) \pm \frac{6EI}{L^2}(\Delta) + M_{CE}^F$$

$$= \frac{4EI}{3}(\theta_C) \qquad \ldots (viii)$$

Step IV : Moment equilibrium condition for joint :

At joint B; $M_{BA} + M_{BC} + M_{BD} = 0$ \qquad … (A)

At joint C; $M_{CB} + M_{CE} = 0$ ... (B)

Step V : Formulation of equilibrium equations in terms of joint displacements :
Substituting equations (ii), (iii) and (vi) in equation (A), we get,

$$[3\,EI\,(\theta_B) - 53.33] + [2.67\,EI\,(\theta_B) + 1.33\,EI\,(\theta_C) + 33.33] + \left[\dfrac{4\,EI}{3}(\theta_B)\right] = 0$$

$7\,EI\,(\theta_B) + 1.33\,EI\,(\theta_C) - 20 = 0.$ ... (I)

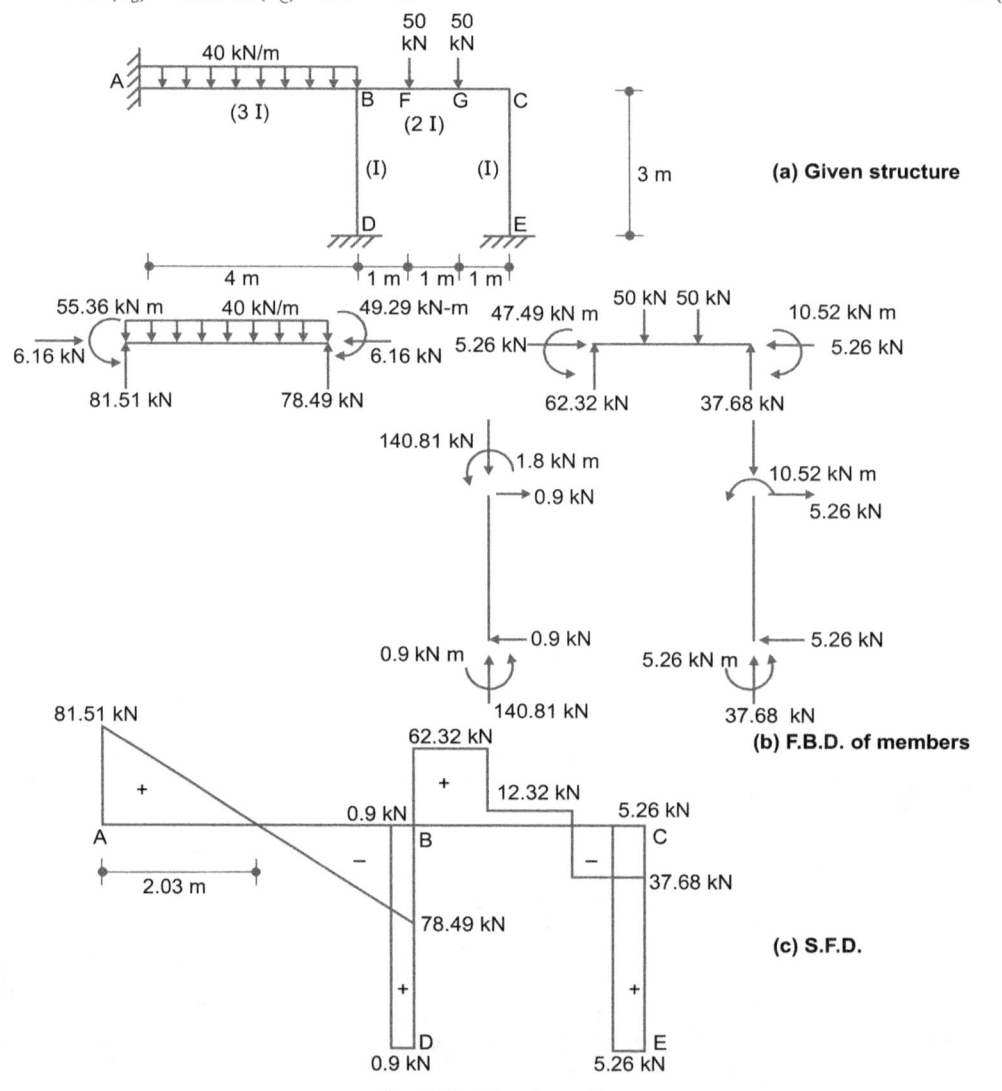

(a) Given structure

(b) F.B.D. of members

(c) S.F.D.

Fig. 1.20 (Continued)

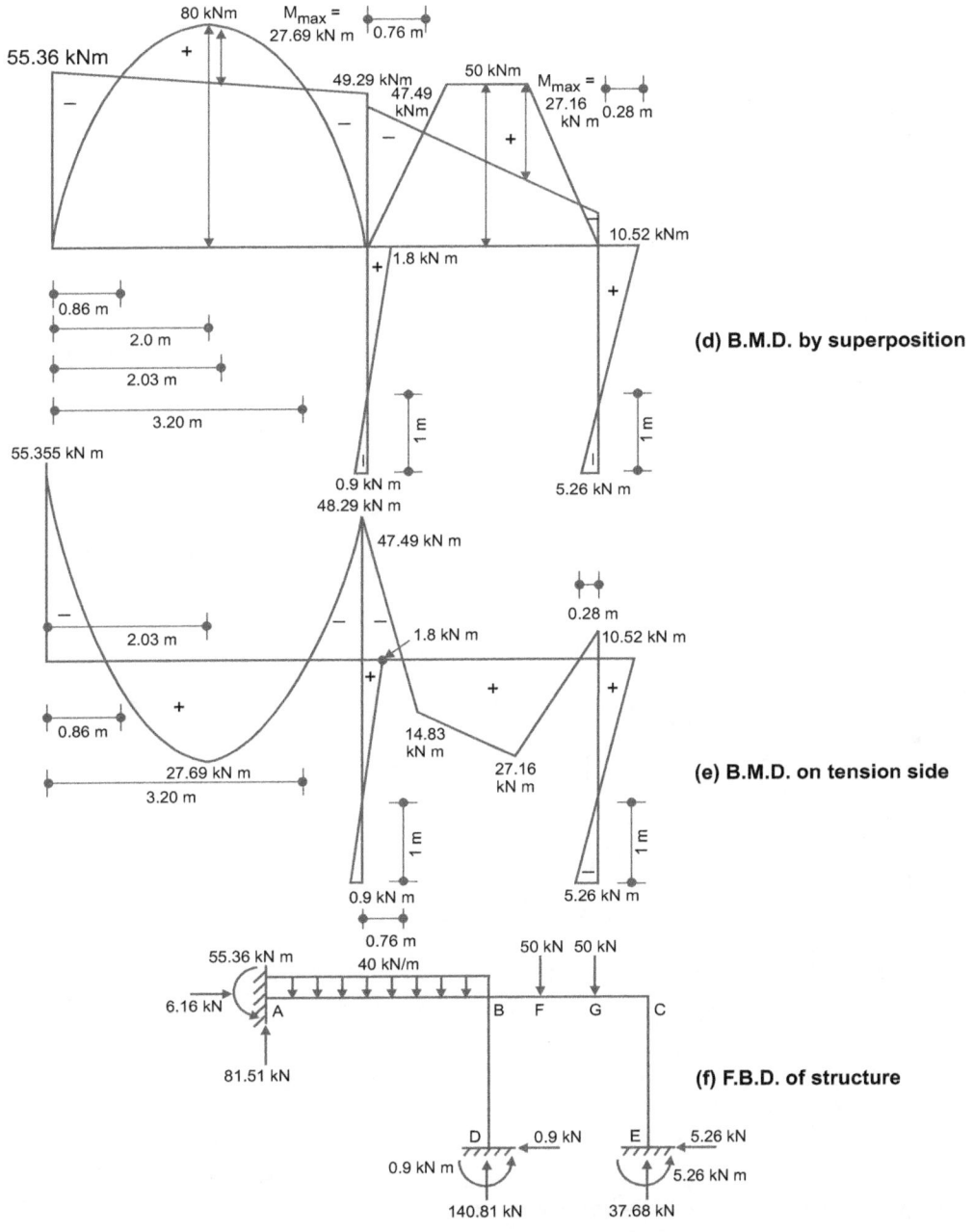

Fig. 1.20 : For Illustrative Example 1.11

Substituting equations (iv) and (viii) in equation (B), we get

$[2.67 \, EI \, (\theta_C) + 1.33 \, EI \, (\theta_B) - 33.33] + \left[\dfrac{4 \, EI}{3} (\theta_C)\right] = 0$

$4 \, EI \, (\theta_C) + 1.33 \, EI \, (\theta_B) - 33.33 = 0$ ... (II)

Step VI : Solution of equations for joint displacements : Solving equations (I) and (II), we get

$$\boxed{\theta_B = \dfrac{1.35}{EI} \quad \text{and} \quad \theta_C = \dfrac{7.89}{EI}}$$

Step VII : Member-end moments :

Substituting the values of above joint displacements in SD equations, member-end moments are obtained as under :

$M_{AB} = 1.5 \, EI \left(\dfrac{1.35}{EI}\right) + 53.33 = 55.36 \text{ kNm}$

$M_{BA} = 3 \, EI \left(\dfrac{1.35}{EI}\right) - 53.33 = -49.29 \text{ kNm}$

$M_{BC} = 2.67 \, EI \left(\dfrac{1.35}{EI}\right) + 1.33 \, EI \left(\dfrac{7.89}{EI}\right) + 33.33 = 47.49 \text{ kNm}$

$M_{CB} = 2.67 \, EI \left(\dfrac{7.89}{EI}\right) + 1.33 \, EI \left(\dfrac{1.35}{EI}\right) - 33.33 = -10.52 \text{ kNm}$

$M_{DB} = \dfrac{2 \, EI}{3} \left(\dfrac{1.35}{EI}\right) = 0.9 \text{ kNm}$

$M_{BD} = \dfrac{4 \, EI}{3} \left(\dfrac{1.35}{EI}\right) = 1.8 \text{ kNm}$

$M_{EC} = \dfrac{2 \, EI}{3} \left(\dfrac{7.89}{EI}\right) = 5.26 \text{ kNm}$

$M_{CE} = \dfrac{4 \, EI}{3} \left(\dfrac{7.89}{EI}\right) = 10.52 \text{ kNm}$

Step VIII : FBD of members is as shown in Fig. 1.20 (b). Considering equilibrium of each member and of complete structure, all reaction components are found out as shown in figure.

Step IX : Axial and shear force diagram is as shown in Fig. 1.20 (c).

Step X : Bending moment diagram.

BMD by superposition is shown in Fig. 1.20 (d). BMD by tension side is shown in Fig. 1.20 (e).

Step XI : FBD of structure is as shown in Fig. 1.20 (f).

Example 1.12 : *Analyse the frame as shown in Fig. 1.21 (a) by slope-deflection method.*

Solution : (1) Data : The beam is loaded and supported as shown in Fig. 1.21 (a).
(2) Frame type : Non-sway frame.

Object : Structural analysis.

Equations : SD equations.

Procedure : Step I : Degree of kinematic indeterminacy = D_{ki} = 2.

Unknown displacements : θ_B, θ_C.

Known displacements : $\theta_A = \theta_D = 0$ and horizontal sway $= \Delta = 0$.

Step II : Fixed-end moments :

$$M_{AB}^F = -M_{BA}^F = 0$$

$$M_{BC}^F = -M_{CB}^F = \frac{WL}{8} = \frac{60 \times 4}{8} = 30 \text{ kN-m}$$

$$M_{CD}^F = -M_{CD}^F = 0$$

Step III : Slope-deflection equations :

Member AB :

$$M_{AB} = \frac{4EI}{L}(\theta_A) + \frac{2EI}{L}(\theta_B) \pm \frac{6EI\Delta}{L^2} + M_{AB}^F$$

$$= \frac{2E\left(\frac{4}{3}I\right)}{4} = 0.667 \, EI \, \theta_B \qquad \ldots (i)$$

$$M_{BA} = \frac{4EI}{L}(\theta_B) + \frac{2EI}{L}(\theta_A) \pm \frac{6EI\Delta}{L^2} + M_{BA}^F$$

$$= \frac{4EI\left(\frac{4}{3}I\right)}{4} \theta_B = 1.33 \, EI \, \theta_B \qquad \ldots (ii)$$

Member BC :

$$M_{BC} = \frac{4EI}{L}(\theta_B) + \frac{2EI}{L}(\theta_C) \pm \frac{6EI\Delta}{L^2} + M_{BC}^F$$

$$= \frac{4EI}{4}(\theta_B) + \frac{2EI}{4}(\theta_C) + 30$$

$$= EI \, \theta_B + 0.5 \, EI \, \theta_C + 30 \qquad \ldots (iii)$$

$$M_{CB} = \frac{4EI}{L}(\theta_C) + \frac{2EI}{L}(\theta_B) \pm \frac{6EI\Delta}{L^2} + M_{CB}^F$$

$$= \frac{4EI}{4}(\theta_C) + \frac{2EI}{4}(\theta_B) - 30$$

$$= EI \, \theta_C + 0.5 \, EI \, \theta_B - 30 \qquad \ldots (iv)$$

Member CD :

$$M_{CD} = \frac{4EI}{L}(\theta_C) + \frac{2EI}{L}(\theta_D) \pm \frac{6EI\Delta}{L^2} + M_{CD}^F$$

$$= \frac{4E\left(\frac{4}{3}I\right)}{4}\theta_C = 1.33\,EI\,\theta_C \qquad \ldots \text{(v)}$$

$$M_{DC} = \frac{4EI}{L}(\theta_D) + \frac{2EI}{L}(\theta_C) \pm \frac{6EI\Delta}{L^2} + M_{DC}^F$$

$$= \frac{2E\left(\frac{4}{3}I\right)}{4}\theta_C = 0.666\,EI\,\theta_C \qquad \ldots \text{(vi)}$$

Step IV : Moment equilibrium conditions for joint.

At joint B : $\quad M_{BA} + M_{BC} = 0$ $\qquad \ldots$ (A)

At joint C : $\quad M_{CB} + M_{CD} = 0$ $\qquad \ldots$ (B)

Step V : Formulation of equilibrium equations in terms of joint displacements. Substituting equations (ii) and (iii) in equation (A),

$1.33\,EI\,\theta_B + EI\,\theta_B + 0.5\,EI\,\theta_C + 30 = 0$

$2.33\,EI\,\theta_B + 0.5\,EI\,\theta_C + 30 = 0$ $\qquad \ldots$ (I)

Substituting equations (iv) and (v) in equation (B),

$EI\,\theta_C + 0.5\,EI\,\theta_B - 30 + 1.33\,EI\,\theta_C = 0$

$2.33\,EI\,\theta_C + 0.5\,EI\,\theta_B - 30 = 0$ $\qquad \ldots$ (II)

Step VI : Solution of equations for joint displacements : Solving equations (I) and (II), we get

$$\theta_B = \frac{-16.39}{EI}, \quad \theta_C = \frac{16.39}{EI}$$

Step VII : Member-end moments :

$$M_{AB} = 0.667\,EI\left(\frac{-16.39}{EI}\right) = -10.9 \text{ kN-m}$$

$$M_{BA} = 1.33\,EI\left(\frac{-16.39}{EI}\right) = -21.79 \text{ kN-m}$$

$$M_{BC} = EI\left(\frac{-16.39}{EI}\right) + 0.5\,EI\left(\frac{16.39}{EI}\right) + 30 = 21.79 \text{ kN-m}$$

$$M_{CB} = EI\left(\frac{16.39}{EI}\right) + 0.5\,EI\left(\frac{-16.39}{EI}\right) - 30 = -21.79 \text{ kN-m}$$

$$M_{CD} = 1.33\,EI\left(\frac{16.39}{EI}\right) = 21.79 \text{ kN-m}$$

$$M_{DC} = 0.666 \, EI \left(\frac{-16.39}{EI} \right) = 10.9 \text{ kN-m}$$

Step VIII : FBD of members is as shown in Fig. 1.21 (b).
Step IX : Shear force diagram is as shown in Fig. 1.21 (c).
Step X : Bending moment diagram.
  BMD by superposition is as shown in Fig. 1.21 (d).
  BMD on tension side is as shown in Fig. 1.21 (e).
Step XI : FBD of structure is as shown in Fig. 1.21 (f).

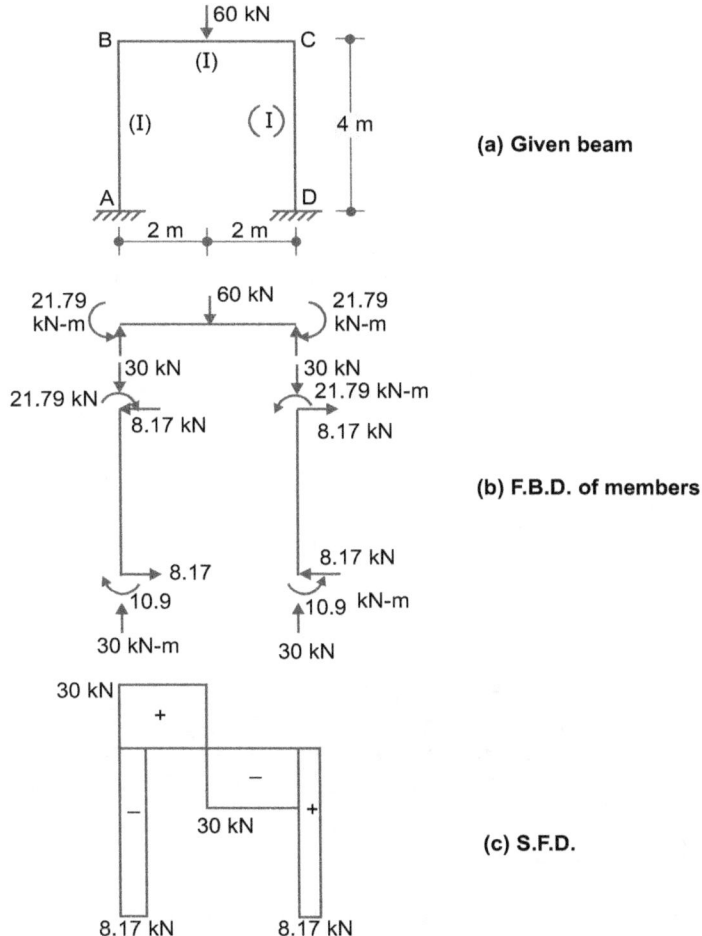

(a) Given beam

(b) F.B.D. of members

(c) S.F.D.

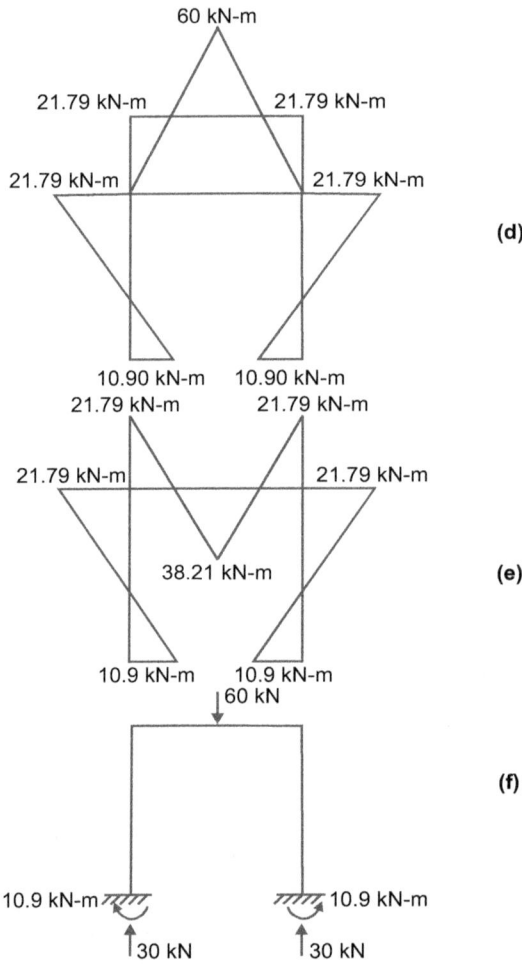

Fig. 1.21 : For Illustrative Example 1.12

Example 1.13 : Using the slope-deflection method, analyse the rigid jointed plane frame supported and loaded as shown in Fig. 1.22 (a). Assume uniform flexural rigidity EI for all the members.

Solution : (1) Data : The frame is loaded and supported as shown in Fig. 1.22 (a).
Object : Structural analysis.
Equation : SD equations.
Procedure : Step I : Degree of kinematic indeterminacy = D_{ki} = 1.
Unknown displacement : θ_B.
Known displacements : $\theta_A = \theta_C = 0$ and horizontal sway = Δ = 0.

Step II : Fixed-end moments.

$$M_{AB}^F = M_{BA}^F = 0$$

$$M_{BC}^F = -M_{CB}^F = \frac{10 \times 5^2}{12} = 20.83 \text{ kN-m}$$

$$M_{BD}^F = -25 \times 2 = -50 \text{ kN-m}$$

Step III : Slope-deflection equations.

Member AB :

$$M_{AB} = \frac{4EI}{L}(\theta_A) + \frac{2EI}{L}(\theta_B) \pm \frac{6EI\Delta}{L^2} + M_{AB}^F = \frac{2EI(\theta_B)}{5}$$

$$= 0.4 \, EI \, \theta_B \qquad \ldots \text{(i)}$$

$$M_{BA} = \frac{4EI}{L}(\theta_B) + \frac{2EI}{L}(\theta_A) \pm \frac{6EI\Delta}{L^2} + M_{BA}^F$$

$$= \frac{4EI}{5}\theta_B = 0.8 \, EI \, \theta_B \qquad \ldots \text{(ii)}$$

Memebr BC :

$$M_{BC} = \frac{4EI}{L}(\theta_B) + \frac{2EI}{L}(\theta_C) \pm \frac{6EI\Delta}{L^2} + M_{BC}^F$$

$$= \frac{4EI}{5}(\theta_B) + 20.83 = 0.8 \, EI \, \theta_B + 20.83 \qquad \ldots \text{(iii)}$$

$$M_{CB} = \frac{4EI}{L}(\theta_C) + \frac{2EI}{L}(\theta_B) \pm \frac{6EI\Delta}{L^2} + M_{CB}^F$$

$$= \frac{2EI}{5}(\theta_B) - 20.83 = 0.4 \, EI \, \theta_B - 20.83 \qquad \ldots \text{(iv)}$$

Member BD : $\quad M_{BD} = -M_{BD}^F = -50 \qquad \ldots \text{(v)}$

Step IV : Moment equilibrium condition for joint.

At joint B : $M_{BA} + M_{BC} + M_{BD} = 0 \qquad \ldots \text{(A)}$

Step V : Formulation of equilibrium equations in terms of joint displacement. Substituting equations (ii), (iii) and (v) in equation (A),

$$0.8 \, EI \, \theta_B + 0.8 \, EI \, \theta_B + 20.83 - 50 = 0$$

$$1.6 \, EI \, \theta_B - 29.17 = 0 \qquad \ldots \text{(I)}$$

Step VI : Solution of equations for joint displacement.

$$\theta_B = \frac{18.23}{EI}$$

Step VII : Member-end moments :

$$M_{AB} = 0.4 \, EI \left(\frac{18.23}{EI}\right) = 7.29 \text{ kN-m}$$

$$M_{BA} = 0.8 \, EI \left(\frac{18.23}{EI}\right) = 14.58 \text{ kN-m}$$

$$M_{BC} = 0.8 \, EI \left(\frac{18.23}{EI}\right) + 20.83 = 35.42 \text{ kN-m}$$

$$M_{CB} = 0.4\, EI \left(\frac{18.23}{EI}\right) - 20.83 = -13.54 \text{ kN-m}$$

$$M_{BD} = -50 \text{ kN-m}$$

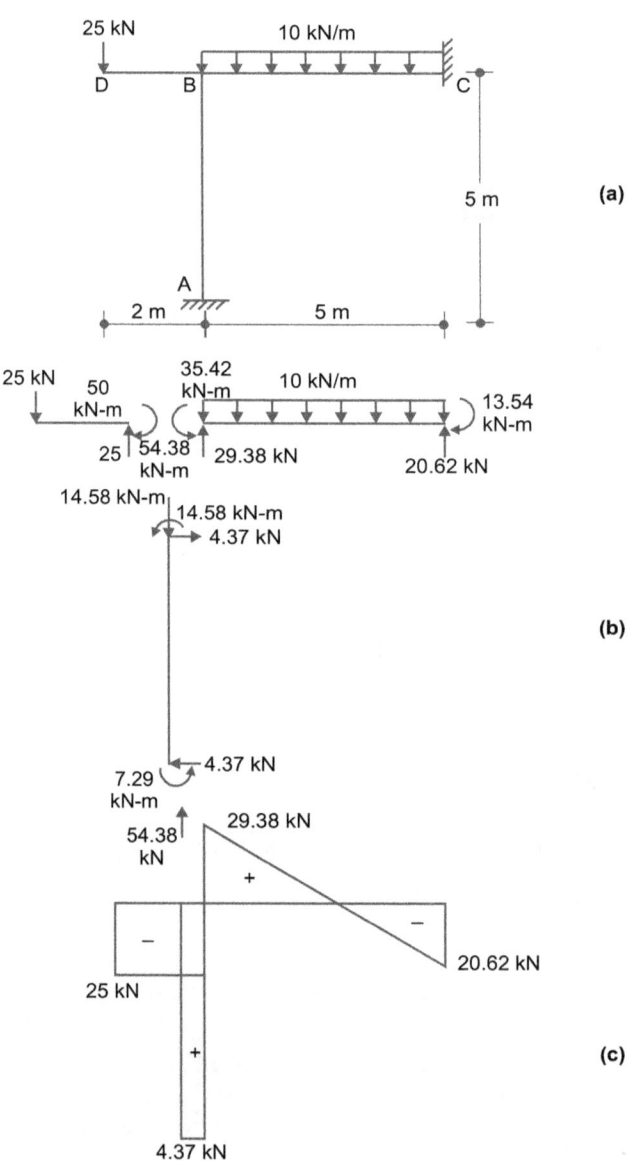

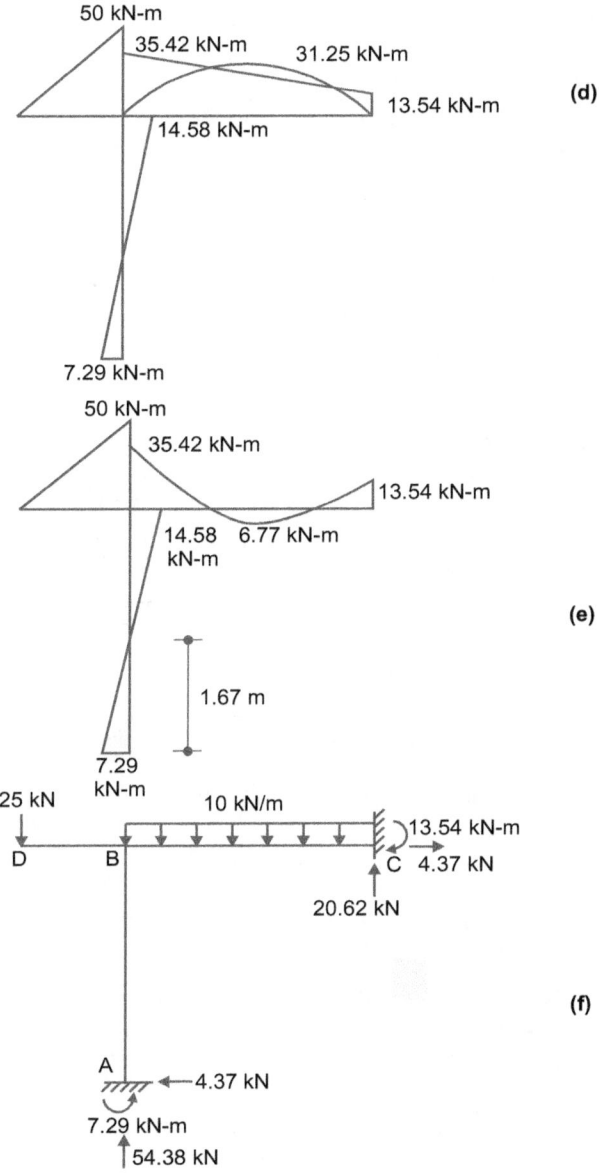

Fig. 1.22 : For Illustrative Example 1.13

Step VIII : FBD of member is as shown in Fig. 1.22 (a).
Step IX : Shear force diagram is as shown in Fig. 1.22 (c).
Step X : Bending moment diagram.

STRUCTURAL ANALYSIS – II   SLOPE-DEFLECTION METHOD

   BMD by superposition is as shown in Fig. 1.22 (d)
   BMD on tension side is as shown in Fig. 1.22 (e).
Step XI : FBD of structure is as shown in Fig. 1.22 (f).

Example 1.14 : *Find the end moments of the frame shown in Fig. 1.23 (a) by slope deflection method. EI = constant.*   **(P.U. May 98)**

Solution : (1) Data : The frame is supported and loaded as shown in Fig. 1.23.
(2) Frame type : Non-sway.
Object : Structural analysis.
Equations : S.D. equations.
Procedure : Step I : Degree of kinematic indeterminacy

$$D_{ki} = 2$$

Unknown displacement $= \theta_B, \theta_C$

Known displacement $= \theta_A = \theta_D = 0$

Step II : Fixed end moments :

$$\overline{M}_{AB} = -\overline{M}_{BA} = -\frac{wl^2}{12} = -\frac{25 \times 4^2}{12} = -33.33 \text{ kN-m}$$

$$\overline{M}_{BC} = -\overline{M}_{CB} = -\frac{wl}{8} = -\frac{45 \times 4}{8} = -22.5 \text{ kN-m}$$

$$\overline{M}_{BD} = -\overline{M}_{DB} = -\frac{wl}{8} = -\frac{25 \times 4}{8} = -12.5 \text{ kN-m}$$

Step III : Slope deflection equations :

$$M_{AB} = -33.33 + \frac{2EI}{l}(2\theta_a + \theta_b)$$

$$M_{AB} = -33.33 + \frac{2EI}{4}(\theta_b)$$

$$M_{BA} = 33.33 + \frac{2EI}{4}(2\theta_b)$$

Span BC :
$$M_{BC} = -22.5 + \frac{2EI}{4}(2\theta_b + \theta_c)$$

$$M_{CB} = 22.5 + \frac{2EI}{4}(2\theta_c + \theta_b)$$

Span BD :
$$M_{BD} = -12.5 + \frac{2EI}{4}(2\theta_b)$$

$$M_{DB} = 12.5 + \frac{2EI}{4}(\theta_b)$$

Step IV : Equilibrium equations:

$$M_{BA} + M_{BC} + M_{BD} = 0$$

Step V : Formulation of equilibrium equations in terms of joint displacements.

$$33.33 + EI\theta_b - 22.5 + EI\theta_b + 0.5\, EI\theta_c - 12.5 + EI\theta_b = 0$$

STRUCTURAL ANALYSIS – II   SLOPE-DEFLECTION METHOD

$$3 EI\theta_b + 0.5 EI\theta_c = 1.67 \quad \ldots(1)$$
$$M_{CB} = 0 \text{ as simple supported end.}$$
$$22.5 + EI\theta_c + 0.5 EI\theta_b = 0 \quad \ldots(2)$$

Step VI : Solution of equations for joint displacements:

$$EI\theta_b = 4.7$$
$$EI\theta_c = -24.85$$

Step VII : Member end moments :

$$M_{AB} = -30.98 \text{ kN-m}$$
$$M_{BA} = 38.03 \text{ kN-m}$$
$$M_{BC} = -30.225 \text{ kN-m}$$
$$M_{BD} = -7.8 \text{ kN-m}$$
$$M_{DB} = 14.6 \text{ kN-m}$$

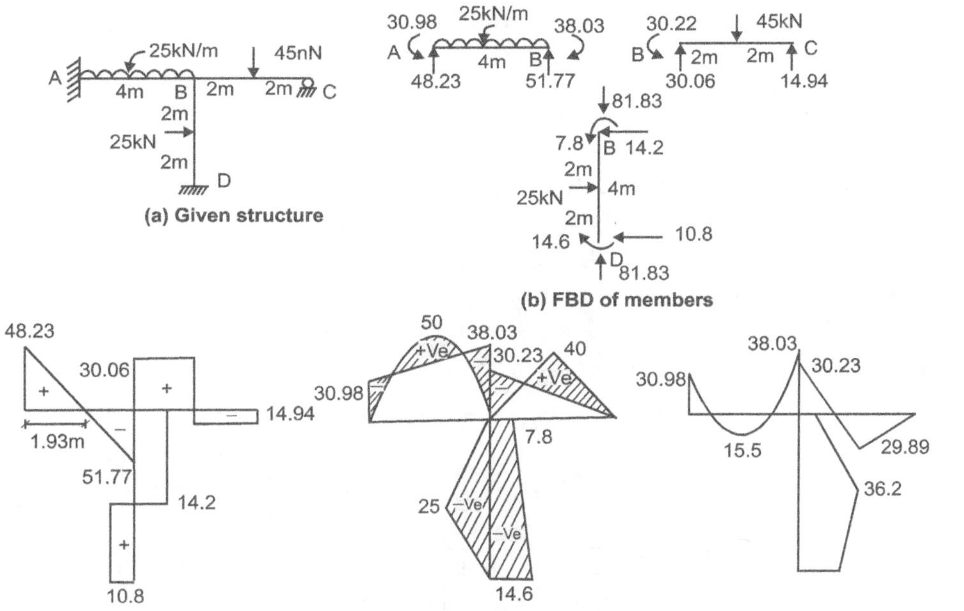

(a) Given structure

(b) FBD of members

(C) S.F.D.

(d) BMD by superposition

(e) BMD on tension side

Fig. 1.23

1.9.3 Sway Frames

The sway i.e. horizontal translation must be considered in unsymmetrical rectangular frames. The sway is same at the horizontal level joints as the axial deformation is neglected. As the sway is horizontal translation, it has effects only on columns i.e. vertical members in SD formulation. There is no effect of sway in horizontal member i.e. beam. The sway, Δ, at the joints at same level is unknown displacement, additional to joint rotations in SD method. The quantity $\frac{6EI}{L^2}(\Delta)$ in SD equation is called the sway moment. The SD equations for vertical members must contain the quantity $\frac{6EI}{L^2}(\Delta)$ in terms of unknown Δ, EI and L of the member. The positive quantity of sway moment means sway to the right. As no effect of sway in horizontal members, the term $\frac{6EI}{L^2}(\Delta)$ is absent in SD equation of the horizontal members. Shear equilibrium is must in sway frame in addition to the joint equilibrium, to formulate the SD method.

1.9.4 Application of SD Method to Frames With Side Sway

Example 1.15 : *Analyse the portal frame shown in Fig. 1.24 (a) by slope-deflection method. Draw SFD, BMD and elastic curve.*

Solution : (1) Data : The frame is supported and loaded as shown in Fig. 1.24 (a).
(2) Frame type : Sway frame.
Object : Structural analysis.
Equations : SD equations.
Procedure :
Step I : Degree of kinematic indeterminacy = D_{ki} = 3.
Unknown displacements : θ_B, θ_C and horizontal sway = Δ
Known displacements : $\theta_A = \theta_D = 0$.
Step II : Fixed-end moments :
$$M_{AB}^F = M_{BA}^F = M_{BC}^F = M_{CB}^F = M_{CD}^F = M_{DC}^F = 0$$
Step III : SD equations : (Assuming horizontal sway = Δ towards right)

Member AB :
$$M_{AB} = \frac{4EI}{L}(\theta_A) + \frac{2EI}{L}(\theta_B) + \frac{6EI}{L^2}(\Delta) + M_{AB}^F$$
$$= \frac{2EI}{4}(\theta_B) + \frac{6EI}{4^2}(\Delta) = 0.5\,EI\,(\theta_B) + 0.375\,EI\,(\Delta) \qquad \ldots (i)$$

$$M_{BA} = \frac{4EI}{L}(\theta_B) + \frac{2EI}{L}(\theta_A) + \frac{6EI}{L^2}(\Delta) + M_{BA}^F$$
$$= \frac{4EI}{4}(\theta_B) + \frac{6EI}{4^2}(\Delta) = EI\,(\theta_B) + 0.375\,EI\,(\Delta) \qquad \ldots (ii)$$

Member BC :
$$M_{BC} = \frac{4EI}{L}(\theta_B) + \frac{2EI}{L}(\theta_C) \pm \frac{6EI}{L^2}(\Delta) + M_{BC}^F$$
$$= \frac{4(2EI)}{4}(\theta_B) + \frac{2(2EI)}{4}(\theta_C) = 2\,EI\,(\theta_B) + EI\,(\theta_C) \qquad \ldots (iii)$$

$$M_{CB} = \frac{4EI}{L}(\theta_C) + \frac{2EI}{L}(\theta_B) \pm \frac{6EI}{L^2}(\Delta) + M_{CB}^F$$

$$= \frac{4(2EI)}{4}(\theta_C) + \frac{2(2EI)}{4}(\theta_B) = 2EI(\theta_C) + EI(\theta_B) \quad \ldots \text{(iv)}$$

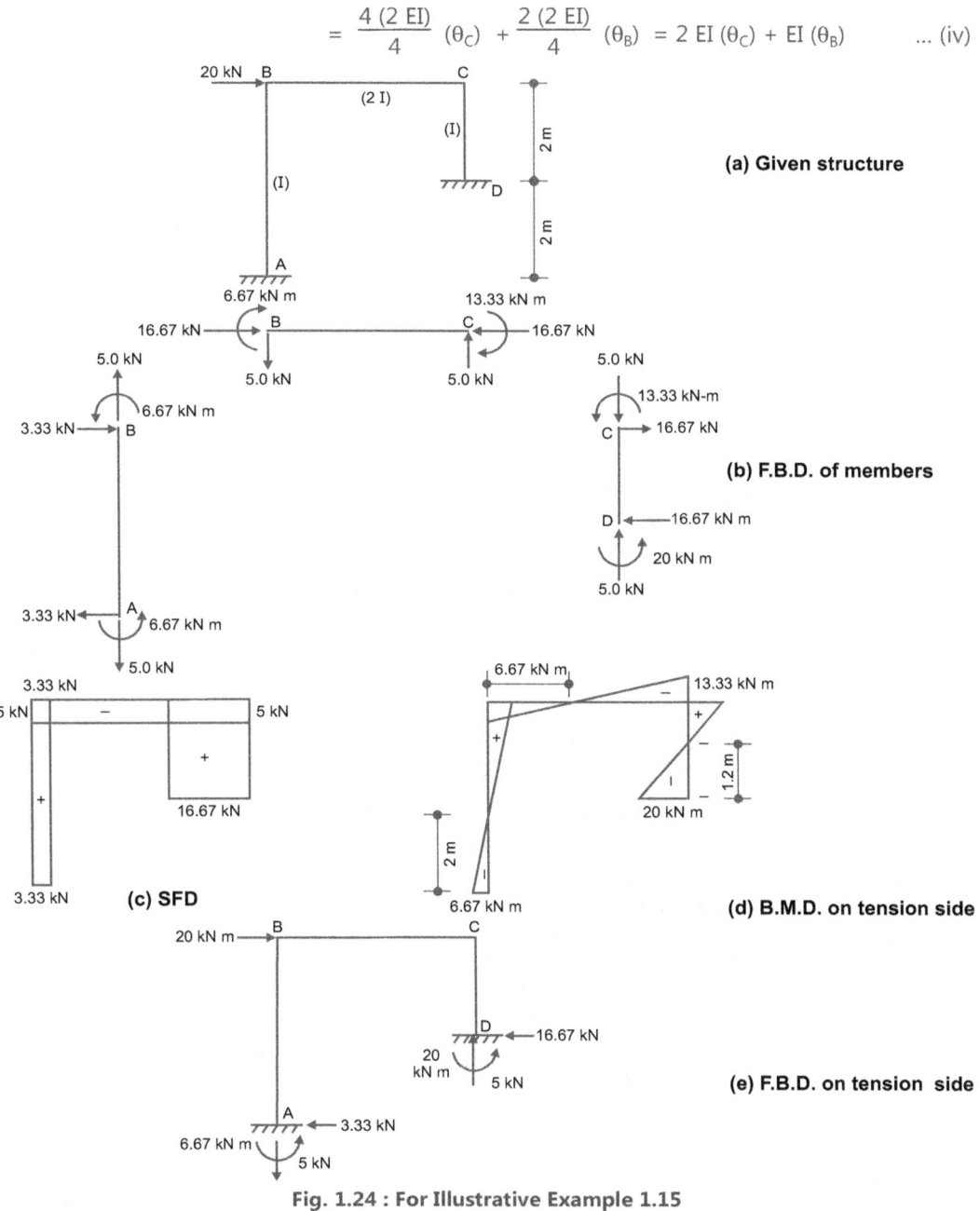

Fig. 1.24 : For Illustrative Example 1.15

STRUCTURAL ANALYSIS – II SLOPE-DEFLECTION METHOD

Member CD :

$$M_{CD} = \frac{4EI}{L}(\theta_C) + \frac{2EI}{L}(\theta_D) + \frac{6EI}{L^2}(\Delta) + M_{CD}^F$$

$$= \frac{4EI}{2}(\theta_C) + \frac{6EI}{2^2}(\Delta) = 2EI(\theta_C) + 1.5EI(\Delta) \quad \ldots (v)$$

$$M_{DC} = \frac{4EI}{L}(\theta_D) + \frac{2EI}{L}(\theta_C) + \frac{6EI}{L^2}(\Delta) + M_{DC}^F$$

$$= \frac{2EI}{2}(\theta_C) + \frac{6EI}{2^2}(\Delta) = EI(\theta_C) + 1.5EI(\Delta) \quad \ldots (vi)$$

Step IV : Equilibrium conditions for joints :
Moment equilibrium of joint B; $M_{BA} + M_{BC} = 0$ ... (A)
Moment equilibrium of joint C; $M_{CB} + M_{CD} = 0$ ... (B)
Horizontal shear equilibrium of structure; $H_A + H_D - 20 = 0$

where, $H_A = \dfrac{M_{AB} + M_{BA}}{4}$ and $H_D = \dfrac{M_{DC} + M_{CD}}{2}$

$$\therefore \quad \frac{M_{AB} + M_{BA}}{4} + \frac{M_{DC} + M_{CD}}{2} = 20$$

$$M_{AB} + M_{BA} + 2(M_{DC} + M_{CD}) = 80 \quad \ldots (C)$$

Step V : Formulation of equilibrium equations in terms of joint displacements :
Substituting equations (ii) and (iii) in equation (A), we get

$$[EI(\theta_B) + 0.375 + EI(\Delta)] [2EI(\theta_B) + EI(\theta_C)] = 0$$
$$3EI(\theta_B) + EI(\theta_C) + 0.375EI(\Delta) = 0 \quad \ldots (I)$$

Substituting equations (iv) and (v) in equation (B), we get

$$[2EI(\theta_C) + EI(\theta_B)] + [2EI(\theta_C) + 1.5EI(\Delta)] = 0$$
$$4EI(\theta_C) + EI(\theta_B) + 1.5EI(\Delta) = 0 \quad \ldots (II)$$

Substituting equations (i), (ii), (v) and (vi) in equation (C), we get

$$[0.4EI(\theta_B) + 0.375EI(\Delta)] + [EI(\theta_B) + 0.375EI(\Delta)]$$
$$+ 2[2EI(\theta_C) + 1.5EI(\Delta) + EI(\theta_C) + 1.5EI(\Delta)] = 80$$
$$1.5EI(\theta_B) + 6EI(\theta_C) + 6.75EI(\Delta) = 80 \quad \ldots (III)$$

Step VI : Solution of equations for joint displacements :
Solving equations (I), (II) and (III), we get

$$\boxed{\theta_B = 0; \quad \theta_C = \frac{-6.67}{EI}; \quad \Delta = \frac{17.77}{EI}}$$

positive sign for Δ indicates that; sway is towards right.

Step VII : Member-end moments : Substituting values of above joint displacements in SD equations; member-end moments are obtained as under :

$$M_{AB} = 0.5EI(0) + 0.375EI\left(\frac{17.77}{EI}\right) = 6.67 \text{ kNm}$$

$$M_{BA} = EI(0) + 0.375\left(\frac{17.77}{EI}\right) = 6.67 \text{ kNm}$$

$$M_{BC} = 2EI(0) + EI\left(-\frac{6.67}{EI}\right) = -6.67 \text{ kNm}$$

$$M_{CB} = 2EI\left(-\frac{6.67}{EI}\right) + 0 = -13.33 \text{ kNm}$$

$$M_{CD} = 2EI\left(-\frac{6.67}{EI}\right) + 1.5EI\left(\frac{17.77}{EI}\right) = 13.33 \text{ kNm}$$

$$M_{DC} = EI\left(-\frac{6.67}{EI}\right) + 1.5EI\left(\frac{17.77}{EI}\right) = 20 \text{ kNm}$$

Step VIII : FBD of members is as shown in Fig. 1.24 (b). Considering equilibrium of each member and of complete structure; all reaction components are found out as shown in the figure.
Step IX : Shear force diagram is as shown in Fig. 1.24 (c).
Step X : Bending moment diagram : BMD on tension side is shown in Fig. 1.24 (d).
Step XI : FBD of structure is as shown in Fig. 1.24 (e).

Example 1.16 : *Analyse the portal frame shown in Fig. 1.25 (a) by slope-deflection method. Draw SFD and BMD.*

Solution : (1) Data : The frame is supported and loaded as shown in Fig. 1.25 (a).
(2) Frame type : Sway frame.
Object : Structural analysis.
Equations : SD equations.
Procedure : Step I : Degree of kinematic indeterminacy for a given structure =
D_{ki} = 5 (θ_B, θ_C, θ_E, Δ_{VE} and horizontal sway Δ)
Degree of kinematic indeterminacy for modified structure
= D_{ki} = 3 (See Fig. 1.25 b).
Unknown displacements : θ_B, θ_C and horizontal sway = Δ
Known displacements : $\theta_A = \theta_D = 0$
Step II : Fixed-end moments :

$$M_{AB}^F = M_{BA}^F = M_{DC}^F = M_{CD}^F = 0$$

$$M_{BC}^F = -M_{CB}^F = \frac{wl^2}{12} = \frac{20 \times 8^2}{12} = 106.67 \text{ kNm}$$

Step III : SD equations : (Assuming horizontal sway = Δ towards right)

Member AB :
$$M_{AB} = \frac{4EI}{L}(\theta_A) + \frac{2EI}{L}(\theta_B) + \frac{6EI}{L^2}(\Delta) + M_{AB}^F$$

$$= \frac{2EI}{6}(\theta_B) + \frac{6EI}{6^2}(\Delta) = \frac{EI}{3}(\theta_B) + \frac{EI}{6}(\Delta) \qquad \ldots \text{(i)}$$

$$M_{BA} = \frac{4EI}{L}(\theta_B) + \frac{2EI}{L}(\theta_A) + \frac{6EI}{L^2}(\Delta) + M_{BA}^F$$

$$= \frac{4EI}{6}(\theta_B) + \frac{6EI}{6^2}(\Delta) = \frac{2EI}{3}(\theta_B) + \frac{EI}{6}(\Delta) \qquad \ldots \text{(ii)}$$

STRUCTURAL ANALYSIS – II   SLOPE-DEFLECTION METHOD

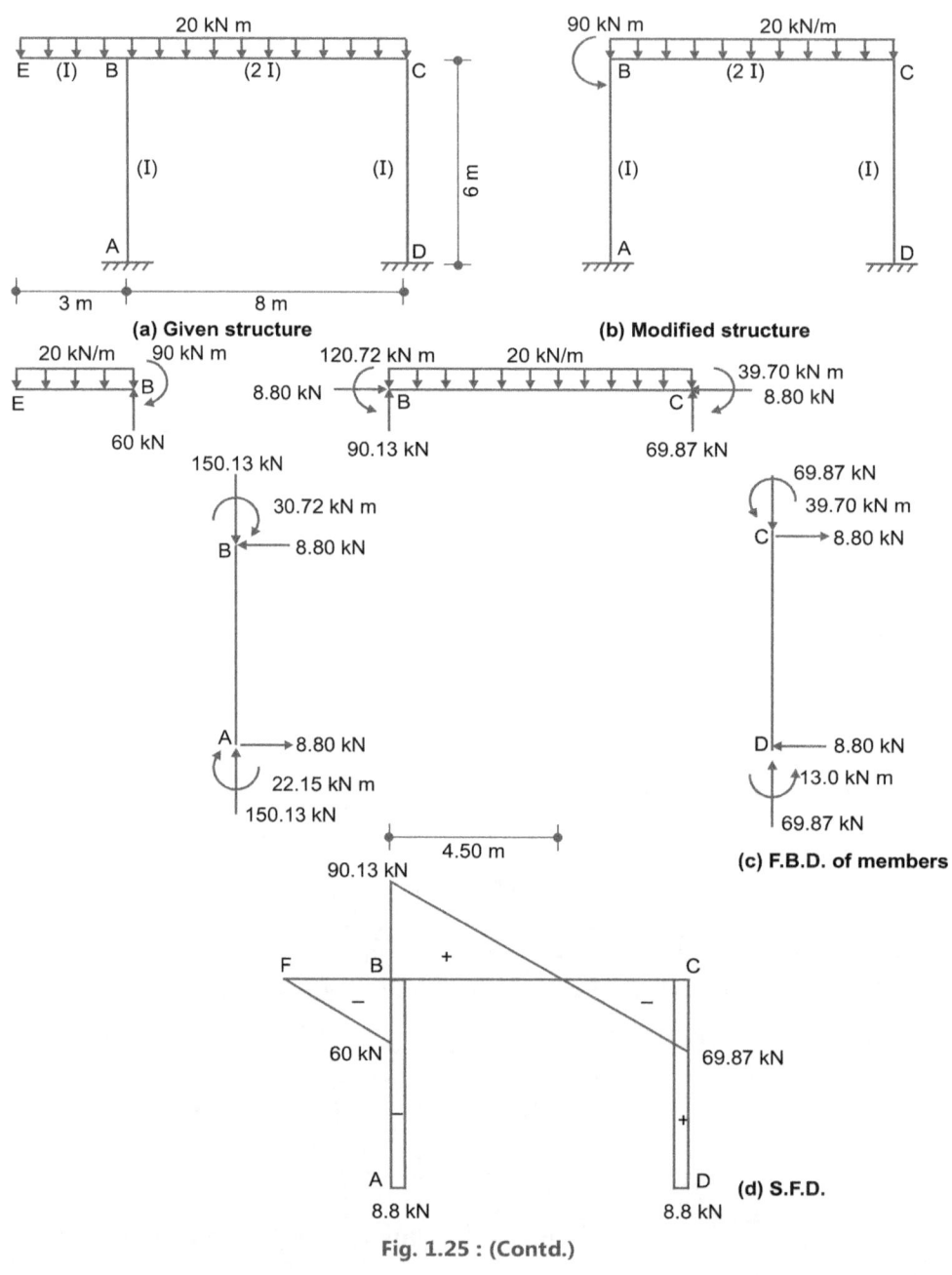

Fig. 1.25 : (Contd.)

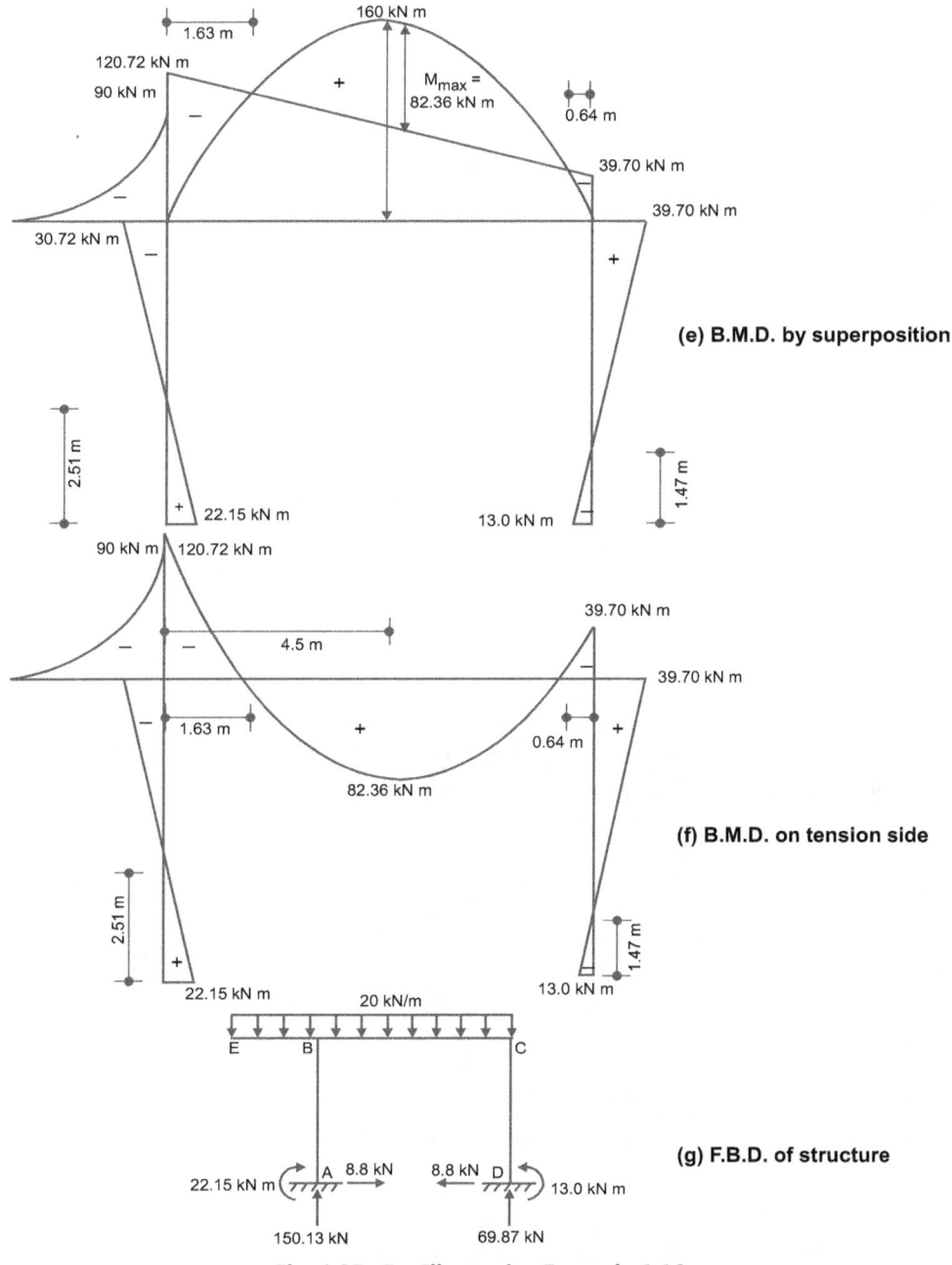

Fig. 1.25 : For Illustrative Example 1.16

Member BC :

$$M_{BC} = \frac{4EI}{L}(\theta_B) + \frac{2EI}{L}(\theta_C) \pm \frac{6EI}{L^2}(\Delta) + M^F_{BC}$$

$$= \frac{4(2EI)}{8}(\theta_B) + \frac{2(2EI)}{8}(\theta_C) + 106.67$$

$$= EI(\theta_B) + 0.5\,EI(\theta_C) + 106.67 \qquad \ldots \text{(iii)}$$

$$M_{CB} = \frac{4EI}{L}(\theta_C) + \frac{2EI}{L}(\theta_B) \pm \frac{6EI}{L^2}(\Delta) + M^F_{CB}$$

$$= \frac{4(2EI)}{8}(\theta_C) + \frac{2(2EI)}{8}(\theta_B) - 106.67$$

$$= EI(\theta_C) + 0.5\,EI(\theta_B) - 106.67 \qquad \ldots \text{(iv)}$$

Member DC :

$$M_{DC} = \frac{4EI}{L}(\theta_D) + \frac{2EI}{L}(\theta_C) + \frac{6EI}{L^2}(\Delta) + M^F_{DC}$$

$$= \frac{2EI}{6}(\theta_C) + \frac{6EI}{6^2}(\Delta) = \frac{EI}{3}(\theta_C) + \frac{EI}{6}\Delta \qquad \ldots \text{(v)}$$

$$M_{CD} = \frac{4EI}{L}(\theta_C) + \frac{2EI}{L}(\theta_D) + \frac{6EI}{L^2}(\Delta) + M^F_{CD}$$

$$= \frac{4EI}{6}(\theta_C) + \frac{6EI}{6^2}(\Delta) = \frac{2EI}{3}(\theta_C) + \frac{EI}{6}(\Delta) \qquad \ldots \text{(vi)}$$

Step IV : Equilibrium conditions for joints :

Moment equilibrium of joint B : $M_{BA} + M_{BC} = 90$ ... (A)

Moment equilibrium of joint C : $M_{CB} + M_{CD} = 0$ ... (B)

Horizontal shear equilibrium of structure :

$$H_A + H_D = 0, \quad \text{where}$$

$$H_A = \frac{M_{AB} + M_{BA}}{6} \quad \text{and} \quad H_D = \frac{M_{CD} + M_{DC}}{6}$$

Substituting :

$$M_{AB} + M_{BA} + M_{CD} + M_{DC} = 0 \qquad \ldots \text{(C)}$$

Step V : Formulation of equilibrium equations in terms of joint displacements.

Substituting equations (ii) and (iii) in equation (A), we get

$$\left[\frac{2EI}{3}(\theta_B) + \frac{EI}{6}(\Delta)\right] + [EI(\theta_B) + 0.5\,EI(\theta_C) + 106.67] = 90$$

$$1.67\,EI(\theta_B) + 0.5\,EI(\theta_C) + 0.167\,EI(\Delta) + 16.67 = 0 \qquad \ldots \text{(I)}$$

Substituting equations (iv) and (vi) in equation (B), we get

$$[EI(\theta_C) + 0.5\,EI(\theta_B) - 106.67] + \left[\frac{2\,EI}{3}(\theta_C) + \frac{EI}{6}(\Delta)\right] = 0$$

$$1.67\,EI(\theta_C) + 0.5\,EI(\theta_B) + 0.167\,EI(\Delta) - 106.67 = 0 \qquad \ldots \text{(II)}$$

Substituting equations (i), (ii), (v) and (vi) in equation (C), we get

$$\left[\frac{EI}{3}(\theta_B) + \frac{EI}{6}(\Delta)\right] + \left[\frac{2\,EI}{3}(\theta_B) + \frac{EI}{6}(\Delta)\right] + \left[\frac{EI}{3}(\theta_C) + \frac{EI}{6}(\Delta)\right] + \left[\frac{2\,EI}{3}(\theta_C) + \frac{EI}{6}(\Delta)\right] = 0$$

$$EI(\theta_B) + EI(\theta_C) + 0.67\,EI(\Delta) = 0 \qquad \ldots \text{(III)}$$

Step VI : Solution of equations for displacements. Solving equations (I), (II) and (III), we get

$$\boxed{\theta_B = -\frac{25.7}{EI}\,;\quad \theta_C = \frac{79.74}{EI}\,;\quad \text{and}\quad \Delta = -\frac{81.52}{EI}}$$

negative sign for Δ indicates that sway is towards left.

Step VII : Member-end moments : Substituting the values of above joint displacements in SD equations, member-end moments are obtained as under :

$$M_{AB} = \frac{EI}{3}\left(-\frac{25.7}{EI}\right) + \frac{EI}{6}\left(-\frac{81.52}{EI}\right) = -22.15\ \text{kNm}$$

$$M_{BA} = \frac{2\,EI}{3}\left(-\frac{25.7}{EI}\right) + \frac{EI}{6}\left(-\frac{81.52}{EI}\right) = -30.72\ \text{kNm}$$

$$M_{BC} = EI\left(-\frac{25.7}{EI}\right) + 0.5\,EI\left(\frac{79.74}{EI}\right) + 106.67 = 120.72\ \text{kNm}$$

$$M_{CB} = EI\left(\frac{79.74}{EI}\right) + 0.5\,EI\left(-\frac{25.7}{EI}\right) - 106.67 = -39.70\ \text{kNm}$$

$$M_{CD} = \frac{2}{3}EI\left(\frac{79.74}{EI}\right) + \frac{EI}{6}\left(-\frac{81.52}{EI}\right) = 39.70\ \text{kNm}$$

$$M_{DC} = \frac{EI}{3}\left(\frac{79.74}{EI}\right) + \frac{EI}{6}\left(-\frac{81.52}{EI}\right) = 13.0\ \text{kNm}$$

Step VIII : FBD of members is as shown in Fig. 1.25 (c). Considering equilibrium of each member and of complete structure; all reaction components are found out as shown in figure.

Step IX : Shear force diagram is as shown in Fig. 1.25 (d).

Step X : Bending moment diagram : BMD by superposition is as shown in Fig. 1.25 (e).

STRUCTURAL ANALYSIS – II   SLOPE-DEFLECTION METHOD

BMD on tension side is as shown in Fig. 1.25 (f).

Step XI : FBD of structure is as shown in Fig. 1.25 (g).

Example 1.17 : *Analyse the portal frame shown in Fig. 1.26 (a) by slope-deflection method. Draw SFD and BMD. Take EI = constant.*

Solution : (1) Data : The frame is supported and loaded as shown in Fig. 1.26 (a).

(2) EI = constant.

(3) Frame type : Sway frame.

Object : Structural analysis.

Equations : SD equations.

Procedure :

Step I : Degree of kinematic indeterminacy = $D_{ki} = 3$

Unknown displacements : θ_B, θ_C and horizontal sway = Δ

Known displacements : $\theta_A = \theta_D = 0$

Step II : Fixed-end moments :

$$M_{AB}^F = -M_{BA}^F = \frac{wl^2}{12} = \frac{25 \times 4^2}{12} = 33.33 \text{ kNm}$$

$$M_{BC}^F = -M_{CB}^F = \frac{WL}{8} = \frac{50 \times 3}{8} = 18.75 \text{ kNm}$$

$$M_{DC}^F = -\frac{Wab^2}{L^2} = -\frac{40 \times 1 \times 2^2}{3^2} = -17.77 \text{ kNm}$$

$$M_{CD}^F = \frac{Wba^2}{L^2} = \frac{40 \times 2 \times 1^2}{3^2} = 8.89 \text{ kNm}$$

Step III : SD equations : (Assuming horizontal sway = Δ towards right)

Member AB :

$$M_{AB} = \frac{4 EI}{L}(\theta_A) + \frac{2 EI}{L}(\theta_B) + \frac{6 EI}{L^2}(\Delta) + M_{AB}^F$$

$$= \frac{2 EI}{4}(\theta_B) + \frac{6 EI}{4^2}(\Delta) + 33.33$$

$$= 0.5 \text{ EI }(\theta_B) + 0.375 \text{ EI }(\Delta) + 33.33 \qquad \ldots \text{(i)}$$

$$M_{BA} = \frac{4 EI}{L}(\theta_B) + \frac{2 EI}{L}(\theta_A) + \frac{6 EI}{L^2}(\Delta) + M_{BA}^F$$

$$= \frac{4EI}{4}(\theta_B) + \frac{6EI}{4^2}(\Delta) - 33.33$$

$$= EI(\theta_B) + 0.375\,EI(\Delta) - 33.33 \quad \ldots \text{(ii)}$$

Member BC :
$$M_{BC} = \frac{4EI}{L}(\theta_B) + \frac{2EI}{L}(\theta_C) \pm \frac{6EI}{L^2}(\Delta) + M^F_{BC}$$

$$= \frac{4EI}{3}(\theta_B) + \frac{2EI}{3}(\theta_C) + 18.75 \quad \ldots \text{(iii)}$$

$$M_{CB} = \frac{4EI}{L}(\theta_C) + \frac{2EI}{L}(\theta_B) \pm \frac{6EI}{L^2}(\Delta) + M^F_{CB}$$

$$= \frac{4EI}{3}(\theta_C) + \frac{2EI}{3}(\theta_B) - 18.75 \quad \ldots \text{(iv)}$$

Member DC :
$$M_{DC} = \frac{4EI}{L}(\theta_D) + \frac{2EI}{L}(\theta_C) + \frac{6EI}{L^2}(\Delta) + M^F_{DC}$$

$$= \frac{2EI}{3}(\theta_C) + \frac{6EI}{3^2}(\Delta) - 17.77$$

$$= 0.67\,EI(\theta_C) + 0.67\,EI(\Delta) - 17.77 \quad \ldots \text{(v)}$$

$$M_{CD} = \frac{4EI}{L}(\theta_C) + \frac{2EI}{L}(\theta_D) + \frac{6EI}{L^2}(\Delta) + M^F_{CD}$$

$$= \frac{4EI}{L}(\theta_C) + \frac{6EI}{3^2}(\Delta) + 8.89$$

$$= 1.33\,EI(\theta_C) + 0.67\,EI(\Delta) + 8.89$$

Step IV : Equilibrium conditions for joints :

Moment equilibrium of joint B : $\quad M_{BA} + M_{BC} = 0 \quad \ldots \text{(A)}$

Moment equilibrium of joint C : $\quad M_{CB} + M_{CD} = 0 \quad \ldots \text{(B)}$

Horizontal shear equilibrium of structure : $H_A + H_D + 40 - 25 \times 4 = 0$

i.e. $\quad H_A + H_D - 60 = 0$

where, $\quad H_A \times 4 = M_{AB} + M_{BA} + 25 \times 4 \times \dfrac{4}{2}$

$$H_A = \frac{M_{AB} + M_{BA}}{4} + 50 \quad \text{and}$$

$$H_D \times 3 + 40 \times 2 = M_{CD} + M_{DC} \quad : \quad H_D = \frac{M_{CD} + M_{DC}}{3} - 26.67$$

STRUCTURAL ANALYSIS – II   SLOPE-DEFLECTION METHOD

Above equation becomes

$$\left[\frac{M_{AB}+M_{BA}}{4}+50\right]+\left[\frac{M_{CD}+M_{DC}}{3}-26.67\right]-60=0$$

$$\frac{M_{AB}+M_{BA}}{4}+\frac{M_{CD}+M_{DC}}{3}-36.67=0$$

$$3(M_{AB}+M_{BA})+4(M_{CD}+M_{DC})-440=0 \qquad \ldots (C)$$

Step V : Formulation of equilibrium equations in terms of displacements :

Substituting equations (ii) and (iii) in equation (A), we get

$$[EI(\theta_B)+0.375\,EI(\Delta)-33.33]+\left[\frac{4EI}{3}(\theta_B)+\frac{2EI}{3}(\theta_C)+18.75\right]=0$$

$$2.33\,EI(\theta_B)+0.67\,EI(\theta_C)+0.375\,EI(\Delta)-14.58=0 \qquad \ldots (I)$$

Substituting equations (iv) and (vi) in equation (B), we get

$$\left[\frac{4EI}{3}(\theta_C)+\frac{2EI}{3}(\theta_B)-18.75\right]+[1.33\,EI(\theta_C)+0.67\,EI(\Delta)+8.89]=0$$

$$2.67\,EI(\theta_C)+0.67\,EI(\theta_B)+0.67\,EI(\Delta)-9.86=0 \qquad \ldots (II)$$

Substituting equations (i), (ii), (v) and (vi) in equation (C), we get

$$3\,[0.5\,EI(\theta_B)+0.375\,EI(\Delta)+33.33+EI(\theta_B)+0.375\,EI(\Delta)-33.33]+$$
$$4\,[0.67\,EI(\theta_C)+0.67\,EI(\Delta)-17.77+1.33\,EI(\theta_C)+0.67\,EI(\Delta)+8.89]-440=0$$

i.e. $4.5\,EI(\theta_B)+8\,EI(\theta_C)+7.58\,EI(\Delta)-475.55=0 \qquad \ldots (III)$

Step VI : Solution of equations for displacements :

Solving equations (I), (II) and (III), we get

$$\boxed{\theta_B=\frac{-2.18}{EI};\quad \theta_C=\frac{-16.08}{EI};\quad \Delta=\frac{81.04}{EI}}$$

positive sign for Δ indicates that sway is towards right.

Step VII : Member-end moments :

Substituting the value of above displacements in SD equations, member-end moments are obtained as under :

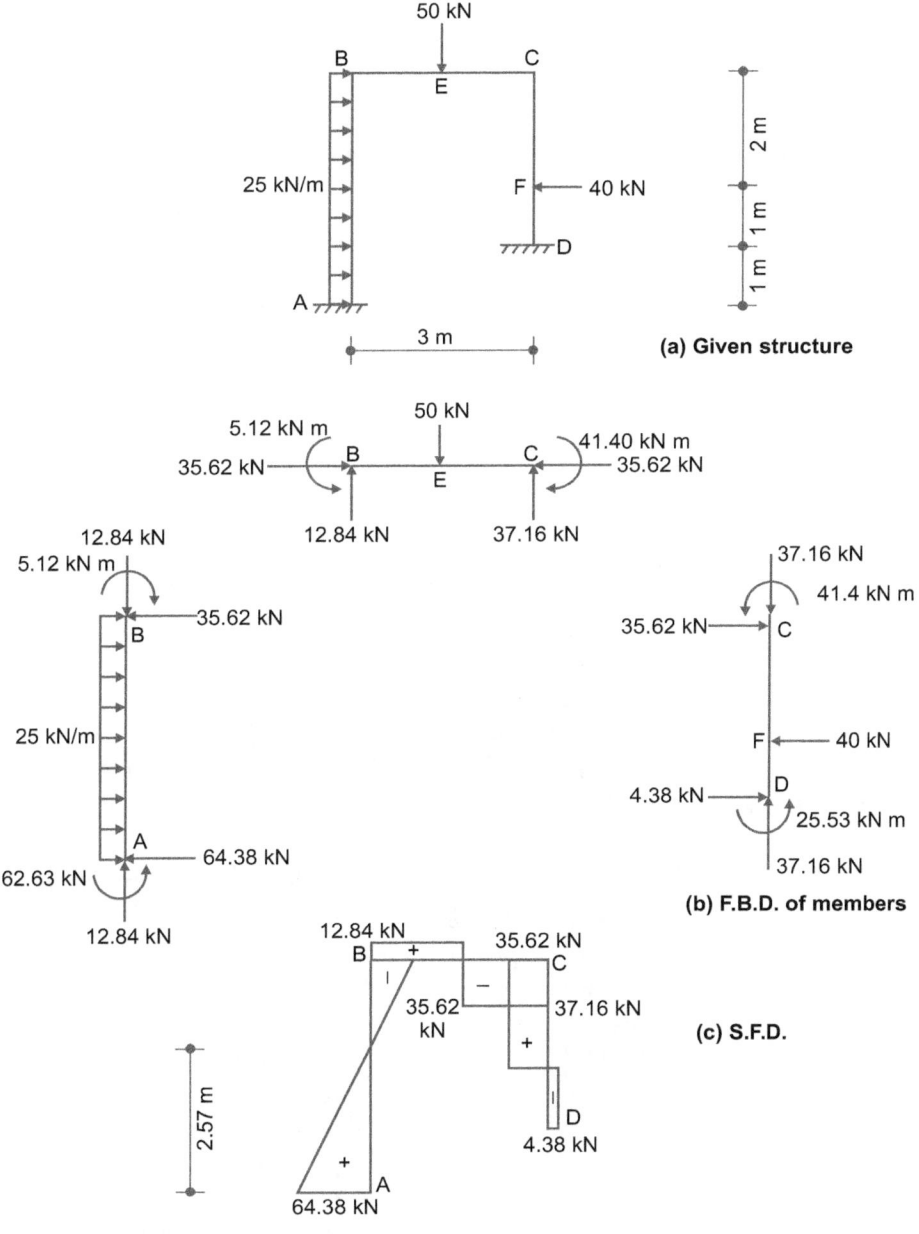

Fig. 1.26 : (Contd.)

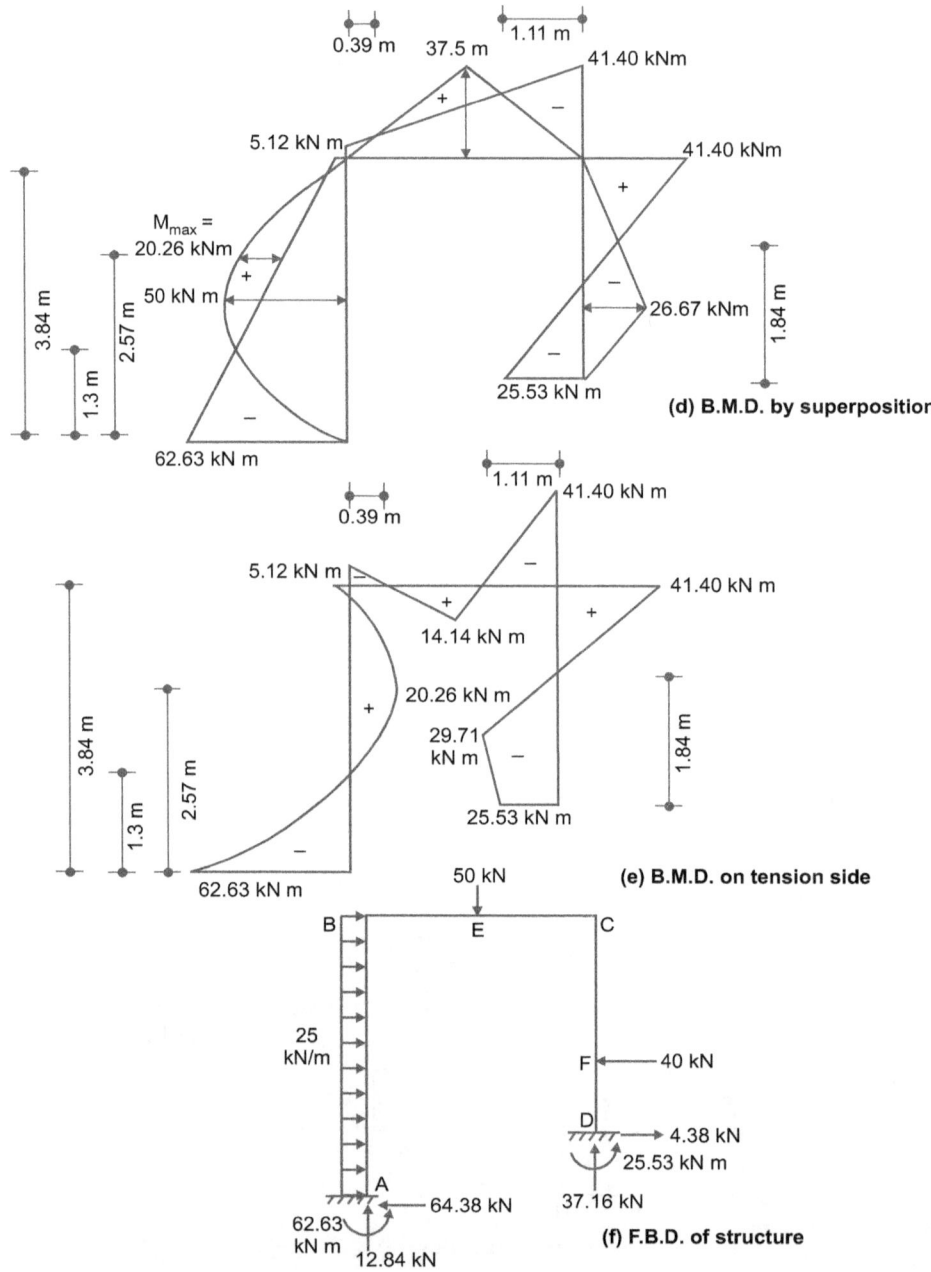

Fig. 1.26 : For Illustrative Example 1.17

STRUCTURAL ANALYSIS – II SLOPE-DEFLECTION METHOD

$$M_{AB} = 0.5\,EI\left(-\frac{2.18}{EI}\right) + 0.375\,EI\left(\frac{81.04}{EI}\right) + 33.33 = 62.63 \text{ kNm}$$

$$M_{BA} = EI\left(-\frac{2.18}{EI}\right) + 0.375\,EI\left(\frac{81.04}{EI}\right) - 33.33 = -5.12 \text{ kNm}$$

$$M_{BC} = \frac{4\,EI}{3}\left(-\frac{2.18}{EI}\right) + \frac{2\,EI}{3}\left(-\frac{16.08}{EI}\right) + 18.75 = 5.12 \text{ kNm}$$

$$M_{CB} = \frac{4\,EI}{3}\left(-\frac{16.08}{EI}\right) + \frac{2\,EI}{3}\left(-\frac{2.18}{EI}\right) - 18.75 = -41.40 \text{ kNm}$$

$$M_{DC} = 0.67\,EI\left(-\frac{16.08}{EI}\right) + 0.67\,EI\left(\frac{81.04}{EI}\right) - 17.77 = 25.53 \text{ kNm}$$

$$M_{CD} = 1.33\,EI\left(-\frac{16.08}{EI}\right) + 0.67\,EI\left(\frac{81.04}{EI}\right) + 8.89 = 41.40 \text{ kNm}$$

Step VIII : FBD of members is as shown in Fig. 1.26 (b). Considering equilibrium of each member and of complete structure; all reaction components are found out as shown in the figure.

Step IX : Shear force diagram is as shown in Fig. 1.26 (c).

Step X : Bending moment diagram.
BMD by superposition is shown in Fig. 1.26 (d).
BMD on tension side is shown in Fig. 1.26 (e).

Step XI : FBD of structure is as shown in Fig. 1.26 (f).

Example 1.18 : *Analyse the portal frame shown in Fig. 1.27 (a) by slope-deflection method. Take EI = constant. Draw SFD and BMD.*

Solution : Data : (1) The frame is supported and loaded as shown in Fig. 1.27 (a).
(2) Frame type : Sway frame.

Object : Structural analysis.

Equations : SD equations.

Procedure :

Step I : Degree of kinematic indeterminacy = D_{ki} = 4.
Unknown displacements : θ_B, θ_C, θ_D and horizontal sway = Δ.
Known displacement : θ_A = 0.

Step II : Fixed-end moments :

$$M^F_{AB} = -M^F_{BA} = \frac{WL}{8} = \frac{160 \times 4}{8} = 80 \text{ kNm}$$

$$M^F_{BC} = -M^F_{CB} = \frac{wl^2}{12} = \frac{20 \times 4^2}{12} = 26.67 \text{ kNm}$$

$$-M^F_{DC} = M^F_{CD} = \frac{wl^2}{12} = \frac{20 \times 3^2}{12} = 15 \text{ kNm}$$

Step III : SD equations : (Assuming horizontal sway = Δ towards right)

Member AB :

$$M_{AB} = \frac{4EI}{L}(\theta_A) + \frac{2EI}{L}(\theta_B) + \frac{6EI}{L^2}(\Delta) + M^F_{AB}$$

$$= \frac{2(2EI)}{4}(\theta_B) + \frac{6(2EI)}{4^2}(\Delta) + 80$$

$$= EI(\theta_B) + 0.75 EI(\Delta) + 80 \qquad \ldots \text{(i)}$$

$$M_{BA} = \frac{4EI}{L}(\theta_B) + \frac{2EI}{L}(\theta_A) + \frac{6EI}{L^2}(\Delta) + M^F_{BA}$$

$$= \frac{4(2EI)}{4}(\theta_B) + \frac{6(2EI)}{4^2}(\Delta) - 80$$

$$= 2EI(\theta_B) + 0.75 EI(\Delta) - 80 \qquad \ldots \text{(ii)}$$

Member BC :

$$M_{BC} = \frac{4EI}{L}(\theta_B) + \frac{2EI}{L}(\theta_C) \pm \frac{6EI}{L^2}(\Delta) + M^F_{BC}$$

$$= \frac{4EI}{4}(\theta_B) + \frac{2EI}{4}(\theta_C) + 26.67$$

$$= EI(\theta_B) + 0.5 EI(\theta_C) + 26.67 \qquad \ldots \text{(iii)}$$

$$M_{CB} = \frac{4EI}{L}(\theta_C) + \frac{2EI}{L}(\theta_B) \pm \frac{6EI}{L^2}(\Delta) + M^F_{CB}$$

$$= \frac{4EI}{4}(\theta_C) + \frac{2EI}{4}(\theta_B) - 26.67$$

$$= EI(\theta_C) + 0.5 EI(\theta_B) - 26.67 \qquad \ldots \text{(iv)}$$

Member DC :

$$M_{DC} = \frac{4EI}{L}(\theta_D) + \frac{2EI}{L}(\theta_C) + \frac{6EI}{L^2}(\Delta) + M^F_{DC}$$

$$= \frac{4EI}{3}(\theta_D) + \frac{2EI}{3}(\theta_C) + \frac{6EI}{3^2}(\Delta) - 15$$

$$= 1.33 EI(\theta_D) + 0.67 EI(\theta_C) + 0.67 EI(\Delta) - 15 \qquad \ldots \text{(v)}$$

$$M_{CD} = \frac{4EI}{L}(\theta_C) + \frac{2EI}{L}(\theta_D) + \frac{6EI}{L^2}(\Delta) + M^F_{CD}$$

$$= \frac{4EI}{3}(\theta_C) + \frac{2EI}{3}(\theta_D) + \frac{6EI}{3^2}(\Delta) + 15$$

$$= 1.33 EI(\theta_C) + 0.67 EI(\theta_D) + 0.67 EI(\Delta) + 15 \qquad \ldots \text{(vi)}$$

Step IV : Equilibrium conditions for joints :

Moment equilibrium of joint B : $\qquad M_{BA} + M_{BC} = 0 \qquad \ldots$ (A)

Moment equilibrium of joint C : $\qquad M_{CB} + M_{CD} = 0 \qquad \ldots$ (B)

Moment equilibrium of joint D : $\qquad M_{DC} = 0 \qquad \ldots$ (C)

Horizontal shear equilibrium of structure :

$$H_A + H_D - 160 + 20 \times 3 = 0$$

i.e. $\qquad H_A + H_D - 100 = 0 \qquad \ldots$ (D)

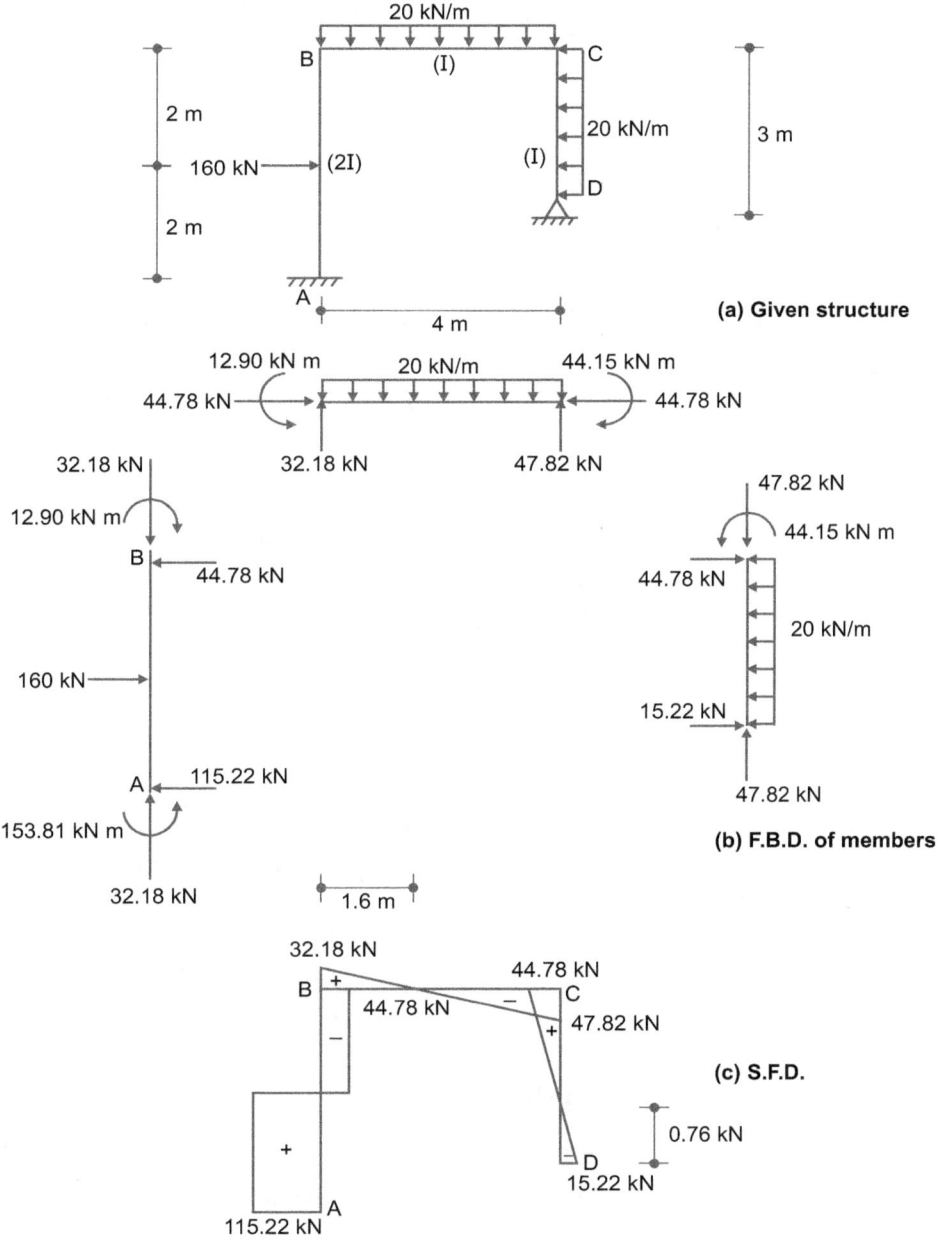

Fig. 1.27 : (Contd.)

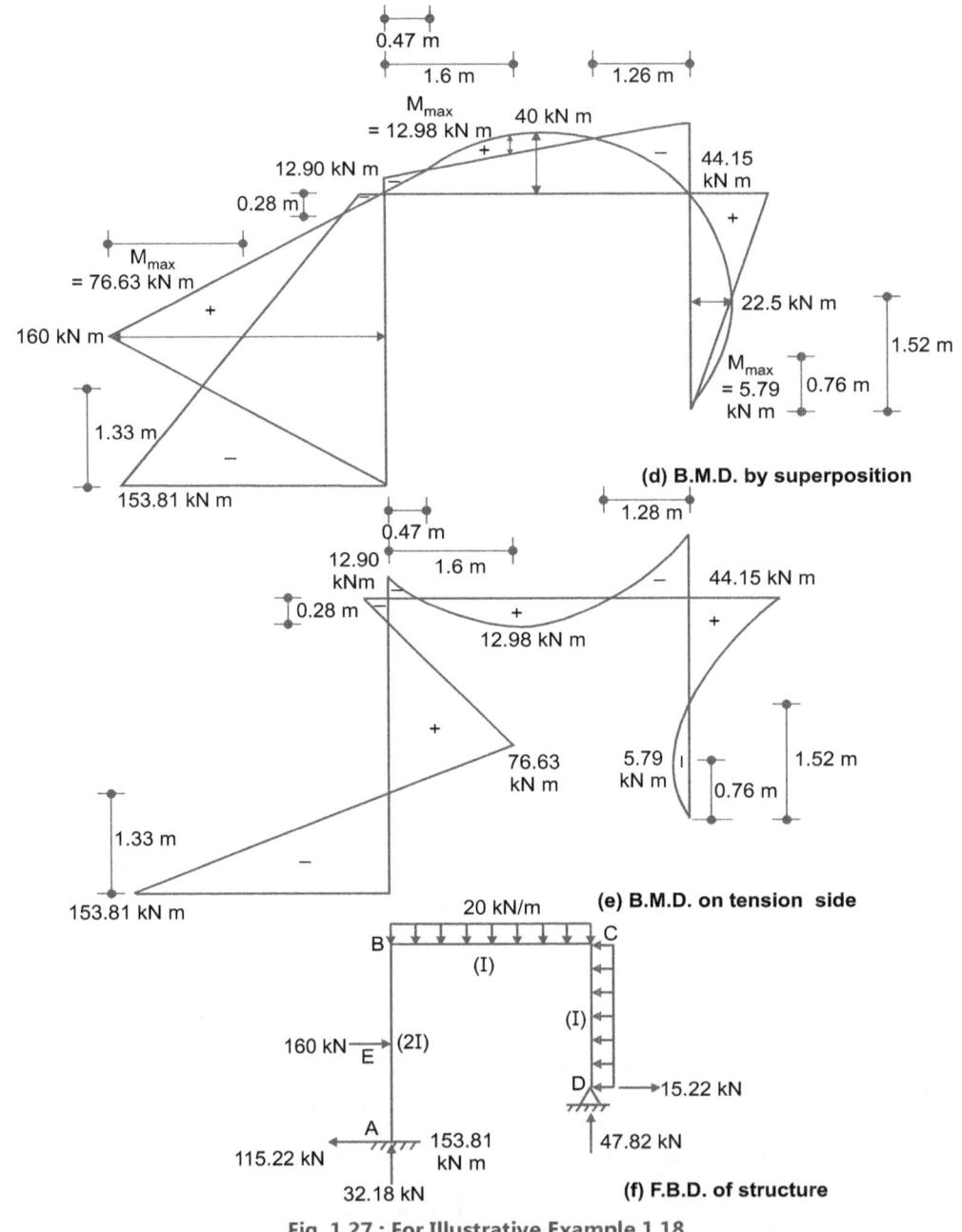

Fig. 1.27 : For Illustrative Example 1.18

STRUCTURAL ANALYSIS – II SLOPE-DEFLECTION METHOD

where,
$$H_A = \frac{M_{AB} + M_{BA}}{4} + 80 \text{ and;}$$

$$H_D = \frac{M_{DC}}{3} - 30, \text{ equation (D) becomes,}$$

$$\frac{M_{AB} + M_{BA}}{4} + 80 + \frac{M_{CD}}{3} - 30 - 100 = 0$$

$$3(M_{AB} + M_{BA}) + 4 M_{CD} - 600 = 0 \quad \ldots (D)$$

Step V : Formulation of equilibrium equations in terms of joint displacements :
Substituting equations (ii) and (iii) in equation (A), we get

$$[2 \, EI \, (\theta_B) + 0.75 \, EI \, (\Delta) - 80] \, [EI \, (\theta_B) + 0.5 \, EI \, (\theta_C) + 26.67] = 0$$

$$3 \, EI \, (\theta_B) + 0.5 \, EI \, (\theta_C) + 0.75 \, EI \, (\Delta) - 53.33 = 0 \quad \ldots (I)$$

Substituting equations (iv) and (vi) in equation (B), we get

$$[EI \, (\theta_C) + 0.5 \, EI \, (\theta_B) - 26.67] \, [1.33 \, EI \, (\theta_C) + 0.67 \, EI \, (\theta_D) + 0.67 \, EI \, (\Delta) + 15] = 0$$

$$2.33 \, EI \, (\theta_C) + 0.5 \, EI \, (\theta_B) + 0.67 \, EI \, (\theta_D) + 0.67 \, EI \, (\Delta) - 11.67 = 0 \quad \ldots (II)$$

Substituting equation (v) in equation (C), we get

$$1.33 \, EI \, (\theta_D) + 0.67 \, EI \, (\theta_C) + 0.67 \, EI \, (\Delta) - 15 = 0 \quad \ldots (III)$$

Substituting equations (i), (ii) and (vi) in equation (D), we get

$$3 \, [EI \, (\theta_B) + 0.75 \, EI \, (\Delta) + 80 + 2 \, EI \, (\theta_B) + 0.75 \, EI \, (\Delta) - 80]$$
$$+ 4 \, [1.33 \, EI \, (\theta_C) + 0.67 \, EI \, (\theta_D) + 0.67 \, EI \, (\Delta) + 15] - 600 = 0$$

$$9 \, EI \, (\theta_B) + 5.33 \, EI \, (\theta_C) + 2.67 \, EI \, (\theta_D) + 7.18 \, EI \, (\Delta) - 540 = 0 \quad \ldots (IV)$$

Step VI : Solution of equations for joint displacements :
Solving equations (I), (II), (III) and (IV), we get

$$\boxed{\theta_B = \frac{-6.70}{EI}, \quad \theta_C = \frac{-14.128}{EI}, \quad \theta_D = \frac{-35.37}{EI}, \quad \Delta = \frac{107.35}{EI}}$$

positive sign for Δ indicates that, sway is towards right.

Step VII : Member-end moments : Substituting the values of above joint displacements in SD equations, member-end moments are obtained as under :

$$M_{AB} = EI \left(\frac{-6.70}{EI}\right) + 0.75 \, EI \left(\frac{107.35}{EI}\right) + 80 = 153.81 \text{ kNm}$$

$$M_{BA} = 2 \, EI \left(\frac{-6.70}{EI}\right) + 0.75 \, EI \left(\frac{107.35}{EI}\right) - 80 = -12.90 \text{ kNm}$$

$$M_{BC} = EI \left(\frac{-6.70}{EI}\right) + 0.5 \, EI \left(-\frac{14.128}{EI}\right) + 26.67 = 12.90 \text{ kNm}$$

$$M_{CB} = EI \left(-\frac{14.128}{EI}\right) + 0.5 \, EI \left(-\frac{6.70}{EI}\right) - 26.67 = -44.15 \text{ kNm}$$

$$M_{DC} = 1.33 \, EI \left(-\frac{35.37}{EI}\right) + 0.67 \, EI \left(-\frac{14.128}{EI}\right) + 0.67 \, EI \left(\frac{107.35}{EI}\right) - 15 = 0$$

$$M_{CD} = 1.33 \, EI \left(-\frac{14.128}{EI}\right) + 0.67 \, EI \left(-\frac{35.37}{EI}\right) + 0.67 \, EI \left(\frac{107.35}{EI}\right) + 15$$
$$= 44.15 \text{ kNm}$$

Step VIII : FBD of members is as shown in Fig. 1.27 (b). Considering equilibrium of each member and of complete structure, all reaction components are found out as shown in the figure.

Step IX : Shear force diagram is as shown in Fig. 1.27 (c).

Step X : Bending moment diagram :

BMD by superposition is shown in Fig. 1.27 (d).

BMD on tension side is shown in Fig. 1.27 (e).

Step XI : FBD of structure is as shown in Fig. 1.27 (f).

***Example 1.19 :** Analyse the portal frame shown in Fig. 1.28 (a) by slope-deflection method. Draw SFD, BMD and elastic curve.*

Solution : Data : (1) The frame is loaded as shown in Fig. 1.28 (a).

(2) Frame type : Sway frame.

Object : Structural analysis.

Equations : SD equations.

Procedure :

Step I : Degree of kinematic indeterminacy = D_{ki} = 4.

Unknown displacements : $\theta_B, \theta_{CB}, \theta_{CD},$ horizontal sway = Δ.

Known displacements : $\theta_A = \theta_D = 0$.

Step II : Fixed-end moments :
$$M_{AB}^F = M_{BA}^F = M_{DC}^F = M_{CD}^F = 0$$
$$M_{BC}^F = -M_{CD}^F = \frac{WL}{8} = \frac{50 \times 4}{8} = 25 \text{ kNm}$$

Step III : SD equations : (Assuming horizontal sway = Δ towards right)

Member AB :
$$M_{AB} = \frac{4 \, EI}{L}(\theta_A) + \frac{2 \, EI}{L}(\theta_B) + \frac{6 \, EI}{L^2}(\Delta) + M_{AB}^F$$
$$= \frac{2 \, EI}{4}(\theta_B) + \frac{6 \, EI}{4^2}(\Delta) = 0.5 \, EI \, (\theta_B) + 0.375 \, EI \, (\Delta) \qquad \ldots \text{(i)}$$

$$M_{BA} = \frac{4 \, EI}{L}(\theta_B) + \frac{2 \, EI}{L}(\theta_A) + \frac{6 \, EI}{L^2}(\Delta) + M_{BA}^F$$
$$= \frac{4 \, EI}{4}(\theta_B) + \frac{6 \, EI}{4^2}(\Delta)$$
$$= EI \, (\theta_B) + 0.375 \, EI \, (\Delta) \qquad \ldots \text{(ii)}$$

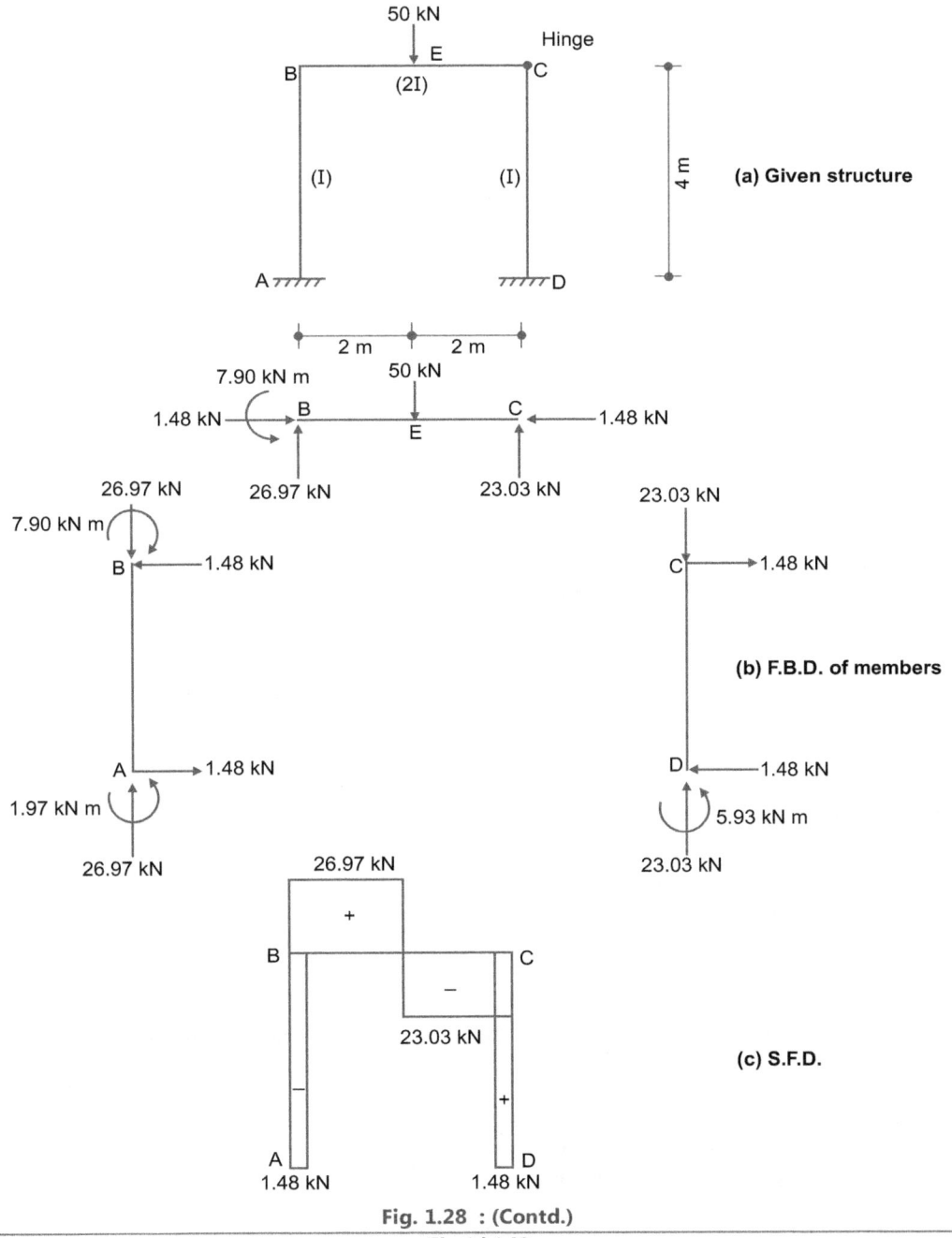

Fig. 1.28 : (Contd.)

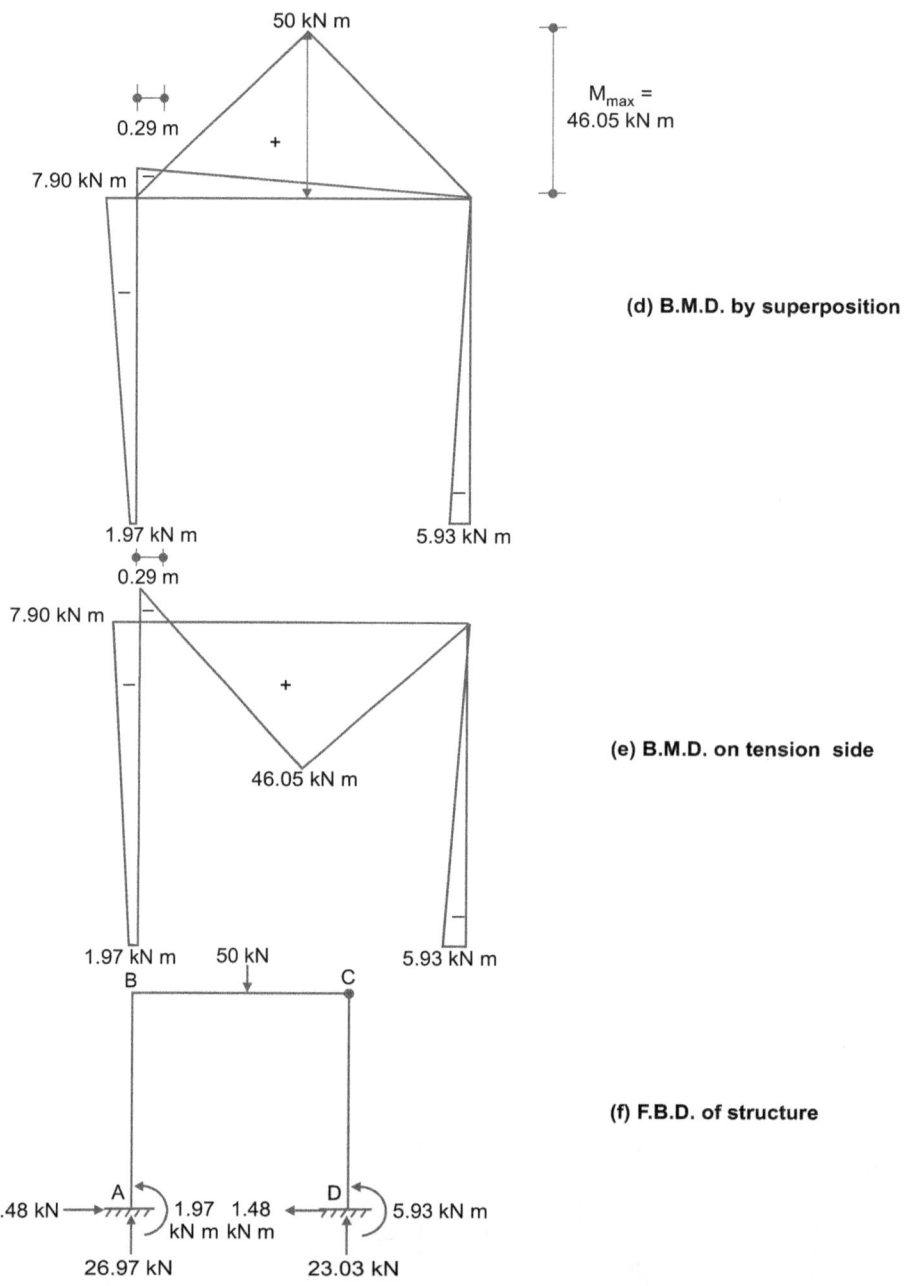

Fig. 1.28 : For Illustrative Example 1.19

Member BC :
$$M_{BC} = \frac{4EI}{L}(\theta_B) + \frac{2EI}{L}(\theta_{CB}) \pm \frac{6EI}{L^2}(\Delta) + M^F_{BC}$$
$$= \frac{4(2EI)}{4}(\theta_B) + \frac{2(2EI)}{4}(\theta_{CB}) + 25$$
$$= 2EI(\theta_B) + EI(\theta_{CB}) + 25 \qquad \ldots \text{(iii)}$$

$$M_{CB} = \frac{4EI}{L}(\theta_{CB}) + \frac{2EI}{L}(\theta_B) \pm \frac{6EI}{L^2}(\Delta) + M^F_{CB}$$
$$= \frac{4(2EI)}{4}(\theta_{CB}) + \frac{2(2EI)}{4}(\theta_B) - 25$$
$$= 2EI(\theta_{CB}) + EI(\theta_B) - 25 \qquad \ldots \text{(iv)}$$

Member DC :
$$M_{DC} = \frac{4EI}{L}(\theta_D) + \frac{2EI}{L}(\theta_{CD}) + \frac{6EI}{L^2}(\Delta) + M^F_{DC}$$
$$= \frac{2EI}{4}(\theta_{CD}) + \frac{6EI}{4^2}(\Delta) = 0.5EI(\theta_{CD}) + 0.375EI(\Delta) \qquad \ldots \text{(v)}$$

$$M_{CD} = \frac{4EI}{L}(\theta_{CD}) + \frac{2EI}{L}(\theta_D) + \frac{6EI}{L^2}(\Delta) + M^F_{CD}$$
$$= \frac{4EI}{L}(\theta_{CD}) + \frac{6EI}{4^2}(\Delta) = EI(\theta_{CD}) + 0.375EI(\Delta) \qquad \ldots \text{(vi)}$$

Step IV : Equilibrium conditions for joints :
Moment equilibrium of joint B : $M_{BA} + M_{BC} = 0$ ... (A)
Moment equilibrium of joint C : $M_{CB} = 0$ ... (B)
and $M_{CD} = 0$ ... (C)
Horizontal shear equilibrium of structure,
$$H_A + H_D = 0 \qquad \ldots \text{(D)}$$
where $H_A = \dfrac{M_{AB} + M_{BA}}{4}$ and $H_D = \dfrac{M_{DC}}{4}$; equation (D) becomes
$$M_{AB} + M_{BA} + M_{DC} = 0 \qquad \ldots \text{(D)}$$

Step V : Formulation of equilibrium equations in terms of joint displacements :
Substituting equations (ii) and (iii) in equation (A), we get
$$[EI(\theta_B) + 0.375EI(\Delta)] + [2EI(\theta_B) + EI(\theta_{CB}) + 25] = 0$$
$$3EI + (\theta_B) + EI(\theta_{CB}) + 0.375EI(\Delta) + 25 = 0 \qquad \ldots \text{(I)}$$
Substituting equation (iv) in equation (B), we get
$$2EI(\theta_{CB}) + EI(\theta_B) - 25 = 0 \qquad \ldots \text{(II)}$$
Substituting equation (vi) in equation (C), we get
$$EI(\theta_{CD}) + 0.375EI(\Delta) = 0 \qquad \ldots \text{(III)}$$
Substituting equations (i), (ii) and (v) in equation (D), we get
$$[0.5EI(\theta_B) + 0.375EI(\Delta)] + [EI(\theta_B) + 0.375EI(\Delta)] + [0.5EI(\theta_{CD}) + 0.375EI(\Delta)] = 0$$
$$1.5EI(\theta_B) + 0.5EI(\theta_{CD}) + 1.125EI(\Delta) = 0 \qquad \ldots \text{(IV)}$$

Step VI : Solution of equations for displacements :
Solving equations (I), (II), (III) and (IV), we get

$$\boxed{\theta_B = \frac{-19.73}{EI}, \quad \theta_{CB} = \frac{22.36}{EI}, \quad \theta_{CD} = \frac{-11.83}{EI} \quad \text{and} \quad \Delta = \frac{31.57}{EI}}$$

positive sign for Δ indicates that; sway is towards right.

Step VII : Member-end moments : Substituting the values of above joint displacements in SD equations, member-end moments are obtained as under :

$$M_{AB} = 0.5\,EI\left(-\frac{19.73}{EI}\right) + 0.375\,EI\left(\frac{31.57}{EI}\right) = 1.973 \text{ kNm}$$

$$M_{BA} = EI\left(-\frac{19.73}{EI}\right) + 0.375\,EI\left(\frac{31.57}{EI}\right) + 25 = -7.9 \text{ kNm}$$

$$M_{BC} = 2\,EI\left(-\frac{19.73}{EI}\right) + EI\left(\frac{22.36}{EI}\right) + 25 = 7.90 \text{ kNm}$$

$$M_{CB} = 2\,EI\left(\frac{22.36}{EI}\right) + EI\left(-\frac{19.73}{EI}\right) - 25 = 0$$

$$M_{DC} = 0.5\,EI\left(-\frac{11.83}{EI}\right) + 0.375\,EI\left(\frac{31.57}{EI}\right) = 5.93 \text{ kNm}$$

$$M_{CD} = EI\left(-\frac{11.83}{EI}\right) + 0.375\,EI\left(\frac{31.57}{EI}\right) = 0.$$

Step VIII : FBD of members is as shown in Fig. 1.28 (b). Considering equilibrium of each member and of complete structure, all reaction components are found out as shown in the figure.

Step IX : Shear force diagram is as shown in Fig. 1.28 (c).

Step X : Bending moment diagram :
BMD by superposition is shown in Fig. 1.28 (d).
BMD on tension side is shown in Fig. 1.28 (e).

Step XI : FBD of structure is as shown in Fig. 1.28 (f).

1.9.5 Frames Having Known Yielding of Supports

The yielding of support, in general, includes rotational yielding of the fixed support θ and translational yielding i.e. settlement of any type of support Δ. Numerical values of yielding of supports i.e. θ and Δ including direction are known.

1.9.6 Application of SD Method to Frames Having Known Yielding of Supports

Numerical values of EI are essential to calculate the moment contributions of $\frac{4\,EI}{L}\,(\theta)$ and $\frac{6\,EI}{L^2}\,(\Delta)$ in SD equations of the corresponding members. The moment contributions must be

STRUCTURAL ANALYSIS – II   SLOPE-DEFLECTION METHOD

taken in correct direction according to the given direction of yielding of support. Rules of sign convention should be strictly observed. Rest of the analysis can be completed as per the procedure of SD method.

The general hints given for beam analysis are also applicable to frame analysis.

Example 1.20 : *Analyse the portal frame shown in Fig. 1.29 (a) by slope-deflection method, if support A sinks by 5 mm and support D is subjected to anticlockwise rotation of 0.002 radians. Take EI = 3000 kNm².*

Solution : Data : (1) The frame is supported and loaded as shown in Fig. 1.29 (a).
                    (2) EI = 3000 kNm2
                    (3) Frame type : Sway frame.

Object : Structural analysis.

Equations : SD equations.

Procedure :

Step I : Degree of kinematic indeterminacy = D_{ki} = 3.

Unknown displacements : θ_B, θ_C and horizontal sway = Δ.

Known displacements : θ_A = 0, Δ_A = 5 mm ($\downarrow$) = Δ_B

                           θ_D = 0.002 (Anticlockwise, hence positive)

                           Δ_D = Δ_C = 0

Step II : Fixed-end moments :

$$M^F_{AB} = M^F_{BA} = M^F_{BC} = M^F_{CB} = M^F_{CD} = M^F_{DC} = 0$$

Step III : SD equations : (Assuming horizontal sway = Δ towards right).

Member AB : $M_{AB} = \dfrac{4EI}{L}(\theta_A) + \dfrac{2EI}{L}(\theta_B) + \dfrac{6EI}{L^2}(\Delta) + M^F_{AB}$

                       $= \dfrac{2EI}{4}(\theta_B) + \dfrac{6EI}{4^2}(\Delta) = 0.5\,EI\,(\theta_B) + 0.375\,EI\,(\Delta)$ ... (i)

               $M_{BA} = \dfrac{4EI}{L}(\theta_B) + \dfrac{2EI}{L}(\theta_A) + \dfrac{6EI}{L^2}(\Delta) + M^F_{BA}$

                       $= \dfrac{4EI}{4}(\theta_B) + \dfrac{6EI}{4^2}(\Delta) = EI\,(\theta_B) + 0.375\,EI\,(\Delta)$ ... (ii)

Note that sinking of support A (also of B by same amount as we shall be neglecting axial deformations of members) does not produce any moment in member AB.

Member BC : $M_{BC} = \dfrac{4EI}{L}(\theta_B) + \dfrac{2EI}{L}(\theta_C) \pm \dfrac{6EI}{L^2}(\Delta) + M^F_{BC}$

                       $= \dfrac{4(2EI)}{5}(\theta_B) + \dfrac{2(2EI)}{5}(\theta_C) - \dfrac{6(2 \times 3000)}{5^2}\left(\dfrac{5}{1000}\right)$

                       $= 1.6\,EI\,(\theta_B) + 0.8\,EI\,(\theta_C) - 7.2$ ... (iii)

STRUCTURAL ANALYSIS – II SLOPE-DEFLECTION METHOD

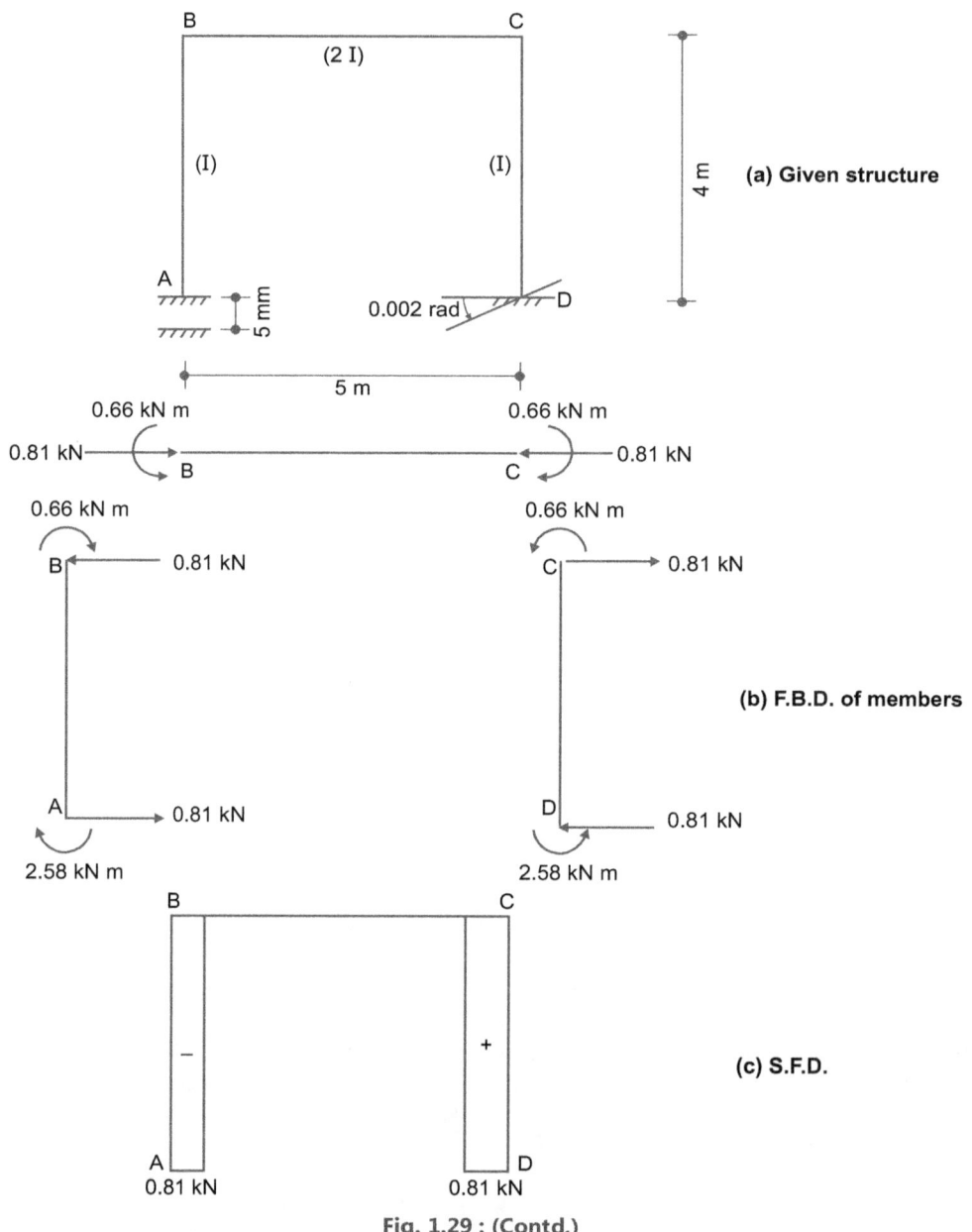

Fig. 1.29 : (Contd.)

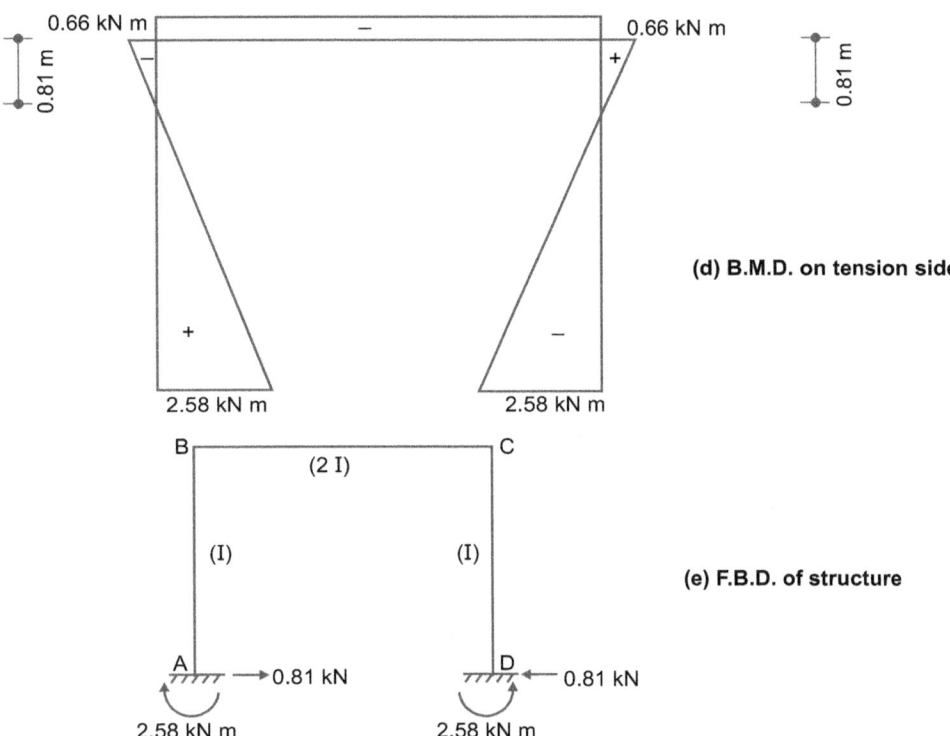

(d) B.M.D. on tension side

(e) F.B.D. of structure

Fig. 1.29 : For Illustrative Example 1.20

$$M_{CB} = \frac{4EI}{L}(\theta_C) + \frac{2EI}{L}(\theta_B) \pm \frac{6EI}{L^2}(\Delta) + M_{CB}^F$$

$$= \frac{4(2EI)}{5}(\theta_C) + \frac{2(2EI)}{5}(\theta_B) - \frac{6 \times 2 \times 3000}{5^2}\left(\frac{5}{1000}\right)$$

$$= 1.6\ EI\ (\theta_C) + 0.8\ EI\ (\theta_B) - 7.2 \quad \ldots \text{(iv)}$$

Note that, sinking of support A (i.e. of B) produces clockwise moments, hence negative for member BC.

Member CD :

$$M_{CD} = \frac{4EI}{L}(\theta_C) + \frac{2EI}{L}(\theta_D) + \frac{6EI}{L^2}(\Delta) + M_{CD}^F$$

$$= \frac{4EI}{4}(\theta_C) + \frac{2 \times 3000}{4}(0.002) + \frac{6EI}{4^2}(\Delta)$$

$$= EI\ (\theta_C) + 0.375\ EI\ (\Delta) + 3 \quad \ldots \text{(v)}$$

STRUCTURAL ANALYSIS – II   SLOPE-DEFLECTION METHOD

$$M_{DC} = \frac{4\,EI}{L}(\theta_D) + \frac{2\,EI}{L}(\theta_C) + \frac{6\,EI}{L^2}(\Delta) + M^F_{DC}$$

$$= \frac{4 \times 3000}{4}(0.002) + \frac{2\,EI}{4}(\theta_C) + \frac{6\,EI}{4^2}(\Delta)$$

$$= 0.5\,EI\,(\theta_C) + 0.375\,EI\,(\Delta) + 6 \qquad \ldots \text{(vi)}$$

Step IV : Equilibrium conditions for joints :

Moment equilibrium for joint B : $M_{BA} + M_{BC} = 0$ ... (A)

Moment equilibrium for joint C : $M_{CB} + M_{CD} = 0$ ... (B)

Horizontal shear equilibrium for structure,

$$H_A + H_D = 0$$

where, $H_A = \dfrac{M_{AB} + M_{BA}}{4}$ and $H_D = \dfrac{M_{DC} + M_{CD}}{4}$

Above equation becomes $M_{AB} + M_{BA} + M_{DC} + M_{CD} = 0$ ... (C)

Step V : Formulation of equilibrium equations in terms of joint displacements :

Substituting equations (ii) and (iii) in equation (A), we get

$$[EI\,(\theta_B) + 0.375\,EI\,(\Delta)] + [1.6\,EI\,(\theta_B) + 0.8\,EI\,(\theta_C) - 7.2] = 0$$

$$2.6\,EI\,(\theta_B) + 0.8\,EI\,(\theta_C) + 0.375\,EI\,(\Delta) - 7.2 = 0 \qquad \ldots \text{(I)}$$

Substituting equations (iv) and (v) in equation (B), we get

$$[1.6\,EI\,(\theta_C) + 0.8\,EI\,(\theta_B) - 7.2] + [EI\,(\theta_C) + 0.375\,EI\,(\Delta) + 3] = 0$$

$$2.6\,EI\,(\theta_C) + 0.8\,EI\,(\theta_B) + 0.375\,EI\,(\Delta) - 4.2 = 0 \qquad \ldots \text{(II)}$$

Substituting equations (i), (ii), (v) and (vi) in equation (C), we get

$$[0.5\,EI\,(\theta_B) + 0.375\,EI\,(\Delta)] + [EI\,(\theta_B) + 0.375\,EI\,(\Delta)] +$$

$$[EI\,(\theta_C) + 0.375\,EI\,(\Delta) + 3]\,[0.5\,EI\,(\theta_C) + 0.375\,EI\,(\Delta) + 6] = 0$$

$$1.5\,EI\,(\theta_B) + 1.5\,EI\,(\theta_C) + 1.5\,EI\,(\Delta) + 9 = 0 \qquad \ldots \text{(III)}$$

Step VI : Solution of equations for joint displacements :

Solving equations (I), (II) and (III), we get,

$$\boxed{\theta_B = \frac{3.834}{EI},\quad \theta_C = \frac{2.163}{EI},\quad \Delta = -\frac{12}{EI}}$$

negative sign for Δ indicates that, sway is towards left.

Step VII : Member-end moments :

STRUCTURAL ANALYSIS – II   SLOPE-DEFLECTION METHOD

Substituting the values of above displacements in SD equations, member-end moments are obtained as under :

$$M_{AB} = 0.5\,EI\left(\frac{3.834}{EI}\right) + 0.375\,EI\left(-\frac{12}{EI}\right) = -2.58 \text{ kNm}$$

$$M_{BA} = EI\left(\frac{3.834}{EI}\right) + 0.375\,EI\left(-\frac{12}{EI}\right) = -0.66 \text{ kNm}$$

$$M_{BC} = 1.6\,EI\left(\frac{3.834}{EI}\right) + 0.8\,EI\left(\frac{2.163}{EI}\right) - 7.2 = 0.66 \text{ kNm}$$

$$M_{CB} = 1.6\,EI\left(\frac{2.163}{EI}\right) + 0.8\,EI\left(\frac{3.834}{EI}\right) - 7.2 = -0.66 \text{ kNm}$$

$$M_{CD} = EI\left(\frac{2.163}{EI}\right) + 0.375\,EI\left(-\frac{12}{EI}\right) + 3 = 0.66 \text{ kNm}$$

$$M_{DC} = 0.5\,EI\left(\frac{2.163}{EI}\right) + 0.375\,EI\left(-\frac{12}{EI}\right) + 6 = 2.58 \text{ kNm}$$

Step VIII : FBD of members is as shown in Fig. 1.29 (b). Considering equilibrium of each member and of complete structure, all reaction components are found out as shown in the figure.

Step IX : Shear force diagram is as shown in Fig. 1.29 (c).

Step X : Bending moment diagram :

BMD on tension side is shown in Fig. 1.29 (d).

Step XI : FBD of structure is as shown in Fig. 1.29 (e).

Example 1.21 : *Analyse the rigid frame shown in Fig. 1.30 using slope-deflection method. Draw BMD.*

Solution : **(1) Data :** The frame is supported and loaded as shown in Fig. 1.30.

(2) Frame type : Sway frame.

Object : Structural analysis.

Equations : SD equations.

Procedure :

Step I : Degree of kinematic indeterminacy = D_{ki} = 3.

Unknown displacements : θ_B, θ_C and horizontal sway = Δ

Known displacements : $\theta_A = \theta_D = 0$

STRUCTURAL ANALYSIS – II SLOPE-DEFLECTION METHOD

Step II : Fixed-end moments :

$$M_{AB}^F = M_{BA}^F = M_{CD}^F = M_{DC}^F = 0$$

$$M_{BC}^F = -M_{CB}^F = \frac{30 \times 3^2}{12} = 22.5 \text{ kN-m}$$

Step III : SD equations :

(Assuming sway = Δ towards right)

Member AB :

$$M_{AB} = \frac{4EI}{L}\theta_A + \frac{2EI}{L}\theta_B + \frac{6EI\Delta}{L^2} + M_{AB}^F$$

$$= \frac{2EI}{4}\theta_B + \frac{6EI\Delta}{4^2} + 0 = 0.5\, EI\, \theta_B + 0.375\, EI\, \Delta \qquad \ldots (i)$$

$$M_{BA} = \frac{4EI}{L}\theta_B + \frac{2EI}{L}\theta_A + \frac{6EI\Delta}{L^2} + M_{BA}^F$$

$$= \frac{4EI}{4}\theta_B + \frac{6EI\Delta}{4^2} = EI\, \theta_B + 0.375\, EI\, \Delta \qquad \ldots (ii)$$

Member BC :

$$M_{BC} = \frac{4E(2I)}{L}\theta_B + \frac{2E(2I)}{L}\theta_C + \frac{6EI\Delta}{L^2} + M_{BC}^F$$

$$= \frac{8EI}{3}\theta_B + \frac{4EI}{3}\theta_C + 22.5$$

$$= 2.67\, EI\, \theta_B + 1.33\, EI\, \theta_C + 22.5 \qquad \ldots (iii)$$

$$M_{CB} = \frac{4E(2I)}{L}\theta_C + \frac{2E(2I)}{L}\theta_B + \frac{6EI\Delta}{L^2} + M_{CB}^F$$

$$= \frac{8EI}{3}\theta_C + \frac{4EI}{3}\theta_B - 22.5$$

$$= 2.67\, EI\, \theta_C + 1.33\, EI\, \theta_B - 22.5 \qquad \ldots (iv)$$

Member CD :

$$M_{CD} = \frac{4EI}{L}\theta_C + \frac{2EI}{L}\theta_D - \frac{6EI\Delta}{L^2} + M_{CD}^F$$

$$= \frac{4EI}{4}\theta_C + \frac{2EI}{4}\theta_D - \frac{6EI\Delta}{4^2} + 0$$

$$M_{CD} = EI\, \theta_C - 0.375\, EI\, \Delta \qquad \ldots (v)$$

$$M_{DC} = \frac{4EI}{L}\theta_D + \frac{2EI}{L}\theta_C - \frac{6EI\Delta}{L^2} + M_{DC}^F$$

$$= \frac{4\,EI}{4}\theta_D + \frac{2\,EI}{4}\theta_C - \frac{6\,EI\,\Delta}{4^2} + 0$$

$$= 0.5\,EI\,\theta_C - 0.375\,EI\,\Delta \qquad \ldots \text{(vi)}$$

Step IV : Equilibrium conditions for joints :

Moment of equilibrium of joint B

$$M_{BA} + M_{BC} = 0 \qquad \ldots \text{(A)}$$

Moment of equilibrium of joint C

$$M_{CB} + M_{CD} = 0 \qquad \ldots \text{(B)}$$

Horizontal shear equilibrium of structure

$$H_A + H_D = 0$$

where, $\quad H_A = \dfrac{M_{AB} + M_{BA}}{4} \quad$ and $\quad H_D = \dfrac{M_{DC} + M_{CD}}{4}$

$$\frac{M_{AB} + M_{BA}}{4} - \frac{M_{DC} + M_{CD}}{4} = 0$$

$$M_{AB} + M_{BA} + M_{DC} + M_{CD} = 0 \qquad \ldots \text{(C)}$$

Step V : Formulation of equilibrium equations in terms of joint displacements :

Substituting equations (ii) and (iii) in equation (A), we get

$$EI\,\theta_B + 0.375\,EI\,\Delta + 2.67\,EI\,\theta_B + 1.33\,EI\,\theta_C + 22.5 = 0$$

$$3.67\,EI\,\theta_B + 1.33\,EI\,\theta_C + 0.375\,EI\,\Delta = -22.5 \qquad \ldots \text{(D)}$$

Substituting equations (iv) and (v) in equation (B), we get

$$2.67\,EI\,\theta_C + 1.33\,EI\,\theta_B - 22.5 + EI\,\theta_C - 0.375\,EI\,\Delta = 0$$

$$1.33\,EI\,\theta_B + 3.67\,EI\,\theta_C - 0.375\,EI\,\Delta = 22.5 \qquad \ldots \text{(E)}$$

Substituting equations (i), (ii), (v) and (vi) in equation (C),

$$0.5\,EI\,\theta_B + 0.375\,EI\,\Delta + EI\,\theta_B + 0.375\,EI\,\Delta$$

$$- EI\,\theta_C + 0.375\,EI\,\Delta - 0.5\,EI\,\theta_C + 0.375\,EI\,\Delta = 0$$

$$1.5\,EI\,\theta_B - 1.5\,EI\,\theta_C + 1.5\,EI\,\Delta = 0 \qquad \ldots \text{(F)}$$

Step VI : Solving equations (D), (E) and (F), we get

$$\boxed{\theta_B = -\frac{14.18}{EI}, \quad \theta_C = \frac{14.18}{EI}, \quad \Delta = \frac{28.36}{EI}}$$

$\Delta \rightarrow$ +ve indicates sway is towards right.

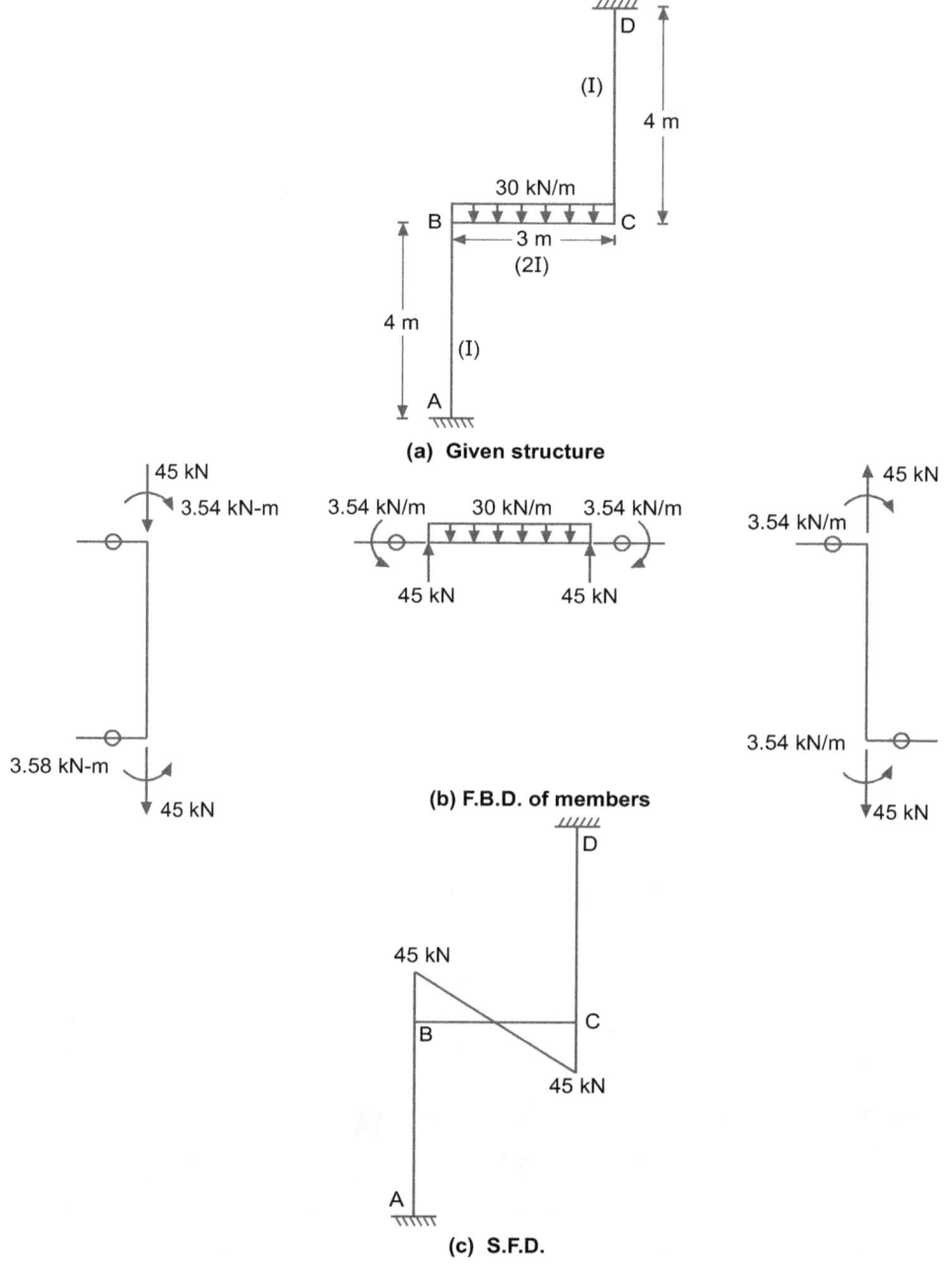

(a) Given structure

(b) F.B.D. of members

(c) S.F.D.

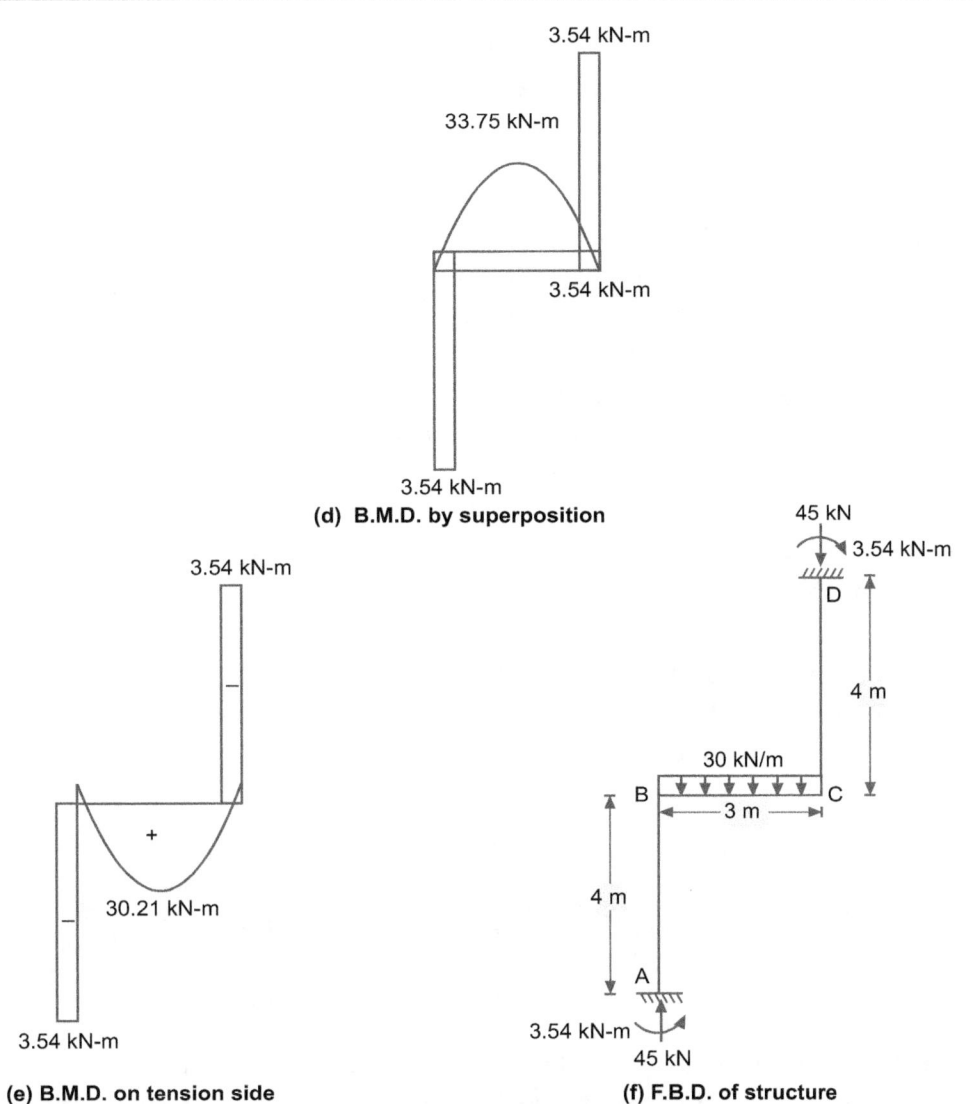

Fig. 1.30 : For Illustrative Example 1.21

Step VII : Member-end moments

M_{AB} = 3.54 kN-m

M_{BA} = − 3.54 kN-m

M_{BC} = 3.54 kN-m

STRUCTURAL ANALYSIS – II SLOPE-DEFLECTION METHOD

$$M_{CB} = -3.54 \text{ kN-m}$$
$$M_{CD} = 3.54 \text{ kN-m}$$

Step VIII : FBD of members is as shown in Fig. 1.30 (b). Considering equilibrium of each member and of complete structure; all reaction components are found out as shown in figure.

Step IX : Shear force diagram is as shown in Fig. 1.30 (c).

Step X : Bending moment diagram : BMD by superposition is shown in Fig. 1.30 (d).

BMD on tension side is shown in Fig. 1.30 (e).

Step XI : F.B.D. of structure is as shown in Fig. 1.30 (f).

Example 1.22 : *Using slope-deflection method, determine the final-end moments for the plane rigid frame shown in Fig. 1.31 (a). Construct BMD.*

Solution : Data : (1) The frame is loaded and supported as shown in Fig. 1.31.

(2) Frame type : Sway frame.

Object : Structural analysis.

Equations : SD equations.

Procedure :

Step I : Degree of kinematic indeterminacy.

Unknown displacements : $\theta_A, \theta_B, \theta_C, \theta_D$ and Δ.

Step II : Fixed-end moments :

$$M_{AB}^F = M_{BA}^F = 0$$

$$M_{BC}^F = -M_{CB}^F = \frac{2.5 \times 4^2}{12} = 3.33 \text{ kN-m}$$

$$M_{CD}^F = \frac{wab^2}{l^2} = \frac{5 \times 1.5 \times 3.5^2}{5^2} = 3.675 \text{ kN-m}$$

$$M_{DC}^F = -\frac{wa^2b}{l^2} = -\frac{5 \times 1.5^2 \times 3.5}{5^2} = -1.575 \text{ kN-m}$$

Step III : SD equations (Assuming horizontal sway = Δ towards right).

Member AB : Modified slope-deflection method :

$$M_{AB} = \frac{3EI}{L}\theta_B + \frac{3EI}{L^2}\Delta + M_{BA}^F$$

$$= \frac{3EI}{4}\theta_B + \frac{3EI}{16}\Delta + 0$$

$$= 0.75 EI \theta_B + 0.1875 EI \Delta \qquad \ldots \text{(I)}$$

Member BC :

$$M_{BC} = \frac{4EI}{L}\theta_B + \frac{2EI}{L}\theta_C + M_{BC}^F$$

$$= \frac{4E(2I)}{4}\theta_B + \frac{2E(2I)}{4}\theta_C + 3.33$$

$$= 2EI\theta_B + EI\theta_C + 3.33 \quad \ldots \text{(II)}$$

$$M_{CB} = \frac{4EI}{L}\theta_C + \frac{2EI}{L}\theta_B + M_{CB}^F$$

$$= \frac{4E(2I)}{4}\theta_C + \frac{2E(2I)}{4}\theta_B - 3.33$$

$$= 2EI\theta_C + EI\theta_B - 3.33 \quad \ldots \text{(III)}$$

Member CD : Using modified slope-deflection method,

$$M_{CD} = M_{CD}^F - \left(\frac{M_{DC}^F}{2}\right) + \frac{3EI}{L}\theta_C + \frac{3EI\Delta}{L^2}$$

$$= 3.675 - \left(-\frac{1.575}{2}\right) + \frac{3E(1.25)}{5}\theta_C + \frac{3E(1.25I)\Delta}{5^2}$$

$$= 4.4625 + 0.75 EI\Delta + 0.15 EI\Delta \quad \ldots \text{(IV)}$$

Step IV : Equilibrium conditions for joints and formulation of equilibrium equations :

Moment equilibrium of joint B

$$M_{BA} + M_{BC} = 0$$

$$0.75 EI\theta_B + 0.1875 EI\Delta + 2EI\theta_B + EI\theta_C + 3.33 = 0$$

$$2.75 EI\theta_B + EI\theta_C + 0.1875 EI\Delta = -3.33 \quad \ldots \text{(A)}$$

Moment equilibrium of joint C

$$M_{CB} + M_{CD} = 0$$

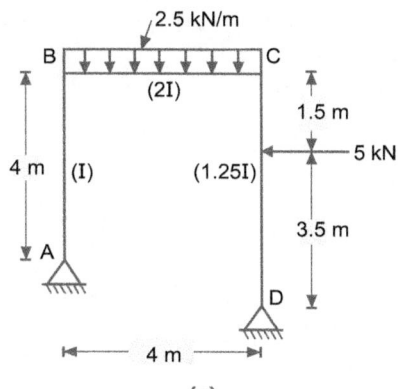

(a)

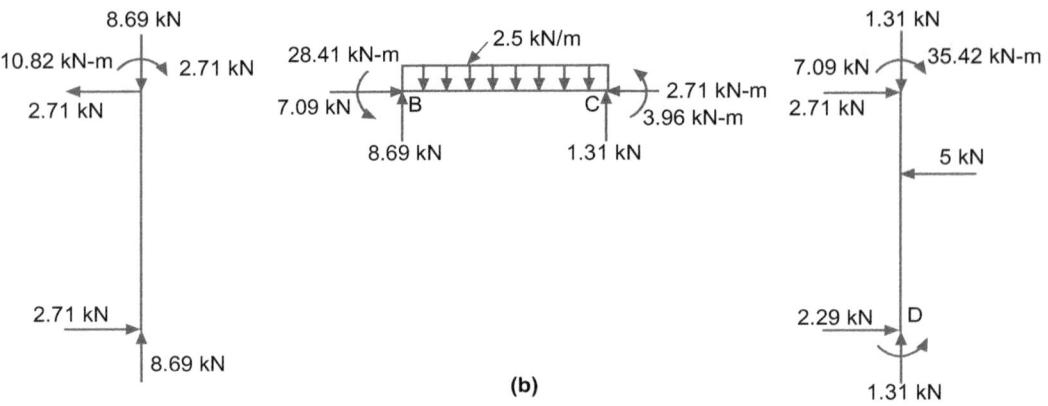

(b)

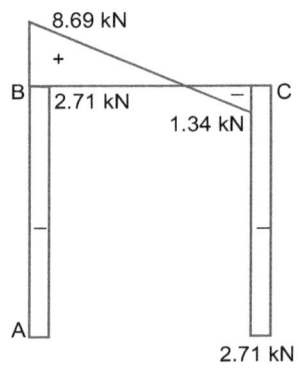

(c)

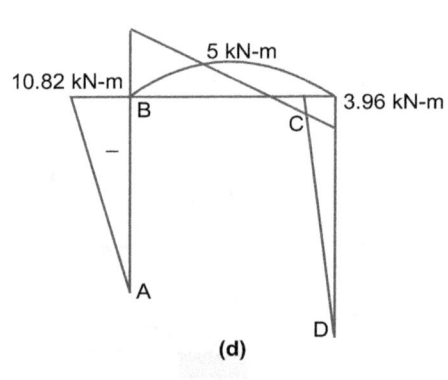

(d)

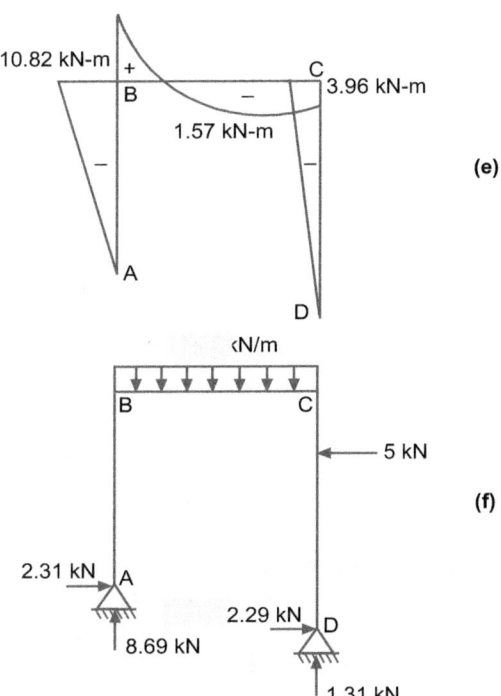

Fig. 1.31 : For Illustrative Example 1.22

$2 EI \theta_C + EI \theta_B - 3.33 + 4.4625 + 0.75 EI \Delta + 0.15 EI \Delta = 0$

$EI \theta_B + 2.75 EI \theta_C + 0.15 EI \Delta = -1.132$ ... (B)

Horizontal shear equilibrium of structure,

$$H_A + H_D + 5 = 0$$

$$H_A = \frac{M_{AB} + M_{BA}}{4}, \quad H_D = \frac{M_{CD} + M_{DC} - 5 \times 1.5}{5}$$

$$\therefore \quad \frac{0.75 EI \theta_B + 0.1875 EI \Delta}{4} + \frac{4.4625 + 0.75 EI \theta_C + 0.15 EI \Delta - 7.5}{5} = -5$$

$3.75 EI \theta_B + 3 EI \theta_C + 1.5375 EI \Delta - 30 = -100$

$3.75 EI \theta_B + 3 EI \theta_C + 1.5375 EI \Delta = -87.85$ ... (C)

Step V : Solving equations (A), (B) and (C),

$$\boxed{\theta_B = \frac{2.57}{EI}, \quad \theta_C = \frac{2.36}{EI}, \quad \Delta = -\frac{68.01}{EI}}$$

Step VI : Member-end moments :
$$M_{AB} = 0$$
$$M_{BA} = -10.82 \text{ kN-m}$$
$$M_{BC} = 10.82 \text{ kN-m}$$
$$M_{CB} = 3.96 \text{ kN-m}$$
$$M_{CD} = -3.96 \text{ kN-m}$$
$$M_{DC} = 0$$

Step VII : FBD of members is as shown in Fig. 1.31 (b). Considering equilibrium of each member and of complete structure; all reaction components are found out as shown in figure.

Step VIII : Shear force diagram is as shown in Fig. 1.31 (c).

Step IX : Bending moment diagram : BMD by superposition is shown in Fig. 1.31 (d). BMD on tension side is shown in Fig. 1.31 (e).

Step X : FBD of structure is as shown in Fig. 1.31 (f).

1.10 INTRODUCTION

The analysis of structure by SD method is carried out conventionally by using the general SD equations and the required equilibrium equations. However, the minimization of the number of unknown joint displacements is very much desirable for easy and speedy working of SD method. This is possible in certain cases by simple modifications in the formulation as per fundamental concepts of structural analysis. In this context, some of the tricks are suggested here for its effective use in the specific problems of analysis.

1.10.1 Structure with the Overhanging Part

The unknown joint displacements i.e. translation and rotation at the end of the overhanging part of a structure, can be conveniently eliminated by removing the overhanging part and replacing the same by the statically equivalent loads on the corresponding joint. The equivalent load generally includes the joint force and the joint moment.

1.10.2 Symmetrical Structure

The joint translations are absent in perfectly symmetrical structure (i.e. symmetry with all respects) and there is specific relationship between the joint rotations. The general rules of symmetry with respect to the joint rotations are as follows :

(i) The joint rotations on the opposite sides of the axis of symmetry are equal but opposite in direction as shown in Fig. 1.31.

(ii) The joint rotations on the axis of symmetry are zero as shown in Fig. 1.31.

The information of joint rotations because of symmetry are taken help of reducing the unknown displacements of the structure and further simplifying the SD method for analysis of structure. This is illustrated in the following example.

STRUCTURAL ANALYSIS – II   SLOPE-DEFLECTION METHOD

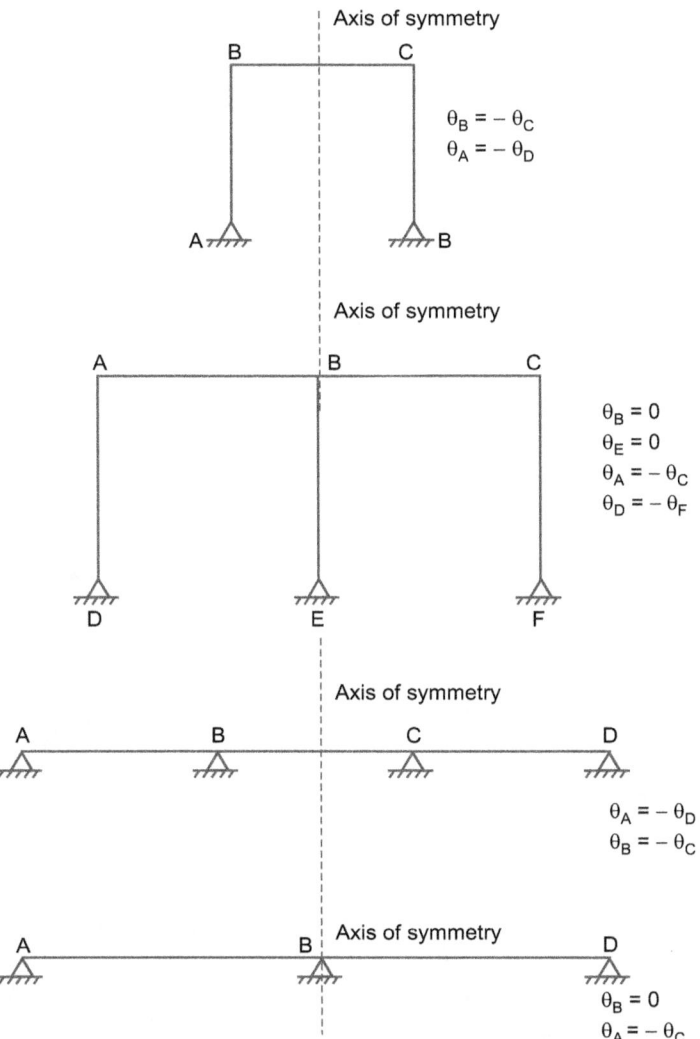

Fig. 1.32 : Symmetrical structures

Example 1.23 : *Analyse the frame shown in Fig. 1.33 (a) by slope-deflection method. Take EI = constant.*

Solution : Data : (1) The frame is supported and loaded as shown in Fig. 1.33 (a).

        (2) EI = constant.

        (3) Frame type : Non-sway frame (symmetrical).

Object : Structural analysis.

Equations : SD equations.

Procedure :

Step I : Degree of kinematic indeterminacy for given structure = D_{ki} = 2.

But, by symmetry, $\theta_B = -\theta_C$.

∴ Degree of kinematic indeterminacy = D_{ki} = 1.

Unknown displacement : θ_B.

Known displacements : $\theta_A = \theta_D = 0$.

Step II : Fixed-end moments :

$$M_{AB}^F = M_{BA}^F = M_{CD}^F = M_{DC}^F = 0$$

$$M_{BC}^F = -M_{CB}^F = \frac{wL^2}{12}$$

Step III : SD equations :

Member AB :
$$M_{AB} = \frac{4EI}{L}(\theta_A) + \frac{2EI}{L}(\theta_B) \pm \frac{6EI}{L^2}(\Delta) + M_{AB}^F$$
$$= \frac{2EI}{L}(\theta_B) \qquad \ldots (i)$$

$$M_{BA} = \frac{4EI}{L}(\theta_B) + \frac{2EI}{L}(\theta_A) \pm \frac{6EI}{L^2}(\Delta) + M_{BA}^F$$
$$= \frac{4EI}{L}(\theta_B) \qquad \ldots (ii)$$

Member BC :
$$M_{BC} = \frac{4EI}{L}(\theta_B) + \frac{2EI}{L}(\theta_C) \pm \frac{6EI}{L^2}(\Delta) + M_{BC}^F$$
$$= \frac{4EI}{L}(\theta_B) + \frac{2EI}{L}(-\theta_B) + \frac{wL^2}{12} = \frac{2EI}{L}(\theta_B) + \frac{wL^2}{12} \qquad \ldots (iii)$$

$$M_{CB} = \frac{4EI}{L}(\theta_C) + \frac{2EI}{L}(\theta_B) \pm \frac{6EI}{L^2}(\Delta) + M_{CB}^F$$
$$= \frac{4EI}{L}(-\theta_B) + \frac{2EI}{L}(\theta_B) - \frac{wL^2}{12} = -\frac{2EI}{L}(\theta_B) - \frac{wL^2}{12} \qquad \ldots (iv)$$

Member CD :
$$M_{CD} = \frac{4EI}{L}(\theta_C) + \frac{2EI}{L}(\theta_D) \pm \frac{6EI}{L^2}(\Delta) + M_{CD}^F$$
$$= -\frac{4EI}{L}(\theta_B) \qquad \ldots (v)$$

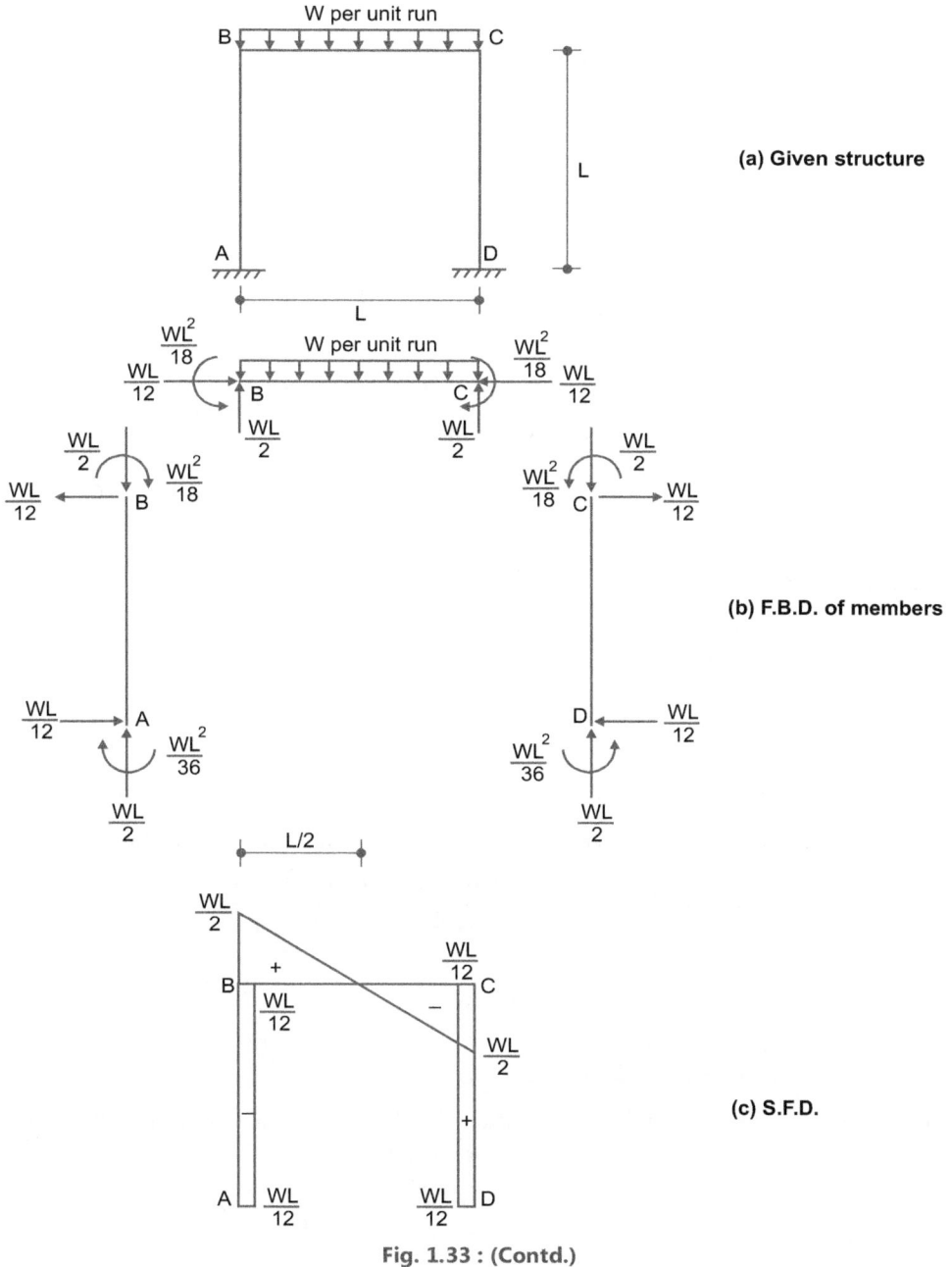

Fig. 1.33 : (Contd.)

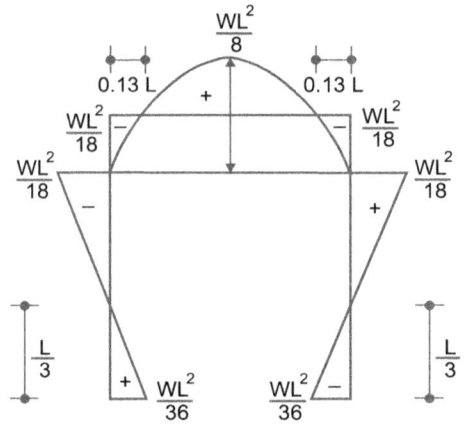
(d) B.M.D. by superposition

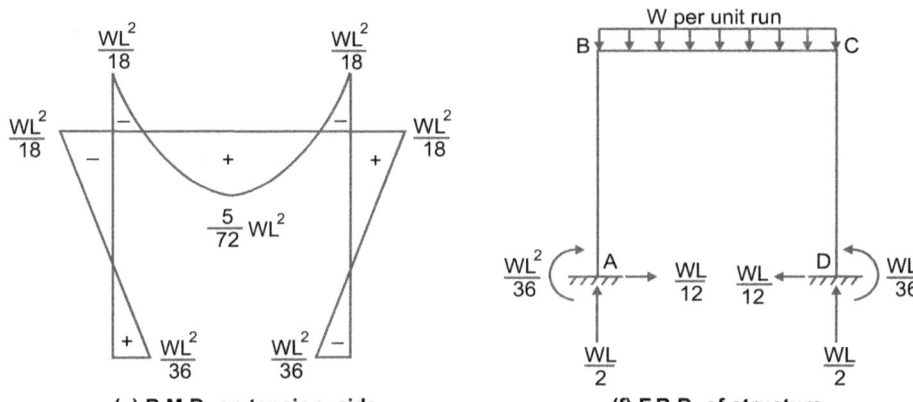
(e) B.M.D. on tension side (f) F.B.D. of structure

Fig. 1.33 : For Illustrative Example 1.23

$$M_{DC} = \frac{4EI}{L}(\theta_D) + \frac{2EI}{L}(\theta_C) \pm \frac{6EI}{L^2}(\Delta) + M_{DC}^F$$

$$= -\frac{2EI}{L}(\theta_B) \qquad \ldots \text{(vi)}$$

Step IV : Equilibrium conditions for joints :

Moment equilibrium of joint B : $M_{BA} + M_{BC} = 0$ ... (A)

Step V : Formulation of equilibrium equations in terms of joint displacements :

Substituting equations (ii) and (iii) in equation (A), we get

$$\frac{4EI}{L}(\theta_B) + \frac{2EI}{L}(\theta_B) + \frac{wL^2}{12} = 0 \quad \text{i.e.} \quad \frac{6EI}{L}(\theta_B) + \frac{wL^2}{12} = 0 \qquad \ldots \text{(A)}$$

Step VI : Solution of equations for displacements :

Solving equation (A), we get

$$\boxed{\theta_B = -\frac{wL^3}{72\,EI}}$$

Step VII : Member-end moments : Substituting the values of above displacements in SD equations; member-end moments are obtained as under :

$$M_{AB} = \frac{2\,EI}{L}\left(-\frac{wL^3}{72\,EI}\right) = -\frac{wL^2}{36}$$

$$M_{BA} = \frac{4\,EI}{L}\left(-\frac{wL^3}{72\,EI}\right) = -\frac{wL^2}{18}$$

$$M_{BC} = \frac{2\,EI}{L}\left(-\frac{wL^3}{72\,EI}\right) + \frac{wL^2}{12} = \frac{wL^2}{18}$$

$$M_{CB} = -\frac{2\,EI}{L}\left(-\frac{wL^3}{72\,EI}\right) - \frac{wL^2}{12} = -\frac{wL^2}{18}$$

$$M_{CD} = -\frac{4\,EI}{L}\left(-\frac{wL^3}{72\,EI}\right) = \frac{wL^2}{18}$$

$$M_{DC} = -\frac{2\,EI}{L}\left(-\frac{wL^3}{72\,EI}\right) = \frac{wL^2}{36}$$

Step VIII : FBD of members is as shown in Fig. 1.33 (b). Considering equilibrium of each member and of complete structure, all reaction components are found out as shown in the figure.

Step IX : Shear force diagram is as shown in Fig. 1.33 (c).

Step X : Bending moment diagram :

BMD by superposition is shown in Fig. 1.33 (d).

BMD on tension side is shown in Fig. 1.33 (e).

Step XI : FBD of structure is as shown in Fig. 1.33 (f).

1.10.3 Structure Without Joint Translation and With Hinge or Roller Support At Ends

1.10.3.1 Unloaded Hinge or Roller Support

The unknown rotations at the unloaded hinged/roller supports can be eliminated if desired so. To achieve this, the SD equation of the member connected to the hinged/roller support is modified and expressed in terms of the near-end rotation only. This modification is based on the following concepts :

- The final member-end moment at the hinged/roller support is zero.

- The flexural rotational stiffness of the member having the far end hinged is $\frac{3\,EI}{L}$.

The SD equation of such member is developed by the superposition technique as illustrated in Fig. 1.34.
- Fig. 1.34 (a) shows the member AB connected to the rigid joint at A and the non-yielding hinged support at B. The member loads are also shown.
- The final deformed shape, rotation of joints and member-end moments are shown in Fig. 1.34 (b). It may be noted that MBA should be zero.
- FEM due to member loads in the restrained beam are shown in Fig. 1.34 (c).

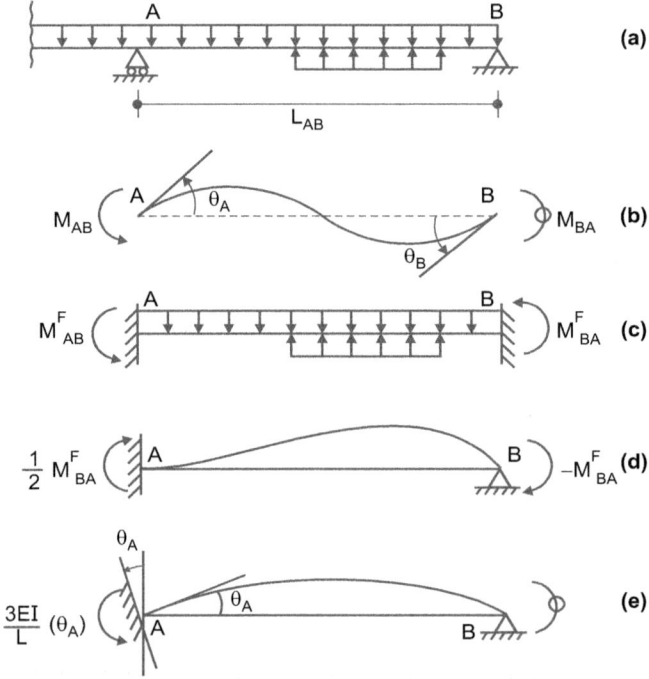

Fig. 1.34 : Development of modified SD equation

- As the condition of hinged support indicates that there should be no moment, the M_{BA}^F in reversed direction is applied at B as shown in Fig. 1.34 (d). The effect of this moment at A is $-\frac{1}{2} M_{BA}^F$ as the carry-over moment.
- The joint A is released for θ_A as shown in Fig. 1.34 (e). Keeping the joint B as hinged.

The member-end moment in this case is $\dfrac{3\,EI_{AB}}{L_{AB}} (\theta_B)$ according to the rotational stiffness of member when the far end is hinged.

Superposing all the member-end moments at A, the modified SD equation of the member is obtained as # STRUCTURAL ANALYSIS – II — SLOPE-DEFLECTION METHOD

$$M_{AB} = M_{AB}^F - \frac{1}{2} M_{BA}^F + \frac{3 EI_{AB}}{L_{AB}} (\theta_A)$$

It is clear from Fig. 1.33 that $M_{BA} = 0$, even after superposition. In generalized form, SD equation becomes

$$M_{ij} = M_{ij}^F - \frac{1}{2} M_{ji}^F + \frac{3 EI_{ij}}{L_{ij}} (\theta_i) \qquad \ldots (1.6)$$

Using the modified equation for the member having the hinged support at either of its ends, the SD method greatly simplifies the analysis of the structure. This is illustrated for two-span uniform beam ABC in example (1.22).

1.10.3.2 Application of modified SD equations to structures without joint translations and with unloaded hinged or roller support at the end

Example 1.24 : *Analyse the beam shown in Fig. 1.35 (a) by using modified SD equations.*

Solution : Step I : Basically the unknown joint displacements are θ_A, θ_B and θ_C. These three unknowns can be reduced to only one i.e. θ_B if the trick of modified SD equation is used in SD method. Following important steps complete the solution easily and quickly.

Unknown displacement : θ_B.

Step II : Fixed-end moments :

$$M_{AB}^F = +\frac{wL^2}{12}$$

$$M_{BA}^F = -\frac{wL^2}{12}$$

$$M_{BC}^F = +\frac{wL^2}{12}$$

$$M_{CB}^F = -\frac{wL^2}{12}$$

Step III : Modified SD equations : Modified SD equations are applicable to the members AB and BC as both the members are connected to the hinged or roller support.

$$M_{BA} = M_{BA}^F - \frac{1}{2} M_{AB}^F + \frac{3 EI_{AB}}{L_{AB}} (\theta_B)$$

i.e. $\quad M_{BA} = -\dfrac{wL^2}{12} - \dfrac{1}{2}\left(+\dfrac{wL^2}{12}\right) + \dfrac{3 EI}{L} (\theta_B)$

and $\quad M_{BC} = M_{BC}^F - \dfrac{1}{2} M_{CB}^F + \dfrac{3 EI_{BC}}{L_{BC}} (\theta_B)$

i.e. $\quad M_{BC} = +\dfrac{wL^2}{12} - \dfrac{1}{2}\left(-\dfrac{wL^2}{12}\right) + \dfrac{3 EI}{L} (\theta_B)$

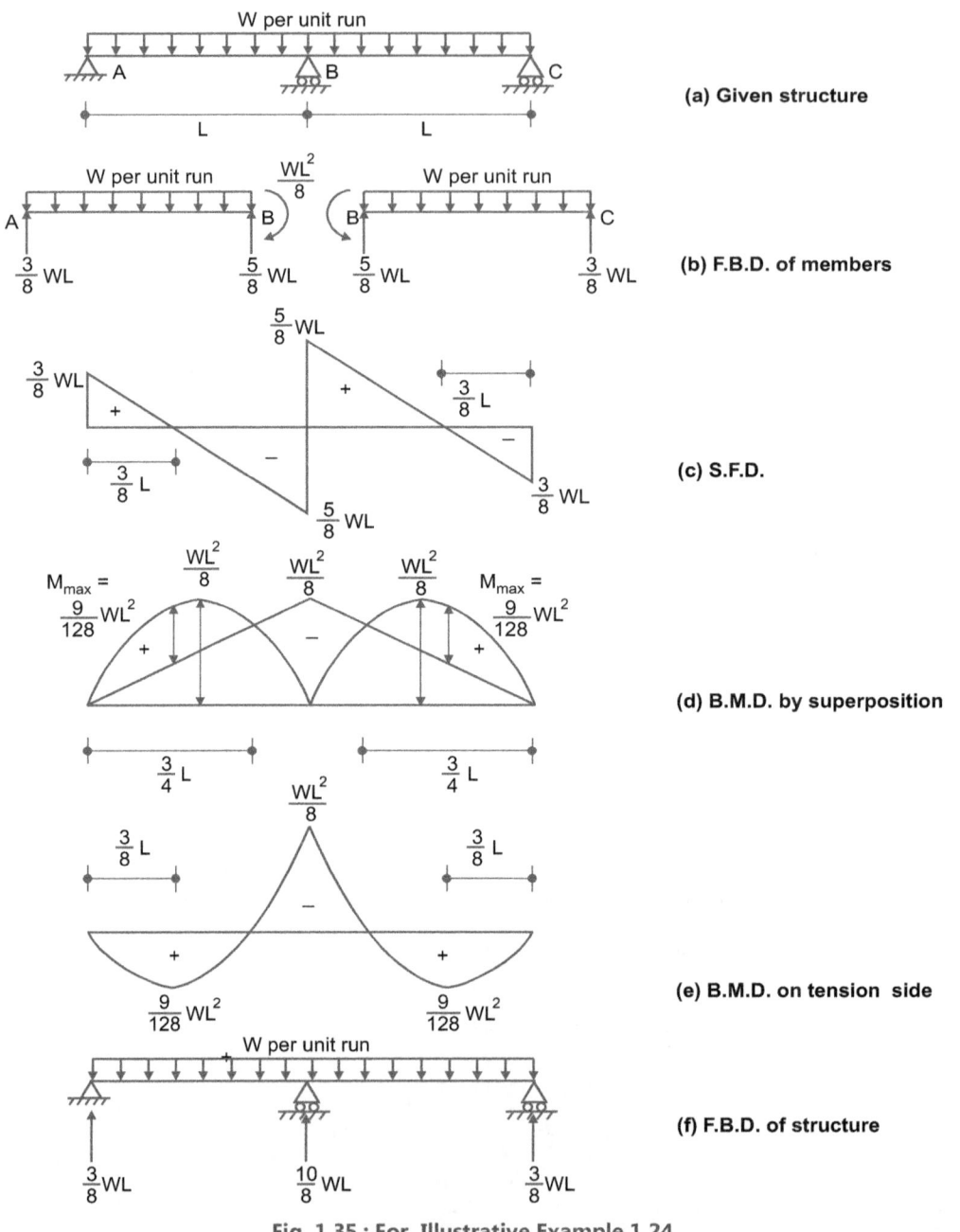

Fig. 1.35 : For Illustrative Example 1.24

Step IV : Equilibrium equation :
For joint B : $M_{BA} + M_{BC} = 0$
Step V : Substituting SD equations in equilibrium equation :
$$\left[-\frac{wL^2}{12} - \frac{wL^2}{24} + 3\frac{EI}{L}\theta_B\right] + \left[\frac{wL^2}{12} + \frac{wL^2}{24} + 3\frac{EI}{L}\theta_B\right] = 0$$
Step VI : Formation of equation for unknown :
$$\frac{6EI}{L}\theta_B = 0$$
$$\therefore \quad \theta_B = 0$$
The result of θ_B verifies the result tallies zero θ_B because of symmetry.

Step VII : Member-end moments :
$$M_{AB} = 0 = M_{CB}$$
$$M_{BA} = -\frac{wL^2}{12} - \frac{wL^2}{24} + \frac{3EI}{L}(0)$$
$$= -\frac{wL^2}{8}$$
$$M_{BC} = +\frac{wL^2}{8}$$

Step VIII : FBD of members is as shown in Fig. 1.35 (b). Considering equilibrium of each member, other reaction components are found out as shown in the figure.

Step IX : Shear force diagram is as shown in Fig. 1.35 (c).

Step X : Bending moment diagram :
BMD by superposition is shown in Fig. 1.35 (d).
BMD on tension side is shown in Fig. 1.35 (e).

Step XI : FBD of structure is as shown in Fig. 1.35 (f).

Example 1.25 : *Analyse the beam shown in Fig. 1.36 (a) using modified SD equations.*
Solution : Step I : $D_{ki} = 3$, Unknown displacements : θ_A, θ_B and θ_C. [Modified $D_{ki} = 1$ (θ_B)].

Step II : Fixed-end moments :
$$M_{AB}^F = 18.33 \text{ kNm}, \qquad M_{BA}^F = -8.33 \text{ kNm}$$
$$M_{BC}^F = 13.06 \text{ kNm}, \qquad M_{CB}^F = -26.93 \text{ kNm}$$

Step III : Modified SD equations :
$$M_{BA} = \frac{3EI}{L}(\theta_B) + M_{BA}^F - \frac{M_{AB}^F}{2}$$
$$= \frac{3EI}{4}(\theta_B) - 8.33 - \frac{1}{2}(18.33) = \frac{3EI}{4}(\theta_B) - 17.5 \qquad \ldots \text{(i)}$$

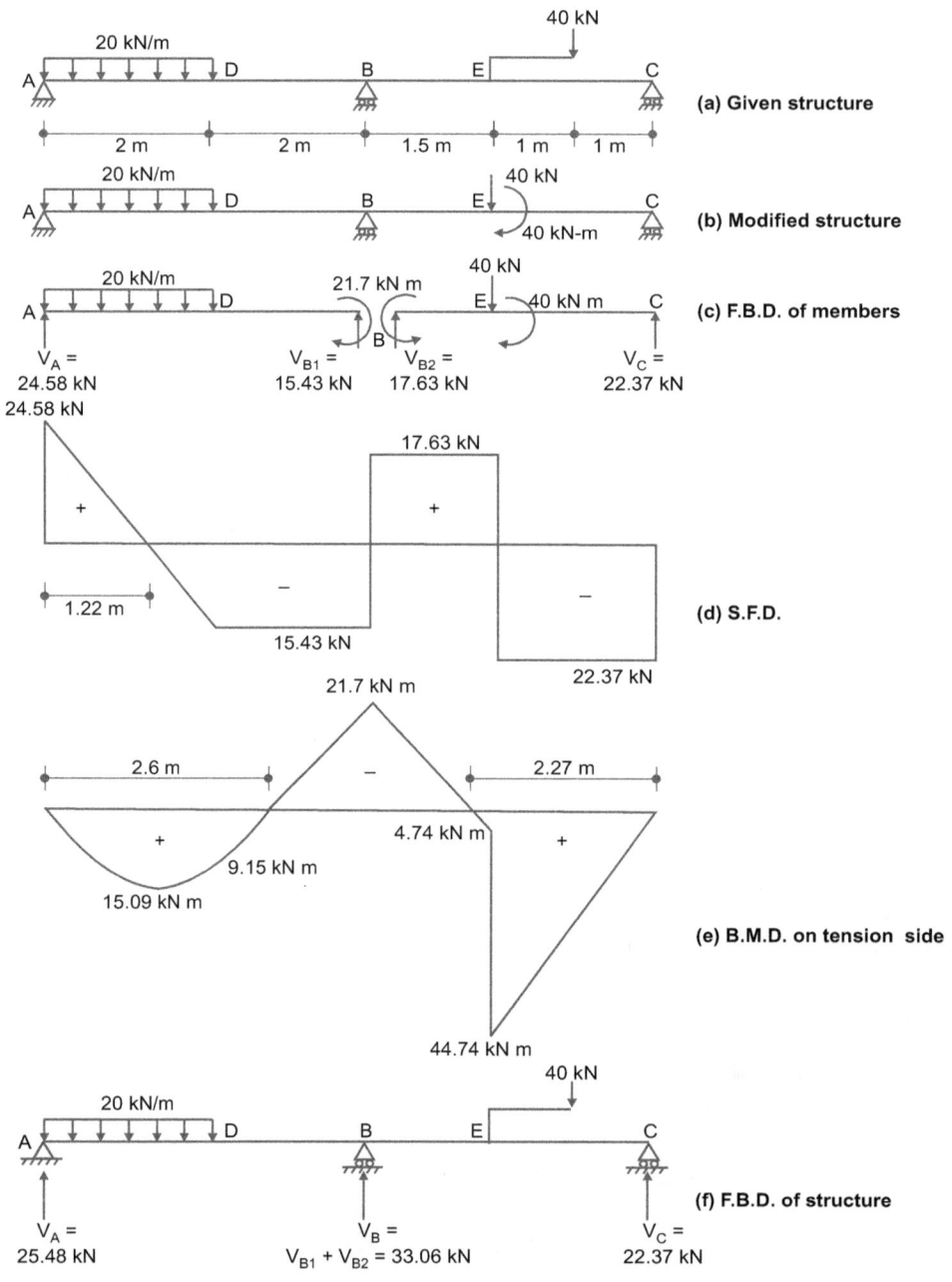

Fig. 1.36 : For Illustrative Example 1.25

$$M_{BC} = \frac{3\,EI}{L}(\theta_B) + M_{BC}^F - \frac{M_{CB}^F}{2}$$

$$= \frac{3\,EI}{3.5}(\theta_B) + 13.06 - \frac{1}{2}(-26.93)$$

$$= \frac{3\,EI}{3.5}(\theta_B) + 26.525 \qquad \ldots \text{(ii)}$$

Step IV : Moment equilibrium condition for joints :
At joint B : $\quad M_{BA} + M_{BC} = 0 \qquad \ldots$ (A)
Step V : Formulation of equilibrium equations in terms of joint displacements :
Substituting equations (i) and (ii) in equation (A), we get
$\quad (1.607)\,EI\,(\theta_B) + 9.025 = 0 \qquad \ldots$ (B)
Step VI : Solution of equations for joint displacements : Solving equation (B), we get

$$\boxed{\theta_B = -\frac{5.62}{EI}}$$

Step VII : Member-end moments :

$$M_{AB} = 0 = M_{CB}$$

$$M_{BA} = \frac{3}{4}\,EI\left(-\frac{5.62}{EI}\right) - 17.5 = -21.7 \text{ kNm}$$

$$M_{BC} = \frac{3\,EI}{3.5}\left(-\frac{5.62}{EI}\right) + 26.525 = 21.7 \text{ kNm}$$

Rest of the analysis is the same as explained earlier.

It should be noted that, by using modified SD equations, the three unknown problems are reduced to only one unknown problem.

1.10.3.3 Loaded Hinged or Roller Support

Even if the end hinged/roller support is loaded, may be due to the equivalent loads of the overhanging part, the SD method could be tailored accordingly. Under such situation, the modified SD equation for the member having the hinged support is given by,

$$M_{AB} = M_{AB}^F - \frac{1}{2}M_{BA}^F + \frac{1}{2}M_{BA} + \frac{3\,EI_{AB}}{L_{AB}}(\theta_A) \qquad \ldots (1.7)$$

The additional term $\frac{1}{2}M_{BA}$ in the equation is the known applied moment at the hinged support, say M_B.

1.10.3.4 Application of modified SD equations to structures without joint translation and with loaded hinged or roller support at the ends

Example 1.26 : *Analyse the beam shown in Fig. 1.37 (a) using modified SD equation.*

Solution : **Step I :** $D_{ki} = 2$ for modified structure.

STRUCTURAL ANALYSIS – II SLOPE-DEFLECTION METHOD

Unknown displacements: θ_B, θ_C. [Modified $D_{ki} = 1\ (\theta_B)$]

Step II: Fixed end moments:

$$M^F_{AB} = -M^F_{BA} = \frac{WL^2}{12} = \frac{6 \times 5^2}{12} = 12.5 \text{ kNm}$$

$$M^F_{BC} = -M^F_{CB} = \frac{WL^2}{12} = \frac{10 \times 4^2}{12} = 13.33 \text{ kNm}$$

Step III: Modified SD equations:

Span AB: $\quad M_{AB} = \dfrac{2EI}{5}(\theta_B) + 12.5$ ... (i)

$\qquad\qquad M_{BA} = \dfrac{4EI}{5}(\theta_B) - 12.5$ ... (ii)

Span BC: $\quad M_{BC} = \dfrac{3EI}{L}(\theta_B) + M^F_{BC} - \dfrac{1}{2}M^F_{CB} + \dfrac{1}{2}M_{CB}$

$\qquad\qquad = \dfrac{3EI}{4}(\theta_B) + 13.33 - \dfrac{1}{2}(-13.33) - \dfrac{1}{2}(20) = 0.75\, EI\,(\theta_B) + 10$ ... (iii)

Step IV: Moment equilibrium condition for joints:

At joint B: $M_{BA} + M_{BC} = 0$ ... (A)

Step V: Formulation of equilibrium equations in terms of joint displacements:

Substituting equations (ii) and (iii) in equation (A), we get

$\qquad 1.5\, EI\,(\theta_B) - 2.5 = 0$ ... (B)

Step VI: Solution of equations for joint displacements: Solving equation (B), we get

$$\boxed{\theta_B = \frac{1.61}{EI}}$$

Step VII: Member-end moments:

$$M_{AB} = \frac{2EI}{5}\left(\frac{1.61}{EI}\right) + 12.5 = 13.14 \text{ kNm}$$

$$M_{BA} = \frac{4EI}{5}\left(\frac{1.61}{EI}\right) - 12.5 = -11.21 \text{ kNm}$$

$$M_{BC} = 0.75\, EI \left(\frac{1.61}{EI}\right) + 10 = 11.21 \text{ kNm}$$

$$M_{CB} = 0$$

Rest of the analysis is the same as explained earlier. It should be noted that two unknown problems reduced to one unknown problem by using modified SD equations.

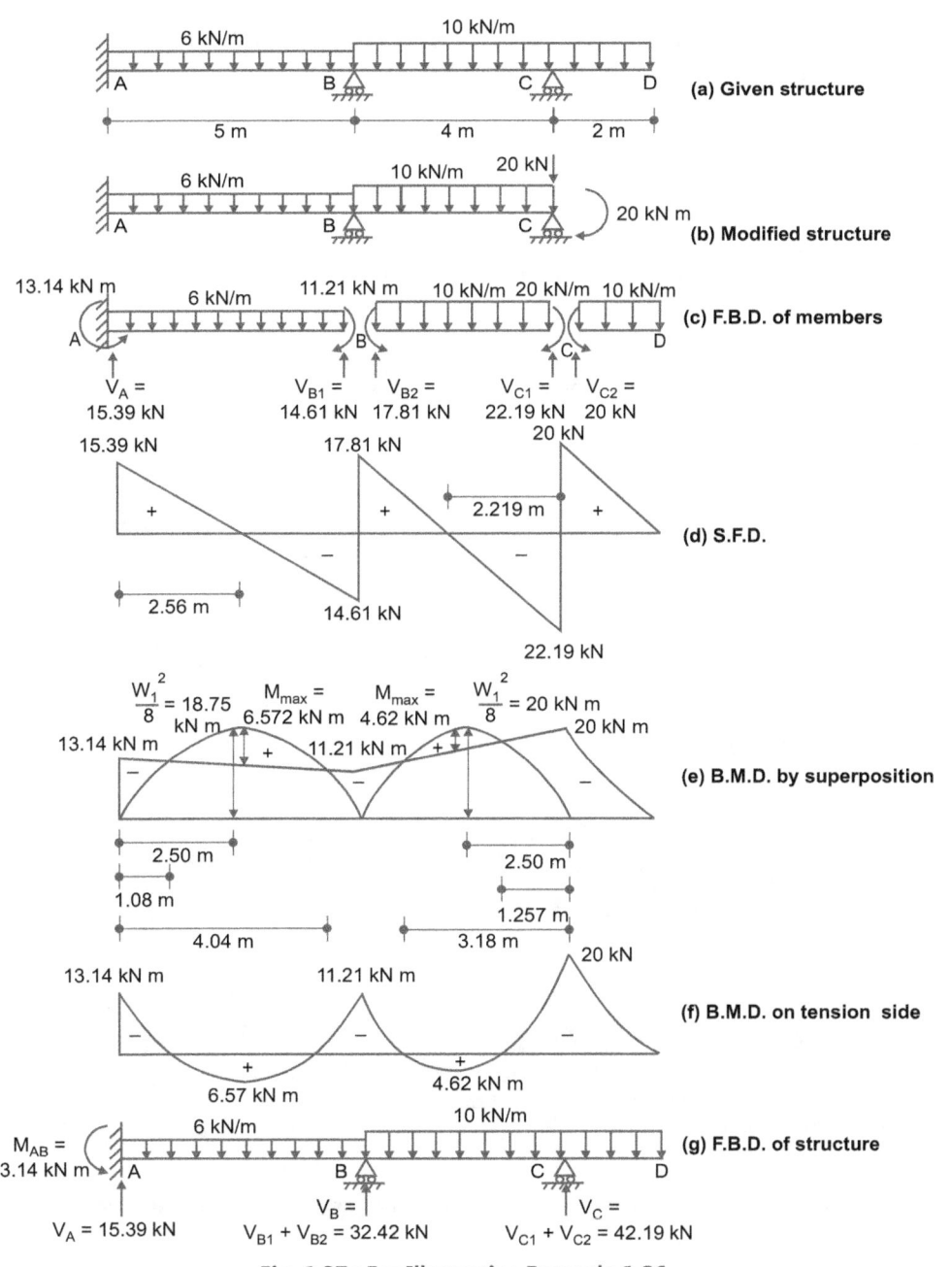

Fig. 1.37 : For Illustrative Example 1.26

1.10.4 Structure with Joint Translation and with Hinged or Roller Support at the End

Analogous tricks may be used to develop the SD equation for the member having joint translations and hinged/roller support to reduce the unknown displacements and simplify the SD method. This is very much useful especially in sway frames supported by hinged/roller support.

The modified SD equation for the member with joint translations can be derived on the same principles of superposition as shown in Fig. 1.38 and expressed as

$$M_{AB} = M^F_{AB} - \frac{1}{2} M^F_{BA} + \frac{1}{2} M_B + 3\frac{EI_{AB}}{L_{AB}}(\theta_A) - 3\frac{EI_{AB}}{L^2_{AB}}(\Delta)_{B/A} \quad \ldots (1.8)$$

where M_B is known applied joint moment if any and $\Delta_{B/A}$ is the relative joint translation, and $\frac{3\,EI}{L^2}$ is the translational stiffness of the member when the far end is hinged.

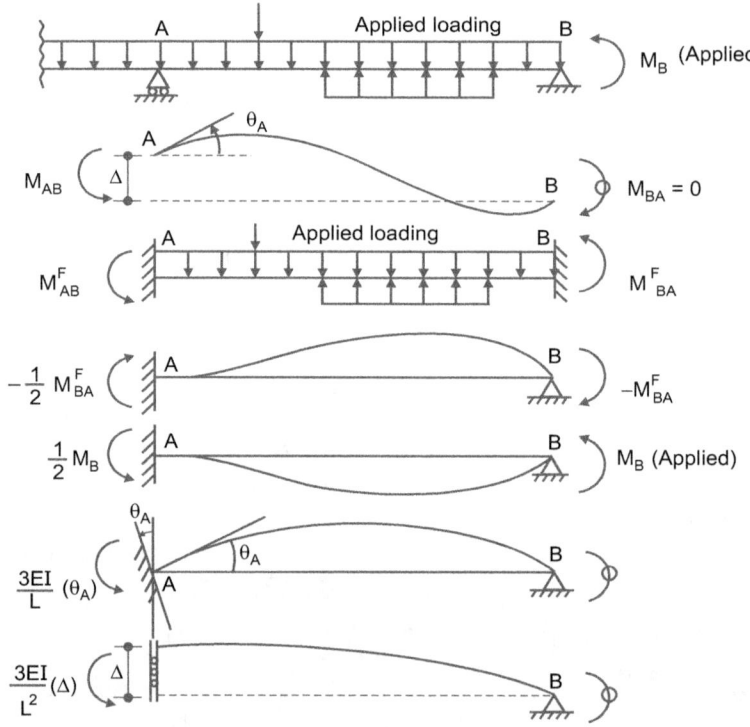

Fig. 1.38 : Development of modified SD equation considering translation

STRUCTURAL ANALYSIS – II SLOPE-DEFLECTION METHOD

1.10.5 Application of Modified SD Equations to Structures with Joint Translations and with Hinged or Roller Support at the Ends

Example 1.27 : *Analyse the beam shown in Fig. 1.39 (a) using modified SD equation.*

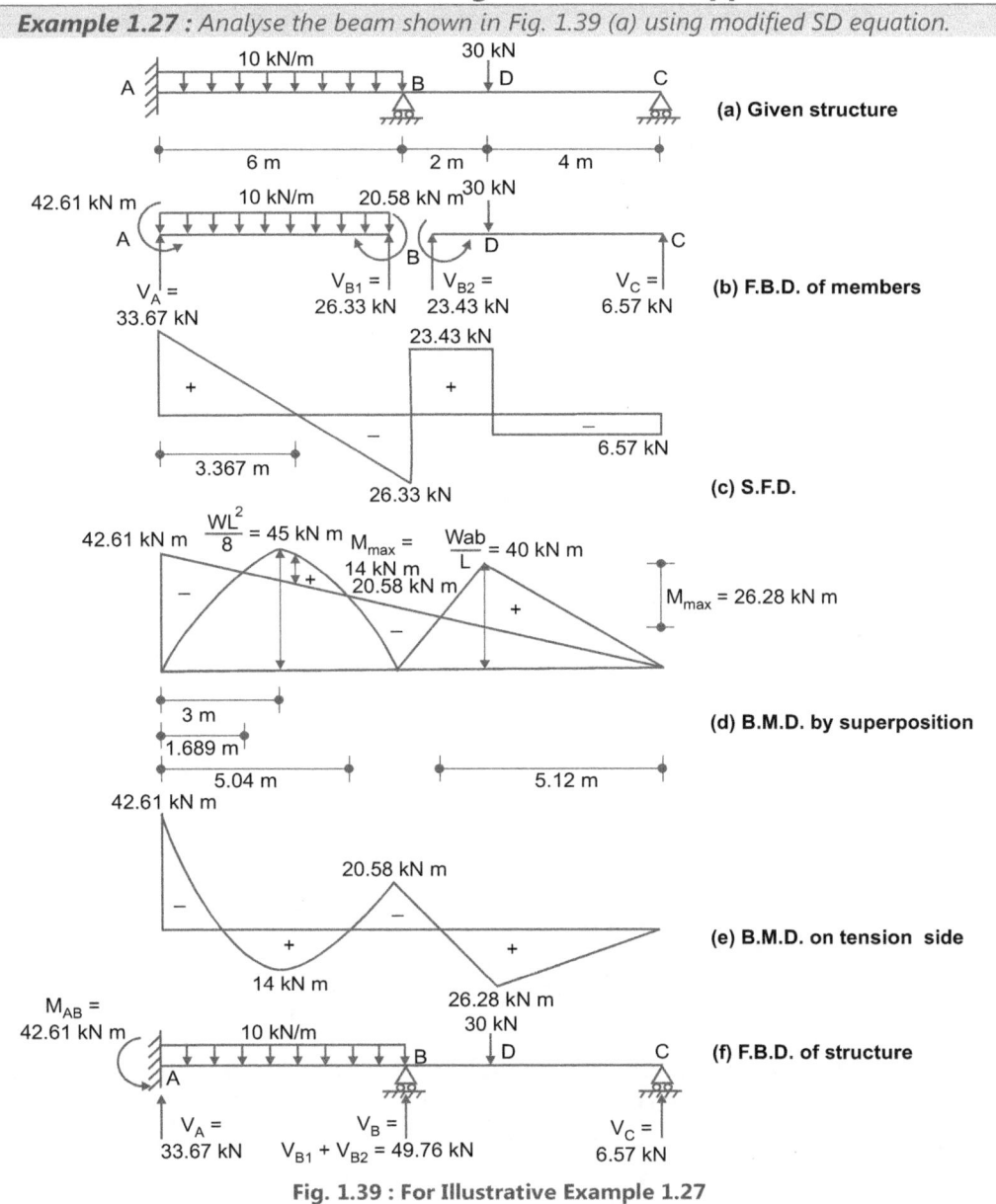

Fig. 1.39 : For Illustrative Example 1.27

Solution : Step I : $D_{ki} = 2$, Unknown displacements : θ_B, θ_C. [Modified $D_{ki} = 1 \,(\theta_B)$].
Step II : Fixed-end moments :
$$M^F_{AB} = -M^F_{BA} = 30 \text{ kNm}$$
$$M^F_{BC} = 26.67 \text{ kNm}$$
$$M^F_{CB} = -13.33 \text{ kNm}$$

Step III : Modified SD equations :

Span AB :
$$M_{AB} = \frac{EI}{3}(\theta_B) + 45.83 \quad \ldots (i)$$

$$M_{BA} = \frac{2EI}{3}(\theta_B) - 14.16 \quad \ldots (ii)$$

Span BC :
$$M_{BC} = \frac{3EI}{L}(\theta_B) + M^F_{BC} - \frac{1}{2}M^F_{CB} - \frac{3EI}{L^2}(\Delta)$$

$$= \frac{3EI}{6}(\theta_B) + 26.67 - \frac{1}{2}(-13.33) - \frac{3 \times 3800}{6^2}\left(\frac{25}{1000}\right)$$

$$= 0.5 \, EI \, (\theta_B) + 25.41 \quad \ldots (iii)$$

Step IV : Moment equilibrium condition for joint :
At joint B, $\quad M_{BA} + M_{BC} = 0 \quad \ldots (A)$

Step V : Substituting equations (ii) and (iii) in equation (A), we get
$$1.167 \, EI \, (\theta_B) + 11.25 = 0 \quad \ldots (B)$$

Step VI : Solution of equations for joint displacements :
Solving equation (A), we get

$$\boxed{\theta_B = -\frac{9.64}{EI}}$$

Step VII : Member end moments :

$$M_{AB} = \frac{EI}{3}\left(-\frac{9.64}{EI}\right) + 45.83 = 42.61 \text{ kNm}$$

$$M_{BA} = \frac{2EI}{3}\left(-\frac{9.64}{EI}\right) - 14.16 = -20.58 \text{ kNm}$$

$$M_{BC} = 0.5 \, EI\left(-\frac{9.64}{EI}\right) + 25.41 = 20.58 \text{ kNm}$$

$$M_{CB} = 0$$

Rest of the analysis is the same as explained earlier. It should be noted that; two unknown problems are reduced to one unknown problem by using modified SD equations.

Example 1.28 : *Analyse the beam shown in Fig. 1.40 using modified slope deflection method.*

STRUCTURAL ANALYSIS – II   SLOPE-DEFLECTION METHOD

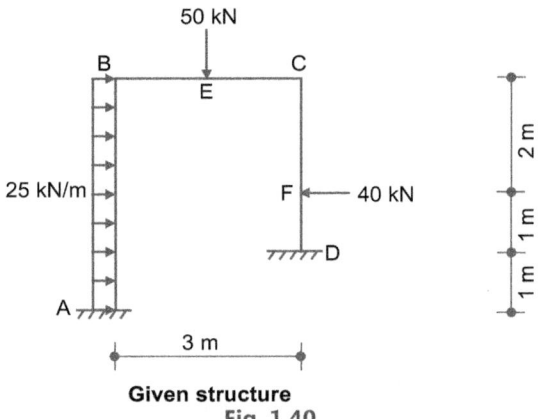

Given structure
Fig. 1.40

Solution : Step I : $D_{ki} = 4$, Unknown displacements : θ_B, θ_C, θ_D and horizontal sway $= \Delta$.
Modified $D_{ki} = 3$ (θ_B, θ_C and Δ). Known displacement : $\theta_A = 0$.

Step II : Fixed-end moments :

$$M^F_{AB} = -M^F_{BA} = 80 \text{ kNm}$$
$$M^F_{BC} = -M^F_{CB} = 26.67 \text{ kNm}$$
$$-M^F_{DC} = M^F_{CD} = 15 \text{ kNm}$$

Step III : Modified SD equations : (Assuming horizontal sway $= \Delta$ towards right).

Member AB :
$M_{AB} = EI(\theta_B) + 0.75 EI(\Delta) + 80$ ... (i)
$M_{BA} = 2 EI(\theta_B) + 0.75 EI(\Delta) - 80$ ... (ii)

Member BC :
$M_{BC} = EI(\theta_B) + 0.5 EI(\theta_C) + 26.67$ ... (iii)
$M_{CB} = EI(\theta_C) + 0.5 EI(\theta_B) - 26.67$ ... (iv)

Member CD :
$$M_{CD} = \frac{3EI}{L}(\theta_C) + \frac{3EI}{L^2}(\Delta) + M^F_{CD} - \frac{1}{2}M^F_{DC}$$

$$= \frac{3EI}{3}(\theta_C) + \frac{3EI}{3^2}(\Delta) + 15 - \frac{1}{2}(-15)$$

$$= EI(\theta_C) + \frac{EI}{3}(\Delta) + 22.5 \quad ...(v)$$

Step IV : Equilibrium conditions for joints :
Moment equilibrium of joint B : $M_{BA} + M_{BC} = 0$ ... (A)
Moment equilibrium of joint C : $M_{CB} + M_{CD} = 0$ ... (B)
Horizontal shear equilibrium of structure,

$$H_A + H_D - 100 = 0$$

i.e. $3(M_{AB} + M_{BA}) + 4 M_{CD} - 600 = 0$ ... (C)

Step V : Formulation of equilibrium equations in terms of joint displacements :
Substituting equations (ii) and (iii) in equation (A), we get

$3 \, EI \, (\theta_B) + 0.5 \, EI \, (\theta_C) + 0.75 \, EI \, (\Delta) - 52.33 = 0$ ... (A)

Substituting equations (iv) and (v) in equation (B), we get,

$0.5 \, EI \, (\theta_B) + 2 \, EI \, (\theta_C) + \dfrac{EI}{3} (\Delta) - 4.17 = 0$ ... (B)

Substituting equations (i), (ii) and (v) in equation (C), we get

$3 \, [EI \, (\theta_B) + 0.75 \, EI \, (\Delta) + 80 + 2 \, EI \, (\theta_B) + 0.75 \, EI \, (\Delta) - 80] +$
$\qquad\qquad\qquad\qquad 4 \left[EI \, (\theta_C) + \dfrac{EI}{3} (\Delta) + 22.5 \right] - 600 = 0$

i.e. $9 \, EI \, (\theta_B) + 4 \, EI \, (\theta_C) + 5.83 \, EI \, (\Delta) - 510 = 0$ ... (C)

Step VI : Solution of equations for joint displacements : Solving equations (A), (B) and (C), we get

$$\theta_B = -\dfrac{6.7}{EI}, \quad \theta_C = -\dfrac{14.128}{EI}, \quad \Delta = \dfrac{107.35}{EI}$$

Step VII : Member-end moments : Substituting the values of above joint displacements in modified SD equations, member-end moments are obtained as under :

$M_{AB} = EI \left(-\dfrac{6.7}{EI} \right) + 0.75 \, EI \left(\dfrac{107.35}{EI} \right) + 80$
$\qquad = 153.81 \text{ kNm (Hogging)}$

$M_{BA} = 2 \, EI \left(-\dfrac{6.7}{EI} \right) + 0.75 \, EI \left(\dfrac{107.35}{EI} \right) - 80$
$\qquad = -12.9 \text{ kNm}$
$\qquad = 12.9 \text{ kNm (Hogging)}$

$M_{BC} = EI \left(-\dfrac{6.7}{EI} \right) + 0.5 \, EI \left(-\dfrac{14.128}{EI} \right) + 26.67$
$\qquad = 12.9 \text{ kNm (Hogging)}$

$M_{CB} = EI \left(-\dfrac{14.128}{EI} \right) + 0.5 \, EI \left(-\dfrac{6.70}{EI} \right) - 26.67$
$\qquad = -44.15 \text{ kNm}$
$\qquad = 44.15 \text{ kNm (Hogging)}$

$M_{DC} = 0$

$M_{CD} = EI \left(-\dfrac{14.128}{EI} \right) + \dfrac{EI}{3} \left(\dfrac{107.35}{EI} \right) + 22.5$
$\qquad = 44.15 \text{ kNm (Sagging)}$

Rest of the analysis is the same as explained earlier. It should be noted that, by using modified SD equations, four unknown problems reduced to three unknown problems.

Chapter 2

MOMENT DISTRIBUTION METHOD

2.1 Stiffness and Carryover Factor

The moment distribution method is used to analyse the statically indeterminate rigid jointed structures. The method will be denoted hereafter as MD method. Unlike SD method, MD method is also the stiffness method or displacement method. However, the technique of MD method is quite different than SD method. Without calculating the values of unknown joint displacements, the member-end moments are obtained by successive approximations. The simultaneous equations need not to be formulated and solved. Restraining and releasing the joints of the member is the main characteristic of the stiffness method, may be SD method or MD method. In this context, following two basic cases as shown in Fig. 2.1 and Fig. 2.2 are very important and hence reviewed again to develop the technique of MD method.

Case I :

The prismatic member AB of length L and flexural rigidity EI is restrained against rotation at joints A and B as shown in Fig. 2.1 (a). One end i.e. near end A of AB is released when the far end B is fixed. To release the joint for rotation, the moment M_{AB} is to be applied at the joint A, to cause the rotation θ_A as shown in Fig. 2.1 (b). The moment M_{AB} is related to the rotation θ_A by the standard results of $M_{AB} = (4\ EI/L)\ \theta_A$. If θ_A is unity i.e. one radian, then $M_{AB} = (4\ EI/L)$ as shown in Fig. 2.1 (c). The quantity $4\ EI/L$ is called as flexural rotational stiffness of a member and defined as the moment required to be applied at A to cause an unit rotation at A when the far end B is fixed.

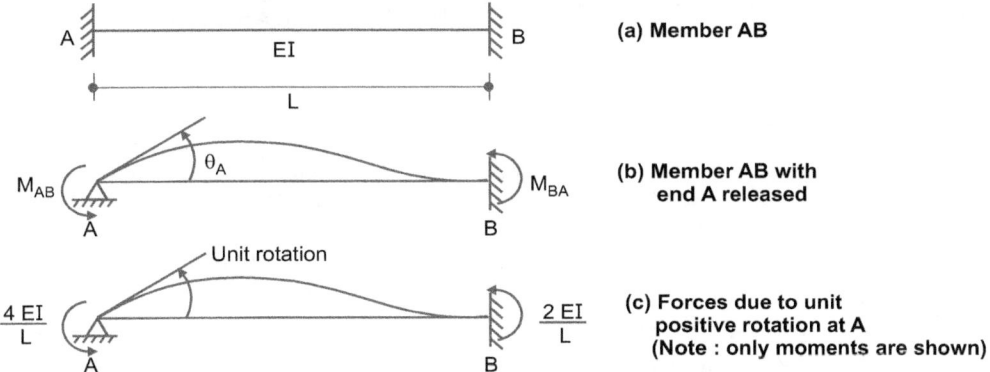

Fig. 2.1 : Releasing the near end when far end is fixed

When M_{AB} is applied at A to release the joint A, the moment M_{BA} is developed far or end B, being fixed as shown in Fig. 2.1 (b). M_{BA} is related to M_{AB} as $M_{BA} = \frac{1}{2} M_{AB}$. The direction of M_{BA} is same as M_{AB}.

$$\therefore \quad \frac{M_{BA}}{M_{AB}} = \frac{1}{2}$$

The moment M_{BA} is called carryover moment and it is defined as the moment developed at far end when the moment is applied at near end. The carryover moment is denoted by COM. The ratio of M_{BA} to M_{AB} is 1/2. This ratio is called carryover factor and defined as the ratio of moment developed at far end to the moment applied at near end. The carryover factor is denoted by COF.

Case II :

Fig. 2.2 (a) shows a prismatic member AB of length L and flexural rigidity EI, restrained at A and hinged at B. To release the joint A, the moment M_{AB} is applied at A to cause the rotation θ_A as shown in Fig. 2.2 (b). From the standard results already derived, M_{AB} is known to be $M_{AB} = (3\ EI/L)\ \theta_A$. If θ_A is unity then $M_{AB} = (3\ EI/L)$ as shown in Fig. 2.2 (c). The quantity (3 EI/L) is considered as the stiffness of a member and defined as the moment required to be applied at A to cause an unit rotation at A when the far end B is hinged.

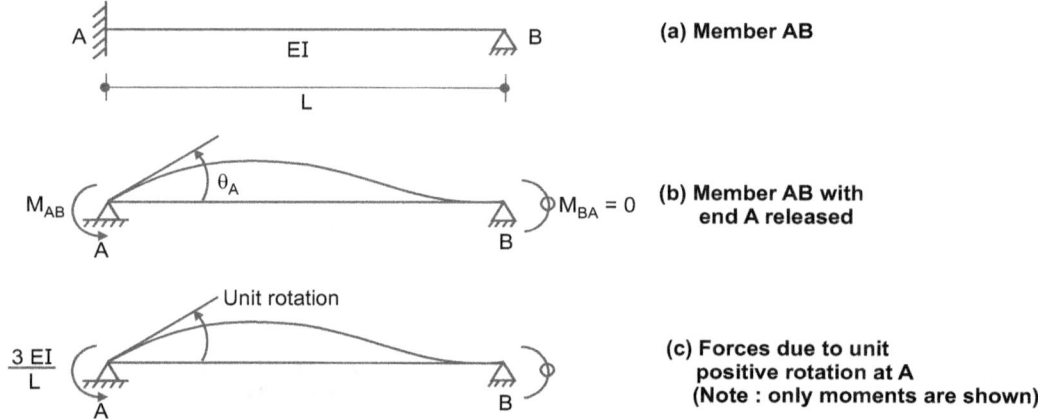

Fig. 2.2 : Releasing the near end when far end is hinged

As the joint B is already given as hinged support, the moment can not be developed at B and therefore there is no carryover moment at B and $M_{BA} = 0$. The ratio M_{BA}/M_{AB} is zero. Thus, carryover factor for this case is zero.

The comparison of these two cases reveals that (i) the stiffness of the member of second case is 3/4 of the stiffness of the member of first case.

For the analysis of structure by MD method, the flexural stiffnesses of members of same material are considered in terms of relative stiffness factor i.e. I/L of the members.

(ii) The carryover factor is 1/2 in first case and zero in second case. Therefore, COF is either 1/2 or 0.

It will be seen further that the carryover factor from one end to other end of the member and relative stiffness of the member play pivotal role in MD method. Therefore, following information will be very useful as prerequisite of MD method.

(1) COF

Type of the member end	COF
(a) Fixed support (FS or EFS)	$\frac{1}{2}$
(b) Intermediate support (IS or ISS)	$\frac{1}{2}$
(c) Rigid joint (RJ)	$\frac{1}{2}$
(d) Exterior simple, roller hinged support (ESS or ES or EHS)	0
(e) Internal pin	0

Thus (a) fixed support, (b) interior support, (c) rigid joint are considered as carryover end of the member and COF is 1/2.

Exterior simple, or roller or hinged support (may be with overhanging part) is taken as non-carryover end of the member and COF is zero.

(2) Relative Stiffness I/L factor

Type of member	Relative stiffness factor
(a) Member having both ends as carryover ends	(I/L)
(b) Member having one of the ends as non-carryover end.	(3/4) (I/L)
(c) Member having one of the ends as free.	0

It may be noted that the relative stiffness factor for the member having one of the ends as exterior simple or roller or hinged support, is required to be modified as (3/4) (I/L). This is called as modified relative stiffness factor. Further, the relative stiffness factors are normalized proportionately and are expressed in numbers by eliminating 1. Therefore, normalized relative stiffness factors of the members are taken in MD method for convenience. The normalized relative stiffness factor is denoted by K.

2.2 Distribution Factor

The concept of distribution of load or moment at the joint, to the members meeting at the joint is the key consideration. The distribution of load or moment is very well formulated using the fundamental principles of (i) equilibrium, (ii) compatibility, and (iii) force-displacement relations in terms of stiffnesses of the members.

The forces acting on the structure are resisted by the members through the joints. The resistance of a member is proportional to its stiffness. The stiffness is the force required to cause unit displacement. The basic stiffness of a member is AE/L for axial deformation and 4 EI/L for flexural rotation. The stiffness of a member is related to :

(i) its cross-sectional and material properties, (ii) length of the member, and (iii) end conditions of the member. More the stiffness of a member, more will be its resistance i.e. contribution to load sharing.

The phenomenon of distribution of load or moment is illustrated as follows :

Case I :

The load W is supported by the structural system as shown in Fig. 2.3 (a). The information of the members is given as :

A_1 = Area of cross-section of member AB
A_2 = Area of cross-section of member CD
E_1 = Modulus of elasticity of material of member AB
E_2 = Modulus of elasticity of material of member CD
L_1 = Length of member AB
L_2 = Length of member CD

It is assumed that the connection of the members at the joint of the load is rigid, ensuring that the displacement at the joint is only vertical translation. The equilibrium of the joint as shown in Fig. 2.3 (b) gives the equation $W = W_1 + W_2$. The compatibility of the rigid joint stipulates the equation of deformation as $dL_1 = dL_2$. Force-displacement relations lead to

$$dL_1 = \frac{W_1 L_1}{A_1 E_1} \quad \text{and} \quad dL_2 = \frac{W_2 L_2}{A_2 E_2}$$

Therefore, we get,

$$\frac{W_1 L_1}{A_1 E_1} = \frac{W_2 L_2}{A_2 E_2} \quad \text{i.e.} \quad \frac{W_1}{\left(\frac{A_1 E_1}{L_1}\right)} = \frac{W}{\left(\frac{A_2 E_2}{L_2}\right)}$$

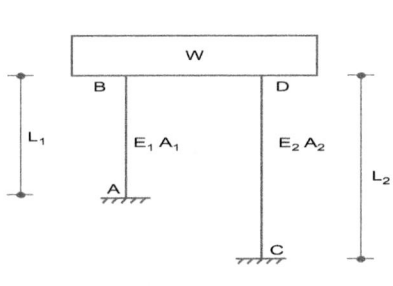
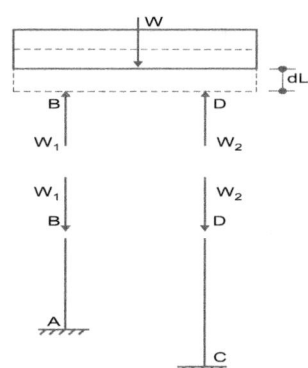

(a) Structural system **(b) Equilibrium of joints**

Fig. 2.3 : Distribution of load

It is to be noted that load sharing is proportional to the stiffness. If the material for two bars is same and A/L is considered as relative stiffness, K then the above equation becomes

$$\frac{W_1}{K_1} = \frac{W_2}{K_2}$$

$$\therefore \quad W_2 = \frac{K_2}{K_1} W_1$$

Substituting this in equilibrium equation,

$$W = W_1 + \frac{K_2}{K_1} W_1 = \left(1 + \frac{K_2}{K_1}\right) W_1 = \left(\frac{K_1 + K_2}{K_1}\right) W_1$$

$$\therefore \quad W_1 = \left(\frac{K_1}{K_1 + K_2}\right) W$$

Similarly, $\quad W_2 = \left(\dfrac{K_2}{K_1 + K_2}\right) W$

The term $\left(\dfrac{K_1}{K_1 + K_2}\right)$ is called the distribution factor DF_1 for the member 1 and $\left(\dfrac{K_2}{K_1 + K_2}\right)$ is DF_2 for the member 2.

$$\therefore \quad W_1 = (DF_1) W$$
$$\therefore \quad W_2 = (DF_2) W$$

Thus, it is concluded that the load is distributed according to the distribution factor which is function of the relative stiffnesses of the members. The distribution factor can also be expressed as

$$DF_1 = \left(\frac{K_1}{\Sigma K}\right)$$

$$DF_2 = \left(\frac{K_2}{\Sigma K}\right)$$

Case II :

The structure as shown in Fig. 2.4 (a) is subjected to the moment M_B applied at the rigid joint B. Other details are :

I_{AB} = Moment of inertia of cross-section of member AB about bending axis

I_{BC} = Moment of inertia of cross-section of member BC about bending axis

E_{AB} = Modulus of elasticity of material of member AB

E_{BC} = Modulus of elasticity of material of member BC

L_{AB} = Length of member AB

L_{BC} = Length of member BC

The member-end moment contributions are M_{BA} and M_{BC}.

From equilibrium of joint B as shown in Fig. 2.4 (b),

$$M_B = M_{BA} + M_{BC}$$

From compatibility of rigid joint,

$$\theta_{BA} = \theta_{BC}$$

From flexural rotational stiffness of the members,

$$M_{BA} = \frac{4 E_{AB} I_{AB}}{L_{AB}} \theta_{BA} \qquad \therefore \theta_{BA} = \frac{M_{BA} L_{AB}}{4 E_{AB} I_{AB}}$$

$$M_{BC} = \frac{4 E_{BC} I_{BC}}{L_{BC}} \theta_{BC} \qquad \therefore \theta_{BC} = \frac{M_{BC} L_{BC}}{4 E_{BC} I_{BC}}$$

$$\therefore \frac{M_{BA} L_{BA}}{4 E_{BA} I_{BA}} = \frac{M_{BC} L_{BC}}{4 E_{BC} I_{BC}}$$

$$\therefore \frac{M_{BA}}{\left(\frac{4 E_{BA} I_{BA}}{L_{BA}}\right)} = \frac{M_{BC}}{\left(\frac{4 E_{BC} I_{BC}}{L_{BC}}\right)}$$

Moment contributions of members are proportional to its stiffness 4 EI/L. If the material of members is same and I/L is taken as relative stiffness K of the member, then

$$\frac{M_{BA}}{K_{BA}} = \frac{M_{BC}}{K_{BC}}$$

$$\therefore \quad M_{BC} = \left(\frac{K_{BC}}{K_{BA}}\right) M_{BA}$$

Putting M_{BC} in equilibrium equation,

$$M_B = M_{BA} + \left(\frac{K_{BC}}{K_{BA}}\right) M_{BA}$$

$$M_B = \left(1 + \frac{K_{BC}}{K_{BA}}\right) M_{BA} = \left(\frac{K_{BA} + K_{BC}}{K_{BA}}\right) M_{BA}$$

$$\therefore \quad M_{BA} = \left(\frac{K_{BA}}{K_{BA} + K_{BC}}\right) M_B$$

$$M_{BC} = \left(\frac{K_{BC}}{K_{BA} + K_{BC}}\right) M_B$$

Again the distribution factors are expressed as

$$DF_{BA} = \frac{K_{BA}}{K_{BA} + K_{BC}} = \frac{K_{BA}}{\Sigma K}$$

$$DF_{BC} = \frac{K_{BC}}{K_{BA} + K_{BC}} = \frac{K_{BC}}{\Sigma K}$$

$$\therefore \quad M_{BA} = (DF_{BA})(M_B)$$

$$M_{BC} = (DF_{BC})(M_B)$$

Case III : For the same structure of case II except the support condition at A as hinged is considered as shown in Fig. 2.4 (c). The distribution of moment at the joint B in this case is formulated on similar lines as follows :

$$M_B = M_{BA} + M_{BC} \text{ from equilibrium of joint B, as shown in Fig. 2.4 (d)}$$

$$\theta_{BA} = \theta_{BC} \text{ from compatibility of joint B}$$

$$\left.\begin{array}{l} \theta_{BA} = \dfrac{M_{BA} L_{AB}}{3 E_{AB} I_{AB}} \\[2mm] \theta_{BC} = \dfrac{M_{BC} L_{BC}}{4 E_{BC} I_{BC}} \end{array}\right\} \text{ from flexural rotational stiffness}$$

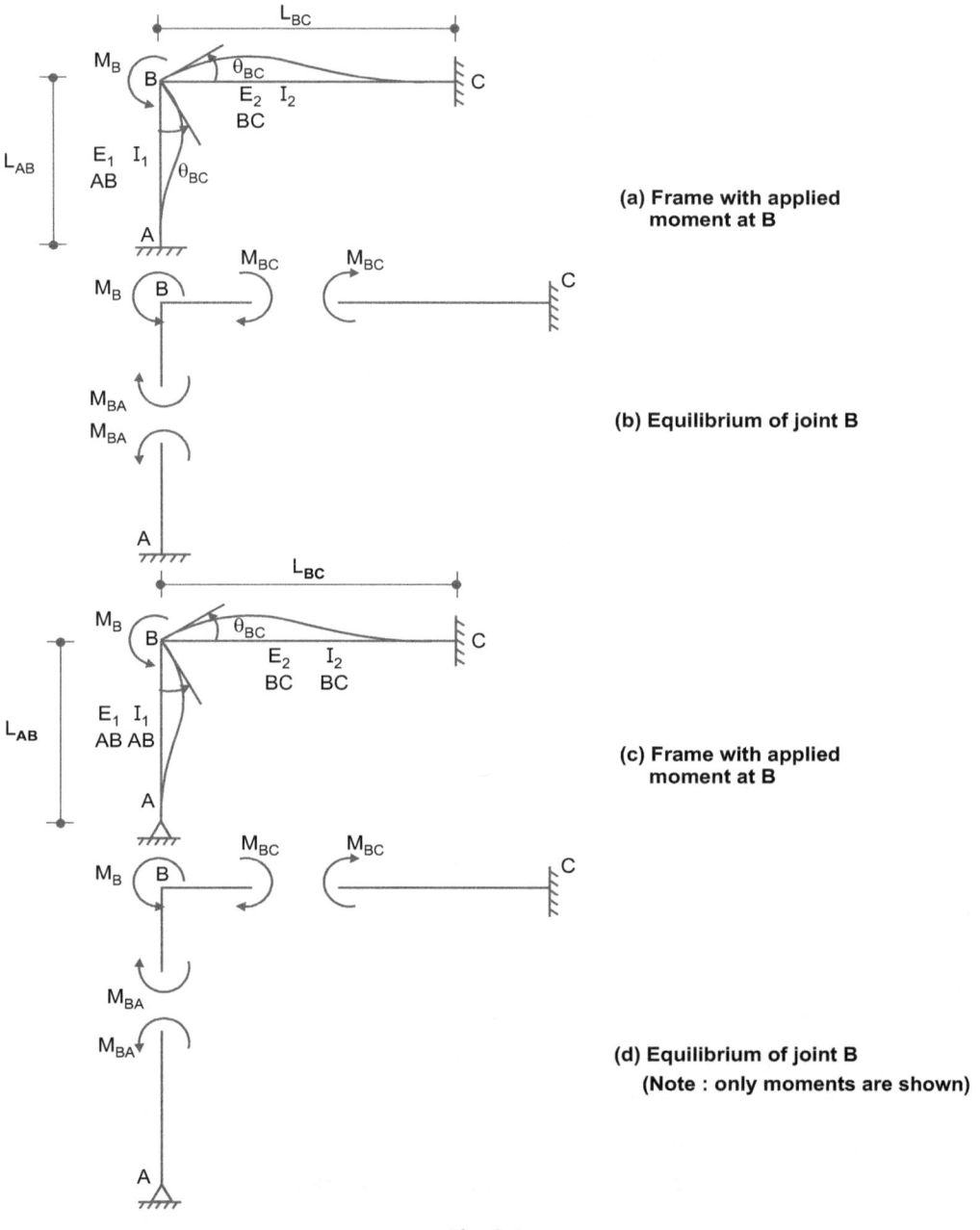

Fig. 2.4

STRUCTURAL ANALYSIS – II MOMENT DISTRIBUTION METHOD

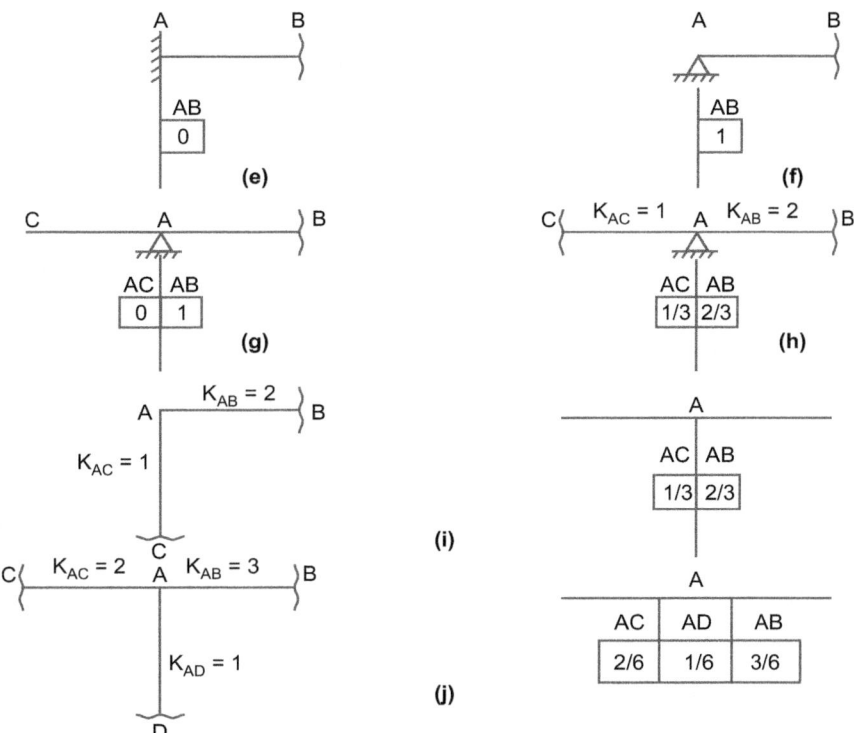

Fig. 2.4 : Distribution of moment

$$\therefore \quad \frac{M_{BA} L_{AB}}{3 E_{AB} I_{AB}} = \frac{M_{BC} L_{BC}}{4 E_{BC} I_{BC}}$$

$\therefore$ If $\quad E_{AB} = E_{BC}$

$$\frac{M_{BA}}{K_{AB}} = \frac{M_{BC}}{K_{BC}}$$

where K_{AB} is the modified relative stiffness i.e. (3/4) (I/L) for the member having hinged end.

$\therefore \quad M_{BA} = (DF_{BA}) (M_B)$
$\therefore \quad M_{BC} = (DF_{BC}) (M_B)$

where $\quad DF_{BA} = \dfrac{K_{BA}}{\Sigma K}$

$\quad DF_{BC} = \dfrac{K_{BC}}{K}$

Thus, the moment at a rigid joint is distributed to the members meeting at the joint, in proportion to the distribution factors of the member at the joint. This is the basic phenomenon of moment distribution. The distribution factor plays vital role in moment distribution. The distribution factor is related to the relative stiffness of the member and sum of the relative stiffnesses of all members meeting at the joint.

The ratio $\dfrac{\text{Relative stiffness of the member}}{\text{Sum of relative stiffnesses of all the members meeting at the joint}}$

is called the distribution factor for the member end meeting at the joint. In general, the distribution factor is expressed as

$$DF_{ij} = \dfrac{K_{ij}}{\sum_i K_{ij}} \qquad \ldots (2.1)$$

Following hints will be useful in connection with DF :
    (i)   At fixed support, the distribution factor for the member end is zero.
    (ii)   At end simple or roller or hinged support, the distribution factor for the member end is one.
    (iii) At exterior simple or roller or hinged support, the distribution factor for the member end is one for inside member end and zero for overhanging member end.
    (iv) At interior simple or roller or hinged support and at intermediate rigid joint, the distribution factor for the member end is less than one and to be obtained from

$$DF_{ij} = \dfrac{K_{ij}}{\sum_i K_{ij}}$$

    (v)   The sum of the distribution factors for the member ends meeting at the joint is one.

2.3 Introduction to MD Method

The MD method mainly consists of successive operations of (i) restraining the joints, and (ii) releasing the joints. The effect of restraining the joints is fixed-end moments i.e. FEM in the first cycle and carryover moments i.e. COM in subsequent cycles. With FEM or COM, the joints may not satisfy the equilibrium conditions. Therefore, there is unbalanced moment at the joint. The balancing moment at the joint is equal and opposite to the unbalanced moment at the joint. The releasing of the joint means balancing the joints. In the operation of releasing the joint, the balancing moment is distributed to the members meeting at the joint. This is called as the distribution of moment in proportion to the normalized relative stiffness factors of the members meeting at the joint. In the first cycle, the FEM due to member loads, is the effect of restraining all the joints. The balancing of all joints means the distribution of moments. In subsequent cycles, the restraining of joints is equivalent to the carryover moments. Carryover and balancing operations are repeated in each cycles. Number of such cycles are performed till required degree of accuracy. Thus, MD method is iterative. The iterations of cycles should be discontinued only when the balancing moments are very small as compared to the initial FEM. The final member-end moments are obtained by adding all member-end moments of all cycles.

STRUCTURAL ANALYSIS – II   MOMENT DISTRIBUTION METHOD

Initially, MD method is explained to analyse the indeterminate structures without joint transitions. In general, the MD method involves restraining of joints against rotation and releasing the joints for rotation. If the joint translations exist in the structure, the restraining of joints against translation will be additional concept, to be considered at the beginning of MD method, as dealt with at later stages.

MD method works with member-end moments as FEM, COM and DM (distributed moments). Compatibility and equilibrium of joints are indirectly taken care of in MD technique. MD method does not require the information of degree of static and kinematic indeterminacy of the structure. Kinematically determinate structures cannot be analysed by MD method.

2.3.1 Sign Conventions for Member-End Moments

Same sign conventions as used in SD method are used for MD method. This is restated as : Anticlockwise member-end moment is positive and clockwise member-end moment is negative.

2.4 PROCEDURE OF MD METHOD

The primary information of FEM, COF, K, and DF, are initially obtained from data and then the cycles of restraining, releasing and balancing the joints, are systematically carried out in the tabular form. The moment distribution table will be denoted hereafter by MD table. The procedure of MD method is formulated in tabular form with reference to the following illustrated example 2.1.

Example 2.1 : *Analyse the beam shown in Fig. 2.5 (a) by MD method.*

Solution : Data : The structure is supported and loaded as shown in Fig. 2.5 (a). The data includes the following information.

(1) Structural configuration – Type of members; joints; supports; dimensions; cross-sectional properties and material properties of members.
(2) Applied loads : Magnitude, direction and position.
(3) Type of structure : Continuous beam without joint translations.

Object :

In general, the objective is the analysis of structure in all respects. However, the immediate objective i.e. target is to obtain member-end moments by MD method. Knowing the member-end moments, other results of analysis can be obtained easily using the equations of equilibrium.

Concepts and Equations :

MD technique based on normalized relative stiffness factors, carryover factors, and distribution factors.

Procedure :

The process of MD method consists of the following steps :

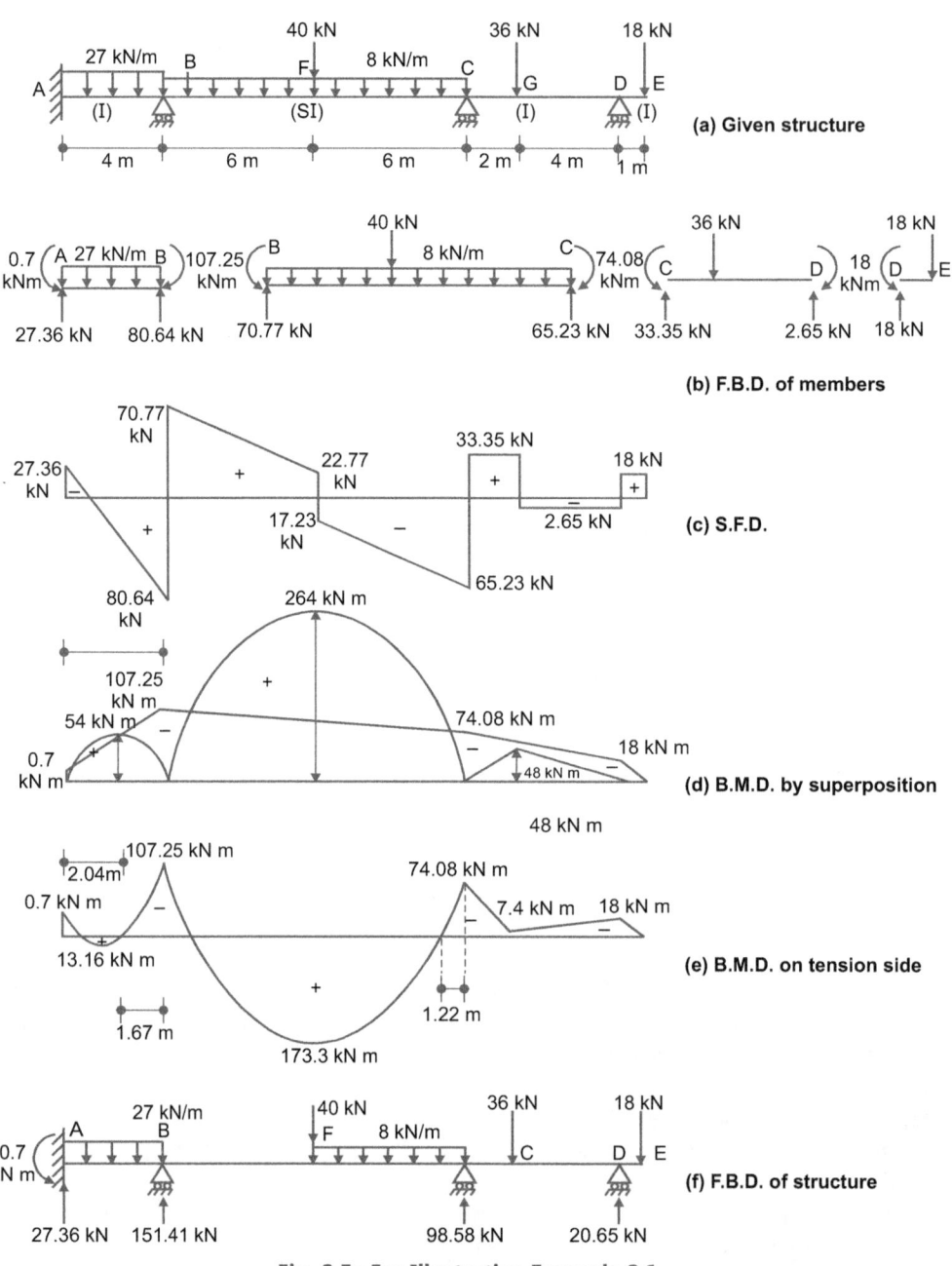

Fig. 2.5 : For Illustrative Example 2.1

Step I : FEM : The fixed-end moments for all members of the structure due to the transverse loads on the member are calculated using the standard results. If the member is not loaded, FEM will be zero. MD begins with the FEM, therefore correctness of FEM is important. For the given data, the FEM are calculated and presented in the following format.

Member	FEM with calculations
AB	$M^F_{AB} = +\left(\dfrac{27 \times 4 \times 4}{12}\right) = +36$ kNm $M^F_{BA} = -M^F_{AB} = -36$ kNm
BC	$M^F_{BC} = +\left(\dfrac{8 \times 12 \times 12}{12}\right) + \left(\dfrac{40 \times 12}{8}\right)$ $= +156$ kNm $M^F_{CB} = -M^F_{BC} = -156$ kNm
CD	$M^F_{CD} = +\left(\dfrac{36 \times 2 \times 4 \times 4}{6 \times 6}\right) = +32$ kNm $M^F_{DC} = -\left(\dfrac{36 \times 2 \times 2 \times 4}{6 \times 6}\right) = -16$ kNm
DE	$M^F_{DE} = +(18 \times 1) = +18$ kNm

Step II : Distribution factors :

Joint	Member	K	ΣK	DF = $\dfrac{K}{\Sigma K}$
A	AB	—	—	0
B	BA	$\dfrac{4EI}{L} = 1$	2.67	0.375
	BC	$\dfrac{4EI}{L} = 1.67$		0.625
C	CB	$\dfrac{4EI}{L} = 1.67$	2.17	0.769
	CD	$\dfrac{3EI}{L} = 0.5$		0.231
D	DC	—	—	1
	DE	—	—	0

Step III : MD Table : The information of joints, type of joints, members meeting the joint, COF, K, DF are consolidated in concise manner in the beginning of cycles of moment distribution as shown in MD table.

The cycles of successive restraining and releasing and balancing the joints are then carried out and accordingly the distributed moments at ends of members are entered row-wise in every cycles of MD table. The operation of balancing of joints is represented by MD in MD

STRUCTURAL ANALYSIS – II MOMENT DISTRIBUTION METHOD

table. The working procedure of MD table is explained below, noting that the method works with member-end moments, which are equal and opposite to the joint moments.

First Cycle :

(a) **Restraining all joints against rotation :** The restraining moments are FEM due to member loads and are entered in first row of this cycle in respective column as shown in MD table.

(b) **Releasing and balancing the joints and distributing the moments :**

Joint A : It is the fixed support, the rotation at A is zero and hence it is not to be released. This is also clear from zero DF for the member AB at A.

Joint B : It is the interior support or rigid joint. This is to be released as there is rotation at B. At this joint, moments equal and opposite to member-end moments, M_{BA}^F and M_{BC}^F are acting as shown in Fig. 2.6 (a). Thus, there is unbalanced moment of 120 kNm clockwise as shown in Fig. 2.6 (b). For balancing the joint B, moment of – 120 kNm is distributed to the member ends of BA and BC in proportion to the distribution factors. The distributed member-end moments are calculated as follows :

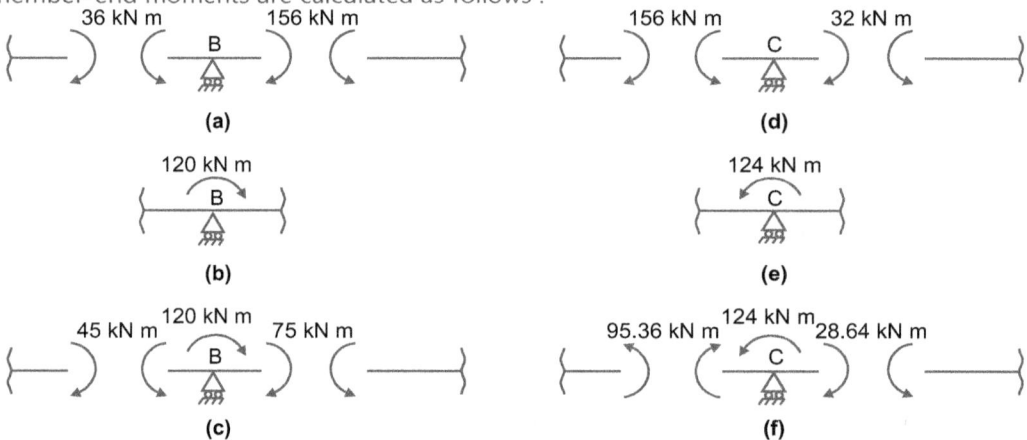

Fig. 2.6 : Balancing the joint

$$M_{BA}^D = (-120)(0.375) = -45 \text{ kNm}$$
$$M_{BC}^D = (-120)(0.625) = -75 \text{ kNm}$$

Balancing of the joint B is demonstrated in Fig. 2.6 (c). Alternatively the distribution of moments is mechanically done according to the following steps :

(1) Unbalanced member-end moment :
$$M_B^{ub} = -36 + 156 = +120 \text{ kNm}$$

(2) Change the sign of M^{ub} and obtain the balancing moment :
$$M_B^b = -120 \text{ kNm}$$

(3) Multiply by DF to obtain the distributed member-end moments :

$$M_{BA}^D = (-120) \times (0.375) = -45 \text{ kNm}$$
$$M_{BC}^D = (-120) \times (0.625) = -75 \text{ kNm}$$

Joint C : This is also to be released and balanced as demonstrated in Fig. 2.6 (d) as the physical phenomenon of distribution. However, the mechanical and mathematical procedure is given below :

(1) $M_C^{ub} = -156 + 32 = -124$ kNm

(2) $M_C^b = -M_C^{ub} = +124$ kNm

(3) $M_{CB}^D = M_C^b \times DF_{CB} = +124 \times 0.769 = +95.36$ kNm

$M_{CD}^D = M_C^b \times DF_{CD} = +124 \times 0.231 = +28.64$

Joint D : This is exterior simple or hinged support and therefore it is to be released and balanced only once in the first cycle.

(1) $M_D^{ub} = -16 + 18 = +2$ kNm

(2) $M_D^b = -M_D^{ub} = -2$ kNm

(3) $M_{DC}^D = (-2)(1) = -2$

(4) $M_{DE}^D = (-2)(0) = 0$

All distributed moments obtained above by balancing all the joints are entered in second row of first cycle in the respective columns as shown in MD table. This completes the first cycle.

Second Cycle :

(a) **Restraining the Joint :** Restraining moments are carryover moments, COM of the distributed moments of first cycle. M^D at one end is carried over to the other end of the member.

$M^{COM} = M^D \times COF$ as shown by crossed arrows in MD table.

i.e. $M_{BA}^{COM} = (-45)\left(\dfrac{1}{2}\right) = -22.5$ kNm

$M_{BC}^{COM} = (+95.36)\left(\dfrac{1}{2}\right) = +47.68$ kNm

and so on. It may be noted that there is no carryover to the exterior simple/hinged support D. It is balanced completely in first cycle itself and hence distribution at D is stopped at this stage.

Carryover moments are entered in first row of this cycle in the respective columns as shown in MD table.

(b) **Releasing and balancing the joints and distributing the moments :** Same procedure as in first cycle is followed. The balancing of one joint is illustrated again.

Joint B :

(1) $M_B^{ub} = 0 + 47.68 = + 47.68$

(2) $M_B^b = - M^{ub} = - 47.68$

(3) $M_{BA}^D = (- 47.68) \times (0.375) = - 17.88$ kNm

(4) $M_{BC}^D = (- 47.65) \times (0.625) = - 29.80$ kNm

Other Cycles :

The operations of carryover and balancing for further cycles are repeated till the desired degree of accuracy. In this sense, the iterations of MD table could be stopped at the end of any cycle so that the distributed moments are small compared to the initial FEM. Accuracy of the results will depend on the stage of terminating MD table. In the particular situations, MD table stops automatically as there may be no moments for distribution. The operations in MD table are represented by COM, DM.

Final Results of MD Tables :

Total member-end moments are obtained by adding the moments in the respective columns.

MD Table

Joint	A		B		C		D
Type of joint	EFS		ISS/RJ		ISS/RJ		ESS
Member	AB	BA	BC	CB	CD	DC	DE
COF	→1/2 1/2←		→1/2 1/2←		→0 1/2←		
DF	0	0.375	0.625	0.769	0.231	1	0
First cycle FEM	+ 36	− 36	+ 156	− 156	+ 32	− 16	+ 18
DM	−	− 45	− 75	+ 95.36	+ 28.64	− 2	−
Second cycle COM	− 22.5	−	+ 47.68	− 37.5	− 1.0	ST	OP
DM	−	− 17.88	− 29.80	+ 29.61	+ 8.89		
Third cycle COM	− 8.94	−	+ 14.80	− 14.90	−		
DM	−	− 5.55	− 9.25	+ 11.46	+ 3.44		
Fourth cycle COM	− 2.78	−	+ 5.73	− 4.62	−		
DM	−	− 2.15	− 3.58	+ 3.55	+ 1.07		
Fifth cycle COM	− 1.08	−	+ 1.78	− 1.79	−		
DM	−	− 0.67	− 1.11	+ 1.38	+ 0.41		
Total final moments	+ 0.7	− 107.25	+ 107.25	− 74.08	+ 74.08	− 18	+ 18

Step IV : FBD of members and member forces : Member-end moments are known from MD table. Member-end forces are obtained from equations of equilibrium applied to FBD of the member as shown in Fig. 2.6 (b).

STRUCTURAL ANALYSIS – II   MOMENT DISTRIBUTION METHOD

Step V : SFD : With known values of member-end shears and member loads, the SFD is drawn as shown in Fig. 2.6 (c).

Step VI : BMD : Member-end moments are considered as bending moments at the supports. Span bending moments are obtained from member loads.

BMD by superposition and BMD on tension side is as shown in Fig. 2.6 (d) and Fig. 2.6 (e) respectively.

Step VII : FBD of structure and reactions : Member-end moments and forces at the support end of the member will correspond to the reactions of the supports.

For interior support, the reactions will be the sum of member-end forces meeting the support joint. FBD of structure is as shown in Fig. 2.6 (f).

Following rules of MD method are worth to be noted for further applications :

1. The relative stiffness factor for members with one exterior simple or roller or hinged support is to be modified as (3/4) (I/L).
2. The fixed support need not be released.
3. The exterior simple or roller or hinged support need to be balanced only once in the first cycle.
4. No carryover moments will ever be brought to the exterior simple or roller or hinged supports.

Example 2.2 : *A continuous beam ABCD with ends A and D is simply supported. A couple of 50 kN-m is acting at centre on AB having span 3m. BC is loaded with UDL of 15 kN/m and span 3.5m. A point load of 60 kN is acting on CD having span 4.5 m at 1 m from D. Draw S.F.D. and B.M.D.*

Solution : Data : The beam is loaded and supported as shown in Fig. 2.7.

Object. Structural analysis.

Concepts and Equations : MD technique based on normalized relative stiffness factors, carryover factors and distribution factors.

Procedure : Step I : Fixed end moments :

$$\overline{M}_{AB} = +\frac{M}{4} = \frac{50}{4} = 12.5 \text{ kN-m}$$

$$\overline{M}_{BA} = +\frac{M}{4} = 12.5 \text{ kN-m}$$

$$\overline{M}_{BC} = -\frac{wl^2}{12} = -\frac{15 \times 3.5^2}{12} = -15.31 \text{ kN-m}$$

$$\overline{M}_{CB} = 15.31 \text{ kN-m}$$

$$\overline{M}_{CD} = -\frac{wab^2}{l^2} = -\frac{60 \times 3.5 \times 1^2}{4.5^2} = -10.37 \text{ kN-m}$$

$$\overline{M}_{DC} = \frac{wa^2b}{l^2} = \frac{60 \times 3.5^2 \times 1}{4.5^2} = 36.3 \text{ kN-m}$$

STRUCTURAL ANALYSIS – II   MOMENT DISTRIBUTION METHOD

Step II : Distribution factors :

Joint	Member	Type of Support	Carry over factor	K	∑K	D.F.
A	AB	Simple support	A → B $1/2$	–	–	–
B	BA	Continuous support	B → A 0	3/4 × I/3	11.5I/14	0.3
	BC		B → C $1/2$	2I/3.5		0.7
C	CB	Continuous support	C → B $1/2$	2I/3.5	41.5I/42	0.58
	CD		C → D 0	3/4 × 2.5I/4.5		0.42
D	DC	Simple support	D → C $1/2$	–	–	–

Step III : MD Table :

Joint	A	B		C		D
Member	AB	BA	BC	CB	CD	DC
D.F.	–	0.3	0.7	0.58	0.42	–
F.E.M.	12.5	12.5	–15.31	15.31	–10.37	36.3
Release Jt. A and D as S.S.	–12.5					–36.3
C.O.		–6.25			–18.15	
Total moments	0	6.25	–15.31	15.31	–28.52	0
Distribution		2.72	6.34	7.66	5.55	
C.O.			3.83	3.17		
Distribution		–1.15	–2.68	–1.84	–1.33	
C.O.			–0.92	–1.34		
		0.28	0.64	0.78	0.56	
Total moments	0	8.1	–8.1	23.74	–23.74	0

Ch. 2 | 2.18

STRUCTURAL ANALYSIS – II   MOMENT DISTRIBUTION METHOD

Step IV : FBD of members is an shown in Fig. Considering equilibrium of each member and of complete structure, all reaction components are found out as shown in Fig. 2.7.

Step V : Shear force diagram is as shown in Fig. 2.7.

Step VI : Bending moment diagrams are as shown in Fig. 2.7 (d) and (e).

Step VII : FBD of structure is as shown in Fig. 2.7.

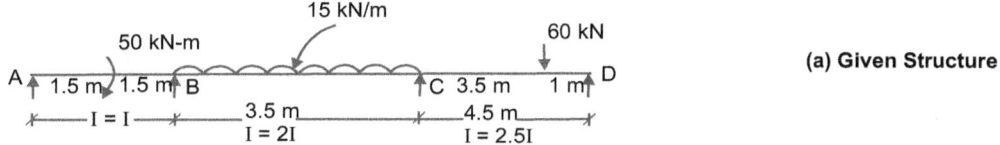

(a) Given Structure

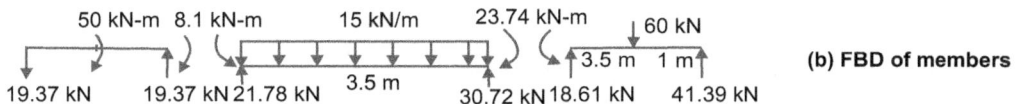

(b) FBD of members

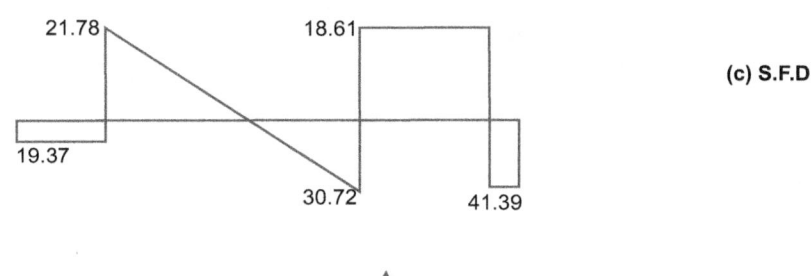

(c) S.F.D

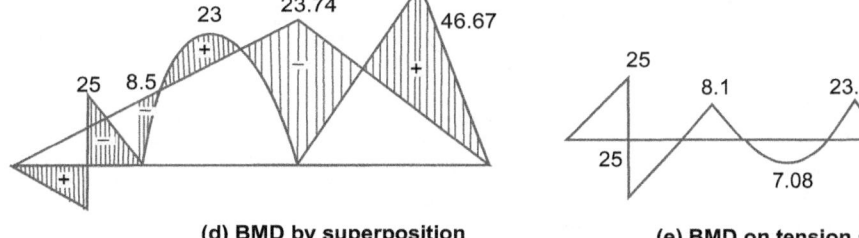

(d) BMD by superposition   (e) BMD on tension side

Fig. 2.7

Example 2.3 : A continuous beam ABC is fixed at A and simply supported at B and C. The span AB is 6 m and carries UDL of 2 kN/m. The span BC is 4 m and carries UDL load of 3 kN/m. Determine the fixed end moments. (I is same throughout).

STRUCTURAL ANALYSIS – II   MOMENT DISTRIBUTION METHOD

Solution : Data : The beam is loaded and supported as shown in Fig. 2.8

Object. Structural analysis :

Concepts and Equations : MD technique based on normlized relative stiffness factors, carry over factors and distribution factors.

Procedure : Step I : Fixed End Moments :

$$M_{AB} = -\frac{wl^2}{12} = -\frac{2 \times 6 \times 6}{12} = -6 \text{ kN-m}$$

$$M_{BA} = +6 \text{ kN-m}$$

$$M_{BC} = -\frac{wl^2}{2} = -\frac{3 \times 4 \times 4}{12} = -4 \text{ kN-m}$$

$$M_{CB} = +4 \text{ kN-m}$$

Step II : Distribution Factors :

Joint	Member	Type of support	Carryover factor	K	ΣK	D. F.
A	AB	Fixed	A → B 0	—	—	—
B	BA	Continuous	B → A 1/2	I/6	34I/96	0.471
	BC	Support	B → C 0	3/4 × I/4		0.529
C	CB	Simple	C → B 1/2	—	—	—

Step III : MD Table :

Joint	A	B		D
Member	AB	BA	BC	DC
D. F.	-	0.471	0.529	-
F.E.M.	−6	+6	−4	+4
Release moment at C				−4
C.O.			−2	
Total moments	−6	+6	−6	0

Ch. 2 | 2.20

STRUCTURAL ANALYSIS – II   MOMENT DISTRIBUTION METHOD

Step IV : FBD of members is an shown in Fig. 2.8 Considering equilibrium of each member and of complete structure, all reaction components are found out as shown in Fig. 2.8.

Step V : Shear force diagram is as shown in Fig. 2.8.

Step VI : Bending moment diagrams are as shown in Fig. 2.8.

Step VII : FBD of structure is as shown in Fig. 2.8.

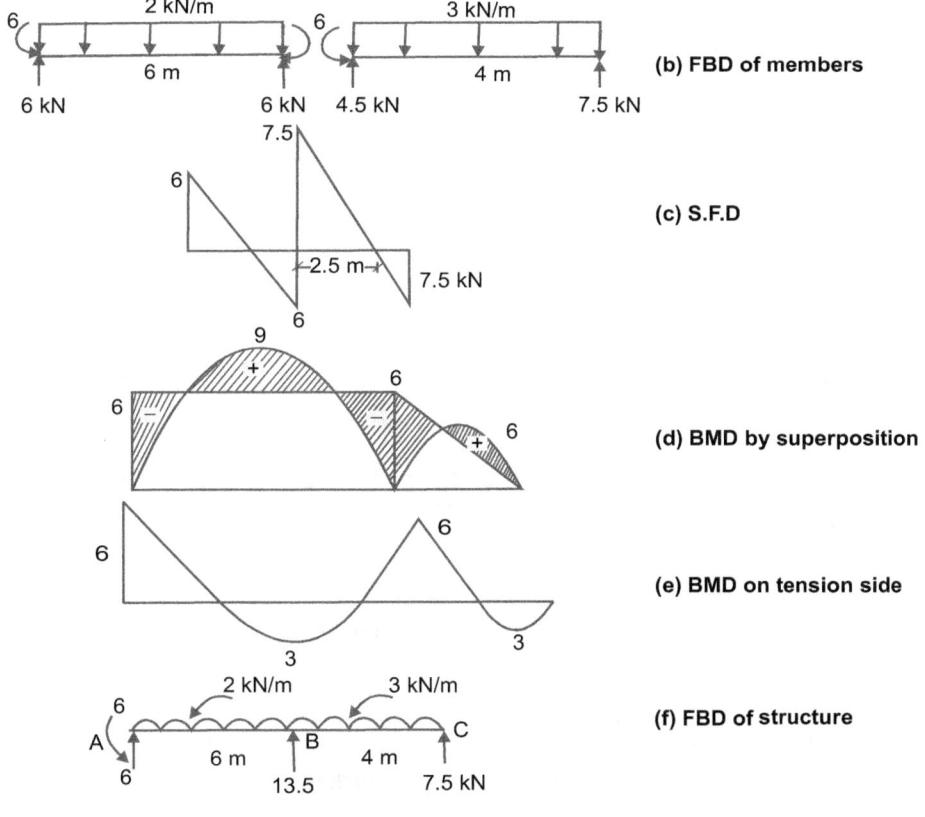

Fig. 2.8

Example 2.4 : *Find the reaction at the prop for the beam AB loaded with U.D.L. of intenstiy w/m run and span of AB is l metres.*

Solution : Data : The beam is loaded and supported as shown in Fig. 2.9.

Object. Structural analysis :

Concepts and Equations : MD technique based on normalized relative stiffness factors, carryover factors and distribution factors.

Procedure : Step I : Fixed End Moments :

$$M_A = -\frac{wl^2}{12}, M_B = -\frac{wl^2}{12}$$

Step II : As no continuation at joint B and joint A is fixed, then there is no relative stiffness and there will not be any distribution factor.

Step III : MD Table :

Joint	A	B
F.E.M.	$-wl^2/12$	$+wl^2/12$
Released B		$-wl^2/12$
C.O.	$-wl^2/24$	
Final moments	$-wl^2/8$	0

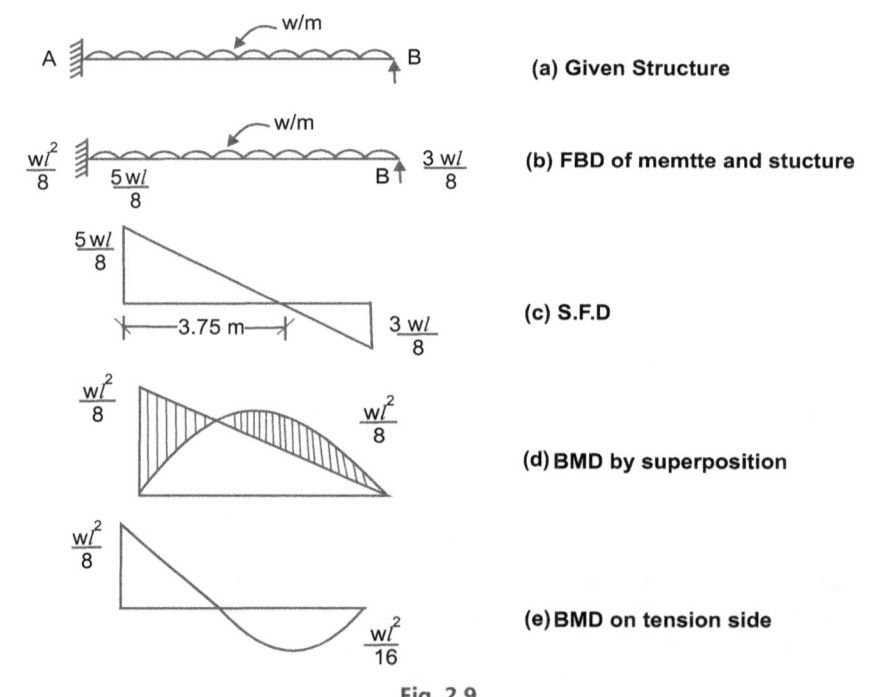

(a) Given Structure

(b) FBD of memtte and stucture

(c) S.F.D

(d) BMD by superposition

(e) BMD on tension side

Fig. 2.9

STRUCTURAL ANALYSIS – II   MOMENT DISTRIBUTION METHOD

Step IV : FBD of members is as shown in Fig. 2.9 Considering equilibrium of each member and of complete structure, all reaction components are found out as shown in Fig.

Step V : Shear force diagram is as shown in Fig. 2.9

Step VI : Bending moment diagrams are as shown in Fig. 2.9

Step VII : FBD of structure is as shown in Fig. 2.9

Example 2.5 : *Analyse the beam shown in Fig. 2.10 (a) using moment distribution method.*

Solution : Data : The beam is supported and loaded as shown in Fig. 2.10 (a).

Object : Structural analysis.

Concepts and Equations : MD technique based on normalized relative stiffness factors, carryover factors and distribution factors.

Procedure : Step I : Fixed-end moments :

Member	FEM with calculations
AB	$M_{AB}^F = \dfrac{WL^2}{12} = \dfrac{20 \times 9^2}{12} = 135$ kN-m
	$M_{BA}^F = \dfrac{-WL^2}{12} = -\dfrac{20 \times 9^2}{12} = -135$ kN-m
BC	$M_{BC}^F = \dfrac{WL}{8} = \dfrac{80 \times 6}{8} = 60$ kN-m
	$M_{CB}^F = -\dfrac{WL}{8} = -\dfrac{80 \times 6}{8} = -60$ kN-m
CD	$M_{CD}^F = \dfrac{WL^2}{12} = \dfrac{15 \times 8^2}{12} = 80$ kN-m
	$M_{DC}^F = \dfrac{-WL^2}{12} = -\dfrac{15 \times 8^2}{12} = -80$ kN-m

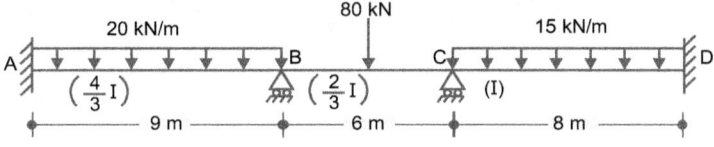

(a) Given structure

STRUCTURAL ANALYSIS – II

MOMENT DISTRIBUTION METHOD

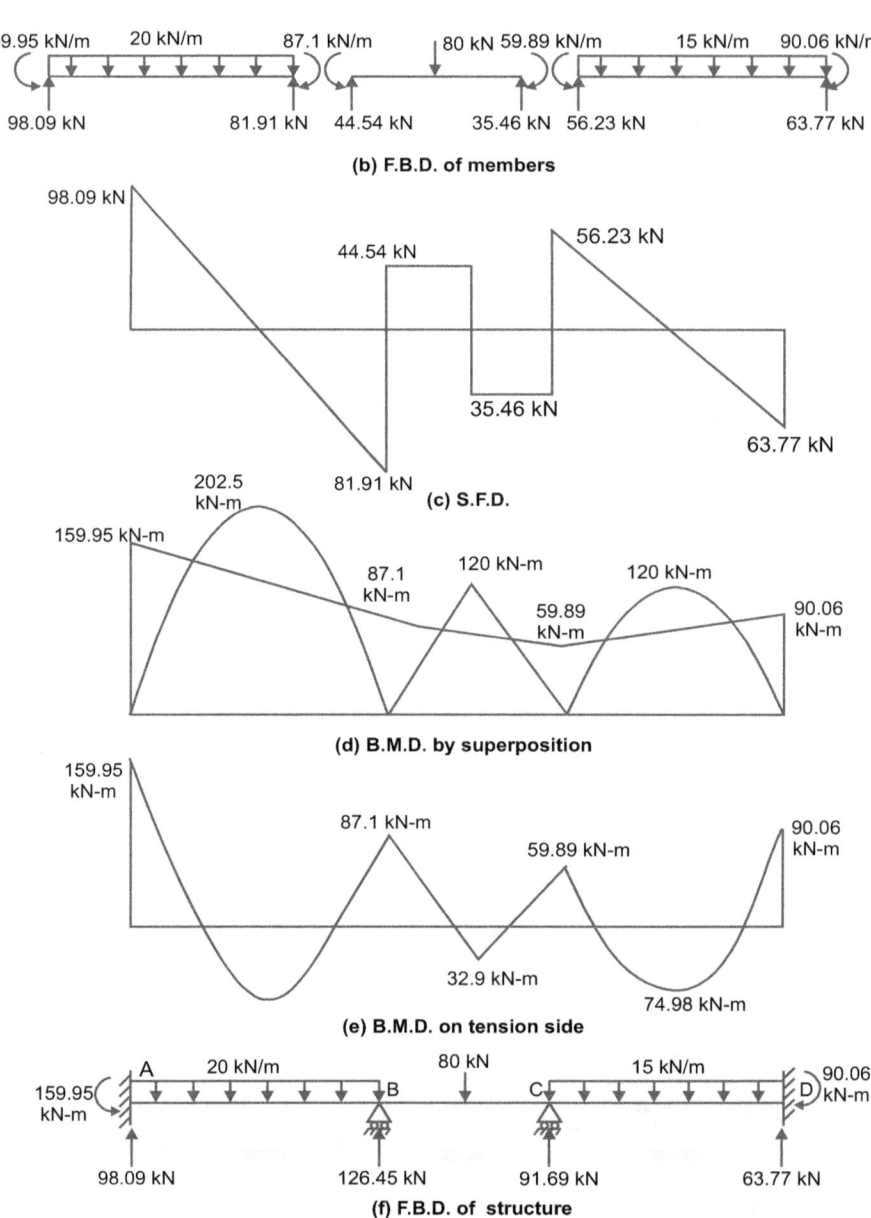

Fig. 2.10 : For Illustrative Example 2.5

STRUCTURAL ANALYSIS – II   MOMENT DISTRIBUTION METHOD

Step II : Distribution factors :

Joint	Member	K	ΣK	D.F.
A	AB	–	–	0
B	BA	$\frac{4EI}{L} = 0.59$	1.03	0.57
	BC	$\frac{4EI}{L} = 0.44$		0.43
C	CB	$\frac{4EI}{L} = 0.44$	0.94	0.47
	CD	$\frac{4EI}{L} = 0.5$		0.53
D	DC	–	–	0

Step III : MD table :

Joint		A	B		C		D
Type of joint		EFS	RJ		RJ		EFS
Member		AB	BA	BC	CB	CD	DC
COF			→ 1/2		→ 1/2		→ 1/2
DF			1/2 ←		1/2 →		1/2 →
		0	0.57	0.43	0.47	0.53	0
First cycle	FEM	135	– 135	60	– 60	80	– 80
	DM	–	42.75	32.25	– 9.4	– 10.6	–
Second cycle	COM	21.38	–	– 4.7	16.12	–	– 5.3
	DM	–	2.69	2.02	– 7.58	– 8.54	–
Third cycle	COM	1.35	–	– 3.79	1.01	–	– 4.27
	DM	–	2.16	1.63	– 0.49	– 0.52	–
Fourth cycle	COM	1.08		– 0.24	0.81		– 0.26
	DM		0.14	0.10	– 0.38	– 0.43	
Fifth cycle	COM	0.07		– 0.19	0.05		– 0.21
	DM		0.11	0.08	– 0.024	– 0.026	
Sixth cycle	COM	0.060		– 0.012	0.04		– 0.013
	DM		0.007	0.005	– 0.019	– 0.021	
Seventh cycle	COM	0.004		– 0.009	0.002		– 0.010
	DM		0.005	0.004	– 0.001	– 0.001	
Total final moment		158.95	– 87.1	87.10	– 59.86	59.86	– 90.06

Step IV : FBD of members is as shown in Fig. 2.10 (b). Considering equilibrium of each member and of complete structure, all reaction components are found out as shown in Fig. 2.10 (d).

Step V : Shear force diagram is as shown in Fig. 2.10 (c).

Step VI : Bending moment diagrams are as shown in Fig. 2.10 (d) and Fig. 2.10 (e).

Step VII : FBD of structure is as shown in Fig. 2.10 (f).

Example 2.6 : *The beam is loaded and supported as shown in Fig. 2.11 (a). Analyse the beam using moment distribution method.*

Solution : Data : The beam is loaded and supported as shown in Fig. 2.11 (a).

Object : Structural analysis.

Concepts and Equations : MD technique based on normalized relative stiffness factors, carryover factors and distribution factors.

Procedure :

Step I : Fixed-end moments :

Member	FEM with calculations		Total FEM
	FEM due to external loads	FEM due to sinking of support D	
AB	$M^F_{BA} = -10 \times 2 = -20$ kN-m	0	-20 kN-m
BC	$M^F_{BC} = \dfrac{WL^2}{12} = \dfrac{16 \times 6^2}{12}$ $= 48$ kN-m	0	48 kN-m
	$M^F_{CB} = -\dfrac{WL^2}{12} = -\dfrac{16 \times 6^2}{12}$ $= -48$ kN-m	0	-48 kN-m
CD	$M^F_{CD} = \dfrac{WL}{8} = \dfrac{8 \times 4}{8}$ $= 4$ kN-m	$M^F_{CD} = \dfrac{6EI\delta}{L^2}$ $= \dfrac{6 \times 2 \times 10^4 \times 2 \times 10^{-3}}{4^2}$ $= 15$ kN-m	19 kN-m
	$M^F_{DC} = -\dfrac{WL}{8} = -\dfrac{8 \times 4}{8}$ $= -4$ kN-m	$M^F_{DC} = \dfrac{6EI\delta}{L^2}$ $= \dfrac{6 \times 2 \times 10^4 \times 2 \times 10^{-3}}{4^2}$ $= 15$ kN-m	11 kN-m

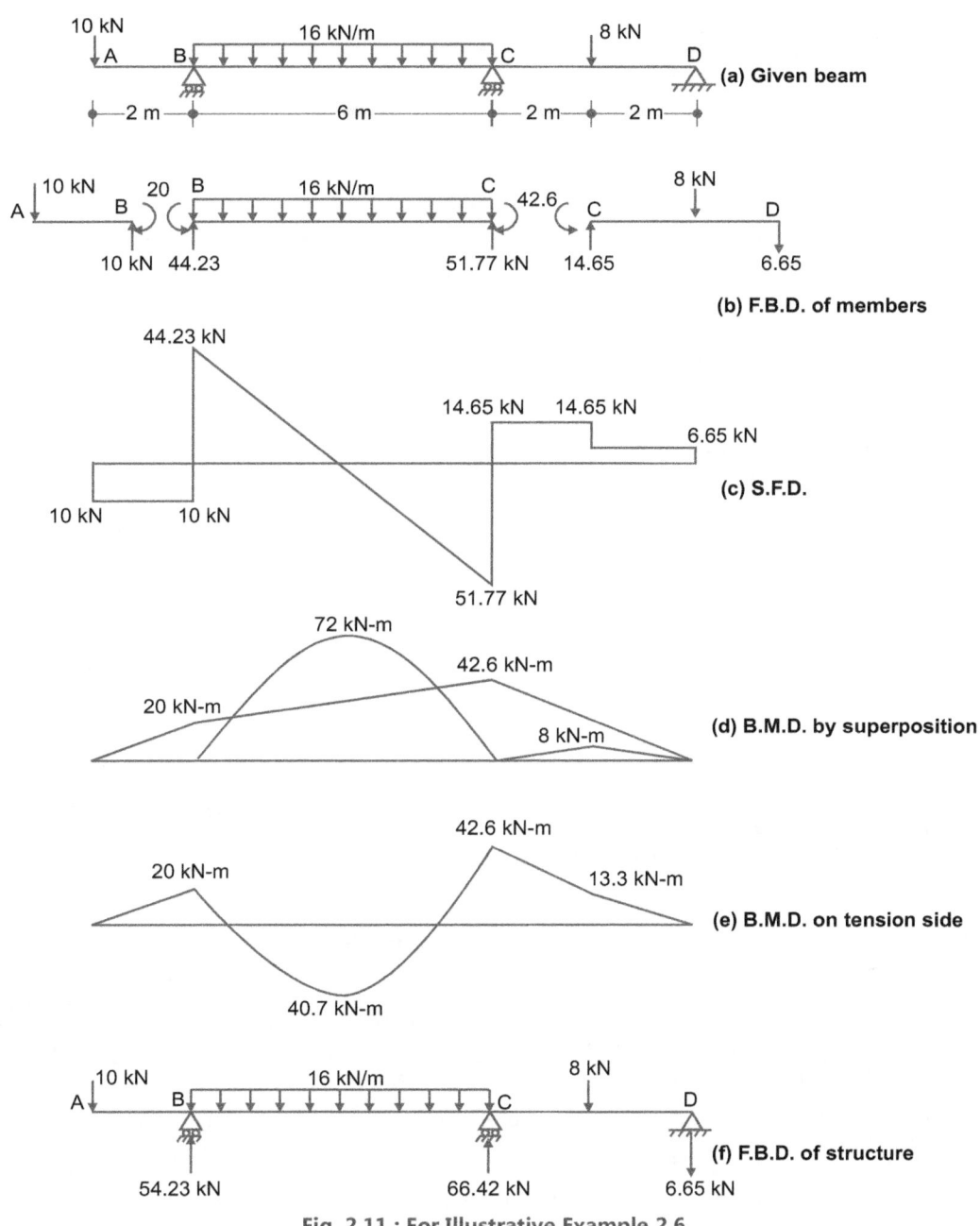

Fig. 2.11 : For Illustrative Example 2.6

Step II : Distribution factors :

Joint	Member	K	ΣK	D.F.
B	BA	–	–	–
	BC	–	–	0
C	CB	$\frac{3EI}{L} = 0.5$	1.25	0.40
	CD	$\frac{3EI}{L} = 0.75$		0.60
D	DC	–	–	0

Step III : MD table :

Joint Type of joint		B EFS			C ISS/RJ		D ESS
Member		BA	BC	CB	CD		DC
COF			→ 1/2			→ 0	
D.F.			0 ←			1/2 →	
			0	0.40	0.60		0
First cycle	FEM	– 20	48	– 48	19		11
	DM	–	– 28	11.6	17.4		– 11
Second cycle	COM			– 14	– 5.5		
	DM			7.8			
Total final moment		– 20	20	– 42.6	42.6		0

Step IV : FBD of members is as shown in Fig. 2.11 (b).

Step V : Shear force diagram is as shown in Fig. 2.11 (c).

Step VI : Bending moment diagrams are as shown in Fig. 2.11 (d) and Fig. 2.11 (e).

Step VII : FBD of structure is as shown in Fig. 2.11 (f).

Example 2.7 : *A beam is loaded and supported as shown in Fig. 2.12 (a). The support B sinks by 25 mm. EI of the beam is 3800 kNm². Using moment distribution method, analyse the beam and draw SFD and BMD.*

Solution : Data : The frame is supported and loaded as shown in Fig. 2.12 (a).

Object : Structural analysis.

Concepts and Equations : MD technique based on normalized relative stiffness factors, carryover factors and distribution factors.

STRUCTURAL ANALYSIS – II   MOMENT DISTRIBUTION METHOD

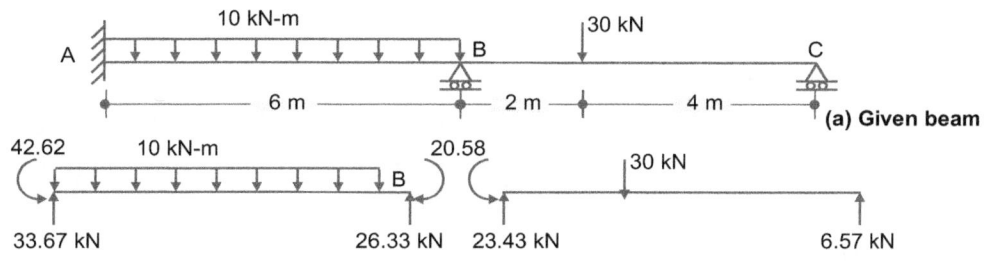
(a) Given beam

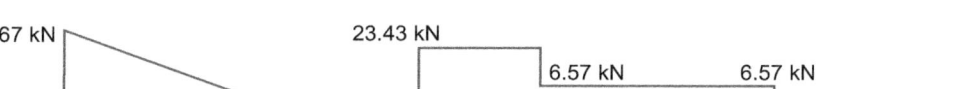
(b) F.B.D. of members

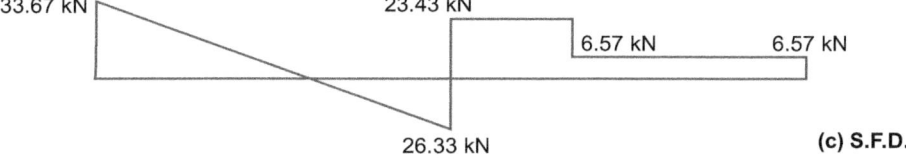
(c) S.F.D.

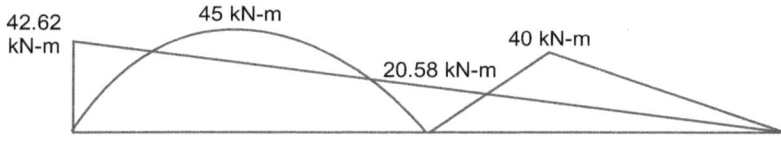
(d) B.M.D. by superposition

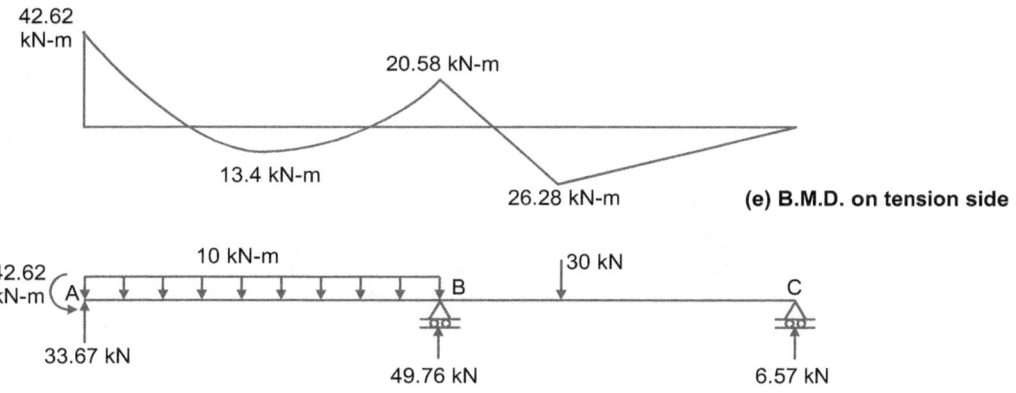
(e) B.M.D. on tension side

(f) F.B.D. of structure

Fig. 2.12 : For Illustrative Example 2.7

Procedure :

Step I : Fixed-end moments :

Member	FEM with calculations		Total FEM
	FEM due to external loads	FEM due to sinking of support B	
AB	$M^F_{AB} = \dfrac{WL^2}{12}$ $= \dfrac{10 \times 6^2}{12} = 30 \text{ kN-m}$	$M^F_{AB} = \dfrac{6EI\Delta}{L^2}$ $= \dfrac{6 \times 3800 \times 25 \times 10^{-3}}{6^2}$ $= 15.83 \text{ kN-m}$	$M^F_{AB} = 45.83 \text{ kN-m}$
	$M^F_{BA} = -\dfrac{WL^2}{12}$ $= -\dfrac{10 \times 6^2}{12}$ $= -30 \text{ kN-m}$	$M^F_{BA} = \dfrac{6EI\Delta}{L^2}$ $= \dfrac{6 \times 3800 \times 25 \times 10^{-3}}{6^2}$ $= 15.83 \text{ kN-m}$	$M^F_{BA} = -14.17 \text{ kN-m}$
BC	$M^F_{BC} = \dfrac{Wab^2}{L^2}$ $= \dfrac{30 \times 2 \times 4^2}{6^2}$ $= 26.67 \text{ kN-m}$	$M^F_{BC} = -\dfrac{6EI\Delta}{L^2}$ $= -\dfrac{6 \times 3800 \times 25 \times 10^{-3}}{6^2}$ $= -15.83 \text{ kN-m}$	$M^F_{BC} = 10.84 \text{ kN-m}$
	$M^F_{CB} = -\dfrac{Wa^2b}{L^2}$ $= -\dfrac{30 \times 2^2 \times 4}{6^2}$ $= -13.33 \text{ kN-m}$	$M^F_{CB} = -\dfrac{6EI\Delta}{L^2}$ $= -\dfrac{6 \times 3800 \times 25 \times 10^{-3}}{6^2}$ $= -15.83 \text{ kN-m}$	$M^F_{CB} = -29.16 \text{ kN-m}$

Step II : Distribution factors :

Joint	Member	K	ΣK	D.F.
A	AB	–	0	0
B	BA	$\dfrac{4EI}{L} = 0.67$		0.57
	BC	$\dfrac{3EI}{L} = 0.50$	1.17	0.43
C	CB	–	–	0

Step III : MD table :

Joint Type of joint	A EFS		B RS		C RS
Member	AB	BA	BC		CB
COF	→ 1/2		→ 0		
		1/2 ←		1/2 ←	
DF					
	0	0.57	0.43		0
First cycle FEM	45.83	– 14.17	10.84		– 29.16
DM	–	1.90	1.43		29.16
Second cycle COM	0.95	–	14.58		–
DM	–	– 8.31	– 6.27		
Third cycle COM	– 4.16	–	–		
Total final moments	42.62	– 20.58	20.58		0

Step IV : FBD of member is as shown in Fig. 2.12 (b).

Consider equilibrium of each member and of complete structure, all reaction components are found out as shown in Fig. 2.12 (b).

Step V : Shear force diagram is as shown in Fig. 2.12 (c).

Step VI : Bending moment diagrams are as shown in Fig. 2.12 (d) and Fig. 2.12 (e).

Step VII : FBD of structure is as shown in Fig. 2.12 (f).

2.5 APPLICATION OF MD METHOD TO BEAMS WITH UNKNOWN JOINT TRANSLATIONS

When flexural rigidity (EI) of the beam member suddenly changes, additional node (joint) is required to be assumed at such points, which is subjected to unknown translation in addition to rotation. Also in case, if the members of the beam are connected by unsupported internal hinge, this joint is subjected to translation in addition to rotation. The procedure to analyse such beams is similar to that of analysis of sway frames and is illustrated in following examples.

Example 2.8 : *Analyse the beam shown in Fig. 2.13 (a) by MD method.*

Solution : Data : The beam is supported and loaded as shown in Fig. 2.13 (a).

Object : Structural analysis.

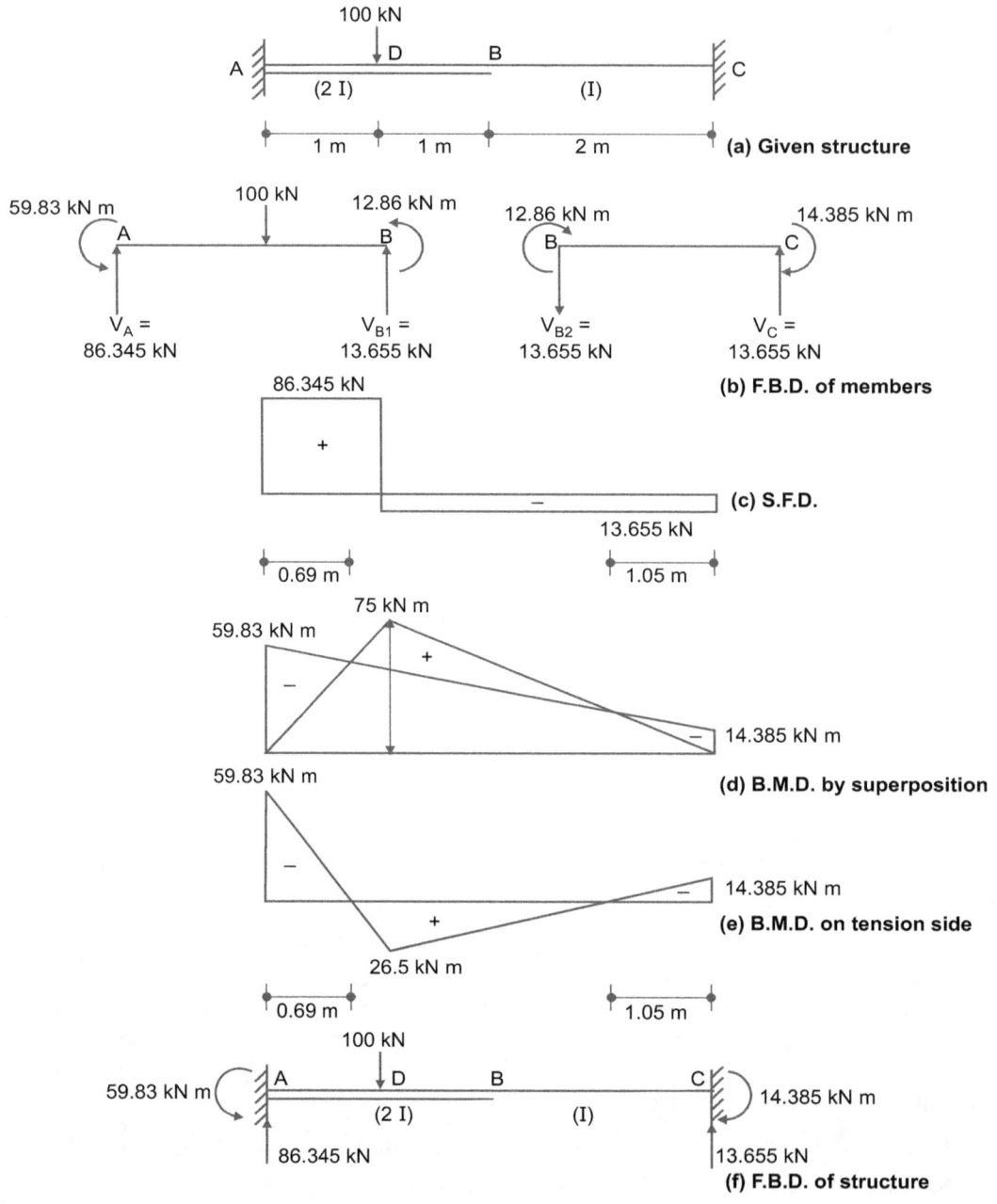

Fig. 2.13 : For Illustrative Example 2.8

STRUCTURAL ANALYSIS – II   MOMENT DISTRIBUTION METHOD

Procedure :

Step I : Fixed-end moments (considering additional node at B).

Member	FEM with calculations
AB	$M^F_{AB} = \dfrac{WL}{8} = \dfrac{100 \times 2}{8} = 25$ kNm $M^F_{BA} = -M^F_{AB} = -25$ kNm
BC	$M^F_{BC} = 0$ $M^F_{CB} = 0$

Step II : Distribution factors :

Joint	Member	K	ΣK	DF = $\dfrac{K}{\Sigma K}$
A	AB	–	–	0
B	BA	$\dfrac{4EI}{L} = 4$	6	0.67
	BC	$\dfrac{4EI}{L} = 2$		0.33
C	CB	–	–	0

Step III : MD Table (I) for moments without joint translation at B :

Joint		A	B			C
Type of Joint		EFS	RJ			EFS
Member		AB	BA	BC		CB
COF			→ 1/2 1/2 ←	→ 1/2 1/2 ←		
DF		0	0.67	0.33		0
First cycle	FEM	25	–25	0		0
	DM	–	16.75	8.25		–
Second cycle	COM	8.38	–	–		4.13
	DM	–	–	–		–
First set of final moments		33.38	–8.25	8.25		4.13

Step IV : MD for moments due to joint translation at B :

(a) The basic information of K, COF and DF remains the same.

(b) Normalized relative translational stiffness factors (K_s). Assuming negative joint translation at B i.e. downwards, which produces anticlockwise i.e. positive moments for member AB and clockwise i.e. negative moments for member BC.

Member	Relative translational stiffness factor	Normalized relative translational stiffness factor (K_s)
AB	$\dfrac{2I}{2^2} = \dfrac{I}{2}$	2
BC	$\dfrac{I}{2^2} = \dfrac{I}{4}$	1

(c) Moments due to translation at B :

Member	Arbitrary relative FEM due to translation
AB	$M_{AB}^{FS} = 200$ kNm $M_{BA}^{FS} = 200$ kNm
BC	$M_{BC}^{FS} = -100$ kNm $M_{CB}^{FS} = -100$ kNm

Step V : MD Table (II) for moments due to translation :

Joint	A	B		C
Type of joint	EFS	RJ		EFS
Member	AB	BA	BC	CB
COF	→ 1/2 1/2 ←		→ 1/2 1/2 ←	
DF	0	0.67	0.33	0
First cycle — FEM	200	200	−100	−100
DM	—	−67	−33	—
Second cycle — COM	−33.5	—	—	−16.5
DM	—	—	—	—
Second set of final moments	166.5	133	−133	−116.5

Let, actual moments due to translation be 'C' times the above moments.

$\therefore$
$$M_{AB} = M_{AB}^{I} + C \cdot M_{AB}^{II} = 33.38 + C\,(166.5)$$
$$M_{BA} = M_{BA}^{I} + C \cdot M_{BA}^{II} = -8.25 + C\,(133)$$
$$M_{BC} = M_{BC}^{I} + C \cdot M_{BC}^{II} = 8.25 + C\,(-133)$$
$$M_{CB} = M_{CB}^{I} + C \cdot M_{CB}^{II} = 4.13 + C\,(-116.5)$$

where, C = Correction factor to be evaluated from the condition of shear equilibrium of the structure.

Step VI : Shear equilibrium : Shear equilibrium of structure gives,

$$V_A - V_C - 100 = 0 \quad \ldots (A)$$

where, $\quad V_A = \dfrac{M_{AB} + M_{BA}}{2} + 50$

and $\quad V_C = \dfrac{M_{BC} + M_{CB}}{2}$

Substituting in equation (A), we get,

$$\left[\dfrac{M_{AB} + M_{BA}}{2} + 50\right] - \left[\dfrac{M_{BC} + M_{CB}}{2}\right] - 100 = 0$$

$$M_{AB} + M_{BA} - M_{BC} - M_{CB} - 100 = 0$$

Substituting the values of moments, we get,

$$33.38 + C(166.5) - 8.25 + C(133) - 8.25 - C(-133) - 4.13 - C(-116.5) - 100 = 0$$

$$\Rightarrow \quad \boxed{C = 0.159}$$

Positive sign for 'C' indicates that translation at 'B' will be in the direction assumed i.e. downwards.

Step VII : Final results :

Member	AB	BA	BC	CB
Corrected moments of second set	26.45	2.11	−2.11	−18.515
Moments of first set	33.38	−8.25	8.25	4.13
Net final moments	59.83	12.86	−12.86	14.385

Step VIII : FBD of members is as shown in Fig. 2.13 (b). Considering equilibrium of each member and of complete structure, all reaction components are found out as shown in figure.

Step IX : Shear force diagram is as shown in Fig. 2.13 (c).

Step X : Bending moment diagram is as shown in Fig. 2.13 (d) and Fig. 2.13 (e).

Step XI : FBD of structure is as shown in Fig. 2.13 (f).

Example 2.9 : *Analyse the beam shown in Fig. 2.14 (a) by MD method.*

Solution : Data : The beam is supported and located as shown in Fig. 2.14 (a).

Object : Structural analysis.

Procedure :

Step I : Fixed-end moments :

Member	FEM with calculations
AB	$M^F_{AB} = \dfrac{wL^2}{12} = \dfrac{60 \times 1^2}{12} = 5$ kNm $M^F_{BA} = -M^F_{AB} = -5$ kNm
BC	$M^F_{BC} = \dfrac{60 \times 2^2}{12} = 20$ kNm $M^F_{CB} = -M^F_{BC} = -20$ kNm

Step II : Distribution factors :

Joint	Member	K	ΣK	DF = $\dfrac{K}{\Sigma K}$
A	AB	–	–	0
B	BA	–	–	1
	BC	–	–	1
C	CB	–	–	0

Step III : MD Table (I) for moments without joint translation at B :

Joint		A EFS	B IH		C EFS
Type of joint					
Member		AB	BA	BC	CB
COF		→ 0 1/2 ←		→ 1/2 0 ←	
DF		0	1	1	0
First cycle	FEM	5	– 5	20	– 20
	DM	–	5	– 20	–
Second cycle	COM	2.5	–	–	– 10
	DM	–	–	–	–
First set of final moments		7.5	0	0	– 30

Step IV : MD for moments due to joint translation at B :

(a) The basic information of K, COF and DF remains the same.

(b) Normalized relative translational stiffness factors (K_S). Assuming negative joint translation at B i.e. downwards, which produces anticlockwise i.e. positive moments for member AB and clockwise i.e. negative moments for member BC.

STRUCTURAL ANALYSIS – II MOMENT DISTRIBUTION METHOD

Member	Relative translational stiffness factor	Normalized relative translational stiffness factor (K_s)
AB	$\dfrac{I}{1^2}$	4
BC	$\dfrac{I}{2^2}$	1

(c) Moments due to translation at B :

Member	Arbitrary relative FEM due to translation
AB	$M_{AB}^{FS} = 40$ kNm $M_{BA}^{FS} = 40$ kNm
BC	$M_{BC}^{FS} = -10$ kNm $M_{CB}^{FS} = -10$ kNm

Step V : MD Table (II) for moments due to translation :

Joint		A	B		C
Type of joint		EFS	EHS		EFS
Member		AB	BA	BC	CB
COF		$\to 0$ $1/2 \leftarrow$		$\to 1/2$ $0 \leftarrow$	
K		6	6	3	3
DF		0	1	1	0
First cycle	FEM	40	40	−10	−10
	DM	−	−40	10	−
Second cycle	COM	−20	−	−	5
	DM	−	−	−	−
Second set of final moments		20	0	0	−5

Let, actual moments due to translation be 'C' times the above moments.

$$M_{AB} = M_{AB}^{I} + C \cdot (M_{AB}^{II}) = 7.5 + C(20)$$
$$M_{BA} = M_{BA}^{I} + C \cdot (M_{BA}^{II}) = 0$$
$$M_{BC} = M_{BC}^{I} + C \cdot (M_{BC}^{II}) = 0$$
$$M_{CB} = M_{CB}^{I} + C \cdot (M_{CB}^{II}) = -30 + C(-5)$$

where, C = Correction factor to be evaluated from the condition of shear equilibrium of the structure.

STRUCTURAL ANALYSIS – II MOMENT DISTRIBUTION METHOD

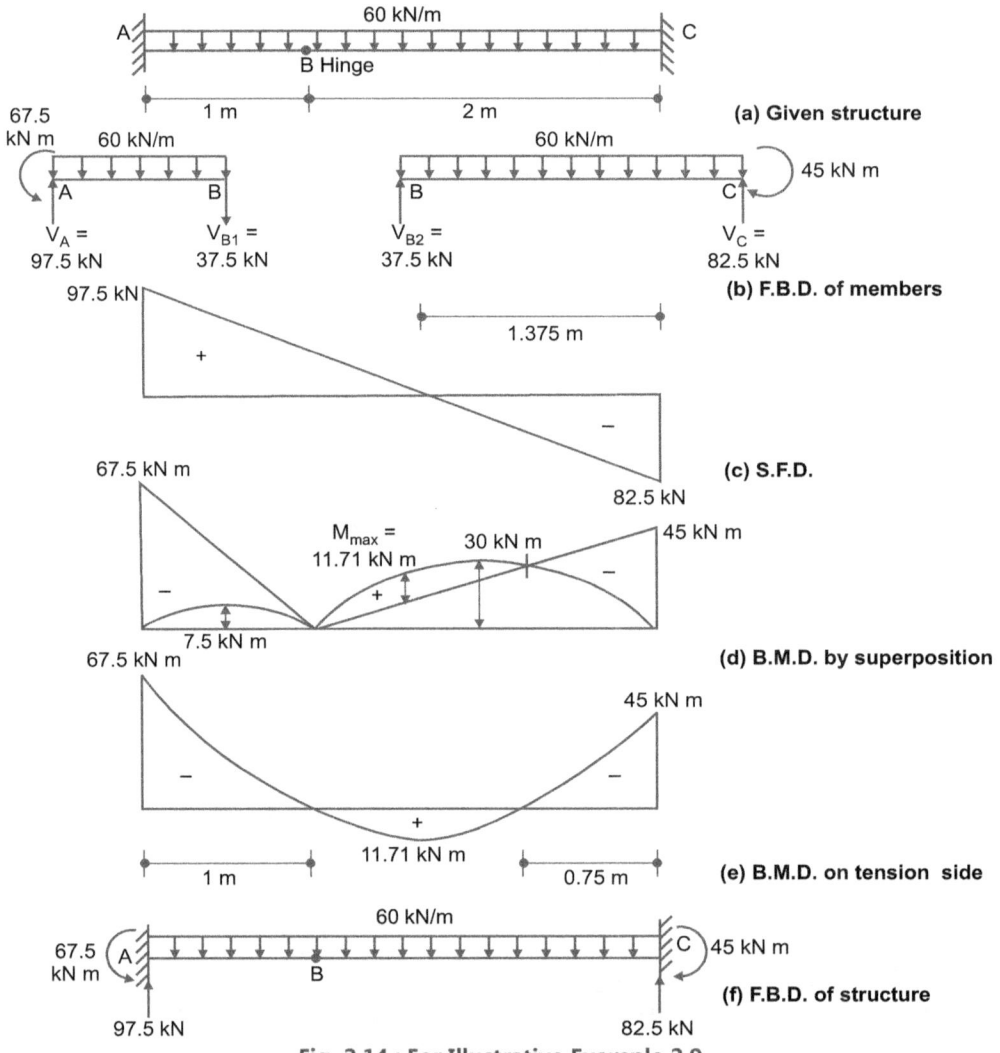

Fig. 2.14 : For Illustrative Example 2.9

Step VI : Shear equilibrium : Shear equilibrium of structure gives,

$$V_A - V_C - 60 \times 3 = 0$$

i.e. $\quad V_A - V_C - 180 = 0 \quad \ldots (A)$

where, $\quad V_A = M_{AB} + 60 \times 1 \times 0.5$

$\quad\quad\quad\quad = M_{AB} + 30$

and $\quad V_C = \dfrac{M_{CB} - 60 \times 2 \times 1}{2} = \dfrac{M_{CB}}{2} - 60$

Substituting in equation (A), we get

$$M_{AB} + 30 - \frac{M_{CB}}{2} + 60 - 180 = 0$$

i.e. $\quad 2 M_{AB} - M_{CB} - 180 = 0$

Substituting the values of moments, we get

$2 (7.5 + C (20)) - (- 30 + C (- 5)) - 180 = 0$

$$45 (C) = 135$$

$$\boxed{C = 3}$$

Positive sign for 'C' indicates that translation at 'B' will be in the direction assumed i.e. downwards.

Step VII : Final results :

Member	AB	BA	BC	CB
Corrected moments of second set	60	0	0	− 15
Moments of first set	7.5	0	0	− 30
Net final moments	67.5	0	0	− 45

Step VIII : FBD of members is as shown in Fig. 2.14 (b). Considering equilibrium of each member and of complete structure, all reaction components are found out as shown in figure.

Step IX : Shear force diagram is as shown in Fig. 2.14 (c).

Step X : Bending moment diagram is as shown in Fig. 2.14 (d) and Fig. 2.14 (e).

Step XI : FBD of structure is as shown in Fig. 2.14 (f).

2.6 APPLICATION OF MD METHOD TO FRAMES WITHOUT JOINT TRANSLATIONS

Rigid jointed indeterminate rectangular plane frames consisting of horizontal and vertical members are only covered in this text. MD method has been the convenient and powerful method to analyse the large frames with high degree of indeterminacy till introduction of computers and its application to matrix stiffness method. The rectangular frames without joint translations are common in the following situations with the assumption of the axial deformations are neglected.

1. The horizontal and vertical members of the rectangular frames are supported by the fixed or hinged support so that horizontal and vertical translations at supports are prevented.
2. The frames are symmetrical in all respects.

MD method applied to such frames is identical to beam problems except the configuration of the structure. The number of members meeting at a joint of frames may be more than two. Therefore, the MD table for frame analysis must be arranged to suit the requirements of (a) distribution factors of member ends meeting at the joint, (b) distribution of moments

STRUCTURAL ANALYSIS – II   MOMENT DISTRIBUTION METHOD

at the joint to the members meeting at the joint, and (c) carryover moments to be brought from one end to other end of the member. With the due attention to this, the process of MD method is tacitly used for the analysis of frames as illustrated in the following examples.

Example 2.10 : *Analyse the frame shown in Fig. 2.15 (a) by MD method.*
Solution : Data : The frame is supported and loaded as shown in Fig. 2.15 (a).
Object : Structural analysis.

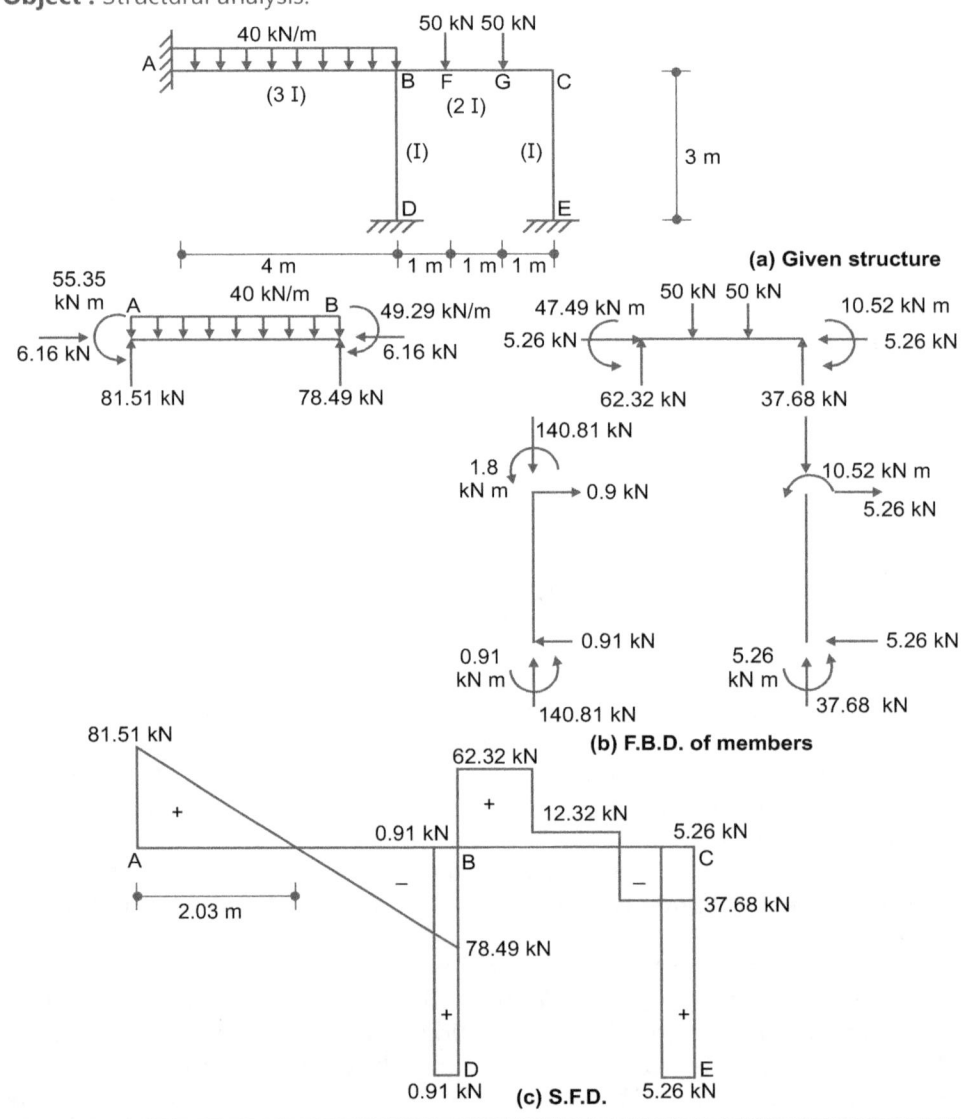

(a) Given structure

(b) F.B.D. of members

(c) S.F.D.

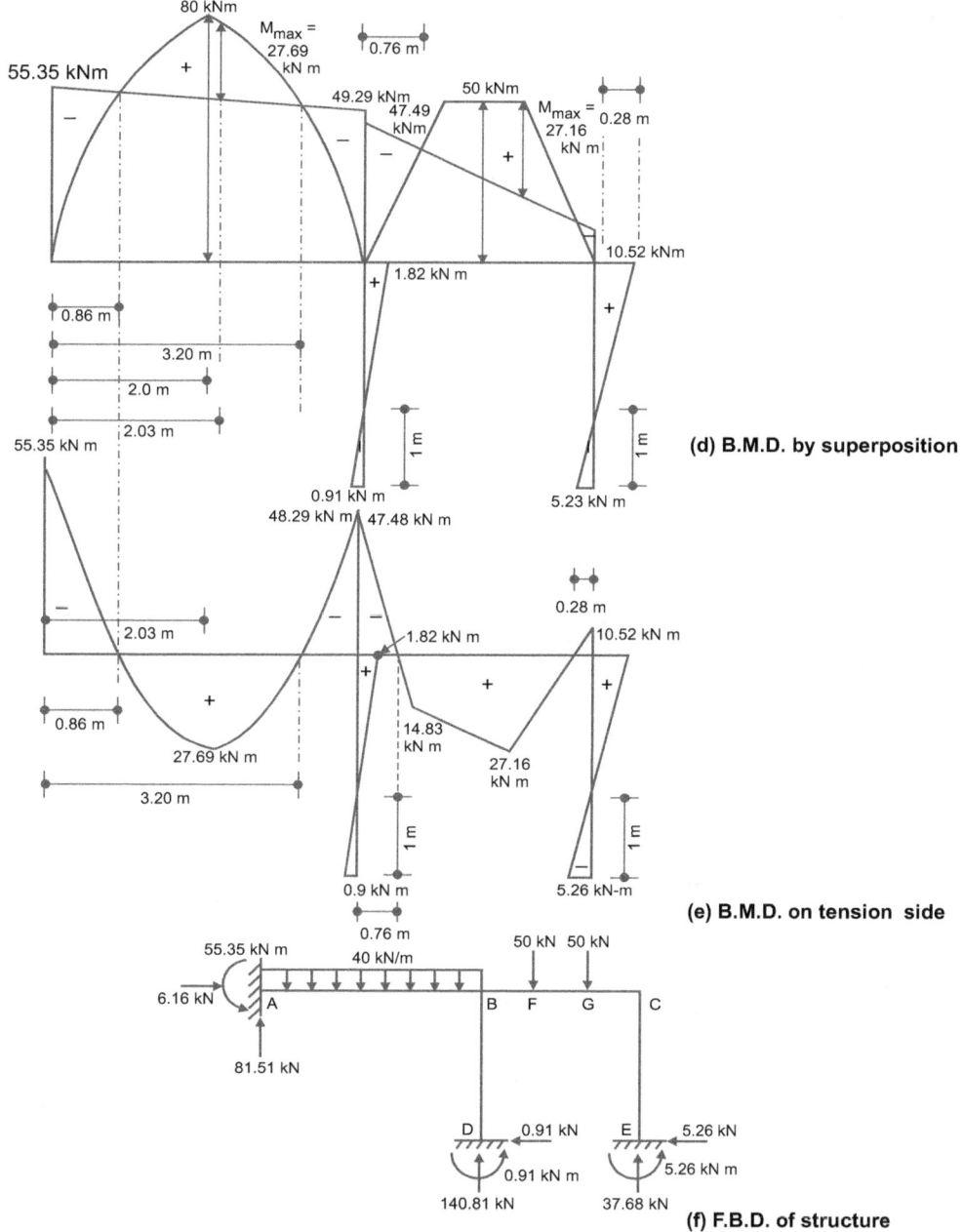

Fig. 2.15 : For Illustrative Example 2.10

STRUCTURAL ANALYSIS – II   MOMENT DISTRIBUTION METHOD

Concepts and Equations : MD technique based on normalized relative stiffness factors and distribution factors.

Procedure :

Step I : Fixed-end moments :

Member	FEM with calculations
AB	$M_{AB}^F = \dfrac{wL^2}{12} = \dfrac{40 \times 4^2}{12} = 53.33$ kNm $M_{BA}^F = -M_{AB}^F = -53.33$ kNm
BC	$M_{BC}^F = \dfrac{50 \times 1 \times 2^2}{3^2} + \dfrac{50 \times 2 \times 1^2}{3^2} = 33.33$ kNm $M_{CB}^F = -M_{BC}^F = -33.33$ kNm
DB	$M_{DB}^F = M_{BD}^F = 0$
EC	$M_{EC}^F = M_{CE}^F = 0$

Step II : Distribution factors :

Joint	Member	K	ΣK	DF = $\dfrac{K}{\Sigma K}$
A	AB	–	–	0
B	BA	$\dfrac{4EI}{L} = 3$	7.01	0.43
	BD	$\dfrac{4EI}{L} = 1.34$		0.19
	BC	$\dfrac{4EI}{L} = 2.67$		0.38
C	CB	$\dfrac{4EI}{L} = 2.67$	4.01	0.67
	CE	$\dfrac{4EI}{L} = 1.34$		0.33
D	DB	–	–	0
E	EC	–	–	0

Step III : MD Table :

Joint	A		B		C		D	E
Type of joint	EFS		RJ		RJ		EFS	EFS
Member	AB	BA	BD	BC	CB	CE	DB	EC
COF	→ 1/2		→ 1/2	→ 1/2		→1/2	1/2 ←	1/2 ←
		1/2 ←	To D		1/2 ←	To E	To B	To C
DF	0	0.43	0.19	0.38	0.67	0.33	0	0
First cycle FEM	53.33	– 53.33	0	33.33	– 33.33	0	0	0
DM		– 8.60	3.80	7.60	22.22	11.11		
Second cycle COM	4.30			11.11	3.80		1.90	5.55
DM		– 4.77	– 2.11	– 4.23	– 2.55	– 1.25		
Third cycle COM	– 2.39			– 1.28	– 2.11		– 1.05	– 0.63
DM		0.55	0.24	0.49	1.41	0.70		
Fourth cycle COM	0.27			0.70	0.25		0.12	– 0.35
DM		– 0.30	– 0.13	– 0.27	– 0.17	– 0.08		
Fifth cycle COM	– 0.15			– 0.09	– 0.14		– 0.06	– 0.04
DM		0.04	0.02	0.03	0.09	0.05		
Total final moments	55.36	– 49.21	1.82	47.39	– 10.53	10.53	0.91	5.23

Step IV : FBD of members : as shown in Fig. 2.15 (b). Considering equilibrium of each member and of complete structure, all reaction components are found out as shown in figure.

Step V : Shear force diagram : as shown in Fig. 2.15 (c).

Step VI : Bending moment diagrams as shown in Fig. 2.15 (d) and Fig. 2.15 (e).

Step VII : FBD of structure : as shown in Fig. 2.15 (f).

Example 2.11 : *Analyse the frame as shown in Fig. 2.16 (a) by moment distribution method.*

Solution : Data : The frame is loaded and supported as shown in Fig. 2.16 (a).

Object : Structural analysis.

Concepts and Equations : MD technique based on normalized relative stiffness factors, carryover factors and distribution factors.

Procedure : Step I : Fixed-end moments :

Member	FEM with calculations
AB	$M^F_{AB} = 0$ $M^F_{BA} = 0$
BC	$M^F_{BC} = \dfrac{WL}{8} = \dfrac{60 \times 4}{8} = 30$ kN-m $M^F_{CB} = -\dfrac{WL}{8} = -\dfrac{60 \times 4}{8} = -30$ kN-m
CD	$M^F_{CD} = 0$ $M^F_{DC} = 0$

Step II : Distribution factors :

Joint	Member	K	ΣK	D.F.
A	AB	–	–	0
B	BA	$\dfrac{4EI}{L} = 1.33$	2.33	0.57
	BC	$\dfrac{4EI}{L} = 1$		0.43
C	CB	$\dfrac{4EI}{L} = 1$	2.33	0.43
	CD	$\dfrac{4EI}{L} = 1.33$		0.57
D	DC	–	–	0

Step III : MD table :

Joint		A	B			C		D
Type of joint		EFS	RJ			RJ		EFS
Member		AB	BA	BC		CB	CD	DC
COF		→ 1/2 1/2 ←		→ 1/2 1/2 ←			→ 1/2 1/2 →	
DF		0	0.57	0.43		0.43	0.57	0
First cycle	FEM	0	0	30		– 30	0	0
	DM		– 17.10	– 12.9		12.9	17.10	
Second cycle	COM	– 8.55		6.45		– 6.45	–	8.55
	DM		– 3.68	– 2.77		2.77	3.68	
Third cycle	COM	– 1.84		1.39		– 1.39	–	1.84
	DM		– 0.79	– 0.6		0.6	0.79	
Fourth cycle	COM	– 0.40		0.3		– 0.3	–	0.40
	DM		– 0.17	– 0.13		0.13	0.17	
Fifth cycle	COM	– 0.09		0.065		– 0.065		
	DM		– 0.04	– 0.025		0.025	0.04	0.02
Sixth cycle	COM	– 0.02		0.013		– 0.013		0.02
	DM		– 0.007	– 0.006		0.006	0.007	
Total final moment		–10.9	–21.79	21.79		– 21.79	21.79	10.9

STRUCTURAL ANALYSIS – II   MOMENT DISTRIBUTION METHOD

Step IV : FBD of members is as shown in Fig. 2.16 (b).
Step V : Shear force diagram is as shown in Fig. 2.16 (c).
Step VI : Bending moment diagrams are as shown in Fig. 2.16 (d) and Fig. 2.16 (e).
Step VII : FBD of structure is as shown in Fig. 2.16 (f).

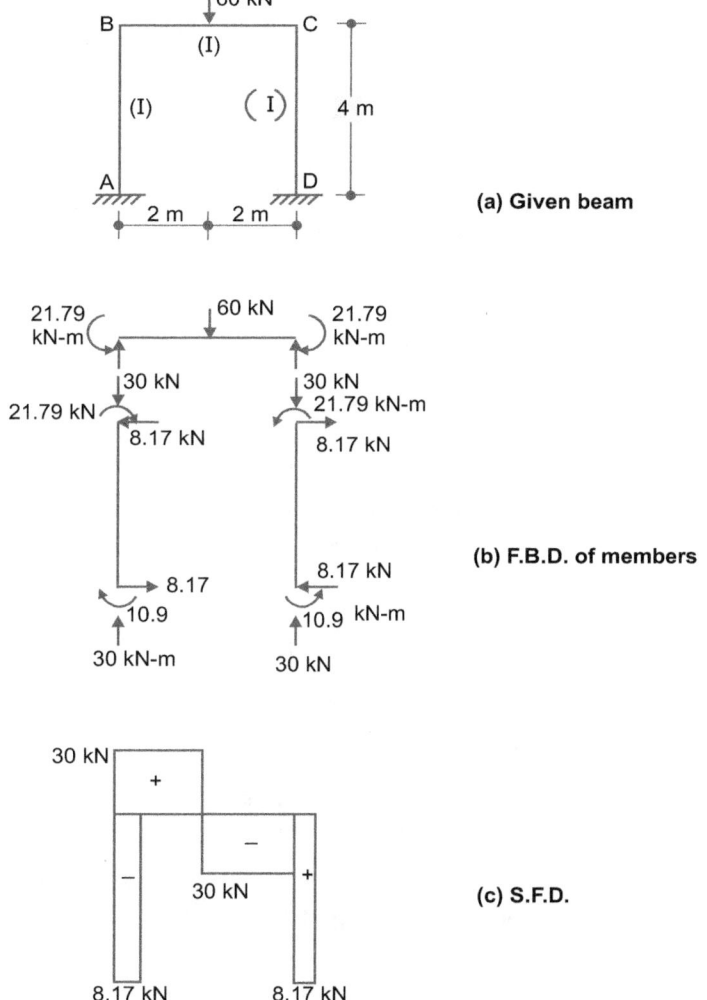

Fig. 2.16 (Continued)

Ch. 2 | 2.45

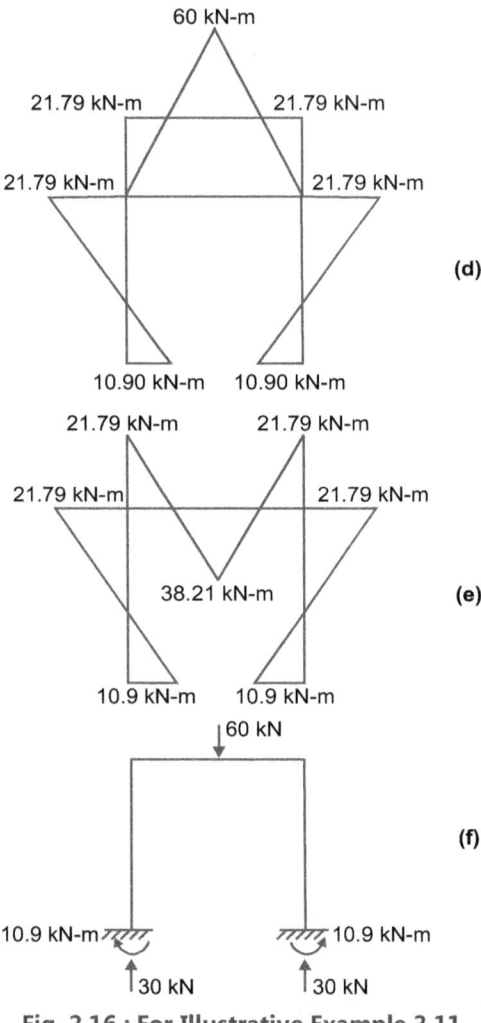

Fig. 2.16 : For Illustrative Example 2.11

Example 2.12 : Using the slope-deflection method, analyse the rigid jointed plane frame supported and loaded as shown in Fig. 2.17 (a). Assume uniform flexural rigidity EI for all the members.

Solution : Data : The frame is supported and loaded as shown in Fig. 2.17 (a).

Object : Structural analysis.

Concepts and Equations : MD technique based on normalized relative stiffness factors, carryover factors and distribution factors.

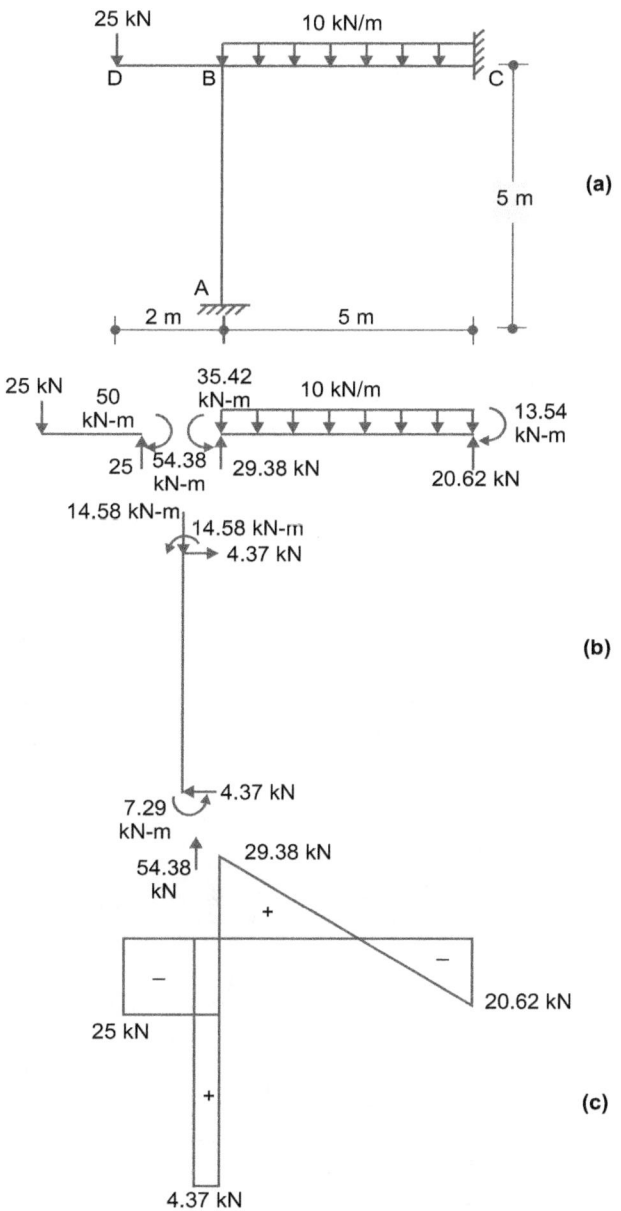

Fig. 2.17 (Continued)

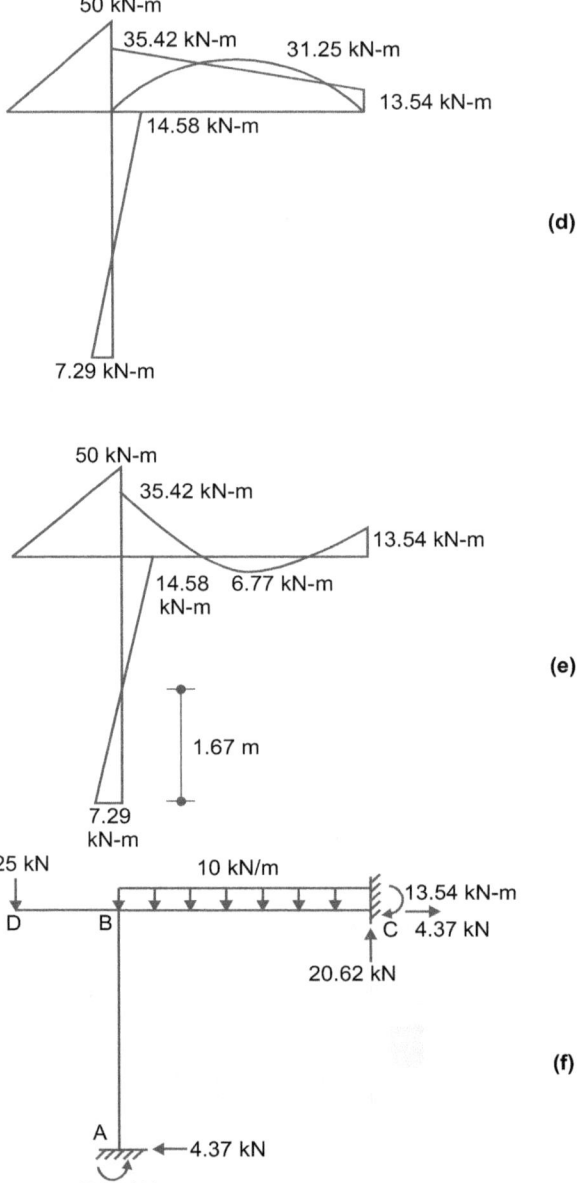

Fig. 2.17 : For Illustrative Example 2.12

Procedure : Step I : Fixed-end moments :

Member	FEM with calculations
AB	$M^F_{AB} = 0$ $M^F_{BA} = 0$
BC	$M^F_{BC} = \dfrac{10 \times 5^2}{12} = 20.83$ kN-m $M^F_{CB} = -\dfrac{10 \times 5^2}{12} = -20.83$ kN-m
BD	$M^F_{BD} = -25 \times 2 = -50$ kN-m

Step II : Distribution factors :

Joint	Member	K	ΣK	D.F.
A	AB	–	–	0
B	BA	$\dfrac{4EI}{L} = 0.8$	1.6	0.50
	BC	$\dfrac{4EI}{L} = 0.8$		0.50
	BD	–	–	0

Step III : MD table :

Joint	A	B			C	
Type of joint	EFS	RJ			EFS	
Member	AB	BA	BD	BC	CB
COF	→1/2 1/2 ←		–	→ 1/2 1/2 ←	
D.F.	0	0.50	0	0.50	0
First cycle FEM	0	0	– 50	20.83	– 20.83
DM		14.58		14.59	
Second cycle COM	7.29				7.29
Total final moments	7.29	14.58	– 50	35.42	– 13.54

Step IV : FBD of members is as shown in Fig. 2.17 (b).

Step V : Shear force diagram is as shown in Fig. 2.17 (c).

Step VI : Bending moment diagrams are as shown in Fig. 2.17 (d) and Fig. 2.17 (e).

Step VII : FBD of structure is as shown in Fig. 2.17 (f).

Example 2.13 : *Analyse the portal frame as shown in Fig. 2.18 by moment distribution method.*

Solution : Data : The frame is supported and loaded as shown in Fig. 2.18.

Object. Structural Analysis :

Concepts and Equations : MD technique based on normalized relative stiffness factors and distribution factors.

Procedure : Step I :

$$\overline{M}_{AB} = -\frac{wab^2}{l^2} = -\frac{50 \times 1 \times 2 \times 2}{3^2} = -22.22 \text{ kN-m}$$

$$\overline{M}_{BA} = \frac{wa^2b}{l^2} = \frac{50 \times 1 \times 1 \times 2}{3^2} = 11.11 \text{ kN-m}$$

$$\overline{M}_{BC} = -\overline{M}_{CB} = -\frac{wl^2}{12} = -\frac{30 \times 4^2}{12} = -40 \text{ kN-m}$$

$$\overline{M}_{BD} = \overline{M}_{DB} = 0$$

Step II : Distribution factors :

Joint	Member	Relative Stiffness	Total Stiffness	D. F.
B	BA	3/4 × 2I/3	5I/4	2/5
	BC	2I/4		2/5
	BD	I/4		1/5

Step III : MD Table :

Joint	A	B			C	D
Member	AB	BA	BD	BC	CB	DB
D.F.	-	2/5	1/5	2/5	-	-
F.E.M.	−22.22	11.11	0	−40	40	0
Release A C.O.	+ 11.11					
Total moments	0	22.22	0	−40	40	0
Distribution		7.11	3.56	7.11		
C.O.					3.55	1.78
Net moments	0	29.33	3.56	−32.89	43.55	1.78

Step IV : FBD of members as shown in Fig. 2.18(b) considering equilibrium of each member and of complete structure all reaction components are found out as shown in Fig. 2.18.

Step V : Shear force diagram is as shown in Fig. 2.18.

STRUCTURAL ANALYSIS – II MOMENT DISTRIBUTION METHOD

Step VI : Bending moment diagrams are as shown in Fig. 2.18 (d) and Fig. 2.18 (c).

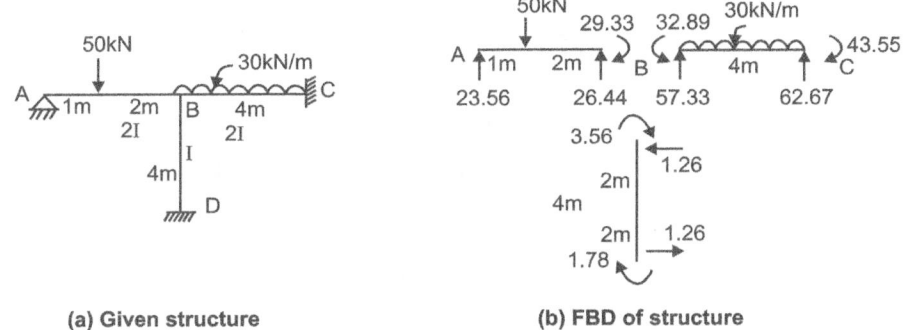

(a) Given structure

(b) FBD of structure

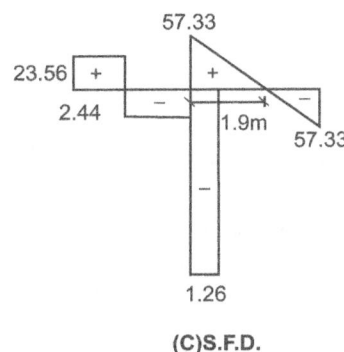

(C) S.F.D.

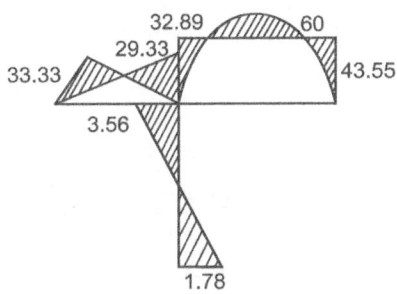

(d) BMD by superposition

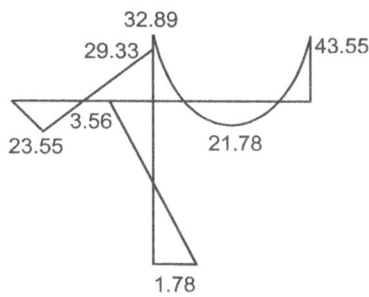

(e) BMD on tension side

Fig. 2.18 : Illustrative Example 2.13

Example 2.14 : *Analyse the non-sway frame as shown below in Fig. 2.19.*

$$I_{ab} : I_{bc} : I_{cd} = 1 : 2 : 1$$

Solution : Data : The frame is supported and coded as shown in Fig. 2.19.

Object : Structural Analysis :

Concepts and Equations : MD technique based on normalized relative stiffness factors and distribution factors.

Procedure : Step I : Fixed End Moments :

$$\overline{M}_{ab} = -\frac{wab^2}{l^2} = -\frac{6 \times 3 \times 1 \times 1}{4^2}$$

$$= 1.125 \text{ kN-m}$$

$$\overline{M}_{ba} = \frac{wa^2b}{l^2} = \frac{6 \times 3 \times 3 \times 1}{4^2}$$

$$= 3.375 \text{ klN-m}$$

$$\overline{M}_{bc} = -\overline{M}_{CB} = -\frac{wl^2}{12} = -\frac{20 \times 2 \times 2}{12}$$

$$= -6.67 \text{ kN-m}$$

$$\overline{M}_{cd} = -\frac{wab^2}{l^2} = -\frac{6 \times 1 \times 3 \times 3}{4^2}$$

$$= -3.375 \text{ kN-m}$$

$$\overline{M}_{dc} = \frac{wa^2b}{l^2} = \frac{6 \times 1 \times 1 \times 3}{4^2}$$

$$= 1.125 \text{ kN-m}$$

Step II : Distribution factors :

Joint	Member	Relative Stiffness	Total Stiffness	D. F.
B	BA	(I/4)	5I/4	1/5
	BC	(2I/2)		4/5
C	CB	(2I/2)	5I/4	4/5
	CD	(I/4)		1/5

Step III : MD table :

Joint	A	B		C		D
Member	AB	BA	BC	CB	CD	DC
D.F.	-	1/5	4/5	4/5	1/5	-
F.E.M.	−1.125	3.375	−6.67	6.67	−3.375	1.125
Distribution		0.629	2.636	−2.636	−0.659	
C.O.	0.33		−1.318	1.318		−0.33
Distribution		0.26	1.05	−1.05	−0.26	
C.O.	0.13		−0.53	0.53		−0.13
Distribution		0.106	0.424	−0.424	−0.106	
C.O.	0.053		−0.212	0.212		0.053
Distribution		0.042	−0.172	−0.172	−0.0424	
Net moments	−0.612	4.44	−4.44	4.44	−4.44	0.612

$$\text{Horizontals thrust (H) } (\rightarrow) = \frac{\text{(Fixed end moment + Moment due to external force)}}{\text{Length of column}}$$

$$= -\frac{0.612 + 4.44 - 6 \times 1}{4}$$

$$= -0.54 \text{ kN}$$

$$H = 0.54 \text{ kN } (\leftarrow)$$

Step IV : FBD of members as shown in figure, considering equilibrium of each member and of complete structure all reaction components are found out as shown in Fig. 2.19 (b).

Step V : Shear force diagram is as shown in Fig. 2.19 (c).

Step VI : Bending moment diagrams are as shown in Fig. 2.19 (d) and Fig. 2.19 (e).

STRUCTURAL ANALYSIS – II MOMENT DISTRIBUTION METHOD

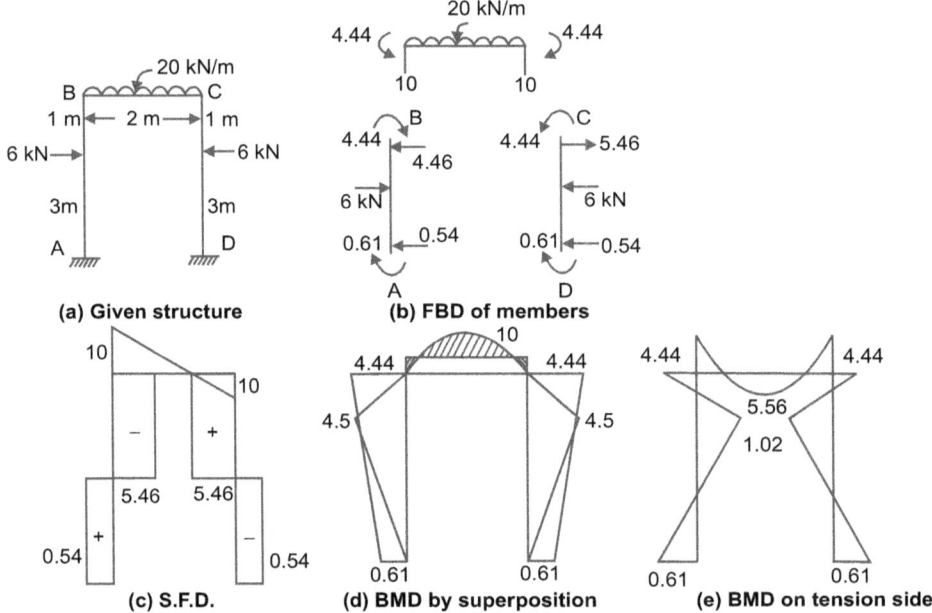

Fig. 2.19 : Illustrative Example 2.14

Example 2.15 : *Analyse the frame as shown in Fig. 2.20 (a) using moment distribution method.*

(P.U. May 2000)

Solution : Data : The frame is supported and loaded as shown in Fig. 2.20 (a).
Object : Structural Analysis :
Concepts and Equations : MD technique based on normalized relative stiffness factors and distribution factors.
Procedure : Step I : Fixed end moments :

$$\overline{M}_{AB} = -\frac{wl^2}{12} = -\frac{30 \times 4^2}{12} = -40 \text{ kN-m}$$

$$\overline{M}_{BA} = 40 \text{ kN-m}$$

$$\overline{M}_{BC} = -\frac{wab^2}{l^2} = -\frac{180 \times 1 \times 2^2}{3^2} = -80 \text{ kN-m}$$

Step II : Distribution factors :

$$\overline{M}_{CB} = \frac{wa^2b}{l^2} = \frac{180 \times 1^2 \times 2}{3^2} = 40 \text{ kN-m}$$

$$\overline{M}_{BE} = \overline{M}_{EB} = 0$$

$$\overline{M}_{CD} = \overline{M}_{DC} = 0$$

Ch. 2 | 2.54

STRUCTURAL ANALYSIS – II   MOMENT DISTRIBUTION METHOD

Joint	Member	Type of support	Carryover factor	K	Σ K	D. F.
A	AB	Fixed	A → B 0	-	-	-
B	BA	Continuous	B → A 1/2	I/4	10I/12	0.3
	BC		B → C 1/2	I/3		0.4
	BE		B → E 0	3/4 × I/3		0.3
C	CB	Continuous	C → B 1/2	I/3	5I/6	0.4
	CD		C → D 1/2	I/2		0.6
D	DC	Fixed	D → C 0	-	-	-
E	EB	Simple	E → B 1/2	-	-	-

Step III : MD Table :

Joint	A	B			C		D	E
Mem.	AB	BA	BE	BC	CB	CD	CD	EB
D.F.	-	0.3	0.3	0.4	0.4	0.6	-	-
F.E.M.	− 40	40	0	− 80	40	0	0	0
Dist.		12	12	16	− 16	− 24	0	0
C.O.	6			− 8	8		− 12	
Dist.		+ 2.4	+ 2.4	+ 3.2	− 3.2	− 4.8		
C.O.	+ 1.2			− 1.6	+ 1.6		− 2.4	
Dist.		0.48	0.48	0.64	− 0.64	− 0.96		
C.O.	0.24			− 0.32	0.32		− 0.48	
Dist.		+ 0.096	+0.128	− 0.128	− 0.128	− 0.192		
Final moments	− 32.56	54.98	14.98	− 69.95	29.95	− 29.95	− 14.95	0

STRUCTURAL ANALYSIS – II MOMENT DISTRIBUTION METHOD

Step IV : FBD of members as shown in figure, considering equilibrium of each member and of complete structure all reaction components are found out as shown in Fig. 2.20 (b).

Step V : Shear force diagram is as shown in figure. 2.20 (c).

Step VI : Bending moment diagrams are as shown in figure 2.20 (d) and figure. 2.20 (e).

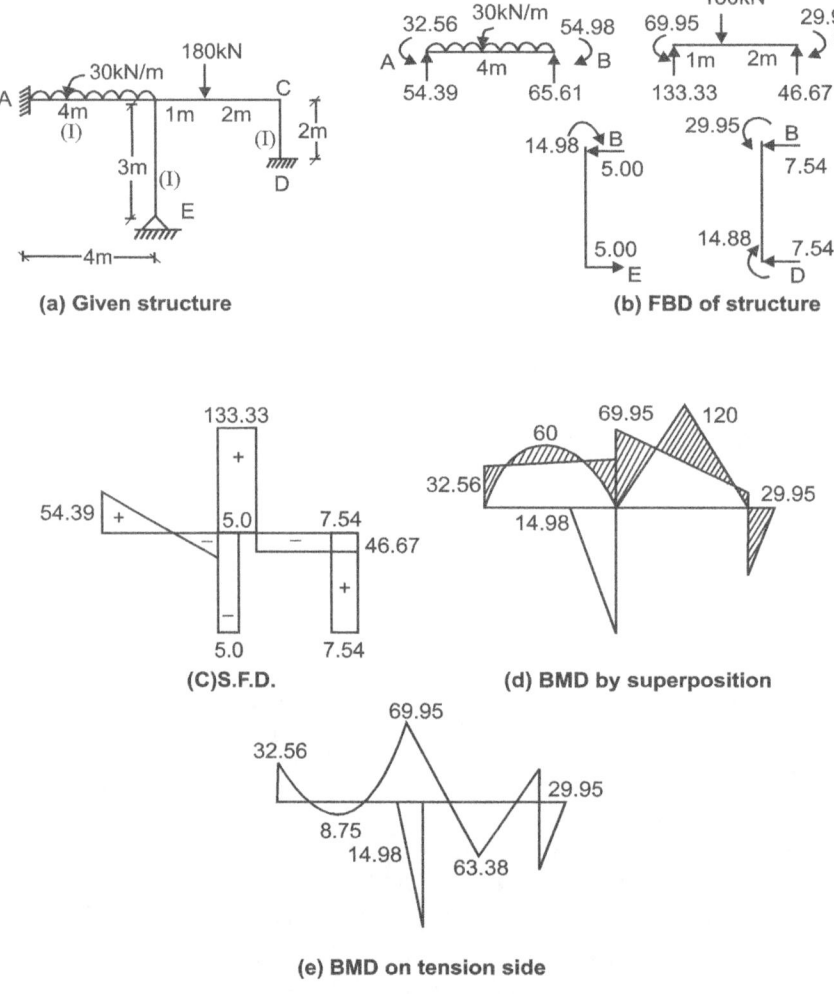

Fig. 2.20 : Illustrative Example 2.15

STRUCTURAL ANALYSIS – II   MOMENT DISTRIBUTION METHOD

2.7 APPLICATION OF MD METHOD TO FRAMES WITH JOINT TRANSLATIONS

The MD method has been so far mainly dealt with the structures with joint rotations only. There may be joint translations in a structure in addition to joint rotations. This is the most general case of unsymmetrical frame. The joint translations along the members do not affect the MD method. But the joint translations perpendicular to the members are required to be considered and hence need special treatment in MD method.

In the rectangular frame, the horizontal translation of joints is termed as sway and the frame is called *sway frame*. In general, the unsymmetrical frames are sway frames. The sway of joints at the same level is assumed to be of same magnitude and direction because axial deformations are neglected. For the analysis of sway frames by MD method, the process of moment distribution is to be carried out twice. First MD is conventional starting with FEM due to member loads, as if no joint translations. First set of member-end moments are the results of first MD table. First MD is also called non-sway MD. In a particular case, if no loads are acting on the members of the structure, then first MD is null and void.

In second MD called as sway MD, arbitrary sway moments proportional to I/L^2 of members having sway, are distributed as per second MD table. The results of second set of arbitrary member-end moments are corrected by the correction factor obtained by shear equilibrium condition. This is the second set of corrected member-end moments. Final member-end moments are the sum of first set of moments and second set of corrected moments.

The procedure of analysis of sway frames by MD method is elaborated with the illustrated example 2.16, highlighting the special treatment, as follows :

Example 2.16 : *Analyse the frame shown in Fig. 2.21 (a) by MD method.*

Solution : Data : The rectangular frame is supported and loaded as shown in Fig. 2.21 (a). The data includes the following information :

(1) Structural configuration : Type of members, joints and supports, dimensions, cross-sectional properties and material properties of members.

(2) Applied loads : Magnitude, direction and position.

(3) Type of structure – Sway frame.

Object : Member-end moments.

Concepts and Equations :

(1) MD technique based on normalized stiffness factors, carryover factors and distribution factors.

(2) Normalized relative sway factors, sway moments.

(3) Shear equilibrium condition and correction factor.

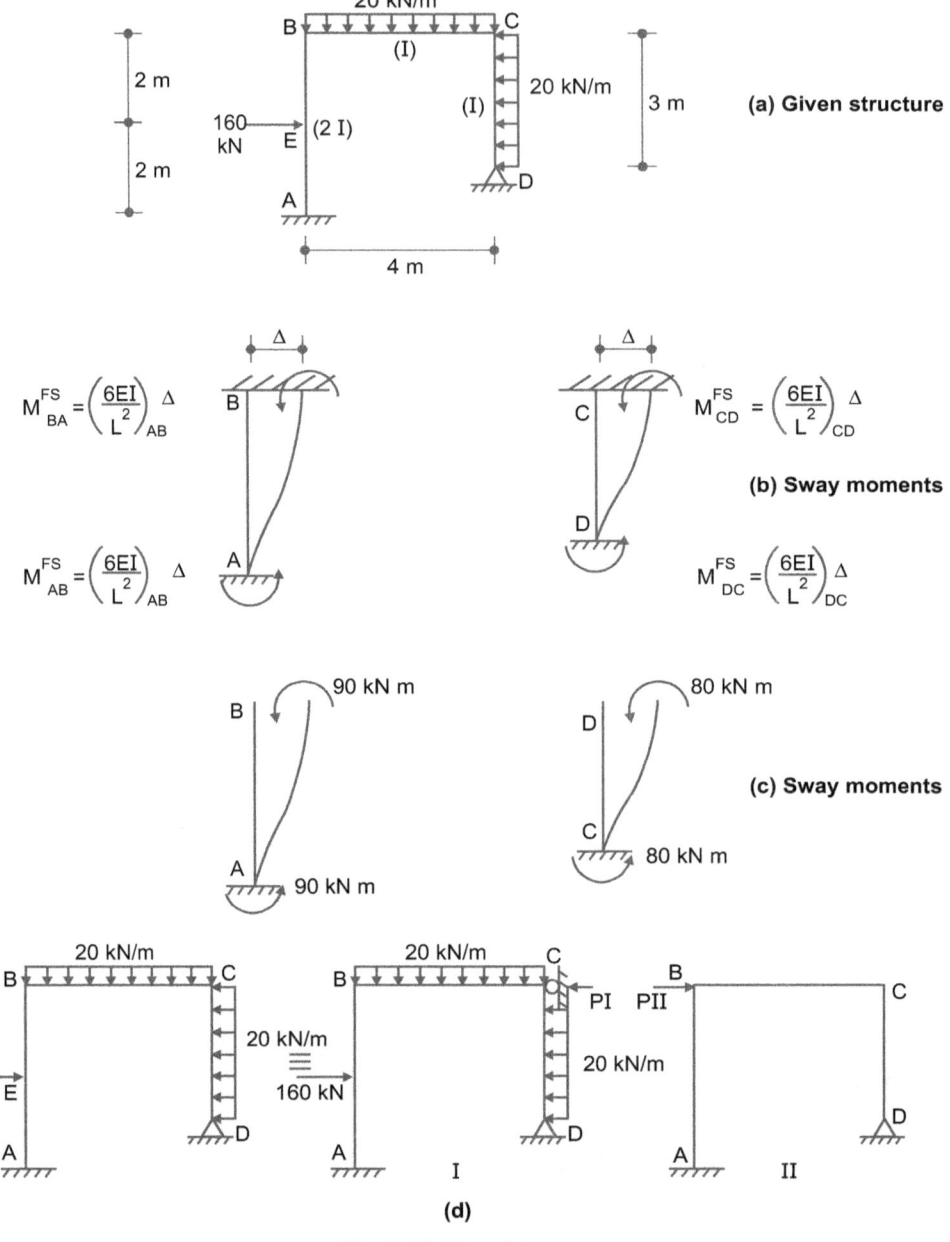

Fig. 2.21 (Contd.)

STRUCTURAL ANALYSIS – II
MOMENT DISTRIBUTION METHOD

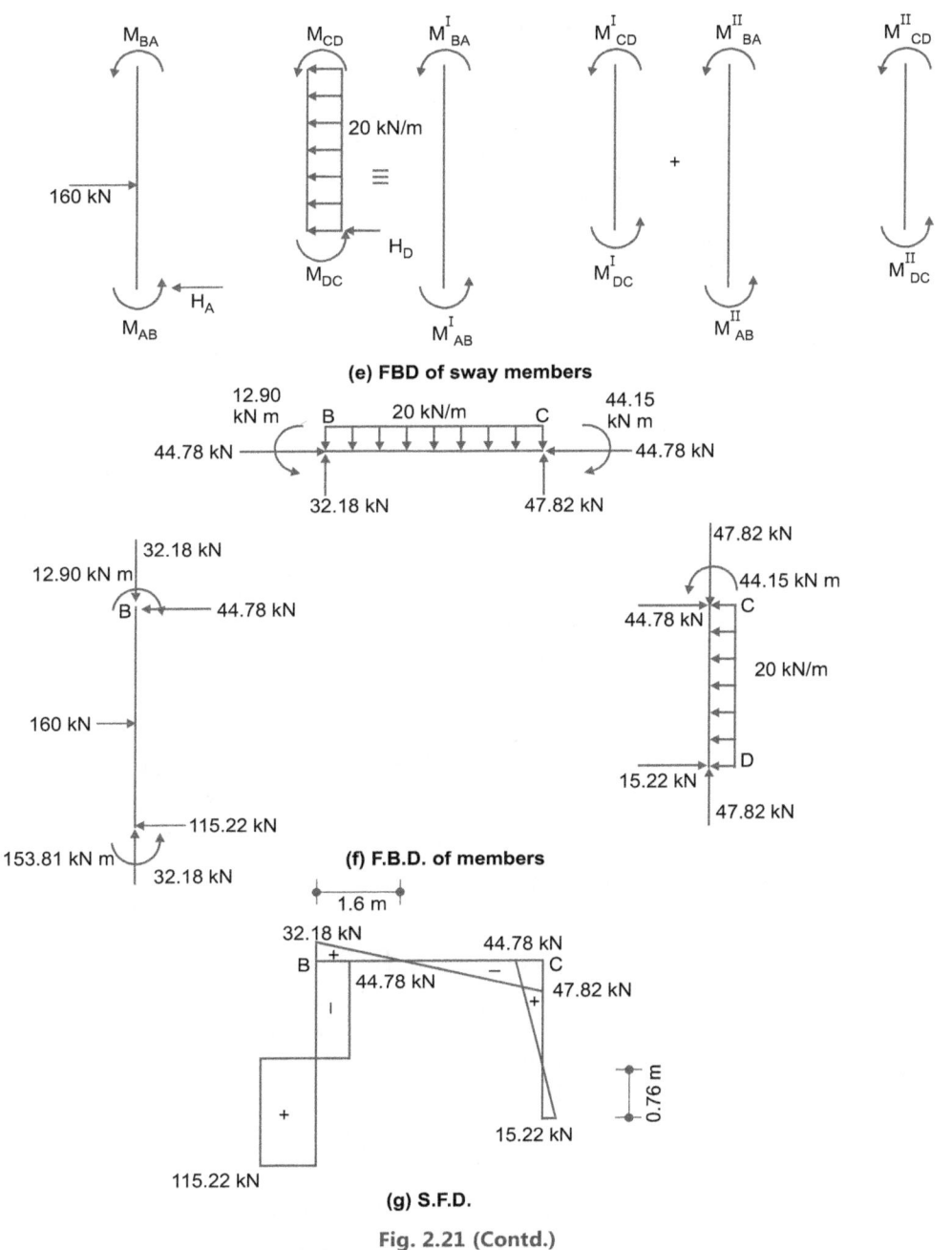

(e) FBD of sway members

(f) F.B.D. of members

(g) S.F.D.

Fig. 2.21 (Contd.)

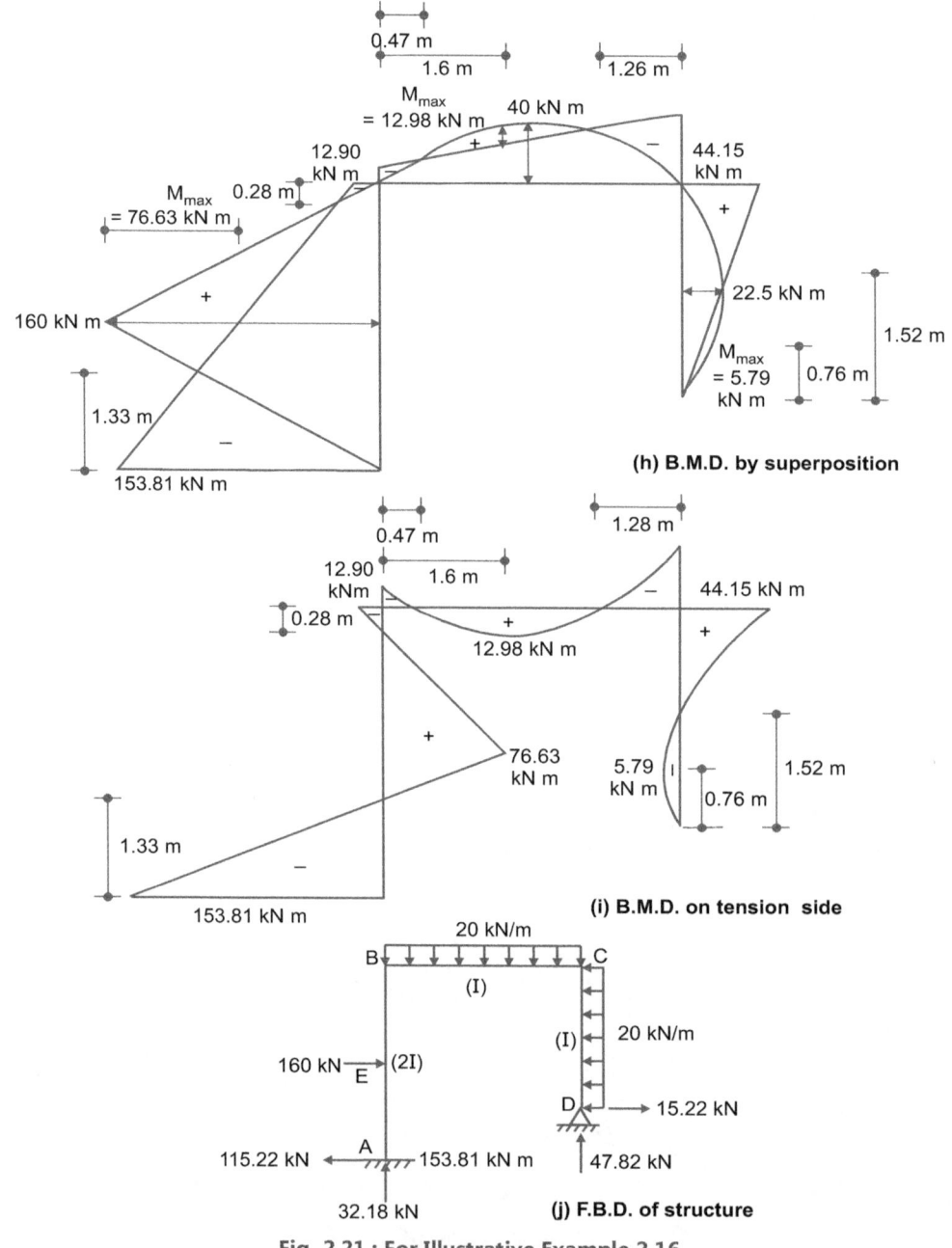

Fig. 2.21 : For Illustrative Example 2.16

Procedure : Step I : Fixed-end moments :

Member	FEM with calculations
AB	$M_{AB}^F = \left(\dfrac{160 \times 4}{8}\right) = +80$ kNm $M_{BA}^F = -M_{AB}^F = -80$ kNm
BC	$M_{BC}^F = +\left(\dfrac{20 \times 4 \times 4}{12}\right) = +26.67$ kNm $M_{CB}^F = -M_{BC}^F = -26.67$ kNm
CD	$M_{CD}^F = +\left(\dfrac{20 \times 3 \times 3}{12}\right) = +15$ kNm $M_{DC}^F = -M_{CD}^F = -15$ kNm

Step II : Distribution factors :

Joint	Member	K	ΣK	$DF = \dfrac{K}{\Sigma K}$
A	AB	–	–	0
B	BA	$\dfrac{4EI}{L} = 2$	3	0.67
	BC	$\dfrac{4EI}{L} = 1$		0.33
C	CB	$\dfrac{4EI}{L} = 1$	2	0.5
	CD	$\dfrac{3EI}{L} = 1$		0.5
D	DC	–	–	1

Step III : MD Table 1 for non-sway moments :

Joint		A	B		B	C		C	D
Type of joint		EFS	RJ			RJ			EHS
Member		AB	BA	BC		CB	CD		DC
COF			→ 1/2 1/2 ←	→ 1/2 1/2 ←			→ 0 1/2 ←		
DF		0	0.67	0.33		0.5	0.5		0
First cycle	FEM	+ 80	− 80	+ 26.67		− 26.67	+ 15		− 15
	DM	–	+ 35.33	18		5.84	5.84		+ 15
Second cycle	COM	+ 17.66	–	2.92		9	7.5		–
	DM	–	− 1.94	− 0.97		− 8.25	− 8.25		–
Third cycle	COM	− 0.97	–	− 4.13		− 0.48	–		–
	DM	–	2.75	1.37		0.24	0.24		–
Fourth cycle	COM	1.38	–	0.12		0.68	–		–
	DM	–	− 0.08	− 0.04		− 0.34	0.34		–
First set of final moments		98.07	− 43.94	43.94		− 19.98	19.98		0.0

Step IV : MD for sway moments :

(a) The basic information of K, COF and DF remains the same.

(b) Sway - There is equal sway Δ at joints B and C. The sway Δ is not known in magnitude and direction. The sway is also not required to be found in MD method.

(c) **Effect of sway :** The sway moments of $\left(\dfrac{6\,EI}{L^2}\right) \times \Delta$ exist at both ends of the member having sway as shown in Fig. 2.21 (b). The arbitrary sway moments are considered for the members having sway. For the same sway and same material of the member, the sway moments are proportional to I/L^2. To decide the arbitrary sway moments, relative I/L^2 are obtained.

(d) **Relative sway-stiffness factor :** The quantity I/L^2 of the member is defined as the relative sway-stiffness factor of the member. The relative sway-stiffness factors are expressed in the normalized form i.e. proportionate numerals eliminating I. The relative sway-stiffness factor of the member is considered as independent of the end conditions for the formulation of MD method. The end conditions of members are already accounted for in K.

Therefore, it is suggested that the relative sway-stiffness factors are taken as I/L^2 irrespective of end conditions of member. The sway moments are developed at ends of members AB and CD
as shown in Fig. 2.21 (b). There is no effect of sway on the member BC. In rectangular frames with sway, the columns only are subjected to sway moments. Normalized relative sway-stiffness factors K_S are obtained as given in the following table.

Member	Relative sway-stiffness factor	Normalized relative sway-stiffness factor, K_S
AB	$\dfrac{2I}{4 \times 4} = \dfrac{I}{8}$	9
CD	$\dfrac{I}{3 \times 3} = \dfrac{I}{9}$	8

(e) **Sway moments :** Corresponding to the normalized relative sway-stiffness factors of the members, the arbitrary but relative sway moments are considered at the ends of the members having sway as shown in Fig. 2.21 (c). These sway moments are treated as FEM to begin with second MD table and denoted as M_{ij}^{FS}. They are assumed as positive corresponding to Δ shown. M_{ij}^{FS} are given in the following table :

Member	Arbitrary relative FEM due to sway
AB	$M_{AB}^{FS} = + 90$ kNm $M_{BA}^{FS} = + 90$ kNm
CD	$M_{CD}^{FS} = + 80$ kNm $M_{DC}^{FS} = + 80$ kNm

STRUCTURAL ANALYSIS – II

MOMENT DISTRIBUTION METHOD

Step V : MD Table for sway moments :

Joint		A		B		C		D
Type of joint		EFS		RJ		RJ		EHS
Member		AB	BA	BC	CB	CD		DC
COF		→ 1/2		→ 1/2		→ 0		
		1/2 ←		1/2 ←		1/2 ←		
DF		1	0	0.67	0.33	0.5	0.5	1
First cycle	FEM	+ 90	+ 90	–	–	+ 80		+ 80
	DM	–	– 60	– 30	– 40	– 40		– 80
Second cycle	COM	– 30	–	– 20	– 15	– 40		
	DM	–	+ 13.33	+ 6.67	+ 27.5	+ 27.5		
Third cycle	COM	+ 6.67	–	+ 13.25	3.33	–		
	DM	–	– 8.83	– 4.42	– 1.67	– 1.67		
Fourth cycle	COM	– 4.42	–	– 0.84	– 2.21	–		
	DM	–	0.56	0.28	1.11	1.11		
Second set of arbitrary final moments		+ 62.25	+ 35.06	– 35.06	– 26.94	26.94		0.0

$$P^I = C \times P^{II}$$

$$M_{AB} = M^I_{AB} + C \cdot M^{II}_{AB}$$

$$M_{BA} = M^I_{BA} + C \cdot M^{II}_{BA}$$

$$M_{CD} = M^I_{CD} + C \cdot M^{II}_{CD}$$

$$M_{DC} = M^I_{DC} + C \cdot M^{II}_{DC}$$

where C is the correction factor to be obtained from shear equilibrium equation developed as follows :

Step VI : Shear Equilibrium Condition :

The arbitrary final moments obtained from second MD table are to be corrected to satisfy the shear equilibrium condition for the structure. The given structure is considered as the equivalent of the superposition of :

(i) Sway prevented structure.
(ii) Sway structure with the correction factor C as shown in Fig. 2.21 (d).

The FBD of sway members are as shown in Fig. 2.21 (e) to formulate the shear equilibrium condition in terms of member-end moments and correction factor C. The formulation based on superposition equations, determines C, as follows :

FBD and shear equilibrium :
FBD of AB

$$\sum M_B = 0$$

$$\therefore M_{BA} + M_{AB} + 160 \times 2 + H_A \times 4 = 0$$

STRUCTURAL ANALYSIS – II   MOMENT DISTRIBUTION METHOD

$$\therefore \quad H_A = \frac{M_{AB} + M_{BA} + 320}{4}$$

$$\therefore \quad H_A = \frac{(M^I_{AB} + CM^{II}_{AB}) + (M^I_{BA} + CM^{II}_{BA}) + 320}{4}$$

FBD of CD

$$\sum M_C = 0$$

$$\therefore \quad M_{CD} + M_{DC} - 20 \times 3 \times 1.5 - H_D \times 3 = 0$$

$$\therefore \quad H_D = \frac{M_{CD} + M_{DC} - 90}{3}$$

$$= \frac{(M^I_{CD} + CM^{II}_{CD}) + (M^I_{DC} + CM^{II}_{DC}) - 90}{3}$$

FBD of frame
$$\sum H = 0$$
$$+ 160 - 20 \times 3 - H_A - H_D = 0$$
$$\therefore \quad H_A + H_D = 100$$

The shear equilibrium equation is therefore expressed in terms of member-end moments

$$\frac{(M^I_{AB} + CM^{II}_{AB}) + (M^I_{BA} + CM^{II}_{BA}) + 320}{4} + \frac{(M^I_{CD} + CM^{II}_{CD}) + (M^I_{DC} + CM^{II}_{DC}) - 90}{3} = 100$$

Substituting the first set of moments and second set of moments obtained from first MD and second MD, in the expression

$$\frac{(+98.07 + C \times 62.25) + (-43.94 + C \times 35.06) + 320}{4} + \frac{(+19.98 + C \times 26.94) + (0 + C \times 0) - 90}{3} = 100$$

i.e. $(33.30) C = 29.80$

$$\boxed{C = 0.894}$$

Step VII : Final results : Corrected moments of second set will be obtained by multiplying by C and then added to first moments to get the net final moments :

	AB	BA	BC	CB	CD	DC
Second set of corrected moments	55.74	31.04	– 31.04	– 24.17	24.17	0
First set of moments	+ 98.07	– 43.94	+ 43.94	– 19.98	19.98	0
Net final moments	153.81	– 12.90	12.90	– 44.15	44.15	0

Step VIII : FBD of Members : as shown in Fig. 2.21 (f). Considering equilibrium of each member and of complete structure, all reaction components are found out as shown in Fig. 2.21.

Step IX : Shear force diagram is as shown in Fig. 2.21 (g).

Step X : Bending moment diagrams are as shown in Fig. 2.22 (h) and Fig. 2.21 (i).

Step XI : FBD of structure is as shown in Fig. 2.21 (j).

STRUCTURAL ANALYSIS – II   MOMENT DISTRIBUTION METHOD

Example 2.17 : Analyse the frame shown in Fig. 2.22 (a) by MD method.

Solution : Data : (1) The frame is supported and loaded as shown in Fig. 2.22 (a).

(2) Type of frame : Sway frame.

Object : Structural analysis.

Concepts and Equations : (1) MD technique based on normalized relative-stiffness factors and distribution factors.

(2) Normalized relative sway factors.

(3) Shear equilibrium condition and correction factors.

Procedure :

Step I : Fixed end-moments :

$$M^F_{AB} = M^F_{BA} = M^F_{BC} = M^F_{CB} = M^F_{CD} = M^F_{DC} = 0$$

Step II : Distribution factors :

Joint	Member	K	ΣK	$DF = \dfrac{K}{\Sigma K}$
A	AB	–	–	0
B	BA	$\dfrac{4EI}{L} = 1$	3	0.33
	BC	$\dfrac{4EI}{L} = 2$		0.67
C	CB	$\dfrac{4EI}{L} = 2$	4	0.5
	CD	$\dfrac{4EI}{L} = 2$		0.5
D	DC	–	–	0

Step III : MD Table (I) for non-sway moments : As member loads are absent, all FEMs are zero and hence MD for non-sway moments is not required.

Step IV : MD for sway moments :

(a) The basic information of K, COF and DF remains the same.

(b) Normalized relative-sway stiffness factors (K_S).

Member	Relative sway stiffness factor	Normalized relative-sway stiffness factor, K_S
AB	$\dfrac{I}{4^2}$	1
DC	$\dfrac{I}{2^2}$	4

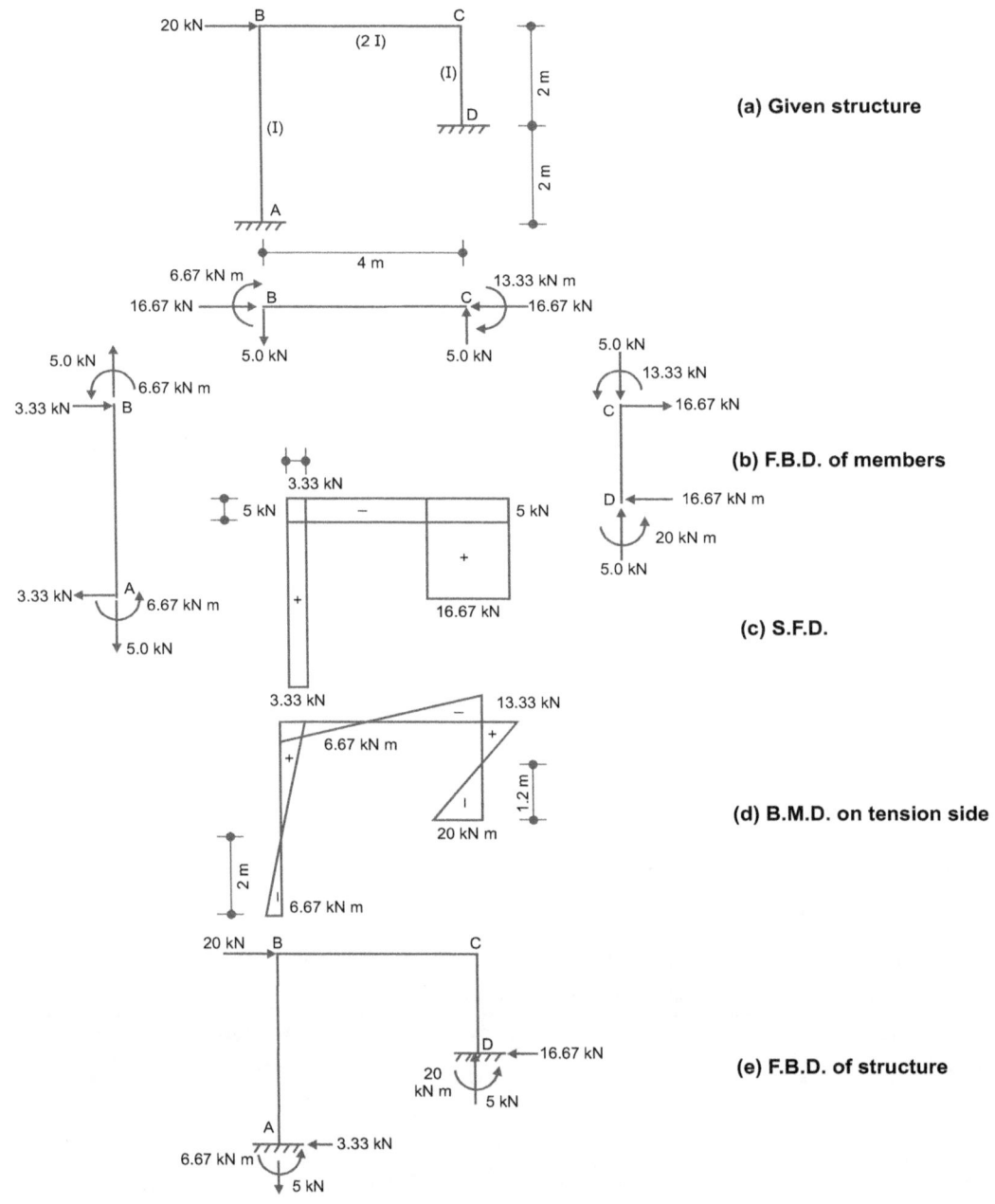

Fig. 2.22 : For Illustrative Example 2.17

STRUCTURAL ANALYSIS – II MOMENT DISTRIBUTION METHOD

(c) Sway moments :

Member	Arbitrary relative FEM due to sway
AB	$M_{AB}^{FS} = 10$ kNm
	$M_{BA}^{FS} = 10$ kNm
DC	$M_{DC}^{FS} = 40$ kNm
	$M_{CD}^{FS} = 40$ kNm

Step V : MD Table (II) for sway moments :

Joint		A	B			C		D
Type of joint		EFS	RJ			RJ		EHS
Member		AB	BA	BC		CB	CD	DC
COF			$\to 1/2$			$\to 1/2$		$\to 1/2$
			$1/2 \leftarrow$			$1/2 \leftarrow$		$1/2 \leftarrow$
DF		0	0.33	0.67		0.5	0.5	0
First cycle	FEM	10	10				40	40
	DM	–	– 3.33	– 6.67		– 20	– 20	–
Second cycle	COM	– 1.67	–	– 10		– 3.33	–	– 10
	DM	–	3.33	6.67		1.67	1.67	–
Third cycle	COM	1.67	–	0.84		3.33	–	0.84
	DM	–	– 0.28	– 0.56		– 1.67	– 1.67	–
Fourth cycle	COM	– 0.14	–	– 0.84		– 0.28	–	– 0.84
	DM	–	0.28	– 0.56		0.14	0.14	–
Fifth cycle	COM	0.14	–	0.07		0.28	–	0.08
	DM	–	– 0.02	– 0.05		– 0.14	– 0.14	–
Second set of final moments		10	9.98	– 9.98		– 20	20	30.08

Let, actual sway moments be 'C' times above sway moments.

$$\therefore \quad M_{AB} = M_{AB}^{I} + C \cdot M_{AB}^{II} = C(10)$$

$$M_{BA} = M_{BA}^{I} + C \cdot M_{BA}^{II} = C(9.98)$$

$$M_{DC} = M_{DC}^{I} + C \cdot M_{DC}^{II} = C(30.08)$$

$$M_{CD} = M_{CD}^{I} + C \cdot M_{CD}^{II} = C(20)$$

where, C = Correction factor to be evaluated from the condition of horizontal shear equilibrium for the structure.

Step VI : Horizontal shear equilibrium :

Horizontal shear equilibrium of structure gives,

$$H_A + H_D - 20 = 0 \qquad \ldots (A)$$

where, $\quad H_A = \dfrac{M_{AB} + M_{BA}}{4}$ and

$$M_D = \dfrac{M_{DC} + M_{CD}}{2}$$

Substituting in equation (A), we get

$$\left(\dfrac{M_{AB} + M_{BA}}{4}\right) + \left(\dfrac{M_{DC} + M_{CD}}{2}\right) - 20 = 0$$

$$(M_{AB} + M_{BA}) + 2(M_{DC} + M_{CD}) - 80 = 0$$

Substituting values of moments, we get

$$[C(10) + C(9.98)] + 2[C(30.08) + C(20)] - 80 = 0$$

$$(120.14)C - 80 = 0 \quad \boxed{C = 0.667}$$

Step VII : Final result :

Member	AB	BA	BC	CB	CD	DC
Corrected moments of second set	6.67	6.67	− 6.67	− 13.33	13.33	20.0
Moments of first set	−	−	−	−	−	−
Net final moments	6.67	6.67	− 6.67	− 13.33	13.33	20.0

Step VIII : FBD of members is as shown in Fig. 2.22 (b). Considering equilibrium of each member and of complete structure, all reaction components are found out as shown in Fig. 2.23.

Step IX : Shear force diagram is as shown in Fig. 2.22 (c).

Step X : Bending moment diagrams are as shown in Fig. 2.16 (d) and Fig. 2.22 (e).

Step XI : FBD of structure is as shown in Fig. 2.22 (f).

Example 2.18 : Analyse the frame shown in Fig. 2.23 (a) by MD method.

Solution : Data : (1) The frame is supported and loaded as shown in Fig. 2.23 (a).

(2) Type of frame : Sway frame.

Object : Structural analysis.

Concepts and Equations :

(1) MD technique based on normalized relative stiffness factors and distribution factors.

(2) Normalized relative sway factors.

(3) Shear equilibrium condition and correction factor.

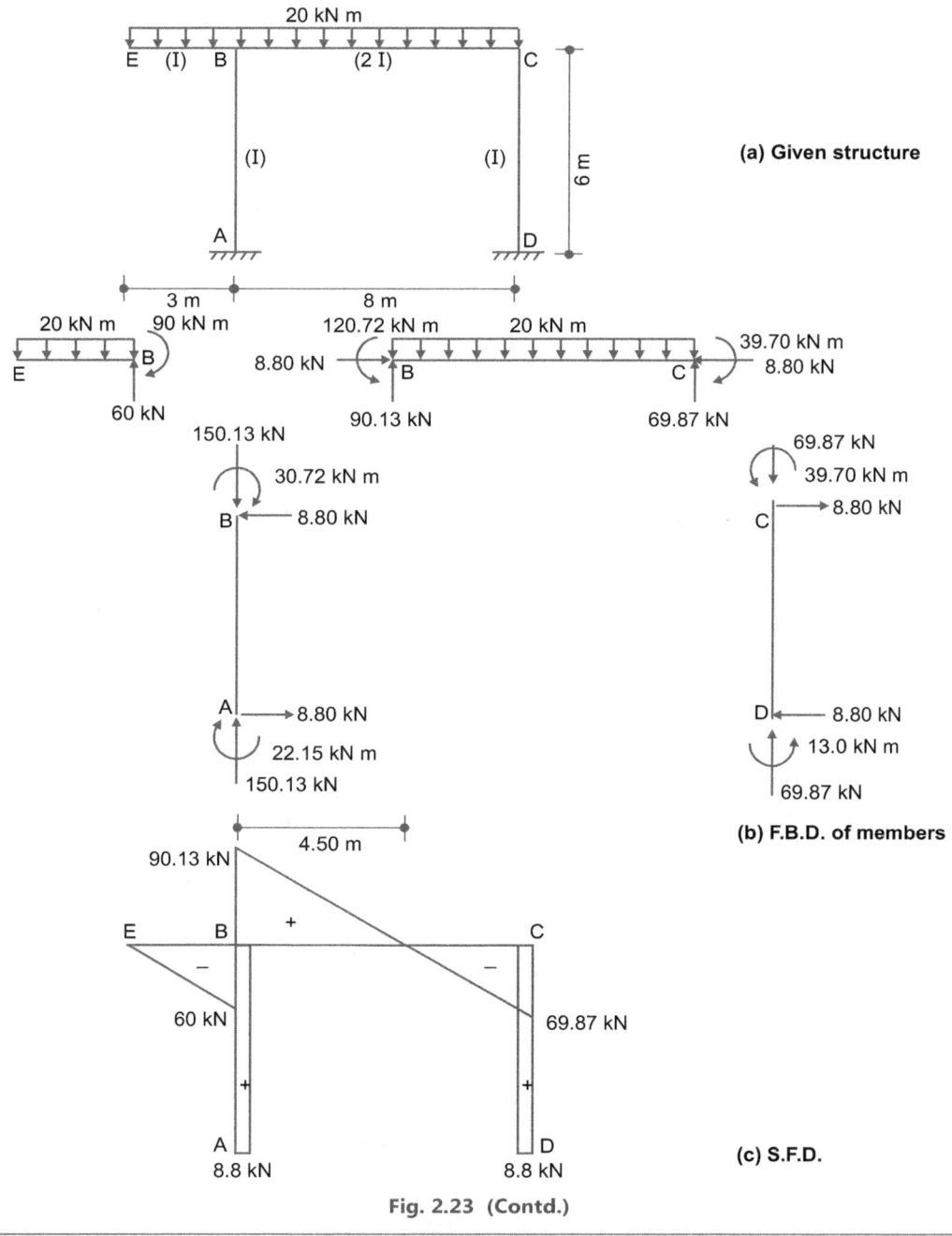

Fig. 2.23 (Contd.)

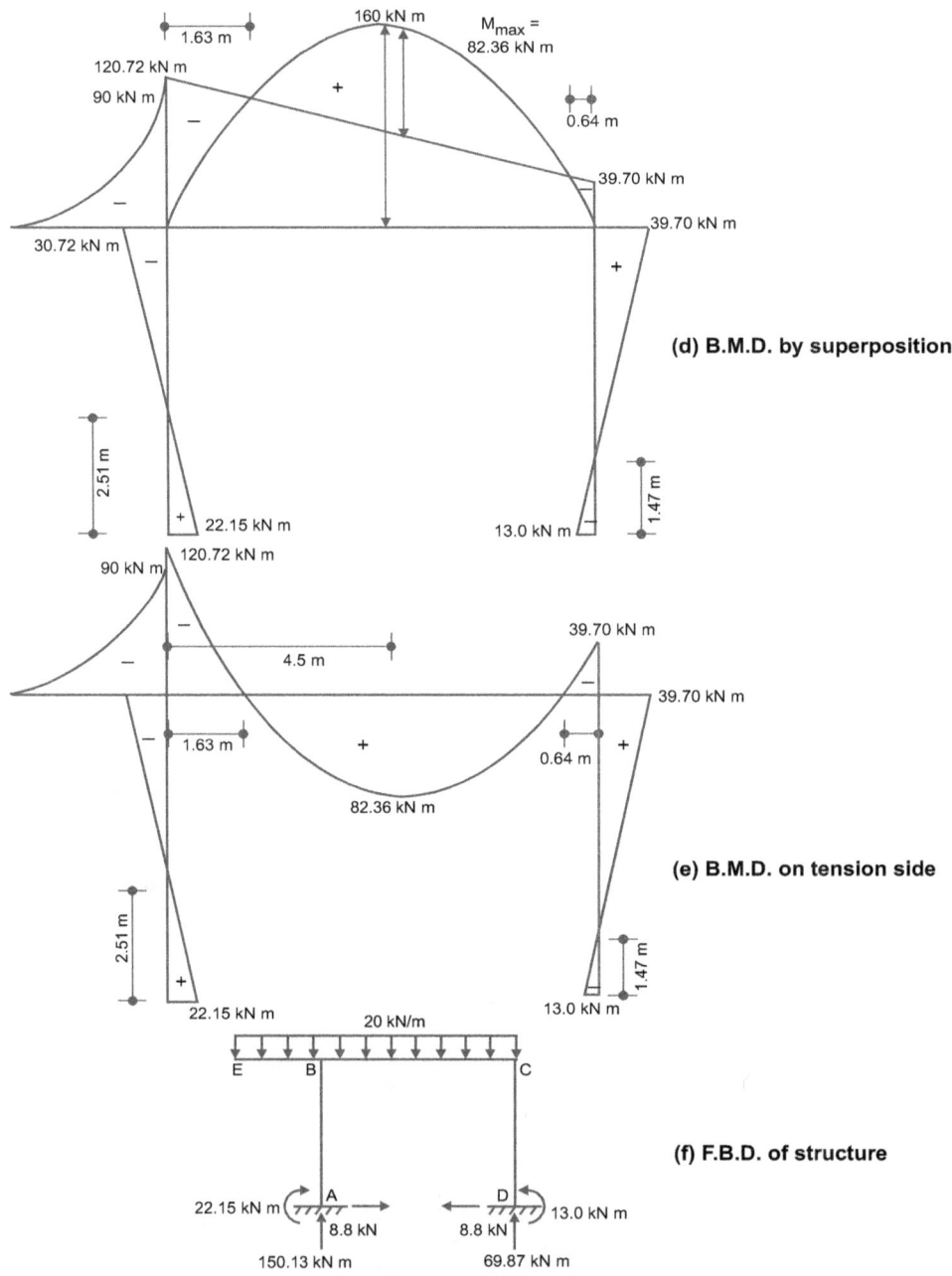

Fig. 2.23 : For Illustrative Example 2.18

STRUCTURAL ANALYSIS – II MOMENT DISTRIBUTION METHOD

Procedure :

Step I : Fixed-end moments :

Member	FEM with calculations
AB	$M^F_{AB} = 0$ $M^F_{BA} = 0$
BC	$M^F_{BC} = \dfrac{wL^2}{12} = \dfrac{20 \times 8^2}{12}$ $= 106.67$ kNm $M^F_{CB} = -M^F_{BC}$ $= -106.67$
DC	$M^F_{DC} = 0$ $M^F_{CD} = 0$
BE	$M^F_{BE} = -\dfrac{wL^2}{2}$ $= \dfrac{-20 \times 3^2}{2}$ $= -90$ kNm

Step II : Distribution factors :

Joint	Member	K	ΣK	DF = $\dfrac{K}{\Sigma K}$
A	AB	–	–	0
B	BA	$\dfrac{4EI}{L} = 0.67$	1.67	0.4
	BC	$\dfrac{4EI}{L} = 1$		0.6
	BE	–		0
C	CB	$\dfrac{4EI}{L} = 1$	1.67	0.6
	CD	$\dfrac{4EI}{L} = 0.67$		0.4
D	DC	–	–	0

Step III : MD Table (I) for non-sway moments :

Joint	A			B		C		D
Type of joint	EFS			RJ		RJ		EFS
Member	AB		BA	BE	BC	CB	CD	DC
COF		→1/2				→1/2	→1/2	
			1/2←			1/2←	1/2←	
DF	0		0.4	0	0.6	0.6	0.4	0
First cycle FEM	0		0	−90	106.67	−106.67	0	0
DM	−		−6.67		−10.0	64	42.67	−
Second cycle COM	−3.33				32	−5.0		21.34
DM	−		−12.8		−19.2	3	2	−
Third cycle COM	−6.4		−		1.5	−9.6		1.0
DM	−		−0.6		−0.9	5.76	3.84	−
Fourth cycle COM	−0.3				2.88	−0.45		1.92
DM	−		−1.15		−1.73	0.27	0.18	−
Fifth cycle COM	−0.56				0.14	−0.87		0.09
DM	−		−0.06		−0.08	0.5	0.37	−
First set of final moments	−10.59		−21.28	−90	111.28	−49.06	49.06	24.35

Step IV : MD for sway moments :

(a) The basic information of K, COF and DF remains the same.

(b) Normalized relative sway stiffness factors (K_s).

Member	Relative sway stiffness factor	Normalized relative sway stiffness factor (K_s)
AB	$\dfrac{I}{6^2}$	1
DC	$\dfrac{I}{6^2}$	1

(c) Sway moments :

Member	Arbitrary relative FEM due to sway
AB	$M_{AB}^{FS} = 100$ kNm
	$M_{BA}^{FS} = 100$ kNm
DC	$M_{DC}^{FS} = 100$ kNm
	$M_{CD}^{FS} = 100$ kNm

Step V : MD Table (II) for sway moments :

Joint		A		B			C		D
Type of joint		EFS		RJ			RJ		EFS
Member		AB	BA	BE	BC	CB	CD		DC
COF		$\rightarrow 1/2$ $1/2 \rightarrow$			$\rightarrow 1/2$ $1/2 \rightarrow$		$\rightarrow 1/2$ $1/2 \rightarrow$		
DF		0	0.4	0	0.6	0.6	0.4		0
First cycle	FEM	100	100	–	–	–	100		100
	DM	–	– 40		– 60	– 60	– 40		–
Second cycle	COM	– 20	–		– 30	– 30	–		– 20
	DM	–	12		18	18	12		–
Third cycle	COM	6	–		9	9	–		6
	DM	–	– 3.6		– 5.4	– 5.4	– 3.6		–
Fourth cycle	COM	– 1.8	–		– 2.7	– 2.7	–		– 1.8
	DM	–	1.08		1.62	1.62	1.08		–
Fifth cycle	COM	0.54	–		0.81	0.81	–		0.54
	DM	–	– 0.32		– 0.49	– 0.49	– 0.32		–
Sixth cycle	COM	– 0.16	–		– 0.25	– 0.25	–		– 0.16
	DM	–	0.10		0.15	0.15	0.10		–
Second set of final moments		84.58	69.26	0	– 69.26	– 69.26	69.26		84.58

Let the actual sway moments be 'C' times the above sway moments.

$\therefore$

$$M_{AB} = M_{AB}^{I} + C \cdot M_{AB}^{II} = -10.59 + C(84.58)$$

$$M_{BA} = M_{BA}^{I} + C \cdot M_{BA}^{II} = -21.28 + C(69.26)$$

$$M_{DC} = M_{DC}^{I} + C \cdot M_{DC}^{II} = 24.35 + C(84.58)$$

$$M_{CD} = M_{CD}^{I} + C \cdot M_{CD}^{II} = 49.08 + C(69.26)$$

where, C = Correction factor to be evaluated from the condition of horizontal shear equilibrium of the structure.

Step VI : Horizontal shear equilibrium : Horizontal shear equilibrium of structure gives,

$$H_A + H_D = 0 \qquad \ldots (A)$$

where, $\quad H_A = \dfrac{M_{AB} + M_{BA}}{6}$

and $\quad H_D = \dfrac{M_{DC} + M_{CD}}{6}$

Substituting in equation (A), we get

$$M_{AB} + M_{BA} + M_{DC} + M_{CD} = 0$$

Substituting values of moments, we get

$$-10.59 + C(84.58) - 21.28 + C(69.26) + 24.35 + C(84.58) + 49.08 + C(69.26) = 0$$

$$\boxed{C = -0.135}$$

Step VII : Final results :

Member	AB	BA	BE	BC	CB	CD	DC
Corrected moments of second set	− 11.56	− 9.44	0	9.44	9.36	− 9.36	− 11.35
Moments of first set	− 10.59	− 21.28	− 90	111.28	− 49.06	49.06	24.35
Net final moments	− 22.15	− 30.72	− 90	120.72	− 39.70	39.70	13.0

Step VIII : FBD of members is as shown in Fig. 2.23 (b). Considering equilibrium of each member and of complete structure, all reaction components are found out as shown in Fig. 2.23.

Step IX : Shear force diagram is as shown in Fig. 2.23 (c).

Step X : Bending moment diagrams are as shown in Fig. 2.23 (d) and Fig. 2.23 (e).

Step XI : FBD of structure is as shown in Fig. 2.23 (f).

Example 2.19 : *Analyse the frame shown in Fig. 2.24 (a) by MD method. Take EI = constant.*

Solution : Data : (1) The frame is supported and loaded as shown in Fig. 2.24 (a).

(2) Type of frame : Sway frame.

Object : Structural analysis.

Concepts and Equations :

(1) MD technique based on normalized relative stiffness factors and distribution factors.

(2) Normalized relative sway factors.

(3) Shear equilibrium condition and correction factor.

Procedure :

Step I : Fixed-end moments :

Member	FEM with calculations
AB	$M_{AB}^F = \dfrac{wL^2}{12} = \dfrac{25 \times 4^2}{12}$ $= 33.33$ kNm $M_{BA}^F = -M_{AB}^F$ $= -33.33$ kNm
BC	$M_{BC}^F = \dfrac{WL}{8} = \dfrac{50 \times 3}{8}$ $= 18.75$ kNm $M_{CB}^F = -M_{BC}^F$ $= -18.75$ kNm
DC	$M_{DC}^F = \dfrac{-Wab^2}{L^2} = \dfrac{-40 \times 1 \times 2^2}{3^2}$ $= -17.77$ kNm $M_{CD}^F = \dfrac{Wba^2}{L^2} = \dfrac{40 \times 2 \times 1^2}{3^2} = 8.88$ kNm

Step II : Distribution factors :

Joint	Member	K	ΣK	DF = $\dfrac{K}{\Sigma K}$
A	AB	–	–	0
B	BA	$\dfrac{4EI}{L} = 1$	2.34	0.43
	BC	$\dfrac{4EI}{L} = 1.34$		0.57
C	CB	$\dfrac{4EI}{L} = 1.34$	2.68	0.5
	CD	$\dfrac{4EI}{L} = 1.34$		0.5
D	DC	–	–	0

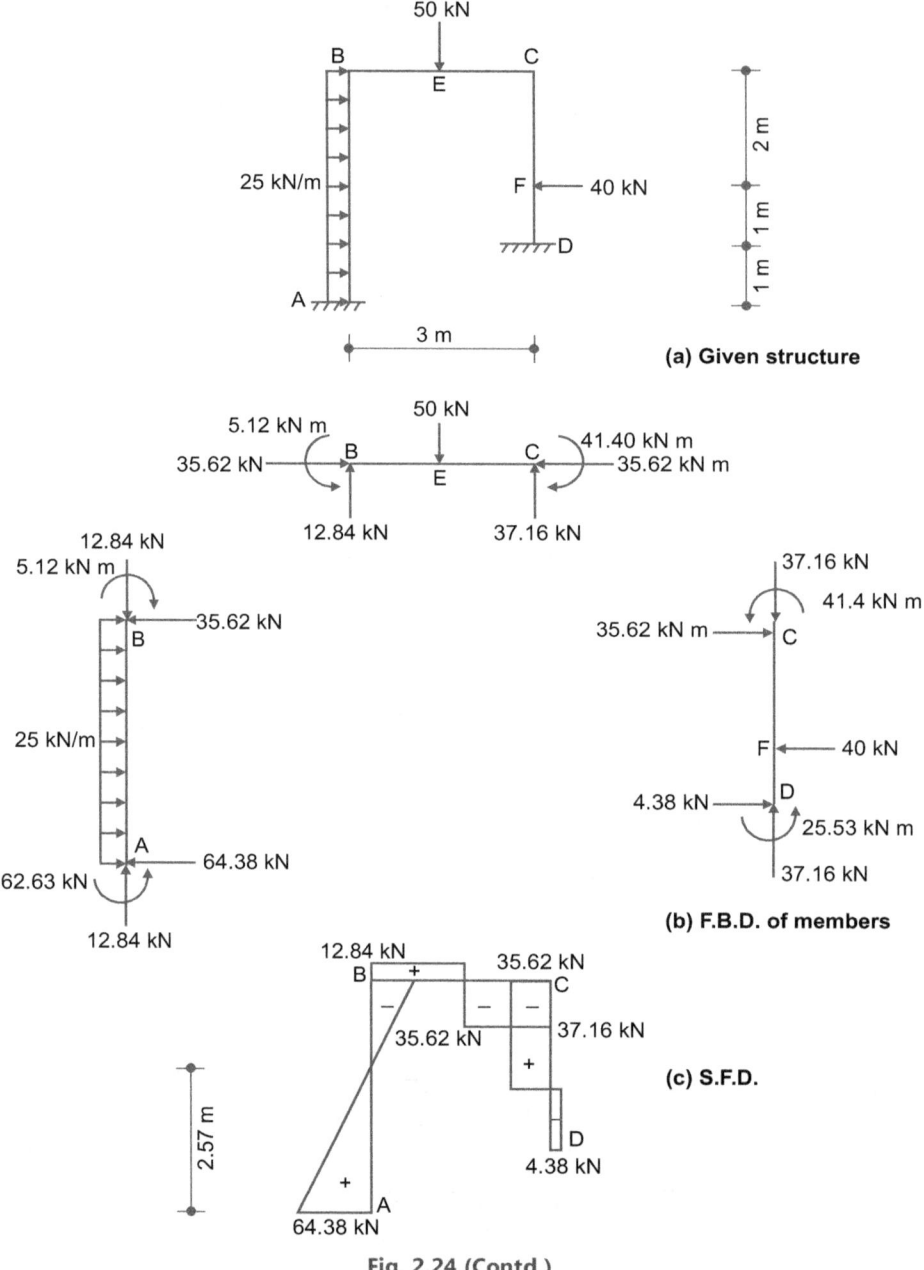

Fig. 2.24 (Contd.)

STRUCTURAL ANALYSIS – II

MOMENT DISTRIBUTION METHOD

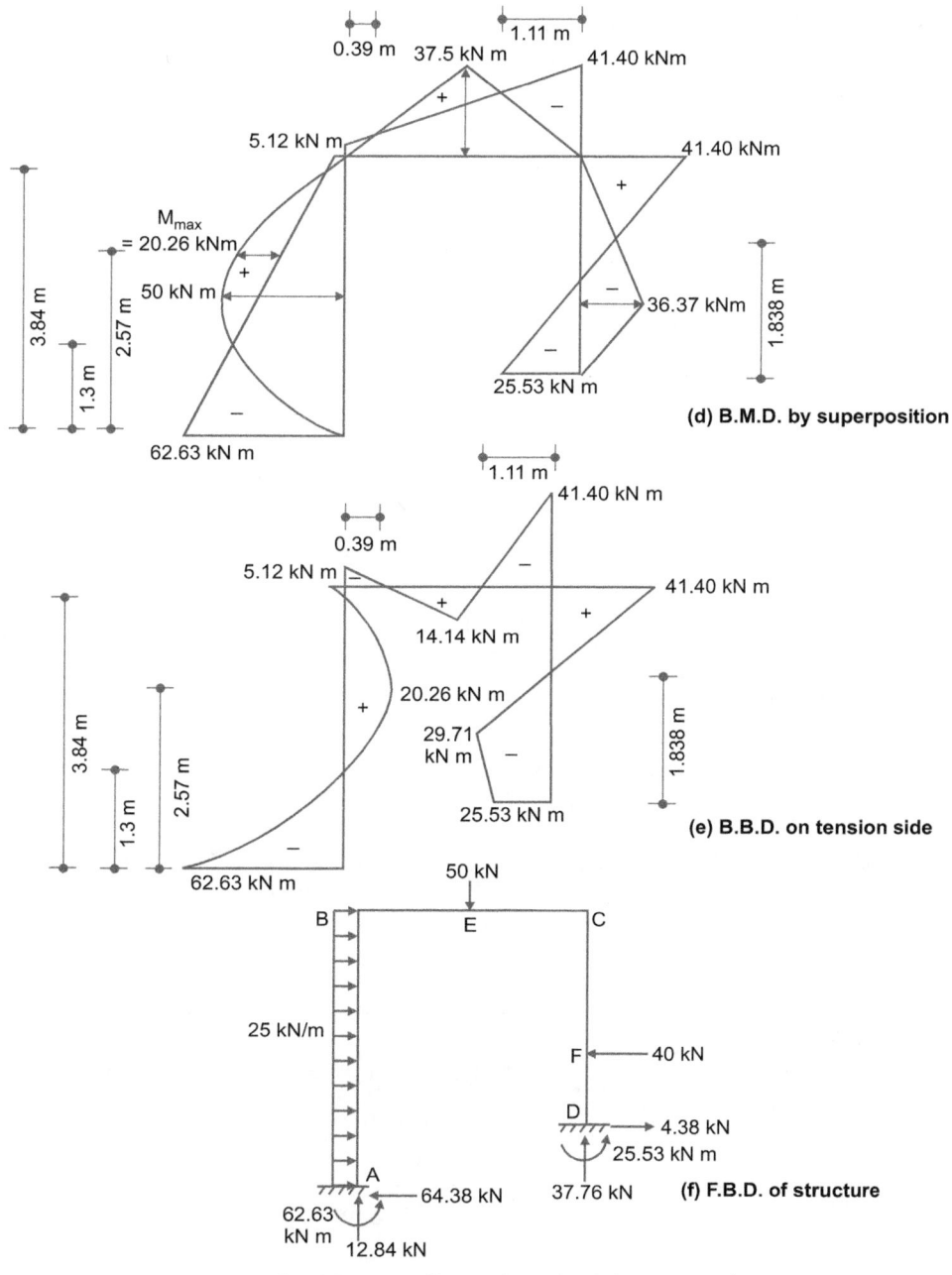

Fig. 2.24 : For Illustrative Example 2.19

STRUCTURAL ANALYSIS – II MOMENT DISTRIBUTION METHOD

Step III : MD Table (I) for non-sway moments :

Joint		A	B			C		D
Type of joint		EFS	RJ			RJ		EFS
Member		AB	BA	BC		CB	CD	DC
COF		→1/2		→1/2			→0	
		1/2←		1/2←			1/2←	
DF		0	0.43	0.57		0.5	0.5	0
First cycle	FEM	33.33	−33.33	18.75		−18.75	8.88	−17.77
	DM	−	6.27	8.31		4.94	4.94	−
Second cycle	COM	3.14	−	2.47		4.16	−	2.47
	DM	−	−1.06	−1.41		−2.08	−2.08	−
Third cycle	COM	−0.53	−	−1.04		−0.70	−	−1.04
	DM	−	0.45	0.59		0.35	0.35	−
Fourth cycle	COM	0.23	−	0.18		0.30	−	0.18
	DM	−	−0.08	−0.10		−0.15	−0.15	−
Fifth cycle	COM	−0.04	−	−0.08		−0.05	−	−0.08
	DM	−	0.03	0.05		0.03	0.03	−
First set of final moments		36.13	−27.72	27.72		−11.97	11.97	−16.24

Step IV : MD for sway moments :

(a) The basic information of K, COF and DF remains the same.

(b) Normalized relative sway stiffness factors (K_S).

Member	Relative sway stiffness factor	Normalized relative sway stiffness factor (K_S)
AB	$\dfrac{I}{4^2}$	9
DC	$\dfrac{I}{3^2}$	16

(c) Sway moments :

Member	Arbitrary relative FEM due to sway
AB	$M_{AB}^{FS} = 90$ kNm
	$M_{BA}^{FS} = 90$ kNm
DC	$M_{DC}^{FS} = 160$ kNm
	$M_{CD}^{FS} = 160$ kNm

STRUCTURAL ANALYSIS – II MOMENT DISTRIBUTION METHOD

Step V : MD Table (II) for sway moments :

Joint		A		B		C		D
Type of joint		EFS		RJ		RJ		EHS
Member		AB	BA	BC	CB	CD		DC
COF			→1/2		→1/2		→1/2	
		1/2←		1/2←		1/2←		
DF		0	0.43	0.57	0.5	0.5		0
First cycle	FEM	90	90	–	–	160		160
	DM	–	– 38.70	– 51.30	– 80	– 80		–
Second cycle	COM	– 19.35		– 40	– 25.65	–		– 40
	DM	–	17.20	– 3.66	12.83	12.83		–
Third cycle	COM	8.60		6.42	11.40	–		6.42
	DM	–	– 2.76	– 3.66	– 5.70	– 5.70		–
Fourth cycle	COM	– 1.38		– 2.85	– 1.83	–		– 2.85
	DM	–	1.23	1.62	0.92	0.92		–
Fifth cycle	COM	0.62		0.46	0.81	–		0.46
	DM	–	– 0.22	– 0.24	– 0.41	– 0.41		–
Second set of final moments		78.49	66.75	– 66.75	– 87.63	– 87.63		124.03

Let, the actual sway moments be 'C' times the above sway moments :

$$\therefore \quad M_{AB} = M_{AB}^{I} + C \cdot M_{AB}^{II} = 36.13 + C\,(78.49)$$

$$M_{BA} = M_{BA}^{I} + C \cdot M_{BA}^{I} = -27.72 + C\,(66.75)$$

$$M_{DC} = M_{DC}^{I} + C \cdot M_{DC}^{II} = -16.24 + C\,(124.03)$$

$$M_{CD} = M_{CD}^{I} + C \cdot M_{CD}^{II} = 11.97 + C\,(87.63)$$

where, C = Correction factor to be evaluated from the condition of horizontal shear equilibrium for the structure.

Step VI : Horizontal shear equilibrium :

Horizontal shear equilibrium of structure gives :

$$H_A + H_D - 25 \times 4 + 40 = 0$$

i.e. $\quad H_A + H_D - 60 = 0 \quad \ldots (A)$

where, $\quad H_A = \dfrac{M_{AB} + M_{BA}}{4} + 50$

and $\quad H_D = \dfrac{M_{DC} + M_{CD}}{3} - 26.67$

Substituting in equation (A), we get

$$\left(\dfrac{M_{AB} + M_{BA}}{4} + 50\right) + \left(\dfrac{M_{DC} + M_{CD}}{3} - 26.67\right) - 60 = 0$$

i.e. $3(M_{AB} + M_{BA}) + 4(M_{DC} + M_{CD}) - 440 = 0$

Substituting values of moments, we get

$3[36.13 + C(78.49) - 27.72 + C(66.75)]$

$\qquad\qquad + 4[-16.24 + C(124.03) + 11.97 + C(87.63)] - 440 = 0$

$C(1282.36) - 431.85 = 0$

$\Rightarrow \boxed{C = 0.337}$

Step VII : Final results : Corrected moments of second set will be obtained by multiplying these moments by C and when added to first set of moments gives net final moments.

Member	AB	BA	BC	CB	CD	DC
Corrected moments of second set	26.50	22.60	− 22.60	− 29.43	29.43	41.77
Moments of first set	36.13	− 27.72	27.72	− 11.97	11.97	− 16.24
Net final moments	62.63	− 5.12	5.12	− 41.40	41.40	25.53

Step VIII : FBD of members is as shown in Fig. 2.24 (b). Considering equilibrium of each member and of complete structure, all reaction components are found out as shown in Fig. 2.24.

Step IX : Shear force diagram is as shown in Fig. 2.24 (c).

Step X : Bending moment diagrams are as shown in Fig. 2.24 (d) and Fig. 2.24 (e).

Step XI : FBD of structure is as shown in Fig. 2.24 (f).

STRUCTURAL ANALYSIS – II   MOMENT DISTRIBUTION METHOD

Example 2.20 : *Analyse the frame shown in Fig. 2.25 (a) by MD method.*

Solution : Data : (1) The frame is supported and loaded as shown in Fig. 2.25 (a).

(2) Type of frame : Sway frame.

Object : Structural analysis.

Concepts and Equations : (1) MD technique based on normalized relative stiffness factors and distribution factors.

(2)   Normalized relative sway factor.

(3)   Shear equilibrium condition and correction factor.

Procedure :

Step I : Fixed-end moments :

Member	FEM with calculations
AB	$M^F_{AB} = 0$ $M^F_{BA} = 0$
BC	$M^F_{BC} = \dfrac{WL}{8} = \dfrac{50 \times 4}{8} = 25$ kNm $M^F_{CB} = -M^F_{BC} = -25$ kNm
DC	$M^F_{DC} = 0$ $M^F_{CD} = 0$

Step II : Distribution factors :

Joint	Member	K	ΣK	DF = $\dfrac{K}{\Sigma K}$
A	AB	–	–	0
B	BA	$\dfrac{4EI}{L} = 1$	2.5	0.4
	BC	$\dfrac{3EI}{L} = 1.5$		0.6
C	CB	–	–	1
	CD	–	–	1
D	DC	–	–	0

Ch. 2 | 2.81

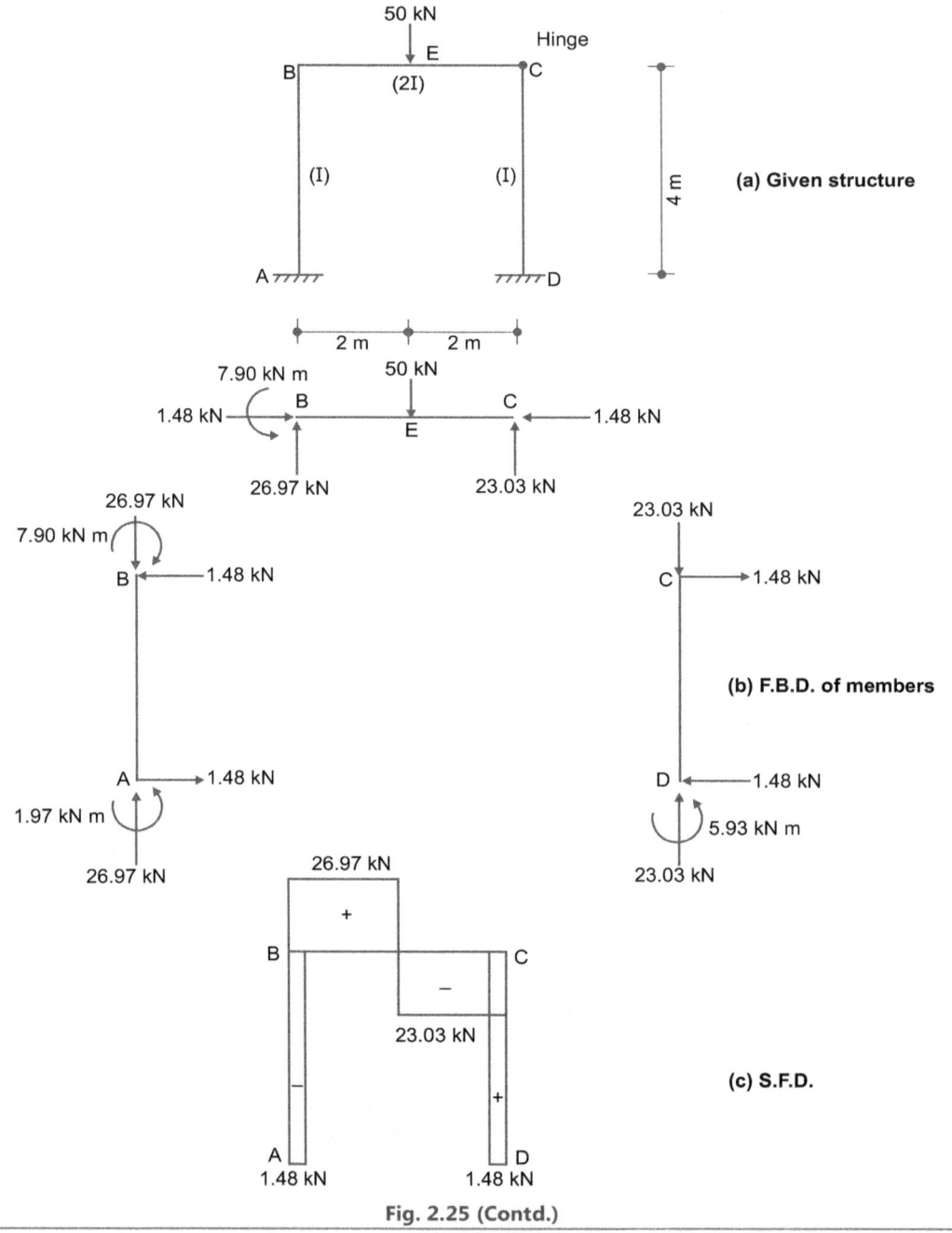

Fig. 2.25 (Contd.)

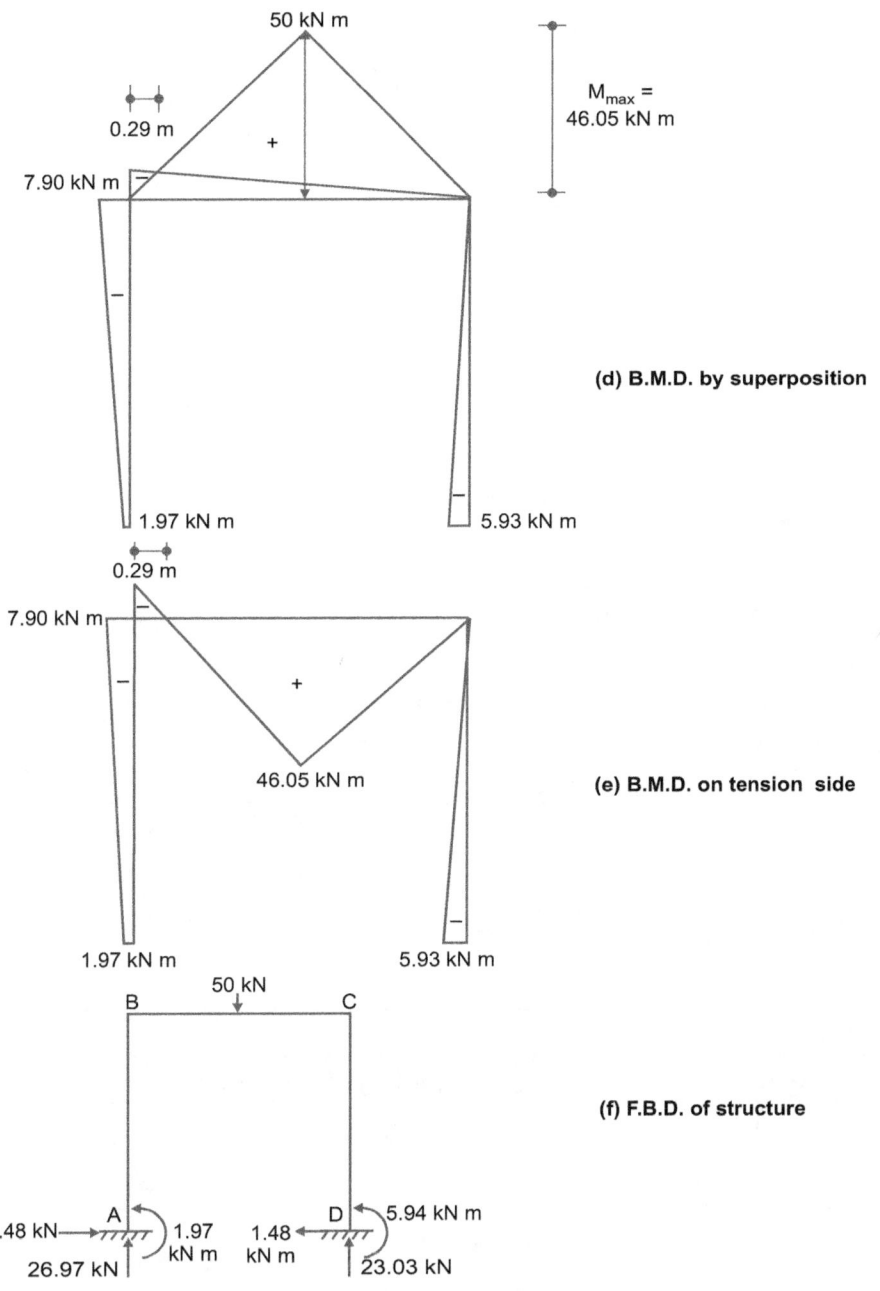

Fig. 2.25 : For Illustrative Example 2.20

STRUCTURAL ANALYSIS – II MOMENT DISTRIBUTION METHOD

Step III : MD Table (I) for non-sway moments :

Joint		A	B			C		D
Type of joint		EFS	RJ			IH		EFS
Member		AB	BA	BC		CB	CD	DC
COF			→ 1/2		→ 0		→ 1/2	
			1/2 ←		1/2 ←		0 ←	
DF		0	0.4	0.6		1	1	0
First cycle	FEM	0	0	25		−25	0	0
	DM	−	−10	−15		25		
Second cycle	COM	−5	−	12.5		−		
	DM	−	−5.0	−7.50		−		
Third cycle	COM	−2.5	−	−		−		
	DM	−	−	−		−		
First set of final moments		−7.50	−15.0	15.0		0	0	0

Step IV : MD for sway moments :

(a) The basic information of K, COF, and DF remains the same.

(b) Normalized relative sway stiffness factors (K_s).

Member	Relative sway stiffness factor	Normalized relative sway stiffness factor (K_s)
AB	$\dfrac{I}{4^2}$	1
DC	$\dfrac{I}{4^2}$	1

(c) Sway moments :

Member	Arbitrary relative FEM due to sway
AB	M_{AB}^{FS} = 100 kNm
	M_{BA}^{FS} = 100 kNm
DC	M_{DC}^{FS} = 100 kNm
	M_{CD}^{FS} = 100 kNm

STRUCTURAL ANALYSIS – II   MOMENT DISTRIBUTION METHOD

Step V : MD Table (II) for sway moments :

Joint	A		B		C		D
Type of joint	EFS		RJ		IH		EFS
Member	AB	BA		BC	CB	CD	DC
COF		$\rightarrow 1/2$		$\rightarrow 0$		$\rightarrow 1/2$	
		$1/2 \leftarrow$		$1/2 \leftarrow$		$0 \leftarrow$	
DF	0	0.4	0.6		1	1	0
First cycle FEM	100	100	0		0	100	100
DM	–	–40	–60		–	–100	–
Second cycle COM	–20	–	–		–	–	–50
DM	–	–	–		–	–	–
Second set of final moments	80	60	–60		0	0	50

Let, the actual sway moments be 'C' times the above sway moments.

$\therefore$
$$M_{AB} = M_{AB}^{I} + C \cdot M_{AB}^{II}$$
$$M_{BA} = M_{BA}^{I} + C \cdot M_{BA}^{II}$$
$$M_{DC} = M_{DC}^{I} + C \cdot M_{DC}^{II}$$

where, C = Correction factor to be evaluated from the condition of horizontal shear equilibrium of the structure.

Step VI : Horizontal shear equilibrium :

Horizontal shear equilibrium of structure gives

$$H_A + H_D = 0 \qquad \ldots(A)$$

where, $\qquad H_A = \dfrac{M_{AB} + M_{BA}}{4}$

and $\qquad H_D = \dfrac{M_{DC}}{4}$

Substituting in equation (A), we get

$$\dfrac{M_{AB} + M_{BA}}{4} + \dfrac{M_{DC}}{4} = 0$$

i.e. $\qquad M_{AB} + M_{BA} + M_{DC} = 0$

Substituting the values of moments, we get

$(-7.50) + C(80) - 15 + C(60) + C(50) = 0$

$$\boxed{C = 0.118}$$

Step VII : Final results :

Member	AB	BA	BC	CB	CD	DC
Corrected moments of second set	9.47	7.10	– 7.10	0	0	5.93
Moments of first set	– 7.50	– 15.0	15.0	0	0	0
Net final moments	1.97	– 7.90	7.90	0	0	5.93

Step VIII : FBD of members is as shown in Fig. 2.25 (b).

Considering equilibrium of each member and of complete structure, all reaction components are found out as shown in Fig. 2.25.

Step IX : Shear force diagram is as shown in Fig. 2.25 (c).

Step X : Bending moment diagrams are as shown in Fig. 2.25 (d) and Fig. 2.25 (e).

Step XI : FBD of structure is as shown in Fig. 2.25 (f).

2.8 APPLICATION OF MD METHOD TO FRAMES WITH YIELDING OF SUPPORTS

Due to yielding of supports, the moments will be developed at the ends of the members having yielding supports :

$$M_{ij}^{FY} = \frac{4 E_{ij} \cdot I_{ij}}{L_{ij}} \theta_{iy} \quad \text{and} \quad M_{ji}^{FY} = \frac{2 EI_{ij}}{L_{ij}} \theta_{iy} \quad \text{due to rotational yielding.}$$

$$M_{ij}^{FY} = \frac{6 E_{ij} I_{ij}}{L_{ij}^2} \Delta_{j/i} \quad \text{and} \quad M_{ji}^{FY} = \frac{6 EI_{ij} I_{ij}}{L_{ij}^2} \Delta_{j/i} \quad \text{due to translational yielding.}$$

These moments are considered as the restraining moments i.e. FEM in the first cycle of MD and the distribution of moments is carried out as per the routine working of MD table. Thus, the effect of yielding of supports can be independently analysed by MD method.

Otherwise combined effect of loads and yielding of supports is obtained. For this FEM due to loads and FEM due to yielding of supports are added and MD table begins with the net FEM. Rest of the procedure of MD method is same. The following example illustrates the analysis of rectangular frames due to yielding of supports.

STRUCTURAL ANALYSIS – II MOMENT DISTRIBUTION METHOD

Example 2.21 : *Analyse the frame shown in Fig. 2.26 (a) by MD method if support A sinks by 5 mm and support D undergoes anticlockwise rotation of 0.002 radians.*

Take EI = 3×10^3 kN.m²

Solution : Data :

(1) The frame is supported and loaded as shown in Fig. 2.26 (a).

(2) Δ_A = 5 mm ($\downarrow$) and θ_D = 0.002 radian.

(3) EI = 3×10^3 kNm²

(4) Type of frame : Sway frame.

Object : Structural analysis.

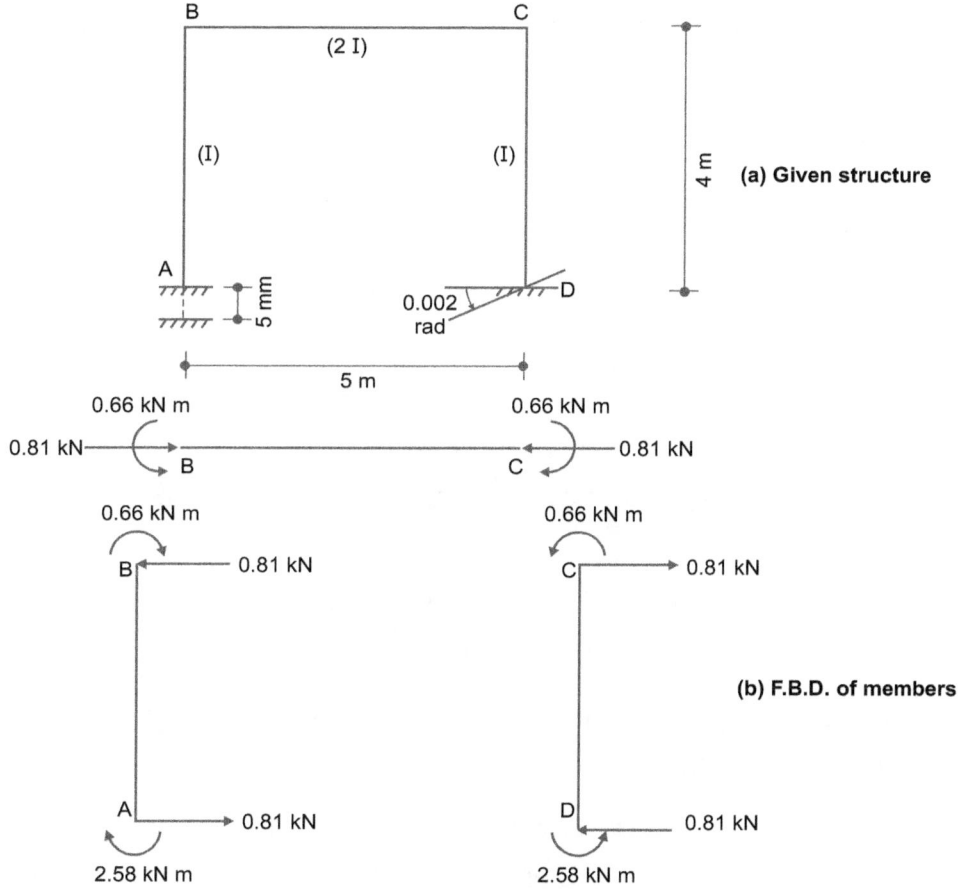

Fig. 2.26 (Contd.)

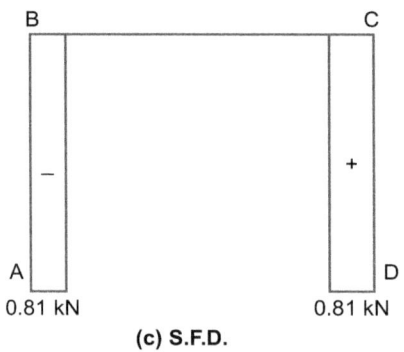

(c) S.F.D.

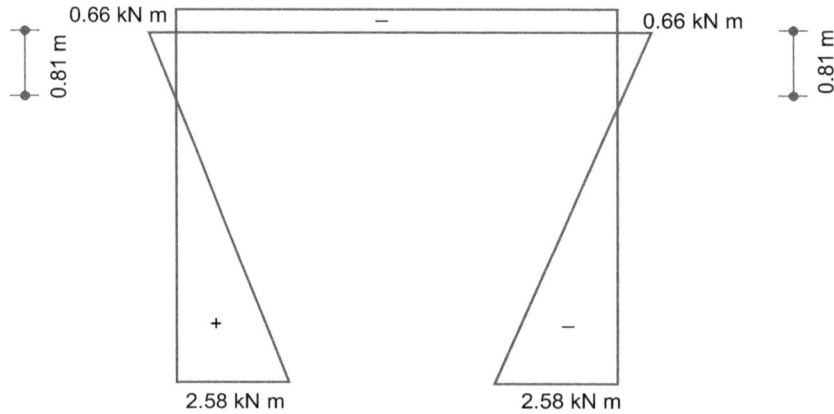

(d) B.M.D. on tension side

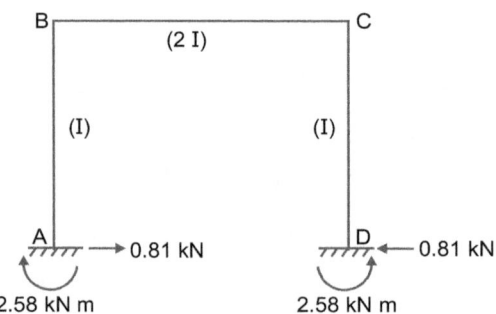

(e) F.B.D. of structure

Fig. 2.26 : For Illustrative Example 2.21

STRUCTURAL ANALYSIS – II   MOMENT DISTRIBUTION METHOD

Procedure :

Step I : Fixed-end moments :

Member	FEM with calculations		Total FEM
	FEM due to sinking of support A	**FEM due to rotation of support D**	
AB	$M^F_{AB} = 0$ $M^F_{BA} = 0$	$M^F_{AB} = 0$ $M^F_{BA} = 0$	$M^F_{AB} = 0$ $M^F_{BA} = 0$
BC	$M^F_{BC} = -6\,EI\,\Delta/L^2$ $= \dfrac{-6 \times 2 \times 3 \times 10^3 \times 0.005}{5^2}$ $= -7.2 \text{ kNm}$ $M^F_{CB} = M^F_{BC} = -7.2 \text{ kNm}$	$M^F_{BC} = 0$ $M^F_{CB} = 0$	$M^F_{BC} = 7.2 \text{ kNm}$ $M^F_{CB} = -7.2 \text{ kNm}$
DC	$M^F_{DC} = 0$ $M^F_{CD} = 0$	$M^F_{DC} = \dfrac{4\,EI\,\theta_D}{L}$ $= \dfrac{4 \times 3 \times 10^3 \times 0.002}{4}$ $= 6 \text{ kNm}$ $M^F_{CD} = \dfrac{2\,EI\theta_D}{L}$ $= 3 \text{ kNm}$	$M^F_{DC} = 6 \text{ kNm}$ $M^F_{CD} = 3 \text{ kNm}$

Step II : Distribution factors :

Joint	Member	K	ΣK	DF = $\dfrac{K}{\Sigma K}$
A	AB	–	–	0
B	BA	$\dfrac{4EI}{L} = 1$	2.6	0.38
	BC	$\dfrac{4EI}{L} = 1.6$		0.62
C	CB	$\dfrac{4EI}{L} = 1.6$	2.6	0.62
	CD	$\dfrac{4EI}{L} = 1$		0.38
D	DC	–	–	0

Step III : MD Table (I) for non-sway moments :

Joint	A		B			C		D
Type of joint	EFS		RJ			RJ		EHS
Member	AB	BA	BC		CB	CD		DC
COF		→ 1/2			→ 1/2			→ 1/2
		1/2 ←			1/2 ←			1/2 ←
DF	0	0.38	0.62		0.62	0.38		0
First cycle FEM	0	0	− 7.2		− 7.2	3.0		6.0
DM	−	2.74	4.46		2.60	1.60		−
Second cycle COM	1.37	−	1.30		2.23	−		0.80
DM	−	− 0.50	− 0.80		− 1.38	− 0.85		−
Third cycle COM	− 0.25	−	− 0.69		− 0.40	−		− 0.43
DM	−	0.26	0.43		0.25	0.15		−
Fourth cycle COM	0.13	−	0.13		0.22	−		0.08
DM	−	− 0.05	− 0.08		− 0.14	− 0.08		−
First set of final moments	1.25	2.45	− 2.45		− 3.82	3.82		6.45

Step IV : MD for sway moments :

(a) The basic information of K, COF and DF remains the same.

(b) Normalized relative sway stiffness factors (K_S).

Member	Relative sway stiffness factor	Normalized relative sway stiffness factor (K_S)
AB	$\dfrac{I}{4^2}$	1
DC	$\dfrac{I}{4^2}$	1

(c) Sway moments :

Member	Arbitrary relative FEM due to sway
AB	M_{AB}^{FS} = 100 kNm
	M_{BA}^{FS} = 100 kNm
DC	M_{DC}^{FS} = 100 kNm
	M_{CD}^{FS} = 100 kNm

STRUCTURAL ANALYSIS – II   MOMENT DISTRIBUTION METHOD

Step V : MD Table (II) for sway moments :

Joint		A	B			C		D
Type of joint		EFS	RJ			RJ		EFS
Member		AB	BA	BC		CB	CD	DC
COF			→ 1/2			→ 1/2		→ 1/2
			1/2 ←			1/2 ←		1/2 ←
DF		0	0.38	0.62		0.62	0.38	0
First cycle	FEM	100	100	0		0	100	100
	DM	–	– 38	– 62		– 62	– 38	
Second cycle	COM	– 19	–	– 31		– 31	–	– 19
	DM	–	11.78	19.22		19.22	11.78	
Third cycle	COM	5.89	–	9.61		9.61	–	5.89
	DM	–	– 3.65	– 5.96		– 5.96	– 3.65	–
Fourth cycle	COM	– 1.83	–	– 2.98		– 2.98	–	– 1.83
	DM	–	1.13	1.85		1.85	1.13	–
Fifth cycle	COM	0.57	–	0.93		0.93	–	0.57
	DM	–	– 0.35	– 0.58		– 0.58	– 0.35	–
Sixth cycle	COM	– 0.18	–	– 0.29		– 0.29	–	– 0.18
	DM	–	0.11	0.18		0.18	0.11	–
Second set of final moments		85.45	71.02	– 71.02		– 71.02	71.02	85.45

Let, the actual sway moments be 'C' times the above sway moments.

$\therefore$

$$M_{AB} = M_{AB}^{I} + C \cdot M_{AB}^{II} = 1.25 + C\,(85.45)$$

$$M_{BA} = M_{BA}^{I} + C \cdot M_{BA}^{II} = 2.45 + C\,(71.02)$$

$$M_{DC} = M_{DC}^{I} + C \cdot M_{DC}^{II} = 6.45 + C\,(85.45)$$

$$M_{CD} = M_{CD}^{I} + C \cdot M_{CD}^{II} = 3.82 + C\,(71.02)$$

where, C = Correction factor to be evaluated from the condition of horizontal shear equilibrium of the structure.

Step VI : Horizontal shear equilibrium :

Horizontal shear equilibrium of structure gives,

$$H_A + H_D = 0 \quad \ldots (A)$$

where $\quad H_A = \dfrac{M_{AB} + M_{BA}}{4}$

and $\quad H_D = \dfrac{M_{DC} + M_{CD}}{4}$

Substituting in equation (A), we get

$$M_{AB} + M_{BA} + M_{DC} + M_{CD} = 0$$

Substituting the values of moments, we get

$1.25 + C\,(85.45) + 2.45 + C\,(71.02) + 6.45 + C\,(85.45) + 3.82 + C\,(71.02) = 0$

$$\boxed{C = -0.0448}$$

Step VII : Final results :

Member	AB	BA	BC	CB	CD	DC
Corrected moments of second set	– 3.83	– 3.11	3.11	3.16	– 3.16	– 3.87
Moments of first set	1.25	2.45	– 2.45	– 3.82	3.82	6.45
Net final moments	– 2.58	– 0.66	0.66	– 0.66	0.66	2.58

Step VIII : FBD of members is as shown in Fig. 2.26 (b). Considering equilibrium of each member and of complete structure, all reaction components are found out as shown in Fig. 2.26.

Step IX : Shear force diagram is as shown in Fig. 2.26 (c).

Step X : Bending moment diagrams are as shown in Fig. 2.26 (d) and Fig. 2.26 (e).

Step XI : FBD of structure is as shown in Fig. 2.26 (f).

Example 2.22 : *Analyse the rigid frame shown in Fig. 2.27 (a) using moment distribution method.*

Solution : Data : (i) The frame is supported and loaded as shown in Fig. 2.27 (a).

(ii) Frame type : Sway frame.

STRUCTURAL ANALYSIS – II   MOMENT DISTRIBUTION METHOD

Object : Structural analysis.

Concepts and Equations :

(i)   MD technique based on normalized relative stiffness factors and distribution factors.

(ii) Normalized relative sway factors.

(iii) Shear equilibrium condition and correction factors.

Procedure :

Step I : Fixed-end moments.

Member	FEM with calculations
AB	$M_{AB}^F = 0$ $M_{BA}^F = 0$
BC	$M_{BC}^F = \dfrac{wl^2}{12} = \dfrac{30 \times 3^2}{12} = 22.5$ kN-m $M_{CB}^F = -M_{BC}^F = -22.5$ kN-m
DC	$M_{DC}^F = 0$ $M_{CD}^F = 0$

Step II : Distribution factors :

Joint	Member	K	ΣK	DF = $\dfrac{K}{\Sigma K}$
A	AB	–	–	0
B	BA	$\dfrac{4EI}{L} = \dfrac{4EI}{4}$	$\dfrac{11EI}{3}$	3/11
	BC	$\dfrac{4EI}{L} = \dfrac{4E(2I)}{3}$		8/11
C	CB	$\dfrac{4EI}{L} = \dfrac{4E(2I)}{3}$	$\dfrac{11EI}{3}$	8/11
	CD	$\dfrac{4EI}{L} = \dfrac{4EI}{4}$	$\dfrac{11EI}{3}$	3/11
D	DC	–	–	0

STRUCTURAL ANALYSIS – II   MOMENT DISTRIBUTION METHOD

Step III : MD Table (I) for non-sway moments :

Joint	A	B		C		D
Type of joint	EFS	RJ		RJ		EFS
Member	AB	BA	BC	CB	CD	DC
COF	→ 1/2 1/2 ←		→ 1/2 1/2 ←		→ 1/2 1/2 ←	
DF	0	3/11	8/11	8/11	3/11	
First cycle FEM	0	0	22.5	– 22.5	0	0
DM		– 6.14	– 16.36	16.36	6.14	
Second cycle COM	– 3.07		8.18	– 8.18		3.07
DM		– 2.23	– 5.95	5.95	2.23	
Third cycle COM	– 1.12		2.98	– 2.98		1.12
DM		– 0.81	– 2.17	2.17	+ 0.81	
Fourth cycle COM	– 0.41		1.08	– 1.08		+ 0.41
DM		– 0.29	– 0.79	0.79	0.29	
Fifth cycle COM	– 0.14		0.395	– 0.395		0.14
DM		– 0.11	– 0.285	0.285	0.11	
First set of final moments	– 4.74	– 9.58	9.58	– 9.58	9.58	4.74

Step IV : MD for sway moments :

(a) The basic information of K, COF and DF remains the same.

(b) Normalized relative sway stiffness factors $[K_S]$.

Member	Relative sway stiffness factor	Normalized relative sway stiffness factor $[K_S]$
AB	$\dfrac{I}{4^2}$	1
DC	$\dfrac{I}{4^2}$	– 1

(c) **Sway moments :**

Member	Arbitrary relative FEM due to sway
AB	$M_{AB}^{FS} = 100$ $M_{BA}^{FS} = 100$
DC	$M_{DC}^{FS} = -100$ $M_{CD}^{FS} = -100$

STRUCTURAL ANALYSIS – II   MOMENT DISTRIBUTION METHOD

Step V : MD Table II : For sway moments :

Joint		A		B		C		D
Type of joint		EFS		RJ		RJ		EHS
Member		AB	BA	BC	CB	CD		DC
COF		$\rightarrow 1/2$ $1/2 \leftarrow$		$\rightarrow 1/2$ $1/2 \leftarrow$		$\rightarrow 1/2$ $1/2 \leftarrow$		
DF			3/11	8/11	8/11	3/11		
First cycle	FEM	100	100	0	0	– 100		– 100
	DM		– 27.27	– 72.73	72.73	27.27		
Second cycle	COM	– 13.365		36.365	– 36.365			13.365
	DM		– 9.92	– 26.445	26.445	9.92		
Third cycle	COM	– 4.96		13.22	– 13.22			4.96
	DM		– 3.605	– 9.615	9.615	3.605		
Fourth cycle	COM	– 1.802		+ 4.808	– 4.808			–1.802
	DM		– 1.31	– 3.498	3.498	+ 1.31		
Fifth cycle	COM	– 0.655		1.749	– 1.749			0.655
	DM		– 0.477	– 1.272	1.272	0.477		
Second set of final moments		79.218	57.418	– 57.418	57.418	– 57.418		– 79.218

$$M_{AB} = M_{AB}^{I} + C\, M_{AB}^{II} = -4.74 + C \times 79.218$$
$$M_{BA} = M_{BA}^{I} + C\, M_{BA}^{II} = -9.58 + C \times 57.418$$
$$M_{CD} = M_{CD}^{I} + C\, M_{CD}^{II} = 9.58 - C \times 57.418$$
$$M_{DC} = M_{DC}^{I} + C\, M_{DC}^{II} = 4.74 - C \times 79.218$$

where C is a correction factor to be evaluated from the condition of horizontal shear equilibrium for structure.

Step VI : Horizontal shear equilibrium.

Horizontal shear equilibrium gives :

$$H_A - H_D = 0$$
$$H_A = \frac{M_{AB} + M_{BA}}{4}$$
$$H_D = \frac{M_{CD} + M_{DC}}{4}$$
$$M_{AB} + M_{BA} - M_{CD} - M_{DC} = 0$$
$$-4.74 + C \times 79.218 - 9.58 + C \times 57.418$$
$$-9.58 + C \times 57.418 - 4.74 + C \times 79.218 = 0$$
$$273.272\,C = 28.64$$
$$\therefore \quad C = 0.105$$

STRUCTURAL ANALYSIS – II   MOMENT DISTRIBUTION METHOD

Step VII : Corrected moments of second set will be obtained by multiplying these moments by C and then added to first set of moments gives net final moments.

Member	AB	BA	BC	CB	CD	DC
Corrected moments of second set	8.32	6.03	– 6.03	6.03	– 6.03	– 8.32
Moments of first set	– 4.74	– 9.58	9.58	– 9.58	9.58	4.74
Net final moments	3.58	– 3.55	3.55	– 3.55	3.55	– 3.58

Step VIII : FBD of members is as shown in Fig. 2.27 (b). Considering equilibrium of each member and of complete structure all the reaction components are found out as shown in Fig. 2.27.

Step IX : Shear force diagram is as shown in Fig. 2.27 (c).

Step X : Bending moment diagrams are as shown in Fig. 2.27 (d) and Fig. 2.27 (e).

Step XI : FBD of structure is as shown in Fig. 2.27 (f).

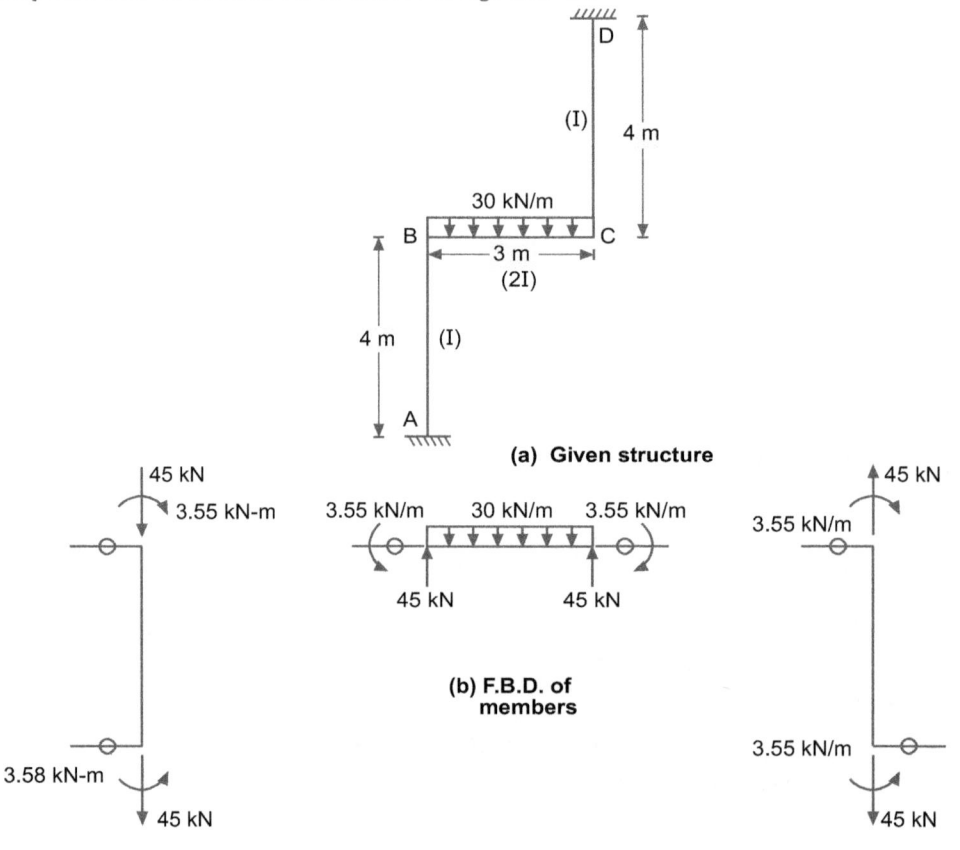

(a) Given structure

(b) F.B.D. of members

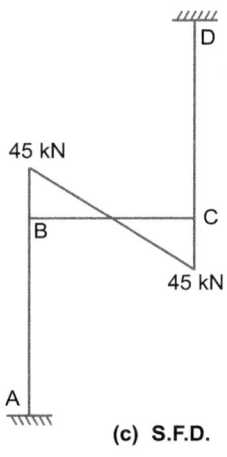

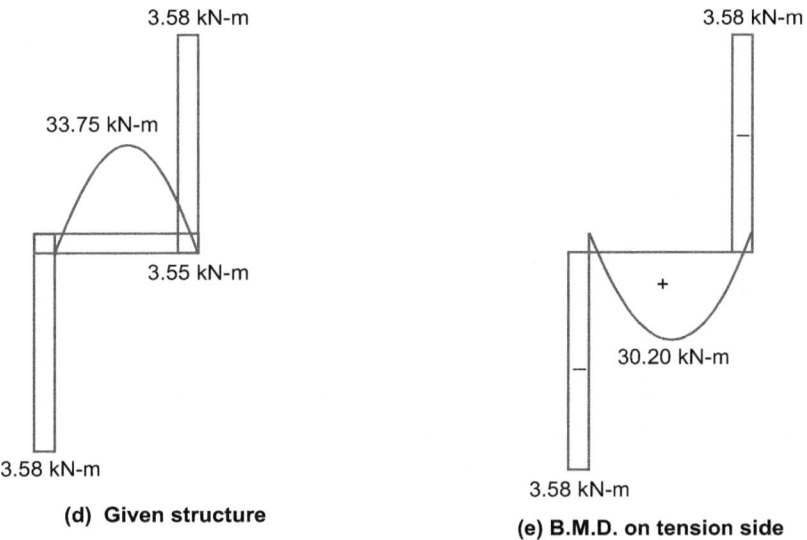

(d) Given structure   (e) B.M.D. on tension side

Fig. 2.27 : For Illustrative Example 2.22

Example 2.23 : A rectangular portal frame is hinged at support A and fixed at support D. AB = CD = 4 m and BC = 5 m. It carries UDL of 2.5 kN/m on horizontal member BC and a horizontal concentrated load of 50 kN on AB towards CD at 3 m from support A. If $I_{AB} = I_{CD} = 0.5\ I_{BC}$, find the moments at B, C and D and draw the BMD. Use moment distribution method only. Use five cycles of iteration for distribution of moments.

STRUCTURAL ANALYSIS – II   MOMENT DISTRIBUTION METHOD

Solution : Data : (1) The frame is supported and loaded as shown in Fig. 2.28 (a).

(2) Type of frame : Sway frame.

Object : Structural analysis.

Concepts and Equations : (1) MD technique based on normalized relative stiffness factors and distribution factors.

(2) Normalized relative sway factors.

(3) Shear equilibrium condition and correction factors.

Procedure :

Step I : Fixed-end moments :

Member	FEM with calculations
AB	$M^F_{AB} = \dfrac{wab^2}{l^2} = \dfrac{50 \times 3 \times 1^2}{4^2} = 9.375$ kN-m $M^F_{BA} = -\dfrac{wa^2b}{l^2} = -\dfrac{50 \times 3^2 \times 1}{4^2} = -28.125$ kN-m
BC	$M^F_{BC} = \dfrac{2.5 \times 5^2}{12} = 5.21$ kN-m $M^F_{CB} = -5.21$ kN-m
CD	$M^F_{CD} = 0$ $M^F_{DC} = 0$

Step II : Distribution factors :

Joint	Member	K	ΣK	$DF = \dfrac{K}{\Sigma K}$
A	AB	–	–	0
B	BA	$\dfrac{3\,EI}{L} = \dfrac{3\,EI}{4}$	$\dfrac{23\,EI}{20}$	$\dfrac{15}{23}$
	BC	$\dfrac{4\,EI}{L} = \dfrac{4\,EI\,(0.5\,I)}{5}$		$\dfrac{8}{23}$
C	CB	$\dfrac{4\,EI}{L} = \dfrac{4\,E\,(0.5\,I)}{5}$	$\dfrac{7\,EI}{5}$	$\dfrac{2}{7}$
	CD	$\dfrac{4\,EI}{L} = \dfrac{4\,EI}{4}$		$\dfrac{5}{7}$
D	DC	–	–	0

STRUCTURAL ANALYSIS – II   MOMENT DISTRIBUTION METHOD

Step III : MD Table (I) for non-sway moments :

Joint		A	B		C		D
Type of joint		EHS	RJ		RJ		EFS
Member		AB	BA	BC	CB	CD	DC
COF			→ 1/2	→ 1/2		→ 1/2	
			0 ←	1/2 ←		1/2 ←	
DF		0	15/23	8/23	2/7	5/7	0
First cycle	FEM	9.375	– 28.125	5.21	– 5.21	0	0
	DM	– 9.375	14.94	7.97	1.49	3.72	
Second cycle	COM		– 4.69	0.75	3.99		1.86
	DM		2.57	1.37	– 1.14	– 2.85	
Third cycle	COM			– 0.57	0.69		– 1.43
	DM		0.37	0.20	– 0.20	– 0.49	
Fourth cycle	COM			– 0.1	0.1		– 0.25
	DM		0.065	0.035	– 0.029	– 0.071	
Fifth cycle	COM			– 0.015	0.017		– 0.035
	DM		0.009	0.005	– 0.005	0.012	
First set of final moments			– 14.86	14.86	– 0.30	0.30	0.14

Step IV : MD for sway moments :

(a) The basic information of K, COF and DF remains the same.
(b) Normalized relative sway stiffness factors (K_S).

Member	Relative sway stiffness factor	Normalized relative sway stiffness factor (K_S)
AB	$\dfrac{I}{4^2}$	1
DC	$\dfrac{I}{4^2}$	1

(c) Sway moments :

Member	Arbitrary relative FEM due to sway
AB	M_{AB}^{FS} = 100 kN-m M_{BA}^{FS} = 100 kN-m
DC	M_{DC}^{FS} = 100 kN-m M_{CD}^{FS} = 100 kN-m

Step V : MD Table (II) for sway moments.

Joint	A	B		C		D
Type of joint	EHS	RJ		RJ		EFS
Member	AB	BA	BC	CB	CD	DC
COF		→ 1/2 0 ←		→ 1/2 1/2 ←		→ 1/2 1/2 ←
DF	0	15/23	8/23	2/7	5/7	
First cycle FEM	100	100	0	0	100	100
DM	− 100	− 65.22	− 34.78	− 28.57	− 71.43	
Second cycle COM		− 50	− 14.28	− 17.39		− 35.72
DM		41.92	22.36	4.97	12.42	
Third cycle COM			2.49	11.18		6.21
DM		− 1.63	− 0.86	− 3.19	− 7.99	
Fourth cycle COM			− 1.6	− 0.43		− 4.0
DM		1.04	0.56	0.12	0.31	
Fifth cycle COM			0.06	0.28		0.15
DM		− 0.039	− 0.021	− 0.08	− 0.2	
First set of final moments		26.07	− 26.07	− 33.11	33.11	66.64

$$M_{AB} = M_{AB}^I + C\, M_{AB}^{II} = 0$$

$$M_{BA} = M_{BA}^I + C\, M_{BA}^{II} = -14.86 + C \times 26.07$$

$$M_{CD} = M_{CD}^I + C\, M_{CD}^{II} = 0.30 + C \times 33.11$$

$$M_{DC} = M_{DC}^I + C\, M_{DC}^{II} = 0.18 + C \times 66.64$$

where C is a correction factor to be evaluated from the condition of horizontal shear equilibrium for structure.

Step VI : Horizontal shear equilibrium.

Horizontal shear equilibrium of structure gives :

$$H_A + H_D - 50 = 0$$

$$H_A = \frac{M_{AB} + M_{BA}}{4} + 50$$

$$H_D = \frac{M_{CD} + M_{DC}}{4}$$

$$\therefore M_{AB} + M_{BA} + 50 + M_{CD} + M_{DC} - 200 = 0$$

$$-14.86 + C \times 26.07 + 0.3 + C \times 33.11 + 0.18 + C \times 66.64 = 150$$

$$125.82\, C = 164.38$$

$$C = 1.31$$

STRUCTURAL ANALYSIS – II   MOMENT DISTRIBUTION METHOD

Step VII : Corrected moments of second set will be obtained by multiplying these moments by C and then added to first set of moments gives net final moments.

Member	AB	BA	BC	CB	CD	DC
Corrected moments of second set	0	34.15	– 34.15	– 43.3	43.31	87.29
Moments of first set	0	– 14.86	14.86	– 0.30	0.30	– 0.14
Net final moments		19.29	– 19.29	– 43.60	43.67	87.15

Step VIII : FBD of members is as shown in Fig. 2.28 (b). Considering equilibrium of each member and of complete structure all the reaction components are found out as shown in Fig. 2.28.

Step IX : Shear force diagram is as shown in Fig. 2.28 (c).

Step X : Bending moment diagrams are as shown in Fig. 2.28 (d) and Fig. 2.28 (e).

Step XI : FBD of structure is as shown in Fig. 2.28 (f).

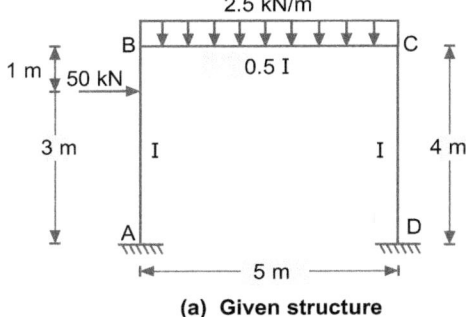

(a) Given structure

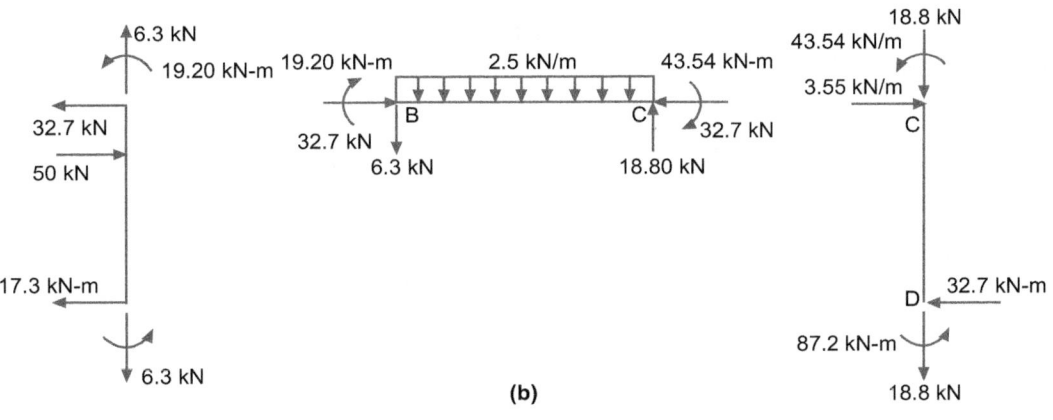

(b)

Ch. 2 | 2.101

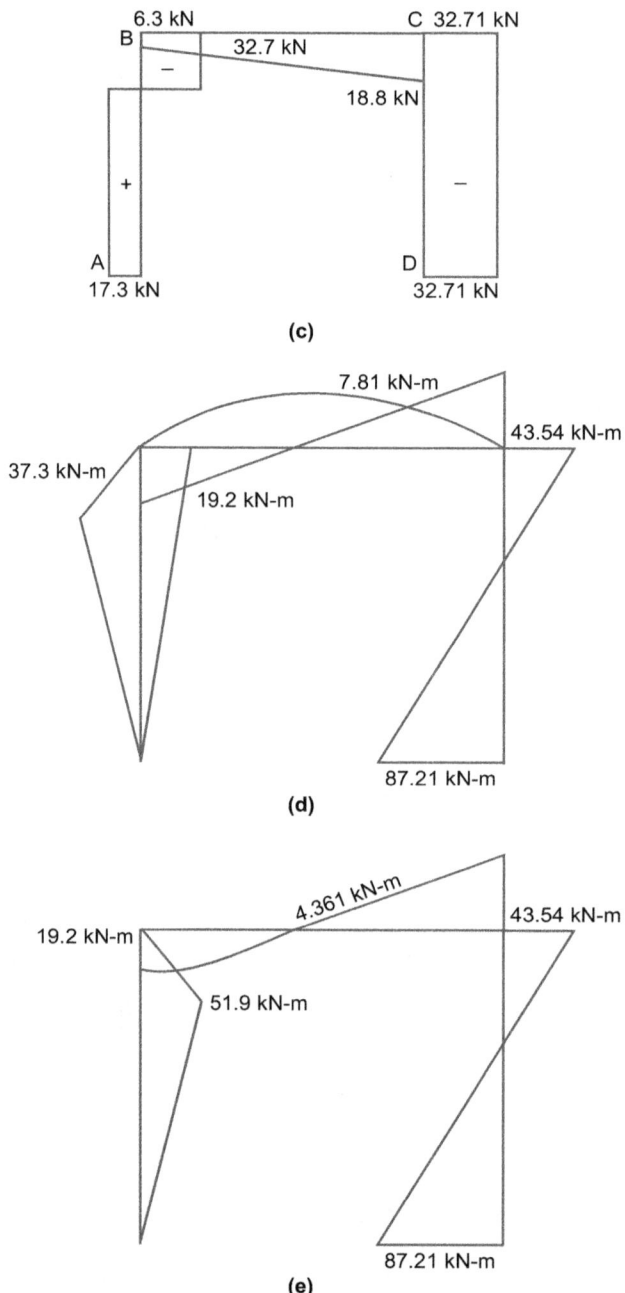

STRUCTURAL ANALYSIS – II MOMENT DISTRIBUTION METHOD

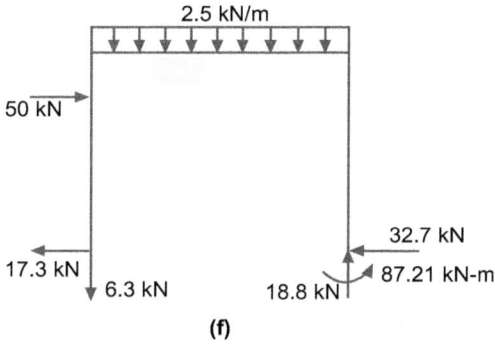

(f)

Fig. 2.28 : For Illustrative Example 2.23

Example 2.24 : *The frame loaded as shown in Fig. 2.29 (a) has members AB, BC and CD with flexural rigidities EI = 60×10^3 kN-m², 40×10^3 kN-m² and 90×10^3 kN-m² respectively. Analyse the frame by slope-deflection method.*

Data : The frame is supported and loaded as shown in Fig. 2.29 (a).

Type of frame : Sway frame.

Object : Structural analysis.

Concepts and Equations : (1) M_D technique based on normalized relative stiffness factors and distribution factors,

(2) Normalized relative sway factors,

(3) Shear equilibrium condition and correction factors.

Procedure :

Step I : Fixed-end moments :

Member	FEM with calculations					
AB	M^F_{AB}	= 0				
	M^F_{BA}	= 0				
BC	M^F_{BC}	$= \dfrac{wab^2}{l^2}$	$+ \dfrac{w \times l^2}{12}$	$= \dfrac{50 \times 1 \times 3^2}{4^2}$	$+ \dfrac{20 \times 4^2}{12}$	= 54.79 kN-m
	M^F_{CB}	$= -\dfrac{wa^2b}{l^2}$	$- \dfrac{wl^2}{12}$	$= -\dfrac{50 \times 1^2 \times 3}{4^2}$	$- \dfrac{20 \times 4^2}{12}$	= – 36.04 kN-m
DC	M^F_{DC}	= 0				
	M^F_{CD}	= 0				

STRUCTURAL ANALYSIS – II MOMENT DISTRIBUTION METHOD

Step II : Distribution factors :

Joint	Member	K	ΣK	$DF = \dfrac{K}{\Sigma K}$
A	AB	–	–	0
B	BA	$\dfrac{4EI}{L} = \dfrac{4E(1.5I)}{5}$		$\dfrac{6}{11}$
	BC	$\dfrac{4EI}{L} = \dfrac{4EI}{4}$	$\dfrac{44}{20} EI$	$\dfrac{5}{11}$
C	CB	$\dfrac{4EI}{L} = \dfrac{4EI}{4}$		$\dfrac{20}{47}$
	CD	$\dfrac{3EI}{L} = \dfrac{3E(2.25I)}{5}$	$\dfrac{47}{20} EI$	$\dfrac{27}{47}$
D	DC	–	–	

Step III : MD Table (I) for non-sway moments :

Joint		A	B		C		D
Type of joint		EFS	RJ		RJ		EFS
Member		AB	BA	BC	CB	CD	DC
COF			$\rightarrow 1/2$		$\rightarrow 1/2$		$\rightarrow 1/2$
			$1/2 \leftarrow$		$1/2 \leftarrow$		$1/2 \leftarrow$
DF		0	6/11	5/11	20/47	27/47	
First cycle	FEM			54.79	–36.04		
	DM		–29.89	–24.9	15.34	20.70	
Second cycle	COM	–14.945		7.67	–12.45		
	DM		–4.18	–3.49	5.29	7.16	
Third cycle	COM	–2.09		2.645	–1.745		
	DM		–1.44	–1.205	0.74	1.005	
Fourth cycle	COM	–0.72		0.37	–0.602		
	DM		–0.20	–0.17	0.26	0.342	
Fifth cycle	COM	–0.10		0.13	–0.085		
	DM		–0.071	–0.059	0.036	0.049	
First set of final moments		–17.855	–35.781	35.781	–29.256	29.256	

Step IV : MD for sway moments.

(a) The basic information of K, COF and DF remains the same.

(b) Normalized relative sway stiffness factors (K_S).

STRUCTURAL ANALYSIS – II   MOMENT DISTRIBUTION METHOD

Member	Relative sway stiffness factor	Normalized relative sway stiffness factor [K_S]
AB	$\dfrac{1.5\,I}{5^2}$	1.5
DC	$\dfrac{2.25\,I}{5^2}$	2.25

Step V : Sway moments :

Member	Arbitrary relative FEM due to sway
AB	$M_{AB}^{FS} = 60$ kN-m
	$M_{BA}^{FS} = 60$ kN-m
DC	$M_{DC}^{FS} = 90$ kN-m
	$M_{CD}^{FS} = 90$ kN-m

Step VI :   MD Table II for sway moments :

Joint		A	B		C		D
Type of joint		EFS	RJ		RJ		EFS
Member		AB	BA	BC	CB	CD	DC
COF			→ 1/2		→ 1/2		→ 1/2
		1/2 ←		1/2 ←		1/2 ←	
DF		0	6/11	5/11	20/47	27/47	0
First cycle	FEM	60	60	0	0	90	90
	DM		– 32.72	– 27.28	– 38.29	– 51.71	– 90
Second cycle	COM	– 16.36		– 19.15	– 13.64	– 45	
	DM		10.45	8.7	24.96	33.69	
Third cycle	COM	5.22		12.48	4.35		
	DM		– 6.81	– 5.67	– 1.85	– 2.5	
Fourth cycle	COM	– 3.41		– 0.92	– 2.83		
	DM		0.50	0.42	1.2	1.63	
Fifth cycle	COM	0.25		0.6	0.21		
	DM		– 0.33	– 0.27	– 0.089	– 0.121	
Second set of final moments		45.7	31.09	– 31.09	– 25.99	25.99	0

$$M_{AB} = M_{AB}^{I} + C\,M_{AB}^{II}$$
$$M_{BA} = M_{BA}^{I} + C\,M_{BA}^{II}$$
$$M_{CD} = M_{CD}^{I} + C\,M_{CD}^{II}$$
$$M_{DC} = M_{DC}^{I} + C\,M_{DC}^{II}$$

where C is a correction factor to be obtained from shear equilibrium equations developed as follows.

Step VII : Shear equilibrium condition : Horizontal shear equilibrium gives :

$$H_A + H_D = 0$$

$$\frac{M_{AB} + M_{BA}}{5} + \frac{M_{CD} + M_{DC}}{5} = 0$$

$$M_{AB} + M_{BA} + M_{CD} + M_{DC} = 0$$

$$-17.855 + C \times 45.7 - 35.781 + C \times 31.09 + 29.256 + 25.99\,C = 0$$

$$102.78\,C = 24.38$$

$$C = 0.237$$

Step VIII : Corrected moments of second set will be obtained by multiplying these moments by C and then added to first set of moments gives net final moments.

Member	AB	BA	BC	CB	CD	DC
Corrected moments of second set	10.83	7.37	– 7.37	– 6.16	6.16	0
Moments of first set	– 17.855	– 35.781	35.781	– 29.256	29.256	0
Net final moments	– 7.02	– 28.41	28.41	– 35.416	35.416	0

Step IX : FBD of members is as shown in Fig. 2.29 (b). Considering equilibrium of each member and of complete structure all the reaction components are found out as shown in figure.

Step X : Shear force diagram is as shown in Fig. 2.29 (c).

Step XI : Bending moment diagrams are as shown in Fig. 2.29 (d) and Fig. 2.29 (e).

Step XII : FBD of structure is as shown in Fig. 2.29 (f).

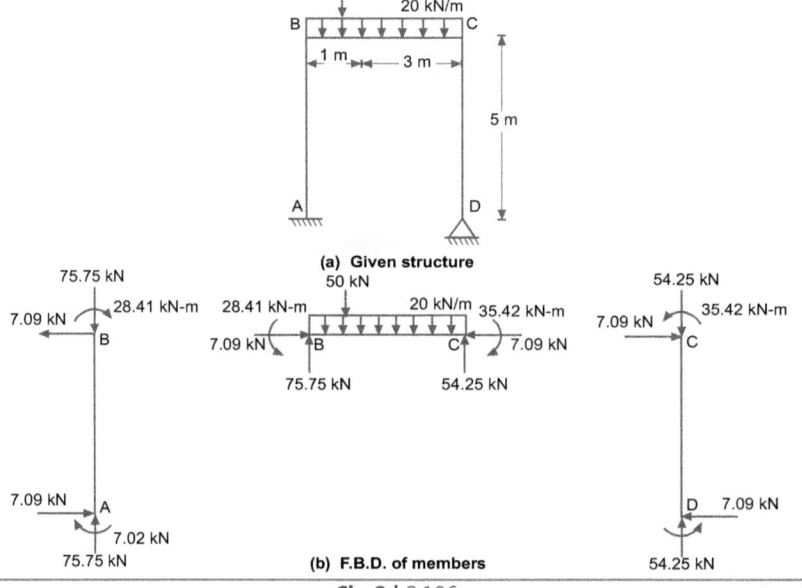

(a) Given structure

(b) F.B.D. of members

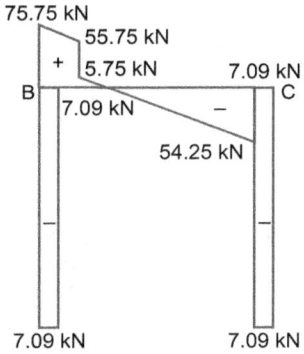

(c) S.F.D.

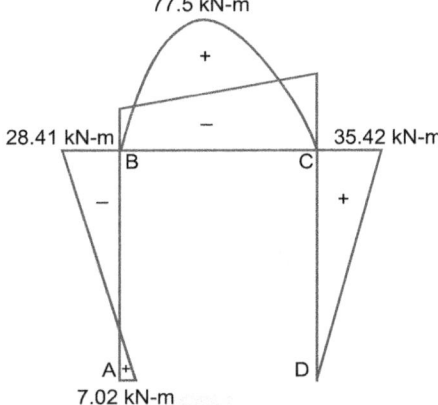

(d) B.M.D. by superposition

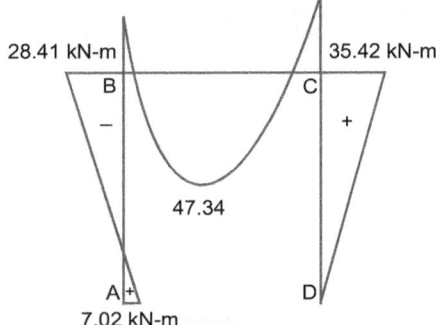

(e) B.M.D. on tension side

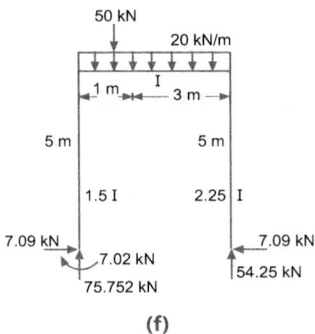

(f)

Fig. 2.29 : For Illustrative Example 2.24

Example 2.25 : Analyse the portal frame shown in Fig. 2.30 (a). All members have the same flexural rigidities.

Solution : Step I : Fixed-end moments :

Member	FEM with calculations
AB	$M^F_{AB} = 0$ $M^F_{BA} = 0$
BC	$M^F_{BC} = \dfrac{wl^2}{12} = \dfrac{30 \times 4^2}{12} = 40$ kN-m $M^F_{CB} = -\dfrac{30 \times 4^2}{12} = -40$ kN-m
DC	$M^F_{DC} = 0$ $M^F_{CD} = 0$

Step II : Distribution factors :

Joint	Member	K	Σ K	DF = $\dfrac{K}{\Sigma K}$
A	AB	–	–	0
B	BA	$\dfrac{3\,EI}{L} = \dfrac{3\,EI}{6} = \dfrac{EI}{2}$	$\dfrac{3}{2}$ I	$\dfrac{1}{3}$
	BC	$\dfrac{4\,EI}{L} = \dfrac{4\,EI}{4} = EI$		$\dfrac{2}{3}$
C	CB	$\dfrac{4\,EI}{L} = \dfrac{4\,EI}{4} = EI$	2 EI	$\dfrac{1}{2}$
	CD	$\dfrac{3\,EI}{L} = \dfrac{3\,EI}{3} = \dfrac{EI}{3}$		$\dfrac{1}{2}$
D	DC	–	–	–

STRUCTURAL ANALYSIS – II   MOMENT DISTRIBUTION METHOD

Step III : MD Table (I) for non-sway moments :

Joint		A		B		C		D
Type of joint		EFS		RJ		RJ		EFS
Member		AB	BA	BC	CB	CD		DC
COF			$\rightarrow 1/2$		$\rightarrow 1/2$		$\rightarrow 1/2$	
			$1/2 \leftarrow$		$1/2 \leftarrow$		$1/2 \leftarrow$	
DF		0	1/3	2/3	1/2	1/2		
First cycle	FEM	0	0	40	– 40	0		0
	DM		– 13.33	– 26.67	20	20		
Second cycle	COM	–		10	– 13.33			–
	DM		– 3.33	– 6.67	6.67	6.67		
Third cycle	COM	–		3.33	– 3.33			–
	DM		– 1.11	– 2.22	+ 1.67	1.67		
Fourth cycle	COM	–		0.84	– 1.11			–
	DM		– 0.28	– 0.56	– 0.55	+ 0.55		
Fifth cycle	COM	–		0.27	– 0.28			–
	DM		– 0.09	– 0.18	0.14	0.14		
First set of final moments		0	– 18.14	18.14	– 29.02	29.02		0

Step IV : MD for sway moments :

(a) The basic information of K, COF and DF remains the same.

(b) Normalized relative sway stiffness factors [K_S].

Member	Relative sway stiffness factor	Normalized relative sway stiffness factor [K_S]
AB	$\dfrac{I}{6^2}$	9
DC	$\dfrac{I}{3^2}$	36

(c) Sway moments :

Member	Arbitrary relative FEM due to sway
AB	$M_{AB}^{FC} = 9$ $M_{BA}^{FC} = 9$
DC	$M_{DC}^{FS} = 36$ $M_{CD}^{FS} = 36$

Ch. 2 | 2.109

STRUCTURAL ANALYSIS – II — MOMENT DISTRIBUTION METHOD

Step V : MD Table (II) for sway moments.

Joint		A	B			C		D
Type of joint		EFS	RJ			RJ		EHS
Member		AB	BA	BC		CB	CD	DC
COF			→ 1/2 1/2 ←			→ 1/2 1/2 ←		→ 1/2 1/2 ←
DF			1/3	2/3		1/2	1/2	
First cycle	FEM	9	9	0		0	36	36
	DM	−9	−3	−6		−18	−18	−36
Second cycle	COM		−4.5	−9		−3	−18	
	DM		4.5	9		10.5	10.5	
Third cycle	COM			5.25		4.5		
	DM		−1.75	−3.5		−2.25	−2.25	
Fourth cycle	COM			−1.13		−1.75		
	DM		0.38	0.75		0.88	0.88	
Fifth cycle	COM			0.44		0.37		
	DM		−0.15	−0.29		−0.19	−0.19	
Second set of final moments			4.48	−4.48		−8.94	8.94	0

$$M_{AB} = M^I_{AB} + C\, M^{II}_{AB} = 0$$

$$M_{BA} = M^I_{BA} + C\, M^{II}_{BA} = -18.14 + C \times 4.48$$

$$M_{CD} = M^I_{CD} + C\, M^{II}_{CD} = 29.02 + C \times 8.94$$

$$M_{DC} = M^I_{DC} + C\, M^{II}_{DC} = 0$$

where C is a correction factor to be evaluated from the condition of horizontal shear equilibrium for structure.

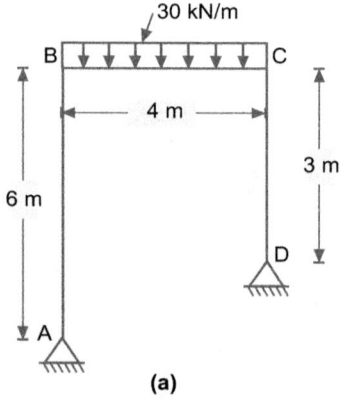

(a)

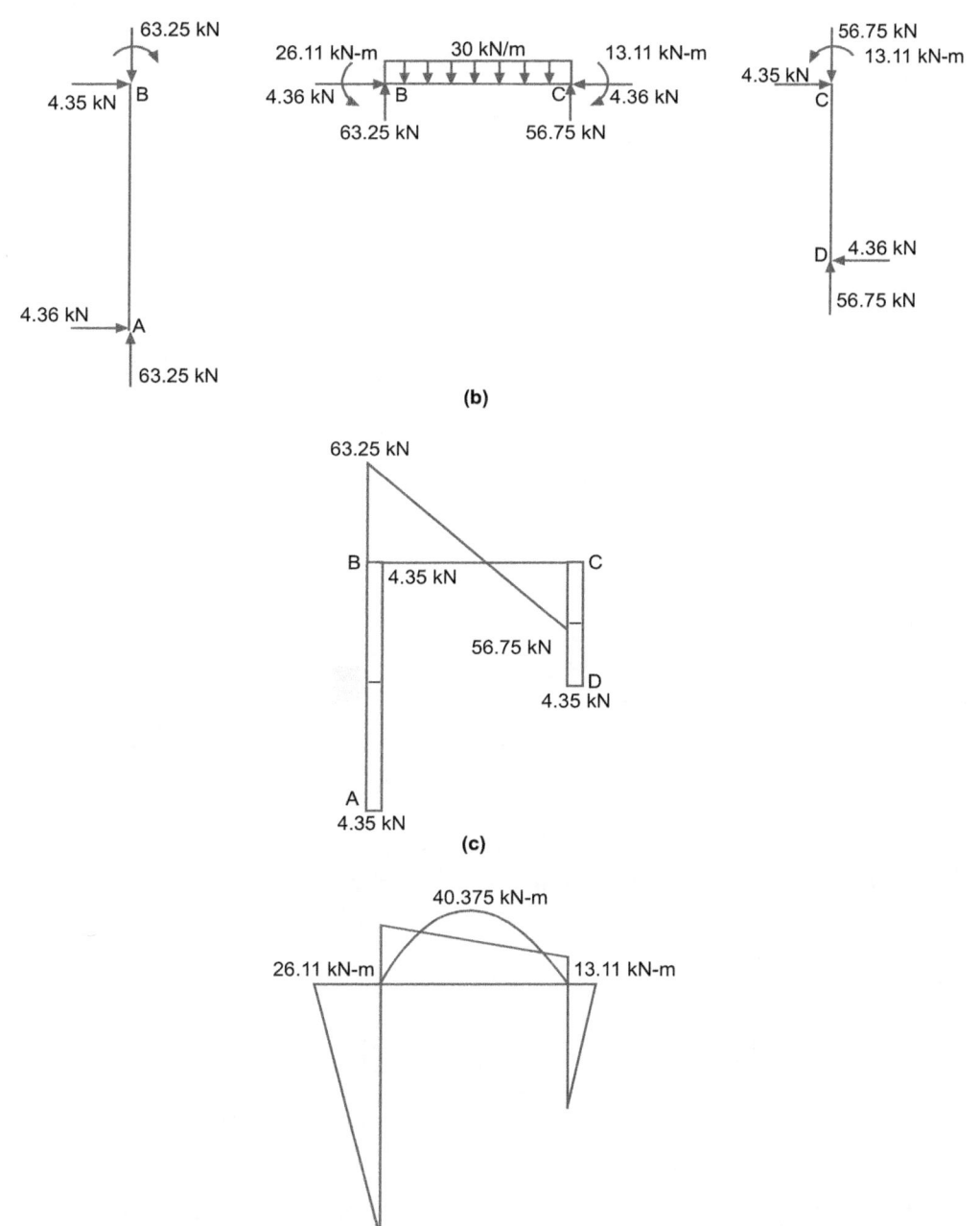

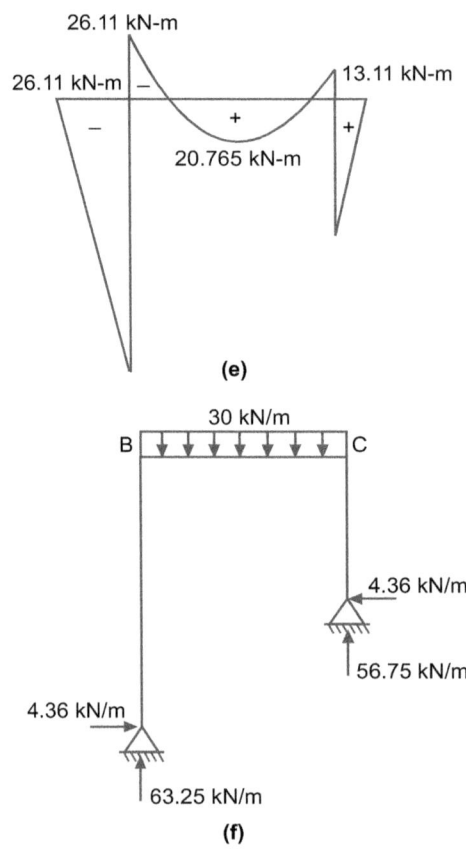

Fig. 2.30 : For Illustrative Example 2.25

Step VI : Horizontal shear equilibrium of structure gives :

$$-H_A + H_D = 0$$

$$\frac{M_{AB} + M_{BA}}{6} + \frac{M_{CD} + M_{DC}}{3} = 0$$

$$M_{BA} + 2 M_{CD} = 0$$

$$-18.14 + C \times 4.48 + (29.02 + 8.94\, C) \times 2 = 0$$

$$22.36\, C = -39.9$$

$$C = -1.784$$

Step VII : Corrected moments of second set will be obtained by multiplying these moments by C and then add to first set of moments gives net final moments.

STRUCTURAL ANALYSIS – II   MOMENT DISTRIBUTION METHOD

Member	AB	BA	BC	CB	CD	DC
Corrected moments of second set		− 8.09	8.09	+ 15.94	− 15.94	
Moments of first set	0	− 18.14	18.14	− 29.02	29.02	
Net final moments		− 26.14	26.14	− 13.08	13.08	

Step VIII : FBD of members is as shown in Fig. 2.30 (b). Considering equilibrium of each member and of complete structure all the reaction components are found out as shown in Fig. 2.30.

Step IX : Shear force diagram is as shown in Fig. 2.30 (c).

Step X : Bending moment diagrams are as shown in Fig. 2.30 (d) and Fig. 2.30 (e).

Step XI : FBD of structure is as shown in Fig. 2.30 (f).

Example 2.26 : *Analyse the frame shown in Fig. 2.31 (a).*

Data : The frame is supported and loaded as shown in Fig. 2.31 (a).

Type of frame : Sway frame.

Object : Structural analysis.

Concepts and Equations : (1) MD technique based on normalized relative stiffness factors and distribution factors, (2) Normalized relative sway factors, (iii) Shear equilibrium condition and correction factor procedure.

Solution : Step I : Fixed-end moments :

Member	FEM with calculations
AB	$M^F_{AB} = 0$ $M^F_{BA} = 0$
BC	$M^F_{BC} = \dfrac{2.5 \times 4^2}{12} = 3.33$ kN-m $M^F_{CB} = -\dfrac{2.5 \times 4^2}{12} = -3.33$ kN-m
DC	$M^F_{DC} = \dfrac{5 \times 1.5 \times 3.5^2}{5^2} = 3.675$ kN-m $M^F_{CD} = \dfrac{-5 \times 1.5^2 \times 3.5}{5^2} = -1.575$ kN-m

STRUCTURAL ANALYSIS – II MOMENT DISTRIBUTION METHOD

Step II : Distribution factors :

Joint	Member	K	ΣK	DF = K/ΣK
A	AB	–	–	0
B	BA	$\frac{3}{4} \times \frac{I}{4} = \frac{3}{16}I$	$\left(\frac{11}{16}I\right)$	$\frac{3}{11}I$
	BC	$\frac{I}{4} = \frac{2I}{4} = \frac{I}{2}$		$\frac{8}{11}I$
C	CB	$\frac{I}{4} = \frac{2I}{4} = \frac{I}{2}$	$\left(\frac{11}{16}I\right)$	$\frac{8}{11}I$
	CD	$\frac{3}{4} \times \frac{I}{4} = \frac{3I}{16}$		$\frac{3}{11}I$
D	DC	–	–	0

Step III : MD Table (I) for non-sway moments :

Joint		A	B		C		D
Type of joint		EFS	RJ		RJ		EFS
Member		AB	BA	BC	CB	CD	DC
COF			→ 1/2	→ 1/2	→ 1/2		
			1/2 ←	1/2 ←	1/2 ←		
DF		0	3/11	8/11	8/11	3/11	0
First cycle	FEM	0	0	3.33	– 3.33	3.675	– 1.575
	DM		– 0.91	– 2.42	– 0.25	– 0.09	+ 1.575
Second cycle	COM			– 0.12	– 1.21	0.78	
	DM		0.032	0.087	0.31	0.11	
Third cycle	COM			0.15	0.043		
	DM		– 0.04	– 0.11	– 0.031	– 0.011	
Fourth cycle	COM			– 0.015	– 0.05		
	DM		0.004	0.011	0.036	0.014	
Fifth cycle	COM			0.018	0.005		
	DM		– 0.005	– 0.013	– 0.0036	– 0.0014	
First set of final moments		0	– 0.92	0.92	– 4.48	4.48	0

Step IV : MD for sway moments :

(a) The basic information of K, COF and DF remains the same.

(b) Normalized relative sway stiffness factors $[K_S]$.

STRUCTURAL ANALYSIS – II   MOMENT DISTRIBUTION METHOD

Member	Relative sway stiffness factor	Normalized relative sway stiffness factor [K_s]
AB	$\dfrac{I}{4^2}$	1.25
DC	$\dfrac{1.25\,I}{5^2}$	1

(c) **Sway moments :**

Member	Arbitrary relative FEM due to sway
AB	$M_{AB}^{FS} =$ $M_{BA}^{FS} =$
DC	$M_{DC}^{FS} =$ $M_{CD}^{FS} =$

Step V : MD Table II for sway moments :

Joint		A	B			C		D
Type of joint		EFS	RJ			RJ		EHS
Member		AB	BA	BC		CB	CD	DC
COF			→ 1/2			→ 1/2		→ 1/2
			1/2 ←			1/2 ←		1/2 ←
DF		0	3/11	8/11		8/11	3/11	0
First cycle	FEM	20	20	0		0	16	16
	DM	– 20	– 5.96	– 14.54		– 11.64	– 4.36	– 16
Second cycle	COM		– 10	– 5.82		– 7.27	– 8	
	DM		4.31	11.51		11.11	4.16	
Third cycle	COM			5.55		5.75		
	DM		– 1.51	– 4.04		– 4.18	– 1.57	
Fourth cycle	COM			– 2.09		– 2.02	1	
	DM		0.57	1.52		1.47	0.55	
Fifth cycle	COM			0.73		0.76		
	DM		– 0.2	– 0.53		– 0.55	– 0.21	
Second set of final moments			– 7.71	7.71		6.57	– 6.57	

$$M_{AB} = M_{AB}^{I} + C\,M_{AB}^{II}$$
$$M_{BA} = M_{BA}^{I} + C\,M_{BA}^{II}$$
$$M_{CD} = M_{CD}^{I} + C\,M_{CD}^{II}$$
$$M_{DC} = M_{DC}^{I} + C\,M_{DC}^{II}$$

STRUCTURAL ANALYSIS – II   MOMENT DISTRIBUTION METHOD

where C is a correction factor to be obtained from shear equilibrium equation developed as follows :

Step VI : Shear equilibrium condition :
Horizontal shear equilibrium gives

$$H_A + H_D = 0$$

$$\frac{M_{AB} + M_{BA}}{4} + \frac{M_{CD} + M_{DC}}{5} + 5 = 0$$

$$\frac{-0.92 - 7.71\,C}{4} + \frac{4.48 - 6.57\,C - 5 \times 1.5}{5} = -5$$

$$-0.23 - 1.93\,C - 0.604 - 1.314\,C = -5$$

$$-3.24\,C = -4.16$$

$$C = 1.284$$

Step VII : Corrected moments of second set will be obtained by multiplying these moments by C and then added to first set of moments gives net final moments.

Member	AB	BA	BC	CB	CD	DC
Corrected moments of second set	0	– 9.90	9.90	8.44	– 8.44	0
Moments of first set	0	– 0.92	0.92	– 4.48	4.48	0
Net final moments	0	– 10.82	10.82	3.96	– 3.96	0

Step VIII : FBD of members is as shown in Fig. 2.31 (b).

Considering equilibrium of each member and of complete structure all the reaction components are found out as shown in Fig. 2.31.

Step IX : Shear force diagram is as shown in Fig. 2.31 (c).
Step X : Bending moment diagrams are as shown in Fig. 2.31 (d) and Fig. 2.31 (e).
Step XI : FBD of structure is as shown in Fig. 2.31 (f).

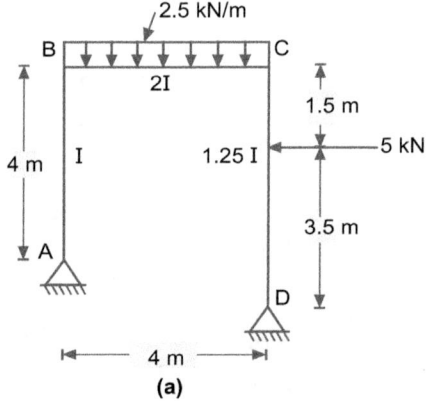

(a)

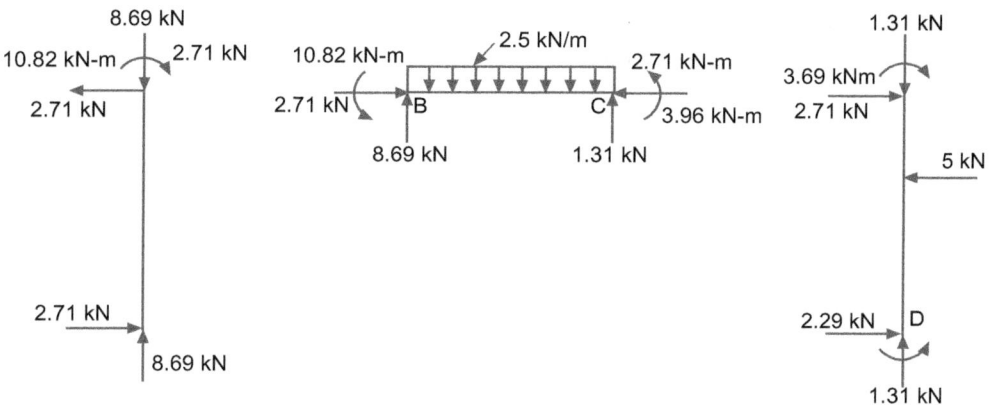

(b)

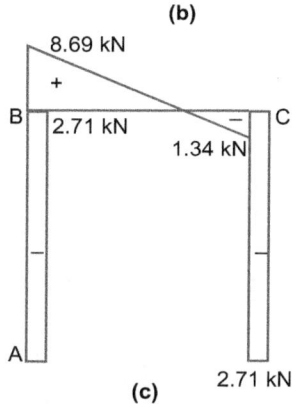

(c)

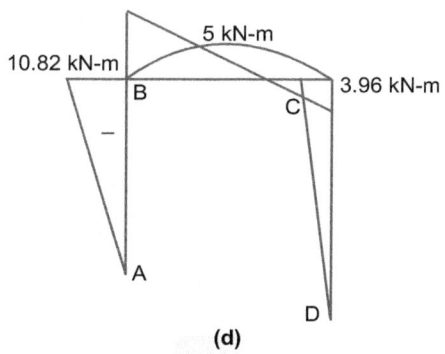

(d)

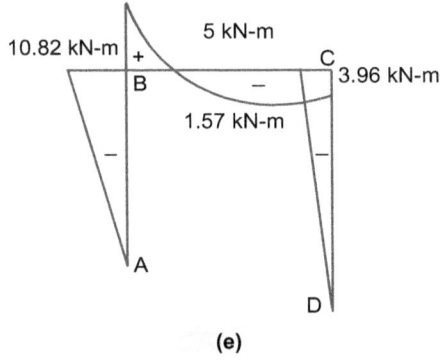

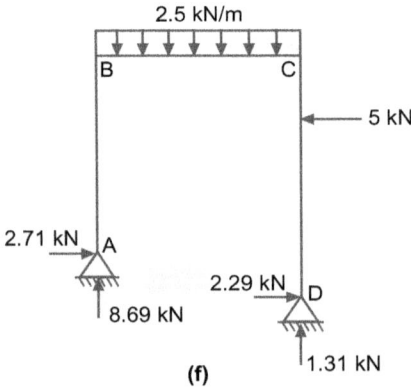

Fig. 2.31 : For Illustrative Example 2.26

Chapter 3
FLEXIBILITY METHOD

3.1 Force Method or Flexibility Method

3.1.1 General

Force method since many years has been the most general and physical approach to analyse statically indeterminate structures. In recent years, it is being replaced by the displacement approach, being systematic and suitable for computers. All types of skeletal structures e.g. beams, plane frames, plane trusses, etc. are analysed by the force method. Redundant forces are considered as unknown in the method. Therefore, the method is called as **force method.** The number of redundant forces is equal to the degree of static indeterminacy. The force method is therefore convenient if the degree of static indeterminacy of the structure is small.

The technique of the method is briefly explained as follows :

- The unknown redundant forces are selected and the basic statically determinate structure is obtained by removing the constraints corresponding the selected redundant forces. The basic determinate structure is also called as the released structure and must be in stable equilibrium. Thus, the equilibrium is indirectly satisfied.
- The displacements of the basic determinate structure at points of and corresponding to redundant forces are computed :
    (i) Due to the given loads on the structure, and
    (ii) Due to the unit force corresponding to the redundant forces. The displacement due to unit force is called as **flexibility.** The displacement due to the unknown redundant force is the product of the flexibility and the unknown force.
- The physical conditions of geometry at the points of redundants, also called as compatibility equations and also called as the superposition equations of displacements are formulated in terms of unknown redundant forces. There are always as many physical conditions of geometry as there are unknown redundant forces. The formulated equations are linear algebraic equations.
- Solution of the equations gives the unknown redundant forces.
- Once the redundant forces are known, the remaining analysis of the structure is completed by equations of statics.

The fundamental principle of the method is the physical requirements of the displacements of the basic determinate structure at the points of removed constraints due to the applied loading and unknown redundants. Basic requirements are listed as follows :

- If a roller support has been removed the translation at the support point in the direction perpendicular to the supporting surface must be zero.
- If a hinge support has been removed, the horizontal and vertical translations at the point must be zero.
- If a fixed support has been removed, the rotational, horizontal and vertical translations at the point must be zero.
- If an axially loaded member has been removed, the relative displacement along the member must be zero.

The force method starts with the equilibrium and ends with the compatibility of displacements, using the flexibility concepts. The force method is also named as :

- Method of consistent deformation as the displacement conditions should be consistent with the given constraints, or
- Compatibility method as the geometrical conditions of displacements are used for the formulation of the method, or
- Flexibility method as the displacement due to unit load corresponding to the redundant force, termed as the flexibility is used to obtain the displacement in terms of unknown redundant force.

3.1.2 Procedure of Force Method

The force method is mainly based on the displacement equation of compatibility. It therefore involves the determination of the following displacements of basic determinate structure corresponding to the redundant force, Q.

- The displacement at Q and corresponding to Q, due to the given loads (L). This is denoted by D_{QL}.
- The displacement at Q and corresponding to Q due to unit force. This is called the flexibility and denoted by F.
- The displacement at Q due to Q. This is denoted by D_{QQ} and is given by,

$$D_{QQ} = F \cdot Q$$

- The displacement at Q because of support condition of the structure. This is denoted by D_Q and D_Q is generally zero.

With these displacements, the compatibility condition is formulated by superposition.

$$\therefore \quad D_Q = D_{QL} + D_{QQ} \quad \ldots (3.1)$$

STRUCTURAL ANALYSIS – II FLEXIBILITY METHOD

$$\therefore \quad D_Q = D_{QL} + F \cdot Q$$
$$\therefore \quad O = D_{QL} + F \cdot Q$$

This is the basic equation of the force method. It is also interested to note that this equation is rearranged and expressed as the fundamental equation of the flexibility.

$$(D_Q - D_{QL}) = FQ$$

i.e.
$$D = FQ$$

The displacement at a point of determinate structure is generally obtained by the unit-load method. In particular cases, standard results of displacements and standard results of flexibilities may be used for convenience. Otherwise, the displacement analysis of determinate structure is itself an exercise. Moreover, the choice of redundant is not unique. Therefore, force method cannot be formulated specifically and hence not well suited to computer programming.

3.1.3 Flexibility Matrix

For multi-redundant structure, the redundant forces are considered as actions and identified by the co-ordinate numbering 1, 2, ... i, j, ... n, where n is the degree of static indeterminancy i.e. number of unknown redundant forces. Accordingly, the basic action-displacement equation D = FQ = FA is formulated in the matrix form in the following manner.

The displacement at the co-ordinate i can be expressed as the sum of the displacements due to actions at different co-ordinates 1, 2, ... i, j, ... n acting separately, only one at a time.

The superposition equations of displacements are

$$D_1 = D_{11} + D_{12} + \ldots + D_{1i} + D_{1j} + \ldots + D_{1n}$$
$$D_2 = D_{21} + D_{22} + \ldots + D_{2i} + D_{2j} + \ldots + D_{2n}$$
$$\vdots \quad \vdots \quad \vdots \quad \vdots \quad \vdots$$
$$D_i = D_{i1} + D_{i2} + \ldots + D_{ii} + D_{ij} + \ldots + D_{in}$$
$$D_j = D_{ji} + D_{j2} + \ldots + D_{ji} + D_{jj} + \ldots + D_{jn}$$
$$\vdots \quad \vdots \quad \vdots \quad \vdots \quad \vdots$$
$$D_n = D_{n1} + D_{n2} + \ldots + D_{ni} + D_{nj} + \ldots + D_{nn}$$

in which D_{ij} is the displacement at co-ordinate i due to the action at the co-ordinate j. As per the concept of flexibility, D_{ij} is given by,

$$D_{ij} = F_{ij} A_j$$

Therefore, displacement equations can be written in terms of actions and flexibility coefficients.

STRUCTURAL ANALYSIS – II   FLEXIBILITY METHOD

$$D_1 = F_{11} A_1 + F_{12} A_2 + \dots + F_{1i} A_i + F_{1j} A_j + \dots + F_{1n} A_n$$

$$\vdots$$

$$D_i = F_{i1} A_1 + F_{i2} A_2 + \dots + F_{ii} A_i + F_{ij} A_j + \dots + F_{in} A_n$$

$$D_j = F_{j1} A_1 + F_{j2} A_2 + \dots + F_{ji} A_i + F_{jj} A_j + \dots + F_{jn} A_n$$

$$\vdots$$

$$D_n = F_{n1} A_1 + F_{n2} A_2 + \dots + F_{ni} A_i + F_{nj} A_j + F_{nn} A_n$$

This set of equations represents the action-displacement relationship of a structure and may be expressed in the matrix form.

$$\begin{Bmatrix} D_1 \\ D_2 \\ \vdots \\ D_i \\ D_j \\ \vdots \\ D_n \end{Bmatrix} = \begin{bmatrix} F_{11} & F_{12} & F_{1i} & F_{ij} & F_{in} \\ F_{21} & F_{22} & F_{2i} & F_{2j} & F_{2n} \\ F_{i1} & F_{i2} & F_{ii} & F_{ij} & F_{in} \\ F_{j1} & F_{j2} & F_{ji} & F_{jj} & F_{jn} \\ F_{n1} & F_{n2} & F_{ni} & F_{nj} & F_{nn} \end{bmatrix} \begin{Bmatrix} A_1 \\ A_2 \\ \vdots \\ A_i \\ A_j \\ \vdots \\ A_n \end{Bmatrix} \quad \dots (3.2)$$

i.e. $\{D\} = [F] \{A\}$
  $n \times 1 \quad n \times n \quad n \times 1$

where,

$\{D\}$ = A column matrix of order $n \times 1$, known as displacement matrix.

$[F]$ = A square matrix of order $n \times n$, known as flexibility matrix.

$\{A\}$ = A column matrix of order $n \times 1$, known as action matrix

In flexibility concept, the cause is the unit positive force and effect is the displacement. For F_{ij}, i stands for effect and j for cause. If j is kept same and i varies then we get the effects i.e. displacements $F_{1j}, F_{2j} \dots F_{ij}$ etc. due to the same cause. These coefficients represent the column coefficients of $[F]$ matrix. Keeping same cause the effects are obtained and column of $[F]$ is generated.

It may be noted that the elements of 'j'th column of the flexibility matrix are the displacements at co-ordinates 1, 2 ... n due to a unit positive force at co-ordinate 'j'. Hence in order to generate the 'j'th column of the flexibility matrix, a unit positive force should be applied at co-ordinate 'j' and the displacements at all co-ordinates are determined. In order to develop the flexibility matrix $[F]$, a unit positive force should be applied successively at co-ordinates 1, 2 ..., n and displacements at all co-ordinates are computed.

Following properties of the flexibility matrix of a linear elastic structure in stable equilibrium will be observed subsequently.

- The flexibility matrix is a square matrix of order n × n where, n is the number of co-ordinates chosen for the example i.e. degree of static indeterminancy.
- The flexibility matrix is a symmetrical matrix i.e. $F_{ij} = F_{ji}$ in accordance with the reciprocal theorem.
- Each flexibility coefficient represents a displacement caused by a unit positive value of the action, while other actions are zero.
- In general, F_{ij} is the ith displacement due to unit value of jth action.
- The coefficient F_{ij} is taken as positive when it is in the positive direction of the ith action.
- F_{ij} that appear on the principal diagonal of [F] are called direct coefficients and represent displacements caused by unit values of the corresponding actions.
- The remaining coefficients are called cross coefficients.
- For direct flexibilities, i = j.
- For indirect flexibilities, i ≠ j.
- Direct flexibilities are always positive.
- Cross flexibilities may be positive or negative.
- For stable equilibrium structure, the flexibility matrix is non-singular, i.e. | [F] | ≠ 0.
- If structure is unstable, the displacements are infinitely large. The flexibility matrix does not exist i.e. singular |F| = 0.

3.1.4 Procedure of Flexibility Matrix Method

The basic equation of the force method developed for one unknown is written in matrix form as $\{D_Q\} = \{D_{QL}\} + [F]\{Q\}$ for more number of unknown redundant forces. This is the key matrix equation of the method. Using this equation, the procedure of the flexibility matrix method is outlined as follows :

- The degree of static indeterminancy D_{si} (= n, say) is determined.
- The redundant i.e. actions are chosen and identified.
- The co-ordinate numbering 1, 2, ... n is assigned to redundants. Thus $Q_1, Q_2 ... Q_n$ are the redundant actions at co-ordinates 1, 2, ... n. This is the matrix $\{Q\}_{n \times 1}$ of unknown redundants. It is to be noted specifically that {Q} is not denoted by {A} because {Q} do not correspond to non-zero joint displacement of a structure. In fact, {Q} corresponds normally to zero displacements.

STRUCTURAL ANALYSIS – II   FLEXIBILITY METHOD

- The redundants are removed and a statically released structure i.e. determinate structure is obtained.
- The displacements at co-ordinates 1, 2, ... n in the released structure caused by applied loads 0 are calculated. This displacement analysis of determinate structure is carried out preferably using unit load method. These displacements are D_{QL1}, D_{QL2}, D_{Ln}. Thus the matrix $\{D_{QL}\}_{n \times 1}$ is obtained.
- The displacements at co-ordinates 1, 2, ... n in the released structure due to positive unit load corresponding to the redundants, applied successively at a time is calculated. These are the flexibility coefficients. The flexibility matrix $[F]_{n \times n}$ is generated column wise.
- The displacement equations are formulated using superposition equations.

   i.e.
   $$D_{Q1} = D_{QL1} + F_{11} Q_1 + F_{12} Q_2 + ... + F_{1n} Q_n$$
   $$D_{Q2} = D_{QL2} + F_{21} Q_1 + F_{22} Q_2 + ... + F_{2n} Q_n$$
   $$D_{Qn} = D_{QLn} + F_{n1} Q_1 + F_{n2} Q_2 + ... + F_{nn} Q_n$$

   i.e. in matrix $\{D_Q\}_{n \times 1} = \{D_{QL}\}_{n \times 1} + [F]_{n \times n} \{Q\}_{n \times 1}$.

- Compatibility conditions that apply to the geometry of the structure are used. If the net displacements at redundants are zero, $\{D_Q\}$ will be null matrix.

   $$\{D_Q\} = \{0\}_{n \times 1}$$

- Formulation of linear simulation equations for unknown redundants is ready at this stage.
- The redundants $Q_1, Q_2, ... Q_n$ are obtained from solution of equations

   $$\{D\}_{n \times 1} = \{D_{QL}\}_{n \times 1} + [F]_{n \times n} \{Q\}_{n \times 1}$$
   i.e.
   $$\{0\}_{n \times 1} = \{D_{QL}\}_{n \times 1} + [F]_{n \times n} \{Q\}_{n \times 1}$$

- Knowing the redundants, the member-end forces i.e. stress resultants i.e. all other actions are obtained by using equations of statics.
- Variations of actions along the structure are plotted as SFD and BMD.
- When the actions throughout the structure have been found, the displacements at any point can also be found and deformed shape of a structure may be shown qualitatively from above information. Thus, the elastic curve is sketched.

In the nutshell, the flexibility matrix method requires the formation of following matrices with the help of elementary concepts of theory of structures.

   1. $\{D_Q\}_{n \times 1}$.
   2. $\{D_{QL}\}_{n \times 1}$.
   3. $[F]_{n \times n}$.
   4. $\{Q\}_{n \times 1}$ – unknown matrix to be obtained from basic equation of flexibility method.

   $$\{D_Q\} = \{D_{QL}\} + [F] \{Q\}$$

3.2 INDETERMINATE TRUSEES

3.2.1 General

A plane truss is a skeletal structure consisting of number of prismatic members, all lying in one plane and hinged together at their ends in such a manner as to form a rigid i.e. stable configuration. The analysis of trusses is simplified by considering the truss as ideal with the following assumptions.

- The members are connected together at their ends by frictionless pin joints though the joints are riveted or welded.
- Loads and reactions are acting only at joints and in the plane of truss.
- The centroidal axis of each member is straight and coincides with the line connecting the centres of joints at each end of the member.
- The members are subjected to only axial forces, though there may be bending moment and shear force as secondary effects.
- The members remain straight even after the deformation.
- A member undergoes either elongation or contraction.
- The displacement of a joint of a truss is specified by the horizontal and vertical translations only.

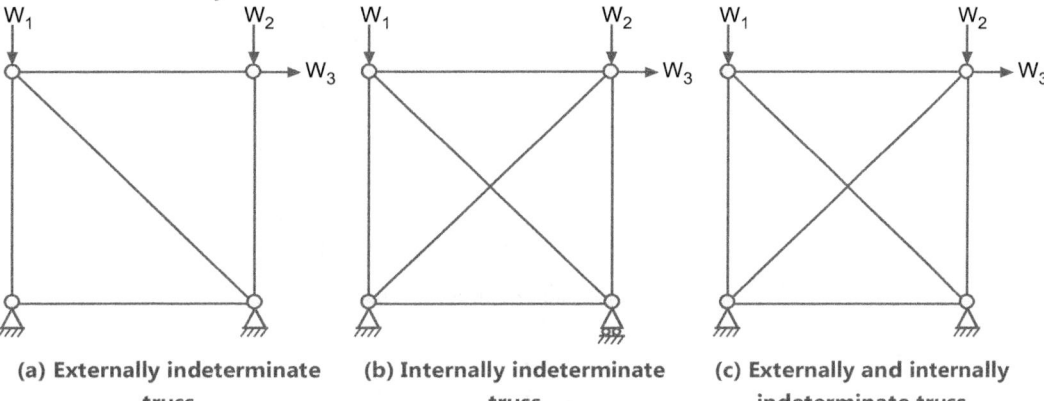

(a) Externally indeterminate truss   (b) Internally indeterminate truss   (c) Externally and internally indeterminate truss

Fig. 3.1 : Statically indeterminate trusses

The analysis of a truss mainly includes the determination of the axial forces in all members of the truss. Trusses may be statically indeterminate externally and/or internally. If the total number of reaction components is more than three, then the truss will be indeterminate externally as shown in Fig. 3.1 (a) and the degree of external indeterminacy is given by (r – 3) where r is the number of reaction components. If the total number of members of a truss is more than that required for stable configuration, the truss will be indeterminate internally as shown in Fig. 3.1 (b) and the degree of internal indeterminacy is given by [m – (2j – 3)] for a simply supported truss and [m − 2j] for a cantilever truss, where m is the number of members and j is the number of joints. Fig. 3.1 (c) shows a truss, indeterminate externally as well as internally. Statically indeterminate trusses are analysed by (i) force or flexibility method, (ii) displacement or stiffness method and (iii) energy method.

3.2.2 Force Method for Analysis of Indeterminate Trusses

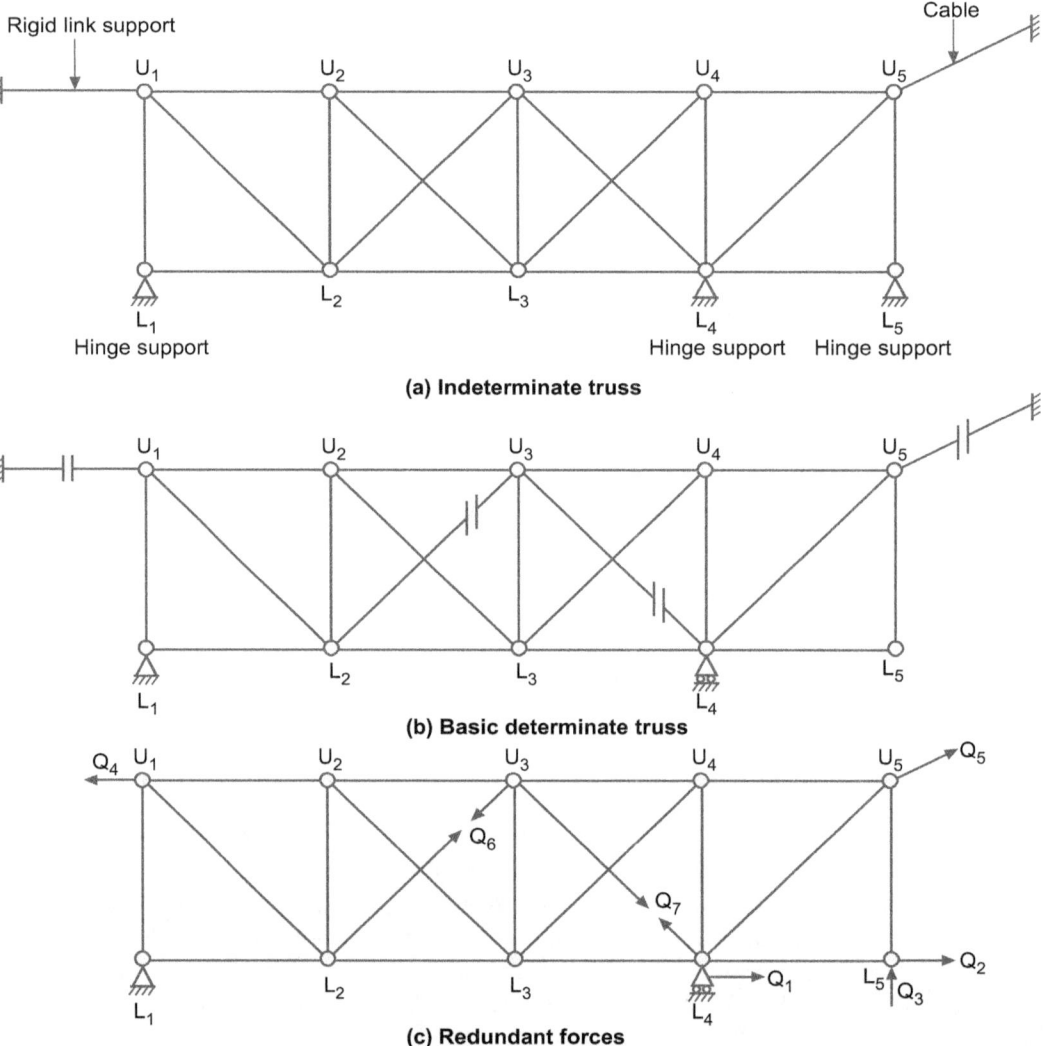

Fig. 3.2 : Released truss and redundant forces

STRUCTURAL ANALYSIS – II   FLEXIBILITY METHOD

Statically indeterminate trusses are generally analysed by the force method. The degree of kinematic indeterminacy of trusses is normally larger than the degree of static indeterminacy. Moreover, a truss consists of inclined members. Therefore displacement method is not convenient for the analysis of trusses by hand calculations.

Table 3.1

Sr. No.	Release	Release of the redundant	Redundant force	Geometrical condition of deformation
1.	One component of reaction at hinged support, at L_4.	Hinge support is replaced by the roller support as shown at L_4.	Force perpendicular to the plane of the roller support, Q_1 as shown at L_4.	The translation in the direction of Q_1 at L_4 is zero in the in-determinate truss.
2.	Hinge support at L_5.	Hinge support is removed as shown at L_5.	Two forces perpendicular to each other Q_2 and Q_3 as shown at L_5.	The translations in the direction of Q_2 and Q_3 at L_5 are zero in the indeterminate truss.
3.	Linked support assuming rigid.	The link is removed as shown at U_1.	Force along the link, Q_4 as shown at U_1.	The translation in the direction of the link at U_1 is zero in the indeterminate truss.
4.	Cable support assuming inextensible	The cable is removed as shown at U_5.	The tensile force in the cable Q_5 as shown at U_5.	The translation in the direction of the cable at U_5 is zero in the indeterminate truss.
5.	Member of the truss (a) Member $L_2 - U_3$ (b) Member $U_3 - L_4$	The member is cut with the gap in the member L_2U_3, in the member U_3L_4 at as shown in Fig. 3.2 (b).	Pair of tensile forces along the member. Q_6 forces acting at L_2 and U_3. Q_7 forces acting at U_3 and L_4.	There is no gap i.e. the relative translation along the member is zero in the in-determinate truss as the member is con-tinuous.
6.	Elastic support having flexibility Fes	The elastic support is removed.	The elastic force at the support say Q.	The translation at elastic support is equal to (Fes × Q).

The basic principle of consistent deformation is used to analyse the statically indeterminate trusses by the force method. The main aim of the method is to obtain redundant forces. The method consists of (i) choosing a basic determinate truss on which the applied loads and the redundant forces act and then (ii) applying the conditions of geometry i.e. compatibility requiring that the displacements in the direction of redundant forces must be zero. The redundant force may be the reaction component at the support and/or the axial force in the member. The basic determinate truss, also called released structure, is obtained from removing the selected redundants. In doing this, care must be taken that the released structure must be stable and determinate. This is particularly critical when the truss is internally indeterminate and a member is to be cut or removed to obtain the determinate truss.

The sign convention for axial force in the member of a truss is as follows :

Tensile force is considered as positive and compressive force as negative.

The selection of the redundants, obtaining the basic determinate i.e. released truss and applying the geometrical conditions of deformations are the primary considerations of the force method. This information, in general, is illustrated in Fig. 3.2 (a) and accordingly consolidated in the Table 3.1. The basic determinate truss after removing the redundant is shown in Fig. 3.2 (b) and the redundant forces are shown in Fig. 3.2 (c).

3.2.3 Basic Formulation of Force Method for Trusses

The superposition equation of the displacements, satisfying the requirement of the compatibility, is the basic equation of the force method as seen previously. This equation is restated in its simplest form of one unknown as

$$D_Q = D_{QL} + F \cdot Q \quad \ldots (3.3)$$

where,

(i) Q is the unknown redundant force.

(ii) D_Q is the displacement in the given structure corresponding to the selected redundant force Q.

(iii) D_{QL} is the displacement corresponding to the redundant force in the basic determinate or released structure due to the applied loads.

(iv) F is the flexibility i.e. the displacement corresponding and due to unit positive redundant force in the basic determinate structure.

As D_Q is zero for the geometrical condition, the basic equation becomes,

$$0 = D_{QL} + FQ \quad \ldots (3.4)$$

and therefore, $Q = -\left(\dfrac{D_{QL}}{F}\right)$ gives the required redundant force.

Analysis of indeterminate trusses of one unknown is based on this equation and it consists of the following important phases.

(1) Basic Determinate Truss :

The selected redundant is removed and the given truss is considered as the equivalent to the superposition of (i) basic determinate truss under given loads and (ii) the basic determinate truss under redundant force 'Q' times unit positive redundant force, as shown in Fig. 3.3.

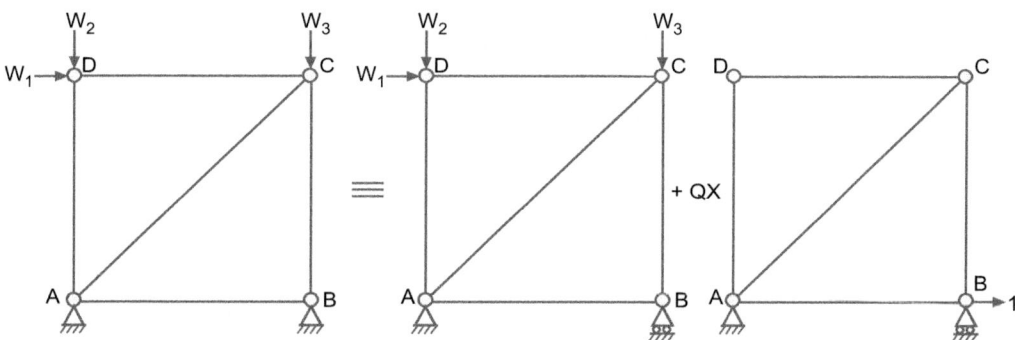

Fig. 3.3 : Superposition technique

(2) P-Analysis of Basic Determinate Truss :

Determination of forces in all members of the basic determinate truss due to the applied loads is called as P-analysis. This is the conventional force analysis of a simple determinate truss by laws of statics i.e. method of joints or method of sections. The technique of isolating a single joint with not more than two unknown forces and applying two conditions of static equilibrium, $\Sigma F_x = 0$ and $\Sigma F_y = 0$ for concurrent forces is called the method of joints to obtain the unknown forces. The technique of isolating a portion of a truss by a section and applying the three conditions of equilibrium, $\Sigma F_x = 0$, $\Sigma F_y = 0$ and $\Sigma M = 0$ for a non-concurrent system of forces including certain known applied loads and unknown member forces cut by the section is called the method of sections to obtain the three unknown forces.

(3) K-analysis :

Determination of forces in all the members including redundant members, which are cut, of the basic determinate truss due to only a unit positive force applied at the location and in the direction of the removed redundant is represented as K-analysis. For this also, method of joints or method of sections is used.

(4) Displacement Analysis of Basic Determinate Truss :

Using the results of P-analysis and K-analysis, the displacement D_{QL} at the location and in the direction of the redundant force due to applied loads is obtained. According to the unit load method, the displacement D_{QL} is given by the equation

$$D_{QL} = \sum_{\text{All members}} \left(\frac{PKL}{AE}\right) \qquad \ldots (3.5)$$

where P is the force in a member of the basic determinate truss due to applied loads.

K is the force in the member of the basic determinate truss due to a unit positive force corresponding to the unknown redundant force.

L is the length of the member.

A is the area of cross-section of the member.

E is the modulus of elasticity of the material of the member. It may be noted that EA is called axial rigidity of a member and $\frac{L}{EA}$ is termed as the flexibility of a member.

(5) Flexibility of the Basic Determinate Truss :

The displacement of basic determinate truss at the location and in the direction of the redundant due to the unit positive force only applied at the location and in the direction of the redundant is called the flexibility 'F'. Thus, the flexibility F is the displacement (effect) due to the unit force (cause) and obtained by the following similar equation of the unit load method.

$$F = \sum_{\text{All members}} \left(\frac{KKL}{EA}\right) = \sum_{\text{All members}} \left(\frac{K^2L}{EA}\right) \qquad \ldots (3.6)$$

(6) Formulation of the Basic Equation of the Force Method :

Applying the condition of consistent deformation that $D_Q = 0$, the unknown redundant force 'Q' is calculated from the equation

$$D_Q = D_{QL} + F \cdot Q$$

$\therefore \quad 0 = D_{QL} + F \cdot Q$

$\therefore \quad Q = -\left(\dfrac{D_{QL}}{F}\right)$

STRUCTURAL ANALYSIS – II

FLEXIBILITY METHOD

$$\therefore \quad Q = -\left(\frac{\sum_{i=1}^{n} \left(\frac{PKL}{EA}\right)_i}{\sum_{i=1}^{n} \left(\frac{K^2L}{EA}\right)_i} \right) \quad \ldots (3.7)$$

This is the key equation of the analysis of indeterminate trusses by the force method to determine the redundant force. This equation is further modified if the information of E or A or L or EA or $\frac{L}{EA}$ of all members of the truss is same. Therefore the basic equation is expressed as

$$Q = -\left(\frac{\sum_{i=1}^{n} \left(\frac{PKL}{EA}\right)_i}{\sum_{i=1}^{n} \left(\frac{K^2L}{EA}\right)_i} \right) \quad \text{for general case}$$

$$= -\left(\frac{\sum_{i=1}^{n} \left(\frac{PKL}{A}\right)_i}{\sum_{i=1}^{n} \left(\frac{K^2L}{A}\right)_i} \right) \quad \text{if E is same for all members}$$

$$= -\left(\frac{\sum_{i=1}^{n} (PKL)_i}{\sum_{i=1}^{n} (K^2L)_i} \right) \quad \text{if EA i.e. axial rigidity is same for all members}$$

$$= -\left(\frac{\sum_{i=1}^{n} (PK)_i}{\sum_{i=1}^{n} (K^2)_i} \right) \quad \text{if } \frac{L}{EA} \text{ i.e. flexibility is same for all members}$$

STRUCTURAL ANALYSIS – II   FLEXIBILITY METHOD

(7) Forces in the Members of a Redundant Truss :

Using the concept of superposition, the final forces in the members are found from the general equation :

$$P_{fj} = P_i + Q \cdot K_j \qquad \ldots (3.8)$$

The above formulation is processed systematically in the tabular form to analyse the indeterminate trusses. The information of A, L and the results of P-analysis and K-analysis, and their products are presented in the tabular format as shown below :

Sr. No.	Member	Length L	Area A	E	P	K	$\dfrac{PKL}{EA}$	$\dfrac{K^2L}{EA}$	Q	KQ	$P_f = P + QK$
							Σ =				

This table should include all the members of the truss including redundant members though they are cut. This is to be noted that this is the general format. If the information of E or A is same for all members, the corresponding columns are not necessary. The algebraic sum of the quantities required are directly obtained from this table to find the redundant force and the final forces in all members as shown in the table.

The detailed procedure of the method is illustrated with the examples of trusses for the following cases.

  Case I   : External indeterminacy.
  Case II : Internal indeterminacy.
  Case III : Lack of fit or fabrication error.
  Case IV : Temperature effects.
  Case V   : Yielding of supports.

Examples of only one unknown redundant force for each of the above cases are common in practice. Therefore, such examples of trusses with only one unknown are illustrated initially explaining the special features.

3.2.4 Externally Indeterminate Trusses

Example 3.1 : *Analyse the truss supported and loaded as shown in Fig. 3.4 (a).*

Take EA = constant.

Solution : Data :

(1) Truss is supported and loaded as shown in Fig. 3.4 (a).
(2) EA = constant.

Objects :

(1) Redundant force,

(2) Forces in all the members of truss and

(3) Reactions at supports.

Concepts and Equations :

(1) Principle of superposition,

(2) Analysis of determinate truss,

(3) Compatibility condition and

(4) $Q = -\left[\dfrac{\sum_{i=1}^{n}\left(\dfrac{PKL}{EA}\right)_i}{\sum_{i=1}^{n}\left(\dfrac{K^2L}{EA}\right)_i}\right]$

Procedure :

Step I : Degree of static indeterminacy (D_{si}) :

(a) Degree of external indeterminacy = $(D_{si})_e$ = r − 3 = 4 − 3 = 1

(b) Degree of internal indeterminacy = $(D_{si})_i$ = m − (2j − 3) = 9 − (2 × 6 − 3) = 0

Total degree of static indeterminacy = D_{si} = $(D_{si})_e$ + $(D_{si})_i$ = 1 + 0 = 1

Step II : Selection of redundant force (Q) :

Let $\quad Q = V_B$ (↑)

Step III : Basic determinate truss : Roller support at B is removed and determinate truss is obtained as shown in Fig. 3.4 (b).

Step IV : Superposition : The given indeterminate truss is considered as superposition of (a) basic determinate truss with given loads [Fig. 3.4 (b)] and (b) unknown redundant force Q times the basic determinate truss with unit positive redundant force [Fig. 3.4 (c)].

Step V : P-analysis of basic determinate truss due to applied loads : Considering static equilibrium of truss all the reaction components (R_p) are found out as shown in Fig. 3.4 (b). Also the forces (P) in all the members of truss are found out and shown in Fig. 3.4 (b).

Step VI : K-analysis of basic determinate truss : Unit positive force corresponding to Q is applied as shown in Fig. 3.4 (c). All the reaction components (R_K) and forces (K) in all the members of truss are found out and are shown in Fig. 3.4 (c).

Step VII : Table for numerical computations :

Sr. No.	Member	Length (m)	P (kN)	K	PKL	K²L	Q (kN)	QK (kN)	P_f = P + QK (kN)
1.	AB	3	47.5	– 1/2	– 71.25	0.75		– 26.35	21.15
2.	BC	3	47.5	– 1/2	– 71.25	0.75		– 26.35	21.15
3.	CD	3	0	0	0	0		0	0
4.	DE	3	0	0	0	0		0	0
5.	EF	3	– 20	0	0	0	52.69	0	– 20
6.	FA	3	0	0	0	0		0	0
7.	EB	3	0	– 1	0	3		– 52.69	– 52.69
8.	AE	3√2	– 27.5 √2	1/√2	– 82.5 √2	3/√2		37.25	– 1.64
9.	CE	3√2	– 47.5 √2	1/√2	– 142.5 √2	3/√2		37.25	– 29.93
				Σ =	– 460.69	8.74			

Step VIII : Calculation of redundant force :

$$Q = -\left[\dfrac{\sum\limits_{i=1}^{n}\left(\dfrac{PKL}{EA}\right)_i}{\sum\limits_{i=1}^{n}\left(\dfrac{K^2L}{EA}\right)_i}\right] = -\left(\dfrac{\Sigma PKL}{\Sigma K^2L}\right) = -\left(\dfrac{-460.69}{8.74}\right)$$

$$= 52.69 \text{ kN } (\uparrow)$$

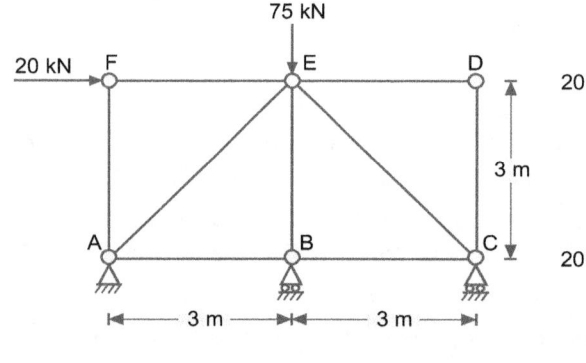

(a) Given truss

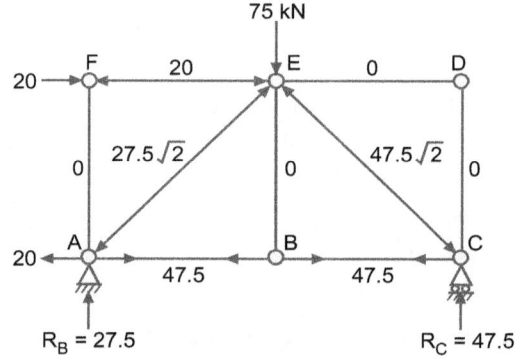

(b) Determinate truss with loads

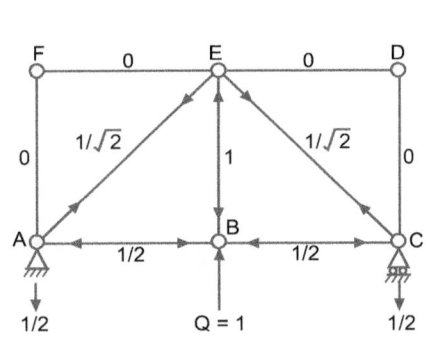
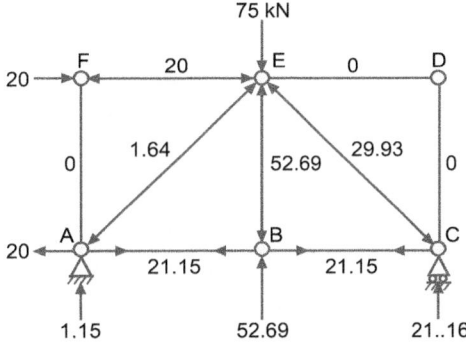

(c) Determinate truss with Q = 1   (d) Final member forces and reactions

Fig. 3.4 : Illustrative Example 3.1

Step IX : Final forces in all the members of truss (P_f) :

Using the equation :
$$P_f = P + QK$$
final forces in all members of truss are computed and are as tabulated above and shown in Fig. 3.4 (d).

Step X : Final reaction components at supports (R) :

Using the equation,
$$R = R_p + Q \cdot R_k$$
final reaction components at supports are computed and are as shown in Fig. 3.4 (d).

Example 3.2 : *Analyse the truss supported and loaded as shown in Fig. 3.5 (a). Cross-sectional area of each member in cm^2 is indicated in brackets. Take E = constant.*

Solution : Data :
(1) Truss is supported and loaded as shown in Fig. 3.5 (a).
(2) E = constant.

Objects :
(1) Redundant force,   (2) Forces in all the members of truss and
(3) Reactions at supports.

Concepts and Equations :
(1) Principle of superposition,   (2) Analysis of determinate truss,
(3) Compatibility condition and

(iv) $Q = - \left[\dfrac{\sum\limits_{i=1}^{n} \left(\dfrac{PKL}{EA} \right)_i}{\sum\limits_{i=1}^{n} \left(\dfrac{K^2 L}{EA} \right)_i} \right]$

STRUCTURAL ANALYSIS – II   FLEXIBILITY METHOD

Procedure : Step I : Degree of static indeterminacy (D_{si}) :
   (a) Degree of external indeterminacy = $(D_{si})_e$ = r − 3 = 4 − 3 = 1
   (b) Degree of internal indeterminacy = $(D_{si})_i$ = m − (2j − 3) = 5 − (2 × 4 − 3) = 0
      Total degree of static indeterminacy = D_{si} = $(D_{si})_e$ + $(D_{si})_i$ = 1 + 0 = 1

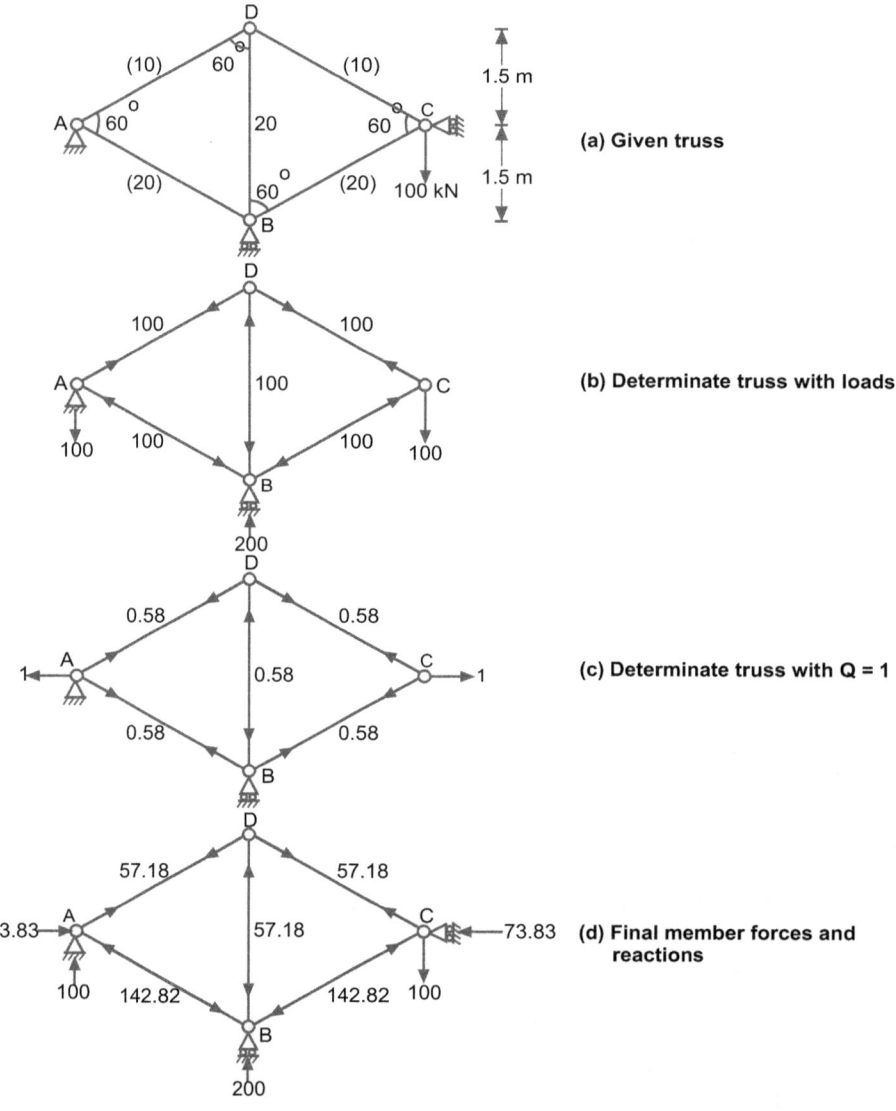

Fig. 3.5 : Illustrative Example 3.2

Step II : Selection of redundant force (Q) :
Let, $\quad Q = H_C (\rightarrow)$

Step III : Basic determinate truss :

Roller support at C is removed and determinate truss is obtained as shown in Fig. 3.5 (b).

Step IV : Superposition : The given indeterminate truss is considered as superposition of (a) basic determinate truss with given loads [Fig. 3.5 (b)] and (b) unknown redundant force Q times the basic determinate truss with unit positive redundant force [Fig. 3.5 (c)].

Step V : P-analysis of basic determinate truss due to applied loads : Considering static equilibrium of truss all the reaction components (R_p) are found out as shown in Fig. 3.5 (b). Also the forces (P) in all the members of truss are found out and are shown in Fig. 3.5 (b).

Step VI : K-analysis of basic determinate truss : Unit positive force corresponding to Q is applied as shown in Fig. 3.5 (c). All the reaction components (R_k) and forces (K) in all the members of truss are found out and are shown in Fig. 3.5 (c).

Step VII : Table for numerical computations :

Sr. No.	Member	Length (mm)	Area (mm^2)	P (kN)	K	$\frac{PKL}{A}$	$\frac{K^2L}{A}$	Q (kN)	QK (kN)	$P_f = P + QK$ (kN)
1.	AB	3000	2000	– 100	0.58	– 87	0.505		– 42.82	– 142.82
2.	BC	3000	2000	– 100	0.58	– 87	0.505		– 42.82	– 142.82
3.	CD	3000	1000	100	0.58	174	1.01	–73.83	– 42.82	57.18
4.	DA	3000	1000	100	0.58	174	1.01		– 42.82	57.18
5.	DB	3000	2000	– 100	– 0.58	87	0.505		42.82	– 57.18
						Σ = 261	3.535			

Step VIII : Calculation of redundant force :

$$Q = -\left[\frac{\sum_{i=1}^{n}\left(\frac{PKL}{EA}\right)_i}{\sum_{i=1}^{n}\left(\frac{K^2L}{EA}\right)_i}\right] = -\left[\frac{\sum\left(\frac{PKL}{A}\right)}{\sum\left(\frac{K^2L}{A}\right)}\right]$$

$$= -\left(\frac{261}{3.535}\right) = -73.83 \text{ kN} = 73.83 \text{ kN} (\rightarrow)$$

Step IX : Final forces in all the members of truss (P_f) :

Using the equation :
$$P_f = P + QK$$

final forces in all the members of truss are computed and are as tabulated above and shown in Fig. 3.5 (d).

Step X : Final reaction components at supports (R) :

Using the equation

$$R = R_p + Q \cdot R_k$$

final reaction components at supports are computed and are as shown in Fig. 3.5 (d).

Example 3.3 : *Analyse the truss supported and loaded as shown in Fig. 3.6 (a). Cross-sectional area of each member in cm² is indicated in brackets. Take E = constant.*

Solution : Data :

(1) Truss is supported and loaded as shown in Fig. 3.6 (a).

(2) E = constant

Objects :

(1) Redundant force,

(2) Forces in all the members of truss and

(3) Reactions at supports,

Concepts and Equations :

(1) Principle of superposition,

(2) Analysis of determinate truss,

(3) Compatibility condition and

(4) $Q = -\left[\dfrac{\sum_{i=1}^{n} \left(\dfrac{PKL}{EA}\right)_i}{\sum_{i=1}^{n} \left(\dfrac{K^2L}{EA}\right)_i} \right]$

Procedure :

Step I : Degree of static indeterminacy (D_{si}) :

(a) Degree of external indeterminacy = $(D_{si})_e$ = r − 3 = 4 − 3 = 1

(b) Degree of internal indeterminacy = $(D_{si})_i$ = m − (2j − 3) = 5 − (2 × 4 − 3) = 0

Total degree of static indeterminacy = D_{si} = $(D_{si})_e$ + $(D_{si})_i$ = 1 + 0 = 1

Step II : Selection of redundant force (Q) :

Let, $\qquad Q = H_B (\rightarrow)$

Step III : Basic determinate truss :

STRUCTURAL ANALYSIS – II　　　　　　　　　　　　　　　　　　FLEXIBILITY METHOD

Hinge support at B is replaced by roller support and determinate truss is obtained as shown in Fig. 3.6 (b).

Step IV : Superposition : The given indeterminate truss is considered as superposition of (a) basic determinate truss with given loads [Fig. 3.6 (b)] and (b) unknown redundant force Q times the basic determinate truss with unit positive redundant force [Fig. 3.6 (c)].

Step V : P-analysis of basic determinate truss due to applied loads : Considering static equilibrium of truss all the reaction components (R_p) are found out as shown in Fig. 3.6 (b). Also the forces (P) in all the members of truss are found out and are shown in Fig. 3.6 (b).

Step VI : K-analysis of basic determinate truss : Unit positive force corresponding to Q is applied as shown in Fig. 3.6 (c). All the reaction components (R_k) and forces (K) in all the members of truss are found out and are shown in Fig. 3.6 (c).

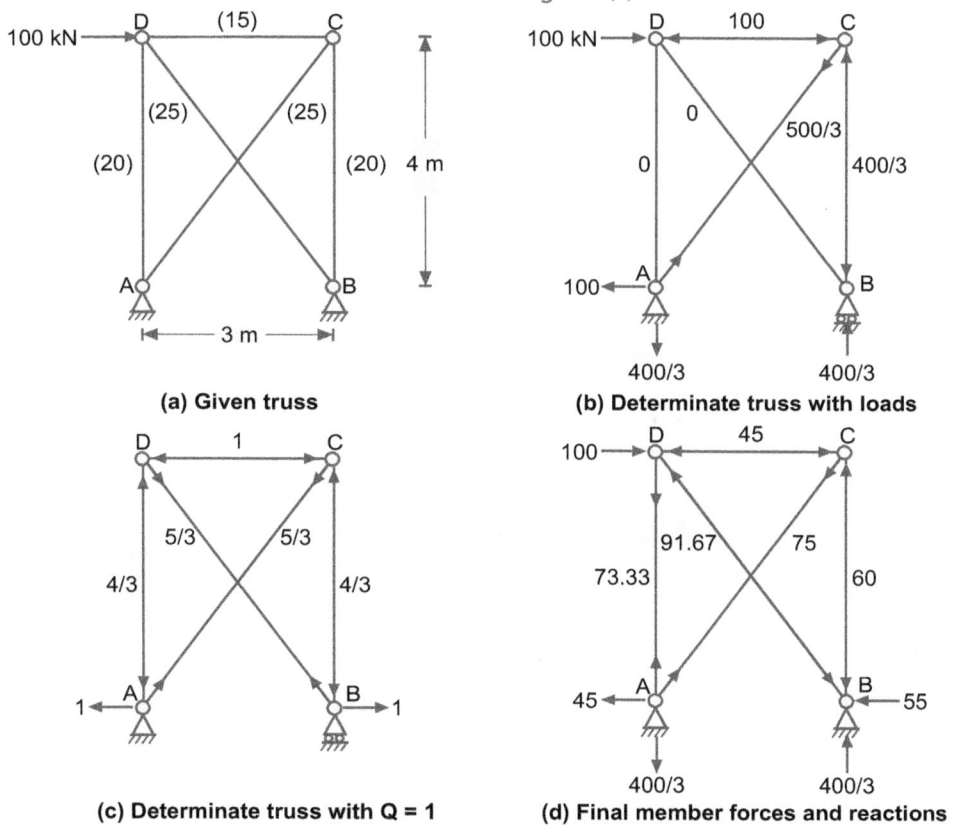

Fig. 3.6 : Illustrative Example 3.3

Step VII : Table for numerical computation :

STRUCTURAL ANALYSIS – II   FLEXIBILITY METHOD

Sr. No.	Member	Length (mm)	Area (mm²)	P (kN)	K	PKL/A	K²L/A	Q (kN)	QK (kN)	$P_f = P + QK$ (kN)
1.	BC	4000	2000	–400/3	–4/3	355.55	3.55		73.33	–60
2.	CD	3000	1500	– 100	–1	200	2.0		55	–45
3.	DA	4000	2000	0	–4/3	0	3.55	–55	73.33	73.33
4.	AC	5000	2500	500/3	5/3	555.55	5.55		–91.67	75
5.	BD	5000	2500	0	5/3	0	5.55		–91.67	–91.67
					Σ =	1111.11	20.2			

Step VIII : Calculation of redundant force :

$$Q = -\left[\frac{\sum_{i=1}^{n}\left(\frac{PKL}{EA}\right)_i}{\sum_{i=1}^{n}\left(\frac{K^2L}{EA}\right)_i}\right] = -\left[\frac{\sum\left(\frac{PKL}{A}\right)}{\sum\left(\frac{K^2L}{A}\right)}\right] = -\left(\frac{1111.11}{20.2}\right)$$

$$= -55 \text{ kN} = 55 \text{ kN} (\leftarrow)$$

Step IX : Final forces in all the members of truss (P_f) :

Using the equation :

$$P_f = P + QK$$

final forces in all the members of truss are computed and are as tabulated above and shown in Fig. 3.6 (d).

Step X : Final reaction components at supports (R) :

Using the equation,

$$R = R_p + Q \cdot R_K$$

final reaction components at supports are computed and are as shown in Fig. 3.6 (d).

Example 3.4 : *Analyse the truss supported and loaded as shown in Fig. 3.7 (a). Cross-sectional area of each member in cm² is indicated in brackets. Take E = constant.*

Solution : Data :
(1) Truss is supported and loaded as shown in Fig. 3.7 (a).
(2) E = constant

Objects :
(1) Redundant force,
(2) Forces in all the members of truss and
(3) Reactions at supports.

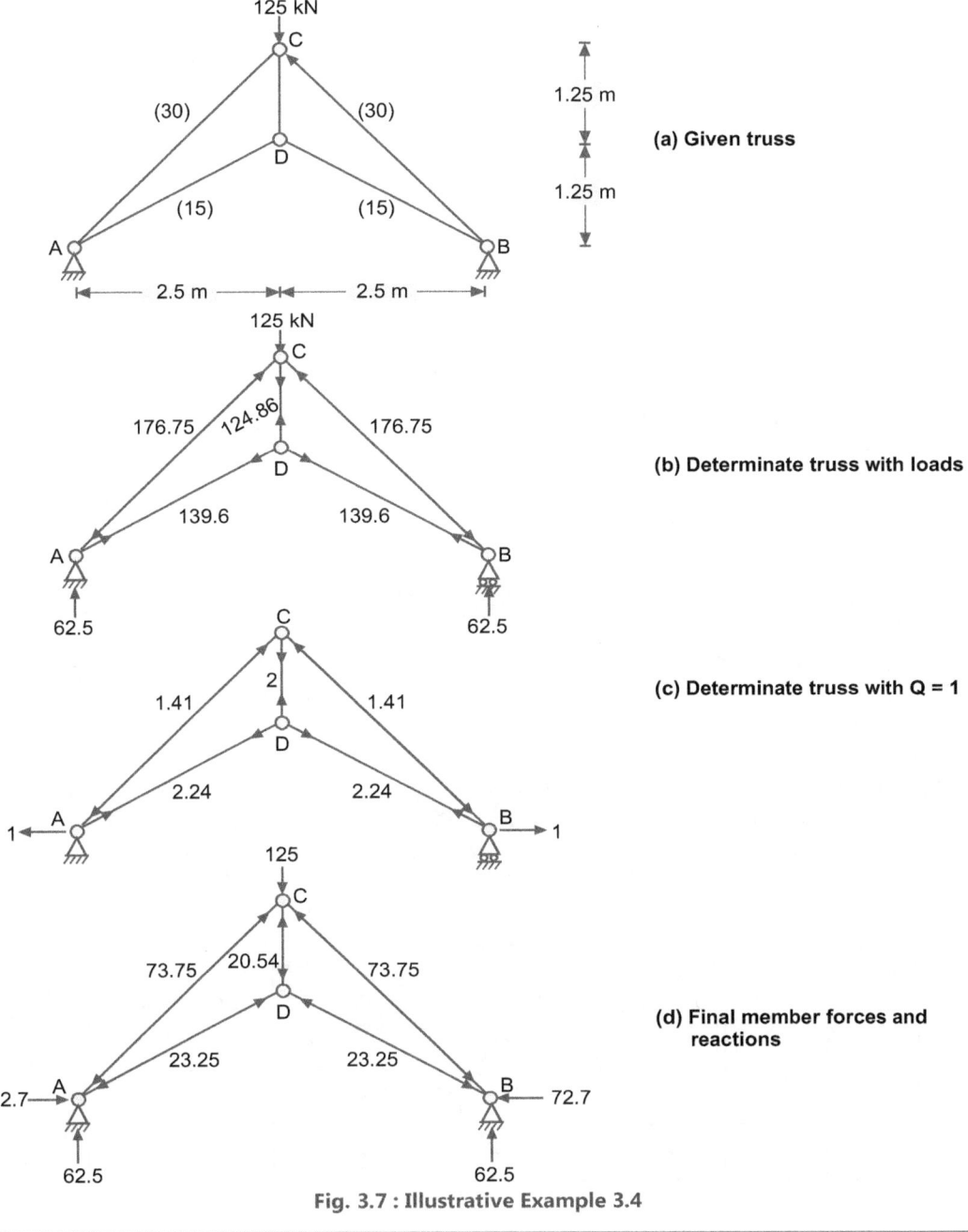

Fig. 3.7 : Illustrative Example 3.4

STRUCTURAL ANALYSIS – II FLEXIBILITY METHOD

Concepts and Equations :
(1) Principle of superposition,
(2) Analysis of determinate truss,
(3) Compatibility condition and

$$\text{(iv)} \quad Q = -\left[\frac{\sum_{i=1}^{n}\left(\frac{PKL}{EA}\right)_i}{\sum_{i=1}^{n}\left(\frac{K^2L}{EA}\right)_i} \right]$$

Procedure :

Step I : Degree of static indeterminacy (D_{si}) :
(a) Degree of external indeterminacy = $(D_{si})_e$ = r – 3 = 4 – 3 = 1
(b) Degree of internal indeterminacy = $(D_{si})_i$ = m – (2j – 3) = 5 – (2 × 4 – 3) = 0
Total degree of static indeterminacy = D_{si} = $(D_{si})_e$ + $(D_{si})_i$ = 1 + 0 = 1

Step II : Selection of redundant force (Q) :
Let, $\quad Q = H_B (\rightarrow)$

Step III : Basic determinate truss : Hinge support at B is replaced by roller support and determinate truss is obtained as shown in Fig. 3.7 (b).

Step IV : Superposition : The given indeterminate truss is considered as superposition of (a) basic determinate truss with given loads [Fig. 3.7 (b)] and (b) unknown redundant force 'Q' times the basic determinate truss with unit positive redundant force. [Fig. 3.7 (c)].

Step V : P-analysis of basic determinate truss due to applied loads : Considering static equilibrium of truss all the reaction components (R_p) are found out as shown in Fig. 3.7 (b). Also the forces (P) in all the members of truss are found out and are shown in Fig. 3.7 (b).

Step VI : K-analysis of basic determinate truss : Unit positive force corresponding to 'Q' is applied as shown in Fig. 3.7 (c). All the reaction components (R_k) and forces (K) in all the members of truss are found out and are shown in Fig. 3.7 (c).

Step VII : Table for numerical computation :

Sr. No.	Member	Length (mm)	Area (mm^2)	P (kN)	K	$\frac{PKL}{A}$	$\frac{K^2L}{A}$	Q (kN)	QK (kN)	P_f = P + QK (kN)
1.	AD	2795	1500	139.6	2.24	582.67	9.35		–18.21	–23.25
2.	BD	2795	1500	139.6	2.24	582.67	9.35		–18.21	–23.25
3.	AC	3535	3000	–176.25	–1.41	292.83	2.34	–72.7	– 76.92	–73.75
4.	BC	3535	3000	–176.25	–1.41	292.83	2.34		– 76.92	–73.75
5.	CD	1250	1000	124.86	2	312.15	5		–16.04	–20.54
					Σ =	2063.15	28.38			

Step VIII : Calculation of redundant force :

$$Q = -\left[\dfrac{\sum_{i=1}^{n}\left(\dfrac{PKL}{EA}\right)_i}{\sum_{i=1}^{n}\left(\dfrac{K^2L}{EA}\right)_i}\right] = -\left(\dfrac{\sum\dfrac{(PKL)}{A}}{(K^2L/A)}\right) = -\left(\dfrac{2063.15}{28.3}\right)$$

$$= -72.70 \text{ kN} = 72.70 \text{ kN} (\leftarrow)$$

Step IX : Final forces in all the members of truss (P_f) :
Using the equation,
$$P_f = P + QK$$
final forces in all the members of truss are computed and are as tabulated above and shown in Fig. 3.7 (d).

Step X : Final reaction components at supports (R) :
Using the equation,
$$R = R_p + Q \cdot R_k$$
final reaction components at supports are computed and are as shown in Fig. 3.7 (d).

3.2.5 Internally Indeterminate Trusses

Example 3.5 : Analyse the truss supported and loaded as shown in Fig. 3.8 (a). Cross-sectional area of each member in cm^2 is indicated in brackets. Take E = constant.

Solution : Data :
(1) Truss is supported and loaded as shown in Fig. 3.8 (a).
Objects :
(1) Redundant force   (2) Forces in all the members of truss and
(3) Reactions at supports.
Concepts and Equations :
(1) Principle of superposition   (2) Analysis of determinate truss,
(3) Compatibility condition and

(iv) $Q = -\left[\dfrac{\sum_{i=1}^{n}\left(\dfrac{PKL}{EA}\right)_i}{\sum_{i=1}^{n}\left(\dfrac{K^2L}{EA}\right)_i}\right]$

Procedure :
Step I : Degree of static indeterminacy (D_{si}) :
(a) Degree of external indeterminacy = $(D_{si})_e$ = r − 3 = 3 − 3 = 0
(b) Degree of internal indeterminacy = $(D_{si})_i$ = m − 2j = 3 − 2 × 1 = 1
  Total degree of static indeterminacy = D_{si} = $(D_{si})_e$ + $(D_{si})_i$ = 0 + 1 = 1

Step II : Selection of redundant force (Q) :

Step III : Basic determinate truss : Member CD is cut and determinate truss is obtained as shown in Fig. 3.8 (b).

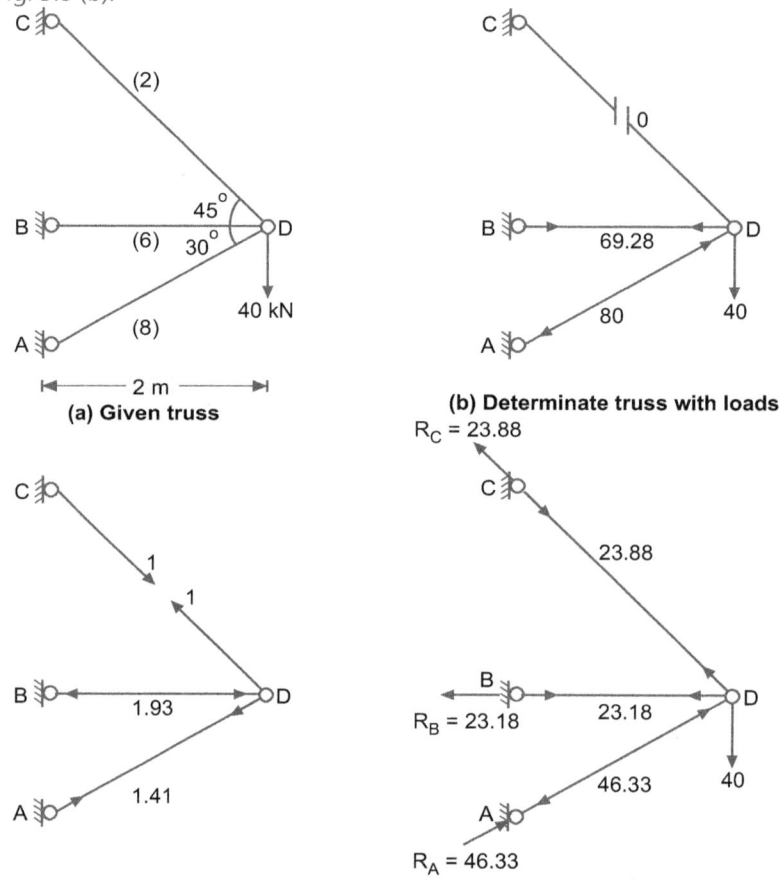

(a) Given truss
(b) Determinate truss with loads
$R_C = 23.88$
(c) Determinate truss with Q = 1
(d) Final member forces and reactions

Fig. 3.8 : Illustrative Example 3.5

Step IV : Superposition : The given indeterminate truss is considered as superposition of (a) basic determinate truss with given loads [Fig. 3.8 (b)] and (b) unknown redundant force 'Q' times the basic determinate truss with unit positive redundant force. [Fig. 3.8 (c)].

Step V : P-analysis of basic determinate truss due to applied loads : The forces (P) in all the members of truss are found out and are shown in Fig. 3.8 (b).

Step VI : K-analysis of basic determinate truss : Unit positive force corresponding to 'Q' is applied as shown in Fig. 3.8 (c) forces (K) in all the members of truss are found out and are shown in Fig. 3.8 (c).

STRUCTURAL ANALYSIS – II   FLEXIBILITY METHOD

Step VII : Table for numerical computations :

Sr. No.	Member	Length (mm)	Area (mm²)	P (kN)	K	$\frac{PKL}{A}$	$\frac{K^2L}{A}$	Q (kN)	QK (kN)	$P_f = P + QK$ (kN)
1.	AD	2310	800	–80	1.41	–325.71	5.74		33.67	–46.33
2.	BD	2000	600	69.28	–1.93	–445.7	12.42	23.88	– 46.10	23.18
3.	CD	2828	200	0	1	0	14.14		– 23.88	–23.88
					Σ =	–771.41	32.3			

Step VIII : Calculation of redundant force :

$$Q = -\left[\frac{\sum_{i=1}^{n}\left(\frac{PKL}{EA}\right)_i}{\sum_{i=1}^{n}\left(\frac{K^2L}{EA}\right)_i}\right] = -\left[\frac{\sum\left(\frac{PKL}{A}\right)}{\sum\left(\frac{K^2L}{A}\right)}\right] = -\left(\frac{-771.41}{32.3}\right)$$

= 23.88 kN (Tensile)

Step IX : Final force in all the members of truss (P_f) :
Using the equation,
$$P_f = P + QK$$
final forces in all the members of truss are computed and are as tabulated above and shown in Fig. 3.8 (d).

Step X : Final reaction components at supports (R) :
Using the equation,
$$R = R_p + Q \cdot R_k$$
final reaction components at supports are computed and are as shown in Fig. 3.8 (d).

Example 3.6 : *Analyse the truss supported and loaded as shown in Fig. 3.9 (a).*
Take EA = constant.
Solution : Data :
(1) Truss is supported and loaded as shown in Fig. 3.9 (a).
(2) EA = constant
Objects :
(1) Redundant force   (2) Forces in all the members of truss and
(3) Reactions at supports.
Concepts and Equations :
(1) Principle of superposition   (2) Analysis of determinate truss,
(3) Compatibility condition and

STRUCTURAL ANALYSIS – II   FLEXIBILITY METHOD

(4) $\quad Q = -\left[\dfrac{\sum\limits_{i=1}^{n}\left(\dfrac{PKL}{EA}\right)_i}{\sum\limits_{i=1}^{n}\left(\dfrac{K^2L}{EA}\right)_i} \right]$

Procedure :

Step I : Degree of static indeterminacy (D_{si}) :
(a) Degree of external indeterminacy = $(D_{si})_e$ = r – 3 = 3 – 3 = 0
(b) Degree of internal indeterminacy = $(D_{si})_i$ = m – (2j – 3) = 8 – (2 × 5 – 3) = 1
  Total degree of static indeterminacy = D_{si} = $(D_{si})_e$ + $(D_{si})_i$ = 0 + 1 = 1

Step II : Selection of redundant force (Q) :
Let,   Q = Force in member BE (Tensile)

Step III : Basic determinate truss :
Member BE is cut and determinate truss is obtained as shown in Fig. 3.9 (b).

Step IV : Superposition : The given indeterminate truss is considered as superposition of (a) basic determinate truss with given loads [Fig. 3.9 (b)] and (b) unknown redundant force 'Q' times the basic determinate truss with unit positive redundant force (Fig. 3.9 (c)).

Step V : P-analysis of basic determinate truss due to applied loads : Considering static equilibrium of truss all the reaction components (R_p) are found out as shown in Fig. 3.9 (b). Also the forces (P) in all the members of truss are found out and are shown in [Fig. 3.9 (b)].

Step VI : K-analysis of basic determinate truss : Unit positive force corresponding to 'Q' is applied as shown in Fig. 3.9 (c).

Forces (K) in all the members of truss are found out and are shown in Fig. 3.9 (c). Reaction components (R_k) are zero for this analysis.

Step VII : Table for numerical computation :

Sr. No.	Member	Length (m)	P (kN)	K	PKL	K^2L	Q (kN)	QK (kN)	P_f = P + QK (kN)
1.	AB	2	25	$-1/\sqrt{2}$	–35.35	1		9.9	34.9
2.	BC	2	25	0	0	0		0	25
3.	CD	$2\sqrt{2}$	$-25\sqrt{2}$	0	0	0		0	$-25\sqrt{2}$
4.	DE	2	–50	$-1/\sqrt{2}$	70.71	1	–14.01	9.9	–40.1
5.	EA	2	0	$-1/\sqrt{2}$	0	1		9.9	9.9
6.	BD	2	0	$-1/\sqrt{2}$	0	1		9.9	9.9
7.	AD	$2\sqrt{2}$	$25\sqrt{2}$	1	100	$2\sqrt{2}$		–14.01	21.35
8.	BE	$2\sqrt{2}$	0	1	0	$2\sqrt{2}$		–14.01	–14.01
				Σ =	135.36	9.66			

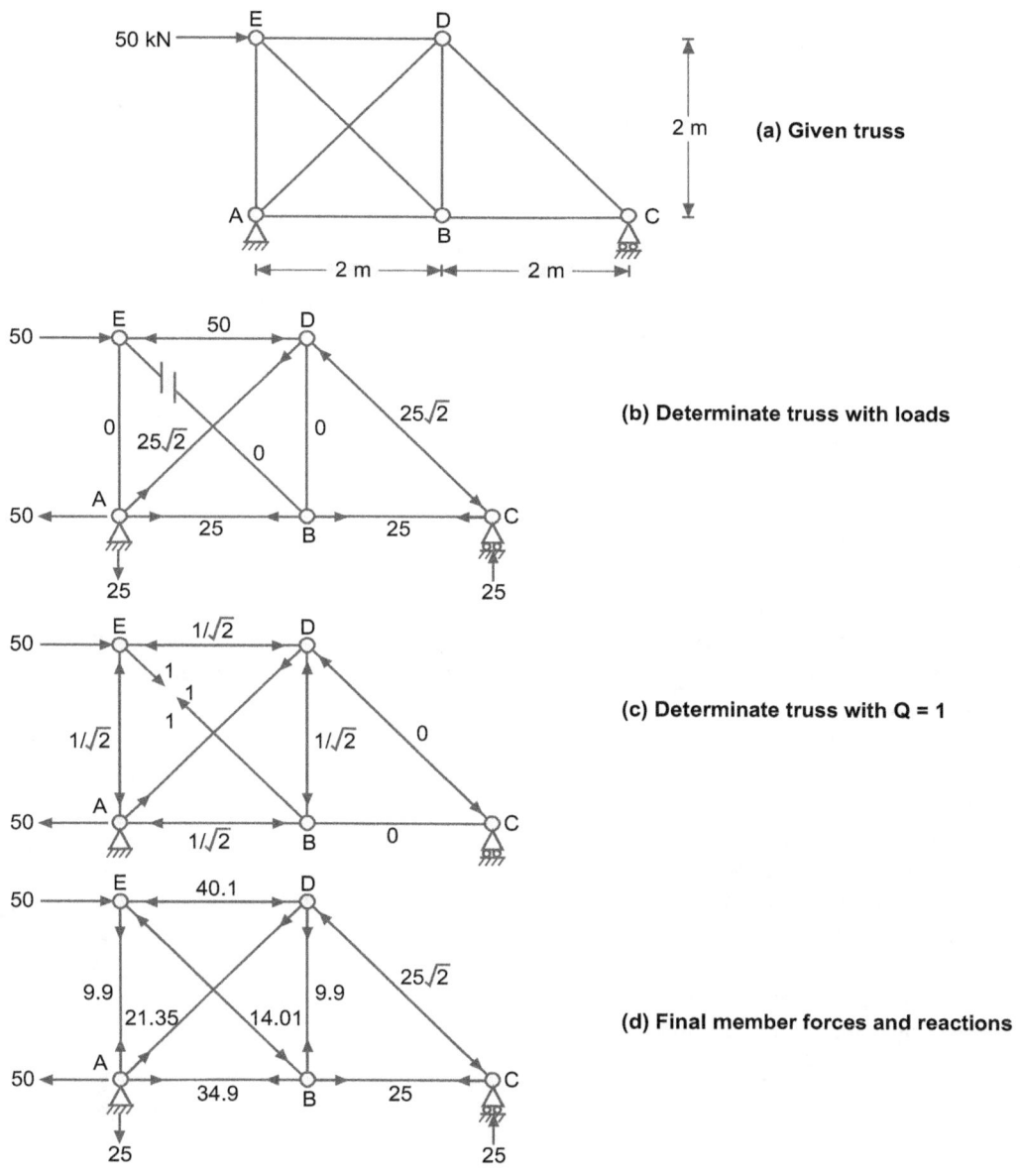

Fig. 3.9 : Illustrative Example 3.6

STRUCTURAL ANALYSIS – II FLEXIBILITY METHOD

Step VIII : Calculation of redundant force :

$$Q = -\left[\dfrac{\sum_{i=1}^{n}\left(\dfrac{PKL}{EA}\right)_i}{\sum_{i=1}^{n}\left(\dfrac{K^2L}{EA}\right)_i}\right]$$

$$= -\left(\dfrac{\sum (PKL)}{\sum (K^2L)}\right) = -\left(\dfrac{135.36}{9.66}\right)$$

$$= -14.01 \text{ kN} = 14.01 \text{ kN (Compressive)}$$

Step IX : Final forces in all the members of truss (P_f) :

Using the equation,

$$P_f = P + QK$$

final forces in all the members of truss are computed and are as tabulated above and shown in Fig. 3.9 (d).

Step X : Final reaction components at supports (R) :

Using the relation,

$$R = R_p + Q \cdot R_k$$

final reaction components at supports are computed and are as shown in Fig. 3.9 (d).

Example 3.7 : *Analyse the truss supported and loaded as shown in Fig. 3.10 (a). Cross-sectional area of each member in cm² is indicated in brackets. Take E = constant.*

Solution : Data :
(1) Truss is supported and loaded as shown in Fig. 3.10 (a).
(2) E = constant

Objects :
(1) Redundant force,
(2) Forces in all the members of truss and
(3) Reactions at supports.

Concepts and Equations :
(1) Principle of superposition,
(2) Analysis of determinate truss,
(3) Compatibility condition and

(4) $Q = -\left[\dfrac{\sum_{i=1}^{n}\left(\dfrac{PKL}{EA}\right)_i}{\sum_{i=1}^{n}\left(\dfrac{K^2L}{EA}\right)_i}\right]$

STRUCTURAL ANALYSIS – II FLEXIBILITY METHOD

Procedure :

Step I : Degree of static indeterminacy (D_{si}) :

(a) Degree of external indeterminacy = $(D_{si})_e$ = r – 3 = 3 – 3 = 0

(b) Degree of internal indeterminacy = $(D_{si})_i$ = m – (2j – 3) = 6 – (2 × 4 – 3) = 1

Total degree of static indeterminacy = D_{si} = $(D_{si})_e$ + $(D_{si})_i$ = 0 + 1 = 1

Step II : Selection of redundant force (Q) :

Let, Q = Force in member AB (Tensile)

Step III : Basic determinate truss :

Member AB is cut and determinate truss is obtained as shown in Fig. 3.10 (b).

Step IV : Superposition : The given indeterminate truss is considered as superposition of (a) basic determinate truss with given loads [Fig. 3.10 (b)] and (b) unknown redundant force 'Q' times the basic determinate truss with unit positive redundant force [Fig. 3.10 (c)].

Step V : P-analysis of basic determinate truss due to applied loads : Considering static equilibrium of truss all the reaction components (R_p) are found out as shown in Fig. 3.10 (b). Also the forces (P) in all the members of truss are found out and are shown in Fig. 3.10 (b).

Step VI : K-analysis of basic determinate truss : Unit positive force corresponding to 'Q' is applied as shown in Fig. 3.10 (c).

Forces (K) in all the members of truss are found out and are shown in Fig. 3.10 (c). Reaction components (R_k) are zero for this analysis.

Step VII : Table for numerical computation :

Sr. No.	Member	Length (mm)	Area (mm²)	P (kN)	K	$\frac{PKL}{A}$	$\frac{K^2L}{A}$	Q (kN)	QK (kN)	P_f = P + QK (kN)
1.	BC	4000	2000	–400/3	4/3	–355.55	3.55		66.67	–66.67
2.	CD	3000	1500	–100	1	–20	2.0		50	–50
3.	DA	4000	2000	0	4/3	0	3.55	50	66.67	66.67
4.	AC	5000	2500	500/3	–5/3	–555.55	5.55		–83.33	83.33
5.	BD	5000	2500	0	–5/3	0	5.55		–83.33	–83.33
6.	AB	3000	1500	0	1	0	2.0		50	50
					Σ =	–1111.11	22.2			

STRUCTURAL ANALYSIS – II   FLEXIBILITY METHOD

Step VIII : Calculation of redundant force :

$$Q = -\left[\frac{\sum_{i=1}^{n}\left(\frac{PKL}{EA}\right)_i}{\sum_{i=1}^{n}\left(\frac{K^2L}{EA}\right)_i}\right]$$

$$= -\left[\frac{\sum\left(\frac{PKL}{A}\right)}{\sum\left(\frac{K^2L}{A}\right)}\right] = -\left(\frac{-1111.11}{22.22}\right) = 50 \text{ kN (Tensile)}$$

Step IX : Final forces in all the members of truss (P_f) :

Using the equation,

$$P_f = P + QK$$

final forces in all the members of truss are computed and are as tabulated above and shown in Fig. 3.10 (d).

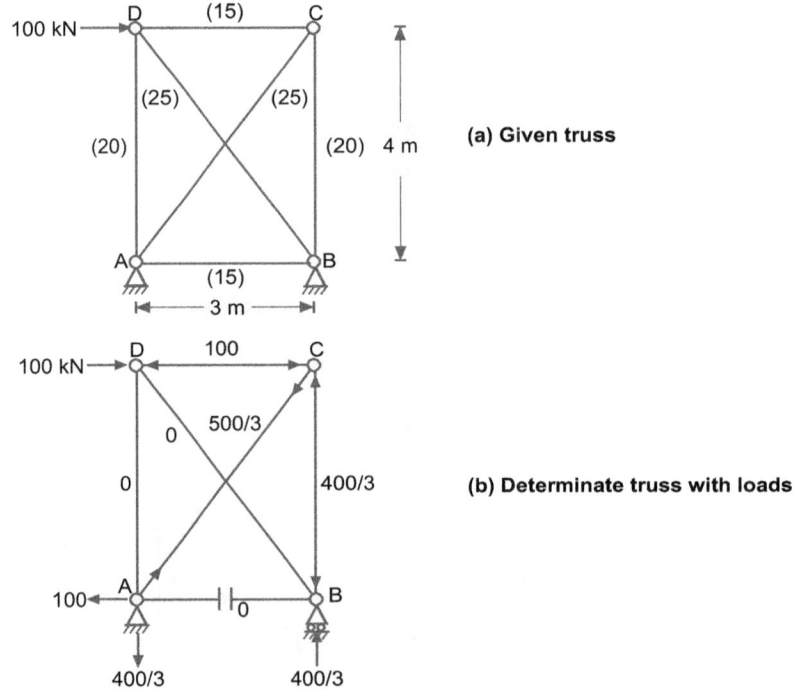

(a) Given truss

(b) Determinate truss with loads

Ch. 3 | 3.32

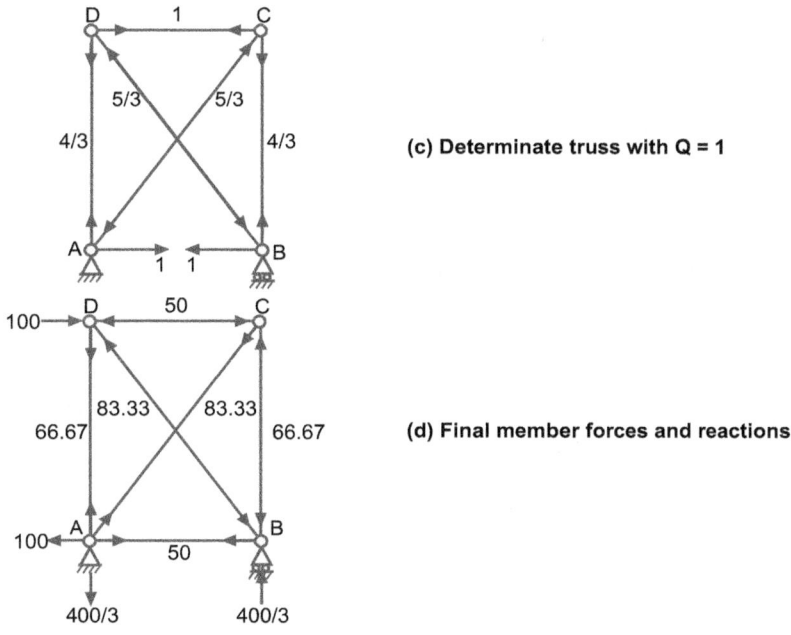

(c) Determinate truss with Q = 1

(d) Final member forces and reactions

Fig. 3.10 : Illustrative Example 3.7

Step X : Final reaction components at supports (R) :
Using the equation,
$$R = R_p + Q \cdot R_k$$
final reaction components at supports are computed and are as shown in Fig. 3.10 (d).

Example 3.8 : *Analyse the truss supported and loaded as shown in Fig. 3.11 (a). Cross-sectional area of each member in cm² is indicated in brackets. Take E = constant.*

Solution : Data :
(1) Truss is supported and loaded as shown in Fig. 3.11 (a). (2) E = constant.

Object :
(1) Redundant force (2) Forces in all the members of truss and
(3) Reactions at supports.

Concepts and Equations :
(1) Principle of superposition, (2) Analysis of determinate truss,
(3) Compatibility condition and

(4) $Q = -\left[\dfrac{\sum\limits_{i=1}^{n} \left(\dfrac{PKL}{EA}\right)_i}{\sum\limits_{i=1}^{n} \left(\dfrac{K^2L}{EA}\right)_i} \right]$

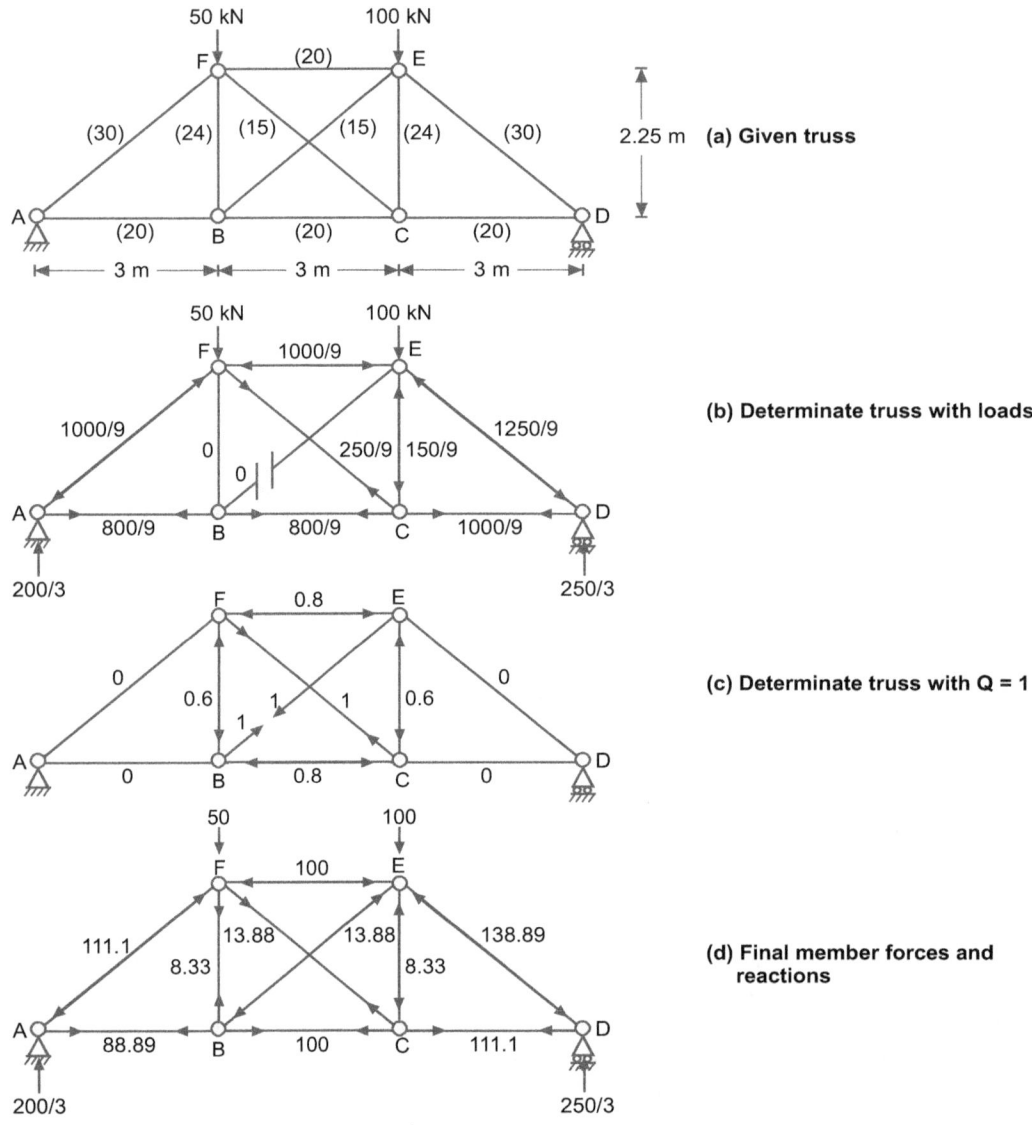

Fig. 3.11 : Illustrative Example 3.8

Procedure :

Step I : Degree of static indeterminacy (D_{si}) :

(a) Degree of external indeterminacy = $(D_{si})_e$ = r − 3 = 3 − 3 = 0

Ch. 3 | 3.34

(b) Degree of internal indeterminacy = $(D_{si})_i$ = m – (2j – 3) = 10 – (2 × 6 – 3) = 1

Total degree of static indeterminacy = D_{si} = $(D_{si})_e$ + $(D_{si})_i$ = 0 + 1 = 1

Step II : Selection of redundant force (Q) :

Let,   Q = Force in member BE (Tensile)

Step III : Basic determinate truss : Member BE is cut and determinate truss is obtained as shown in Fig. 3.11 (b).

Step IV : Superposition : The given indeterminate truss is considered as superposition of (a) basic determinate truss with given loads [Fig. 3.11 (b)] and (b) unknown redundant force 'Q' times the basic determinate truss with unit positive redundant force. [Fig. 3.11 (c)].

Step V : P-analysis of basic determinate truss due to applied loads : Considering static equilibrium of truss all the reaction components (R_p) are found out as shown in Fig. 3.11 (b). Also the forces (P) in all the members of truss are found out and are shown in Fig. 3.11 (b).

Step VI : K-analysis of basic determinate truss : Unit positive force corresponding to 'Q' is applied as shown in Fig. 3.11 (c).

Forces (K) in all the members of truss are found out and are shown in Fig. 3.11 (c). Reaction components (R_k) are zero for this analysis.

Step VII : Table for numerical computation :

Sr. No.	Member	Length (mm)	Area (mm²)	P (kN)	K	$\frac{PKL}{A}$	$\frac{K^2L}{A}$	Q (kN)	QK (kN)	P_f = P + QK (kN)
1.	AB	3000	2000	800/9	0	0	0		0	88.89
2.	BC	3000	2000	800/9	–0.8	–106.67	0.96		11.1	100
3.	CD	3000	2000	1000/9	0	0	0		0	111.1
4.	EF	3000	2000	–1000/9	–0.8	133.33	0.96		11.1	–100
5.	BF	2250	2400	0	–0.6	0	0.34	–13.88	8.33	8.33
6.	CE	2250	2400	–150/9	–0.6	9.375	0.34		8.33	–8.33
7.	AF	3750	3000	–1000/9	0	0	0		0	–111.1
8.	DE	3750	3000	–1250/9	0	0	0		0	–138.89
9.	CF	3750	1500	250/9	1	69.44	2.5		–13.88	13.88
10.	BE	3750	1500	0	1	0	2.5		–13.88	–13.88
					Σ =	105.475	7.6			

Step VIII : Calculation of redundant force :

$$Q = -\left[\dfrac{\sum_{i=1}^{n}\left(\dfrac{PKL}{EA}\right)_i}{\sum_{i=1}^{n}\left(\dfrac{K^2 L}{EA}\right)_i}\right] = -\left[\dfrac{\sum\left(\dfrac{PKL}{A}\right)}{\sum\left(\dfrac{K^2 L}{A}\right)}\right] = -\left(\dfrac{105.475}{7.6}\right)$$

$$= -13.88 \text{ kN} = 13.88 \text{ kN (Compressive)}$$

Step IX : Final forces in all the members of truss (P_f) :

Using the equation,

$$P_f = P + QK$$

final forces in all the members of truss are computed and are as tabulated above and shown in Fig. 3.11 (d).

Step X : Final reaction components at supports (R) :

Using the equation,

$$Q = R_p + Q \cdot R_k$$

final reaction components at supports are computed and are as shown in Fig. 3.11 (d).

3.2.6 Indeterminate Trusses with Lack of Fit

The trusses are fabricated with the specific amount of tolerance in the length of members so that the members fit perfectly. But there may be errors in the fabrication, the length of a member of a truss may be slightly more or less than that required for the perfect assembly of members to form the truss. This is called the lack of fit due to the fabrication error.

The fabrication of a determinate truss with lack of fit can be accommodate this error and adjust itself without stressing. Whereas in an internally indeterminate truss, a member having fabrication error does not fit in well and the truss does not adjust the discrepancy. The member is to be forced for the right fit and the forces are developed in the members of the truss due to this lack of fit, before the external loading. Therefore, it is necessary to analyse indeterminate trusses for the effect of lack of fit independently. The forces in the members of the truss due to (i) lack of fit and (ii) external loads are then superposed to get the final forces.

Analysis of indeterminate trusses having lack of fit is effectively done by the force method with the following additional concepts :

(i) The member which has lack of fit should be selected as the redundant member.

(ii) The known lack of fit of the redundant member is denoted by D_{QF}.

(iii) The sign convention for D_{QF} is important which is as follows :

D_{QF} is positive if the member is too long.

D_{QF} is negative if the member is too short.

(iv) The equation of the force method is used in the following form

$$D_Q = D_{QF} + F \cdot Q$$

$$0 = D_{QF} + \Sigma \left(\frac{K^2 L}{EA}\right) \cdot Q$$

$$\therefore \quad Q = -\left[\frac{D_{QF}}{\sum_{i=1}^{n} \left(\frac{K^2 L}{EA}\right)_i}\right] \quad \ldots (3.9)$$

Following Examples illustrate the procedure. Note that the numerical values of member properties and material properties are required.

Example 3.9 : *Analyse the truss supported as shown in Fig. 3.12 (a), if member AB is short by 5 mm. Take E = 200 GPa. Cross-sectional area of each member in cm² is indicated in brackets.*

Solution : Data :

(1) Truss is supported as shown in Fig. 3.12 (a).

(2) E = 200 GPa.

Objects :

(1) Redundant force,

(2) Forces in all the members of truss and

(3) Reactions at supports.

Concepts and Equations :

(1) Analysis of determinate truss,

(2) Compatibility condition and

(3) $Q = -\left[\dfrac{D_{QF}}{\sum_{i=1}^{n} \left(\frac{K^2 L}{EA}\right)_i}\right]$

Procedure :

Step I : Degree of static indeterminacy (D_{si}) :

(a) Degree of external indeterminacy = $(D_{si})_e$ = $r - 3$ = $4 - 3$ = 1

(b) Degree of internal indeterminacy = $(D_{si})_i$ = $m - (2j - 3)$ = $6 - (2 \times 4 - 3)$ = 1

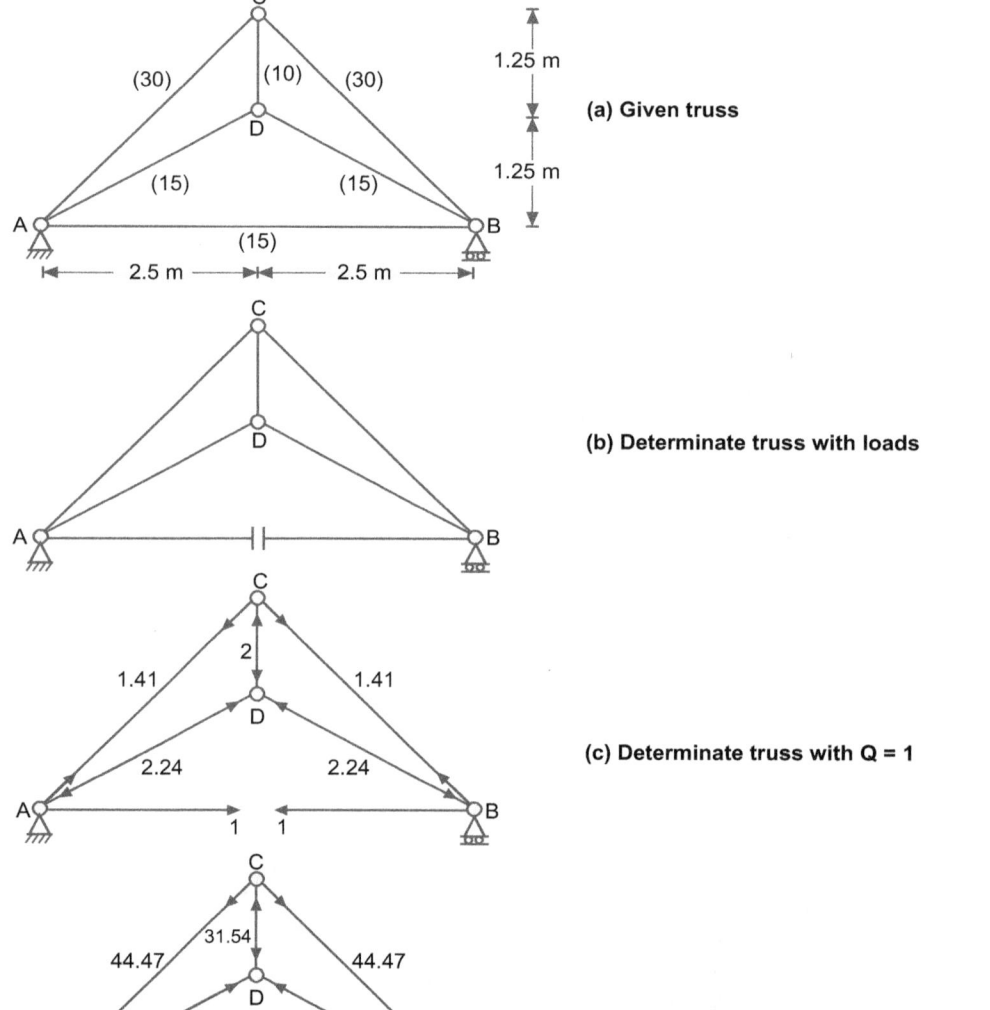

Fig. 3.12 : Illustrative Example 3.9

Step II : Selection of redundant force (Q) :

Let,   Q = Force in member AB (Tensile)

Step III : Basic determinate truss :

Member AB is cut and determinate truss is obtained as shown in Fig. 3.12 (b).

Step IV : K-analysis of basic determinate truss :

Unit positive force corresponding to 'Q' is applied as shown in Fig. 3.12 (c). Reaction components (R_k) are zero for this analysis. Forces (K) in all the members of truss are found out and are shown in Fig. 3.12 (c).

Step V : Table for numerical computation :

Sr. No.	Member	Length (mm)	Area (mm²)	K	$\frac{K^2L}{A}$	Q (kN)	$P_f = QK$ (kN)
1.	AD	2795	1500	− 2.24	9.35		− 70.65
2.	BD	2795	1500	− 2.24	9.35		− 70.65
3.	AC	3535	3000	1.41	2.34	31.54	44.47
4.	BC	3535	3000	1.41	2.34		44.47
5.	CD	1250	1000	− 2	5.00		− 63.08
6.	AB	5000	1500	1	3.33		31.54
				Σ =	31.71		

Step VI : Calculation of redundant force :

$$Q = -\left[\frac{D_{QF}}{\sum_{i=1}^{n}\left(\frac{K^2L}{EA}\right)_i}\right]$$

$$= -\left(\frac{-5}{\frac{31.71}{200}}\right) = 31.54 \text{ kN (Tensile)}$$

Step VII : Final forces in all the members of truss (P_f) :

Using the equation,

$$P_f = QK$$

final forces in all the members of truss are computed and are as tabulated above and shown in Fig. 3.12 (d).

STRUCTURAL ANALYSIS – II FLEXIBILITY METHOD

Step VIII : Final reaction components at supports (R) : Reaction components at supports are zero.

Example 3.10 : *Analyse the truss supported as shown in Fig. 3.13 (a), if member AC is long by 7 mm. Take E = 200 GPa and cross-sectional area of each member = 350 mm².*

Solution : Data :
(1) Truss is supported and loaded as shown in Fig. 3.13 (a).
(2) E = 200 GPa.

Objects :
(1) Redundant force (2) Forces in all the members of truss and
(3) Reactions at supports.

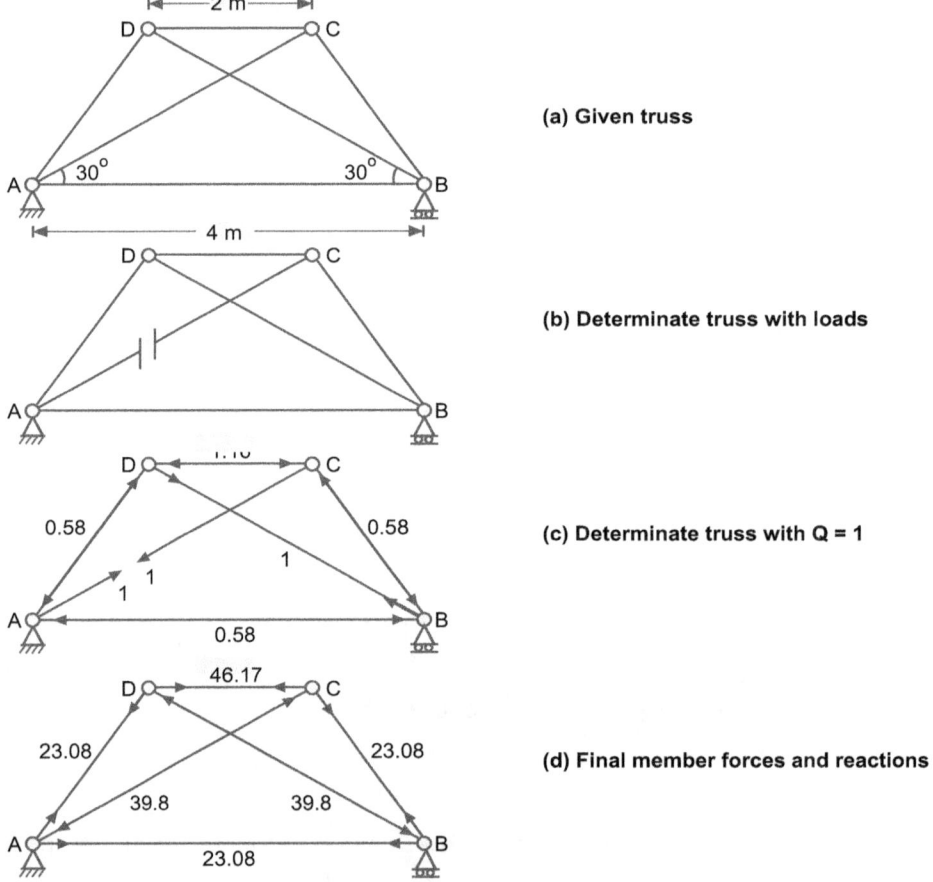

Fig. 3.13 : Illustrative Example 3.10

Concepts and Equations :
(1) Analysis of determinate truss,
(2) Compatibility condition and
(3) $Q = -\left[\dfrac{D_{QF}}{\sum\limits_{i=1}^{n}\left(\dfrac{K^2 L}{EA}\right)_i}\right]$

Procedure :
Step I : Degree of static indeterminacy (D_{si}) :
(a) Degree of external indeterminacy = $(D_{si})_e$ = r − 3 = 4 − 3 = 1
(b) Degree of internal indeterminacy = $(D_{si})_i$ = m − (2j − 3) = 6 − (2 × 4 − 3) = 1

Step II : Selection of redundant force (Q) :
Let,   Q = Force in member AC (Tensile)

Step III : Basic determinate truss :
Member AC is cut and determinate truss is obtained as shown in Fig. 3.13 (b).

Step IV : K-analysis of basic determinate truss : Unit positive force corresponding to 'Q' is applied as shown in Fig. 3.13 (c). Reaction components (R_k) are zero for this analysis. Forces (K) in all the members of truss are found out and are shown in Fig. 3.13 (c).

Step V : Table for numerical computation :

Sr. No.	Member	Length (m)	K	K²L	Q (kN)	P_f = KQ (kN)
1.	AB	4	− 0.58	1.345		23.08
2.	BC	2	− 0.58	0.673		23.08
3.	CD	2	− 1.16	2.691	− 39.80	46.17
4.	DA	2	− 0.58	0.673		23.08
5.	BD	3.464	1	3.464		− 39.80
6.	AC	3.464	1	3.464		− 39.80
				Σ = 12.31		

Step VI : Calculation of redundant force :

$$Q = -\left[\dfrac{D_{QF}}{\sum\limits_{i=1}^{n}\left(\dfrac{K^2 L}{EA}\right)_i}\right] = -\left[\dfrac{7}{12.31 \times \dfrac{1000}{200} \times 350}\right]$$

= − 39.80 kN = 39.80 kN (Compressive)

Step VII : Final forces in all the members of truss (P_f) :
Using the equation
$$P_f = QK$$
final forces in all the members of truss are computed and are as tabulated above and shown in Fig. 3.13 (d).

Step VIII : Final reaction components at supports (R) :
Reaction components at supports are zero.

3.2.7 Temperature Effects in Indeterminate Trusses

The rise in temperature causes the increase in length of a member and the fall in temperature causes the decrease in length of a member if the member is free to expand or contract. This is called free thermal change in the length and given by (αtL) where α is the coefficient of linear expansion of the material, t is the change in temperature and L is the length of the member. If the free thermal expansion or contraction is prevented, then the stresses are developed. This is in general the effect of temperature.

In this context the following hints will be useful to consider the effects of temperature in trusses.

(i) In a statically determinate structure no internal forces are developed due to temperature changes as the thermal expansions or contractions are not prevented.

(ii) Due to uniform temperature variation in an externally determinate structure, no internal forces are induced.

(iii) Due to non-uniform temperature changes in an externally determinate structure, the internal forces are developed.

(iv) In an externally indeterminate structure there are always temperature effects irrespective of uniform or non-uniform temperature variations.

The forces in members of a truss due to temperature effects are obtained by the force method with the following techniques and for the following common situations.

(A) Externally and internally indeterminate truss :

Subjected to the temperature change in a particular member :

- The temperature-affected member is selected as the redundant member.
- The force in the redundant member is Q.
- Free thermal change in the redundant member is calculated as (αtL) and denoted by D_{Qt}.
- D_{Qt} is positive if expansion i.e. rise in temperature and D_{Qt} is negative if contraction i.e. fall in temperature.
- The usual procedure of the force method is used to find Q and the member forces.
- The basic equation is modified as

$$D_Q = D_{Qt} + F \cdot Q$$

$$\therefore \quad 0 = (\alpha tL) + \sum \left(\frac{K^2 L}{EA}\right) \cdot Q$$

$$\therefore \quad Q = -\left[\frac{\alpha tL}{\sum \left(\frac{K^2 L}{EA}\right)}\right] \qquad \ldots (3.10)$$

STRUCTURAL ANALYSIS – II FLEXIBILITY METHOD

(B) Externally indeterminate truss subjected to the uniform temperature change :

- The reaction component in the direction of axis of member connecting two supports is selected as the redundant force Q.
- Free thermal expansion / contraction in the complete length of the member connecting the supports is calculated as (αtL) and denoted by D_{Qt}.
- It is to be noted that this D_{Qt} corresponds to Q.

$$Q = -\left[\frac{(\alpha tL)}{\sum_{i=1}^{n}\left(\frac{K^2L}{EA}\right)_i}\right]$$

Following illustrative examples will clarify the procedure in detail.

Example 3.11 : *Analyse the truss supported as shown in Fig. 3.14 (a), if member AD is subjected to temperature drop of 30°C. Take E = 200 GPa and coefficient of thermal expansion = α = 1.1 ×10^{-5} /°C, cross-sectional area of each member in cm² is indicated in brackets.*

Solution : Data :
(1) Truss is supported and loaded as shown in Fig. 3.14 (a).
(2) E = 200 GPa.
(3) α = 1.1 × 10^{-5} /°C.

Objects :
(1) Redundant force
(2) Forces in all the members of truss and
(3) Reactions of supports :

Concepts and Equations :
(1) Analysis of determinate truss,
(2) Compatibility condition and

(3) $Q = -\left[\dfrac{D_{Qt}}{\sum_{i=1}^{n}\left(\dfrac{K^2L}{EA}\right)_i}\right]$

Procedure :

Step I : Degree of static indeterminacy (D_{si}) :

(a) Degree of external indeterminacy $(D_{si})_e$ = r – 3 = 4 – 3 = 1
(b) Degree of internal indeterminacy $(D_{si})_i$ = m – (2j – 3) = 6 – (2 × 4 – 3) = 1

STRUCTURAL ANALYSIS – II FLEXIBILITY METHOD

Step II : Selection of redundant force (Q) :

Let, $\quad Q$ = Force in member AD (Tensile)

Step III : Basic determinate truss :

Member AD is cut and determinate truss is obtained as shown in Fig. 3.14 (b).

Step IV : K-analysis of basic determinate truss : Unit positive force corresponding to 'Q' is applied as shown in Fig. 3.14 (c). Reaction components (R_k) are zero for this analysis, forces (K) in all the members of truss are found out and are shown in Fig. 3.14 (c).

Step V : Table for numerical computations :

Sr. No.	Member	Length (mm)	Area (mm²)	K	$\frac{K^2 L}{A}$	Q (kN)	$P_f = QK$ (kN)
1.	AB	4000	2000	1.33	3.56		11.84
2.	BC	3000	1500	1	2		8.90
3.	CD	4000	2000	1.33	3.56	8.90	11.84
4.	AC	5000	2500	– 1.67	5.56		– 14.86
5.	BD	5000	2500	– 1.67	5.56		– 14.86
6.	AD	3000	1500	1	2		8.90
				Σ =	22.24		

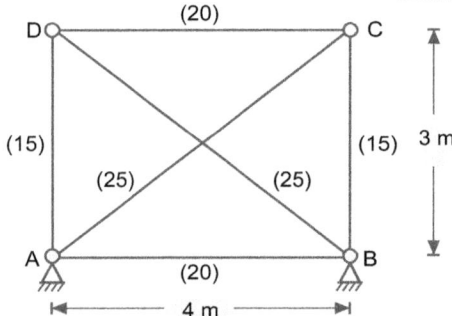

(a) Given truss

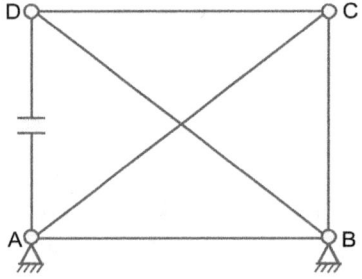

(b) Determinate truss with loads

Ch. 3 | 3.44

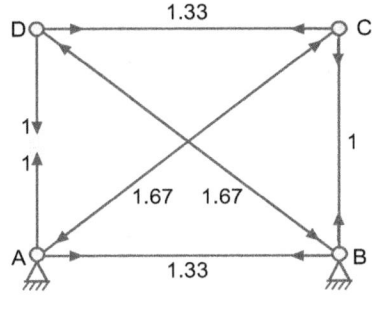

(c) Determinate truss with Q = 1

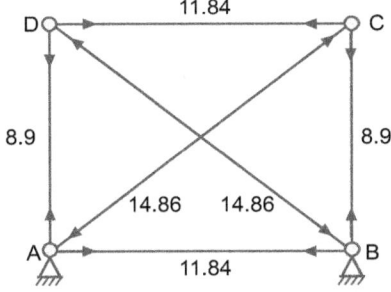

(d) Final member forces and reactions

Fig. 3.14 : Illustrative Example 3.11

Step VI : Calculation of redundant force :

$$Q = -\left[\frac{D_{Qt}}{\sum_{i=1}^{n}\left(\frac{K^2L}{EA}\right)_i}\right] = -\left[\frac{\alpha t L}{\sum K^2 L / EA}\right]$$

$$= -\left[\frac{-1.1 \times 10^{-5} \times 30 \times 3000}{22.24/200}\right] = 8.90 \text{ kN (Tensile)}$$

Step VII : Final forces in all the members of truss (P_f) :

Using the equation

$$P_f = QK$$

final forces in all the members of truss are computed and are as tabulated above and shown in Fig. 3.14 (d).

Step VIII : Final reaction components at supports (R) : Reaction components at supports are zero.

STRUCTURAL ANALYSIS – II FLEXIBILITY METHOD

Example 3.12 : *Analyse the truss supported as shown in Fig. 3.15 (a), if the member AC is subjected to temperature rise of 20ºC. Take E = 200 GPa and coefficient of thermal expansion = α = 1.2 × 10⁻⁵/ºC, cross-sectional area of each member in cm² is indicated in brackets.*

Solution : Data :

(1) Truss is supported and loaded as shown in Fig. 3.15 (a).

(2) E = 200 GPa,

(3) $\alpha = 1.2 \times 10^{-5}$/ ºC.

Objects :

(1) Redundant force,

(2) Forces in all the members of truss and

(3) Reactions at supports.

Concepts and Equations :

(1) Analysis of determinate truss,

(2) Compatibility condition and

(3) $Q = -\left[\dfrac{D_{Qt}}{\sum\limits_{i=1}^{n} \left(\dfrac{K^2 L}{EA}\right)_i} \right]$

Procedure :

Step I : Degree of static indeterminacy (D_{si}) :

(a) Degree of external indeterminacy = $(D_{si})_e$ = r – 3 = 4 – 3 = 1

(b) Degree of internal indeterminacy = $(D_{si})_i$ = m – (2j – 3) = 6 – (2 × 4 – 3) = 1

Step II : Selection of redundant force (Q) :

Let,   Q = Force in member AC (Tensile)

Step III : Basic determinate truss : Member AC is cut and determinate truss is obtained as shown in Fig. 3.15 (b).

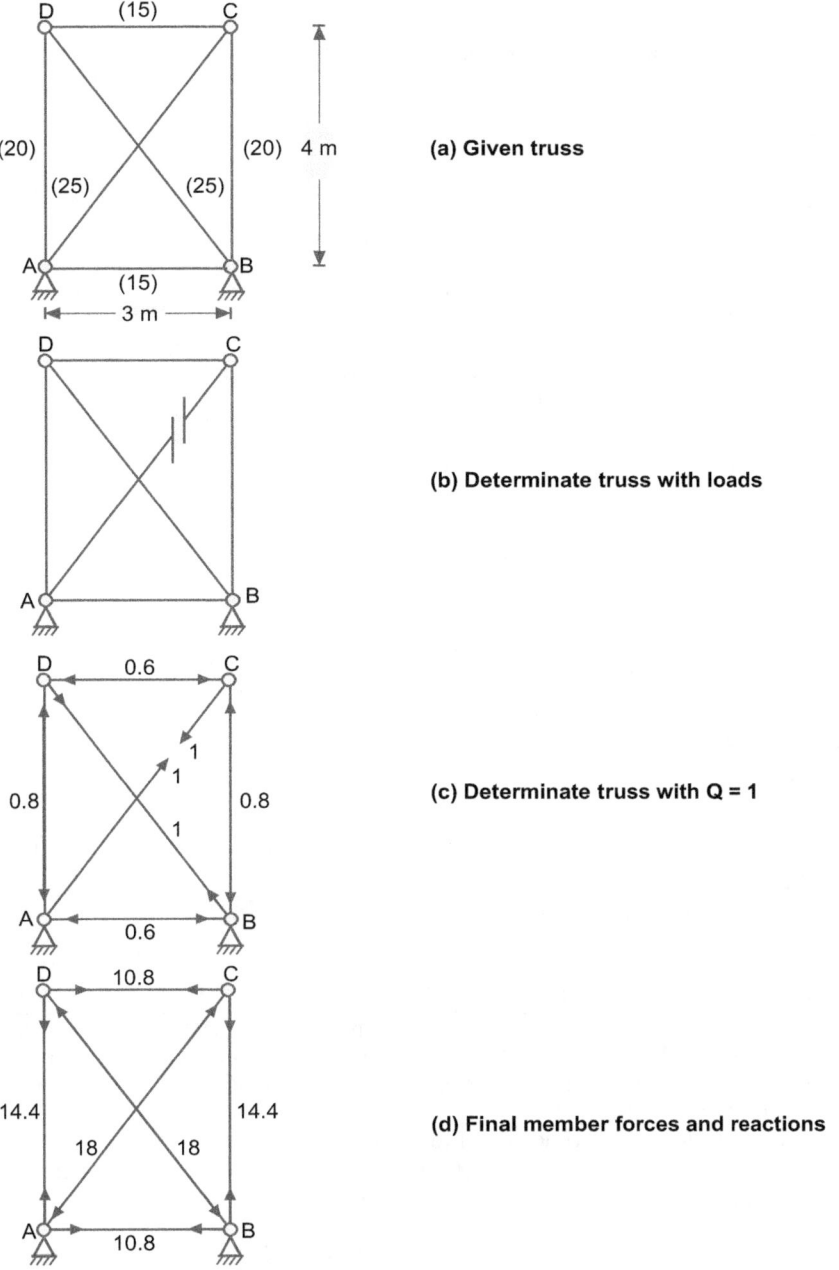

Fig. 3.15 : Illustrative Example 3.12

STRUCTURAL ANALYSIS – II   FLEXIBILITY METHOD

Step IV : K-analysis of basic determinate truss : Unit positive force corresponding to 'Q' is applied as shown in Fig. 3.15 (c). Reaction components (R_k) are zero for this analysis. Force (K) in all the members of truss are found out and are shown in Fig. 3.15 (c).

Step V : Table for numerical computation :

Sr. No.	Member	Length (mm)	Area (mm²)	K	$\frac{K^2L}{A}$	Q (kN)	$P_f = QK$ (kN)
1.	AB	3000	1500	– 0.6	0.72		10.8
2.	BC	4000	2000	– 0.8	1.28		14.4
3.	CD	3000	1500	– 0.6	0.72	– 18	10.8
4.	DA	4000	2000	– 0.8	1.28		14.4
5.	BD	5000	2500	1	2		– 18
6.	AC	5000	2500	1	2		– 18
				Σ =	8		

Step VI : Calculation of redundant force :

$$Q = -\left[\frac{D_{Qt}}{\sum_{i=1}^{n}\left(\frac{K^2L}{EA}\right)_i}\right] = -\left[\frac{\alpha tL}{\sum K^2L / EA}\right]$$

$$= -\left[\frac{1.2 \times 10^{-5} \times 20 \times 3000}{8/200}\right] = -18 \text{ kN}$$

$$= 18 \text{ kN (Compressive)}$$

Step VII : Final forces in all the members of truss (P_f) :

Using the equation,

$$P_f = QK$$

final forces in all the members of truss are computed and are as tabulated above and shown in Fig. 3.15 (d).

Step VIII : Final reaction components at supports (R) :

Reaction components at supports are zero.

3.2.8 Effects of Yielding of Support in Indeterminate Trusses

The yielding of the support of externally indeterminate truss induces the internal forces in the members of truss. The conventional procedure of the force method is used to analyse the externally indeterminate trusses for the effect of the yielding of the support employing the following particular techniques.

- Force corresponding to yielding of support must be selected as the redundant.
- Basic determinate truss is obtained by removing the constraint corresponding to yielding of support. The redundant force is the reaction component corresponding to the yielding.
- The geometrical condition of deformation at the yielding support is that D_Q should be equal to the amount of yielding.

STRUCTURAL ANALYSIS – II   FLEXIBILITY METHOD

- The basic equation of the force method in the following form is applied to determine the redundant force i.e. the reaction component due to the effect of yielding of support only.

$$D_Q = F \cdot Q$$

$$\therefore \quad D_Q = \Sigma \left(\frac{K^2 L}{EA}\right) \cdot Q$$

$$\therefore \quad Q = \left[\frac{D_Q}{\sum_{i=1}^{n} \left(\frac{K^2 L}{EA}\right)_i}\right] \quad \ldots (3.9)$$

where D_Q is the known amount of the yielding of the support i.e. known translation. Generally it is the settlement of support.

- D_Q is considered a positive or negative according to the co-ordinate system i.e. positive in the positive direction of the co-ordinate axes and negative in the negative direction of the co-ordinate axes.

The following example illustrates the procedure for this case.

Example 3.13 : *Analyse the truss supported as shown in Fig. 3.16 (a), if support B sinks by 3 mm. Take E = 210 GPa and cross-sectional area of each member = 400 mm².*

Solution : Data :
(1) Truss is supported and loaded as shown in Fig. 3.16 (a).
(2) E = 210 GPa.

Objects :
(1) Redundant force,   (2) Forces in all the members of truss and
(3) Reactions at supports.

Concepts and Equations :
(1) Analysis of determinate truss, (2) Compatibility condition and

(3) $Q = \left[\dfrac{D_Q}{\sum_{i=1}^{n} \left(\frac{K^2 L}{EA}\right)_i}\right]$

Procedure :

Step I : Degree of static indeterminacy (D_{si}) :
(a) Degree of external indeterminacy = $(D_{si})_e$ = r – 3 = 4 – 3 = 1
(b) Degree of internal indeterminacy = $(D_{si})_i$ = m – (2j – 3) = 9 – (2 × 6 – 3) = 0
    Total degree of static indeterminacy = D_{si} = $(D_{si})_e$ + $(D_{si})_i$ = 1 + 0 = 1

Step II : Selection of redundant force (Q) :
Let,   Q = V_B (↑)

Step III : Basic determinate truss : Roller support at B is removed and determinate truss is obtained as shown in Fig. 3.16 (b).

Step IV : K-analysis of basic determinate truss : Unit positive force corresponding to 'Q' is applied as shown in Fig. 3.16 (c). Reaction components (R_k) and forces (K) in all the members of truss are found out and are shown in Fig. 3.16 (c).

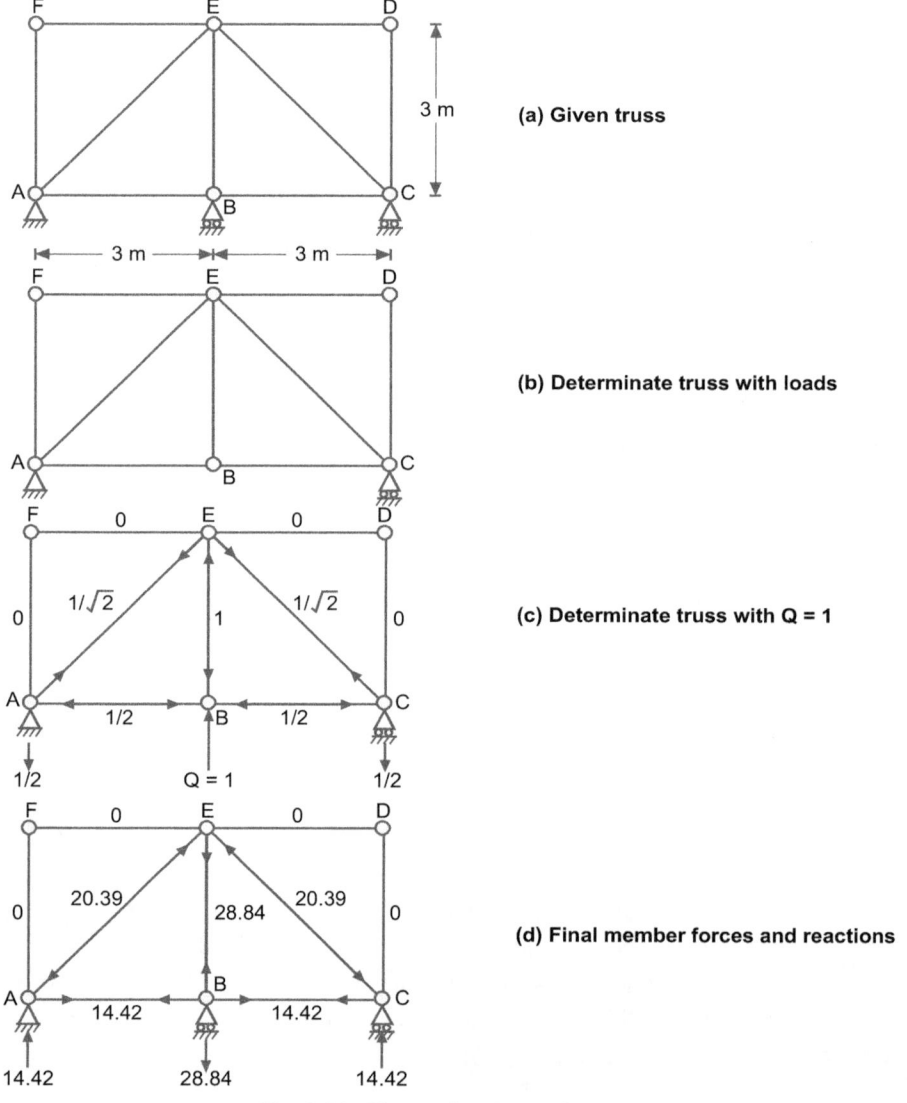

Fig. 3.16 : Illustrative Example 3.13

STRUCTURAL ANALYSIS – II   FLEXIBILITY METHOD

Step V : Table for numerical computation :

Sr. No.	Member	Length (m)	K	K²L	Q (kN)	P_f = KQ (kN)
1.	AB	3	–1/2	0.75		14.42
2.	BC	3	–1/2	0.75		14.42
3.	CD	3	0	0		0
4.	DE	3	0	0	–28.84	0
5.	EF	3	0	0		0
6.	FA	3	0	0		0
7.	EB	3	–1	3		28.84
8.	AE	$3\sqrt{2}$	$1/\sqrt{2}$	$3/\sqrt{2}$		–20.39
9.	CE	$3\sqrt{2}$	$1/\sqrt{2}$	$3/\sqrt{2}$		–20.39
			Σ =	8.74		

Step VI : Calculation of redundant force :

$$Q = \left[\frac{D_Q}{\sum_{i=1}^{n}\left(\frac{K^2 L}{EA}\right)_i}\right]$$

$$= \left[\frac{-3}{8.74 \times 1000/(210 \times 400)}\right] = -28.84 \text{ kN}$$

Step VII : Final forces in all the members of truss (P_f) :

Using the equation

$$P_f = QK$$

final forces in all the members of truss are computed and are as tabulated above and shown in Fig. 3.16 (d).

Step VIII : Final reaction components at supports (R) :

Using the equation

$$R = Q \cdot R_k$$

final reaction components at supports are computed and are as shown in Fig. 3.16 (d).

Example 3.14 : *Analyse the truss supported and loaded as shown in Fig. 3.17 (a). If support B sinks by 3 mm. Take E = 210 GPa and cross-sectional area of each member = 400 mm².*

Solution : Data :
(1) Truss is supported and loaded as shown in Fig. 3.17 (a).
(2) E = 210 GPa

Objects :
(1) Redundant force,   (2) Forces in all the members of truss and
(3) Reactions at supports.

STRUCTURAL ANALYSIS – II FLEXIBILITY METHOD

Concepts and Equations :

(1) Principle of superposition, (2) Analysis of determinate truss,
(3) Compatibility condition and (4) $D_Q = D_{QL} + FQ$

Procedure :

Step I : Degree of static indeterminacy (D_{si}) :

(a) Degree of external indeterminacy = $(D_{si})_e$ = $r - 3$ = $4 - 3$ = 1

(b) Degree of internal indeterminacy = $(D_{si})_i$ = $m - (2j - 3)$ = $9 - (2 \times 6 - 3)$ = 0

Total degree of static indeterminacy = $(D_{si})_e + (D_{si})_i$ = $1 + 0 = 1$

Step II : Selection of redundant force (Q) :

Let, $Q = V_B\ (\uparrow)$

Step III : Basic determinate truss :

Roller support at B is removed and determinate truss is obtained as shown in Fig. 3.17 (b).

Step IV : Superposition : The given indeterminate truss is considered as superposition of (a) basic determinate truss with given loads [Fig. 3.17 (b)] and (b) unknown redundant force 'Q' times the basic determinate truss with unit positive redundant force (Fig. 3.17 (c)).

Step V : P-analysis of basic determinate truss due to applied loads : Considering static equilibrium of truss all the reaction components (R_p) are found out as shown in Fig. 3.17 (b). Also the forces (P) in all the members of truss are found out and are shown in Fig. 3.17 (b).

Step VI : K-analysis of basic determinate truss : Unit positive force corresponding to 'Q' is applied as shown in Fig. 3.17 (c). All the reaction components (R_k) and forces (K) in all the members of truss are found out and are shown in Fig. 3.17 (c).

Step VII : Table for numerical computation :

Sr. No.	Member	Length (m)	P (kN)	K	PKL	K²L	Q (kN)	QK (kN)	$P_f = P + QK$ (kN)
1.	AB	3	47.5	– 1/2	– 71.25	0.75		– 11.93	35.57
2.	BC	3	47.5	– 1/2	– 71.25	0.75		– 11.93	35.57
3.	CD	3	0	0	0	0		0	0
4.	DE	3	0	0	0	0	23.85	0	0
5.	EF	3	– 20	0	0	0		0	– 20
6.	FA	3	0	0	0	0		0	0
7.	EB	3	0	– 1	0	3		– 23.85	– 23.85
8.	AE	$3\sqrt{2}$	$-27.5\sqrt{2}$	$1/\sqrt{2}$	$-82.5\sqrt{2}$	$3/\sqrt{2}$		16.86	– 22.03
9.	CE	$3\sqrt{2}$	$-47.5\sqrt{2}$	$1/\sqrt{2}$	$-142.5\sqrt{2}$	$3/\sqrt{2}$		16.86	– 50.32
				Σ =	– 460.69	8.74			

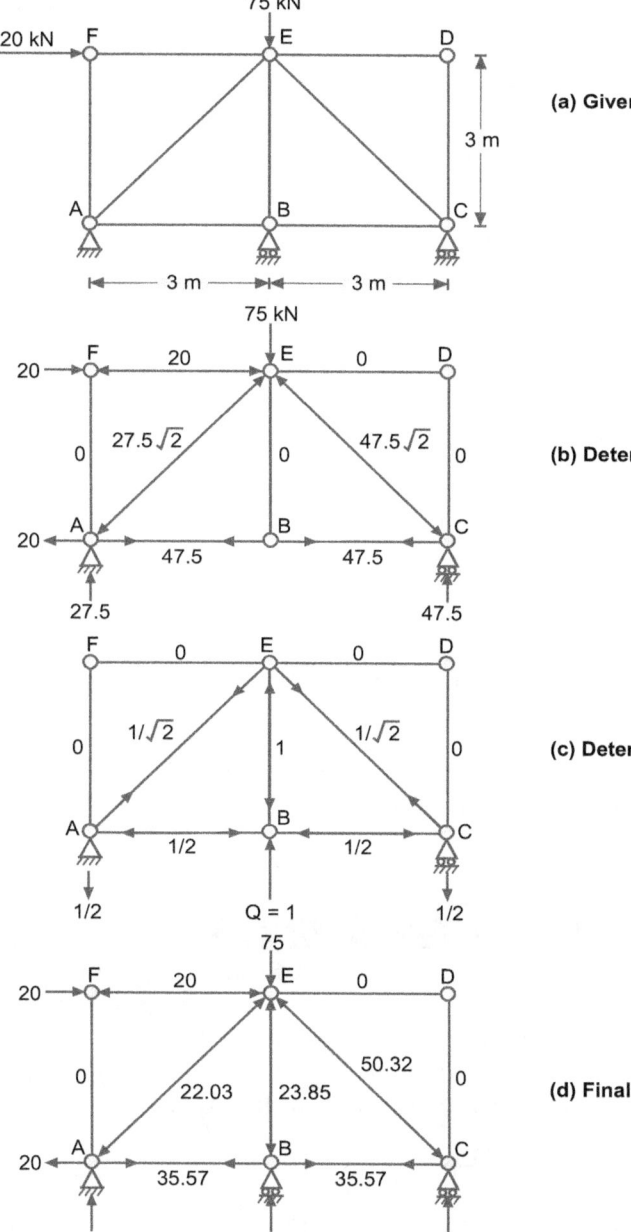

Fig. 3.17 : Illustrative Example 3.14

Step VIII : Physical requirement of displacement (D_Q) : Vertical translation at B in the given structure = 3 mm (↓) ∴ D_Q = – 3 mm.

Step IX : Calculation of redundant force :

$$D_Q = D_{QL} + FQ$$

where, $\quad D_Q = -3$ mm

$$D_{QL} = \sum_{i=1}^{n} \left(\frac{PKL}{EA}\right)_i = \frac{-460.69 \times 1000}{210 \times 400} = -5.48 \text{ mm}$$

$$F = \sum_{i=1}^{n} \left(\frac{K^2 L}{EA}\right)_i = \frac{8.74 \times 1000}{210 \times 400} = 0.104 \text{ mm/kN}$$

Substituting in above equation, we get,

$$Q = 23.85 \text{ kN} (↑)$$

Step X : Final forces in all the members of truss (P_f) :

Using the equation, $\quad P_f = P + QK$

final forces in all the members of truss are computed and are as tabulated above and shown in Fig. 3.17 (d).

Step XI : Final reaction components at supports (R) :

Using the equation, $\quad R = R_p + Q \cdot R_k$

final reaction components at supports are computed and are as shown in Fig. 3.17 (d).

Note : Similar results of above Example can also be obtained by superposition of results of Examples 3.1 and 3.13.

3.3 FLEXIBILITY METHOD APPLIED TO BEAMS AND FRAMES

The method, illustrated for simple problem, is extended to beams and frames in general using matrix formulation. The beams and single storeyed frames are generally indeterminate externally. Displacement analysis of basic determinate structure is the main concern. Unit load method is used to find displacements and forming {D_{QL}} and [F]. The displacement at co-ordinate i in a structure due to applied loads is obtained by the equation

$$D_{QLi} = \int \frac{M \cdot m_i \cdot dx}{EI} \qquad \ldots (3.12\text{ a})$$

where M is the bending moment at a section of the basic determinate structure due to applied loads, m_i is the bending moment at the section of the basic determinate structure due to unit positive force at co-ordinate i.

STRUCTURAL ANALYSIS – II   FLEXIBILITY METHOD

Integration is to be performed over the entire structure with due care of limits and validity of BM equation and origin. The displacement at co-ordinate i due to the unit force at co-ordinate i is the direct flexibility coefficient and given by the equation

$$F_{ii} = \int \frac{m_i \, m_i \, dx}{EI} = \int \frac{(m_i)^2 \, dx}{EI} \qquad \ldots (3.12 \text{ b})$$

The displacement at co-ordinate i, as the effect, due to the unit force at co-ordinate j, as the cause, is the indirect or cross flexibility coefficient and given by equation

$$F_{ij} = \int \frac{m_i \, m_j \, dx}{EI} \qquad \ldots (3.12 \text{ c})$$

$$F_{ij} = F_{ji} \text{ by reciprocal theorem.}$$

The remaining procedure is same. The complete method is illustrated with the examples having 1 to 3 unknown redundant forces.

Example 3.15 : *Analyse the beam shown in Fig. 3.18 (a) by force method. Take EI = constant.*

Solution : Data : The beam is supported and loaded as shown in Fig. 3.18 (a). The data includes the following information :

1. Structural configuration : Type and arrangement of members, joints and supports, dimensions.
2. Cross-sectional properties of members : moment of inertia about bending axis.
3. Material properties of members.
4. Applied loads : Member loads, joint loads - magnitude, direction, position.
5. Type of structure : beam.

Objects :

1. Unknown redundant forces as the initial target.
2. Analysis.

Assumptions :

1. Linear Elastic Analysis.
2. Axial deformations are neglected in beams.

Concepts and Equations :

1. Statically determinate structure (Released structure)
2. Displacement analysis of determinate structure.
3. Superposition equations or compatibility of displacements.

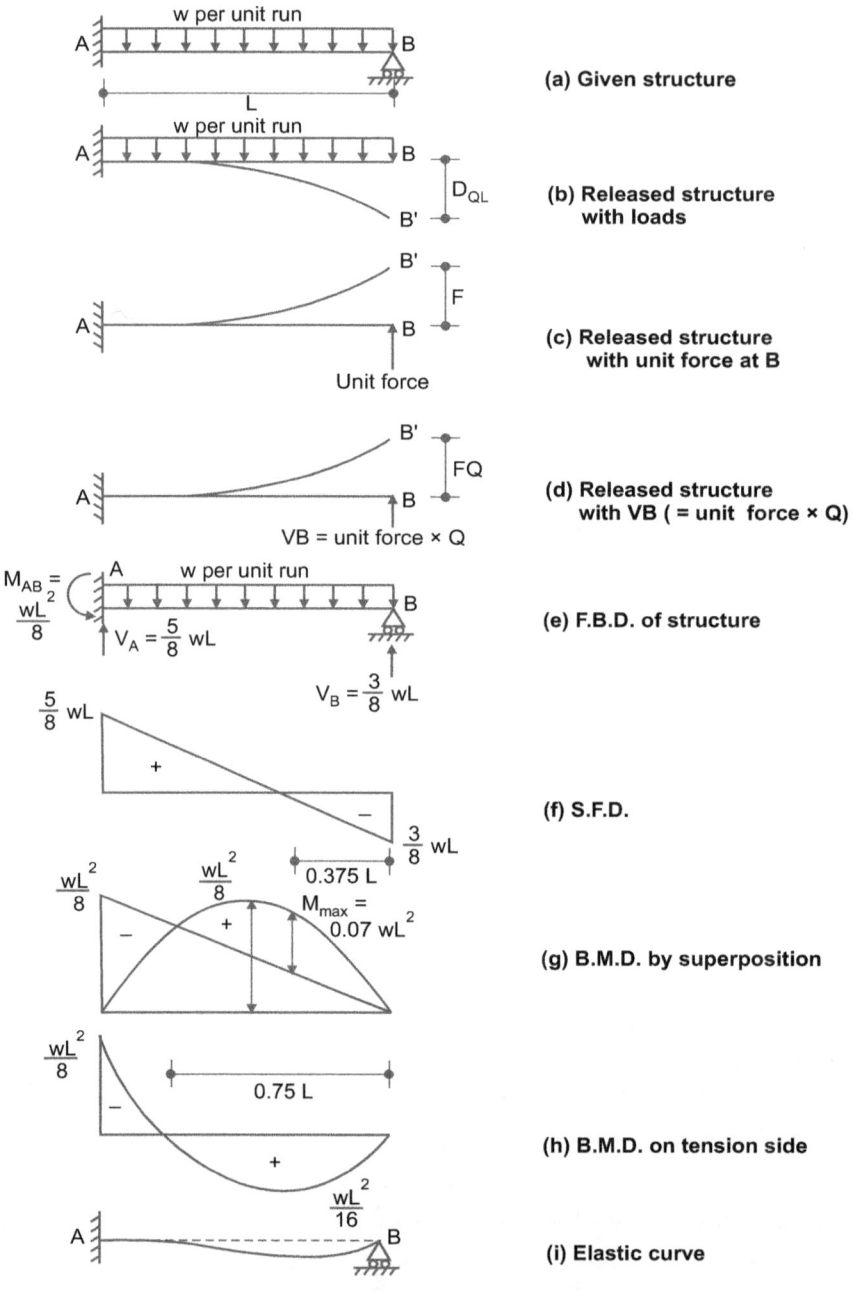

Fig. 3.18 : For Illustrative Example 3.15

STRUCTURAL ANALYSIS – IIFLEXIBILITY METHOD

Procedure :

Step I : The degree of static indeterminacy (D_{si})

(a) External indeterminacy : Total number of reaction components = 3 i.e. V_A, M_A, V_B.

Equations of equilibrium = 2 i.e. $\sum V = 0$, $\sum M = 0$.

∴ Degree of external static indeterminacy $(D_{si})_e = 3 - 2 = 1$.

(b) Internal indeterminacy - once reactions are known the internal forces i.e. SF and BM can be obtained statically.

∴ Degree of internal static indeterminacy = $(D_{si})_i = 0$.

(c) Total degree of static indeterminacy = $(D_{si}) = (D_{si})_e + (D_{si})_i = 1$.

Step II : Selection of unknown redundant force denoted by Q.

∴ $\quad Q = V_B (\uparrow)$ i.e. vertical reaction at B.

Step III : Released structure : The roller support at B is removed and statically determinate structure is obtained. Thus, the given indeterminate beam is considered as equivalent to the superposition of :

(a) Released structure under given loads, and

(b) Released structure under unit force at B and then under V_B as shown in Fig. 3.18 (b), Fig. 3.18 (c) and Fig. 3.18 (d).

Step IV : Displacement analysis of the released structure.

(a) Vertical translation i.e. deflection at B due to given loading is calculated. For this problem, the standard result is used to obtain the deflection at B. This is denoted by D_{QL}.

∴ $\quad Q_{QL} = -\dfrac{wL^4}{8\,EI}$ (downward)

(b) Deflection at B due to unit force at B is the flexibility denoted by F.

∴ $\quad F = \dfrac{L^3}{3\,EI}$

(c) Deflection at B due to the redundant force V_B. This is denoted by D_{QQ} and expressed in terms of F.

∴ $\quad D_{QQ} = FQ$

∴ $\quad D_{QQ} = +\left(\dfrac{L^3}{3\,EI}\right) V_B$ (upward)

STRUCTURAL ANALYSIS – II   FLEXIBILITY METHOD

Step V : The physical requirement of displacement :

In the given structure, the deflection at B must be zero because of support condition. This displacement is denoted by D_Q.

$$\therefore \quad D_Q = 0$$

Step VI : Superposition equation of compatibility of displacements :

$$\therefore \quad D_Q = D_{QL} + D_{QQ} = D_{QL} + FQ$$

$$\therefore \quad 0 = \frac{wL^4}{8EI} + \frac{V_B L^3}{3EI}$$

Step VII : Solution of equation for unknown redundant force

$$\therefore \quad V_B = +\frac{3}{8}(wL)$$

The positive result of V_B indicates that the direction of V_B corresponds to the direction of unit force.

Step VIII : Other reaction components.

For FBD of structure, the equations of equilibrium, $\sum M_A = 0$ and $\sum V = 0$, are applied and the results are obtained.

$$M_A = +\frac{wL^2}{8} \text{ and } V_A = \frac{5}{8}wL$$

FBD of structure is shown in Fig. 3.18 (e).

Step IX : Shear force and Bending moment diagrams :

(a) SFD is as shown in Fig. 3.18 (f).

(b) BMD is drawn by superposition technique. It is shown in Fig. 3.18 (g). BMD can also be drawn on tensile side as shown in Fig. 3.18 (h), however this requires additional ordinates to compute.

Step X : Elastic curve :

As per support conditions and nature of BMD, the deflected shape of the beam i.e. elastic curve is drawn qualitatively as shown in Fig. 3.18 (i).

Alternate Solution to the Simple Problem of Force Method

The choice of the redundant force is not unique, therefore, the solution is altered accordingly, however the procedure remains the same. For the problem in hand if the moment reaction at the support A is selected as the redundant force, the procedure of the solution proceeds through the following important steps :

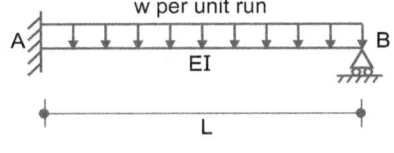

(a) Given structure

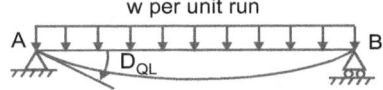

(b) Released structure with loads

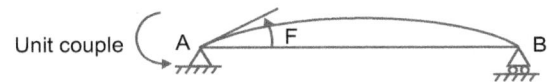

(c) Released structure with unit couple at A

(d) Released structure with M_{AB} (= unit force × Q)

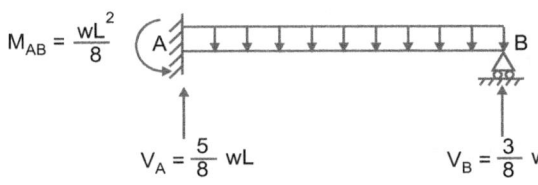

(e) F.B.D. of structure

Fig. 3.19 : Alternate Solution to Example 3.15

Step I : $D_{si} = 1$.

Step II : $Q = M_{AB}$ (↺)

Step III : Released structure – As shown in Fig. 3.19 (b), 3.19 (c) and 3.19 (d).

Step IV : $D_{QL} = -\dfrac{wL^3}{24\,EI}$.

$F = \dfrac{L^3}{3\,EI}$

Step V : $D_Q = \theta_A = 0$.

Step VI : ∴ $D_Q = D_{QL} + F \cdot Q$ i.e. $0 = -\dfrac{wL^3}{24\,EI} + \left(\dfrac{L^3}{3\,EI}\right) Q$

Step VII : $Q = M_{AB} = \dfrac{wL^2}{8}$ (↺)

Step VIII : Other reaction components : As shown in Fig. 3.19 (e).

STRUCTURAL ANALYSIS – II   FLEXIBILITY METHOD

Step IX :   Shear force and bending moment diagrams :

SFD is as shown in Fig. 3.19 (f). BMD by superposition and on tension side are as shown in Fig. 3.19 (g) and 3.18 (h) respectively.

Step X :   **Elastic curve :** As shown in Fig. 3.19 (i).

***Example 3.16** : Analyse the beam shown in Fig. 3.20 (a) by flexibility method. Take EI = constant. The stiffness coefficient of spring at B is as shown in figure.*

Solution : (1) Data : The beam is supported and loaded as shown in Fig. 3.20 (a).

(2) $K_B = (EI/2)$ kN/m.

Object : Structural analysis.

Concepts and Equations :

(1) Statically determinate structure (released structure).

(2) Displacement analysis of released structure.

(3) Superposition equations of compatibility of displacements.

Procedure :

Step I : The degree of static indeterminacy (D_{si}) :

(a) Degree of external static indeterminacy = $(D_{si})_e = 1$.

(b) Degree of internal static indeterminacy = $(D_{si})_i = 0$.

(c) Total degree of static indeterminacy = $D_{si} = (D_{si})_e + (D_{si})_i = 1 + 0 = 1$.

Step II : Selection of unknown redundant force (Q) :

Let, $Q_1 = V_B(\uparrow)$

Step III : Released structure : Elastic support at B is removed and basic released structure is as shown in Fig. 3.20 (b). Also released structure subjected to unit value of Q_1 is shown in Fig. 3.20 (c).

Step IV : Displacement analysis of released structure :

(a) Displacements in the released structure subjected to loads corresponding to redundant actions :

$$D_{QL1} = -\frac{wL^4}{8\,EI} = -\frac{10 \times 3^4}{8\,EI} = -\frac{101.25}{EI}$$

(b) Displacements in the released structure subjected to unit value of Q_1 corresponding to redundant actions :

$$F_{11} = \frac{(Q_1)L^3}{3\,EI} = \frac{3^3}{3\,EI} = \frac{9}{EI}$$

STRUCTURAL ANALYSIS – II   FLEXIBILITY METHOD

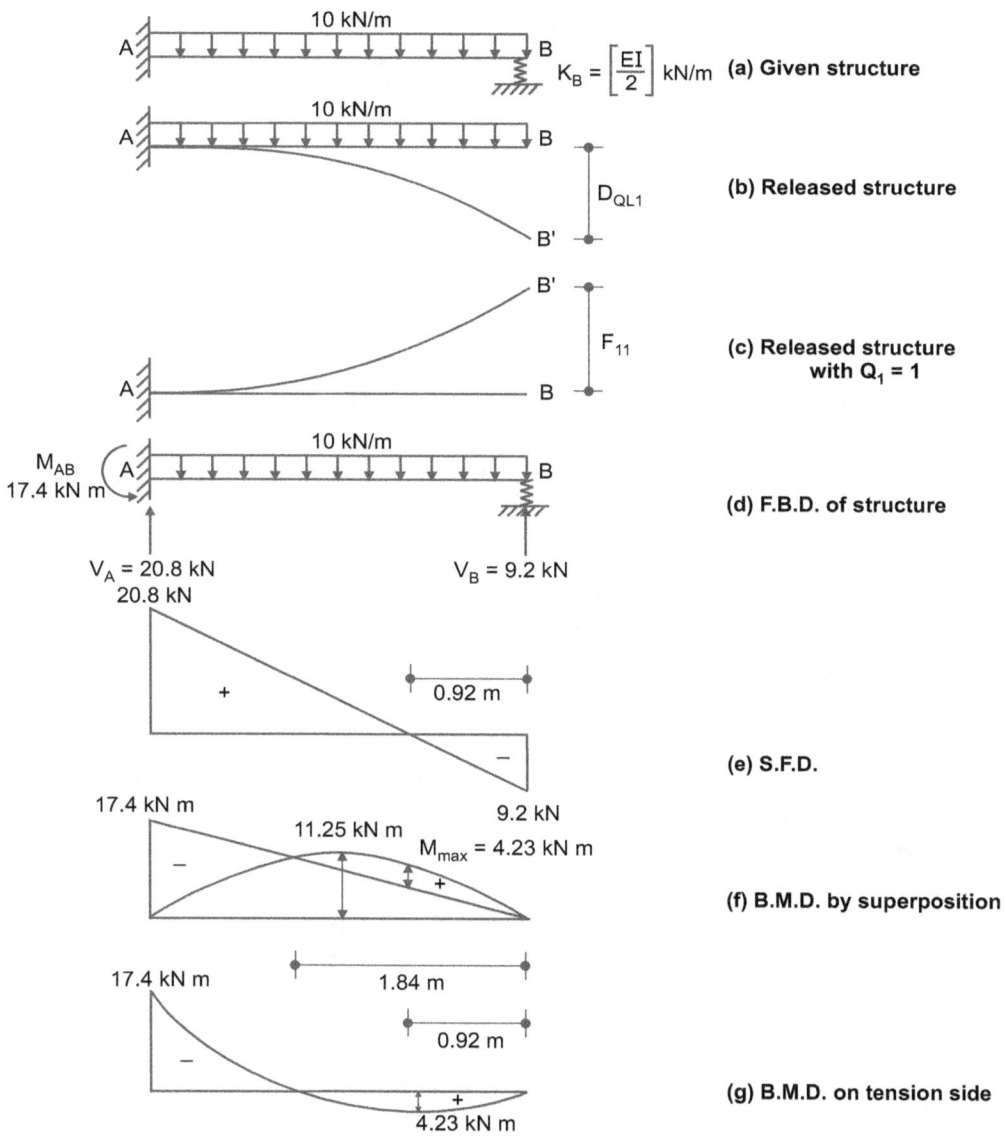

Fig. 3.20 : For Illustrative Example 3.16

Step V : The physical requirement of displacements : The flexibility coefficient of spring at $B = F_B = \dfrac{1}{K_B} = \dfrac{2}{EI}$ m/kN.

STRUCTURAL ANALYSIS – II   FLEXIBILITY METHOD

$\therefore$ Vertical translation at $B = D_{Q1} = \left(\dfrac{2}{EI}\right) Q_1 (\downarrow) = -\left(\dfrac{2}{EI}\right) Q_1$

Step VI : Superposition equation of compatibility of displacements :
$$\{D_Q\} = \{D_{QL}\} + [F] \cdot \{Q\}$$

where $[F] = \left[\dfrac{9}{EI}\right]$

Also, $\{D_{QL}\} = \dfrac{1}{EI}\{-101.25\}$ and $\{D_Q\} = \dfrac{1}{EI}\{-2 Q_1\}$

Substituting, we get,
$$\dfrac{1}{EI}\{-2 Q_1\} = \dfrac{1}{EI}\{-101.25\} + \dfrac{1}{EI}[9]\cdot\{Q_1\}$$

i.e. $-2 Q_1 = -101.25 + 9(Q_1)$ ... (A)

Step VII : Solution of equations for unknown redundant forces :
Solving equation (A), we get

$$\boxed{Q_1 = V_B = 9.20 \text{ kN} = 9.20 \text{ kN} (\uparrow)}$$

Step VIII : Other reaction components : Considering equilibrium of complete structure, other reaction components are found out and FBD of structure is as shown in Fig. 3.20 (d).

Step IX : Shear force and bending moment diagrams : SFD is as shown in Fig. 3.20 (e). BMD by superposition and on tension side is as shown in Fig. 3.20 (f) and Fig. 3.20 (g) respectively.

Example 3.17 : *Analyse the beam shown in Fig. 3.21 (a) by flexibility method. Take EI = constant.*

Solution : Data : The beam is supported and loaded as shown in Fig. 3.21 (a).
Object : Structural analysis.
Concepts and Equations :
(1) Statically determinate structure (Released structure).
(2) Displacement analysis of released structure.
(3) Superposition equations of compatibility of displacements.

Procedure :
Step I : The degree of static indeterminacy (D_{si}) :
(a) Degree of external static indeterminacy = $(D_{si})_e = 1$.
(b) Degree of internal static indeterminacy = $(D_{si})_i = 0$.
(c) Total degree of static indeterminacy = $D_{si} = (D_{si})_e + (D_{si})_i = 1 + 0 = 1$.

Step II : Selection of unknown redundant forces (Q) :
Let, $Q_1 = V_B (\uparrow)$

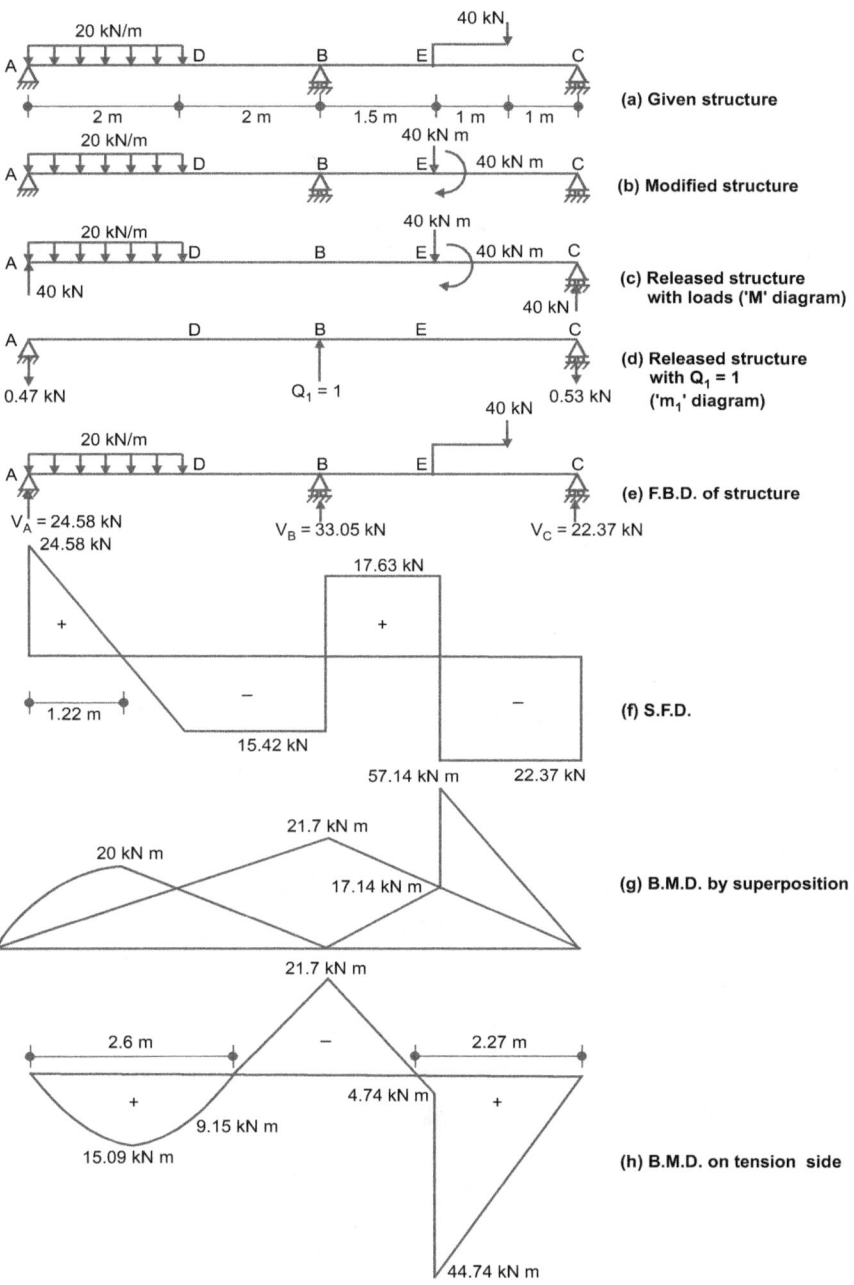

Fig. 3.21 : For Illustrative Example 3.17

STRUCTURAL ANALYSIS – II FLEXIBILITY METHOD

Step III : Released structure : Roller support at B is removed and basic released structure is as shown in Fig. 3.21 (c). Also released structure subjected to unit value of Q_1 is shown in Fig. 3.21 (d).

Step IV : Displacement analysis of released structure :

Zone	Origin	Limits	M	m_1
CE	C	0 – 2	40x	– 0.533 (x)
EB	C	2 – 3.5	40x – 40 – 40 (x – 2) = 40	– 0.533 (x)
AD	A	0 – 2	40x – 20x²/2 = 40x – 10x²	– 0.467 (x)
DB	A	2 – 4	40x – 20 × 2 (x – 1) = 40x – 40 (x – 1) = 40	– 0.467 (x)

(a) Displacement in the released structure subjected to loads corresponding to redundant actions :

$$D_{QL1} = \int_0^L \frac{M m_1 \cdot dx}{EI}$$

$$= \int_0^2 (40x)(-0.533x) \cdot \frac{dx}{EI} + \int_2^{3.5} (40)(-0.533x) \cdot \frac{dx}{EI} + \int_0^2 (40x - 10x^2)(-0.467x) \cdot \frac{dx}{EI}$$

$$+ \int_2^4 (40)(-0.467x) \frac{dx}{EI}$$

$$= -(56.85 + 87.94 + 31.13 = 112.08)/EI = \frac{-288}{EI}$$

(b) Displacement in the released structure subjected to unit value of Q_1 corresponding to redundant actions :

$$F_{11} = \int_0^1 \frac{m_1 \cdot m_1 \cdot dx}{EI}$$

$$= \int_0^2 (-0.533x)^2 \cdot \frac{dx}{EI} + \int_2^{3.5} (-0.533x)^2 \cdot \frac{dx}{EI} + \int_0^2 (-0.477x)^2 \cdot \frac{dx}{EI} + \int_2^4 (-0.467x)^2 \cdot \frac{dx}{EI}$$

$$= \int_0^{3.5} (-0.533x)^2 \cdot \frac{dx}{EI} + \int_0^4 (-0.467x)^2 \cdot \frac{dx}{EI} = \frac{(4.060 + 4.65)}{EI} = \frac{8.71}{EI}$$

Step V : The physical requirement of displacements : The vertical translation at B must be zero i.e. $D_{Q1} = 0$

Step VI : Superposition equation of compatibility of displacements :

$$\{D_Q\} = \{D_{QL}\} + [F] \cdot \{Q\}$$

i.e. $$0 = -\frac{288}{EI} + \left(\frac{8.71}{EI}\right)(Q_1) \quad \ldots (A)$$

STRUCTURAL ANALYSIS – II   FLEXIBILITY METHOD

Step VII : Solution of equations for unknown redundant forces : Solving equation (A), we get,

$$\boxed{Q_1 = V_B = 33.06 \text{ kN } (\uparrow)}$$

Step VIII : Other reaction components : Considering equilibrium of complete structure, other unknown reaction components are found out and FBD of structure is as shown in Fig. 3.21 (e).

Step IX : Shear force and bending moment diagrams : SFD is as shown in Fig. 3.21 (f). BMD by superposition and on tension side are as shown in Fig. 3.21 (g) and (h).

Example 3.18 : *Analyse the beam shown in Fig. 3.22 (a) by flexibility method. Take EI = constant.*

Solution : Data : The beam is supported and loaded as shown in Fig. 3.22 (a).

Object : Structural analysis.

Concepts and Equations :

(1) Statically determinate structure (Released structure).
(2) Displacement analysis of released structure.
(3) Superposition equations of compatibility of displacements.

Procedure :

Step I : The degree of static indeterminacy (D_{si}) :

(a) Degree of external static indeterminacy = $(D_{si})_e$ = 2.
(b) Degree of internal static indeterminacy = $(D_{si})_i$ = 0.
(c) Total degree of static indeterminacy = $D_{si} = (D_{si})_e + (D_{si})_i$ = 2 + 0 = 2.

Step II : Selection of unknown redundant forces (Q) :

Let,
$$Q_1 = V_B(\uparrow) \text{ and}$$
$$Q_2 = V_C(\uparrow)$$

Step III : Released structure : Roller supports at B and C are removed and the basic released structure is as shown in Fig. 3.22 (b). Also released structure subjected to the unit values of Q_1 and Q_2 is shown in Fig. 3.22 (c).

Step IV : Displacement analysis of released structure and Fig. 3.22 (d) respectively.

Zone	Origin	Limits	M	m_1	m_2
DC	D	0 – 2	$-10x^2/2 = -5x^2$	0	0
CB	D	2 – 6	$-10x^2/2 = -5x^2$	0	(x – 2)
BA	D	6 – 11	$-10 \times 6 \times (x-3) - 6(x-6)^2/2$ $= -60(x-3) - 3(x-6)^2$	(x – 6)	(x – 2)

STRUCTURAL ANALYSIS – II FLEXIBILITY METHOD

(a) Displacements in the released structure subjected to loads corresponding to redundant actions:

$$D_{QL1} = \int_0^L \frac{M m_1 \cdot dx}{EI}$$

$$= \int_0^2 (-5x^2)(0)\frac{dx}{EI} + \int_2^6 (-5x^2)(0)\frac{dx}{EI} + \int_6^{11}[-60(x-3) - 3(x-6)^2](x-6)\frac{dx}{EI}$$

$$= \frac{(0 + 0 - 5218.75)}{EI} = -\frac{5218.75}{EI}$$

$$D_{QL2} = \int_0^L \frac{M m_2 \cdot dx}{EI}$$

$$= \int_0^2 (-5x^2)(0)\frac{dx}{EI} + \int_2^6 (-5x^2)(x-2)\cdot\frac{dx}{EI} + \int_6^{11}[-60(x-3) - 3(x-6)^2](x-2)\frac{dx}{EI}$$

$$= \frac{(0.906.67 - 12318.75)}{EI} = -\frac{13225.42}{EI}$$

(b) Displacements in the released structure subjected to unit values of Q_1 and Q_2 corresponding to redundant actions:

$$F_{11} = \int_0^L \frac{m_1 \cdot m_1 \cdot dx}{EI}$$

$$= \int_0^2 (0)\cdot\frac{dx}{EI} + \int_2^6 (0)\cdot\frac{dx}{EI} + \int_6^{11}(x-6)^2\cdot\frac{dx}{EI} = \frac{(0 + 0 + 41.67)}{EI} = \frac{41.67}{EI}$$

$$F_{21} = F_{12} = \int_0^L \frac{m_1 \cdot m_2 \cdot dx}{EI} = \int_0^2 (0)\frac{dx}{EI} + \int_2^6 (0) + (x-2)\frac{dx}{EI} + \int_6^{11}(x-6)(x-2)\frac{dx}{EI}$$

$$= \frac{(0 + 0 + 91.67)}{EI} = \frac{91.67}{EI}$$

$$F_{22} = \int_0^L \frac{m_2 \cdot m_2 \cdot dx}{EI} = \int_0^2 (0)\cdot\frac{dx}{EI} + \int_2^6 (x-2)^2\cdot\frac{dx}{EI} + \int_6^{11}(x-2)^2\cdot\frac{dx}{EI}$$

$$= \int_2^{11}(x-2)^2\cdot\frac{dx}{EI} = \frac{243}{EI}$$

Step V: The physical requirement of displacements: The vertical translations at B and C must be zero. i.e. $D_{Q1} = D_{Q2} = 0$

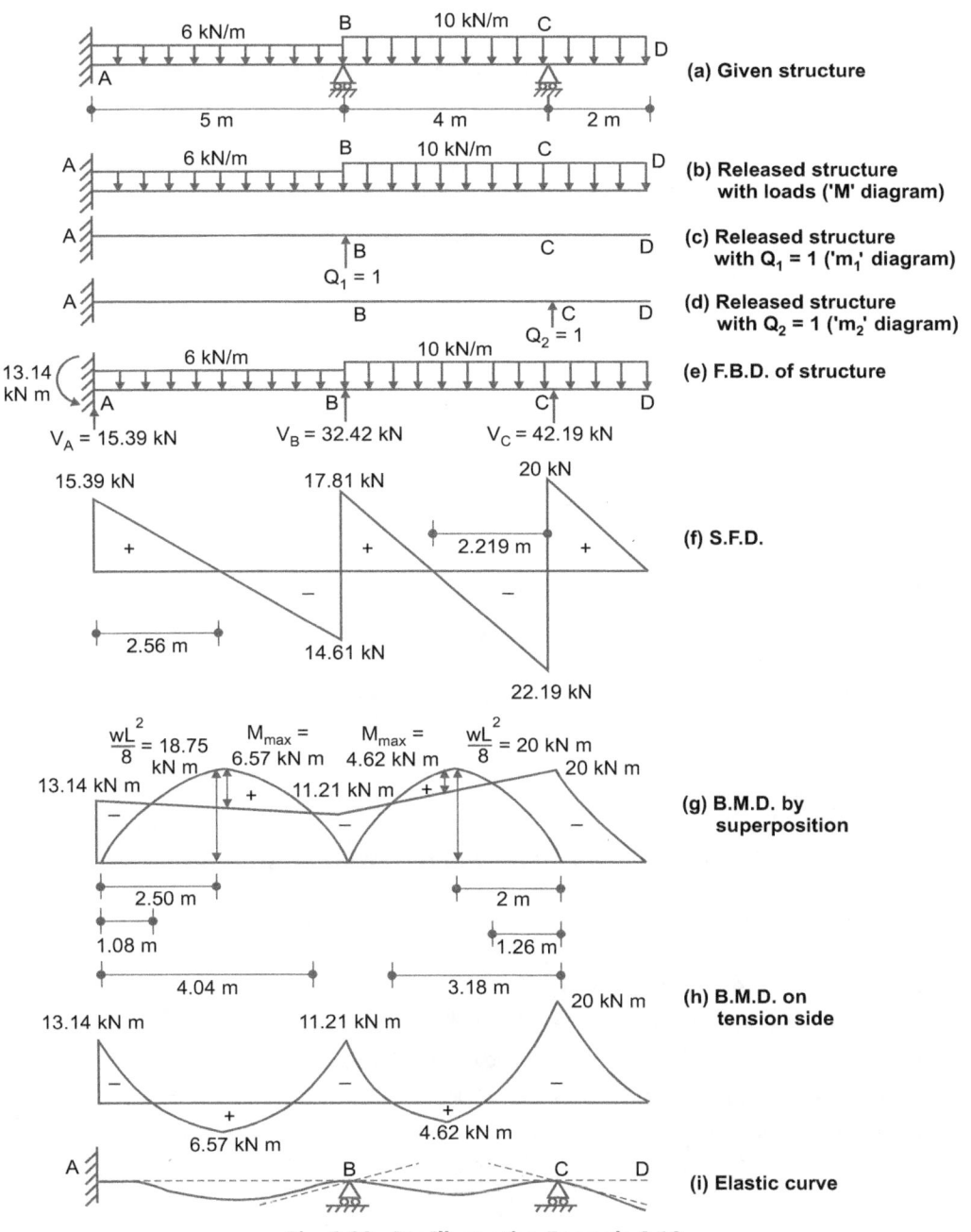

Fig. 3.22 : For Illustrative Example 3.18

STRUCTURAL ANALYSIS – II   FLEXIBILITY METHOD

Step VI : Superposition equation of compatibility of displacements :
$$\{D_Q\} = \{D_{QL}\} + [F]\{Q\}$$

i.e.
$$\begin{Bmatrix} 0 \\ 0 \end{Bmatrix} = \frac{1}{EI}\begin{Bmatrix} -5218.75 \\ -13225.42 \end{Bmatrix} + \frac{1}{EI}\begin{bmatrix} 41.67 & 91.67 \\ 91.67 & 243 \end{bmatrix} \cdot \begin{Bmatrix} Q_1 \\ Q_2 \end{Bmatrix}$$

i.e.
$$0 = -5218.75 + 41.67\,(Q_1) + 91.67\,(Q_2) \quad \ldots (A)$$
$$0 = -13225.42 + 91.67\,(Q_1) + 243\,(Q_2) \quad \ldots (B)$$

Step VII : Solution of equations for unknown redundant forces : Solving equations (A) and (B), we get,
$$Q_1 = V_B = 32.42 \text{ kN} = 32.42 \text{ kN} (\uparrow)$$
$$Q_2 = V_C = 4.2.19 \text{ kN} = 42.19 \text{ kN} (\uparrow)$$

Step VIII : Other reaction components : Considering equilibrium of complete structure, other unknown reaction components are found out and FBD of structure is as shown in Fig. 3.22 (e).

Step IX : Shear force and bending moment diagrams : SFD is as shown in Fig. 3.22 (f). BMD by superposition and on tension side is as shown in Fig. 3.22 (g) and 3.22 (h) respectively.

Step X : Elastic curve : As shown in Fig. 3.22 (i).

Example 3.19 : *Analyse the beam shown in Fig. 3.23 (a) by flexibility method; if support B sinks by 25 mm. Take EI = 3800 kN-m².*

Solution : (1) Data : The beam is supported and loaded as shown in Fig. 3.23 (a),
(2) EI = 3800 kNm²
(3) AB = 25 mm ($\downarrow$).

Object : Structural analysis.

Concepts and Equations :
(1) Statically determinate structure (Released structure).
(2) Displacement analysis of released structure.
(3) Superposition equations of compatibility of displacements.

Procedure :

Step I : The degree of static indeterminacy (D_{si}) :
(a) Degree of external static indeterminacy = $(D_{si})_e$ = 2.
(b) Degree of internal static indeterminacy = $(D_{si})_i$ = 2.
(c) Total degree of static indeterminacy = $D_{si} = (D_{si})_e + (D_{si})_i = 2 + 0 = 2$.

Step II : Selection of unknown redundant forces (Q).
Let,
$$Q_1 = V_B\,(\uparrow) \text{ and }$$
$$Q_2 = V_C\,(\uparrow)$$

STRUCTURAL ANALYSIS – II FLEXIBILITY METHOD

Step III : Released structure : Roller supports at B and C are removed and basic released structure is as shown in Fig. 3.23 (b). Also released structure subjected to unit values of Q_1 and Q_2 is shown in Fig. 3.23 (c) and Fig. 3.23 (d) respectively.

Step IV : Displacement analysis of released structure :

Zone	Origin	Limits	M	m_1	m_2
CD	C	0 – 4	0	0	x
DB	C	4 – 6	– 30 (x – 4)	0	x
BA	C	6 – 12	– 30 (x – 4) – 10 (x – 6)²/2 = – 5x² + 30x – 60	(x – 6)	x

(a) Displacements in the released structure subjected to loads corresponding to redundant actions :

$$D_{QL1} = \int_0^L \frac{M m_1 \cdot dx}{EI}$$

$$= \int_0^4 (0) \cdot \frac{dx}{EI} + \int_4^6 -30(x-4)(0) \cdot \frac{dx}{EI} + \int_6^{12} (-5x^2 + 30x - 60)(x-6) \cdot \frac{dx}{EI}$$

$$= \frac{(0 + 0 - 4860)}{EI} = -\frac{4860}{EI}$$

$$D_{QL2} = \int_0^L \frac{M m_2 \cdot dx}{EI}$$

$$= \int_0^4 (0) \cdot (x) \cdot \frac{dx}{EI} + \int_4^6 -30(x-4)(x) \cdot \frac{dx}{EI} + \int_6^{12} (-5x^2 + 30x - 60)(x) \cdot \frac{dx}{EI}$$

(d) Displacements in the released structure subjected to unit values of Q_1 and Q_2 corresponding to redundant actions.

$$F_{11} = \int_0^L \frac{m_1 \cdot m_1 \cdot dx}{EI}$$

$$= \int_0^4 (0) \cdot \frac{dx}{EI} + \int_4^6 (0) \cdot \frac{dx}{EI} + \int_6^{12} (x-6)^2 \cdot \frac{dx}{EI}$$

$$= \frac{(0 + 0 + 72)}{EI} = \frac{72}{EI}$$

$$F_{21} = F_{12} \int_0^L \frac{m_1 \cdot m_2 \cdot dx}{EI}$$

$$= \int_0^4 (0)(x) \cdot \frac{dx}{EI} + \int_4^6 (0)(x) \cdot \frac{dx}{EI} + \int_6^{12} (x-6)(x) \cdot \frac{dx}{EI}$$

$$= \frac{0 + 0 + 180}{EI} = \frac{180}{EI}$$

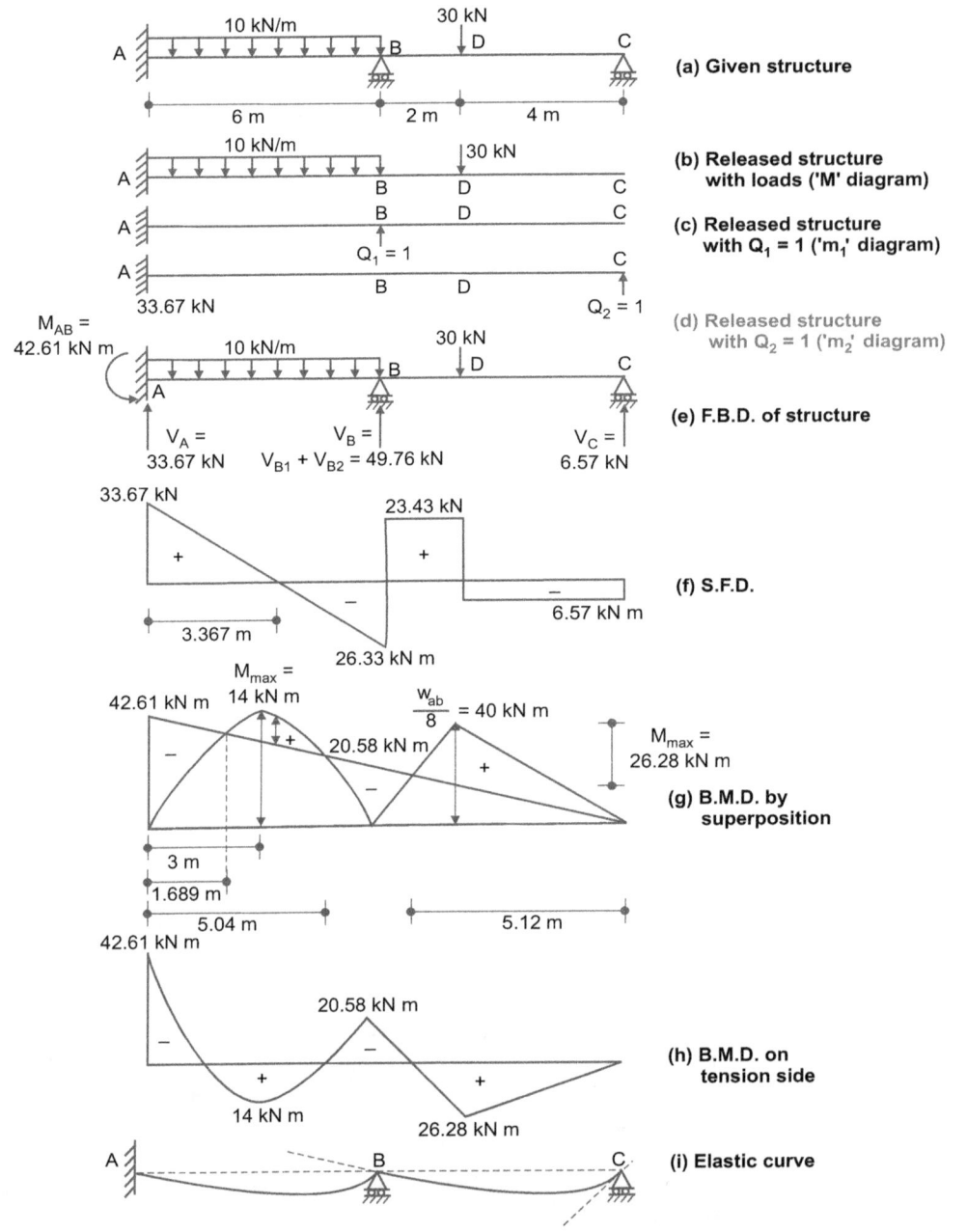

Fig. 3.23 : For Illustrative Example 3.19

$$F_{22} = \int_0^L \frac{m_2 \cdot m_2 \cdot dx}{EI}$$

$$= \int_0^4 (x)^2 \cdot \frac{dx}{EI} + \int_4^6 (x)^2 \cdot \frac{dx}{EI} + \int_6^{12} (x)^2 \cdot \frac{dx}{EI} = \int_0^{12} x^2 \cdot \frac{dx}{EI}$$

$$= \frac{576}{EI}$$

Step V : The physical requirement of displacements :

The vertical translation at B = 25 mm (↓) = – 0.025 m and the vertical translation at C = 0.

i.e. D_{Q1} = – 0.025 m and D_{Q2} = 0

Step VI : Superposition equation of compatibility of displacements :

$$\{D_Q\} = \{D_{QL}\} + [F] \cdot \{Q\}$$

i.e. $\begin{Bmatrix} -0.025 \\ 0 \end{Bmatrix} = \frac{1}{EI}\begin{Bmatrix} -4860 \\ -12740 \end{Bmatrix} + \frac{1}{EI}\begin{bmatrix} 72 & 180 \\ 180 & 576 \end{bmatrix}\begin{Bmatrix} Q_1 \\ Q_2 \end{Bmatrix}$

i.e. $EI \cdot \begin{Bmatrix} -0.025 \\ 0 \end{Bmatrix} = \begin{Bmatrix} -4860 \\ -12740 \end{Bmatrix} + \begin{bmatrix} 72 & 180 \\ 180 & 576 \end{bmatrix} \cdot \begin{Bmatrix} Q_1 \\ Q_2 \end{Bmatrix}$

i.e. $3800 \cdot \begin{Bmatrix} -0.025 \\ 0 \end{Bmatrix} = \begin{Bmatrix} -4860 \\ -12740 \end{Bmatrix} + \begin{bmatrix} 72 & 180 \\ 180 & 576 \end{bmatrix} \cdot \begin{Bmatrix} Q_1 \\ Q_2 \end{Bmatrix}$

i.e. – 95 = – 4860 + 72 (Q_1) + 180 (Q_2)... (A)

0 = – 12740 + 180 (Q_1) + 576 (Q_2)... (B)

Step VII : Solution of equations for unknown redundant forces. Solving equations (A) and (B), we get

$$\boxed{\begin{aligned} Q_1 &= V_B = 49.76 \text{ kN} = 49.76 \text{ kN (↑)} \\ Q_2 &= V_C = 6.57 \text{ kN} = 6.57 \text{ kN (↑)} \end{aligned}}$$

Step VIII : Other reaction components : Considering equilibrium of complete structure, other reaction components are found out and FBD of structure is as shown in Fig. 3.23 (e).

Step IX : Shear force and bending moment diagrams :

SFD is as shown in Fig. 3.23 (f).

BMD by superposition and on tension side is as shown in Fig. 3.23 (g) and Fig. 3.23 (h) respectively.

Step X : Elastic curve : as shown in Fig. 3.23 (i).

STRUCTURAL ANALYSIS – II FLEXIBILITY METHOD

Example 3.20 : *Analyse the beam shown in Fig. 3.24 (a) by flexibility method. Take EI = constant. The stiffness coefficients of spring at B and C are as shown in figure.*

Solution : (1) Data : The beam is supported and loaded as shown in Fig. 3.24 (a).

(2) $K_B = (EI)$ kN/m and $K_C = (EI/2)$ kN/m

Object : Structural analysis.

Concepts and Equations :

(1) Statically determinate structure (Released structure).

(2) Displacement analysis of released structure.

(3) Superposition equations of compatibility of displacements.

Procedure :

Step I : The degree of static indeterminacy (D_{si}) :

(a) Degree of external static indeterminacy = $(D_{si})_e = 2$.

(b) Degree of internal static indeterminacy = $(D_{si})_i = 0$.

(c) Total degree of static indeterminacy = $D_{si} = (D_{si})_e + (D_{si})_i = 2 + 0 = 2$.

Step II : Selection of unknown redundant forces (Q) :

Let, $Q_1 = V_B (\uparrow)$ and

$Q_2 = V_C (\uparrow)$

Step III : Released structure : Elastic supports at B and C are removed and basic released structure is as shown in Fig. 3.24 (b). Also released structure subjected to unit values of Q_1 and Q_2 is shown in Fig. 3.24 (c) and Fig. 3.24 (d) respectively.

Step IV : Displacement analysis of released structure : same as explained in example (3.19), step (iv).

Step V : The physical requirement of displacements :

Flexibility coefficient of spring at B = $F_B = \dfrac{1}{K_B} = \left(\dfrac{1}{EI}\right)$ m/kN

Flexibility coefficient of spring at C = $F_C = \dfrac{1}{K_C} = \left(\dfrac{2}{EI}\right)$ m/kN

The vertical translation at B = $\left(\dfrac{1}{EI}\right) Q_1 (\downarrow)$ $\therefore D_{Q_1} = -\dfrac{Q_1}{EI}$

The vertical translation at C = $\left(\dfrac{2}{EI}\right) Q_2 (\downarrow)$ $\therefore D_{Q_2} = -\left(\dfrac{2}{EI}\right) Q_2$

STRUCTURAL ANALYSIS – II FLEXIBILITY METHOD

Step VI : Superposition equation of compatibility of displacements :

$$\{D_Q\} = \{D_{QL}\} + [F] \cdot \{Q\}$$

where, $[F] = \dfrac{1}{EI}\begin{bmatrix} 72 & 180 \\ 180 & 576 \end{bmatrix}$ as developed in Example 3.19.

Also $\{D_{QL}\} = \dfrac{1}{EI}\begin{Bmatrix} -4860 \\ -12740 \end{Bmatrix}$ and $\{D_Q\} = \dfrac{1}{EI}\begin{Bmatrix} -Q_1 \\ -2Q_2 \end{Bmatrix}$

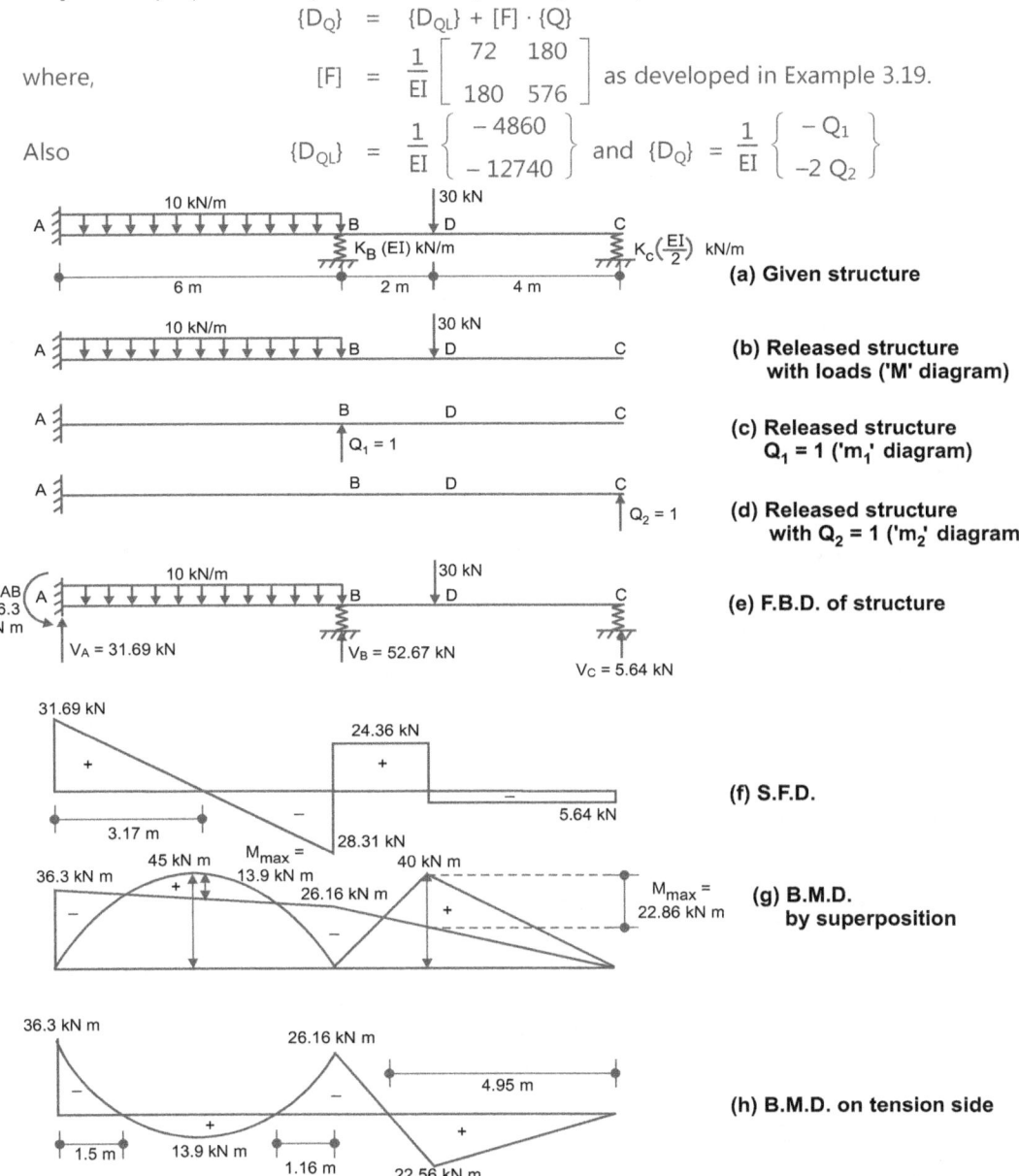

Fig. 3.24 : For Illustrative Example 3.20

Substituting, we get,

$$\frac{1}{EI}\begin{Bmatrix} -Q_1 \\ -2Q_2 \end{Bmatrix} = \frac{1}{EI}\begin{Bmatrix} -4860 \\ -12740 \end{Bmatrix} + \frac{1}{EI} \cdot \begin{bmatrix} 72 & 180 \\ 180 & 576 \end{bmatrix} \begin{Bmatrix} Q_1 \\ Q_2 \end{Bmatrix}$$

i.e.
$$-Q_1 = -4860 + 72(Q_1) + 180(Q_2) \ldots \text{(A)}$$
$$-2Q_2 = -12740 + 180(Q_1) + 576(Q_2) \ldots \text{(B)}$$

Step VII : Solution of equations for unknown redundant forces : Solving equations (A) and (B), we get,

$$\boxed{\begin{aligned} Q_1 &= V_B = 52.67 \text{ kN} = 52.67 \text{ kN} (\uparrow) \\ Q_2 &= V_C = 5.64 \text{ kN} = 5.64 \text{ kN} (\uparrow) \end{aligned}}$$

Step VIII : Other reaction components : Considering equilibrium of complete structure, other reaction components are found out and FBD of structure is as shown in Fig. 3.24 (e).

Step IX : Shear force and bending moment diagrams : SFD is as shown in Fig. 3.24 (f). BMD by superposition and on tension side is as shown in Fig. 3.24 (g) and Fig. 3.24 (h) respectively.

Example 3.21 : *Analyse the beam shown in Fig. 3.25 (a) by flexibility method.*

Solution : Data : The beam is supported and loaded as shown in Fig. 3.25 (a).

Object : Structural analysis.

Concepts and equations :

(1) Statically determinate structure (Released structure).

(2) Displacement analysis of released structure.

(3) Superposition equations of compatibility of displacements.

Procedure :

Step I : The degree of static indeterminacy (D_{si}) :

(a) Degree of external static indeterminacy = $(D_{si})_e$ = 2.

(b) Degree of internal static indeterminacy = $(D_{si})_i$ = 2.

(c) Total degree of static indeterminacy = $D_{si} = (D_{si})_e + (D_{si})_i = 2 + 0 = 2$.

Step II : Selection of unknown redundant forces (Q) :

Let,
$$Q_1 = V_C (\uparrow)$$
$$Q_2 = M_{CB} (\circlearrowleft)$$

Step III : Released structure : Fixed support at C is removed and basic released structure is as shown in Fig. 3.25 (b). Also released structure subjected to unit values of Q_1 and Q_2 is shown in Fig. 3.25 (c) and Fig. 3.25 (d) respectively.

STRUCTURAL ANALYSIS – II FLEXIBILITY METHOD

Step IV : Displacement analysis of released structure.

Zone	Origin	Limits	EI	M	m_1	m_2
CB	C	0 – 2	EI	0	x	1
BD	C	2 – 3	2 EI	0	x	1
DA	C	3 – 4	2 EI	– 100 (x – 3)	x	1

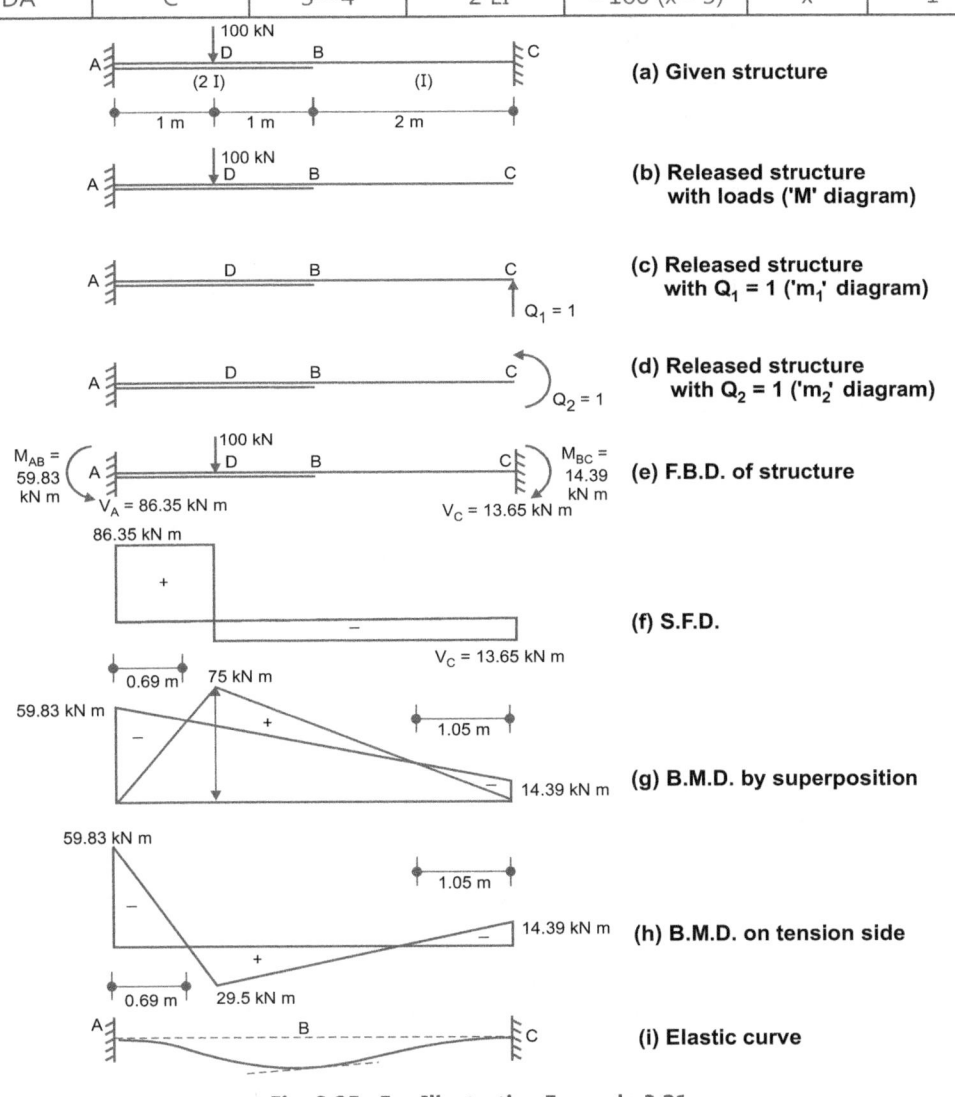

Fig. 3.25 : For Illustrative Example 3.21

(a) Displacements in the released structure subjected to loads corresponding to redundant actions :

$$D_{QL1} = \int_0^L \frac{M m_1 \cdot dx}{EI}$$

$$= \int_0^2 (0) \cdot (x) \cdot \frac{dx}{EI} + \int_2^3 (0)(x) \cdot \frac{dx}{2EI} + \int_3^4 -100(x-3)(x) \cdot \frac{dx}{2EI}$$

$$= \frac{(0 + 0 - 91.67)}{EI} = \frac{-91.67}{EI}$$

$$D_{QL2} = \int_0^L \frac{M m_2 \cdot dx}{EI}$$

$$= \int_0^2 (0)(1) \cdot \frac{dx}{EI} + \int_2^3 (0)(1) \frac{dx}{2EI} + \int_3^4 -100(x-3)(1) \cdot \frac{dx}{2EI}$$

$$= \frac{(0 + 0 - 25)}{EI} = -\frac{25}{EI}$$

(b) Displacements in the released structure subjected to unit values of Q_1 and Q_2 corresponding to redundant actions :

$$F_{11} = \int_0^L \frac{m_1 m_1 \cdot dx}{EI} = \int_0^2 (x)^2 \cdot \frac{dx}{EI} + \int_2^3 (x)^2 \cdot \frac{dx}{2EI} + \int_3^4 (x)^2 \cdot \frac{dx}{2EI}$$

$$= \int_0^2 (x)^2 \cdot \frac{dx}{EI} + \int_2^4 (x)^2 \cdot \frac{dx}{2EI} = \frac{(2.67 + 9.33)}{EI} = \frac{12}{EI}$$

$$F_{21} = F_{12} = \int_0^L \frac{m_1 \cdot m_2 \cdot dx}{EI}$$

$$= \int_0^2 (x)(1) \frac{dx}{EI} + \int_2^3 (x)(1) \cdot \frac{dx}{2EI} + \int_3^4 (x)(1) \cdot \frac{dx}{2EI}$$

$$= \int_0^2 x \cdot \frac{dx}{EI} + \int_2^4 x \cdot \frac{dx}{2EI} = \frac{(2+3)}{EI} = \frac{5}{EI}$$

$$F_{22} = \int_0^L \frac{m_2 \cdot m_2 \cdot dx}{EI} = \int_0^2 (1)^2 \cdot \frac{dx}{EI} + \int_2^3 (1)^2 \cdot \frac{dx}{2EI} + \int_3^4 (1)^2 \cdot \frac{dx}{2EI}$$

STRUCTURAL ANALYSIS – II FLEXIBILITY METHOD

$$= \int_0^2 (1) \cdot \frac{dx}{EI} + \int_2^4 (1) \cdot \frac{dx}{2EI} = \frac{(2+1)}{EI} = \frac{3}{EI}$$

Step V : The physical requirement of displacements : The vertical translation and rotation at C must be zero.

i.e. $D_{Q1} = D_{Q2} = 0$

Step VI : Superposition equation of compatibility of displacements :

$$\{D_Q\} = \{D_{QL}\} + [F] \cdot \{Q\}$$

i.e. $\begin{Bmatrix} 0 \\ 0 \end{Bmatrix} = \frac{1}{EI} \cdot \begin{Bmatrix} -91.67 \\ -25 \end{Bmatrix} + \frac{1}{EI} \begin{bmatrix} 12 & 5 \\ 5 & 3 \end{bmatrix} \begin{Bmatrix} Q_1 \\ Q_2 \end{Bmatrix}$

i.e. $0 = -91.67 + 12(Q_1) + 5(Q_2)$

$0 = -25 + 5(Q_1) + 3(Q_2)$

Step VII : Solution of equations for unknown redundant forces : Solving equations (A) and (B), we get

$Q_1 = V_B = 13.65$ kN $= 13.65$ kN ($\uparrow$)

$Q_2 = M_{CB} = -14.385$ kNm $= 14.39$ kNm ($\circlearrowleft$)

Step VIII : Other reaction components : Considering equilibrium of complete structure, other reaction components are found out and FBD of structure is as shown in Fig. 3.25 (e).

Step IX : Shear force and bending moment diagrams : SFD is as shown in Fig. 3.25 (f). BMD by superposition and on tension side is as shown in Fig. 3.25 (g) and Fig. 3.25 (h) respectively.

Step X : Elastic curve : As shown in Fig. 3.25 (i).

Example 3.22 : Analyse the frame shown in Fig. 3.26 (a) by flexibility method. Take EI = constant.

Solution : Data : The frame is supported and loaded as shown in Fig. 3.26 (a).

Object : Structural analysis.

Concepts and Equations :

(1) Statically determinate structure (Released structure).

STRUCTURAL ANALYSIS – II   FLEXIBILITY METHOD

(2) Displacement analysis of released structure.

(3) Superposition equations of compatibility of displacements.

Procedure :

Step I : The degree of static indeterminacy (D_{si})

(a) Degree of external static indeterminacy = $(D_{si})_e = 2$

(b) Degree of internal static indeterminacy = $(D_{si})_i = 0$

(c) Total degree of static indeterminacy = $D_{si} = (D_{si})_e + (D_{si})_i = 2 + 0 = 2$.

Step II : Selection of unknown redundant forces (Q) :

Let, $Q_1 = V_C (\uparrow)$ and

$Q_2 = H_C (\rightarrow)$

Step III : Released structure : Hinged support at C is removed and the basic released structure is shown in Fig. 3.26 (b). Also released structure subjected to unit values of Q_1 and Q_2 is shown in Fig. 3.26 (c) and Fig. 3.27 (d) respectively.

Step IV : Displacement analysis of released structure :

Zone	Origin	Limits	M	m_1	m_2
CB	C	0 – 3	$-\dfrac{25x^2}{2}$	x	0
BD	B	0 – 2	– 112.5	3	– x
DA	B	2 – 4	– 112.5 – 50 (x – 2) = – 50x – 12.5	3	– x

(a) Displacements in the released structure subjected to loads corresponding to redundant actions :

$$D_{QL1} = \int_0^L \frac{M m_1 \cdot dx}{EI}$$

$$= \int_0^3 \left(-\frac{25x^2}{2}\right)(x) \cdot \frac{dx}{EI} + \int_0^2 (-112.5)(3) \cdot \frac{dx}{EI} + \int_2^4 (-50x - 12.5)(3) \cdot \frac{dx}{EI}$$

$$= \frac{(-253.125 - 675 - 975)}{EI} = \frac{(-1903.125)}{EI}$$

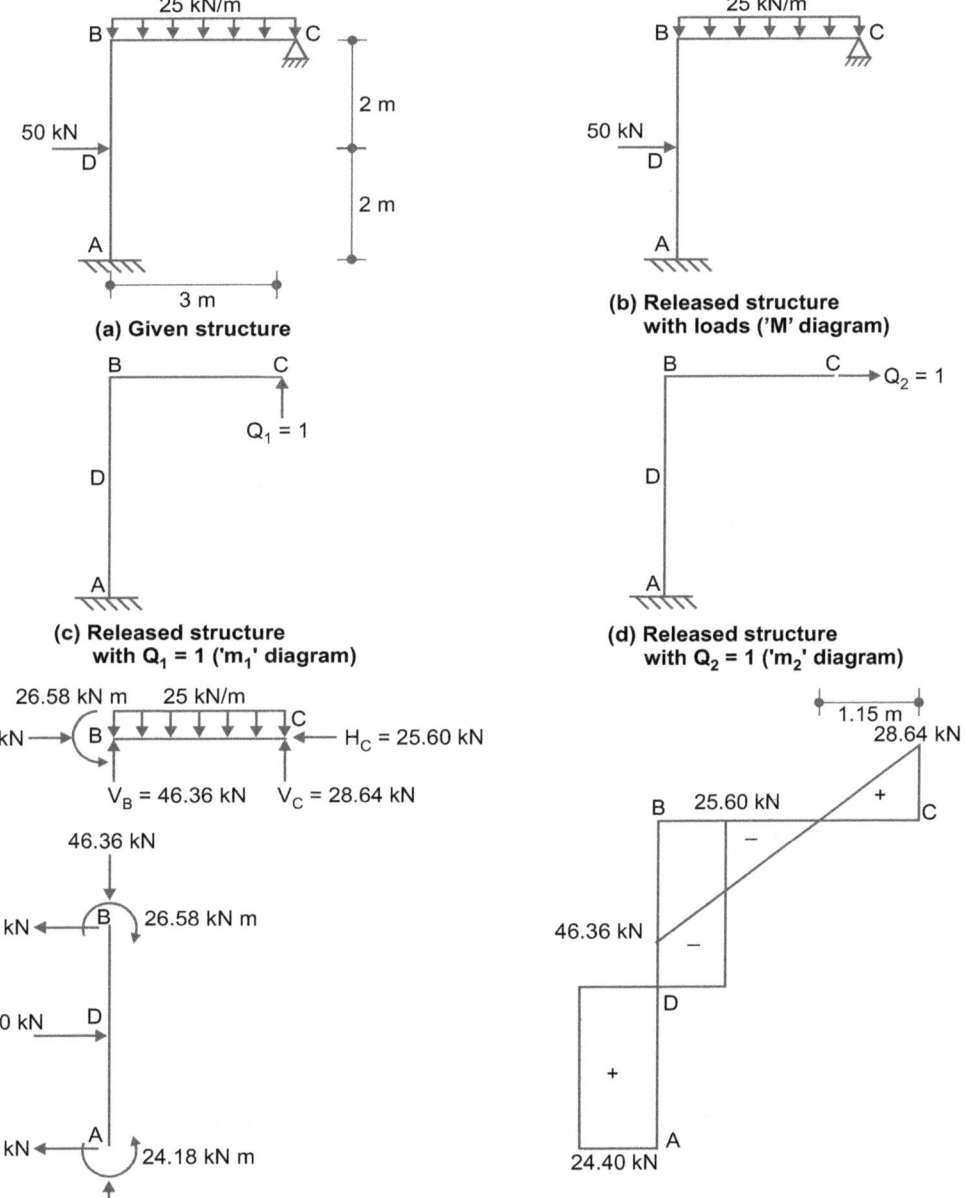

Fig. 3.26 : (Continued)

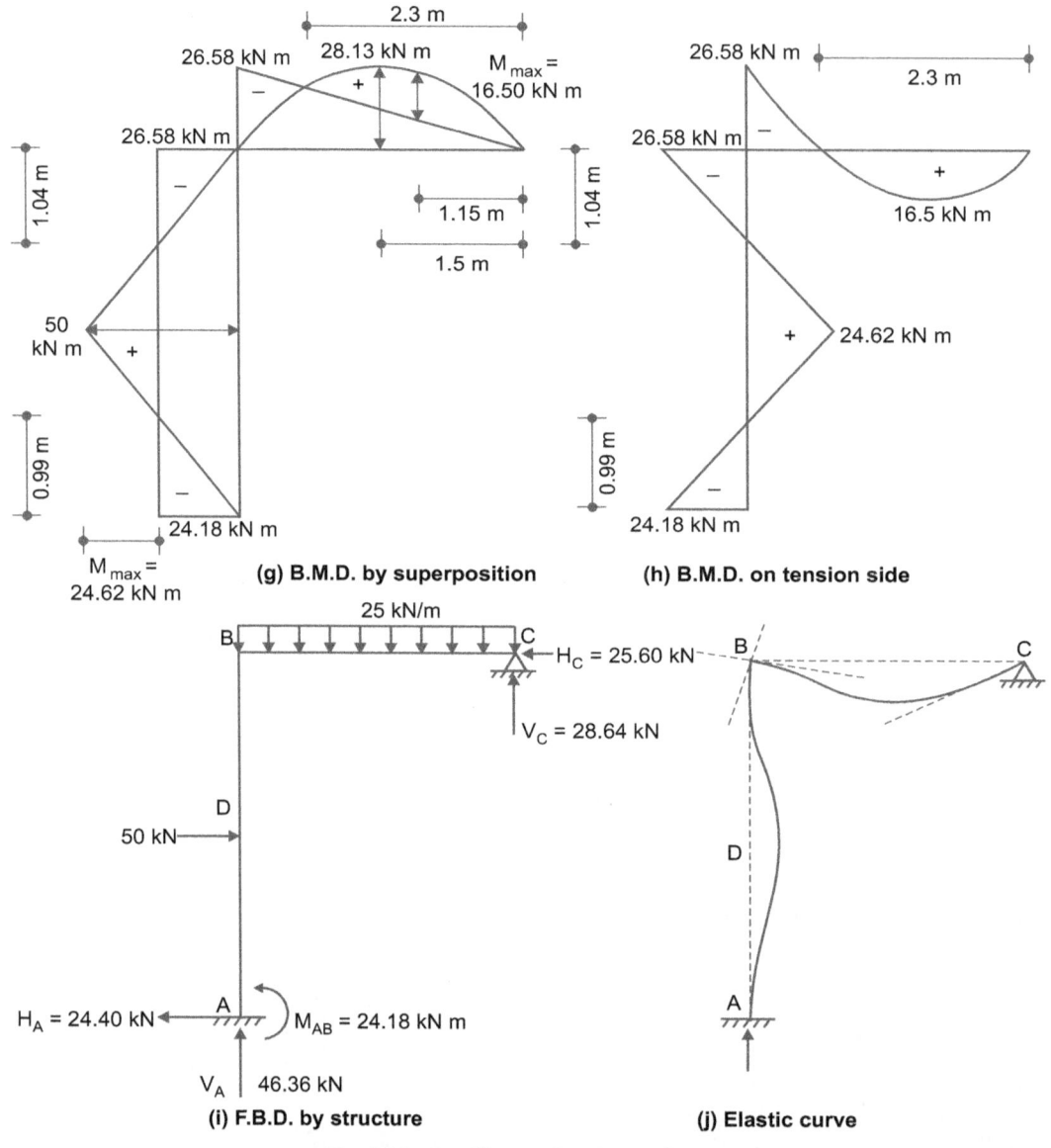

Fig. 3.26 : For Illustrative Example 3.22

$$D_{QL2} = \int_0^L \frac{Mm_2 \cdot dx}{EI}$$

$$= \int_0^3 \left(-\frac{25x^2}{2}\right)(0)\frac{dx}{EI} + \int_0^2 (-112.5)(-x)\cdot\frac{dx}{EI} + \int_2^4 (-50x - 12.5)(-x)\cdot\frac{dx}{EI}$$

$$= \frac{(0 + 225 + 1008.83)}{EI}$$

$$= \frac{1233.33}{EI}$$

(b) Displacements in the released structure subjected to unit values of Q_1 and Q_2 corresponding to redundant actions :

$$F_{11} = \int_0^L \frac{m_1 \cdot m_1 \cdot dx}{EI}$$

$$= \int_0^3 (x)^2 \cdot \frac{dx}{EI} + \int_0^2 (3)^2 \cdot \frac{dx}{EI} + \int_2^4 (3)^2 \cdot \frac{dx}{EI}$$

$$= \frac{(9 + 18 + 18)}{EI} = \frac{45}{EI}$$

$$F_{21} = F_{12} = \int_0^L \frac{m_1 \cdot m_2 \cdot dx}{EI}$$

$$= \int_0^3 (x)(0)\frac{dx}{EI} + \int_0^2 (3)(-x)\cdot\frac{dx}{EI} + \int_2^4 (3)(-x)\frac{dx}{EI}$$

$$= \int_0^4 (-3x)\frac{dx}{EI} = -\frac{24}{EI}$$

$$F_{22} = \int_0^L \frac{m_2 \cdot m_2 \cdot dx}{EI}$$

$$= \int_0^3 (0)\cdot\frac{dx}{EI} + \int_0^2 (-x)^2\cdot\frac{dx}{EI} + \int_2^4 (-x)^2\cdot\frac{dx}{EI} = \int_0^4 x^2\cdot\frac{dx}{EI} = \frac{21.33}{EI}$$

Step V : The physical requirement of displacements : The vertical and horizontal translation at C must be zero.

i.e. $\quad D_{Q1} = D_{Q2} = 0$

Step VI : Superposition equation of compatibility of displacements :

i.e. $\quad \{D_Q\} = \{D_{QL}\} + [F]\{Q\}$

i.e. $\quad \begin{Bmatrix} 0 \\ 0 \end{Bmatrix} = \frac{1}{EI}\begin{Bmatrix} -1903.125 \\ 1233.33 \end{Bmatrix} + \frac{1}{EI}\begin{bmatrix} 45 & -24 \\ -24 & 21.33 \end{bmatrix}\begin{Bmatrix} Q_1 \\ Q_2 \end{Bmatrix}$

i.e. $\quad 0 = -1903.125 + 45(Q_1) - 24(Q_2)$ ... (A)

$\quad 0 = 1233.33 - 24(Q_1) + 21.33(Q_2)$ ... (B)

STRUCTURAL ANALYSIS – II   FLEXIBILITY METHOD

Step VII : Solution of equations for unknown redundant forces : Solving equations (A) and (B), we get

$$Q_1 = V_C = 28.64 \text{ kN} = 28.64 \text{ kN} (\uparrow)$$
$$Q_2 = H_C = 25.60 \text{ kN} = 25.60 \text{ kN} (\leftarrow)$$

Step VIII : Other reaction components : Considering equilibrium of each member and of complete structure, other reaction components are found out and FBD of members is as shown in Fig. 326 (e).

Step IX : Shear force and bending moment diagrams : SFD is as shown in Fig. 3.26 (f). BMD by superposition and on tension side is as shown in Fig. 3.26 (g) and Fig. 3.26 (h) respectively.

Step X : FBD of structure : as shown in Fig. 3.26 (i).

Step XI : Elastic curve : as shown in Fig. 3.26 (j).

Example 3.23 : *Analyse the frame shown in Fig. 3.27 (a) by flexibility method.*

Solution : Data : The frame is supported and loaded as shown in Fig. 3.27 (a).

Object : Structural analysis.

Concepts and Equations :

(1) Statically determinate structure (released structure).
(2) Displacement analysis of released structure.
(3) Superposition equations of compatibility of displacements.

Procedure :

Step I : The degree of static indeterminacy (D_{si}) :

(a) Degree of external static indeterminacy = $(D_{si})_e = 3$
(b) Degree of internal static indeterminacy = $(D_{si})_i = 0$
(c) Total degree of static indeterminacy = $D_{si} = (D_{si})_e + (D_{si})_i = 3 + 0 = 3$.

Step II : Selection of unknown redundant forces (Q) :
Let,
$$Q_1 = V_C (\uparrow)$$
$$Q_2 = H_C (\rightarrow) \text{ and}$$
$$Q_3 = M_{CB} (\circlearrowleft)$$

Step III : Released structure : Fixed support at C is removed and the basic released structure is shown in Fig. 3.27 (b). Also released structure subjected to unit values of Q_1, Q_2 and Q_3 is shown in Fig. 3.27 (c), Fig. 3.27 (d) and Fig. 3.27 (e) respectively.

Step IV : Displacement analysis of released structure :

Zone	Origin	Limits	EI	M	m_1	m_2	m_3
CB	C	0 – 3	EI	$-\dfrac{25x^2}{2}$	x	0	1
BD	B	0 – 2	2 EI	– 112.5	3	– x	1
DA	B	2 – 4	2 EI	– 112.5 – 50 (x – 2) = – 50x – 12.5	3	– x	1

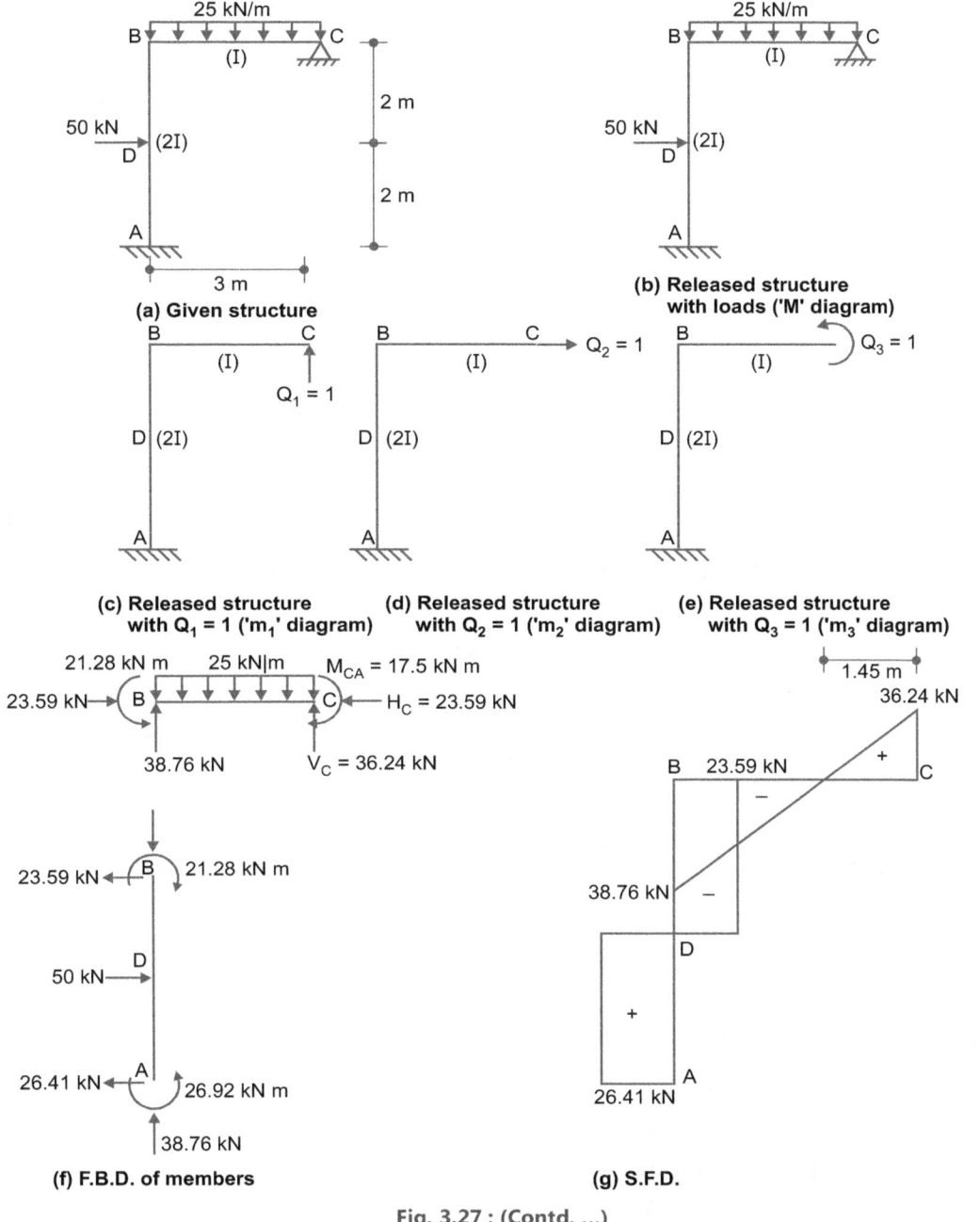

Fig. 3.27 : (Contd. ...)

STRUCTURAL ANALYSIS – II FLEXIBILITY METHOD

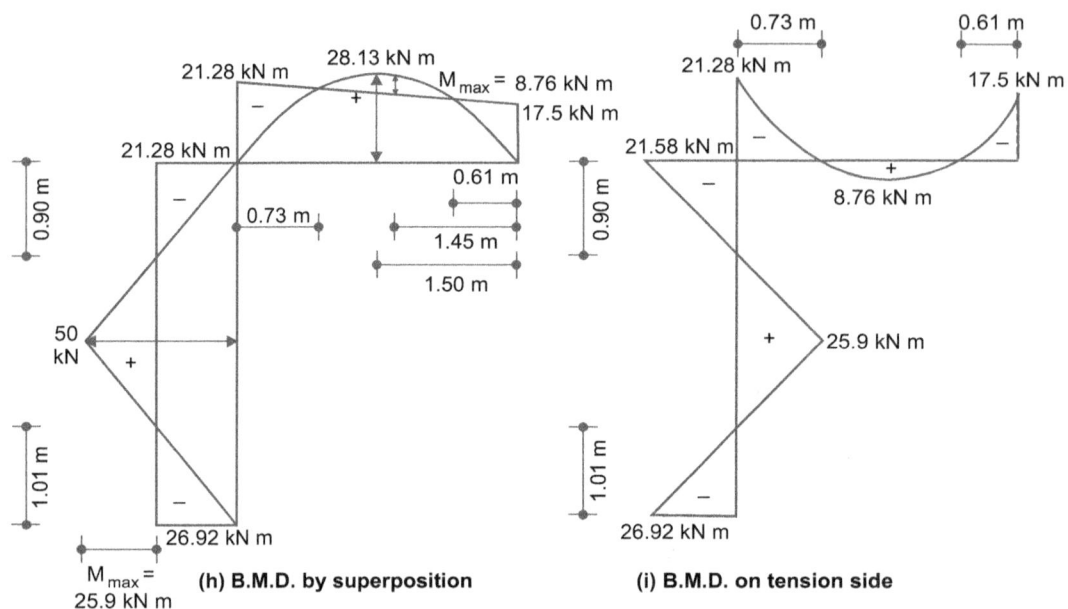

(h) B.M.D. by superposition

(i) B.M.D. on tension side

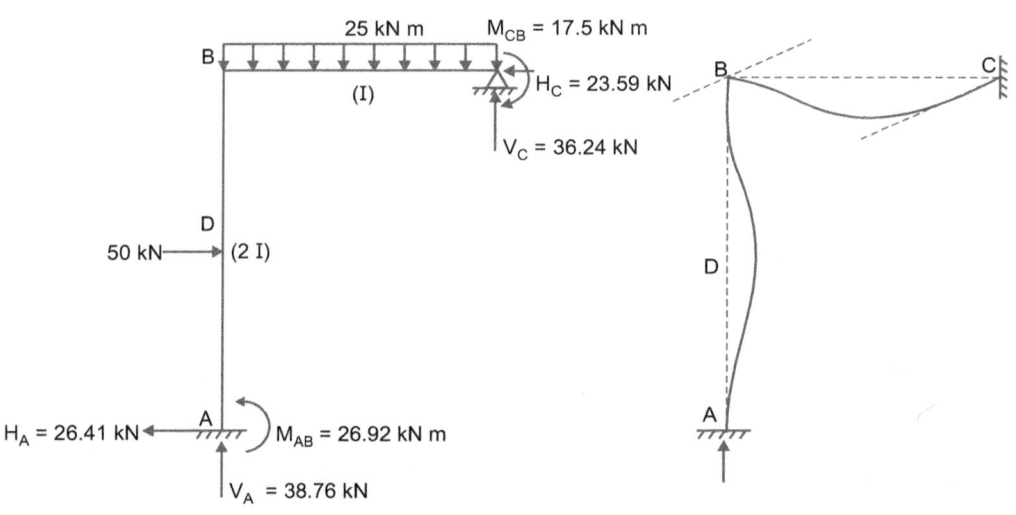

(j) F.B.D. of structure

(k) Elastic curve

Fig. 3.27 : For Illustrative Example 3.23

STRUCTURAL ANALYSIS – II FLEXIBILITY METHOD

(a) Displacements in the released structure subjected to loads corresponding to redundant actions :

$$D_{QL1} = \int_0^L \frac{M m_1 \cdot dx}{EI}$$

$$= \int_0^3 \left(-\frac{25x^2}{2}\right)(x) \cdot \frac{dx}{EI} + \int_0^2 (-112.5)(3) \cdot \frac{dx}{2EI} + \int_2^4 (-50x - 12.5)(3) \cdot \frac{dx}{2EI}$$

$$= \frac{(-253.125 - 337.5 - 487.5)}{EI} = \frac{-1078.125}{EI}$$

$$D_{QL2} = \int_0^L \frac{M m_2 \cdot dx}{EI}$$

$$= \int_0^3 \left(-\frac{25x^2}{2}\right)(0) \cdot \frac{dx}{EI} + \int_0^2 (-112.5)(-x) \cdot \frac{dx}{2EI} + \int_2^4 (-50x - 12.5)(-x) \cdot \frac{dx}{2EI}$$

$$= \frac{(0 + 112.5 + 504.165)}{EI} = \frac{616.665}{EI}$$

$$D_{QL3} = \int_0^L \frac{M m_3 \cdot dx}{EI}$$

$$= \int_0^3 \left(-\frac{25x^2}{2}\right)(1) \cdot \frac{dx}{EI} + \int_0^2 (-112.5)(1) \cdot \frac{dx}{2EI} + \int_2^4 (-50x - 12.5)(1) \cdot \frac{dx}{2EI}$$

$$= \frac{(-112.5 - 112.5 - 162.5)}{EI} = \frac{-387.5}{EI}$$

(b) Displacements in the released structure subjected to unit values of Q_1, Q_2 and Q_3 corresponding to redundant actions :

$$F_{11} = \int_0^L \frac{m_1 \cdot m_1 \cdot dx}{EI}$$

$$= \int_0^3 (x)^2 \cdot \frac{dx}{EI} + \int_0^2 (3)^2 \cdot \frac{dx}{2EI} + \int_2^4 (3)^2 \cdot \frac{dx}{2EI} = \frac{(9 + 9 + 9)}{EI} = \frac{27}{EI}$$

$$F_{21} = F_{12} = \int_0^L \frac{m_1 \cdot m_2 \cdot dx}{EI}$$

$$= \int_0^3 (x)(0) \cdot \frac{dx}{EI} + \int_0^2 (3)(-x) \frac{dx}{2EI} + \int_2^4 (3)(-x) \cdot \frac{dx}{2EI}$$

$$= \int_0^4 (3)(-x) \frac{dx}{2EI} = \frac{-12}{EI}$$

STRUCTURAL ANALYSIS – II   FLEXIBILITY METHOD

$$F_{31} = F_{13} = \int_0^L \frac{m_1 \cdot m_3 \cdot dx}{EI}$$

$$= \int_0^3 (x)(1) \cdot \frac{dx}{EI} + \int_0^2 (3)(1) \cdot \frac{dx}{2EI} + \int_2^4 (3)(1) \frac{dx}{2EI} = \frac{(4.5 + 3 + 3)}{EI} = \frac{10.5}{EI}$$

$$F_{22} = \int_0^L \frac{m_2 \cdot m_2 \cdot dx}{EI}$$

$$= \int_0^3 (0) \cdot \frac{dx}{EI} + \int_0^2 (-x)^2 \cdot \frac{dx}{2EI} + \int_2^4 (-x)^2 \cdot \frac{dx}{2EI}$$

$$= \int_0^4 x^2 \cdot \frac{dx}{2EI} = \frac{10.67}{EI}$$

$$F_{32} = F_{23} = \int_0^L \frac{m_2 \cdot m_3 \cdot dx}{EI}$$

$$= \int_0^3 (0)(1) \cdot \frac{dx}{EI} + \int_0^2 (-x)(1) \cdot \frac{dx}{2EI} + \int_2^4 (-x)(1) \cdot \frac{dx}{2EI}$$

$$= \int_0^4 (-x) \cdot \frac{dx}{2EI} = -\frac{4}{EI}$$

$$F_{33} = \int_0^L \frac{m_3 \cdot m_3 \cdot dx}{EI}$$

$$= \int_0^3 (1)^2 \cdot \frac{dx}{EI} + \int_0^2 (1)^2 \cdot \frac{dx}{2EI} + \int_2^4 (1)^2 \cdot \frac{dx}{2EI}$$

$$= \frac{(3 + 1 + 1)}{EI} = \frac{5}{EI}$$

Step V : The physical requirement of displacements : The vertical and horizontal translation at C must be zero. Also rotation at C must be zero.

i.e. $D_{Q1} = D_{Q2} = D_{Q3} = 0$

Step VI : Superposition equation of compatibility of displacements :

$$\{D_Q\} = \{D_{QL}\} + [F]\{Q\}$$

i.e. $\begin{Bmatrix} 0 \\ 0 \\ 0 \end{Bmatrix} = \frac{1}{EI} \begin{Bmatrix} -1078.125 \\ 616.665 \\ -387.5 \end{Bmatrix} + \frac{1}{EI} \begin{bmatrix} 27 & -12 & 10.5 \\ -12 & 10.67 & -4 \\ 10.5 & -4 & 5 \end{bmatrix} \begin{Bmatrix} Q_1 \\ Q_2 \\ Q_3 \end{Bmatrix}$

i.e. $0 = -1078.125 + 27(Q_1) - 12(Q_2) + 10.5(Q_3)$ ... (A)

STRUCTURAL ANALYSIS – II   FLEXIBILITY METHOD

$$0 = 616.665 - 12(Q_1) + 10.67(Q_2) - 4(Q_3) \quad \ldots (B)$$
$$0 = -387.50 + 10.5(Q_1) - 4(Q_2) + 5(Q_3) \quad \ldots (C)$$

Step VII : Solution of equations for unknown redundant forces : Solving equations (A), (B), and (C), we get,

$$Q_1 = V_C = 36.24 \text{ kN} = 36.24 \text{ kN } (\uparrow)$$
$$Q_2 = H_C = -23.59 \text{ kN} = 23.59 \text{ kN } (\leftarrow)$$
$$Q_3 = M_C = -17.5 \text{ kNm} = 17.5 \text{ kNm } (\circlearrowleft)$$

Step VIII : Other reaction components : Considering equilibrium of each member and of complete structure, other reaction components are found out and FBD of members is as shown in Fig. 3.27 (f).

Step IX : Shear force and bending moment diagrams : SFD is as shown in Fig. 3.27 (g). BMD by superposition and on tension side is as shown in Fig. 3.27 (h) and Fig. 3.27 (i) respectively.

Step X : FBD of structure : as shown in Fig. 3.27 (j).

Step XI : Elastic curve : as shown in Fig. 3.27 (k).

Example 3.24 : *Analyse the frame shown in Fig. 3.28 (a) by flexibility method.*

Solution : Data : The frame is supported and loaded as shown in Fig. 3.28 (a).

Object : Structural analysis.

Concepts and Equations :

(1) Statically determinate structure (Released structure).
(2) Displacement analysis of released structure.
(3) Superposition equations of compatibility of displacements.

Procedure :

Step I : The degree of static indeterminacy (D_{si}) :

(a) Degree of external static indeterminacy = $(D_{si})_e = 2$.
(b) Degree of internal static indeterminacy = $(D_{si})_i = 0$.
(c) Total degree of static indeterminacy = $D_{si} = (D_{si})_e + (D_{si})_i = 2 + 0 = 2$.

Step II : Selection of unknown redundant forces (Q) :
Let,
$$Q_1 = V_D (\uparrow) \text{ and}$$
$$Q_2 = H_D (\rightarrow)$$

Step III : Released structure : Hinged support at D is removed and the basic released structure is as shown in Fig. 3.28 (b). Also released structure subjected to unit values of Q_1 and Q_2 is shown in Fig. 3.28 (c) and Fig. 3.28 (d) respectively.

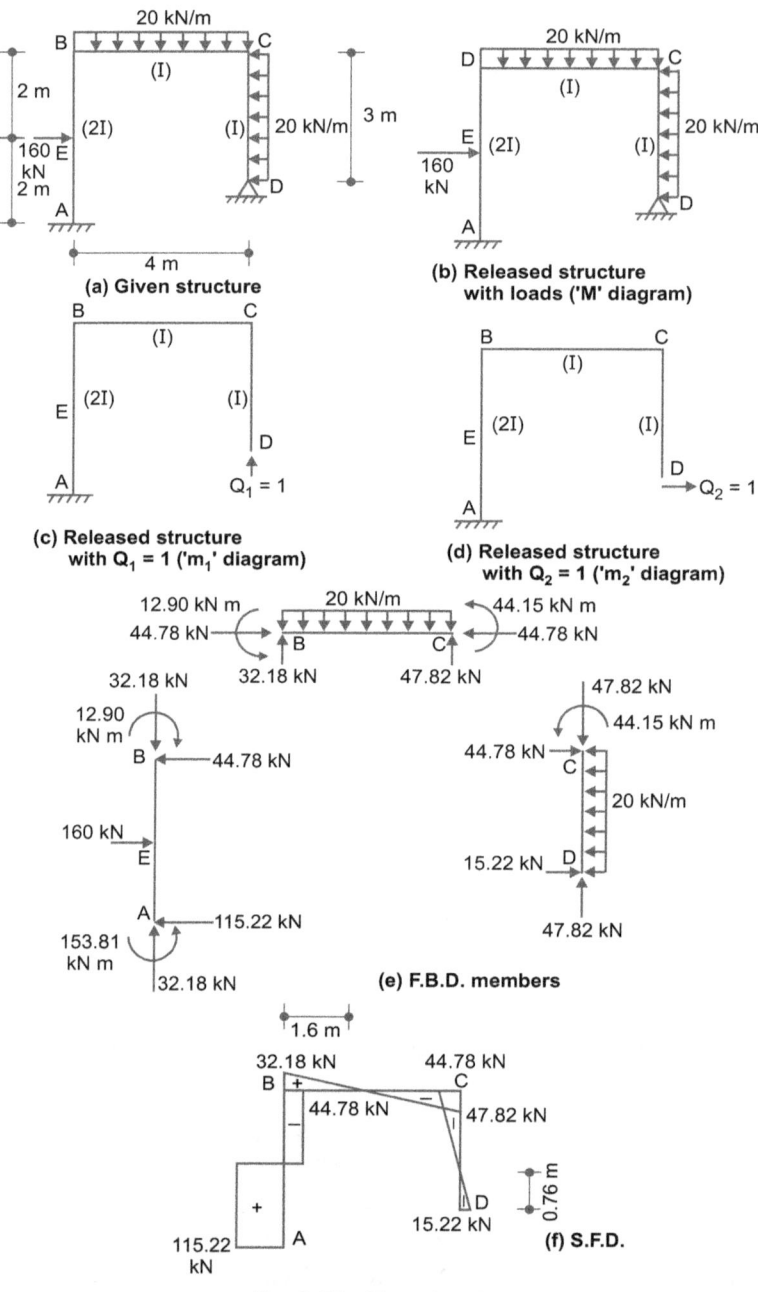

Fig. 3.28 : (Contd. ...)

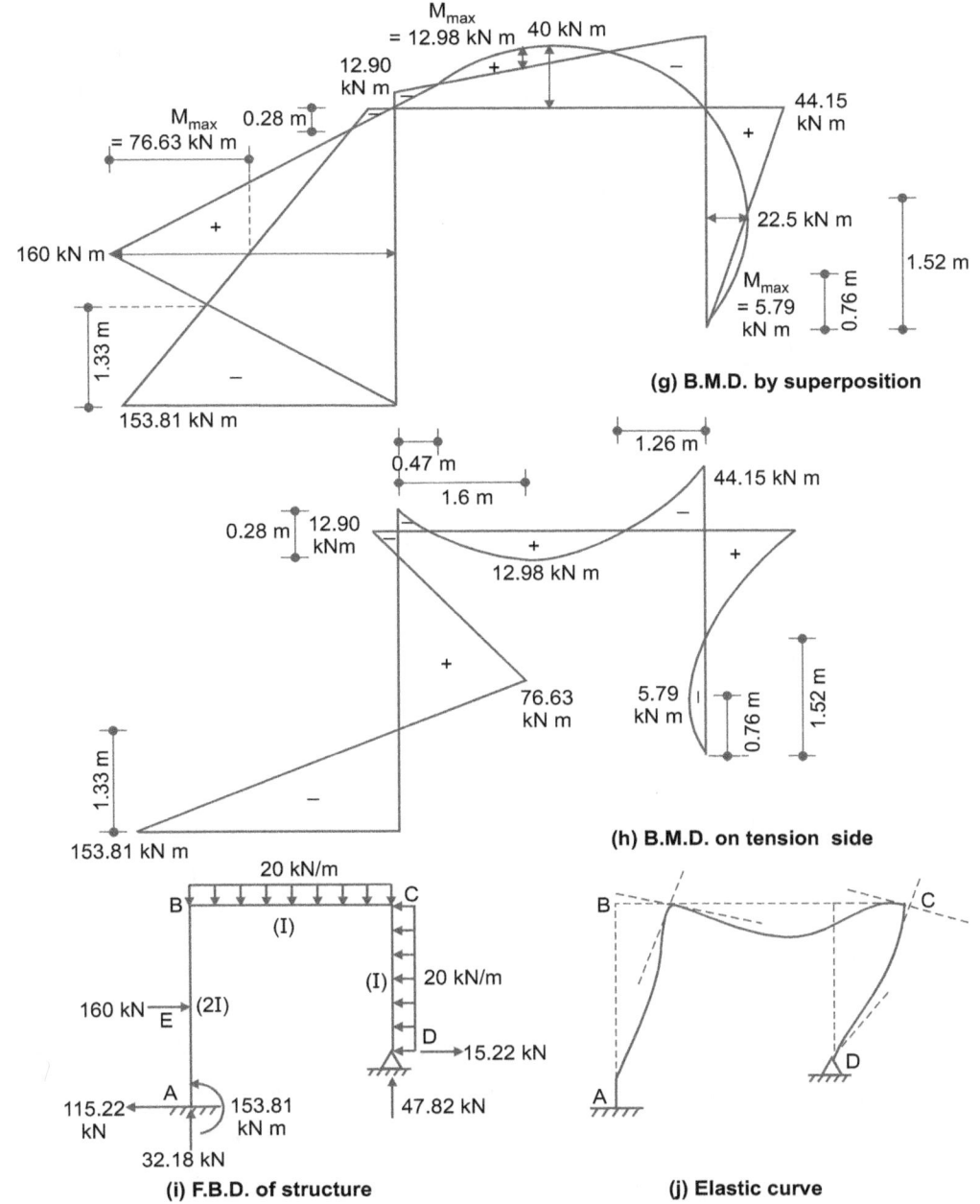

Fig. 3.28 : For Illustrative Example 3.24

Step IV : Displacement analysis of released structure :

Zone	Origin	Limits	EI	M	m_1	m_2
DC	D	0 – 3	EI	$-20\dfrac{x^2}{2}$	0	x
CB	C	0 – 4	EI	$-90 - \dfrac{20x^2}{2}$	x	3
BE	B	0 – 2	2 EI	$-250 + 60x$	4	3 – x
EA	B	2 – 4	2 EI	$-250 + 60 - 160(x-2) = 70 - 100(x)$	4	3 – x

(a) Displacements in the released structure subjected to loads corresponding to redundant actions :

$$D_{QL1} = \int_0^L \frac{M m_1 \cdot dx}{EI}$$

$$= \int_0^3 \left(\frac{20x^2}{2}\right)(0) \cdot \frac{dx}{EI} + \int_0^4 (-90 - 20x^2/2)(x) \cdot \frac{dx}{EI}$$

$$+ \int_0^2 (-250 + 60x)(4) \cdot \frac{dx}{2EI} + \int_2^4 (70 - 100x)(4) \cdot \frac{dx}{2EI}$$

$$= \frac{(0 - 1360 - 760 - 920)}{EI} = \frac{-3040}{EI}$$

$$D_{QL2} = \int_0^L \frac{M m_2 \cdot dx}{EI}$$

$$= \int_0^3 \left(\frac{20x^2}{2}\right)(-x) \cdot \frac{dx}{EI} + \int_0^4 (-90 - 20x^2/2)(3) \cdot \frac{dx}{EI} + \int_0^2 (-250 + 60x)(3-x) \cdot \frac{dx}{2EI}$$

$$+ \int_2^4 (70 - 100x)(3-x) \cdot \frac{dx}{2EI}$$

$$= \frac{(-202.5 - 1720 - 400 + 33.33)}{EI} = \frac{-2289.16}{EI}$$

(b) Displacements in the released structure subjected to unit values of Q_1 and Q_2 corresponding to redundant actions :

$$F_{11} = \int_0^L \frac{m_1 \cdot m_1 \cdot dx}{EI}$$

$$= \int_0^3 (0) \cdot \frac{dx}{EI} + \int_0^4 (x)^2 \cdot \frac{dx}{EI} + \int_0^2 (4)^2 \cdot \frac{dx}{2EI} + \int_2^4 (4)^2 \cdot \frac{dx}{2EI}$$

$$= \frac{(0 + 21.33 + 16 + 16)}{EI} = \frac{53.33}{EI}$$

$$F_{21} = F_{12} = \int_0^L \frac{m_1 \cdot m_2 \cdot dx}{EI}$$

$$= \int_0^3 (0)(-x)\frac{dx}{EI} + \int_0^4 (x)(3)\frac{dx}{EI} + \int_0^2 4(3-x)\frac{dx}{2EI} + \int_2^4 4(3-x)\frac{dx}{2EI}$$

$$= \frac{(0+24+8+0)}{EI} = \frac{32}{EI}$$

$$F_{22} = \int_0^L \frac{m_2 \cdot m_2 \cdot dx}{EI}$$

$$= \int_0^3 (-x)^2 \cdot \frac{dx}{EI} + \int_0^4 (3)^2 \cdot \frac{dx}{EI} + \int_0^2 (3-x)^2 \cdot \frac{dx}{2EI} + \int_2^4 (3-x)^2 \cdot \frac{dx}{2EI}$$

$$= \frac{(9+36+4.33+0.33)}{EI} = \frac{49.67}{EI}$$

Step V : The physical requirement of displacements :
The vertical and horizontal translation at D must be zero.
i.e. $D_{Q1} = D_{Q2} = 0$

Step VI : Superposition equation of compatibility of displacements :

$$\{D_Q\} = \{D_{QL}\} + [F]\{Q\}$$

i.e. $\begin{Bmatrix} 0 \\ 0 \end{Bmatrix} = \frac{1}{EI} \cdot \begin{Bmatrix} -3040 \\ -2289.16 \end{Bmatrix} + \frac{1}{EI} \begin{bmatrix} 53.33 & 32 \\ 32 & 49.67 \end{bmatrix} \begin{Bmatrix} Q_1 \\ Q_2 \end{Bmatrix}$

i.e. $0 = -3040 + 53.33(Q_1) + 32(Q_2)$ ... (A)
$0 = -2289.16 + 32(Q_1) + 49.67(Q_2)$ ... (B)
$Q_2 = H_D = 15.22 \text{ kN} = 15.22 \text{ kN} (\rightarrow)$

Step VII : Solution of equations for unknown redundant forces. Solving equations (A) and (B), we get,

$$\boxed{\begin{aligned} Q_1 &= V_D = 47.82 \text{ kN} = 47.82 \text{ kN} (\uparrow) \\ Q_2 &= H_D = 15.22 \text{ kN} = 15.22 \text{ kN} (\rightarrow) \end{aligned}}$$

Step VIII : Other reaction components : Considering equilibrium of each member and of complete structure, other reaction components are found out and FBD of members is as shown in Fig. 3.28 (e).

Step IX : Shear force and bending moment diagrams : SFD is as shown in Fig. 3.28 (f). BMD by superposition and on tension side is as shown in Fig. 3.28 (g) and Fig. 3.28 (h) respectively.

Step X : FBD of structure : as shown in Fig. 3.28 (i).

Step XI : Elastic curve : as shown in Fig. 3.28 (j).

Example 3.25 : Analyse the frame shown in Fig. 3.29 (a) by flexibility method.

STRUCTURAL ANALYSIS – II   FLEXIBILITY METHOD

        Take EI = constant.
Solution : Data : The frame is supported and loaded as shown in Fig. 3.29 (a).
Object : Structural analysis.
Concepts and Equations :
(1)   Statically determinate structure (Released structure).
(2)   Displacement analysis of released structure.
(3)   Superposition equations of compatibility of displacements.

Procedure :
Step I : The degree of static indeterminacy (D_{si}) :
(a)   Degree of external static indeterminacy = $(D_{si})_e$ = 3.
(b)   Degree of internal static indeterminacy = $(D_{si})_i$ = 0.
(c)   Total degree of static indeterminacy = $D_{si} = (D_{si})_e + (D_{si})_i = 3 + 0 = 3$.

Step II : Selection of unknown redundant forces (Q) :
Let, $Q_1 = V_D(\uparrow)$
          $Q_2 = H_D(\rightarrow)$ and
          $Q_3 = M_{DC}$

Step III : Released structure : Fixed support at D is removed and the basic released structure is as shown in Fig. 3.29 (b). Also released structure subjected to unit values of Q_1; Q_2 and Q_3 is shown in Fig. 3.29 (c), Fig. 3.29 (d), and Fig. 3.29 (e) respectively.

Step IV : Displacement analysis of released structure :

Zone	Origin	Limits	M	m_1	m_2	m_3
DF	D	0 – 1	0	0	x	1
FC	D	1 – 3	40 (x – 1)	0	x	1
CE	C	0 – 1.5	– 80	x	3	1
EB	C	1.5 – 3	– 50 (x – 1.5) – 80	x	3	1
BA	B	0 – 4	$-25\dfrac{x^2}{2} - 155 + 40x$	3	3 – x	1

(a) Displacements in the released structure subjected to loads corresponding to redundant actions :

$$D_{QL1} = \int_0^L \frac{M m_1 \cdot dx}{EI}$$

$$= \int_0^1 (0) \cdot \frac{dx}{EI} + \int_1^3 40(x-1)(0) \cdot \frac{dx}{EI} + \int_0^{1.5} (-80)(x) \cdot \frac{dx}{EI} + \int_{1.5}^3 [-50(x-1.5) - 80](x) \cdot \frac{dx}{EI}$$

$$+ \int_0^4 \left(-25\frac{x^2}{2} - 155 + 40x\right)(3) \cdot \frac{dx}{EI}$$

$$= \frac{(0 + 9 - 90 - 410.625 - 1700)}{EI} = \frac{-2200.625}{EI}$$

STRUCTURAL ANALYSIS – II FLEXIBILITY METHOD

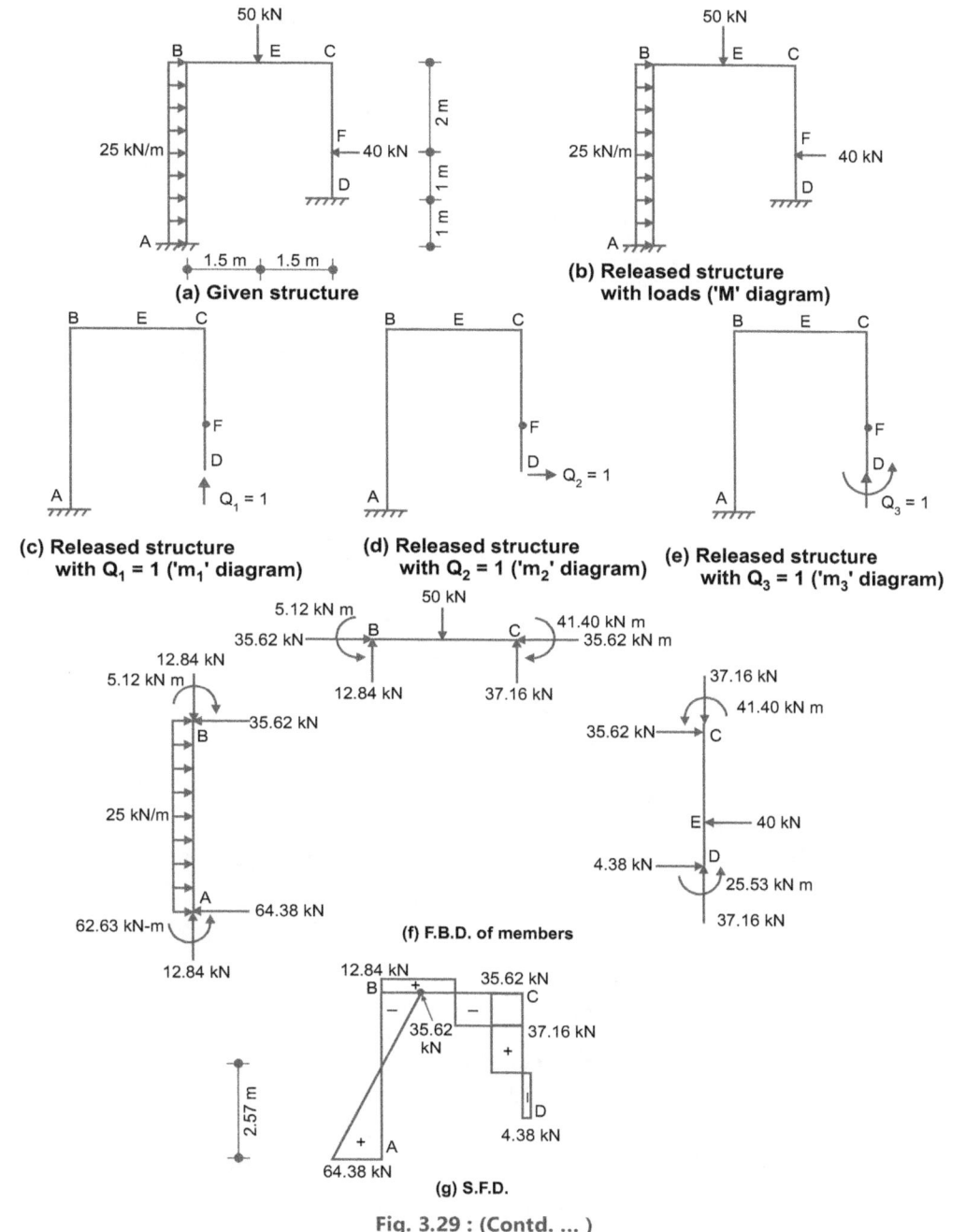

Fig. 3.29 : (Contd. ...)

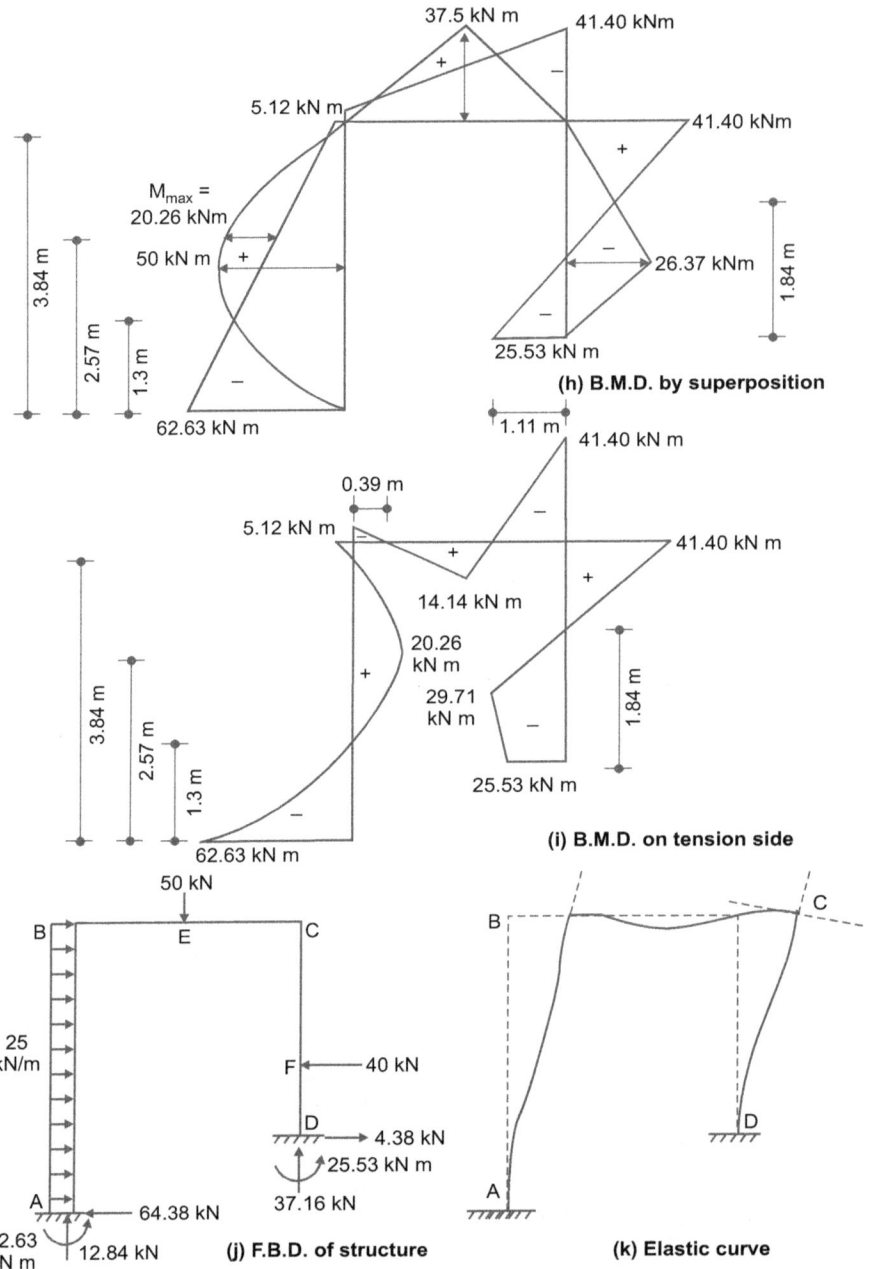

Fig. 3.29 : For Illustrative Example 3.25

STRUCTURAL ANALYSIS – II   FLEXIBILITY METHOD

$$D_{QL2} = \int_0^L \frac{Mm_2 \cdot dx}{EI}$$

$$= \int_0^1 (0)(-x) \cdot \frac{dx}{EI} + \int_1^3 40(x-1)(-x) \cdot \frac{dx}{EI} + \int_0^{1.5} (-80)(3) \frac{dx}{EI}$$

$$+ \int_{1.5}^3 [-50(x-1.5) - 80](3) \cdot \frac{dx}{EI} + \int_0^4 \left(-\frac{25x^2}{2} - 155 + 40x\right)(3-x)\frac{dx}{EI}$$

$$= \frac{(0 - 186.67 - 360 - 528.75 - 513.33)}{EI} = -\frac{1588.75}{EI}$$

$$D_{QL3} = \int_0^L \frac{Mm_3 \cdot dx}{EI}$$

$$= \int_0^1 (0)(-1) \cdot \frac{dx}{EI} + \int_1^3 40(x-1)(-1) \cdot \frac{dx}{EI} + \int_0^{1.5} (-80)(1) \cdot \frac{dx}{EI}$$

$$+ \int_{1.5}^3 [-50(x-1.5) - 80](1) \cdot \frac{dx}{EI} + \int_0^4 \left(-\frac{25x^2}{2} - 155 + 40x\right)(1) \cdot \frac{dx}{EI}$$

$$= \frac{(0 - 80 - 120 - 176.25 - 566.67)}{EI} = -\frac{942.92}{EI}$$

(b) Displacements in the released structure subjected to unit values of Q_1, Q_2 and Q_3 corresponding to redundant actions :

$$F_{11} = \int_0^L \frac{m_1 \cdot m_1 \cdot dx}{EI}$$

$$= \int_0^1 (0) \cdot \frac{dx}{EI} + \int_1^3 (0) \cdot \frac{dx}{EI} + \int_0^{1.5} (x)^2 \cdot \frac{dx}{EI} + \int_{1.5}^3 (x)^2 \cdot \frac{dx}{EI} + \int_0^4 (3)^2 \cdot \frac{dx}{EI}$$

$$= \frac{(0 + 0 + 1.125 + 7.875 + 36)}{EI} = \frac{45}{EI}$$

$$F_{21} = F_{12} = \int_0^L \frac{m_1 \cdot m_2 \cdot dx}{EI}$$

$$= \int_0^1 (0)(-x) \cdot \frac{dx}{EI} + \int_1^3 (0)(-x) \cdot \frac{dx}{EI} + \int_0^{1.5} (x)(3) \cdot \frac{dx}{EI} + \int_{1.5}^3 (x)(3) \cdot \frac{dx}{EI} + \int_0^4 (3)(3-x) \frac{dx}{EI}$$

$$= \frac{0 + 0 + 3.375 + 10.125 + 12}{EI} = \frac{25.5}{EI}$$

Ch. 3 | 3.95

STRUCTURAL ANALYSIS – II FLEXIBILITY METHOD

$$F_{31} = F_{13} = \int_0^L \frac{m_1 \cdot m_3 \cdot dx}{EI}$$

$$= \int_0^1 (0)(-1) \cdot \frac{dx}{EI} + \int_1^3 (0)(-1) \cdot \frac{dx}{EI} + \int_0^{1.5} (x)(1) \cdot \frac{dx}{EI} + \int_{1.5}^3 (x)(1) \cdot \frac{dx}{EI} + \int_0^4 (3)(1) \cdot \frac{dx}{EI}$$

$$= \frac{(0 + 0 + 1.125 + 3.375 + 12)}{EI} = \frac{16.5}{EI}$$

$$F_{22} = \int_0^L \frac{m_2 \cdot m_2 \cdot dx}{EI}$$

$$= \int_0^1 (-x)^2 \cdot \frac{dx}{EI} + \int_1^3 (-x)^2 \cdot \frac{dx}{EI} + \int_0^{1.5} (3)^2 \cdot \frac{dx}{EI} + \int_{1.5}^3 (3)^2 \cdot \frac{dx}{EI} + \int_0^4 (3-x)^2 \cdot \frac{dx}{EI}$$

$$= \frac{0.33 + 8.67 + 13.5 + 13.5 + 9.33}{EI} = \frac{45.33}{EI}$$

$$F_{32} = F_{23} = \int_0^L \frac{m_2 \cdot m_3 \cdot dx}{EI}$$

$$= \int_0^1 (-x)(-1) \cdot \frac{dx}{EI} + \int_1^3 (-x)(-1) \cdot \frac{dx}{EI} + \int_0^{1.5} (3)(1) \cdot \frac{dx}{EI}$$

$$+ \int_{1.5}^3 (3)(1) \cdot \frac{dx}{EI} + \int_0^4 (3-x)(1) \cdot \frac{dx}{EI}$$

$$= \frac{(0.5 + 4 + 4.5 + 4.5 + 4)}{EI} = \frac{17.5}{EI}$$

$$F_{33} = \int_0^L \frac{m_3 \cdot m_3 \cdot dx}{EI}$$

$$= \int_0^1 (-1)^2 \frac{dx}{EI} + \int_1^3 (-1)^2 \cdot \frac{dx}{EI} + \int_0^{1.5} (1)^2 \cdot \frac{dx}{EI} + \int_{1.5}^3 (1)^2 \cdot \frac{dx}{EI} + \int_0^4 (1)^2 \cdot \frac{dx}{EI}$$

$$= \frac{(1 + 2 + 1.5 + 1.5 + 4)}{EI} = \frac{10}{EI}$$

Step V : The physical requirement of displacements : The vertical and horizontal translation at D must be zero. Also rotation at D must be zero.

i.e. $D_{Q1} = D_{Q2} = D_{Q3} = 0$

Step VI : Superposition equation of compatibility of displacements :

$$\{D_Q\} = \{D_{QL}\} + [F]\{Q\}$$

STRUCTURAL ANALYSIS – II   FLEXIBILITY METHOD

i.e. $\quad \begin{Bmatrix} 0 \\ 0 \\ 0 \end{Bmatrix} = \dfrac{1}{EI} \begin{Bmatrix} -2200.625 \\ -1588.75 \\ -942.91 \end{Bmatrix} + \dfrac{1}{EI} \begin{bmatrix} 45 & 25.5 & 16.5 \\ 25.5 & 45.33 & 17.5 \\ 16.5 & 17.5 & 10 \end{bmatrix} \begin{Bmatrix} Q_1 \\ Q_2 \\ Q_3 \end{Bmatrix}$

i.e. $\quad 0 = -2200.625 + 45\,(Q_1) + 25.5\,(Q_2) + 16.5\,(Q_3)$ ... (A)
$\qquad 0 = -1588.75 + 25.5\,(Q_1) + 45.33\,(Q_2) + 17.5\,(Q_3)$ ... (B)
$\qquad 0 = -942.91 + 16.5\,(Q_1) + 17.5\,(Q_2) + 10\,(Q_3)$ ... (C)

Step VII : Solution of equations for unknown redundant forces : Solving equations (A), (B) and (C). we get,

$\qquad Q_1 = V_D = 37.16$ kN $= 37.16$ kN (↑)
$\qquad Q_2 = H_D = 4.38$ kN $= 4.38$ kN (→)
$\qquad Q_3 = M_{DC} = 25.33$ kNm $= 25.33$ kNm (↻)

Step VIII : Other reaction components : Considering equilibrium of each member and of complete structure, other reaction components are found out and FBD of members is as shown in Fig. 3.29 (f).

Step IX : Shear force and bending moment diagrams : SFD is as shown in Fig. 3.29 (g). BMD by superposition and on tension side is as shown in Fig. 3.29 (h) and Fig. 3.29 (i) respectively.

Step X : FBD of structure : as shown in Fig. 3.29 (j).

Step XI : Elastic curve : as shown in Fig. 3.29 (k).

Example 3.26 : *Analyse the portal frame as shown in Fig. 3.30 by flexibility method.*
EI = constant.

Solution : Data : The frame is supported and loaded as shown in Fig. 3.30 (a).
Object : Structural analysis.
Concepts and equations :
(1) Statically determinate structure (released structure).
(2) Displacement analysis of released structure.
(3) Superposition equations of compatability of displacements.
Procedure : Step I : The degree of static indeterminacy
(a) Degree of external static indeterminacy = $(D_{si})_e = 1$
(b) Degree of internal static indeterminacy = $(D_{si})_i = 0$
(c) Total degree of static indeterminacy = $(D_{si}) = (D_{si})_e + (D_{si})_i = 1 + 0 = 1$
Step II : Selection of unknown redundant forces (Q_1) :
Let, $\qquad Q = V_B$ (↑)
Step III : Released Structure : Roller support at B is removed and basic released structure is as shown in Fig. 3.30 (c). Also released structure is subjected to unit value of θ_1 is as shown in Fig. 3.30 (d).

Step IV : Displacement analysis of released structure :

Zone	Origin	Limit	EI	M	m_1
CB	C	0 – 2.4	2EI	0	x
BA	B	0 – 4.8	EI	$-20x^2/2 = -10x^2$	2.4

(a) Displacement in the released structure subjected to loads corresponding to redundant actions :

$$D_{QL1} = \int_0^L Mm_1 \frac{dx}{EI}$$

$$= \int_0^{2.4} 0(x) = \frac{dx}{2EI} + \int_0^{4.8} (-10x^2)(2.4) \frac{dx}{EI}$$

$$= -\frac{884.74}{EI}$$

(b) Displacement in the released structure subjected to unit value of Q_1 corresponding to redundant actions :

$$F_{11} = \int_0^L m_1 m_1 \frac{dx}{EI}$$

$$= \int_0^{2.4} x \cdot x \frac{dx}{2EI} + \int_0^{4.8} 2.4 \times 2.4 \frac{dx}{EI}$$

$$= \frac{2.30}{EI} + \frac{27.65}{EI} = \frac{29.95}{EI}$$

Step V : The physical requirement of displacements :

The vertical translation at must be zero i.e.

$$D_{Q1} = 0$$

Step VI : Superposition equation of compatibility of displacements :

$$\{D_Q\} = \{D_{QL}\} + [F]\{Q\}$$

$$0 = \frac{-884.74}{EI} + \left(\frac{29.95}{EI}\right) Q_1 \quad \ldots A$$

Step VII : Solution of equations for redundant forces :

Solving equation (A), we get,

$$Q_1 = 29.54 \text{ kN } (\uparrow)$$

STRUCTURAL ANALYSIS – II   FLEXIBILITY METHOD

Step VIII : Other reaction components : Consider equilibrium of complete structure, other unknown reaction components are found. FBD of structure is as shown in Fig. 3.30 (e).

Step IX : Shear force and bending moment diagrams : SFD is as shown in Fig. 3.30 (f), BMD by superposition and tension side as shown in Fig. 3.30 (g) and (h).

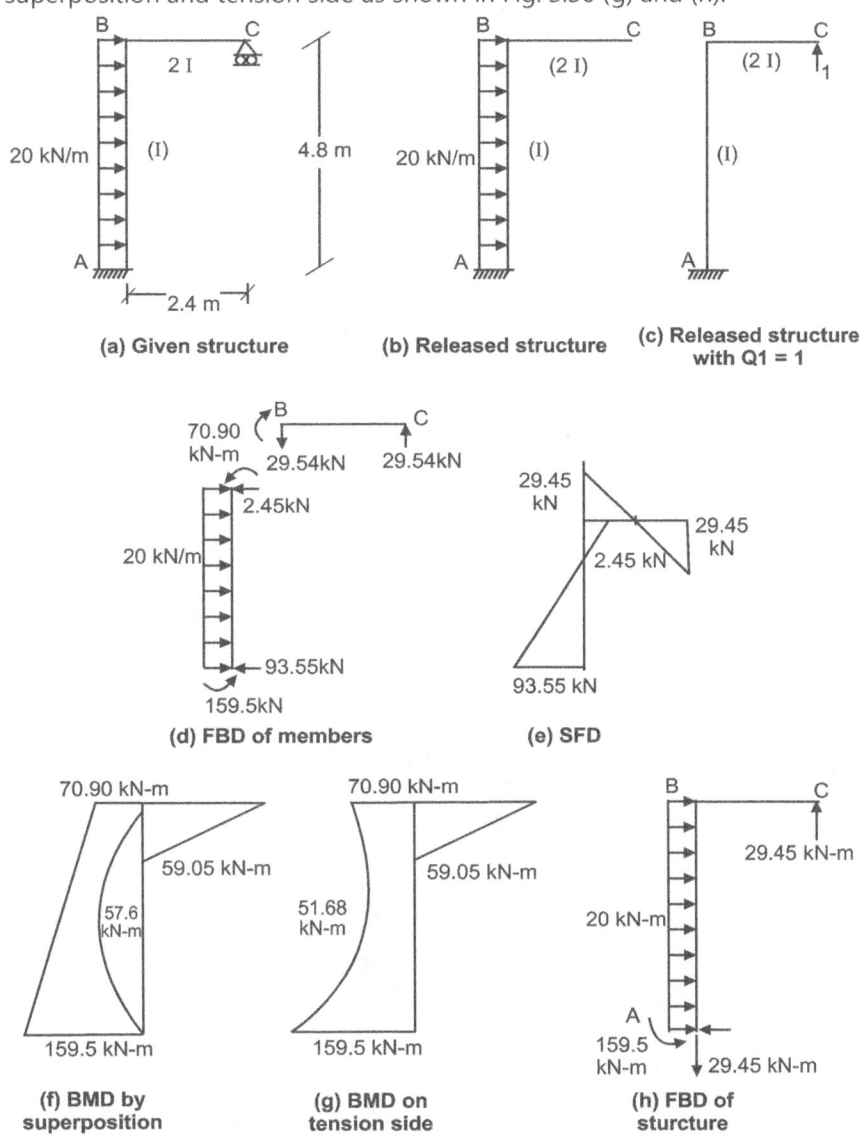

Fig. 3.30 : For Illustration – Example 3.26

EXERCISE

For pin jointed plane trusses in problems 1 to 17, find forces in all the members. Take E = constant. Figures in the bracket indicate cross-sectional areas of members in cm², wherever mentioned. Otherwise A shall be taken constant.

1.

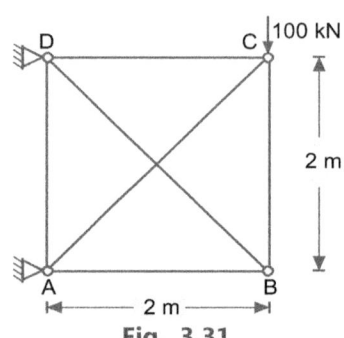

Fig. 3.31

(**Ans.** $F_{AB} = -54.84$ kN, $F_{BC} = -54.84$ kN, $F_{CD} = 45.16$ kN, $F_{AD} = 45.16$ kN, $F_{AC} = -63.87$ kN, $F_{DB} = 77.55$ kN)

2.

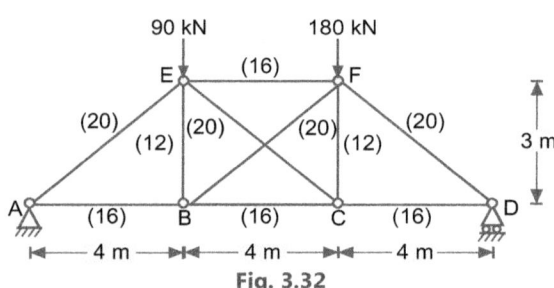

Fig. 3.32

(**Ans.** $F_{AE} = -200$ kN, $F_{AB} = 160$ kN, $F_{BC} = 175.65$ kN, $F_{BE} = 171.74$ kN, $F_{EF} = -184.35$ kN, $F_{EC} = 30.44$ kN, $F_{CF} = -18.26$ kN, $F_{DF} = -250$ kN, $F_{DC} = 200$ kN, $F_{BF} = -19.56$ kN)

3.

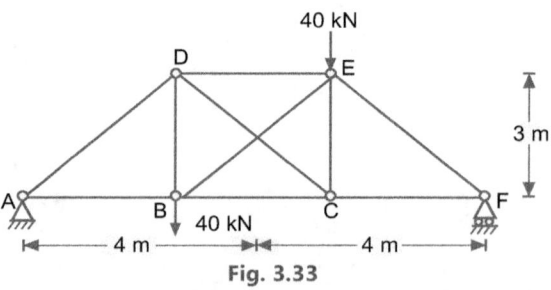

Fig. 3.33

(**Ans.** F_{AB} = 26.6 kN, F_{AD} = – 33.2 kN, F_{BD} = 31.2 kN, F_{DC} = – 18.7 kN, F_{BE} = 14.4 kN, F_{DE} = – 11.6 kN, F_{BC} = 15 kN, F_{EC} = – 48.8 kN)

4.

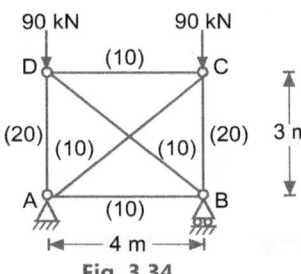

Fig. 3.34

(**Ans.** F_{AB} = 8 kN, F_{DC} = 8 kN, F_{AD} = – 84 kN, F_{BC} = – 84 kN, F_{AC} = – 10 kN, F_{BD} = – 10 kN)

5.

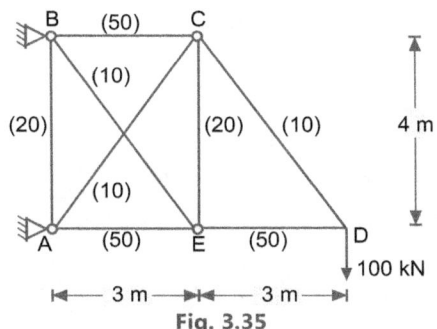

Fig. 3.35

(**Ans.** F_{AB} = – 40.14 kN, F_{AE} = – 105.11 kN, F_{BE} = 50.18 kN, F_{BC} = 119.89 kN, F_{CE} = – 40.14 kN, F_{DE} = – 75 kN, F_{DC} = 125 kN, F_{AC} = – 74.82 kN)

6.

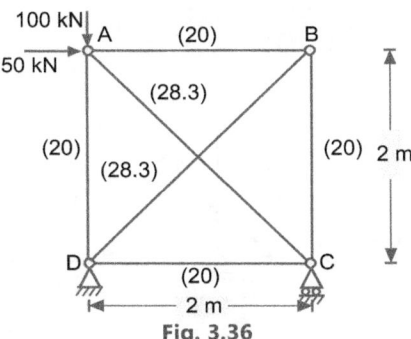

Fig. 3.36

(**Ans.** F_{AB} = – 12.5 kN, F_{BC} = 12.5 kN, F_{AC} = – 53 kN, F_{AD} = – 62.5 kN, F_{DC} = 37.5 kN, F_{DB} = 17.68 kN)

7.

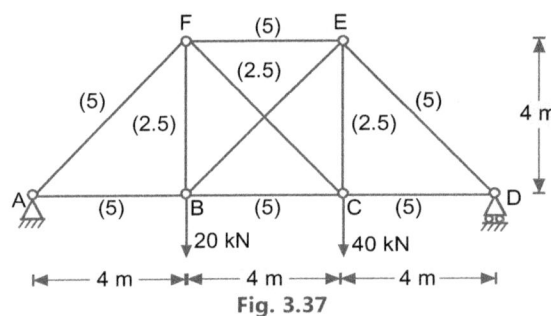

Fig. 3.37

(**Ans.** F_{AB} = 26.67 kN, F_{BC} = 23.06 kN, F_{CD} = 33.33 kN, F_{FE} = – 36.93 kN, F_{AF} = – 37.73 kN, F_{ED} = – 47.06 kN, F_{BF} = 23.06 kN, F_{CE} = 29.73 kN, F_{BE} = 5.08 kN, F_{CF} = 14.5 kN)

8.

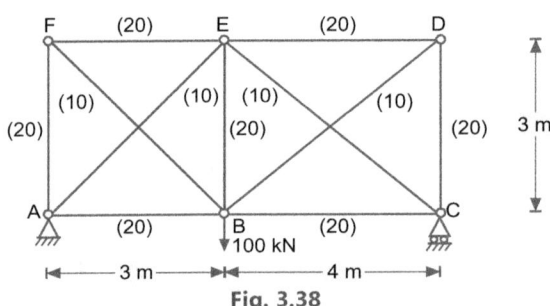

Fig. 3.38

(**Ans.** F_{AB} = 27.2 kN, F_{BC} = 27.2 kN, F_{FE} = – 29.95 kN, F_{ED} = – 30 kN, F_{AF} = 29.95 kN, F_{BE} = 47.55 kN, F_{CD} = – 22.5 kN, F_{AE} = – 38.5 kN, F_{FB} = – 42.3 kN, F_{BD} = – 37.55 kN, F_{EC} = – 33.9 kN)

9.

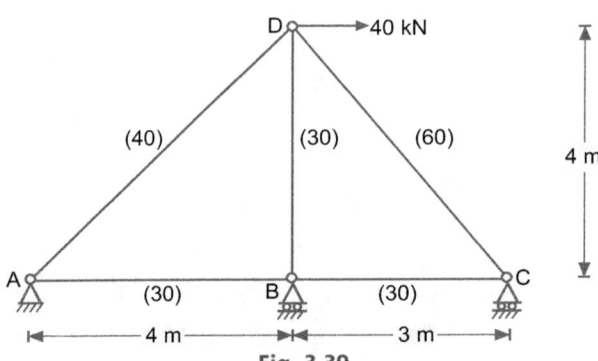

Fig. 3.39

(**Ans.** F_{AB} = 16.12 kN, F_{BC} = 16.12 kN, F_{AD} = 33.77 kN, F_{BD} = – 23.80 kN, F_{CD} = – 26.87 kN)

10.

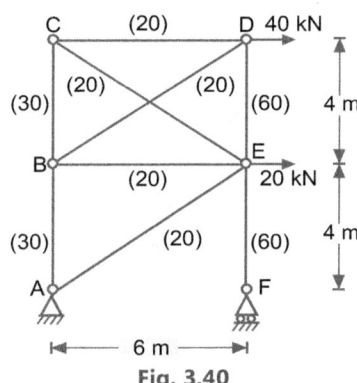

Fig. 3.40

(**Ans.** $F_{AB} = 26.67$ kN, $F_{AE} = 72.11$ kN, $F_{EF} = -72.11$ kN, $F_{BE} = -40$ kN, $F_{BC} = 0$, $F_{BD} = 48.1$ kN, $F_{CE} = 0$, $F_{DE} = -26.67$ kN, $F_{DC} = 0$)

11.

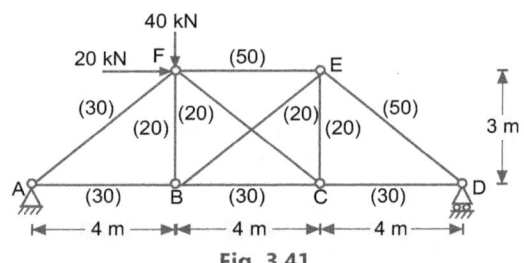

Fig. 3.41

(**Ans.** $F_{AB} = 48.89$ kN, $F_{AF} = -36.11$, $F_{BF} = -10.43$ kN, $F_{FE} = -38.35$ kN, $F_{FC} = -13.18$ kN, $F_{BE} = 17.38$ kN, $F_{BC} = 35$ kN, $F_{DE} = -30.55$ kN, $F_{CE} = 7.91$ kN, $F_{CD} = 24.44$ kN)

12.

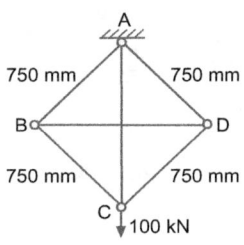

Fig. 3.42

(**Ans.** $F_{AB} = 20.72$ kN, $F_{BC} = 20.72$ kN, $F_{CD} = 20.72$ kN, $F_{DA} = 20.72$ kN, $F_{BD} = -29.3$ kN, $F_{AC} = 70.7$ kN)

13.

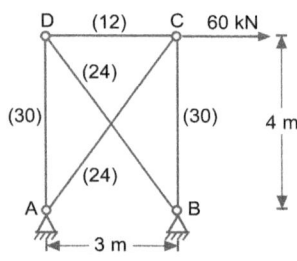

Fig. 3.43

(**Ans.** $F_{AD} = 34.58$ kN, $F_{DC} = 26$ kN, $F_{CB} = -45.42$ kN, $F_{AC} = 56.58$ kN, $F_{BD} = -43.4$ kN)

14.

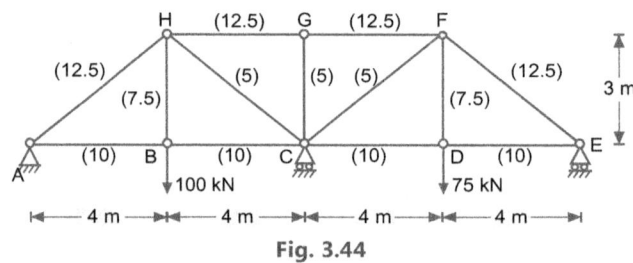

Fig. 3.44

(**Ans.** $F_{AH} = -85.75$ kN, $F_{HG} = -3.92$ kN, $F_{GF} = -3.92$ kN, $F_{FE} = -64.91$ kN, $F_{AB} = 68.625$ kN, $F_{BC} = 68.625$ kN, $F_{CD} = 51.88$ kN, $F_{DE} = 51.88$ kN, $F_{BH} = 100$ kN, $F_{CH} = 80.75$ kN, $F_{CG} = 0$, $F_{CF} = 60.125$ kN, $F_{DF} = 75$ kN)

15.

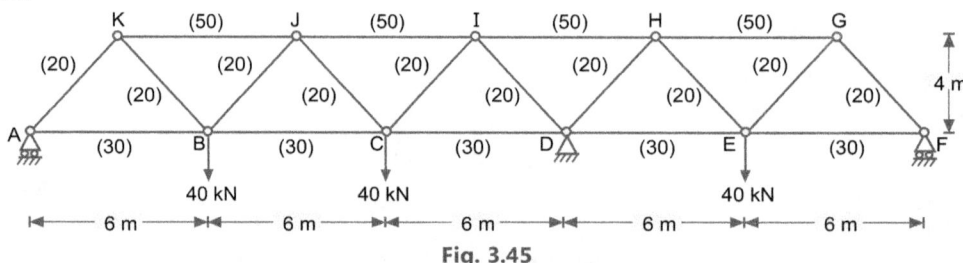

Fig. 3.45

(**Ans.** $F_{AB} = 25.15$ kN, $F_{AK} = -41.92$ kN, $F_{KB} = 41.92$ kN, $F_{KJ} = -50.31$ kN, $F_{BC} = 45.46$ kN, $F_{BJ} = 8.1$ kN, $F_{CJ} = -8.1$ kN, $F_{JI} = -40.62$ kN, $F_{CD} = 5.77$ kN, $F_{CI} = 58.1$ kN, $F_{DI} = -58.1$ kN, $F_{IH} = 29.1$ kN, $F_{DE} = -6.81$ kN, $F_{DH} = -37.11$ kN, $F_{EH} = 37.11$ kN, $F_{HG} = -15.46$ kN, $F_{EF} = 7.73$ kN, $F_{EG} = 12.9$ kN, $F_{FG} = -12.9$ kN)

16.

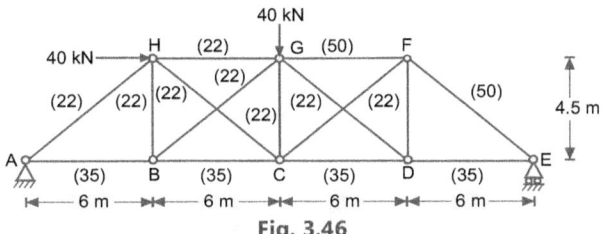

Fig. 3.46

(**Ans.** F_{AB} = 56.67 kN, F_{AH} = – 20.83 kN, F_{HB} = 10.17 kN, F_{HG} = – 59.78 kN, F_{HC} = 3.89 kN, F_{BG} = – 16.95 kN, F_{BC} = 70.22 kN, F_{GC} = – 17.22 kN, F_{DG} = – 21 kN, F_{GF} = – 56.53 kN, F_{CD} = 53.47 kN, F_{CF} = 24.83 kN, F_{DF} = 12.60 kN, F_{EF} = –45.83 kN, F_{DE} = 36.67 kN)

17.

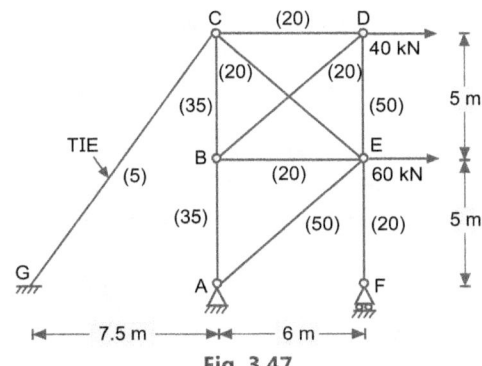

Fig. 3.47

(**Ans.** F_{AB} = 9.73 kN, F_{BC} = – 3.18 kN, F_{CD} = 24.50 kN, F_{CE} = – 17.72 kN, F_{BD} = 20.17 kN, F_{ED} = – 12.91 kN, F_{BE} = – 15.50 kN, F_{EF} = – 98.51 kN, F_{AE} = 115.99 kN, F_{GC} = 18.16 kN)

18. A pin jointed rectangular truss is as shown in Fig. 3.47. The member AD is last to be added and is short by 4 mm. Find the forces in all the members when it is forced into position. Take E = 200 GPa. Figures in the bracket indicate cross-sectional areas of members in cm².

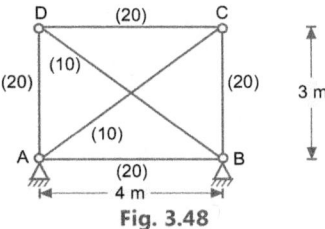

Fig. 3.48

(**Ans.** F_{AB} = 28.04 kN, F_{BC} = 21.08 kN, F_{CD} = 28.04 kN, F_{DA} = 21.08 kN, F_{DB} = – 35.2 kN, F_{AC} = – 35.2 kN)

19. A pin jointed truss is as shown in Fig. 3.48. The member EF is last to be added and is long by 2 mm. Find forces in all the members of truss when it is forced into position. Take E = 200 GPa. Figures in the bracket indicate cross-sectional areas of members in cm².

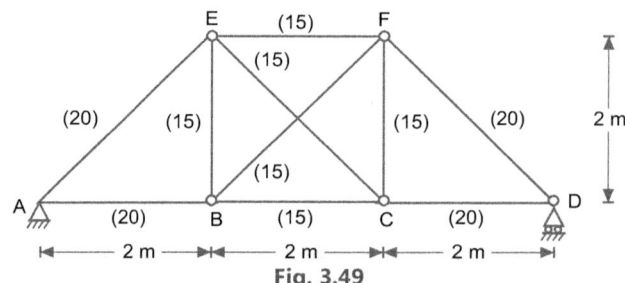

Fig. 3.49

(**Ans.** F_{AE} = 0, F_{AB} = 0, F_{BE} = – 31.1 kN, F_{EF} = – 31.3 kN, F_{EC} = 43.97 kN, F_{BF} = 43.97 kN, F_{BC} = – 31.1 kN, F_{CF} = – 31.1 kN, F_{FD} = 0, F_{CD} = 0)

20. A pin jointed truss is shown in Fig. 3.49. All members has cross-sectional area of 10 cm². If there is a rise of temperature of member BD by 30°C, determine forces due to change in temperature. Coefficient of linear expansion α = 12 × 10⁻⁶ per °C and E = 200 GPa.

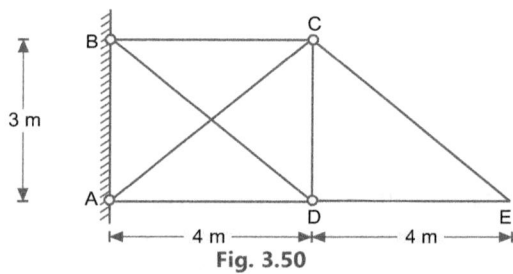

Fig. 3.50

(**Ans.** F_{BC} = 17.77 kN, F_{CD} = 13.33 kN, F_{AD} = 17.77 kN, F_{AC} = – 22.22 kN, F_{BD} = – 22.22 kN, F_{DE} = 0, F_{CE} = 0).

Chapter 4

STIFFNESS METHOD

4.1 DISPLACEMENT METHOD OR STIFFNESS METHOD

4.1.1 General

Displacement method, now-a-days has been an effective tool for structural analysis because of its specific and disciplined characteristics conducive to computer programming. Non-zero point displacements of a structure are considered as unknown. Therefore, the method is named as the displacement method. The number of non-zero point displacements is also called as the degree of kinematic indeterminacy or degree of freedom of the structure. It is not necessary to identify the redundant in this method, therefore the method does not require the information of degree of static indeterminacy of the structure.

The method mainly consists of restraining, releasing and balancing the points of the structure. The logic of the displacement method is almost parallel to that of the force method and briefly described as follows :

- The unknown joint displacements of a structure are identified by which the compatibility is implied. All points are restrained i.e. locked and kinematically determinate structure is obtained. Kinematically determinate structure is also called as restrained structure.
- The forces of kinematically determinate structure at points of and corresponding to the unknown joint displacements, due to the given loads are found.
- The structure is released successively for the displacements corresponding to unknown. To do this, unit displacement, only one at a time is given to the kinematically indeterminate structure and forces due to this cause are obtained. The force required for unit displacement is termed as stiffness. The force due to unknown displacement is the product of the stiffness and the unknown displacement.
- The conditions of balancing the joints also called as the equilibrium equations also called as the superposition equations of forces are formulated in terms of unknown point displacements. There are always as many conditions of equilibrium as there are unknown displacements. The formulated equations are linear and algebraic.
- The solution of the equations gives the unknown joint displacements.
- Once the displacements are known the remaining analysis of the structure is completed by known force-displacement relations.

The fundamental principle of the method is the equilibrium requirements of the forces of the kinematically determinate structure at joints which are released for unknown displacements. Basic equilibrium requirements are as follows :
- If a joint is released for horizontal translation, then $\Sigma H = 0$.
- If a joint is released for vertical translation, then $\Sigma V = 0$.
- If a joint is released for rotation then $\Sigma M = 0$.

The displacement method begins with the compatibility and ends with the equilibrium of forces using the stiffness concept. The displacement method is also called as :
- Equilibrium method because the conditions of equilibrium are used to formulate the method, or
- Stiffness method because the force required for unit displacement termed as the stiffness is used to obtain the force in terms of unknown displacement.

4.1.2 Procedure of Displacement Method

The displacement method is mainly based on the force equations of equilibrium. It therefore involves the determination of the following forces of kinematically determinate structure corresponding to the unknown joint displacement, D :

- The force at D and corresponding to D due to given loads (L). This is denoted by A_{DL}.
- The force at D and corresponding to D due to unit displacement. This is called the stiffness and denoted by S.
- The force at D due to D. This is denoted by A_{DD} and given by

$$A_{DD} = S \cdot D \qquad \ldots (4.1)$$

- The known force at D and corresponding to D. This is denoted by A_D. With these forces the equilibrium of joint is formulated by the superposition principle.

$$\therefore \quad A_D = A_{DL} + A_{DD} \qquad \ldots (4.2)$$
$$\therefore \quad A_D = A_{DL} + S \cdot D$$

This is the basic equation of the displacement method. This equation is rearranged and shown as the fundamental equation of the stiffness.

$$\therefore \quad (A_D - A_{DL}) = S \cdot D$$
$$A = S \cdot D$$

The force at a point of kinematically determinate structure :
(1) Due to given loads is generally obtained from the standard results of fixed beam and
(2) Due to unit displacement is obtained from the standard results of stiffness, as given in Table 1.5.

The displacement method will be subsequently formulated in general as the stiffness matrix method. However the procedure of the displacement method is illustrated with the same

STRUCTURAL ANALYSIS – II   STIFFNESS METHOD

simple problem of beam of the force method to pave the foundation of the stiffness matrix method, for multi-displacement and multi-force system i.e. structure. The problem of displacement method is illustrated by the following steps.

4.1.3 Simple Problem on Displacement Method

Example 4.1 : *Analyse the beam shown in Fig. 4.1 by displacement method. Take EI = Constant.*

Solution : Data : The beam is supported and loaded as shown in Fig. 4.1 (a). As the data is same as the problem of force method, only steps are listed.
1. Structural configuration
2. Cross-sectional properties of members
3. Material properties of members
4. Applied loads
5. Type of structure.

Objects :
1. Unknown joint displacements as the initial target
2. Analysis of structure.

Assumptions :
1. Linear Elastic Analysis
2. Axial deformations are neglected in beams

Concepts and Equations :
1. Kinematically determinate structure (Restrained structure).
2. Force analysis of restrained structure.
3. Superposition equations of equilibrium of forces.

Procedure :

Step I : The degree of kinematic indeterminacy i.e. Number of non-zero joint displacement or degree of freedom.

$$\therefore \quad D_{ki} = 1$$

Step II : Unknown point displacement. It is denoted by D

$$\therefore \quad D = \theta_B \text{ i.e. rotation at the joint B.}$$

Step III : The kinematically determinate structure : The joint B is locked and the restrained structure is obtained. Thus, the given beam is considered equivalent to the superposition of :

(a) Restrained beam under given loads as shown in Fig. 4.1 (b) and

(b) Restrained beam under unit rotation at B and then under θ_B, as shown in Fig. 4.1 (c) and Fig. 4.1 (d) respectively.

STRUCTURAL ANALYSIS – II   STIFFNESS METHOD

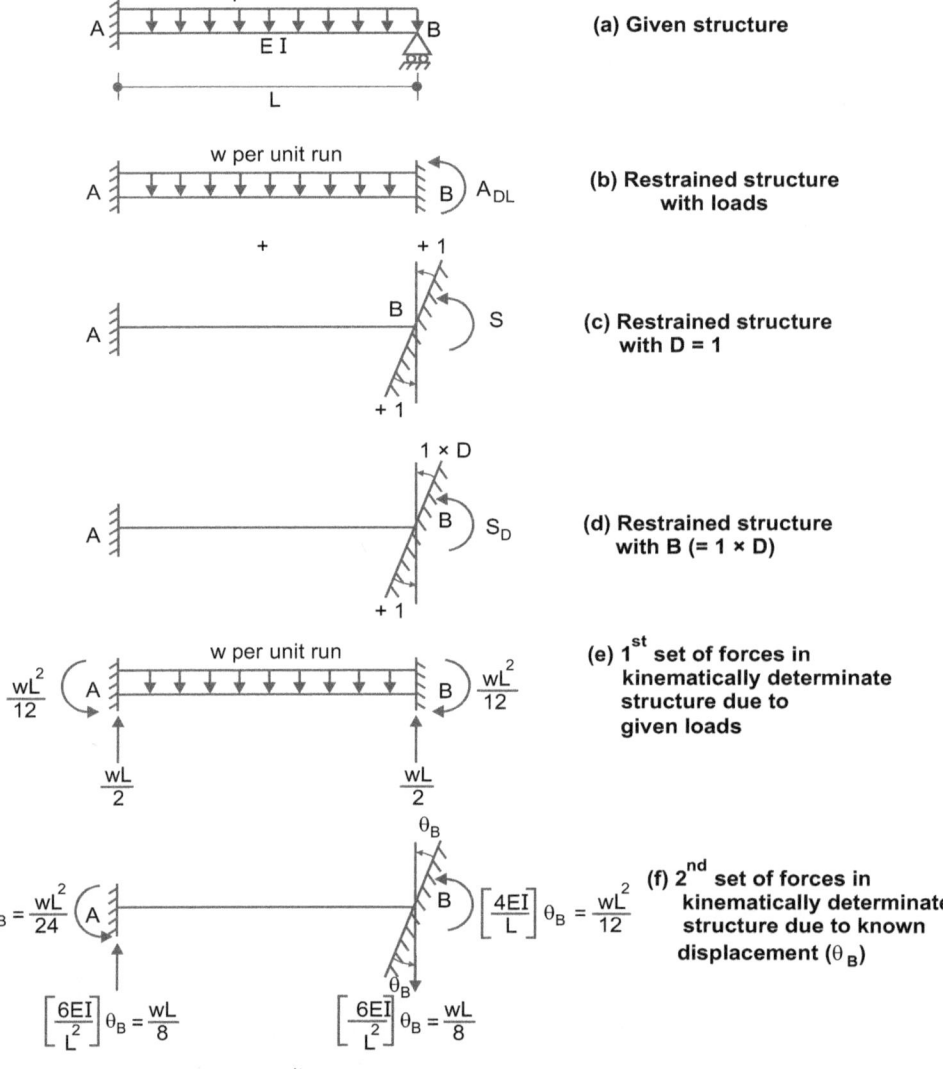

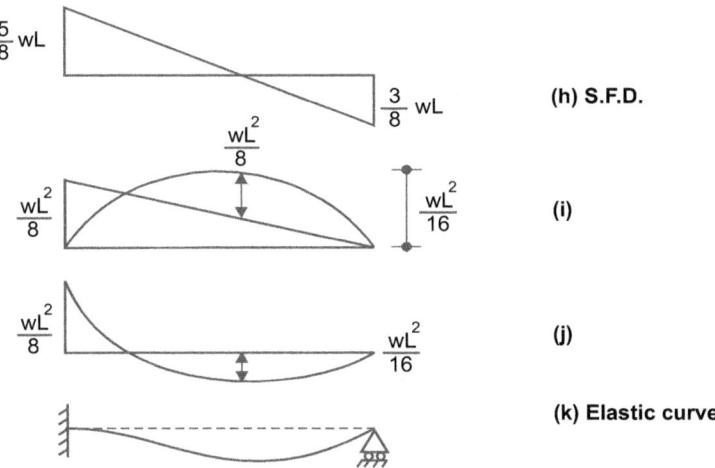

Fig. 4.1 : Illustrative Example 4.1

Step IV : Force analysis of the kinematically determinate i.e. restrained structure.

(a) The member end moment at B due to given loading is calculated. For this problem the standard result of fixed beam with udl is used to obtain the moment at B. This is denoted by A_{DL}.

$$\therefore \quad A_{DL} = -\frac{wL^2}{12} \text{ (clockwise)}$$

(b) The moment at B required for unit rotation at B is the flexural rotational stiffness taken from the standard result. This is denoted by S.

$$\therefore \quad S = \frac{4EI}{L}$$

(c) The moment at B due to unknown rotation θ_B is denoted by A_{DD} and obtained in terms of θ_B from stiffness.

$$\therefore \quad A_{DD} = S \cdot D$$

$$\therefore \quad A_{DD} = \left(\frac{4EI}{L}\right) D$$

Step V : The equilibrium requirement of force. In the given structure there is no applied moment at B. This moment at B is known to be zero and denoted by A_D.

$$\therefore \quad A_D = 0$$

Step VI : Superposition equation of equilibrium of forces :

$$\therefore \quad A_D = A_{DL} + A_{DD}$$

$$\therefore \quad A_D = A_{DL} + S \cdot D$$

$$\therefore \quad 0 = -\frac{wL^2}{12} + \left(\frac{4\,EI}{L}\right)\theta_B$$

Step VII : Solution of equation for unknown displacement

$$\therefore \quad \theta_B = +\frac{wL^3}{48\,EI}$$

The positive result of θ_B indicates that the direction of θ_B corresponds to the direction of unit rotation.

Step VIII : Other forces : First set of other forces in the kinematically determinate structure due to given loads are obtained as shown in Fig. 4.1 (e).

Second set of other forces in the kinematically determinate structure due to now known θ_B are computed by the standard results of force-displacement relations of beam as shown in Fig. 4.1 (f).

The two sets of forces are superimposed and the analysis of beam is completed. The final results are as shown in Fig. 4.1 (g).

Step IX : SFD and BMD.

(a) SFD is same as shown in Fig. 4.1 (h).

(b) BMD drawn by two methods are same as shown in Fig. 4.1 (i) and Fig. 4.1 (j).

Step X : Elastic curve : Qualitative nature of the elastic curve is also same as shown in Fig. 4.1 (k).

4.2 STIFFNESS MATRIX

The action equations for the structure with 1, 2, ... n co-ordinates for actions $A_1, A_2 ... A_n$ producing displacements $D_1, D_2 ... D_n$ can be obtained similarly by using the principle of superposition, where n is the degree of kinematic indeterminacy.

If a unit positive displacement is given at co-ordinate i without any displacement at other co-ordinates, the forces required at co-ordinates 1, 2, ... n are represented by $S_{1i}, S_{2i}, ... S_{ii}, S_{ji}, S_{ni}$. S_{ij} is the force at co-ordinate i due to a unit positive displacement at co-ordinates j only. This is called stiffness coefficient. As per superposition principle, the total action at co-ordinate i due to displacements $D_1, D_2 ... D_n$ is given by

$$A_i = S_{i1} + S_{i2} D_2 + S_{ii} D_i + S_{ij} D_j + ... + S_{in} D_n$$

Therefore, action equations for a structure are :

$$A_1 = S_{11} D_1 + S_{12} D_2 + S_{1i} D_i + S_{ij} D_j + ... + S_{1n} D_n$$
$$A_2 = S_{21} D_1 + S_{22} D_2 + ... + S_{2i} D_i + S_{2j} D_j + ... + S_{2n} D_n$$
$$\vdots \qquad \vdots \qquad\qquad\qquad \vdots \qquad \vdots$$
$$A_i = S_{i1} D_1 + S_{i2} D_2 + ... + D_{ii} D_i + S_{ij} D_j + ... + S_{in} D_n$$

$$A_j = S_{j1} D_1 + S_{j2} D_2 + \ldots + S_{ji} D_i + S_{jj} D_j + \ldots + D_{jn} D_n$$
$$\vdots \qquad \vdots \qquad \qquad \vdots \qquad \qquad \vdots$$
$$A_n = S_{n1} D_1 + S_{n2} D_2 + \ldots + S_{ni} D_i + S_{ni} D_j + \ldots + S_{nn} D_n$$

The action displacement equations in matrix form are :

$$\begin{Bmatrix} A_1 \\ A_2 \\ \vdots \\ A_i \\ A_j \\ \vdots \\ A_n \end{Bmatrix} = \begin{bmatrix} S_{11} & S_{12} & \ldots & S_{1i} & S_{ij} & \ldots & S_{in} \\ S_{21} & S_{22} & \ldots & S_{2i} & S_{2j} & \ldots & S_{2n} \\ S_{i1} & S_{i2} & \ldots & S_{ii} & S_{ij} & \ldots & S_{in} \\ S_{j1} & S_{j2} & \ldots & S_{ji} & S_{jj} & \ldots & S_{jn} \\ S_{n1} & S_{n2} & \ldots & S_{ni} & S_{ni} & \ldots & S_{nn} \end{bmatrix} \begin{Bmatrix} D_1 \\ D_2 \\ \vdots \\ D_i \\ D_j \\ \vdots \\ D_n \end{Bmatrix} \qquad \ldots (4.4)$$

i.e. $\{A\} = [S] \{D\}$
$\quad n \times 1 = n \times n \quad n \times 1$

where, $\{A\}_{n \times 1}$ = A column matrix of order n × 1, known as action matrix

$[S]_{n \times n}$ = A square matrix of order n × n, known as stiffness matrix

$\{D\}_{n \times 1}$ = A column matrix of order n × 1, known as displacement matrix

In the concept of stiffness, cause is the unit positive displacement and the effect is the force. For S_{ij}, i stands for effect and j for cause. If j is kept same and i varies we get the effects i.e. forces at different coordinates as $S_{1j}, S_{2j}, \ldots S_{ij}, S_{jj}, S_{nj}$. These are column coefficients of [S]. The column of [S] is generated by this technique i.e. keeping same cause the effects are obtained.

Each stiffness coefficient S_{ij} can be defined as the ith action due to a unit value of the jth 0 displacement assuming that the remaining displacements are zero. The jth column of the stiffness matrix are the forces at co-ordinates 1, 2, ... n due to unit positive displacement at coordinate j. Hence in order to generate the jth column of the stiffness matrix, a unit displacement must be given at coordinate j without any displacement at other coordinates and the forces required at all the co-ordinates are determined. These forces are the elements of the jth column of the stiffness matrix. Hence in order to develop the stiffness matrix of a structure, unit positive displacement should be given successively at coordinates 1, 2 ... n and forces at all the coordinates are calculated.

Properties of the stiffness matrix are :

- The stiffness matrix is a square matrix of order n × n where n is the number of coordinates for the problem, i.e. degree of kinematic indeterminacy.
- The stiffness matrix is a symmetrical matrix and hence $S_{ij} = S_{ji}$.

- Each stiffness coefficient S_{ij} represents a action caused by a unit positive displacement, while other displacements are zero.
- In general, S_{ij} is i^{th} action due to unit value of jth displacement.
- The coefficient S_{ij} is taken as positive when it is in positive direction of the ith coordinate.
- S_{ii} that appear on the principal diagonal of [S] are called direct coefficients and remaining coefficients are cross coefficients.
- For direct stiffness i = j.
- For indirect or cross stiffness i ≠ j.
- Direct stiffnesses are always positive.
- Cross stiffnesses may be positive or negative.
- For stable equilibrium structure, the stiffness matrix is non-singular i.e. | [S] | ≠ 0.
- If structure is unstable, the stiffness matrix does not exist or | [S]| = 0 i.e. singular.
- Stiffness matrix [S] of the given structure is invariant as it is the property of the structure.

If the flexibility and stiffness matrices have a common system of coordinates, the product of [F] and [S] is a unit matrix i.e. [F] [S] = [I]. For this condition the flexibility and stiffness matrices are reciprocal of each other or inverse of each other.

It is to be noted that the flexibility matrix [F] for a structure being analysed by the flexibility method is not the inverse of the stiffness matrix [S] for the same structure being analysed by the stiffness method. The reason is that different co-ordinate systems are used in the two methods.

4.3 PROCEDURE OF STIFFNESS MATRIX METHOD

The basic equation of the displacement method developed for one unknown is given a matrix form as $\{A_D\} = \{A_{DL}\} + [S] \{D\}$ for more number of unknowns. This is the governing matrix equation of the method. Using this equation the procedure of the stiffness method is outlined as follows :

- The degree of kinematic indeterminacy D_{ki} (= n, say) is determined.
- The independent joint displacements are identified.
- The coordinate numbering 1, 2 ... n is systematically assigned to unknown joint displacements. Thus $D_1, D_2 ... D_n$ are the displacements at coordinates 1, 2 ... n. This is the matrix $\{D\}_{n \times 1}$ of unknown displacements.
- The restrained structure i.e. kinematically determinate structure is obtained by restraining all joints i.e. preventing all the independent displacements.

- The restrained actions corresponding to coordinates 1, 2 ... n in the restrained structure due to applied member loads are calculated using fixed beam analysis. If number of members are meeting at a joint, the restrained actions for these members are cummulated. This is also termed as assembly of load vector. The assembled actions are $A_{DL1}, A_{DL2} ... A_{DLn}$. Thus the matrix $\{A_{DL}\}_{n \times 1}$ is formed.

- The restrained actions corresponding to coordinates 1, 2 . . . n in the restrained structure due to unit positive displacement imposed one at a time are calculated, memberwise and summed up for the members meeting at the joint. These are the stiffness coefficients generated columnwise. The technique is repeated and thus the stiffness matrix of a structure $[S]_{n \times n}$ is assembled.

- Given joint actions (forces and couples) corresponding to coordinates 1, 2 ... n form the matrix $\{A_D\}_{n \times 1}$.

- The action equations are formulated using superposition equations.

$$A_{D1} = A_{DL1} + S_{11} D_1 + S_{12} D_2 + ... + S_{1n} D_n$$
$$D_{D2} = A_{DL2} + S_{21} D_1 + S_{22} D_2 + ... + S_{2n} D_n$$
$$D_{Dn} = A_{DLn} + S_{n1} D_1 + S_{n2} D_2 + ... + S_{nn} D_n$$

i.e. in matrix form,

$$\{A_D\}_{n \times 1} = \{A_{DL}\}_{n \times 1} + [S]_{n \times n} \{D\}_{n \times 1}$$

- Equilibrium equations applicable to the joint actions corresponding to coordinates 1, 2 ... n are written. If there are no given joint loads at all coordinates then $\{A_D\}$ matrix will be null matrix. Otherwise as the case may be.

- Formulation of linear simultaneous equations for unknown joint displacements $\{D\}$ is ready at this stage.

- The joint displacements $D_1, D_2 ... D_n$ are obtained from solution of equations.

$$\{A_D\}_{n \times 1} = \{A_{DL}\}_{n \times 1} + [S]_{n \times n} \{D\}_{n \times 1}$$

- Knowing the displacements, all actions at member ends are obtained from cummulative effects of displacements according to the stiffness coefficients of member. In general the member end moments for member are obtained as :

$$M_{ij} = \left(\frac{4 EI}{L}\right) \theta_i + \left(\frac{2 EI}{L}\right) \theta_j \pm \left(\frac{6 EI}{L^2}\right) \Delta + M_{ij}^F$$

- Variations of actions along the member and structure are plotted as SFD and BMD.

- Deformed shape of a structure may be shown qualitatively from the information of joint displacements, compatibility and BMD. This is the elastic curve.

STRUCTURAL ANALYSIS – II   STIFFNESS METHOD

In short, the stiffness method involves the formation of following matrices.

(1) $\{A_D\}_{n \times 1}$
(2) $\{A_{DL}\}_{n \times 1}$
(3) $[S]_{n \times n}$
(4) $\{D\}_{n \times 1}$ – unknown joint displacement matrix to be obtained from basic equation of stiffness method

$$\{A_D\} = \{A_{DL}\} + [S]\{D\}$$

4.4 STIFFNESS COEFFICIENTS OF MEMBER

A stiffness matrix [S] of a structure is developed columnwise by considering the unit positive joint displacement, only one at a time, in the restrained structure. For the development of [S], the stiffness coefficients of the members meeting the joint, are required to be added and hence very important. Therefore it is the prerequisite of the stiffness method to know the standard results of stiffness coefficients of a member of a structure.

4.4.1 A Beam Member or Frame Member

In general, a prismatic member AB of length L and flexural rigidity EI as shown in Fig 4.2 (a) is considered having rigid joints at A and B. According to the possible joint displacements i.e. translations and rotations, the coordinate numbering is shown in Fig. 4.2 (b) to represent member end actions and joint displacements. The member is restrained and then released successively. The desired unit positive displacement, as the cause, is given, only one at a time, and corresponding member end actions, as the effects, are obtained. These effects are called the member stiffness coefficients and are developed as follows :

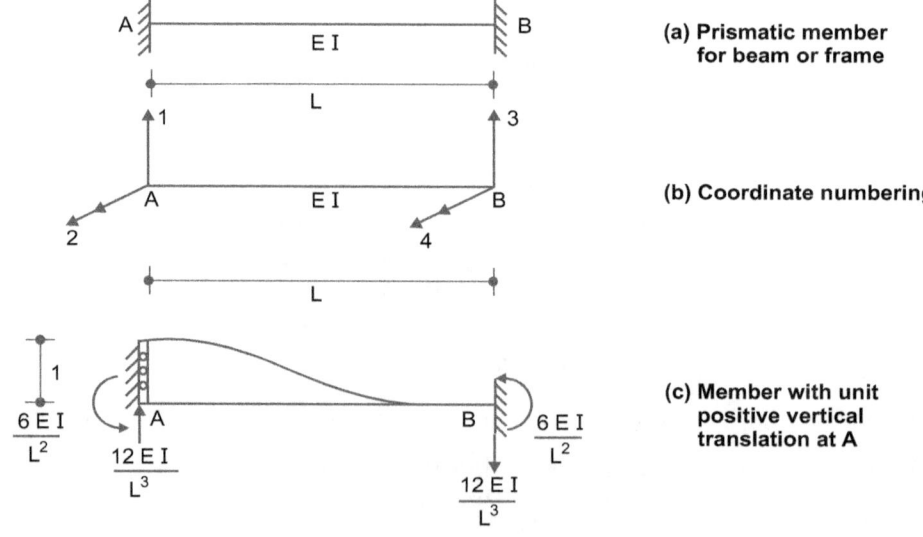

(a) Prismatic member for beam or frame

(b) Coordinate numbering

(c) Member with unit positive vertical translation at A

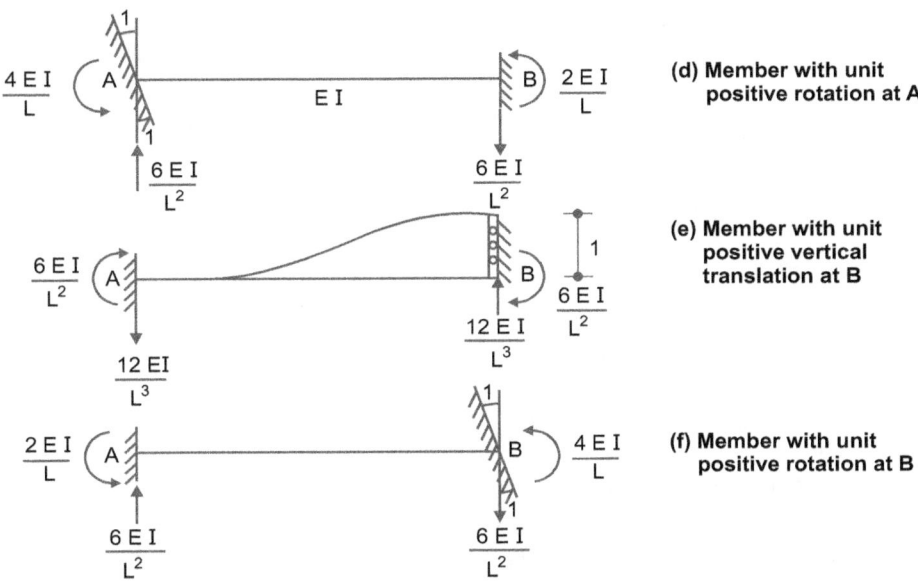

Fig. 4.2 : Generation of stiffness for beam or frame

(i) **Cause** : Unit positive displacement i.e. transverse translation at coordinate 1 as shown in Fig. 4.2 (c).

Effects : Force at coordinate 1 = S_{11} = $\dfrac{12\,EI}{L^3}$

(from basic relation already derived)

Moment at coordinate 2 (from equilibrium) = S_{21} = $6\,EI/L^2$
Force at coordinate 3 (from equilibrium) = S_{31} = $-12\,EI/L^3$
Moment at coordinate 4 (from equilibrium) = S_{41} = $6\,EI/L^2$

(ii) **Cause** : Unit positive displacement i.e. rotation at co-ordinate 2 as shown in Fig. 4.2 (d).

Effects : Force at coordinate 1 = S_{12} = $6\,EI/L^2$

(from equilibrium)

Moment at coordinate 2 = S_{22} = $\dfrac{4\,EI}{L}$

(from basic relation already derived)

Force at coordinate 3 = S_{32} = $-6\,EI/L^2$
Moment at coordinate 4 = S_{42} = $2\,EI/L$

(iii) Cause : Unit positive displacement i.e. transverse translation at coordinate 3 as shown in Fig. 4.2 (e).

Effects : This is the mirror image of case (i). Therefore

Force at coordinate   1 = S_{13} = $-12\ EI/L^3$

Moment at coordinate   2 = S_{23} = $-6\ EI/L^2$

Force at coordinate   3 = S_{33} = $12\ EI/L^3$

Moment at coordinate   4 = S_{43} = $-6\ EI/L^2$

(iv) Cause : Unit positive displacement i.e. rotation at coordinate 4 as shown in Fig. 4.2 (f).

Effects : This is the mirror image of case (ii) therefore,

Force at coordinate   1 = S_{14} = $6\ EI/L^2$

Moment at coordinate   2 = S_{24} = $2\ EI/L$

Force at coordinate   3 = S_{34} = $-6\ EI/L^2$

Moment at coordinate   4 = S_{44} = $4\ EI/L$

The stiffness coefficients thus obtained can be represented in the matrix form. This is the standard stiffness matrix of a beam member or a frame member with respect to the member coordinate and denoted by $[S_M]$. The size of the matrix is 4×4.

$$\therefore \quad [S_M]_{4 \times 4} = \begin{bmatrix} \dfrac{12\ EI}{L^3} & \dfrac{6\ EI}{L^2} & -\dfrac{12\ EI}{L^3} & \dfrac{6\ EI}{L^2} \\ \dfrac{6\ EI}{L^2} & \dfrac{4\ EI}{L} & -\dfrac{6\ EI}{L^2} & \dfrac{2\ EI}{L} \\ -\dfrac{12\ EI}{L^3} & -\dfrac{6\ EI}{L^2} & \dfrac{12\ EI}{L^3} & -\dfrac{6\ EI}{L^2} \\ \dfrac{6\ EI}{L^2} & \dfrac{2\ EI}{L} & -\dfrac{6\ EI}{L^2} & \dfrac{4\ EI}{L} \end{bmatrix}$$

It is to be noted that

1. Axial deformation is neglected.
2. $[S_m]$ is symmetrical.
3. Diagonal coefficients are direct stiffnesses.
4. Off-diagonal coefficients are indirect stiffnesses as side effects.
5. The determinant of $[S_m]$ is zero i.e. $|[S_M]| = 0$.
6. Thus $[S_M]$ is singular because all displacements are given and hence the member is not in stable equilibrium. This is not possible in case of the structure. The structure stiffness matrix should be non-singular as the structure is stable.

STRUCTURAL ANALYSIS – II   STIFFNESS METHOD

4.5 Stiffness Method Applied to Beams and Frames

Beams and frames mainly consist of rigid joints and bending members. The unknown joint displacements are rotations and or translations as per coordinate numbering to form the matrix $\{D\}_{n\times 1}$. The sizes of matrices is governed by 'n', the degree of kinematic indeterminacy. The given joint loads form the matrix $\{A\}_{n\times 1}$ directly. The analysis of fixed beam for the applied member loads will help in preparing the matrix $\{A_{DL}\}_{n\times 1}$. At a joint, if number of members are meeting then corresponding to the coordinate i, A_{DLi} is given by the equation

$$A_{DLi} = \sum_{\text{All members}} \text{Fixed end member actions at i}$$

The most critical part of the stiffness method is to generate stiffness matrix of a structure. $[S]_{n\times n}$. However it can be done very systematically as illustrated below.

Consider the frame shown in Fig. 4.3 (a).

- Unknown displacements
  - (a) Rotations at B, C and D i.e. θ_B, θ_C and θ_D.
  - (b) Horizontal translation at B i.e. $\Delta_B = \Delta_C = \Delta$.

  It may be noted specifically that $\Delta_B = \Delta_C$ as the axial deformations are neglected.

- Degree of kinematic indeterminacy

  $$n = 4$$

- Coordinate numbering

  Corresponding to unknown displacements it is shown in Fig. 4.3 (b). Again note that the coordinate number 4 is given to both Δ_B and Δ_C.

- The size of stiffness matrix

  $$[S]_{4\times 4}$$

- Generation of [S]

  Note that [S] is independent of loading and it only requires the information of structural configuration, dimensions, cross-sectional properties and material properties.

- Restrain the structure. This is shown in Fig. 4.3 (c).
- Release the structure only for one displacement at a time.

  (a) Cause : Unit positive displacement at coordinate 1 i.e. $D_1 = \theta_B = +1$ as shown in Fig. 4.3 (c).

  (b) Effects : Member end actions in terms of stiffness coefficients for all members at all coordinates 1, 2, 3 and 4. Note that if the member does not deform there is no resistance to deformation and stiffness coefficients of the member will be zero. The effects are shown in Fig. 4.3 (d).

STRUCTURAL ANALYSIS – II   STIFFNESS METHOD

(c) Stiffness coefficients of column 1 of [S] :

$$S_{11} = \sum \text{Stiffness coefficients at 1 of contributing members}$$

$$= \left(\frac{4\,EI}{L}\right)_{BA} + \left(\frac{4\,EI}{L}\right)_{BC} = \frac{4\,EI}{4} + \frac{4\,(2\,EI)}{6} = 2.33\,EI$$

$$S_{21} = \sum \text{Stiffness coefficients at 2 members}$$

$$= \left(\frac{2\,EI}{L}\right)_{BC} = \frac{2\,(2\,EI)}{6} = 0.67\,EI$$

$$S_{31} = \sum \text{Stiffness coefficients at 3 of members} = 0$$

$$S_{41} = \sum \text{Stiffness coefficients at 4 of contributing member}$$

$$= \left(\frac{6\,EI}{L^2}\right)_{BA} = \frac{6\,EI}{4^2} = 0.375\,EI$$

Thus the coefficients of first column of [S] are obtained. The technique of columnwise generation of [S] is repeated for all coordinates, using the general concept.

$$S_{ij} = \sum \text{Stiffness coefficients at i of contributing members}$$

where j is kept constant and i varies.

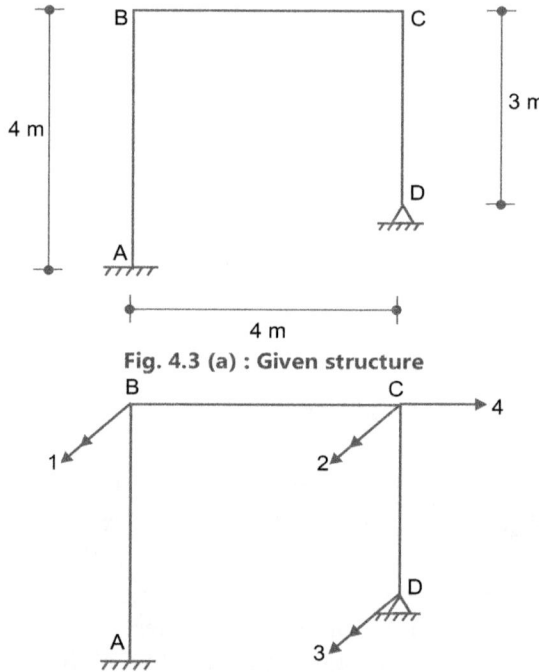

Fig. 4.3 (a) : Given structure

Fig. 4.3 (b) : Co-ordinate numbering for given structure

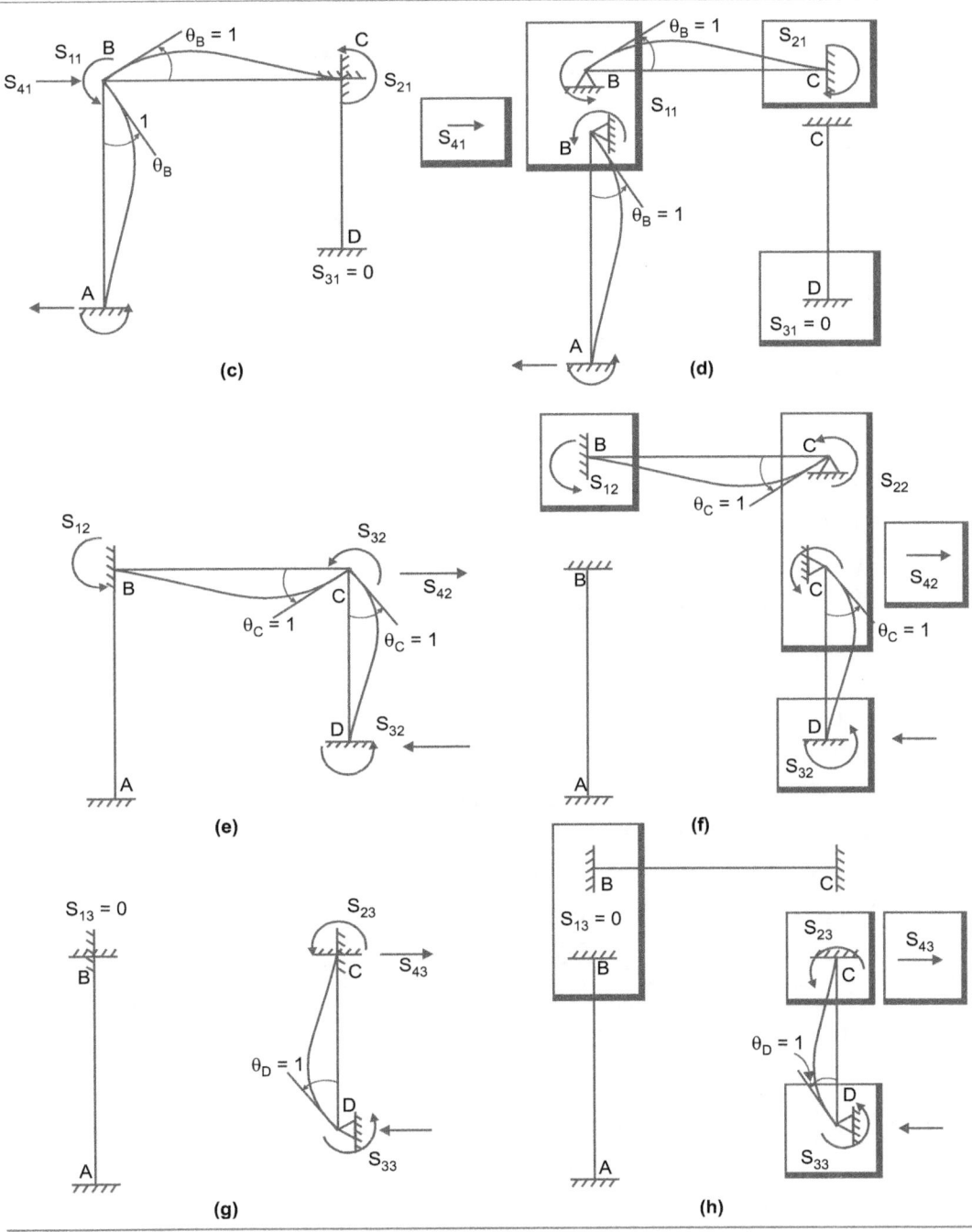

STRUCTURAL ANALYSIS – II   STIFFNESS METHOD

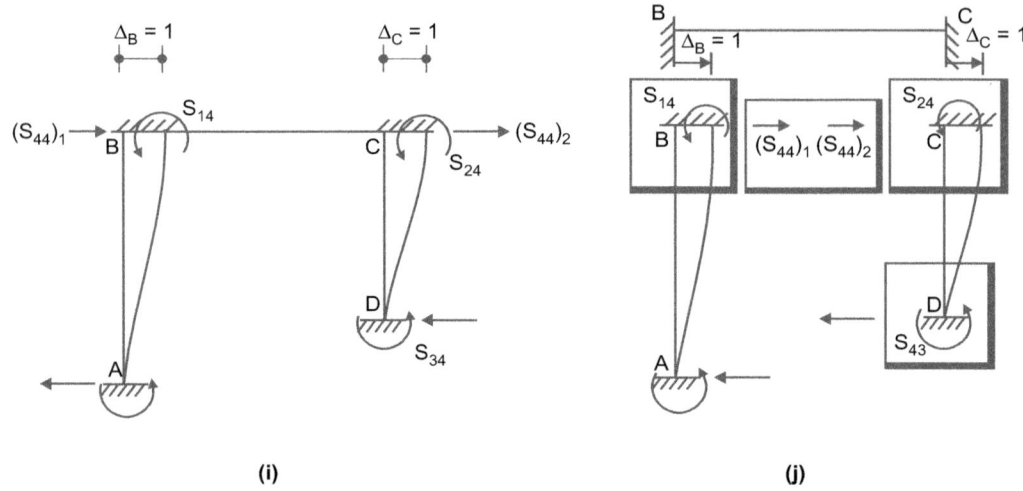

        (i)   (j)

(c)   Restrained Structure with $D_1 = 1$
(d)   Effects of $D_1 = 1$ for Restrained Structure
(e)   Restrained Structure with $D_2 = 1$
(f)   Effects of $D_2 = 1$ for Restrained Structure
(g)   Restrained Structure with $D_3 = 1$
(h)   Effects of $D_3 = 1$ for Restrained Structure
(i)   Restrained Structure with $D_4 = 1$
(j)   Effects of $D_4 = 1$ for Restrained Structure

Fig. 4.3 : Generation of Stiffness Matrix of Structure

- (a) **Cause :** $D_2 = \theta_C = +1$ as shown in Fig. 4.3 (e).
  (b) **Effects :** Member end actions as shown in Fig. 4.3 (f).
  (c) Stiffness coefficients of column 2 of (S).

$$S_{12} = \left(\frac{2\,EI}{L}\right)_{BC} = \frac{2 \times 2\,EI}{6} = 0.67\,EI$$

$$S_{22} = \left(\frac{4\,EI}{L}\right)_{CB} + \left(\frac{4\,EI}{L}\right)_{CD} = \frac{4 \times 2\,EI}{4} = 2.33\,EI$$

$$S_{32} = \left(\frac{2\,EI}{L}\right)_{DC} = \frac{2\,EI}{4} = 0.5\,EI$$

$$S_{42} = \left(\frac{6\,EI}{42}\right)_{CD} = \frac{6\,EI}{42} = 0.375\,EI$$

- (a) **Cause** : $D_3 = \theta_D = +1$ as shown in Fig. 4.3 (g).
- (b) **Effects** : Member end actions as shown in Fig. 4.3 (h).
- (c) Stiffness coefficients of column 3 of [S].

$$S_{13} = 0$$

$$S_{23} = \left(\frac{2EI}{L}\right)_{CD} = \frac{2EI}{4} = 0.5 \, EI$$

$$S_{33} = \left(\frac{4EI}{L}\right)_{CD} = \frac{4EI}{4} = EI$$

$$S_{43} = \left(\frac{6EI}{L^2}\right) = \frac{6EI}{4^2} = 0.375 \, EI$$

- (a) **Cause** : $D_4 = \Delta = +1$ as shown in Fig. 4.3 (i).
- (b) **Effects** : Member end actions as shown in Fig. 4.3 (j).
- (c) Stiffness coefficients of column 4 of [S]

$$S_{14} = \left(\frac{6EI}{L^2}\right)_{BA} = \frac{6EI}{4^2} = 0.375 \, EI$$

$$S_{24} = \left(\frac{6EI}{L^2}\right)_{CD} = \frac{6EI}{4^2} = 0.375 \, EI$$

$$S_{34} = \left(\frac{6EI}{L^2}\right)_{DC} = \frac{6EI}{4^2} = 0.375 \, EI$$

$$S_{44} = \left(\frac{12EI}{L^3}\right)_{BA} + \left(\frac{12EI}{L^3}\right)_{CD} = \frac{12EI}{4^3} + \frac{12EI}{4^3} = 0.375 \, EI$$

This is to be noted that there is resistance i.e. stiffness contributions to A from members AB and CD. Therefore, transverse translation is resisted by the members perpendicular to the translation. For the rectangular frame this horizontal translation is called sway and sway is resisted by column members of the frame. Note that there is no effect of sway on beam as translation is along the member.

- Stiffness matrix of the structure

$$[S]_{4 \times 4} = EI \begin{bmatrix} 2.33 & 0.67 & 0 & 0.375 \\ 0.67 & 2.33 & 0.5 & 0.375 \\ 0 & 0.5 & 1 & 0.375 \\ 0.375 & 0.375 & 0.375 & 0.375 \end{bmatrix}$$

STRUCTURAL ANALYSIS – II   STIFFNESS METHOD

Note that :
1. The matrix is square symmetrical.
2. The diagonal coefficients of [S] are positive and definite and dominant.
3. The matrix [S] is non-singular as the structure is stable i.e. | [S]| ≠ 0.
4. The stiffness matrix [S] of the structure for given data is invariant as it is the property of the structure.

The general procedure of the stiffness matrix method formulated earlier is applicable to the beams and frames and analysis can be completed. This is illustrated with the following examples. For problems of one unknown the matrix formulation is not necessary.

Example 4.2 : *Analyse the beam shown in Fig. 4.4 (a) by stiffness method. Take EI = constant. Stiffness coefficient of spring at B is as shown in the figure.*

Solution : (1) Data : The beam is supported and loaded as shown in Fig. 4.4 (a).

(2) Stiffness coefficient of spring at B = $\left(\dfrac{EI}{2}\right)$ kN/m.

Object : Structural analysis.

Concepts and Equations :

(1) Kinematically determinate structure (Restrained structure).
(2) Force analysis of restrained structure.
(3) Superposition equations of equilibrium of forces.

Procedure :

Step I : Degree of kinematic indeterminacy (D_{ki}) :

Degree of kinematic indeterminacy = D_{ki} = 2.

Step II : Unknown joint displacements (D) :

Let, $D_1 = \theta_B\,(\circlearrowright)$ and $D_2 = \Delta_B\,(\uparrow)$

Step III : Restrained Structure : Joint B is locked and the restrained structure is as shown in Fig. 4.4 (b). Also restrained structure with unit values of D_1 and D_2 is shown in Fig. 4.4 (c) and 4.4 (d) respectively.

Step IV : Force analysis of restrained structure :

(a) Fixed end moments :

$$M_{BA}^{F} = -M_{BA}^{F} = \dfrac{wL^2}{12} = \dfrac{10 \times 3^2}{12} = 7.5 \text{ kNm}$$

(b) Forces in the restrained structure subjected to loads corresponding to unknown displacements :

$$A_{DL1} = M_{BA}^{F} = -7.5 \text{ kNm}$$

A_{DL2} = Vertical reaction component at B in the restrained structure subjected to loads = 15 kN.

(c) Forces in the restrained structure subjected to unit values of D_1 and D_2 corresponding to unknown displacements.

$$S_{11} = \left(\frac{4EI}{L}\right)_{AB} = \frac{4EI}{3} = 1.33\,EI$$

$$S_{12} = S_{21} = \left(-\frac{6EI}{L^2}\right) = \frac{-6EI}{3^2} = -0.67\,EI$$

$$S_{22} = \left(\frac{12EI}{L^3}\right)_{AB} = \frac{12EI}{3^3} = 0.44\,EI$$

Step V : The equilibrium requirement of force :

There is no applied couple at B $\therefore A_{D1} = 0$

There is no applied point load at B $\therefore A_{D2} = 0$

Step VI : Superposition equation of equilibrium of forces :

$$\{A_D\} = \{A_{DL}\} + [S]\{D\}$$

i.e.
$$\begin{Bmatrix} 0 \\ 0 \end{Bmatrix} = \begin{Bmatrix} -7.5 \\ 15 \end{Bmatrix} + EI \begin{bmatrix} 1.33 & -0.67 \\ -0.67 & 0.44 \end{bmatrix} \begin{Bmatrix} D_1 \\ D_2 \end{Bmatrix}$$

* Because of the elastic support at B 'S_{22}' is to be modified as

$$S_{22} = \left(0.44 + \frac{1}{2}\right) EI = 0.94\,EI$$

∴ Superposition equation of equilibrium of forces becomes,

$$\begin{Bmatrix} 0 \\ 0 \end{Bmatrix} = \begin{Bmatrix} -7.5 \\ 15 \end{Bmatrix} + EI \begin{bmatrix} 1.33 & -0.67 \\ -0.67 & 0.94 \end{bmatrix} \begin{Bmatrix} D_1 \\ D_2 \end{Bmatrix}$$

i.e. $0 = -7.5 + (1.33\,EI)\,D_1 - (0.67\,EI)\,D_2$ ... (A)

$0 = 15 - (0.67\,EI)\,D_1 + (0.94\,EI)\,D_2$ ... (B)

Step VII : Solution of equations for unknown displacements : Solving equations (A) and (B), we get

$$\boxed{\begin{aligned} D_1 &= \frac{-3.7}{EI} = \frac{3.7}{EI}\ (\circlearrowright) \\ D_2 &= -\frac{18.54}{EI} = \frac{18.54}{EI}\ (\downarrow) \end{aligned}}$$

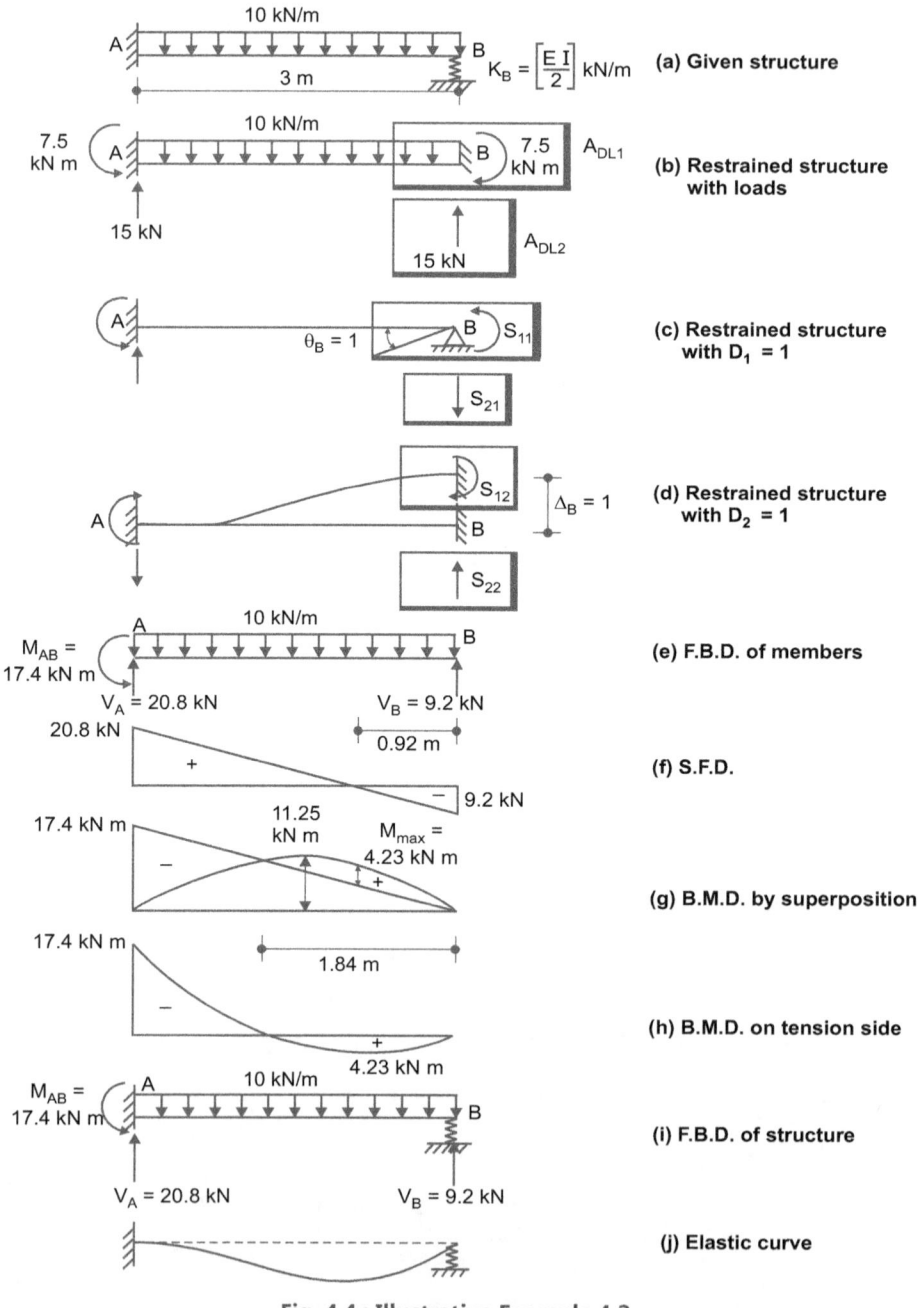

Fig. 4.4 : Illustrative Example 4.2

Step VIII : Other Forces :

$$M_{AB} = \frac{4\,EI}{3}(0) + \frac{2\,EI}{3}\left(-\frac{3.7}{EI}\right) + \frac{6\,EI}{3^2}\left(\frac{18.54}{EI}\right) + 7.5 = 17.4 \text{ kNm}$$

$$M_{BA} = \frac{4\,EI}{3}\left(-\frac{3.7}{EI}\right) + \frac{2\,EI}{3}(0) + \frac{6\,EI}{3^2}\left(\frac{18.54}{EI}\right) - 7.5 = 0$$

FBD of members is as shown in Fig. 4.4 (e).

Considering equilibrium of structure other reaction components are found out as shown in figure.

Step IX : Shear force and bending moment diagrams :

SFD is as shown in Fig. 4.4 (f).

BMD by superposition on tension side is as shown in Fig. 4.4 (g) and Fig. 4.4 (h) respectively.

Step X : FBD of structure : as shown in Fig. 4.4 (i).

Step XI : Elastic curve : as shown in Fig. 4.4 (j).

Example 4.3 : *Analyse the beam shown in Fig. 4.5 (a) by stiffness method. Take EI = Constant.*

Solution : Data : The beam is supported and loaded as shown in Fig. 4.5 (a).

Object : Structural Analysis.

Concepts and Equations : (i) Kinematically determinate structure (Restrained structure).

(ii) Force analysis of restrained structure.

(iii) Superposition equations of equilibrium of forces.

Procedure :

Step I : Degree of kinematic indeterminacy (D_{ki}) : Degree of kinematic indeterminacy = D_{ki} = 1.

Step II : Unknown joint displacements (D) :

Let, $\quad D_1 = \theta_B \; (\circlearrowleft)$

Step III : Restrained structure : The joint B is locked and the restrained structure is obtained as shown in Fig. 4.5 (b). Also restrained structure with unit value of D_1 is as shown in Fig. 4.5 (c).

Step IV : Force analysis of restrained structure :

(a) Fixed End Moments :

$$M^F_{AB} = -M^F_{BA} = \frac{wL^2}{12} = \frac{15 \times 2^2}{12} = 5.0 \text{ kNm}$$

$$M^F_{BC} = \frac{Wab^2}{L^2} = \frac{30 \times 1 \times 2^2}{3^2} = 13.33 \text{ kNm}$$

$$M^F_{CB} = -\frac{Wba^2}{L^2} = -\frac{30 \times 2 \times 1^2}{3^2} = -6.67 \text{ kNm}$$

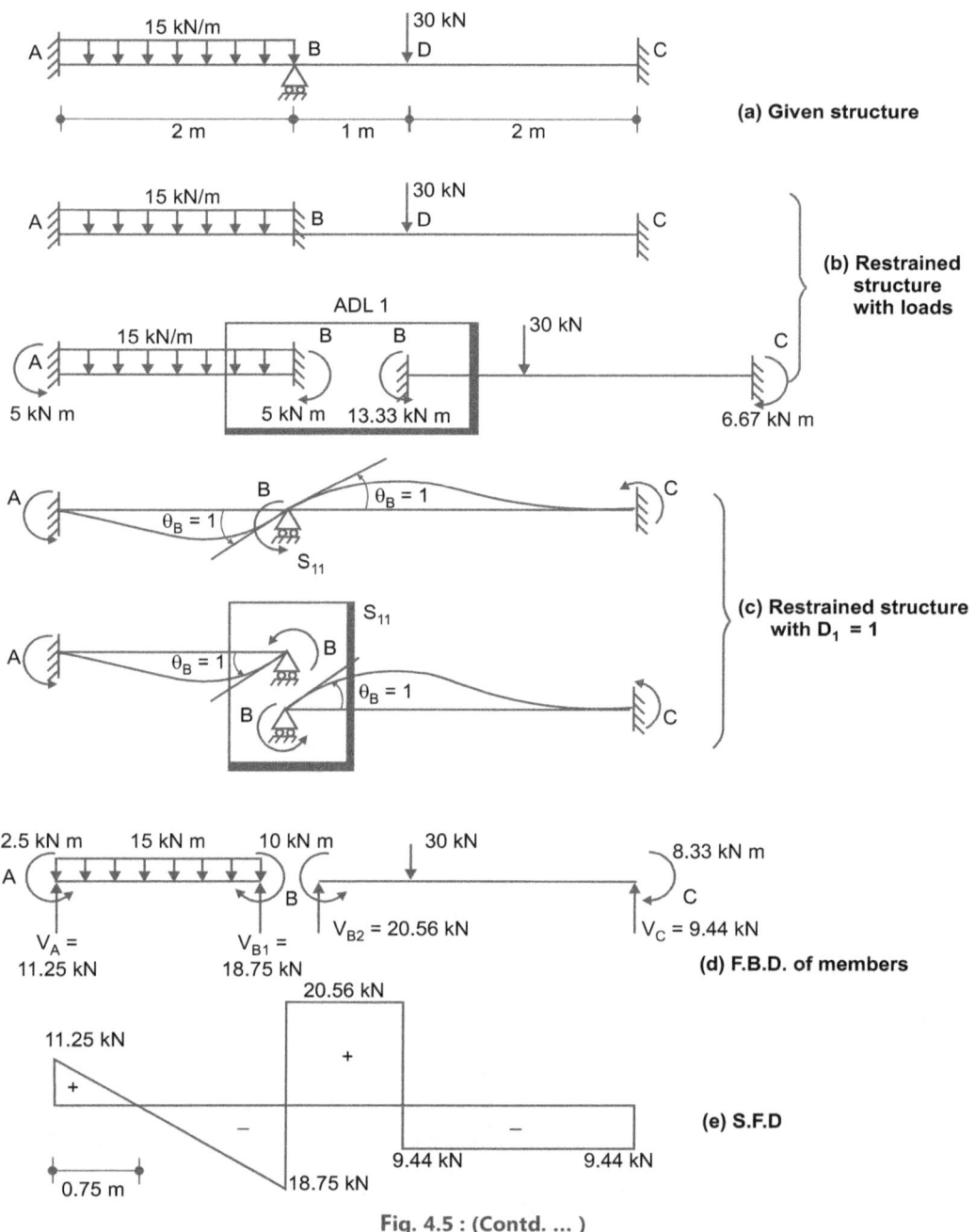

Fig. 4.5 : (Contd. ...)

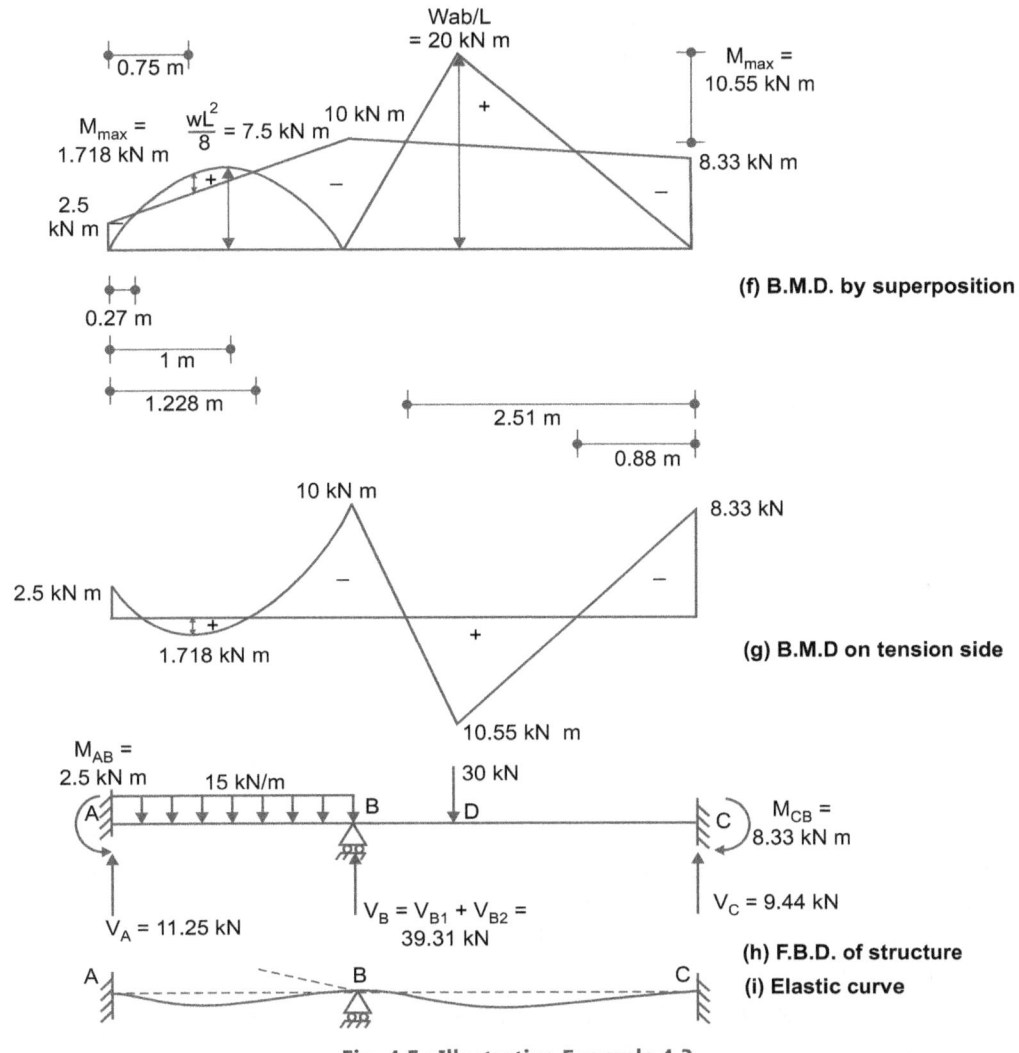

Fig. 4.5 : Illustrative Example 4.3

(b) Forces in the restrained structure subjected to loads corresponding to unknown displacements.

$$A_{DL1} = M^F_{BA} + M^F_{BC} = -5.0 + 13.33 = 8.33 \text{ kNm}$$

(c) Forces in the restrained structure subjected to unit values of D_1 corresponding to unknown displacement.

$$S_{11} = \left(\frac{4EI}{L}\right)_{BA} + \left(\frac{4EI}{L}\right)_{BC} = \frac{4EI}{2} + \frac{4EI}{3} = 3.33 \text{ EI}$$

Step V : The equilibrium requirement of forces :
There is no applied couple at B $\therefore$ $AD_1 = 0$

Step VI : Superposition equation of equilibrium of forces :

$$\{A_D\} = \{A_{DL}\} + [S]\{D\}$$

i.e. $\{0\} = \{8.33\} + EI [3.33] \{D_1\}$ ... (A)

i.e. $0 = 8.33 + 3.33\, EI\, (D_1)$

Step VII : Solution of equations for unknown displacements : Solving equation (A), we get

$$\boxed{D_1 = \theta_B = \frac{-2.5}{EI} = \frac{2.5}{EI}\ (\circlearrowleft)}$$

Step VIII : Other Forces :

$$M_{AB} = \frac{4\,EI}{2}(0) + \frac{2\,EI}{2}\left(-\frac{2.5}{EI}\right) + 5.0 = 2.5 \text{ kNm}$$

$$M_{BA} = \frac{4\,EI}{2}\left(-\frac{2.5}{EI}\right) + \frac{2\,EI}{3}(0) + -5.0 = -10.0 \text{ kNm}$$

$$M_{BC} = \frac{4\,EI}{3}\left(\frac{-2.5}{EI}\right) + \frac{2\,EI}{3}(0) + 13.33 = 10.0 \text{ kNm}$$

$$M_{CB} = \frac{4\,EI}{3}(0) + \frac{2\,EI}{3}\left(\frac{-2.5}{EI}\right) - 6.67 = -8.33 \text{ kNm}$$

FBD of members is as shown in Fig. 4.5 (d).

Considering equilibrium of each member and of complete structure, all the reaction components are found out as shown in figure.

Step IX : Shear force and bending moment diagrams : SFD is shown in Fig. 4.5 (e).

BMD by superposition and on tension side is as shown in Fig. 4.5 (f) and Fig. 4.5 (g) respectively.

Step X : FBD of structure : as shown in Fig. 4.5 (h).

Step XI : Elastic curve : as shown in Fig. 4.5 (i).

Example 4.4 : *Analyse the beam shown in Fig. 4.6 (a) by stiffness method. Take EI = Constant.*

Solution : Data : The beam is supported and loaded as shown in Fig 4.6 (a).

Object : Structural analysis.

Concepts and equations :

(1) Kinematically determinate structure (Restrained structure).

(2) Force analysis of restrained structure.

(3) Superposition equations of equilibrium of forces.

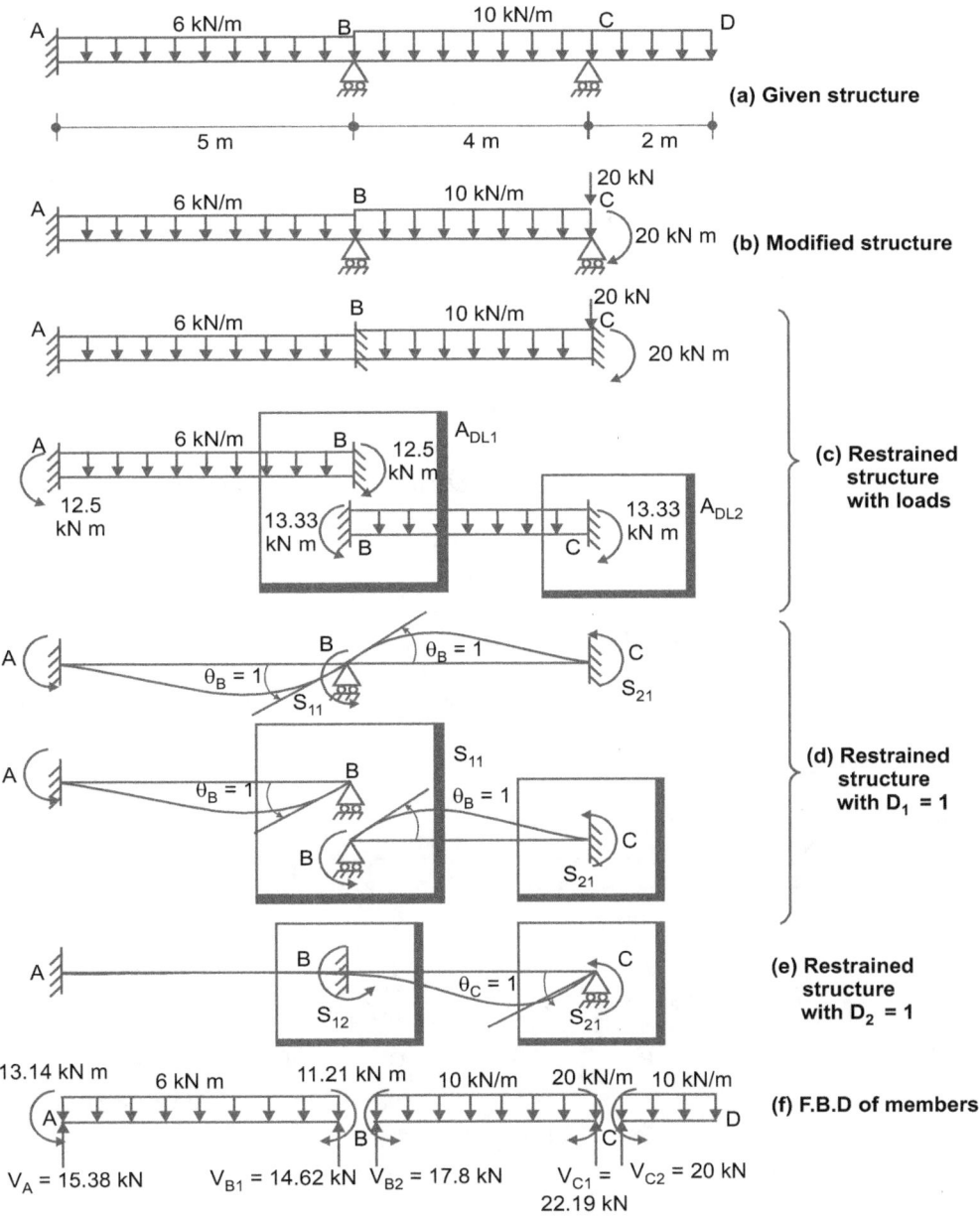

Fig. 4.6 : (Contd. ...)

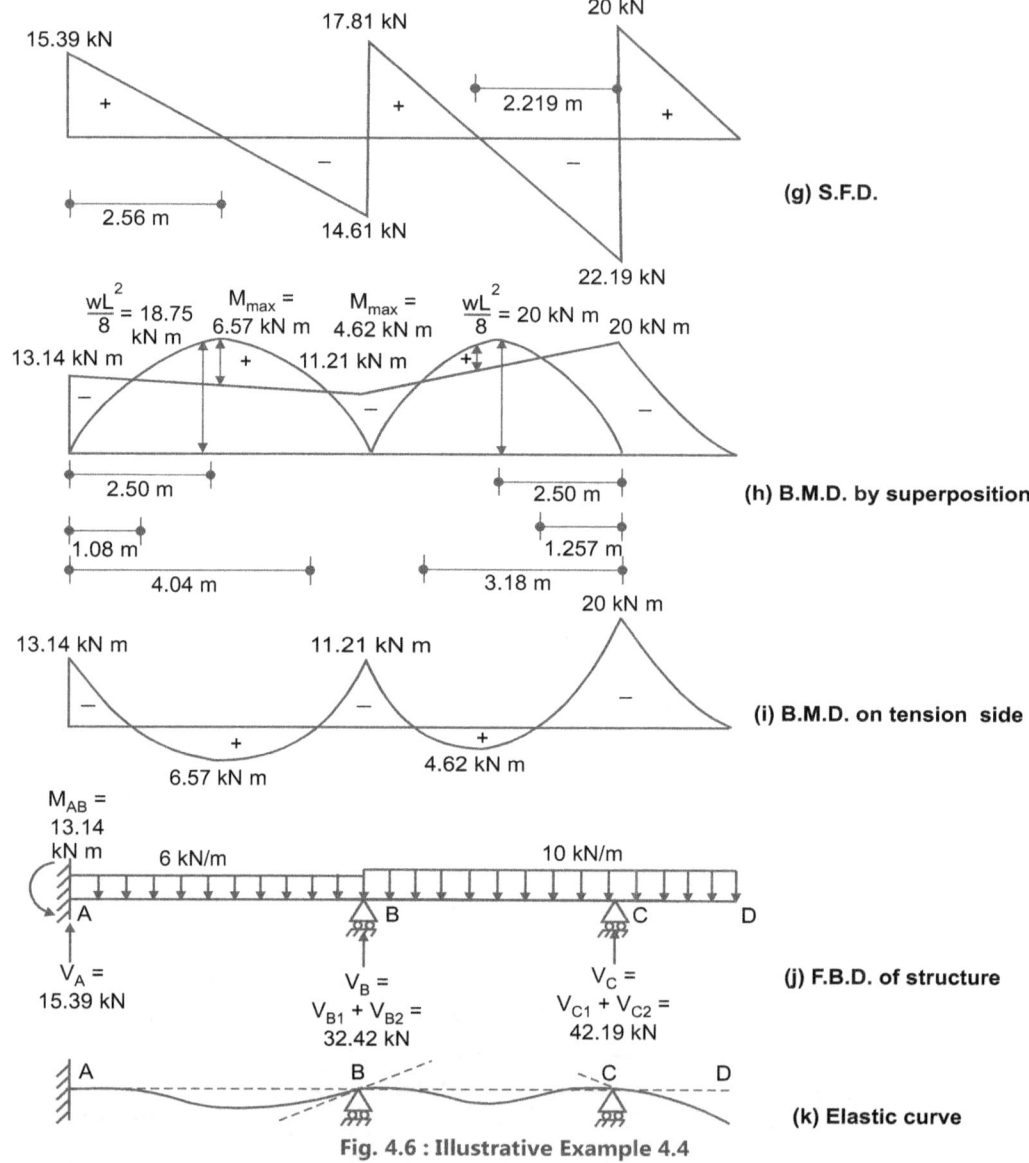

Fig. 4.6 : Illustrative Example 4.4

Procedure :
Step I : Degree of kinematic indeterminacy (D_{ki}) :
Degree of kinematic indeterminacy for given structure = D_{ki} = 4.
Degree of kinematic indeterminacy for modified structure = D_{ki} = 2.

STRUCTURAL ANALYSIS – II STIFFNESS METHOD

Step II : Unknown joint displacements (D) :
Let, $\quad D_1 = \theta_B (\circlearrowleft) \quad \text{and} \quad D_2 = \theta_C (\circlearrowleft)$

Step III : Restrained structure : The joints B and C are locked and the kinematically determinate i.e. restrained structure is obtained as shown in Fig. 4.6 (c). Also restrained structure with unit values of D_1 and D_2 is shown in Fig. 4.6 (d) and 4.6 (e) respectively.

Step IV : Force analysis of restrained structure :

(a) Fixed end moments :

$$M_{AB}^F = -M_{BA}^F = \frac{wL^2}{12} = \frac{6 \times 5^2}{12} = 12.5 \text{ kNm}$$

$$M_{BC}^F = -M_{CB}^F = \frac{wL^2}{12} = \frac{10 \times 4^2}{12} = 13.33 \text{ kNm}$$

(b) Forces in the restrained structure subjected to loads corresponding to unknown displacements.

$$A_{DL1} = M_{BA}^F + M_{BC}^F = -12.5 + 13.33 = 0.83 \text{ kNm}$$

$$A_{DL2} = M_{CB}^F = -13.33 \text{ kNm}$$

(c) Forces in the restrained structure subjected to unit values of D_1 and D_2 corresponding to unknown displacements :

$$S_{11} = \left(\frac{4 EI}{L}\right)_{BA} + \left(\frac{4 EI}{L}\right)_{BC} = \frac{4 EI}{4} + \frac{4 EI}{4} = 1.8 \text{ EI}$$

$$S_{21} = S_{12} = \left(\frac{2 EI}{L}\right)_{BC} = \frac{2 EI}{4} = 0.5 \text{ EI}$$

$$S_{22} = \left(\frac{4 EI}{L}\right)_{CB} = \frac{4 EI}{4} = EI$$

Step V : The equilibrium requirement of forces :
There is no applied couple at B $\therefore$ $A_{D1} = 0$.
Clockwise couple of magnitude 20 kNm is applied at C $\therefore$ $A_{D2} = -20$ kNm.

Step VI : Superposition equation of equilibrium of forces :

$$\{A_D\} = \{A_{DL}\} + [S] \{D\}$$

i.e. $\quad \begin{Bmatrix} 0 \\ -20 \end{Bmatrix} = \begin{Bmatrix} 0.83 \\ -13.33 \end{Bmatrix} + EI \begin{bmatrix} 1.8 & 0.5 \\ 0.5 & 1.0 \end{bmatrix} \cdot \begin{Bmatrix} D_1 \\ D_2 \end{Bmatrix}$

$0 = 0.83 + 1.8 \text{ EI } (D_1) + 0.5 \text{ EI } (D_2)$ ... (A)
$-20 = -13.33 + 0.5 \text{ EI } (D_1) + 1.0 \text{ EI } (D_2)$ ... (B)

Step VII : Solution of equations for unknown displacements : Solving equations (A) and (B), we get

$$D_1 = \theta_B = \frac{1.61}{EI} = \frac{1.61}{EI} \; (\circlearrowleft)$$

$$D_2 = \theta_C = -\frac{7.47}{EI} = \frac{7.47}{EI} \;(\circlearrowleft)$$

Step VIII : Other forces :

$$M_{AB} = \frac{4\,EI}{5}(0) + \frac{2\,EI}{5}\left(\frac{1.61}{EI}\right) + 12.5 = 13.14 \text{ kNm}$$

$$M_{BA} = \frac{4\,EI}{5}\left(\frac{1.61}{EI}\right) + \frac{2\,EI}{5}(0) - 12.5 = -11.21 \text{ kNm}$$

$$M_{BC} = \frac{4\,EI}{4}\left(\frac{1.161}{EI}\right) + \frac{2\,EI}{4}\left(-\frac{7.47}{EI}\right) + 13.33 = 11.21 \text{ kNm}$$

$$M_{CB} = \frac{4\,EI}{4}\left(-\frac{7.47}{EI}\right) + \frac{2\,EI}{4}\left(\frac{1.61}{EI}\right) - 13.33 = -20 \text{ kNm}$$

$$M_{CD} = 20 \text{ kNm}$$

FBD of members is as shown in Fig. 4.6 (f).

Considering equilibrium of each member and of complete structure, all the reaction components are found out as shown in figure.

Step IX : Shear force and bending moment diagrams :

SFD is shown in Fig. 4.6 (g). BMD by superposition and on tension side is as shown in Fig. 4.6 (h) and 4.6 (i) respectively.

Step X : FBD of structure : as shown in Fig. 4.6 (j).

Step XI : Elastic curve : as shown in Fig. 4.6 (k).

Example 4.5 : Analyse the beam shown in Fig. 4.7 (a) by stiffness method. Take EI = Constant.

Solution : Data : The beam is supported and loaded as shown in Fig. 4.7 (a).

Object : Structural Analysis.

Concepts and equations :

(1) Kinematically determinate structure (Restrained structure).
(2) Force analysis of restrained structure.
(3) Superposition equations of equilibrium of forces.

Procedure :

Step I : Degree of kinematic indeterminacy (D_{ki}) :

Degree of kinematic indeterminacy = D_{ki} = 3.

Step II : Unknown joint displacements (D) :

Let, $D_1 = \theta_A$, $D_2 = \theta_B$ and $D_3 = \theta_C$

Step III : Restrained structure :

The joints A, B and C are locked and the restrained structure is obtained as shown in Fig. 4.7 (c). Also restrained structure with unit values of D_1, D_2 and D_3 is shown in Fig. 4.7 (d), Fig. 4.7 (e) and Fig. 4.7 (f) respectively.

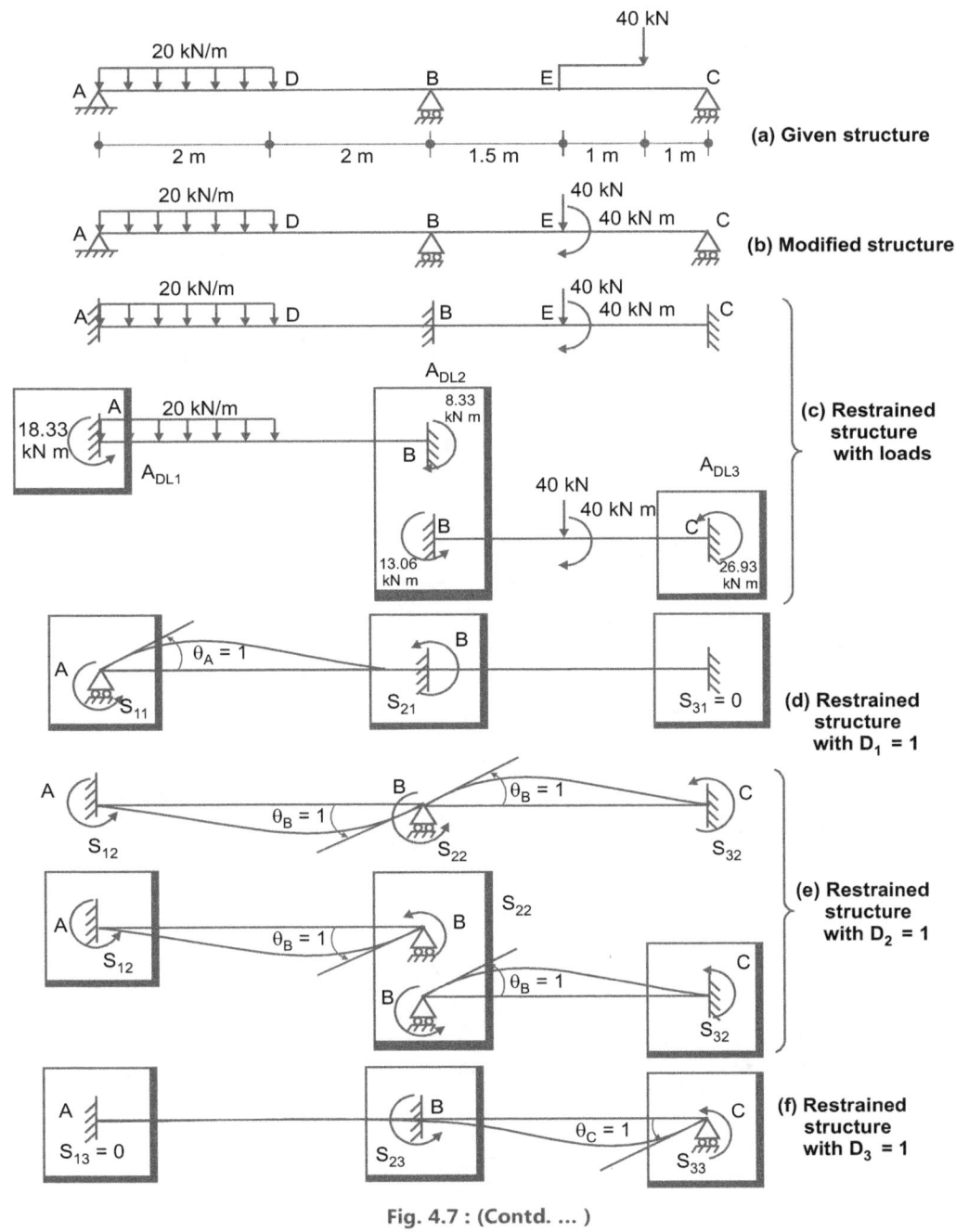

Fig. 4.7 : (Contd. ...)

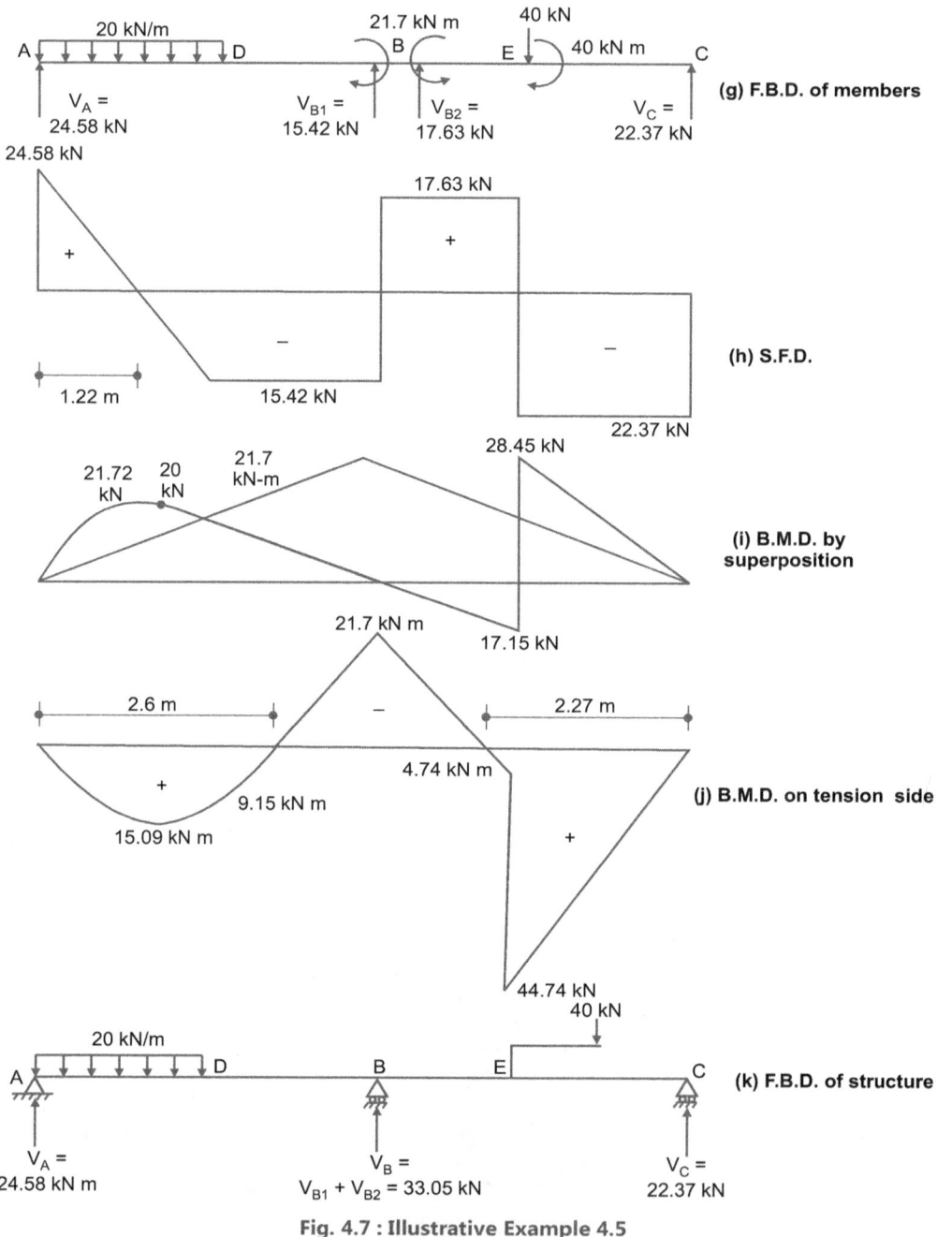

Fig. 4.7 : Illustrative Example 4.5

Step IV : Force analysis of restrained structure :
(a) Fixed End Moments :

$$M_{AB}^F = \frac{wa^2}{12L^2}(6L^2 - 8aL + 3a^2) = \frac{20 \times 2^2}{12 \times 4^2}[6 \times 4^2 - 8 \times 2 \times 4 + 3 \times 2^2]$$

$$= 18.33 \text{ kNm}$$

$$M_{BA}^F = -\frac{wa^3}{12L^2}(4L - 3a) = \frac{-20 \times 2^2}{12 \times 4^2}[4 \times 4 - 3 \times 2] = -8.33 \text{ kNm}$$

$$M_{BC}^F = \frac{Wab^2}{L^2} - \frac{Mb}{L^2}(2a - b) = \frac{40 \times 1.5 \times 2^2}{3.5^2} - \frac{40 \times 2 \times (2 \times 1.5 - 2)}{3.5^2}$$

$$= 13.06 \text{ kNm}$$

$$M_{CB}^F = -\frac{Wba^2}{L^2} - \frac{Ma}{L^2}(2b - a) = -\frac{40 \times 2 \times 1.5^2}{3.5^2} - \frac{40 \times 1.5 (2 \times 2 - 1.5)}{3.5^2}$$

$$= -26.93 \text{ kNm}$$

(b) Forces in the restrained structure subjected to loads corresponding to unknown displacements.

$$A_{DL1} = M_{AB}^F = 18.33 \text{ kNm}$$

$$A_{DL2} = M_{BA}^F + M_{BC}^F = -8.33 + 13.06 = 3.73 \text{ kNm}$$

$$A_{DL3} = M_{CB}^F = -26.93 \text{ kNm}$$

(c) Forces in the restrained structure subjected to unit values of D_1, D_2 and D_3 corresponding to unknown displacements.

$$S_{11} = \left(\frac{4EI}{L}\right)_{AB} = \frac{4EI}{4} = 1 \text{ EI}$$

$$S_{12} = S_{21} = \left(\frac{2EI}{L}\right)_{BA} = \frac{2EI}{4} = 0.5 \text{ EI}$$

$$S_{22} = \left(\frac{5EI}{L}\right)_{BA} + \left(\frac{4EI}{L}\right)_{BC} = \frac{4EI}{4} + \frac{4EI}{3.5} = 2.14 \text{ EI}$$

$$S_{32} = S_{23} = \left(\frac{2EI}{L}\right)_{CB} = \frac{2EI}{3.5} = 0.57 \text{ EI}$$

$$S_{33} = \left(\frac{4EI}{L}\right)_{CB} = \frac{4EI}{3.5} = 2.14 \text{ EI}$$

$$S_{13} = S_{31} = 0$$

Step V : The equilibrium requirement of force :
There is no applied couple at A, B and C.

$$\therefore \quad A_{D1} = A_{D2} = A_{D3} = 0$$

Step VI : Superposition equation of equilibrium of forces :

$$\{A_D\} = \{A_{DL}\} + [S]\{D\}$$

i.e. $\begin{Bmatrix} 0 \\ 0 \\ 0 \end{Bmatrix} = \begin{Bmatrix} 18.33 \\ 4.73 \\ -26.93 \end{Bmatrix} + EI \begin{bmatrix} 1.0 & 0.5 & 0 \\ 0.5 & 2.14 & 0.57 \\ 0 & 0.57 & 2.14 \end{bmatrix} \begin{Bmatrix} D_1 \\ D_2 \\ D_3 \end{Bmatrix}$

i.e.
$0 = 18.33 + 1.0\ EI\ (D_1) + 0.5\ EI\ (D_2) + 0\ EI\ (D_3)$ ... (A)
$0 = 4.73 + 0.5\ EI\ (D_1) + 2.14\ EI\ (D_2) + 0.57\ EI\ (D_3)$ ... (B)
$0 = -256.93 + 0\ EI\ (D_1) + 0.57\ EI\ (D_2) + 2.14\ EI\ (D_3)$ ... (C)

Step VII : Solution of equations for unknown displacements : Solving equations (A), (B) and (c) we get,

$$D_1 = \theta_A = \frac{-15.51}{EI} = \frac{15.51}{EI}\ (\circlearrowright)$$

$$D_2 = \theta_B = \frac{-5.62}{EI} = \frac{5.62}{EI}\ (\circlearrowright)$$

$$D_3 = \theta_C = \frac{26.38}{EI} = \frac{26.38}{EI}\ (\circlearrowleft)$$

Step VIII : Other forces :

$$M_{AB} = \frac{4\ EI}{4}\left(\frac{-15.51}{EI}\right) + \frac{2\ EI}{4}\left(\frac{-5.62}{EI}\right) + 18.33 = 0\ kNm$$

$$M_{BA} = \frac{4\ EI}{4}\left(\frac{-5.62}{EI}\right) + \frac{2\ EI}{4}\left(\frac{-15.51}{EI}\right) + (-8.33) = -21.70\ kNm$$

$$M_{BC} = \frac{4\ EI}{3.5}\left(\frac{-5.62}{EI}\right) + \frac{2\ EI}{3.5}\left(\frac{26.38}{EI}\right) + 13.06 = 21.70\ kNm$$

$$M_{CB} = \frac{4\ EI}{3.5}\left(\frac{26.38}{EI}\right) + \frac{2\ EI}{3.5}\left(\frac{-5.62}{EI}\right) + (-26.93) = 0\ kNm$$

FBD of members is as shown in Fig. 4.7 (g). Considering equilibrium of each member and of complete structure all the reaction components are found out as shown in figure.

Step IX : Shear force and bending moment diagrams : SFD is as shown in Fig. 4.7 (h).

BMD by superposition and on tension side is as shown in Fig. 4.7 (i) and 4.7 (j) respectively.

Step X : FBD of structure: as shown in Fig. 4.7 (k).

Example 4.6 : Analyse the beam shown in Fig. 4.8 (a) by stiffness method. Support B sinks by 25 mm. Take EI = 3800 kNm².

Solution : Data :
(1) The beam is supported and loaded as shown in Fig. 4.8 (a).
(2) $EI = 3800\ kNm^2$
(3) $\Delta_B = 25\ mm\ (\downarrow)$

Object : Structural analysis.

STRUCTURAL ANALYSIS – II STIFFNESS METHOD

Concepts and Equations :
(1) Kinematically determinate structure (Restrained structure).
(2) Force analysis of restrained structure.
(3) Superposition equations of equilibrium of forces.

Procedure :

Step I : Degree of kinematic indeterminacy (D_{ki}) :
Degree of kinematic indeterminacy = D_{ki} = 2.

Step II : Unknown joint displacements (D) :
Let, $D_1 = \theta_B$ and $D_2 = \theta_C$.

Step III : Restrained structure :
The joints B and C are locked and the restrained structure is obtained as shown in Fig. 4.8 (b). Also restrained structure with unit values of D_1 and D_2 is shown in Fig. 4.8 (c) and Fig. 4.8 (d) respectively.

Step IV : Force analysis of restrained structure :

(a) Fixed end moments :

$$M_{AB}^F = \frac{wL^2}{12} + \frac{6EI}{L^2}(\Delta) = \frac{10 \times 6^2}{12} + \frac{6 \times 3800}{6^2}\left(\frac{25}{1000}\right) = 45.83 \text{ kNm}$$

$$M_{BA}^F = -\frac{wL^2}{12} + \frac{6EI}{L^2}(\Delta) = -\frac{10 \times 6^2}{12} + \frac{6 \times 3800}{6^2}\left(\frac{25}{10000}\right) = -14.16 \text{ kNm}$$

$$M_{BC}^F = \frac{Wab^2}{L^2} - \frac{6EI}{L^2}(\Delta) = \frac{30 \times 2 \times 4^2}{6^2} - \frac{6 \times 3800}{6^2}\left(\frac{25}{1000}\right) = 10.83 \text{ kNm}$$

$$M_{CB}^F = -\frac{Wba^2}{L^2} - \frac{6EI}{L^2}(\Delta) = -\frac{30 \times 4 \times 2^2}{6^2} - \frac{6 \times 3800}{6^2}\left(\frac{25}{1000}\right) = -29.16 \text{ kNm}$$

(b) Forces in the restrained structure subjected to loads corresponding to unknown displacements.

$$A_{DL1} = M_{BA}^F + M_{BC}^F = -14.16 + 10.83 = -3.33 \text{ kNm}$$

$$A_{DL2} = M_{CB}^F = -19.16 \text{ kNm}$$

(c) Forces in the restrained structure subjected to unit values of unit values of D_1 and D_2 corresponding to unknown displacements.

$$S_{11} = \left(\frac{4EI}{L}\right)_{BA} + \left(\frac{4EI}{L}\right)_{BC} = \frac{4EI}{6} + \frac{4EI}{6} = 1.33 \text{ EI}$$

$$S_{21} = S_{12} = \left(\frac{2EI}{L}\right)_{CB} = \frac{2EI}{6} = 0.33 \text{ EI}$$

$$S_{22} = \left(\frac{4EI}{L}\right)_{CB} = \frac{4EI}{6} = 0.66 \text{ EI}$$

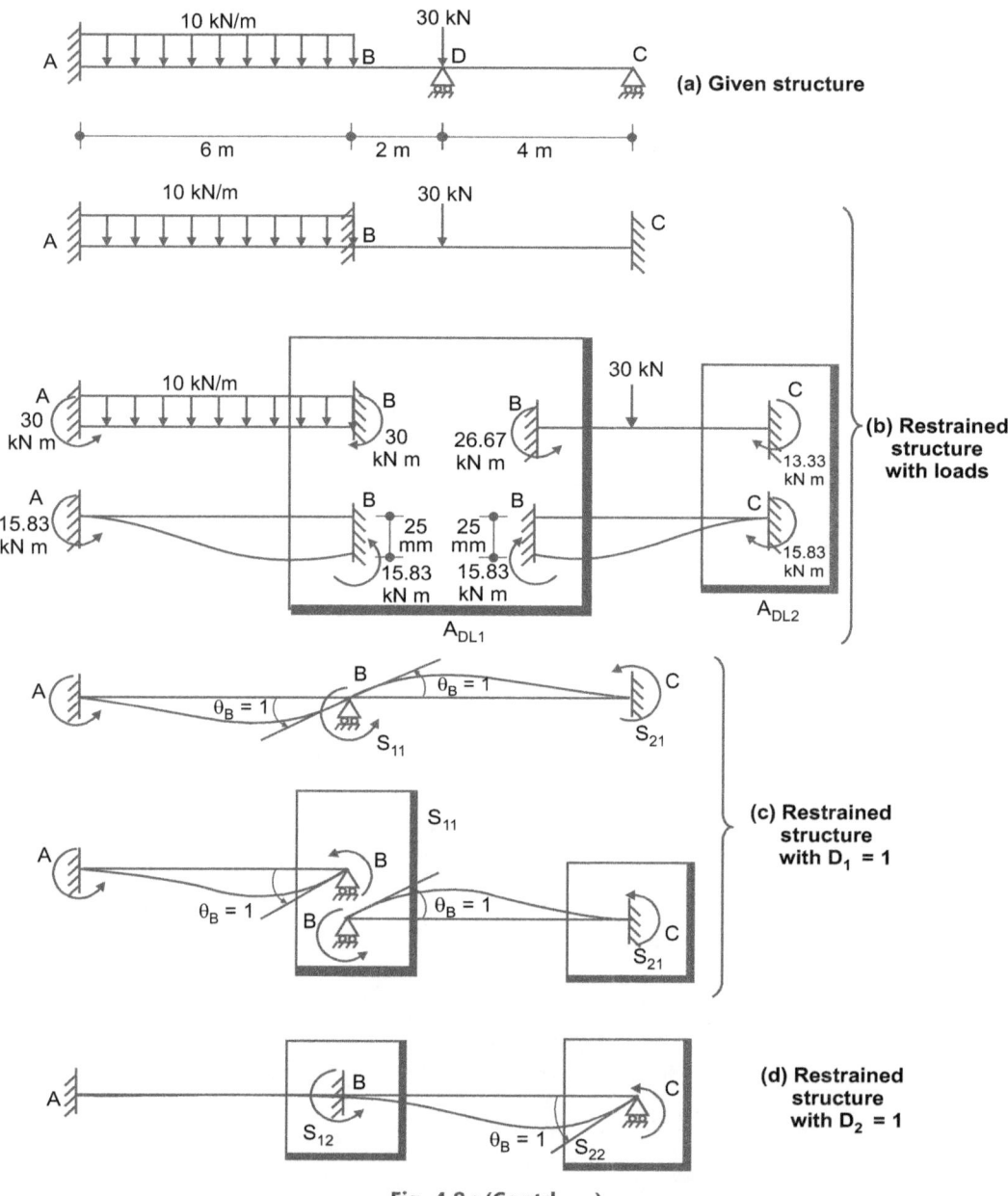

Fig. 4.8 : (Contd. ...)

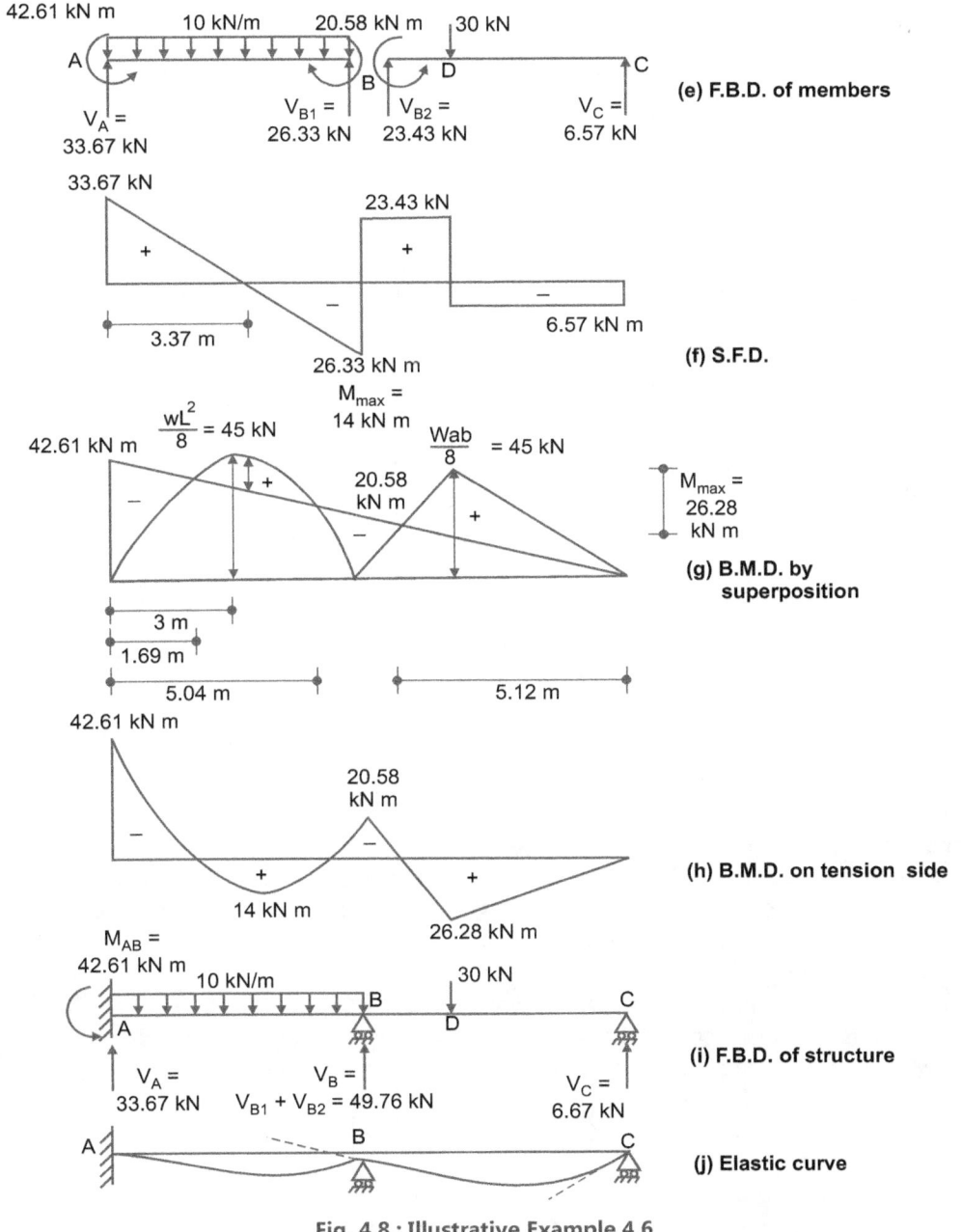

Fig. 4.8 : Illustrative Example 4.6

Step V : The equilibrium requirement of force : There is no applied couple at B and C.
∴ $A_{D1} = A_{D2} = 0$

Step VI : Superposition equations of equilibrium of forces :
$$\{AD\} = \{A_{DL}\} + [S]\{D\}$$

i.e.,
$$\begin{Bmatrix} 0 \\ 0 \end{Bmatrix} = \begin{Bmatrix} -3.33 \\ -29.16 \end{Bmatrix} + EI \begin{bmatrix} 1.33 & 0.33 \\ 0.33 & 0.66 \end{bmatrix} \begin{Bmatrix} D_1 \\ D_2 \end{Bmatrix}$$

i.e.,
$$0 = -3.33 + 1.33\ EI\ (D_1) + 0.33\ EI\ (D_2) \quad \ldots (A)$$
$$0 = -29.16 + 0.33\ EI\ (D_1) + 0.66\ EI\ (D_2) \quad \ldots (B)$$

Step VII : Solution of equations for unknown displacements : Solving equation (A) and (B) we get,

$$\boxed{\begin{aligned} D_1 &= \theta_B = \frac{-9.64}{EI} = \frac{9.64}{EI}\ (\circlearrowleft) \\ D_2 &= \theta_C = \frac{48.56}{EI} = \frac{48.56}{EI}\ (\circlearrowright) \end{aligned}}$$

Step VIII : Other forces :

$$M_{AB} = \frac{4\ EI}{6}(0) + \frac{2\ EI}{6}\left(\frac{-9.64}{EI}\right) + 45.83 = 42.61\ \text{kNm}$$

$$M_{BA} = \frac{4\ EI}{6}\left(\frac{-9.64}{EI}\right) + \frac{2\ EI}{6}(0) + (-14.16) = -20.58\ \text{kNm}$$

$$M_{BC} = \frac{4\ EI}{6}\left(\frac{-9.64}{EI}\right) + \frac{2\ EI}{6}\left(\frac{48.56}{EI}\right) + 10.83 = 20.58\ \text{kNm}$$

$$M_{CB} = \frac{4\ EI}{6}\left(\frac{48.56}{EI}\right) + \frac{2\ EI}{6}\left(\frac{-9.64}{EI}\right) + (-29.16) = 0\ \text{kNm}$$

FBD of members is as shown in Fig. 4.8 (e).
Considering equilibrium of each member and of complete structure all the reaction components are found out as shown in figure.

Step IX : Shear force and bending moment diagrams: SFD is shown in Fig. 4.8 (f).
BMD by superposition and on tension side is as shown in Fig. 4.8 (g) and 4.8 (h) respectively.

Step X : FBD of structure : as shown in Fig. 4.8 (i).

Step XI : Elastic curve : as shown in Fig. 4.8 (j).

Example 4.7 : *Analyse the beam shown in Fig. 4.9 (a) by stiffness method. Take EI = Constant. Stiffness coefficients of spring at B and C are as shown in the figure.*

Solution : (1) Data : The beam is supported and loaded as shown in Fig. 4.9 (a).

(2) $K_B = (EI)$ kN/m and $K_C = \left(\frac{EI}{2}\right)$ kN/m.

Object : Structural analysis.

Concepts and Equations :

(1) Kinematically determinate structure (Restrained structure).

(2) Force analysis of restrained structure.
(3) Superposition equations of equilibrium of forces.

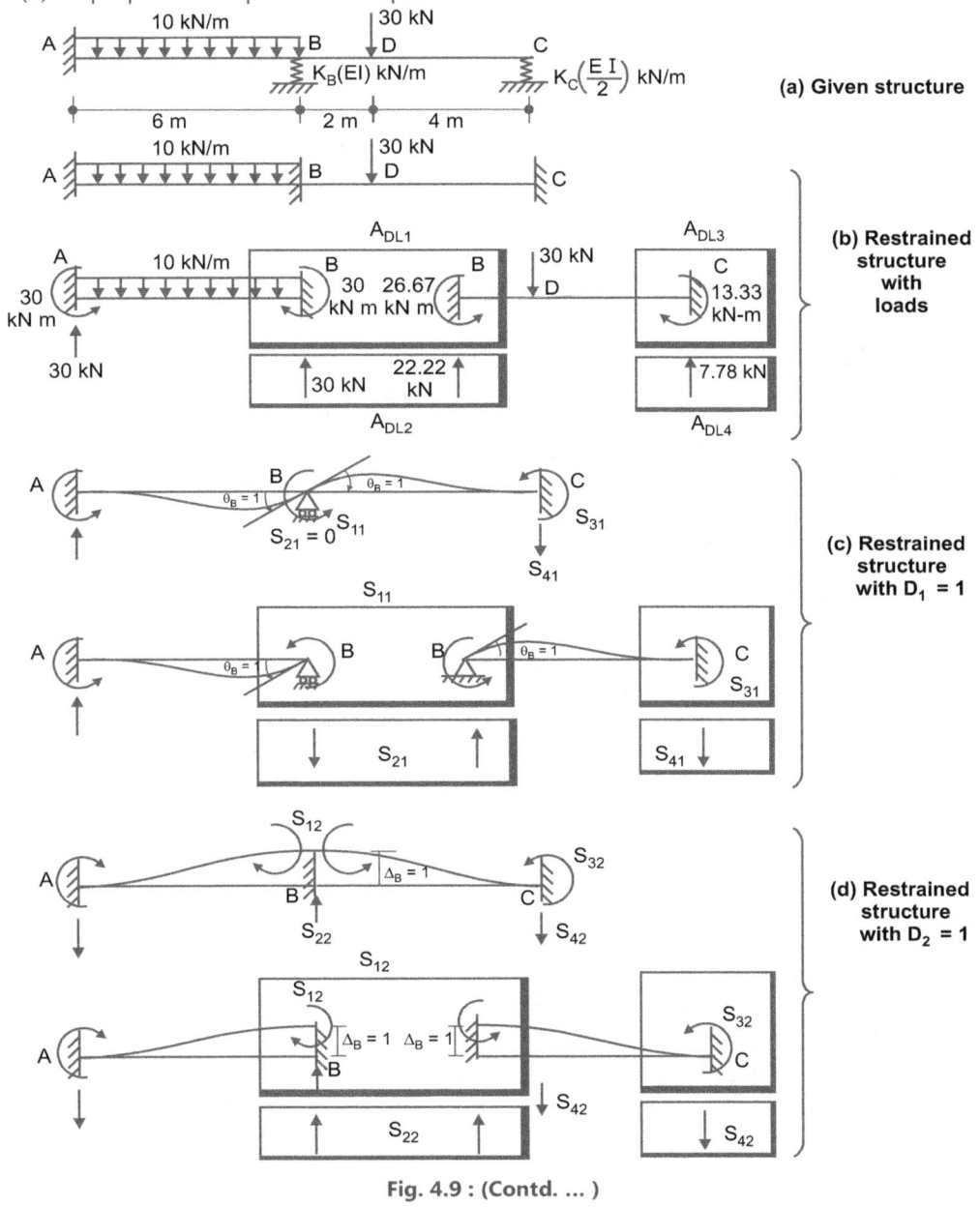

Fig. 4.9 : (Contd. ...)

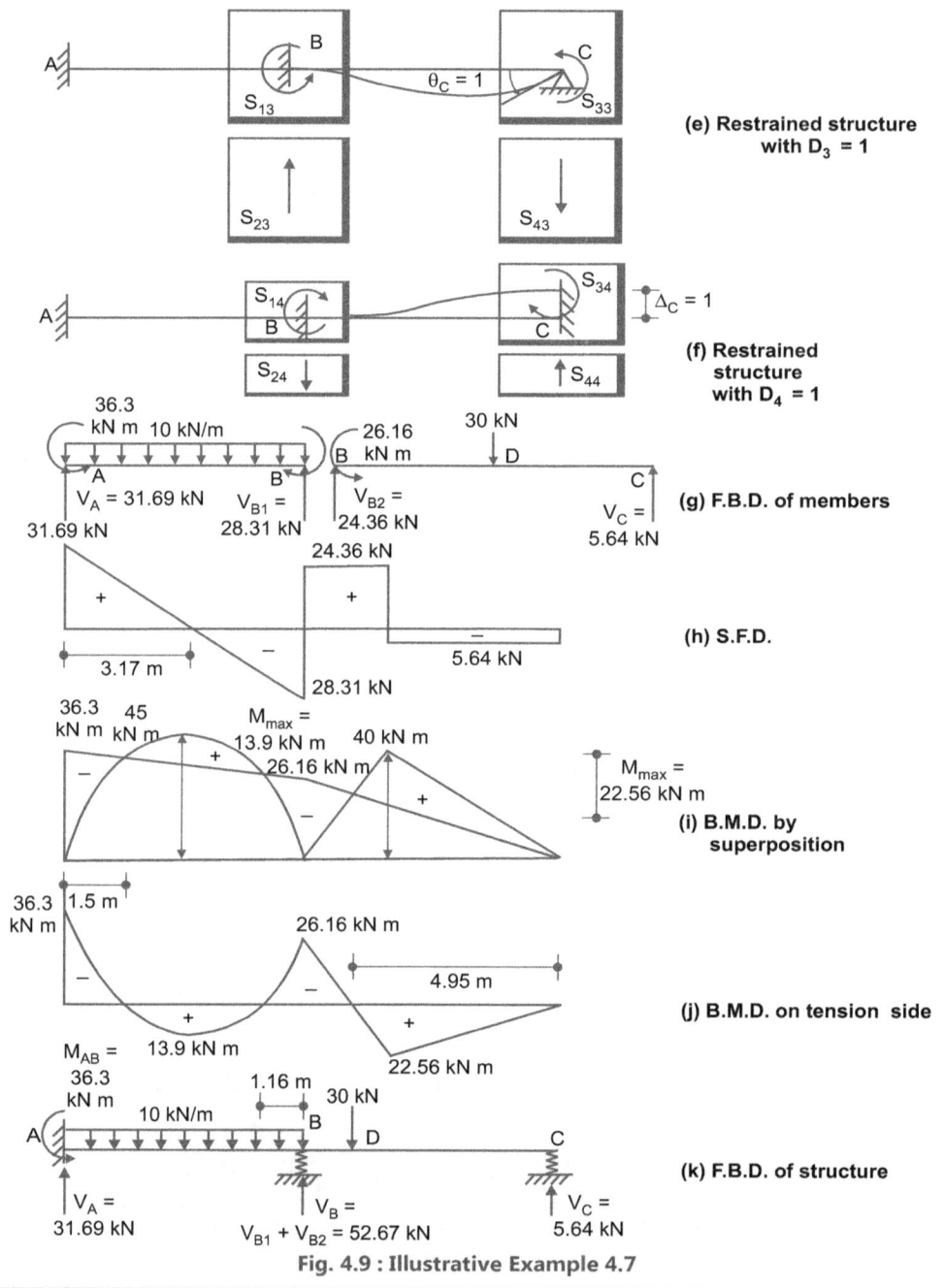

Fig. 4.9 : Illustrative Example 4.7

STRUCTURAL ANALYSIS – II   STIFFNESS METHOD

Procedure :

Step I : Degree of kinematic indeterminacy (D_{ki}) :

Degree of kinematic indeterminacy = D_{ki} = 4.

Step II : Unknown joint displacements (D) :

Let, $D_1 = \theta_B$ (↺), $D_2 = \Delta_B$ (↑), $D_3 = \theta_B$ (↺) and $D_4 = \Delta_C$ (↑)

Step III : Restrained structure : Joints B and C are locked and restrained structure is as shown in Fig. 4.9 (b). Also restrained structure with unit values of D_1, D_2, D_3 and D_4 is shown in Fig. 4.9 (c), Fig. 4.9 (d), Fig. 4.9 (e) and Fig. 4.9 (f) respectively.

Step IV : Force analysis of restrained structure :

(a) Fixed end moments :

$$M_{AB}^F = -M_{BA}^F = \frac{wL^2}{12} = \frac{10 \times 6^2}{12} = 30 \text{ kNm}$$

$$M_{BC}^F = \frac{Wab^2}{L^2} = \frac{30 \times 2 \times 4^2}{6} = 26.67 \text{ kNm}$$

$$M_{CB}^F = -\frac{Wba^2}{L^2} = \frac{30 \times 4 \times 2^2}{6^2} = -13.33 \text{ kNm}$$

(b) Forces in the restrained structure subjected to loads corresponding to unknown displacements :

$A_{DL1} = M_{BA}^F + M_{BC}^F = -30 + 26.67 = -3.33$ kNm

A_{DL2} = Vertical reaction component at B in the restrained structure subjected to loads

    = 30 + 22.22 = 52.22 kN

$A_{DL3} = M_{CB}^F = -13.33$ kNm

A_{DL4} = Vertical reaction component at C in the restrained structure subjected to loads

    = 7.78 kN

(c) Forces in the restrained structure subjected to unit values of D_1, D_2, D_3 and D_4 corresponding to unknown displacements :

$$S_{11} = \left(\frac{4EI}{L}\right)_{BA} + \left(\frac{4EI}{L}\right)_{BC} = \frac{4EI}{6} + \frac{4EI}{6} = 1.33 \, EI$$

$$S_{21} = S_{12} = -\left(\frac{6EI}{L^2}\right)_{BA} + \left(\frac{6EI}{L^2}\right)_{BC} = -\frac{6EI}{6^2} + \frac{6EI}{6^2} = 0$$

$$S_{31} = S_{13} = \left(\frac{2EI}{L}\right)_{BC} = \frac{2EI}{6} = -0.33 \, EI$$

Ch. 4 | 4.39

$$S_{41} = S_{14} = -\left(\frac{6\,EI}{L^2}\right)_{BC} = -\frac{6\,EI}{6^2} = -0.167\,EI$$

$$S_{22} = \left(\frac{12\,EI}{L^3}\right)_{BA} + \left(\frac{12\,EI}{L^3}\right)_{BC} = \frac{12\,EI}{6^3} + \frac{12\,EI}{6^3} = 0.11\,EI$$

$$S_{32} = S_{23} = \left(\frac{6\,EI}{L^2}\right)_{BC} = \frac{6\,EI}{6^2} = 0.167\,EI$$

$$S_{42} = S_{24} = -\left(\frac{12\,EI}{L^3}\right)_{BC} = -\frac{12\,EI}{6^3} = -0.055\,EI$$

$$S_{33} = \left(\frac{4\,EI}{L}\right)_{BC} = \frac{4\,EI}{6} = 0.67\,EI$$

$$S_{43} = S_{34} = -\left(\frac{6\,EI}{L^2}\right)_{BC} = -\frac{6\,EI}{6^2} = -0.167\,EI$$

$$S_{44} = \left(\frac{12\,EI}{L^3}\right)_{BC} = \frac{12\,EI}{6^3} = 0.055\,EI$$

Step V : The equilibrium requirements of forces.

There is no applied couple at B and C. $\therefore$ $A_{D1} = A_{D3} = 0$

There is no applied point load at B and C. $\therefore$ $A_{D2} = A_{D4} = 0$.

Step VI : Superposition equation of equilibrium of forces :

$$\{A_D\} = \{A_{DL}\} + [S]\{D\}$$

i.e.
$$\begin{Bmatrix} 0 \\ 0 \\ 0 \\ 0 \end{Bmatrix} = \begin{Bmatrix} -3.33 \\ 52.22 \\ -13.33 \\ 7.78 \end{Bmatrix} + EI \begin{bmatrix} 1.33 & 0 & 0.33 & -0.167 \\ 0 & 0.11 & 0.167 & -0.055 \\ 0.33 & 0.167 & 0.67 & -0.167 \\ -0.167 & -0.055 & -0.167 & 0.055 \end{bmatrix} \begin{Bmatrix} D_1 \\ D_2 \\ D_3 \\ D_4 \end{Bmatrix}$$

Because of the elastic supports at B and C, S_{22} and S_{44} are to be modified as :

$$S_{22} = (0.11 + 1)\,EI = 1.11\,EI$$

$$S_{44} = \left(0.055 + \frac{1}{2}\right)EI = 0.555\,EI$$

Superposition equation of equilibrium of forces becomes :

$$\begin{Bmatrix} 0 \\ 0 \\ 0 \\ 0 \end{Bmatrix} = \begin{Bmatrix} -3.33 \\ 52.22 \\ -13.33 \\ 7.78 \end{Bmatrix} + EI \begin{bmatrix} 1.33 & 0 & 0.33 & -0.167 \\ 0 & 0.11 & 0.167 & -0.055 \\ 0.33 & 0.167 & 0.67 & -0.167 \\ -0.167 & -0.055 & -0.167 & 0.055 \end{bmatrix} \begin{Bmatrix} D_1 \\ D_2 \\ D_3 \\ D_4 \end{Bmatrix}$$

i.e.
$$0 = -3.33 + (1.33\ EI)\ D_1 + (0)\ D_2 + (0.33\ EI)\ D_3 - (0.167\ EI)\ D_4 \quad \ldots (A)$$
$$0 = 52.22 + (0)\ D_1 + (1.11\ EI)\ D_2 + (0.167\ EI)\ D_3\ (0.055\ EI)\ D_4 \quad \ldots (B)$$
$$0 = -13.33 + (0.33\ EI)\ D_1 + (0.167\ EI)\ D_2 + (0.67\ EI)\ D_3 - (0.167\ EI)\ D_4 \quad \ldots (C)$$
$$0 = 7.78 - (0.167\ EI)\ D_1 + (0.055\ EI)\ D_2 - (0.167\ EI)\ D_3 + (0.55\ EI)\ D_4 \quad \ldots (D)$$

Step VII : Solution of equations for unknown displacements :

Solving equations (A), (B), (C) and (D) we get,

$$D_1 = \theta_B = \frac{-7.23}{EI} = \frac{7.23}{EI}\ (\circlearrowleft)$$

$$D_2 = \Delta_B = \frac{-52.67}{EI} = \frac{52.67}{EI}\ (\downarrow)$$

$$D_3 = \theta_C = \frac{33.54}{EI} = \frac{33.54}{EI}\ (\circlearrowright)$$

$$D_4 = \Delta_C = \frac{-11.28}{EI} = \frac{11.28}{EI}\ (\downarrow)$$

Step VIII : Other forces :

$$M_{AB} = \frac{4\ EI}{6}(0) + \frac{2\ EI}{6}\left(-\frac{7.23}{EI}\right) + \frac{6\ EI}{6^2}\left(\frac{52.67}{EI}\right) + 30 = 36.3\ kNm$$

$$M_{BA} = \frac{4\ EI}{6}\left(-\frac{7.23}{EI}\right) + \frac{2\ EI}{6}(0) + \frac{6\ EI}{6^2}\left(\frac{52.67}{EI}\right) - 30 = -26.16\ kNm$$

$$M_{BC} = \frac{4\ EI}{6}\left(-\frac{7.23}{EI}\right) + \frac{2\ EI}{6}\left(\frac{33.54}{EI}\right) - \frac{6\ EI}{6^2}\left(\frac{52.67 - 11.28}{EI}\right) + 26.67$$
$$= 26.16\ kNm$$

$$M_{CB} = \frac{4\ EI}{6}\left(\frac{33.54}{EI}\right) + \frac{2\ EI}{6}\left(-\frac{7.23}{EI}\right) - \frac{6\ EI}{6^2}\left(\frac{52.67 - 11.28}{EI}\right) - 13.33 = 0$$

FBD of member is as shown in Fig. 4.9.(g). Considering equilibrium of each member and of complete structure other reaction components are found out as shown in figure.

Step IX : Shear force and bending moment diagrams: SFD is as shown in Fig. 4.9 (h). BMD by superposition and on tension side is as shown in Fig. 4.9 (i) and Fig. 4.9 (j) respectively.

Step X : FBD of structure: as shown in Fig. 4.9 (k).

Example 4.8 : *Analyse the beam shown in Fig. 4.10 (a) by stiffness method.*

Solution : Data : The beam is supported and loaded as shown in Fig. 4.10 (a).

Object : Structural analysis.

Concepts and Equations :
(1) Kinematically determinate structure (Restrained structure).
(2) Force analysis of restrained structure.
(3) Superposition equations of equilibrium of forces.

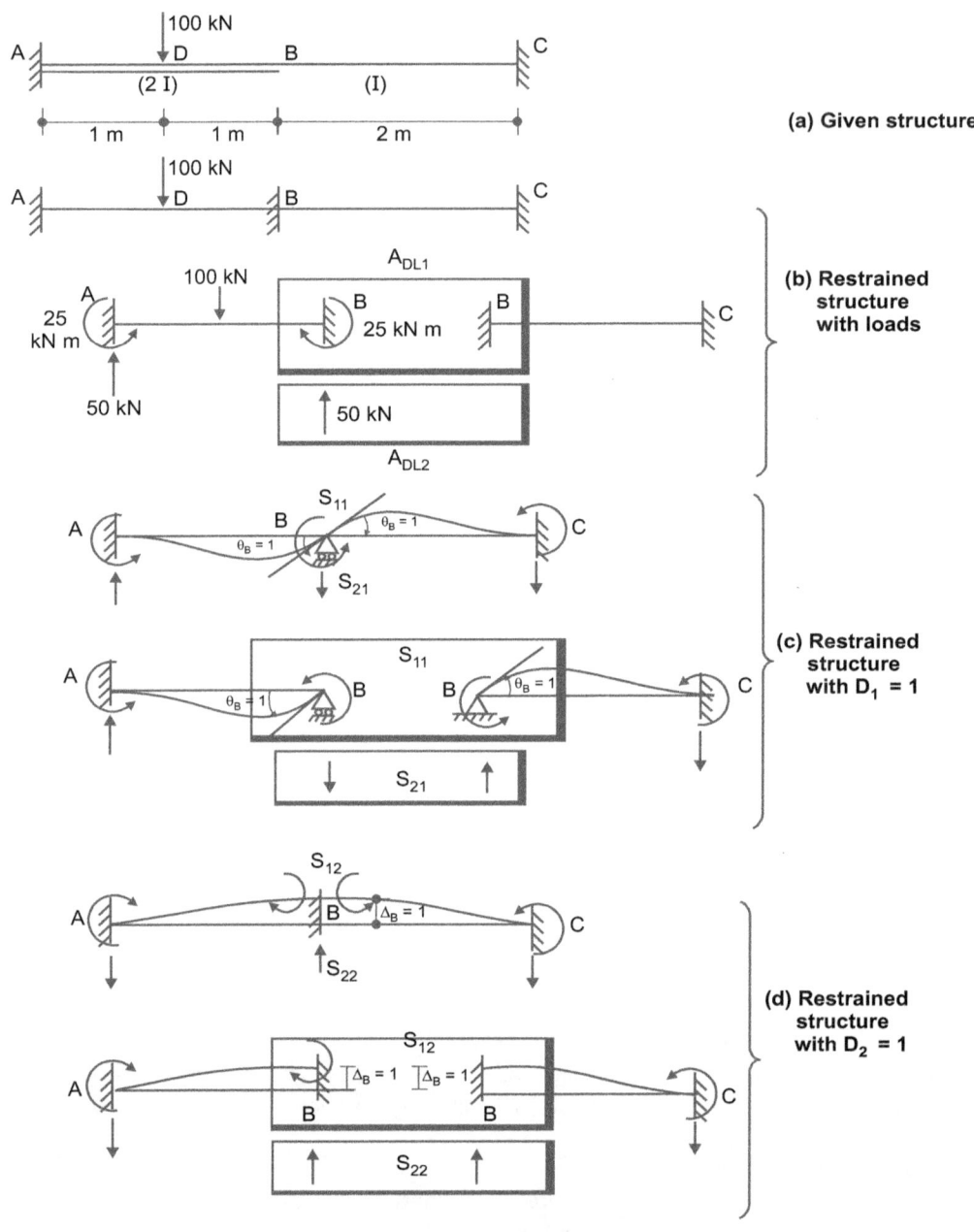

Fig. 4.10 : (Contd. ...)

STRUCTURAL ANALYSIS – II   STIFFNESS METHOD

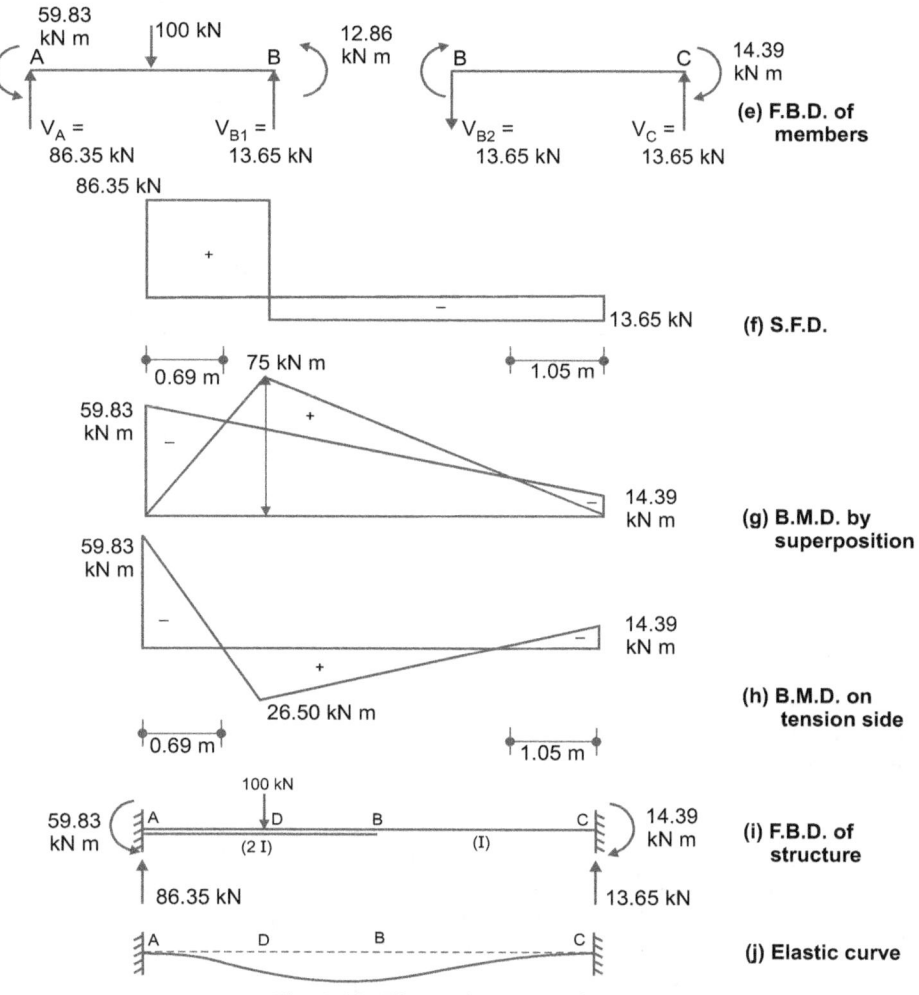

Fig. 4.10 : Illustrative Example 4.8

Procedure :

Step I : Degree of kinematic indeterminacy (D_{ki}) :
  Degree of kinematic indeterminacy = D_{ki} = 2.

Step II : Unknown joint displacements (D).
  Let, $D_1 = \theta_B$ (↻) and $D_2 = \Delta_B$ (↑)

Step III : Restrained structure :

The joint B is locked and the restrained structure is obtained as shown in Fig. 4.10 (b). Also restrained structure with unit values of D1 and D2 is shown in Fig. 4.10 (c) and Fig. 4.10 (d) respectively.

Step IV : Force analysis of restrained structure :
(a) Fixed end moments

$$M_{AB}^F = -M_{BA}^F = \frac{WL}{8} = \frac{100 \times 2}{8} = 25 \text{ kNm}$$

$$M_{BC}^F = M_{CB}^F = 0 \text{ kNm}$$

(b) Forces in the restrained structure subjected to loads corresponding to unknown displacements :

$$A_{DL1} = M_{BA}^F + M_{BC}^F = -25 + 0 = -25 \text{ kNm}$$

A_{DL2} = Vertical reaction component at B in the restrained structure subjected to loads = 50 kN

(c) Forces in the restrained structure subjected to unit values of D_1 and D_2 corresponding to unknown displacements.

$$S_{11} = \left(\frac{4 EI}{L}\right)_{BA} + \left(\frac{4 EI}{L}\right)_{BC} = \frac{4 \times 2 EI}{2} + \frac{4 EI}{2} = 6 EI$$

$$S_{21} = S_{12} = -\left(\frac{6 EI}{L^2}\right)_{BC} = \left(\frac{6 EI}{L^2}\right)_{BC} = -\frac{6 \times 2 EI}{2^2} + \frac{6 EI}{2^2} = -1.5 EI$$

$$S_{22} = \left(\frac{12 EI}{L^3}\right)_{BA} + \left(\frac{12 EI}{L^3}\right)_{BC} = \frac{12 \times 2 EI}{2^2} + \frac{12 EI}{2^3} = 4.5 EI$$

Step V : The equilibrium requirement of force :
There is no applied couple at B. $\therefore A_{D1} = 0$
There is no applied point load at B. $\therefore A_{D2} = 0$.

Step VI : Superposition equation of equilibrium of forces :

$$\{A_D\} = \{A_{DL}\} + [S]\{D\}$$

i.e.
$$\begin{Bmatrix} 0 \\ 0 \end{Bmatrix} = \begin{Bmatrix} -25 \\ 50 \end{Bmatrix} + EI \begin{bmatrix} 6 & -1.5 \\ -1.5 & 4.5 \end{bmatrix} \begin{Bmatrix} D_1 \\ D_2 \end{Bmatrix}$$

i.e.
$$0 = -25 + (6 EI) D_1 - (1.5 EI) D_2 \qquad \ldots (A)$$
$$0 = 50 - (1.5 EI) D_1 + (4.5 EI) D_2 \qquad \ldots (B)$$

Step VII : Solution of equations for unknown displacements : Solving equations (A) and (B), we get

$$D_1 = \theta_B = \frac{1.52}{EI} = \frac{1.52}{EI} \ (\circlearrowleft)$$

$$D_2 = \Delta_B = \frac{-10.60}{EI} = \frac{10.60}{EI} \ (\circlearrowright)$$

Step VIII : Other forces :

$$M_{AB} = \frac{4 (2 EI)}{2} (0) + \frac{2 (2 EI)}{2} \left(\frac{1.52}{EI}\right) + \left(\frac{6 (2 EI)}{2^2}\right) \left(\frac{10.60}{EI}\right) + 25$$

$$= 59.83 \text{ kNm}$$

STRUCTURAL ANALYSIS – II   STIFFNESS METHOD

$$M_{BA} = \frac{4(2EI)}{2}\left(\frac{1.52}{EI}\right) + \frac{2(2EI)}{2}(0) + \frac{6(2EI)}{2^2}\left(\frac{10.60}{EI}\right) - 25$$
$$= 12.86 \text{ kNm}$$
$$M_{BC} = \frac{4EI}{2}\left(\frac{1.52}{EI}\right) + \frac{2EI}{2}(0) - \frac{6EI}{2^2}\left(\frac{10.60}{EI}\right) = -12.86 \text{ kNm}$$
$$M_{CB} = \frac{4EI}{2}(0) + \frac{2EI}{2}\left(\frac{1.52}{EI}\right) - \frac{6EI}{2^2}\left(\frac{10.60}{EI}\right) = -14.39 \text{ kNm}$$

FBD of members is as shown in Fig. 4.10 (e). Considering equilibrium of each member and of complete structure all the reaction components are found out as shown in figure.

Step IX : Shear force and bending moment diagrams : SFD is shown in Fig. 4.10 (f).

BMD by superposition and on tension side is as shown in Fig. 4.10 (g) and 4.10 (h) respectively.

Step X : FBD of structure : as shown in Fig. 4.10 (i).

Step XI : Elastic curve : as shown in Fig. 4.10 (j).

Example 4.9 : *Analyse the frame shown in Fig. 4.11 (a) by stiffness method. Take EI = Constant.*

Solution : Data : The frame is supported and loaded as shown in Fig. 4.11 (a).
Object : Structural analysis.
Concepts and Equations :
(1) Kinematically determinate structure (Restrained structure)
(2) Force analysis of restrained structure.
(3) Superposition equations of equilibrium of forces.
Procedure :
Step I : Degree of kinematic indeterminacy (D_{ki}) :
Degree of kinematic indeterminacy = D_{ki} = 2.
Step II : Unknown joint displacements (D) :
Let, $D_1 = \theta_B$ (↻) and $D_2 = \theta_C$ (↻)
Step III : Restrained structure :
The joints B and C are locked and the restrained structure is obtained as shown in Fig. 4.11 (b). Also restrained structure with unit values of D_1 and D_2 is shown in Fig. 4.11 (c) and 4.11 (d) respectively.
Step IV : Force analysis of restrained structure :
(a) Fixed end moments :

$$M_{AB}^F = -M_{BA}^F = \frac{WL}{8} = \frac{50 \times 4}{8} = 25 \text{ kNm}$$
$$M_{BC}^F = -M_{CB}^F = \frac{wL^2}{12} = \frac{25 \times 3^2}{12} = 18.75 \text{ kNm}$$

(b) Forces in the restrained structure subjected to loads corresponding to unknown displacements

$$A_{DL1} = M^F_{BA} + M^F_{BC} = -25 + 18.75 = -6.25 \text{ kNm}$$
$$A_{DL2} = M^F_{CB} = -18.75 \text{ kNm}$$

(c) Forces in the restrained structure subjected to unit values of D_1 and D_2 corresponding to unknown displacements.

$$S_{11} = \left(\frac{4EI}{L}\right)_{BA} + \left(\frac{4EI}{L}\right)_{BC} = \frac{4EI}{4} + \frac{4EI}{3} = 2.33 \, EI$$

$$S_{21} = S_{12} = \left(\frac{2EI}{L}\right)_{CB} = \frac{2EI}{3} = 0.67 \, EI$$

$$S_{22} = \left(\frac{4EI}{L}\right)_{CB} = \frac{4EI}{3} = 1.33 \, EI$$

Step V : The equilibrium requirement of force :
There is no applied couple at B and C $\therefore$ $A_{D1} = A_{D2} = 2$.

Step VI : Superposition equation of equilibrium of forces :

$$\{A_D\} = \{A_{DL}\} + [S]\{D\}$$

i.e. $\begin{Bmatrix} 0 \\ 0 \end{Bmatrix} = \begin{Bmatrix} -6.25 \\ -18.75 \end{Bmatrix} + EI \begin{bmatrix} 2.33 & 0.67 \\ 0.67 & 1.33 \end{bmatrix} \begin{Bmatrix} D_1 \\ D_2 \end{Bmatrix}$

i.e. $0 = -6.25 + 2.33 \, EI \, (D_1) + 0.67 \, EI \, (D_2)$ ... (A)
$\ 0 = -18.75 + 0.67 \, EI \, (D_1) + 1.33 \, EI \, (D_2)$ ... (B)

Step VII : Solution of equations for unknown displacements : Solving equations (A) and (B), we get

$$D_1 = \theta_B = -\frac{1.58}{EI} = \frac{1.58}{EI} \, (\circlearrowright)$$

$$D_2 = \theta_C = \frac{14.84}{EI} = \frac{14.84}{EI} \, (\circlearrowleft)$$

Step VIII : Other forces :

$$M_{AB} = \frac{4EI}{4}(0) + \frac{2EI}{4}\left(\frac{-1.58}{EI}\right) + 25 = 24.18 \text{ kNm}$$

$$M_{BA} = \frac{4EI}{4}\left(\frac{-1.58}{EI}\right) + \frac{2EI}{4}(0) - 25 = -26.58 \text{ kNm}$$

$$M_{BC} = \frac{4EI}{3}\left(\frac{-1.58}{EI}\right) + \frac{2EI}{3}\left(\frac{14.89}{EI}\right) + 18.75 = 26.58 \text{ kNm}$$

$$M_{CB} = \frac{4EI}{3}\left(\frac{14.84}{EI}\right) + \frac{2EI}{3}\left(\frac{-1.53}{EI}\right) - 18.75 = 0 \text{ kNm}$$

FBD of members is as shown in Fig. 4.11 (e).

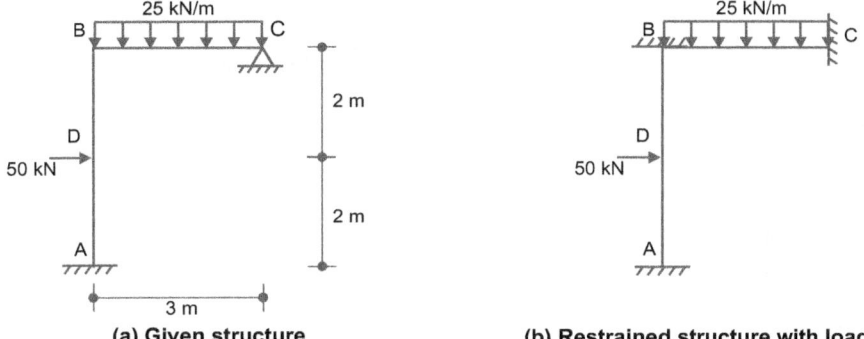

(a) Given structure

(b) Restrained structure with loads

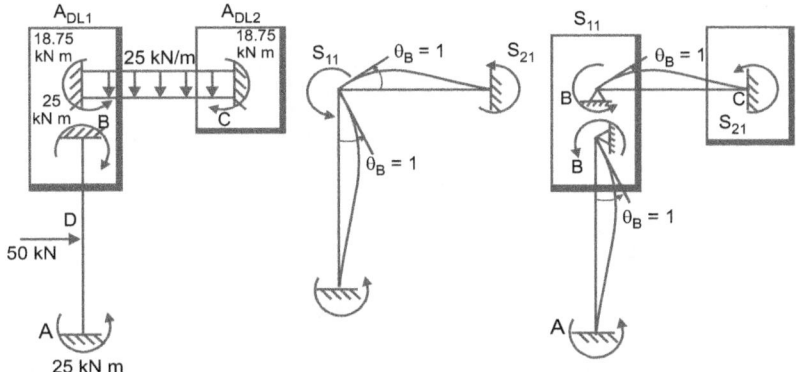

(c) Restrained structure with loads

(d) Restrained structure with $D_1 = 1$

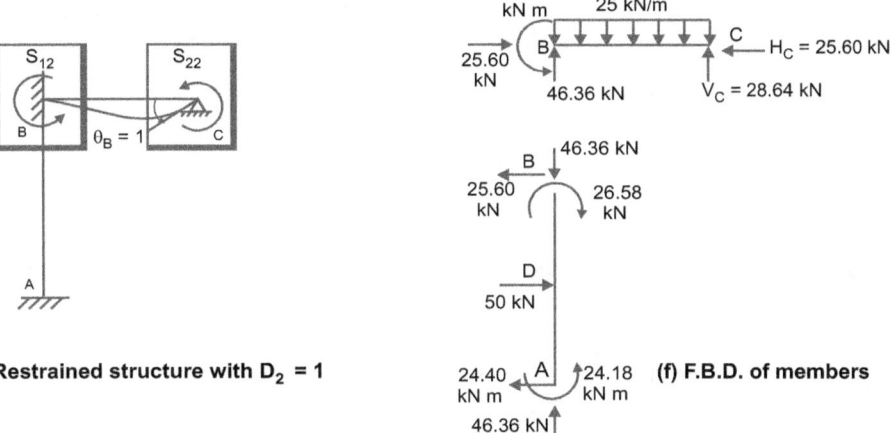

(e) Restrained structure with $D_2 = 1$

(f) F.B.D. of members

Fig. 4.11 : (Contd. ...)

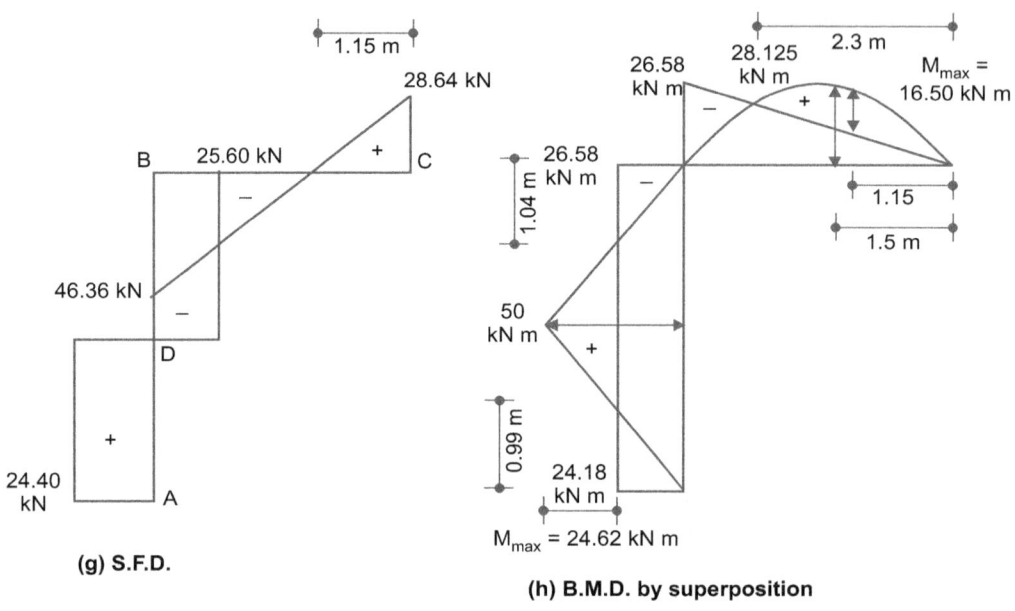

(g) S.F.D.

(h) B.M.D. by superposition

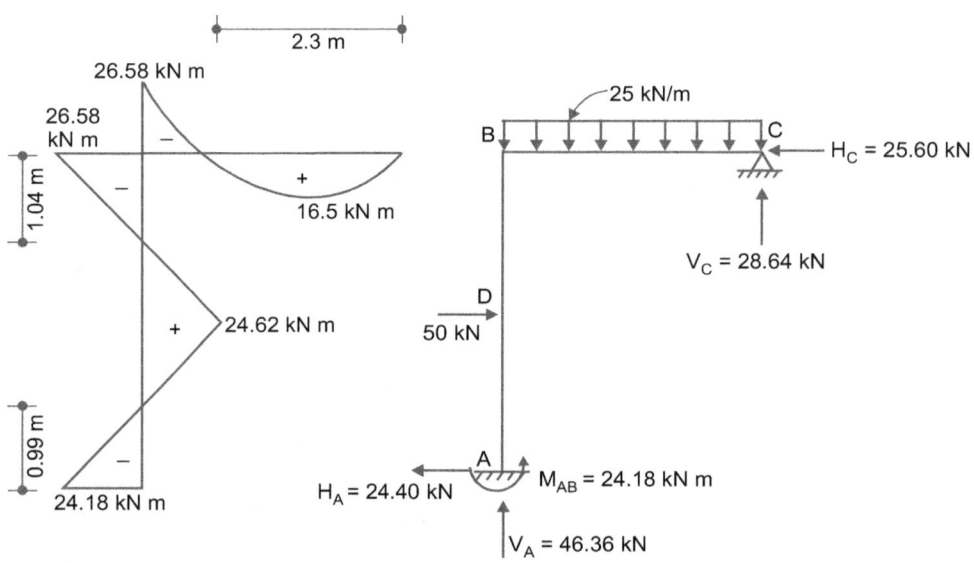

(i) B.M.D. on tension side

(j) F.B.D. of structure

Fig. 4.11 : Illustrative Example 4.9

Considering equilibrium of each member and of complete structure, all the reaction components are found out as shown in figure.

Step IX : Shear force and bending moment diagrams : SFD is as shown in Fig. 4.11 (f).

BMD by superposition and on tension side is as shown in Fig. 4.11 (g) and 4.11 (h) respectively.

Step X : FBD of structure : as shown in Fig. 4.11 (i).

Example 4.10 : *Analyse the frame shown in Fig. 4.12 (a) by stiffness method.*

Solution : Data : The frame is supported and loaded as shown in Fig. 4.12 (a).

Object : Structural analysis.

Concepts and Equations :
(1) Kinematically determinate structure (Restrained structure).
(2) Force analysis of restrained structure.
(3) Superposition equations of equilibrium of forces.

Procedure :

Step I : Degree of kinematic indeterminacy (D_{ki}) :

Degree of kinematic indeterminacy = D_{ki} = 1.

Step II : Unknown joint displacements (D) :

Let, $D_1 = \theta_B$ (↻)

Step III : Restrained structure :

The joint B is locked and the restrained structure is obtained as shown in Fig. 4.12 (b). Also restrained structure with unit value of D_1 is shown in Fig. 4.12 (c).

Step IV : Force analysis of restrained structure :

(a) Fixed end moments :

$$M_{AB}^F = -M_{BA}^F = \frac{WL}{8} = \frac{50 \times 4}{8} = 25 \text{ kNm}$$

$$M_{BC}^F = -M_{CB}^F = \frac{wL^2}{12} = \frac{25 \times 3^2}{12} = 18.75 \text{ kNm}$$

(b) Forces in the restrained structure subjected to loads corresponding to unknown displacements :

$$A_{DL1} = M_{BA}^F + M_{BC}^F = -25 + 18.75 = -6.25 \text{ kNm}$$

(c) Forces in the restrained structure subjected to unit values of D_1 corresponding to unknown displacement.

$$S_{11} = \left(\frac{4(2EI)}{L}\right)_{BA} + \left(\frac{4EI}{L}\right)_{BC} = \frac{8EI}{4} + \frac{4EI}{3} = 3.33\, EI$$

Step V : The equilibrium requirement of force : There is no applied couple at B

∴ $A_{D1} = 0$.

Step VI : Superposition equation of equilibrium of forces :

$$\{A_D\} = \{A_{DL}\} + [S]\{D\}$$

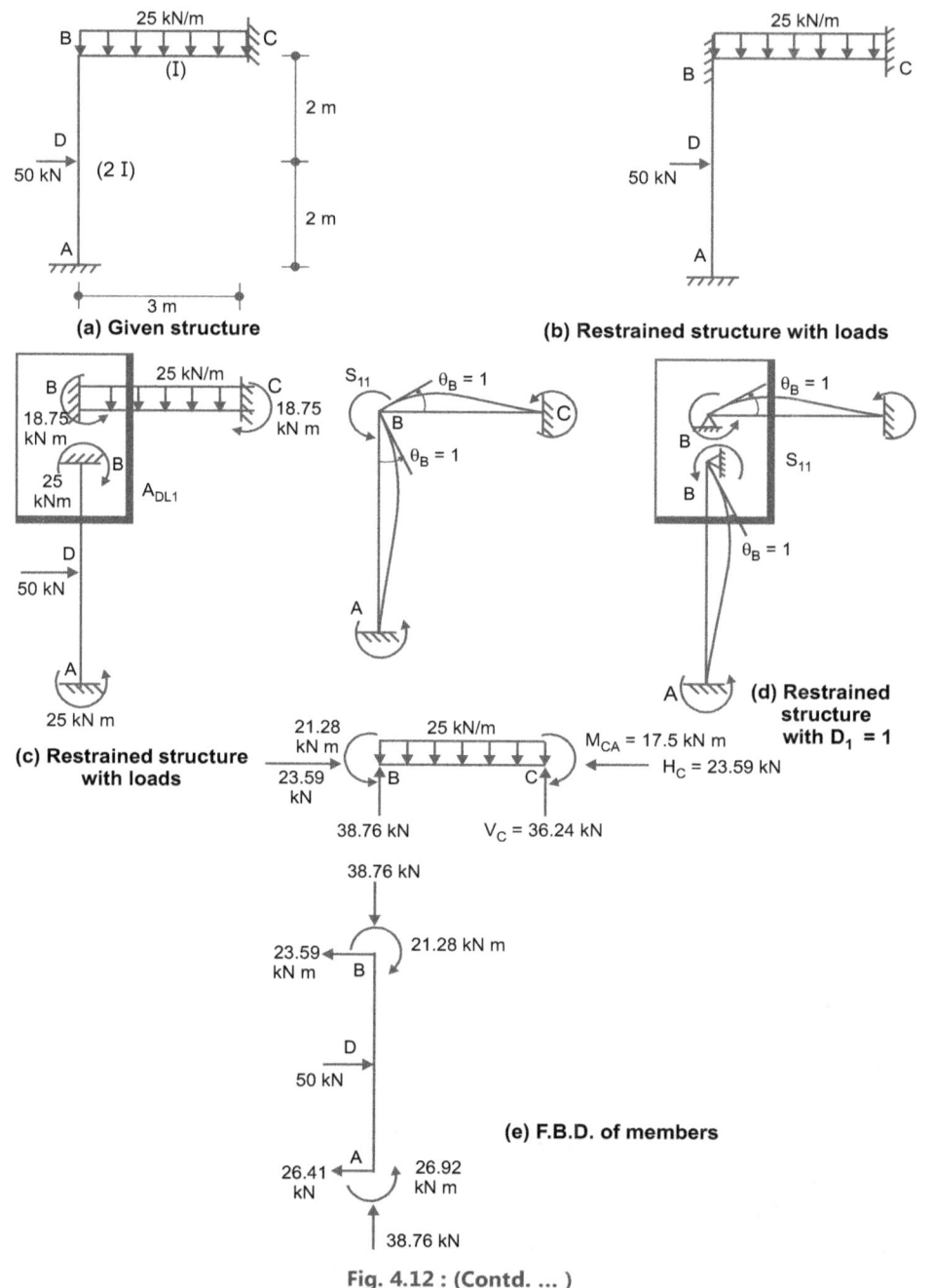

Fig. 4.12 : (Contd. ...)

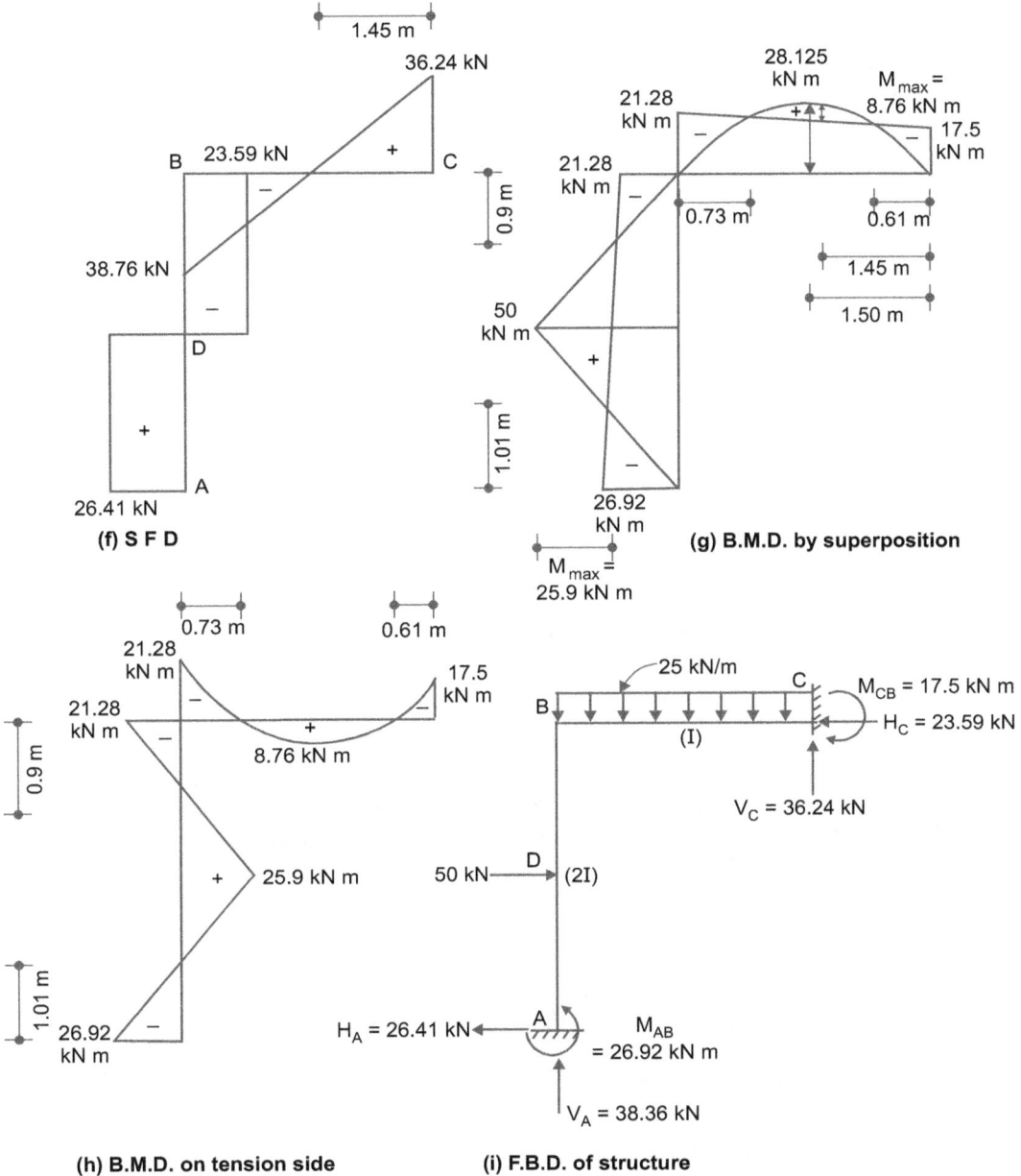

Fig. 4.12 : Illustrative Example 4.10

i.e. $\quad\quad\quad\quad\quad \{0\} = \{-6.25\} + EI [3.33] [D_1]$

i.e. $\quad\quad\quad\quad\quad 0 = -6.25 + 3.33\, EI\, (D_1)$ ... (A)

Step VII : Solution of equations for unknown displacements : solving equation (A) we get,

$$D_1 = \theta_B = \frac{1.87}{EI} = \frac{1.87}{EI}\ (\circlearrowleft)$$

Step VIII : Other forces :

$$M_{AB} = \frac{4(2\,EI)}{4}(0) + \frac{2(2\,EI)}{4}\left(\frac{1.87}{EI}\right) + 25 = 26.92 \text{ kNm}$$

$$M_{BA} = \frac{4(2\,EI)}{4}\left(\frac{1.87}{EI}\right) + \frac{EI}{4}(0) - 25 = -21.28 \text{ kNm}$$

$$M_{BC} = \frac{4\,EI}{3}\left(\frac{1.87}{EI}\right) + \frac{2\,EI}{3}(0) + 18.75 = 21.28 \text{ kNm}$$

$$M_{CB} = \frac{4\,EI}{3}(0) + \frac{2\,EI}{3}\left(\frac{1.87}{EI}\right) - 18.75 = -17.50 \text{ kNm}$$

FBD of members is as shown in Fig. 4.12 (d).

Considering equilibrium of each member and of complete structure all the reaction components are found out as shown in figure.

Step IX : Shear force and bending moment diagrams :

SFD is shown in Fig. 4.12 (e).

BMD by superposition and on tension side is as shown in Fig. 4.12 (f) and 4.12 (g) respectively.

Step X : FBD of structure : as shown in Fig. 4.12 (h).

Example 4.11 : *Analyse the frame shown in Fig. 4.13 (a) by stiffness method.*

Solution : (1) Data : The frame is supported and loaded as shown in Fig. 4.13 (a).

(2) Type of frame : sway frame.

Object : Structural analysis.

Concepts and equations :

(1) Kinematically determinate structure (Restrained structure).

(2) Force analysis of restrained structure.

(3) Superposition equations of equilibrium of forces.

Procedure :

Step I : Degree of kinematic indeterminacy (D_{ki}) :

Degree of kinematic indeterminacy = D_{ki} = 4.

Step II : Unknown joint displacements (D) :

Let, $D_1 = \theta_B\ (\circlearrowleft),\quad D_2 = \theta_C\ (\circlearrowleft),\quad D_3 = \theta_D\ (\circlearrowleft)\text{ and }\quad D_4 = \Delta\ (\rightarrow)$

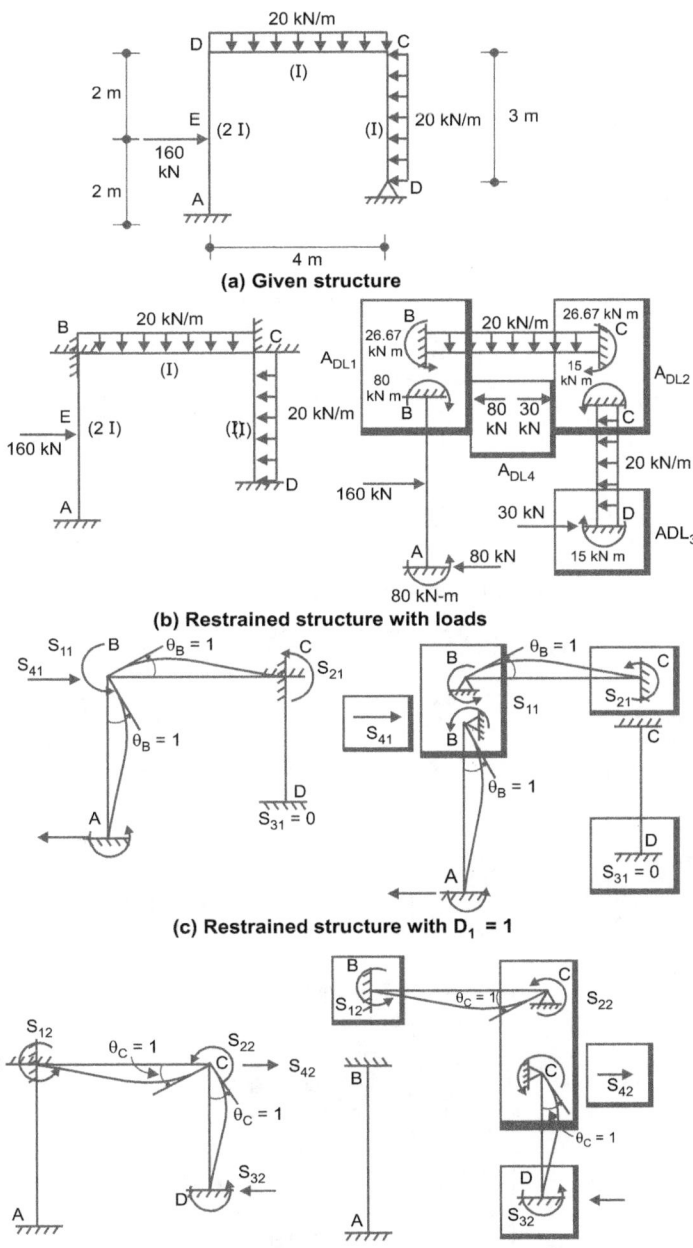

Fig. 4.13 : (Contd. ...)

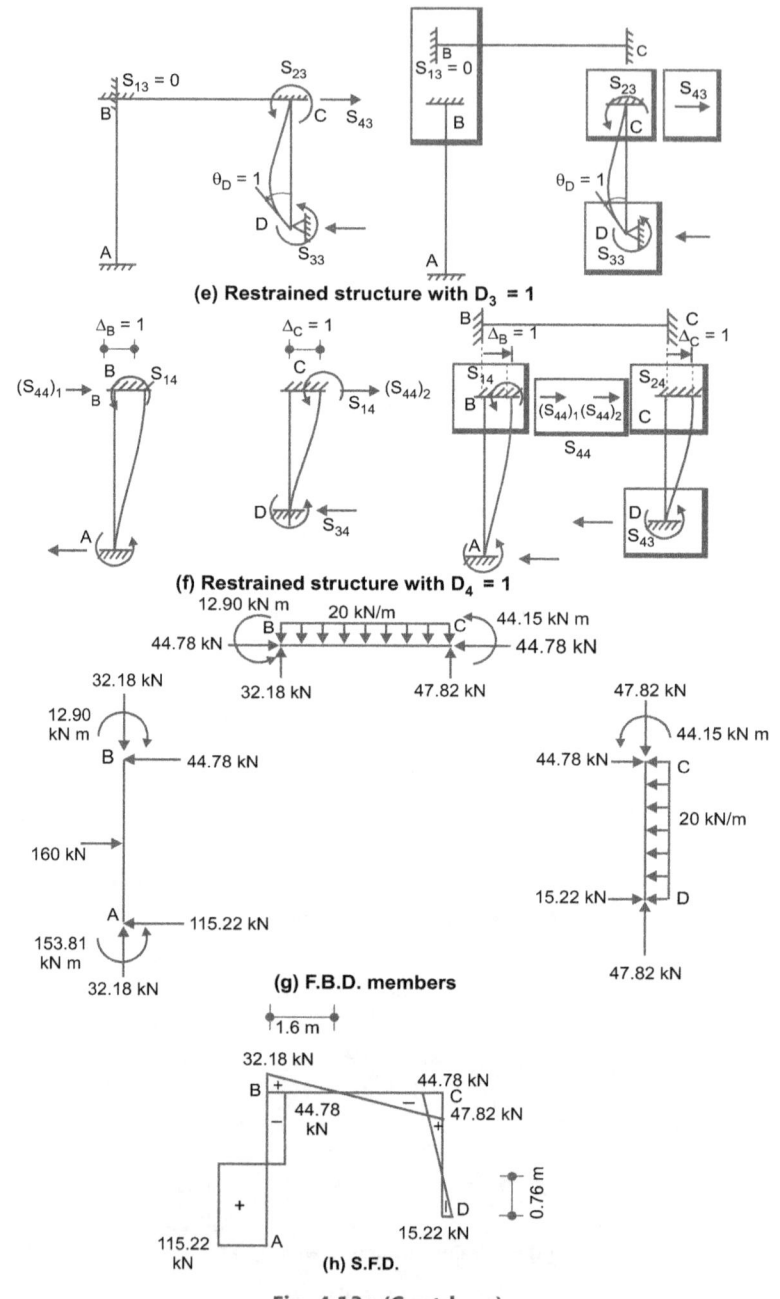

Fig. 4.13 : (Contd. ...)

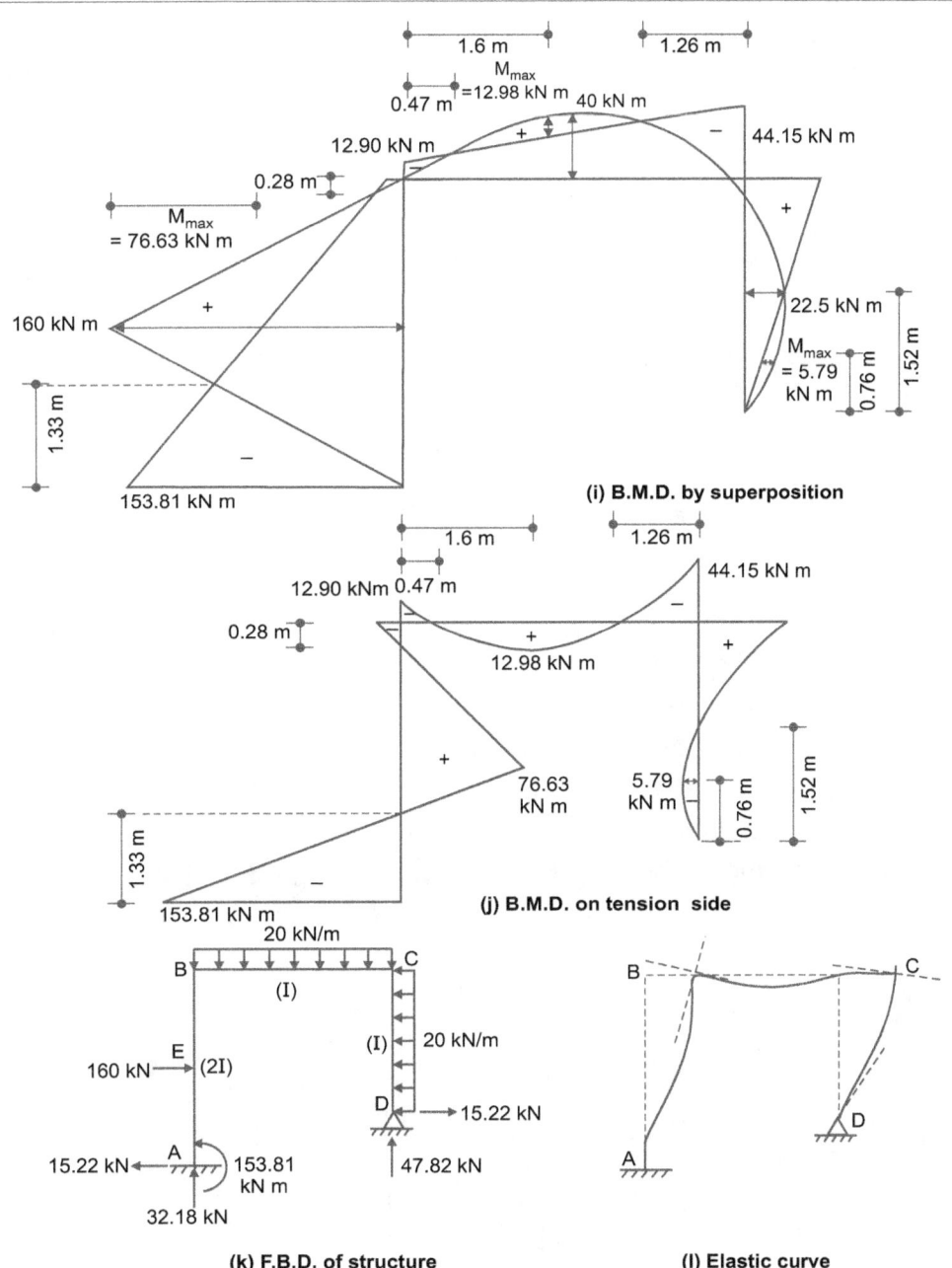

Fig. 4.13 : Illustrative Example 4.11

Step III : Restrained structure : The joints B, C and D are locked and the restrained structure is obtained as shown in Fig. 4.13 (b). Also restrained structure with unit values of D_1, D_2, D_3 and D_4 is shown in Fig. 4.13 (c), Fig. 4.13 (d), Fig. 4.13 (e), and Fig. 4.13 (f) respectively.

Step IV : Force analysis of restrained structure :

(a) Fixed end moments :

$$M^F_{AB} = -M^F_{BA} = \frac{wL}{8} = \frac{160 \times 4}{8} = 80 \text{ kNm}$$

$$M^F_{BC} = -M^F_{CB} = \frac{wL^2}{12} = \frac{20 \times 4^2}{12} = 26.67 \text{ kNm}$$

$$M^F_{CD} = -M^F_{DC} = \frac{wL^2}{12} = \frac{20 \times 3^2}{12} = 15.0 \text{ kNm}$$

(b) Forces in the restrained structure subjected to loads corresponding to unknown displacements.

$$A_{DL1} = M^F_{BA} + M^F_{BC} = -80 + 26.57 = -53.33 \text{ kNm}$$

$$A_{DL2} = M^F_{CB} + M^F_{CD} = -26.67 + 15 = -11.67 \text{ kNm}$$

$$A_{DL3} = M^F_{DC} = -15 \text{ kNm}$$

A_{DL4} = Algebraic sum of horizontal reaction components at B and C in the restrained structure subjected to loads = $-80 + 30 = -50$ kN.

(c) Forces in the restrained structure subjected to unit values of D_1, D_2, D_3 and D_4 corresponding to unknown displacements.

$$S_{11} = \left(\frac{4(2EI)}{L}\right)_{BA} + \left(\frac{4EI}{L}\right)_{BC} = \frac{8EI}{4} + \frac{4EI}{4} = 3EI$$

$$S_{21} = S_{12} = \left(\frac{2EI}{L}\right)_{CB} = \frac{2EI}{4} = 0.5EI$$

$$S_{31} = S_{13} = 0$$

$$S_{41} = S_{14} = \left(\frac{6(2EI)}{L^2}\right)_{AB} = \frac{6(2EI)}{4^2} = 0.75EI$$

$$S_{22} = \left(\frac{4EI}{L}\right)_{CB} + \left(\frac{4(EI)}{L}\right)_{CD} = \frac{4EI}{4} + \frac{4EI}{3} = 2.33EI$$

STRUCTURAL ANALYSIS – II   STIFFNESS METHOD

$$S_{32} = S_{23} = \left(\frac{2\,EI}{L}\right)_{DC} = \frac{2\,EI}{3} = 0.67\,EI$$

$$S_{42} = S_{24} + \left(\frac{6\,EI}{L^2}\right)_{CD} = \frac{6\,EI}{3^2} = 0.67\,EI$$

$$S_{33} = \left(\frac{4\,EI}{L}\right)_{DC} = \frac{4\,EI}{3} = 1.33\,EI$$

$$S_{43} = S_{34} = \left(\frac{6\,EI}{L^2}\right)_{CD} = \frac{6\,EI}{3^2} = 0.67\,EI$$

$$S_{44} = \left(\frac{12\,EI}{L^3}\right)_{AB} + \left(\frac{12\,EI}{L^3}\right)_{CD} = \frac{12\,(2\,EI)}{4^3} + \frac{12\,EI}{3^3} = 0.81\,EI$$

Step V : The equilibrium requirements of force :

There is no applied couple at B, C and D. $\therefore$ $A_{D1} = A_{D2} = A_{D3} = 0$

Also, there is no applied point load at B or C $\therefore$ $A_{D4} = 0$

Step VI : Superposition equation of equilibrium of forces :

$$\{A_D\} = \{A_{DL}\} + [S]\{D\}$$

i.e. $\begin{Bmatrix} 0 \\ 0 \\ 0 \\ 0 \end{Bmatrix} = \begin{Bmatrix} -53.33 \\ -11.67 \\ -15 \\ -50 \end{Bmatrix} + EI \begin{bmatrix} 3 & 0.5 & 0 & 0.75 \\ 0.5 & 2.33 & 0.67 & 0.67 \\ 0 & 0.67 & 1.33 & 0.67 \\ 0.75 & 0.67 & 0.67 & 0.81 \end{bmatrix} \begin{Bmatrix} D_1 \\ D_2 \\ D_3 \\ D_4 \end{Bmatrix}$

i.e. $0 = -53.33 + (3\,EI)\,D_1 + (0.5\,EI)\,D_2 + (0)\,D_3 + (0.75\,EI)\,D_4$ ... (A)

$0 = -11.67 + (0.5\,EI)\,D_1 + (2.33\,EI)\,D_2 + (0.67\,EI)\,D_3 + (0.67\,EI)\,D_4$ ... (B)

$0 = -15 + (0)\,D_1 + (0.67\,EI)\,D_2 + (1.33\,EI)\,D_3 + (0.67\,EI)\,D_4$ ... (C)

$0 = -50 + (0.75\,EI)\,D_1 + (0.67\,EI)\,D_2 + (0.67\,EI)\,D_3 + (0.81\,EI)\,D_4$ ... (D)

Step VII : Solution of equations for unknown displacements : Solving equations (A), (B), (C) and (D), we get

$$D_1 = \theta_B = \frac{-6.70}{EI} = \frac{6.70}{EI}\ (\circlearrowleft)$$

$$D_2 = \theta_C = \frac{-14.128}{EI} = \frac{14.128}{EI}\ (\circlearrowleft)$$

Ch. 4 | 4.57

$$D_3 = \theta_D = \frac{-35.37}{EI} = \frac{35.37}{EI} \; (\circlearrowleft)$$

$$D_4 = \Delta = \frac{107.35}{EI} = \frac{107.35}{EI} \; (\rightarrow)$$

Step VIII : Other forces :

$$M_{AB} = \frac{4\,(2\,EI)}{4}(0) + \frac{2\,(2\,EI)}{4}\left(\frac{-6.70}{EI}\right) + \frac{6\,(2\,EI)}{4^2}\left(\frac{+107.35}{EI}\right) + 80 = 153.81 \text{ kNm}$$

$$M_{BA} = \frac{4\,(2\,EI)}{4}\left(\frac{-6.70}{EI}\right) + \frac{2\,(2\,EI)}{4}(0) + \frac{6\,(2\,EI)}{4^2}\left(\frac{107.35}{EI}\right) - 80 = -12.90 \text{ kNm}$$

$$M_{BC} = \frac{4\,EI}{4}\left(\frac{-6.70}{EI}\right) + \frac{2\,EI}{4}\left(\frac{-14.128}{EI}\right) + 26.66 = 12.90 \text{ kNm}$$

$$M_{CB} = \frac{4\,EI}{4}\left(\frac{-14.128}{EI}\right) + \frac{2\,EI}{4}\left(\frac{-6.70}{EI}\right) - 26.66 = -44.14 \text{ kNm}$$

$$M_{CD} = \frac{4\,EI}{3}\left(\frac{-14.128}{EI}\right) + \frac{2\,EI}{3}\left(\frac{-35.37}{EI}\right) + \frac{6\,EI}{3^2}\left(\frac{107.35}{EI}\right) + 15 = 44.14 \text{ kNm}$$

$$M_{DC} = \frac{4\,EI}{3}\left(\frac{-35.37}{EI}\right) + \frac{2\,EI}{3}\left(\frac{-14.128}{EI}\right) + \frac{6\,EI}{3^2} - 15 = 0 \text{ kNm}$$

FBD of members is as shown in Fig. 4.13 (g).

Considering equilibrium of each member and of complete structure all the reaction components are found out as shown in figure.

Step IX : Shear force and bending moment diagrams : SFD is shown in Fig. 4.13 (h).

BMD by superposition and on tension side is as shown in Fig. 4.13 (i) and 4.13 (j) respectively.

Step X : FBD of structure : as shown in Fig. 4.13 (k).

Step XI : Elastic curve : as shown in Fig. 4.13 (l).

Example 4.12 : *Analyse the frame shown in Fig. 4.14 (a) by stiffness method. Take EI = Constant.*

Solution : Data : The frame is supported and loaded as shown in Fig. 4.14 (a).

Object : Structural analysis.

Concepts and equations :

(1) Kinematically determinate structure (Restrained structure).

STRUCTURAL ANALYSIS – II   STIFFNESS METHOD

(2) Force analysis of restrained structure.

(3) Superposition equations of equilibrium of forces.

Procedure :

Step I : Degree of kinematic indeterminacy (D_{ki}) :

Degree of kinematic indeterminacy = D_{ki} = 3.

Step II : Unknown joint displacements (D) :

Let, $D_1 = \theta_B$ (↻), $D_2 = \theta_C$ (↻) and $D_3 = \Delta$ (→)

Step III : Restrained structure : The joints B and C are locked and the restrained structure is obtained as shown in Fig. 4.14 (b). Also restrained structure with unit values of D_1, D_2 and D_3 is shown in Fig. 4.14 (c), Fig. 4.14 (d) and Fig. 4.14 (e) respectively.

Step IV : Force analysis of restrained structure :

(a) Fixed end moments :

$$M_{AB}^F = -M_{BA}^F = \frac{wL^2}{12} = \frac{25 \times 4^2}{12} = 33.33 \text{ kNm}$$

$$M_{BC}^F = -M_{CB}^F = \frac{wL}{8} = \frac{50 \times 3}{8} = 18.75 \text{ kNm}$$

$$M_{CD}^F = \frac{Wab^2}{L^2} = \frac{40 \times 2 \times 1^2}{3^2} = 8.88 \text{ kNm}$$

$$M_{DC}^F = -\frac{Wab^2}{L^2} = \frac{40 \times 1 \times 2^2}{3^2} = -17.77 \text{ kNm}$$

(b) Forces in the restrained structure subjected to loads corresponding to unknown displacements :

$$A_{DL1} = M_{BA}^F + M_{BC}^F = -33.33 + 18.75 = -14.58 \text{ kNm}$$

$$A_{DL2} = M_{CB}^F + M_{CD}^F = -18.75 + 8.88 = -9.87 \text{ kNm}$$

A_{DL3} = Algebraic sum of horizontal reaction component at B and C in the restrained structure subjected to loads = $-50 + 10.37 = -39.63$ kN

(c) Forces in the restrained structure subjected to unit values of D_1, D_2 and D_3 corresponding to unknown displacements.

$$S_{11} = \left(\frac{4EI}{L}\right)_{BA} + \left(\frac{4EI}{L}\right)_{BC} = \frac{4EI}{4} + \frac{4EI}{3} = 2.33 \text{ EI}$$

$$S_{21} = S_{12} = \left(\frac{2EI}{L}\right)_{CB} = \frac{2EI}{3} = 0.67\ EI$$

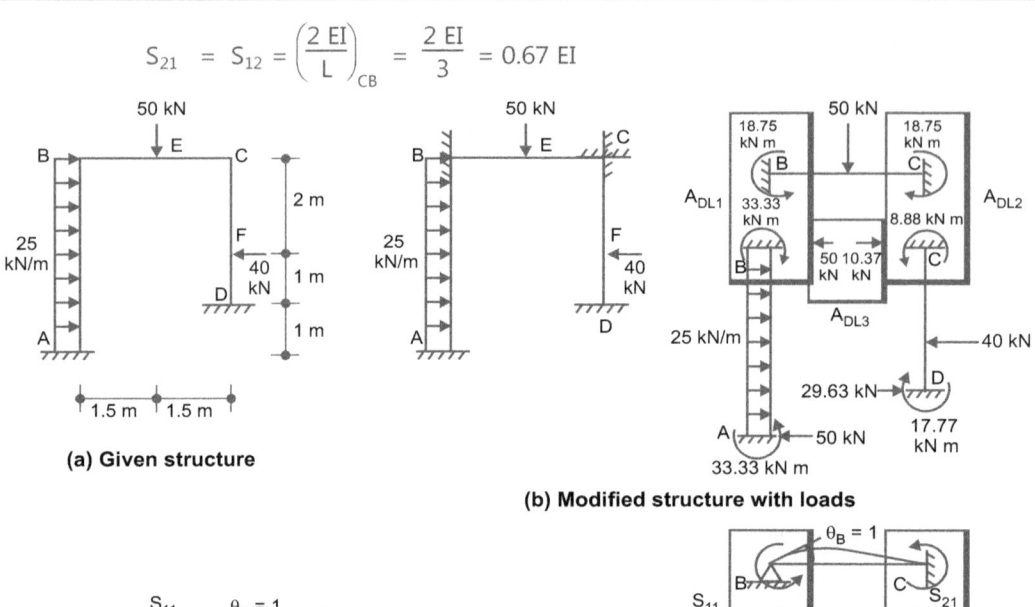

(a) Given structure

(b) Modified structure with loads

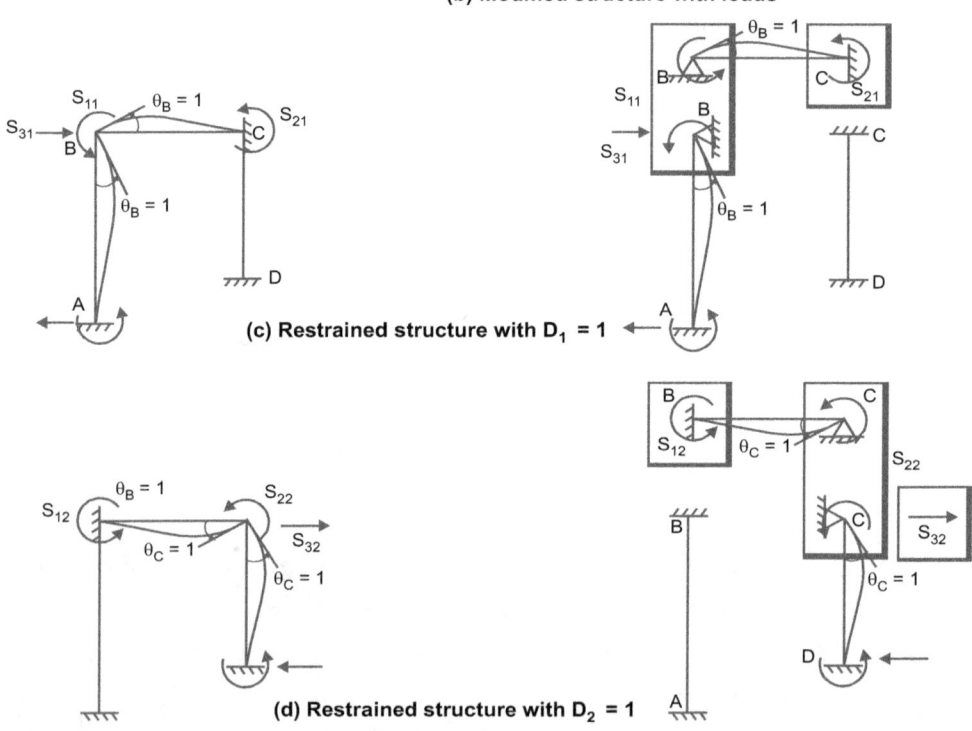

(c) Restrained structure with $D_1 = 1$

(d) Restrained structure with $D_2 = 1$

Fig. 4.14 : (Contd. ...)

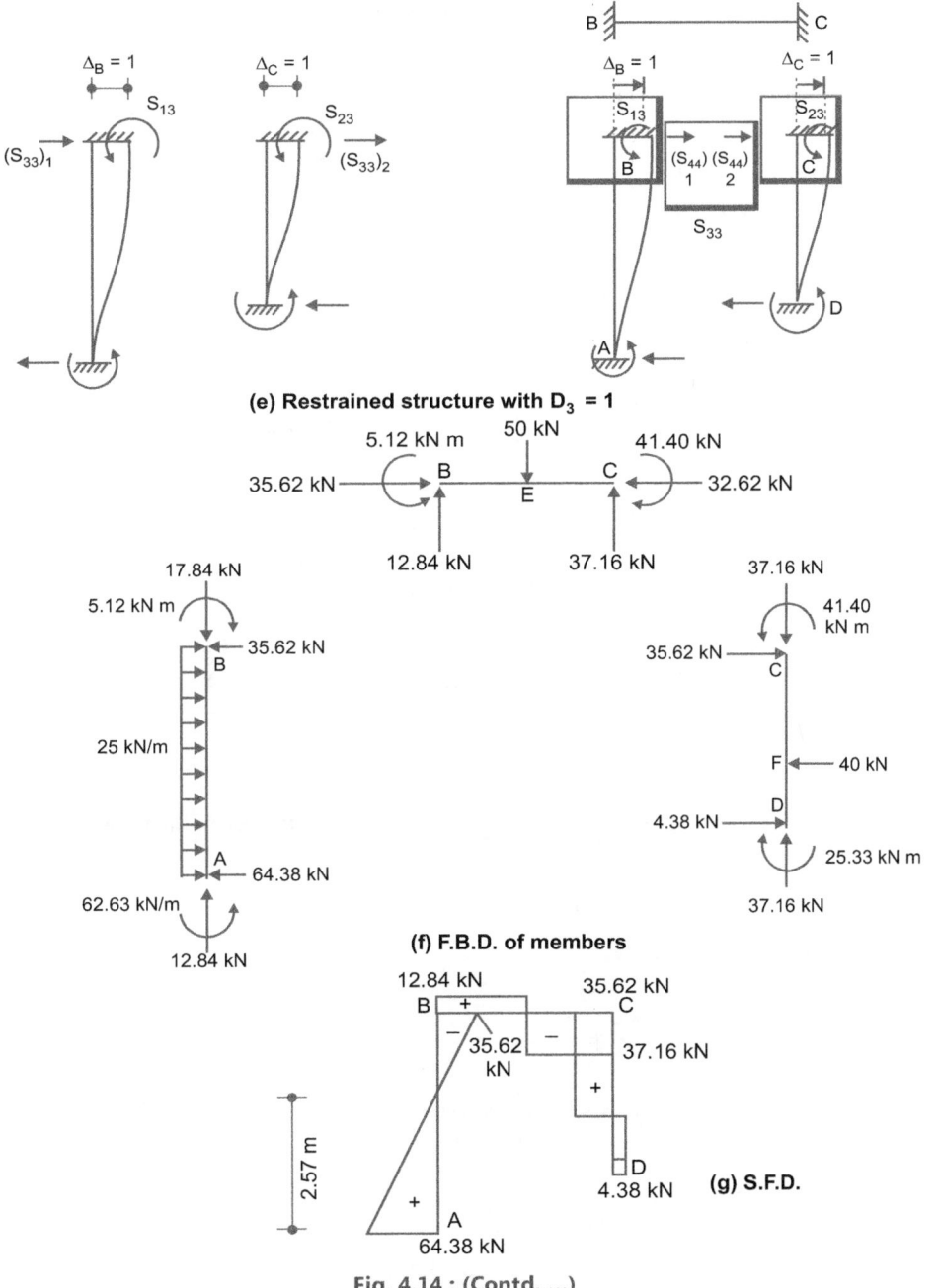

Fig. 4.14 : (Contd. ...)

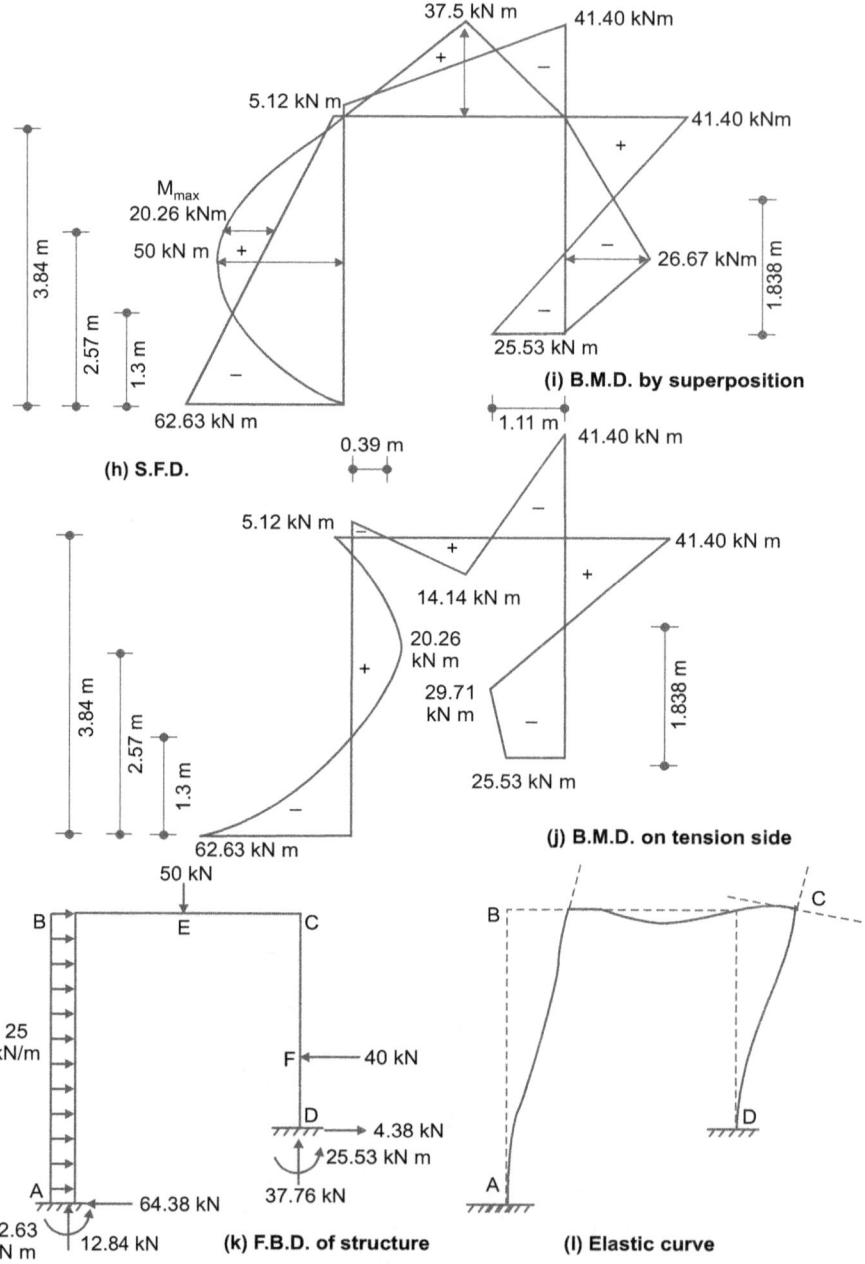

Fig. 4.14 : Illustrative Example 4.12

STRUCTURAL ANALYSIS – II   STIFFNESS METHOD

$$S_{31} = S_{13} = \left(\frac{6\,EI}{L^2}\right)_{AB} = \frac{6\,EI}{4^2} = 0.375\,EI$$

$$S_{22} = \left(\frac{4\,EI}{L}\right)_{CB} + \left(\frac{4\,EI}{L}\right)_{CD} = \frac{4\,EI}{3} + \frac{4\,EI}{3} = 2.67\,EI$$

$$S_{32} = S_{23} = \left(\frac{6\,EI}{L^2}\right)_{DC} = \frac{6\,EI}{3^2} = 0.67\,EI$$

$$S_{33} = \left(\frac{12\,EI}{L^3}\right)_{AB} + \left(\frac{12\,EI}{L^3}\right) = \frac{12\,EI}{4^3} + \frac{12\,EI}{3^3} = 0.63\,EI$$

Step V : The equilibrium requirements of force : There is no applied couple at B and C.

∴ $A_{D1} = A_{D2} = 0$

Also, there is no applied point load at B or C ∴ $A_{D3} = 0$.

Step VI : Superposition equation of equilibrium of forces :

$$\{A_D\} = \{A_{DL}\} + [S]\{D\}$$

i.e.
$$\begin{Bmatrix} 0 \\ 0 \\ 0 \end{Bmatrix} = \begin{Bmatrix} -14.58 \\ -09.87 \\ -39.63 \end{Bmatrix} + EI \begin{bmatrix} 2.33 & 0.67 & 0.375 \\ 0.67 & 2.67 & 0.67 \\ 0.375 & 0.67 & 0.63 \end{bmatrix} \begin{Bmatrix} D_1 \\ D_2 \\ D_3 \end{Bmatrix}$$

i.e. $0 = -14.58 + (2.33\,EI)\,D_1 + (0.67\,EI)\,D_2 + (0.375\,EI)\,D_3$ ... (A)

$0 = -9.87 + (0.67\,EI)\,D_1 + (2.67\,EI)\,D_2 + (0.67\,EI)\,D_3$ ... (B)

$0 = -39.63 + (0.375\,EI)\,D_1 + (0.67\,EI)\,D_2 + (0.63\,EI)\,D_3$ ...(C)

Step VII : Solution of equations for unknown displacements : Solving equations (A) and (B) and (C), we get

$$D_1 = \theta_B = \frac{-2.18}{EI} = \frac{2.18}{EI}\,(\circlearrowleft)$$

$$D_2 = \theta_C = \frac{-16.08}{EI} = \frac{16.08}{E}\,(\circlearrowleft)$$

$$D_3 = \Delta = \frac{81.04}{EI} = \frac{81.04}{EI}\,(\rightarrow)$$

Step VIII : Other forces :

$$M_{AB} = \frac{4\,EI}{4}(0) + \frac{2\,EI}{4}\left(\frac{-2.18}{EI}\right) + \frac{6\,EI}{4^2}\left(\frac{81.04}{EI}\right) + 33.33 = 62.63\text{ kNm}$$

$$M_{BA} = \frac{4\,EI}{4}\left(\frac{-2.18}{EI}\right) + \frac{2\,EI}{4}(0) + \frac{6\,EI}{4^2}\left(\frac{81.04}{EI}\right) - 33.33 = -5.12\text{ kNm}$$

STRUCTURAL ANALYSIS – II   STIFFNESS METHOD

$$M_{BC} = \frac{4EI}{3}\left(\frac{-2.18}{EI}\right) + \frac{2EI}{3}\left(\frac{-16.08}{EI}\right) + 18.75 = 5.12 \text{ kNm}$$

$$M_{CB} = \frac{4EI}{3}\left(\frac{-16.08}{E}\right) + \frac{2EI}{3}\left(-\frac{2.18}{EI}\right) - 18.75 = -41.40 \text{ kNm}$$

$$M_{CD} = \frac{4EI}{3}\left(-\frac{16.08}{EI}\right) + \frac{2EI}{3}(0) + \frac{6EI}{3^2}\left(\frac{81.04}{EI}\right) - 17.77 = 41.40 \text{ kNm}$$

$$M_{DC} = \frac{4EI}{3}(0) + \frac{2EI}{3}\left(\frac{-16.08}{EI}\right) + \frac{6EI}{3^2}\left(\frac{81.04}{EI}\right) + 8.88 = 25.53 \text{ kNm}$$

FBD of members is as shown in Fig. 4.14 (f). Considering equilibrium of each member and of complete structure all the reaction components are found out as shown in figure.

Step IX : Shear force and bending moment diagrams :

SFD is shown in Fig. 4.14 (g). BMD by superposition and on tension side is as shown in Fig. 4.14 (h) and (4.14) (i) respectively.

Step X : FBD of structure : as shown in Fig. 4.14 (j).

Step XI : Elastic curve : as shown in Fig. 4.14 (k).

Example 4.13 : *Analyse the portal frame as shown in Fig. 4.15 by stiffness method. Take EI = constant.*

Solution : Data : The frame is loaded and supported as shown in Fig. 4.15 (a)

Object : Structural analysis.

Concepts and Equations :

(1) Kinematically determinate structure. (Restrained structure).

(2) Force analysis of restrained structure.

(3) Superposition equations of equilibrium of forces.

Procedure : Step I : Degree of kinematic indeterminacy (D_{ki}) :

Degree of kinematic indeterminacy = D_{ki} = 2.

Step II : Unknown joint displacements (D) :

$D_1 = \theta_C$ (↻) and $D_2 = \theta_C$ (↻), $D_3 = \delta_C$ (→)

Step III : Restrained Structure : The joints B and C are locked and the restrained structure is obtained as shown in Fig. 4.15 (b). Also restrained structure with unit values of D_1, D_2 and D_3 is as shown in Fig. 4.15 (c), (d) respectively.

Step IV : Force analysis of restrained structure.

STRUCTURAL ANALYSIS – II
STIFFNESS METHOD

(a) Fixed end moments :

$$M^F_{AB} = -M^F_{BA} = \frac{wL^2}{12} = \frac{20 \times 4.8^2}{12} = 38.4 \text{ kNm}$$

$$M^F_{BC} = -M^F_{CB} = 0$$

(b) Forces in the restrained structure subjected to loads corresponding to unknown displacements :

$$A_{DL1} = M_{FBA} + M_{FBC} = -38.4 + 0$$
$$= -38.4 \text{ kN-m}$$

$$A_{DL2} = M_{FCB} = 0$$

A_{DL3} = Algebric sum of horizontal reaction components at B and C respectively in the restrained structure subjected to loads.

$$= -48 \text{ kN}$$

(c) Forces in the restrained structure subjected to unit values of D_1, D_2 and D_3 corresponding to unknown displacements :

$$S_{11} = \left(\frac{4EI}{L}\right)_{BA} + \left(\frac{4(2EI)}{L}\right)_{BC} = \frac{4EI}{4.8} + \frac{8EI}{2.4}$$

$$= 0.83 \text{ EI} + 3.33 \text{ EI} = 4.16 \text{ EI}$$

$$S_{21} = S_{12} = \left(\frac{2(2EI)}{L}\right)_{CB} = \frac{4EI}{2.4} = 1.67 \text{ EI}$$

$$S_{31} = S_{13} = \left(\frac{6\,EI}{L^2}\right)_{AB} = \frac{6EI}{(4.8)^2} = 0.26$$

$$S_{22} = \left(\frac{4(2EI)}{L}\right)_{CB} = \frac{8EI}{2.4} = 3.33 \text{ EI}$$

$$S_{23} = S_{32} = 0$$

$$S_{33} = \left(\frac{12(EI)}{L^3}\right)_{AB} = \frac{12EI}{(4.8)^3} = 0.11 \text{ EI}$$

Step V : The equilibrium requirement of force :

There is no applied couple at B and C. $A_{D1} = A_{D2} = 0$, there is no applied point load at B.

∴ $\quad A_{D3} = 0$

Step VI : Superposition equation of equilibrium of forces :

$$\{A_D\} = \{A_{DL}\} + [S]\{D\}$$

Ch. 4 | 4.65

STRUCTURAL ANALYSIS – II

STIFFNESS METHOD

$$\begin{Bmatrix} 0 \\ 0 \\ 0 \end{Bmatrix} = \begin{Bmatrix} -38.4 \\ 0 \\ -48 \end{Bmatrix} + EI \begin{bmatrix} 4.16 & 1.67 & 0.26 \\ 1.67 & 3.33 & 0 \\ 0.26 & 0 & 0.11 \end{bmatrix} \begin{Bmatrix} D_1 \\ D_2 \\ D_3 \end{Bmatrix}$$

i.e.
$$0 = -38.4 + (4.16\ EI)\ D_1 + (1.67\ EI)\ D_2 + (0.26\ EI)\ D_3 \quad ...(A)$$
$$0 = 0 + (1.67\ EI)\ D_1 + (3.33\ EI)\ D_2 + (0\ EI)\ D_3 \quad ...(B)$$
$$0 = -48 + (0.26\ EI)\ D_1 + (0\ EI)\ D_2 + (0.11\ EI)\ D_3 \quad ...(C)$$

Step VII : Solution of equations for unknown displacements : Solving equations (A), (B) and (C) we get,

$$D_1 = \theta_B = -\frac{28.35}{EI} = \frac{28.35}{EI} \ (\circlearrowleft)$$

$$D_2 = \theta_C = \frac{14.18}{EI} \ (\circlearrowleft)$$

$$D_3 = \delta_C = \frac{510.42}{EI} \ (\rightarrow)$$

Step VIII : Other forces :

$$M_{AB} = \frac{4\ EI}{4.8}(0) + \frac{2EI}{4.8}\left(\frac{-28.61}{EI}\right) + \frac{6EI}{(4.8)^2}\left(\frac{510.42}{EI}\right) + 38.4$$

$$= 159.50 \text{ kN-m}$$

$$M_{BA} = \frac{4EI(-28.35)}{4.8\ EI} + \frac{2EI(0)}{4.8} + \frac{6EI}{(4.8)^2}\left(\frac{510.42}{EI}\right) - 38.4$$

$$= 709 \text{ kN-m}$$

$$M_{BC} = \frac{4(2EI)(-28.35)}{2.4\ EI} + \frac{2(2EI)}{2.4}\left(\frac{14.18}{EI}\right) = 0$$

$$= -70.90 \text{ kNm}$$

$$M_{CB} = \frac{2(2EI)(-28.35)}{2.4\ EI} + \frac{4(2EI)}{2.4}\left(\frac{14.18}{EI}\right) = 0$$

FBD of members is an shown in Fig. 4.15.

Considering equilibrium of each member and of complete structure all the reaction components are found out as shown in Fig. 4.15.

Step IX : Shear force and bending moment diagrams.

SFD is as shown in Fig. 4.15 (g).

BMD by superposition and on tension side is as shown in Fig. 4.15 (h) and Fig. 4.15 (i) respectively.

Step X : FBD of structure is as shown in Fig. 4.15 (j).

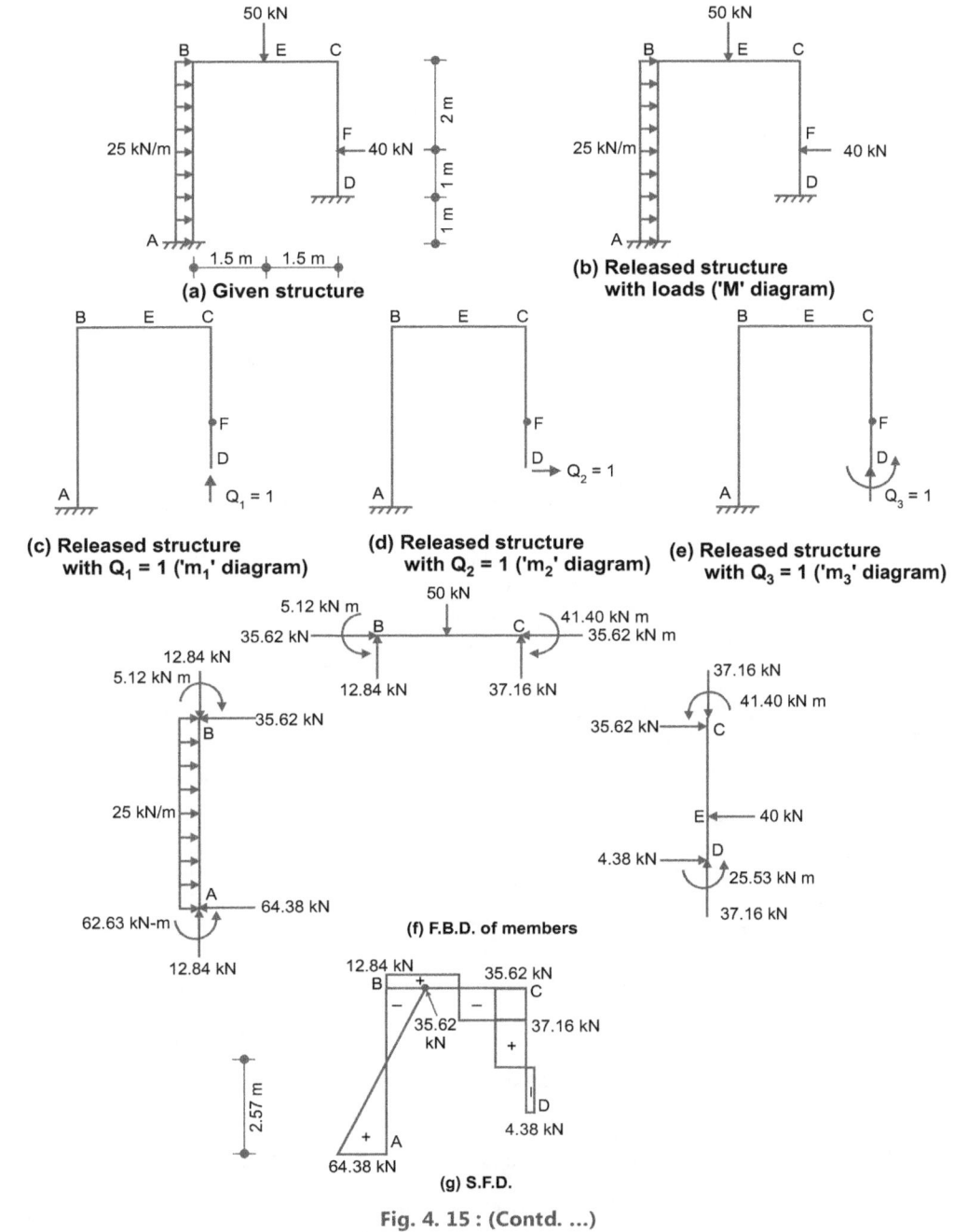

Fig. 4. 15 : (Contd. ...)

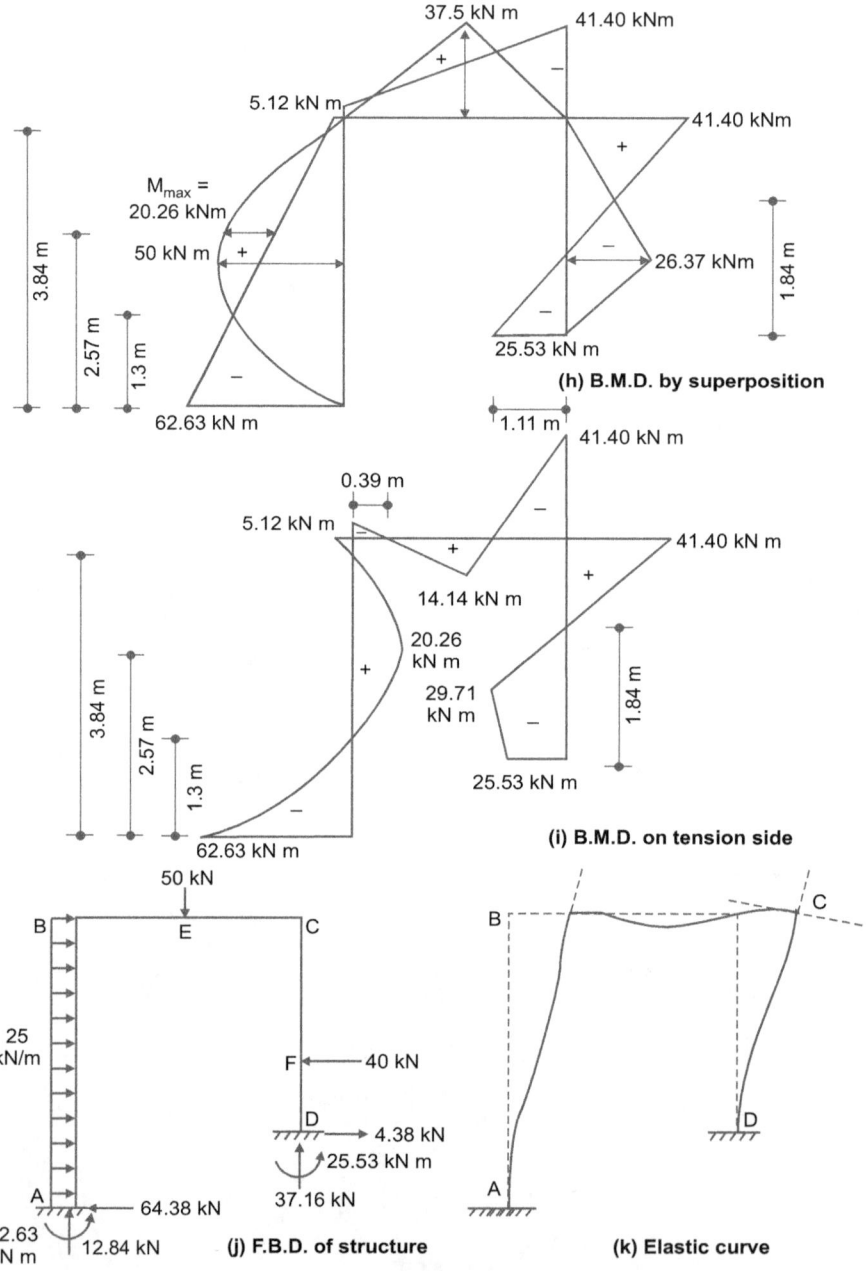

Fig. 4.15 : Illustrative Example 4.13

4.6 COMPARISON OF FLEXIBILITY AND STIFFNESS METHODS

The two methods of structural analysis show striking similarities with respect to the parallel steps in the procedure of solution of a problem. Yet there are also striking differences in the two approaches. The brief comparison between the two methods, given below, clarifies the logic and technique.

Table 4.1

	Flexibility Method		Stiffness Method
1.	Degree of static indeterminacy.	1.	Degree of kinematic indeterminacy.
2.	Unknown redundant forces {Q}.	2.	Unknown joint displacements {D}.
3.	Static admissibility.	3.	Kinematic admissibility.
4.	Equilibrium indirectly satisfied.	4.	Compatibility indirectly satisfied.
5.	Known joint displacement corresponding to {Q} = {D_Q}.	5.	Known joint forces corresponding to D = {A_D}.
6.	Statically determinate structure (SD) i.e. released structure.	6.	Kinematically determinate (KD) structure i.e. restrained structure.
7.	Displacement analysis of SD structure under given loads corresponding to {Q} = {D_{QL}}.	7.	Force analysis of KS structure under given loads corresponding to {D} = {A_{DL}}.
8.	Flexibility coefficient F_{ij} displacement at i due to unit force at j.	8.	Stiffness coefficients – S_{ij} force at i due to unit displacement at j.
9.	Flexibility matrix of the structure [F].	9.	Stiffness matrix of the structure [S].
10.	Superposition equations in terms of displacements as per compatibility conditions of joints.	10.	Superposition equations in terms of forces as per equilibrium conditions of joints.
11.	Linear simultaneous equations {D_Q} = {D_{QL}} + [F] {Q}	11.	Linear simultaneous equations {A_D} = {A_{DL}} + [S] {Q}.
12.	Solution of equations for unknown redundant forces.	12.	Solution of equations for unknown joint displacement.
13.	Choice of {Q} is not unique.	13.	Choice of {D} is unique.
14.	Displacement analysis of SD structure is not simple with respect to {D_{QL}} and [F].	14.	Force analysis of KD structure is simple with respect to {A_{DL}} and [S].
15.	More physics.	15.	More mechanical.
16.	Not well disciplined.	16.	Very well disciplined.
17.	Not suitable to computer programming.	17.	Very much suitable to computer programming.
18.	Complex in case of analysis of continum.	18.	Well extended to analysis of continuum.

EXERCISE

Analyse the following beams and frames using Flexibility matrix, Stiffness matrix, Slope Deflection, Moment distribution and Energy methods. Draw SFD, BMD and elastic curve.

1.

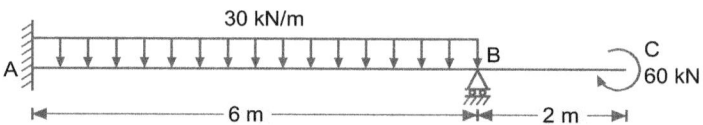

Fig. 4.15

(**Ans.** $M_A = -105$ kNm; $M_B = -60$ kNm)

2.

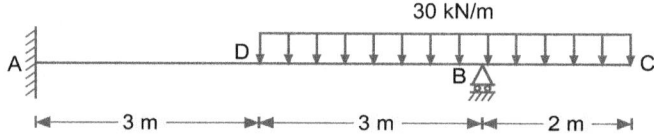

Fig. 4.16

(**Ans.** $M_A = -29.04$ kNm; $M_B = -60$ kNm)

3.

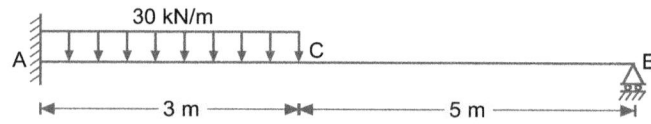

Fig. 4.17

(**Ans.** $M_A = -89.16$ kNm; $M_B = 0$)

4.

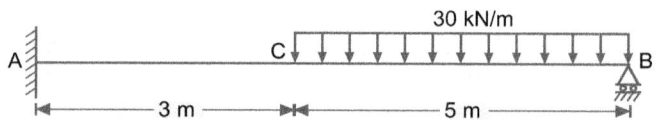

Fig. 4.18

(**Ans.** $M_A = -150.5$ kNm; $M_B = 0$)

5.

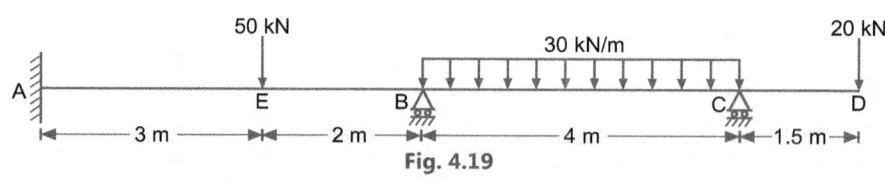

Fig. 4.19

(**Ans.** $M_A = -21.7$ kNm; $M_B = -40.6$ kNm; $M_C = -30$ kNm)

STRUCTURAL ANALYSIS – II   STIFFNESS METHOD

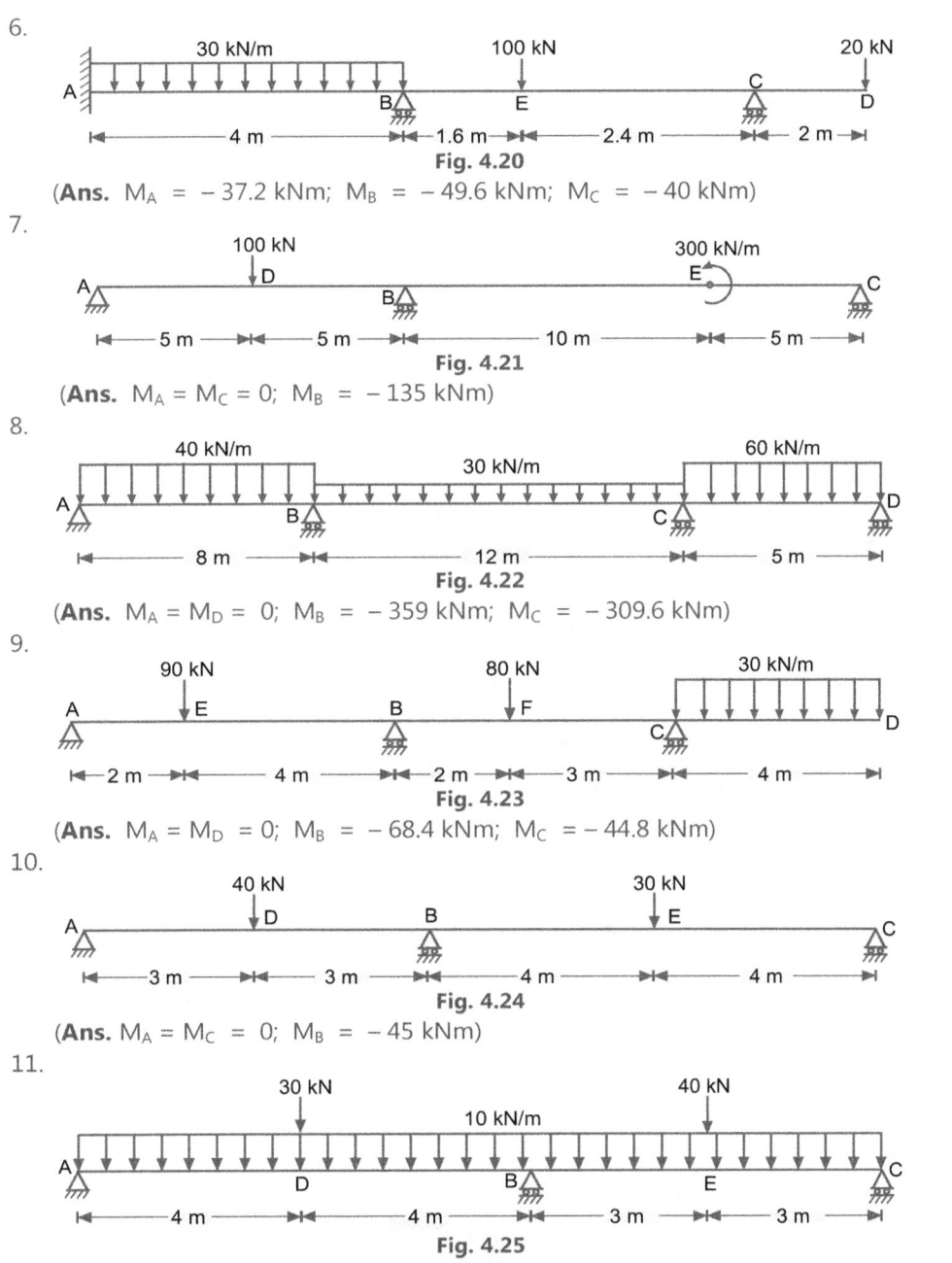

6.
Fig. 4.20
(**Ans.** $M_A = -37.2$ kNm; $M_B = -49.6$ kNm; $M_C = -40$ kNm)

7.
Fig. 4.21
(**Ans.** $M_A = M_C = 0$; $M_B = -135$ kNm)

8.
Fig. 4.22
(**Ans.** $M_A = M_D = 0$; $M_B = -359$ kNm; $M_C = -309.6$ kNm)

9.
Fig. 4.23
(**Ans.** $M_A = M_D = 0$; $M_B = -68.4$ kNm; $M_C = -44.8$ kNm)

10.
Fig. 4.24
(**Ans.** $M_A = M_C = 0$; $M_B = -45$ kNm)

11.
Fig. 4.25
(**Ans.** $M_A = M_C = 0$; $M_B = -110$ kNm)

Ch. 4 | 4.71

12.

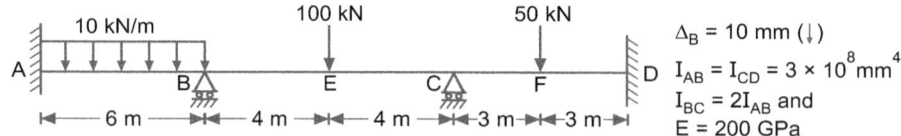

Fig. 4.26

(**Ans.** $M_A = -57.4$ kNm; $M_B = -25.7$ kNm, $M_C = -92$ kNm; $M_D = -20.7$ kNm)

13.

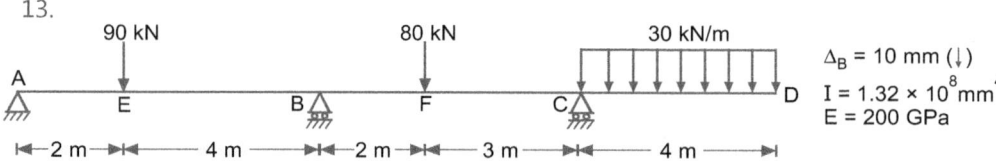

Fig. 4.27

(**Ans.** $M_A = M_D = 0$; $M_B = -35.87$ kNm, $M_C = -71.56$ kNm)

14.

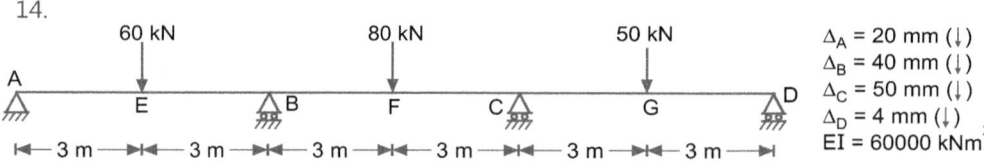

Fig. 4.28

(**Ans.** $M_A = M_D = 0$; $M_B = -68.5$ kNm, $M_C = 59$ kNm)

15.

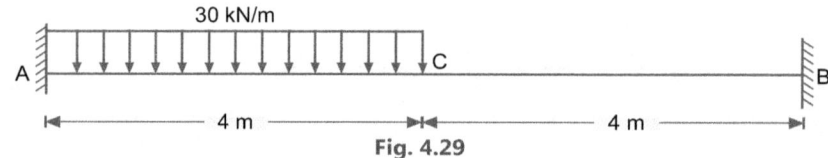

Fig. 4.29

(**Ans.** $M_A = -60$ kNm; $M_B = -180$ kNm; $M_C = 0$)

16.

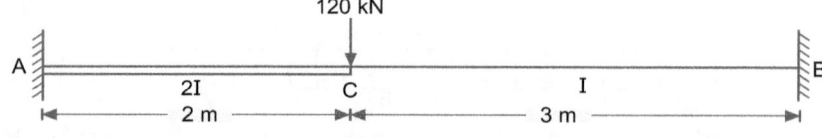

Fig. 4.30

(**Ans.** $M_A = -105.22$ kNm; $M_B = -47.45$ kNm)

17.

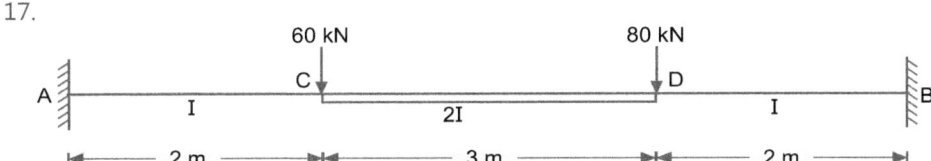

Fig. 4.31

(**Ans.** $M_A = -79.49$ kNm; $M_B = -98.68$ kNm)

18.

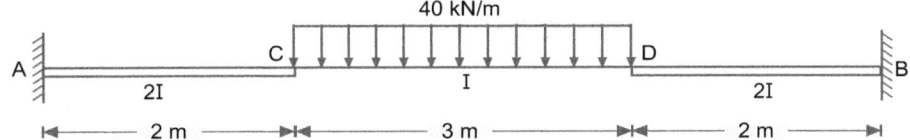

Fig. 4.32

(**Ans.** $M_A = M_B = -114$ kNm)

19.

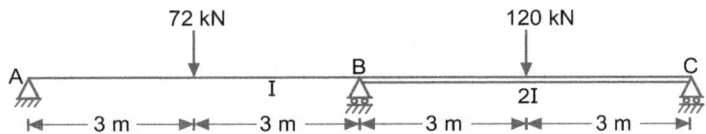

Fig. 4.33

(**Ans.** $M_B = -99$ kNm)

20.

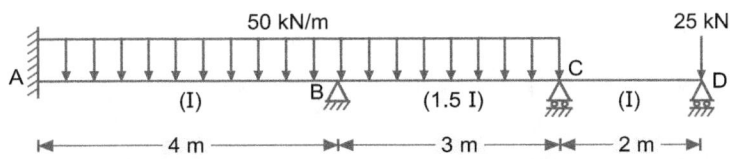

Fig. 4.34

(**Ans.** $M_A = -53.75$ kNm; $M_B = -52.5$ kNm; $M_C = -50$ kNm)

21.

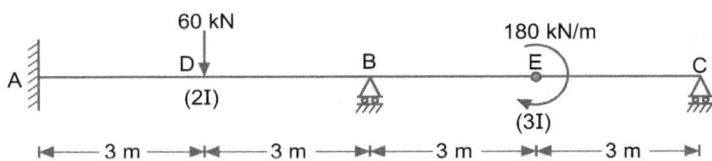

Fig. 4.35

(**Ans.** $M_A = -60.88$ kNm; $M_B = -13.24$ kNm; $M_C = 50$ kNm)

STRUCTURAL ANALYSIS – II STIFFNESS METHOD

22.

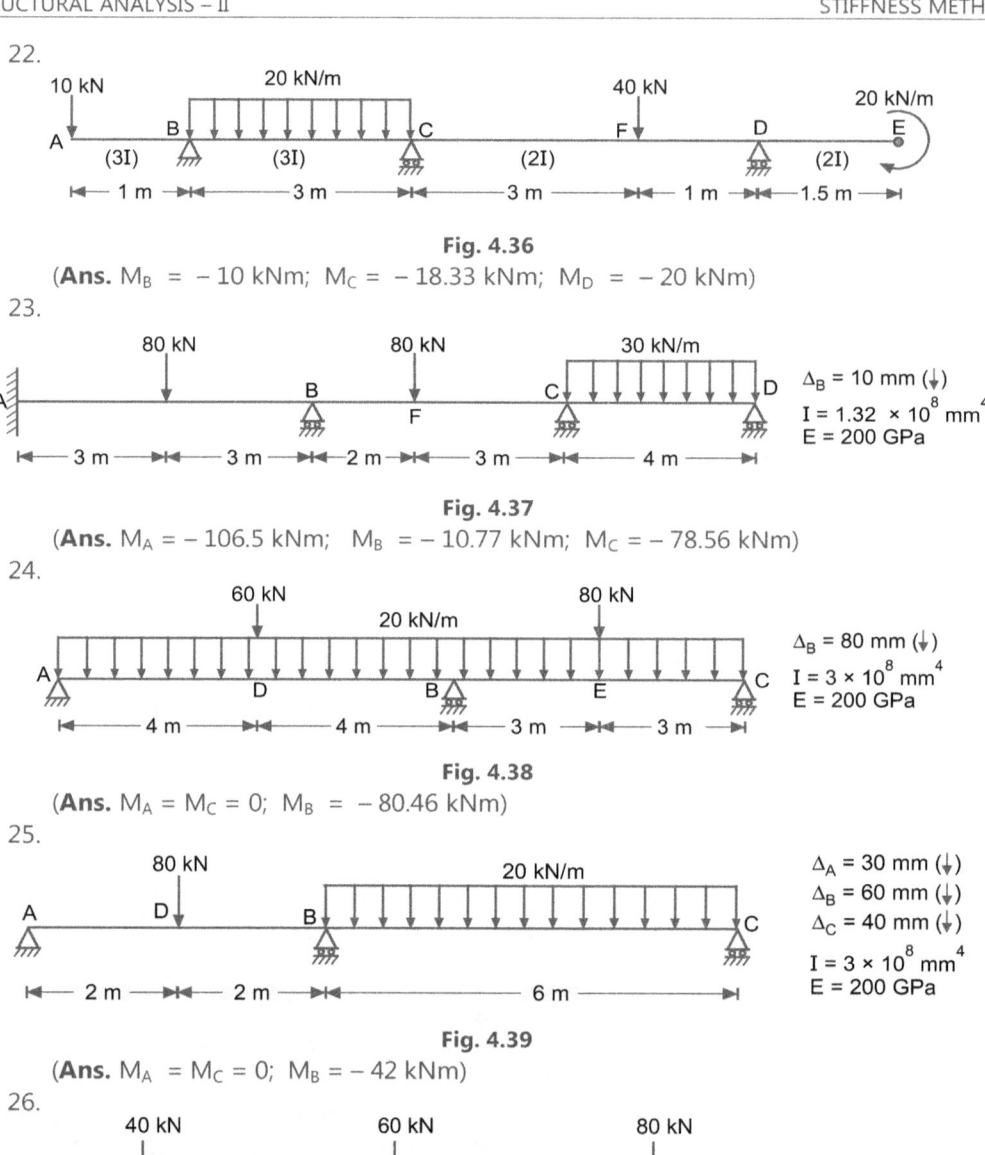

Fig. 4.36

(**Ans.** $M_B = -10$ kNm; $M_C = -18.33$ kNm; $M_D = -20$ kNm)

23.

Fig. 4.37

(**Ans.** $M_A = -106.5$ kNm; $M_B = -10.77$ kNm; $M_C = -78.56$ kNm)

24.

Fig. 4.38

(**Ans.** $M_A = M_C = 0$; $M_B = -80.46$ kNm)

25.

Fig. 4.39

(**Ans.** $M_A = M_C = 0$; $M_B = -42$ kNm)

26.

Fig. 4.40

(**Ans.** $M_A = M_D = 0$; $M_B = -203$ kNm; $M_C = +227$ kNm)

27.

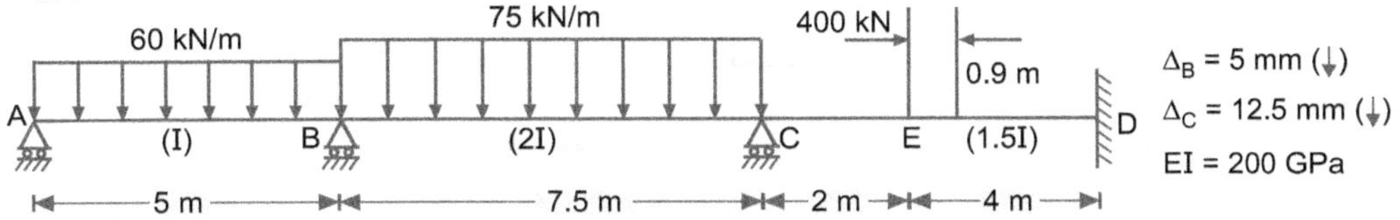

Fig. 4.41

(**Ans.** $M_A = 0$; $M_B = -226.1$ kNm; $M_C = -191.7$ kNm; $M_D = -42$ kNm)

28.

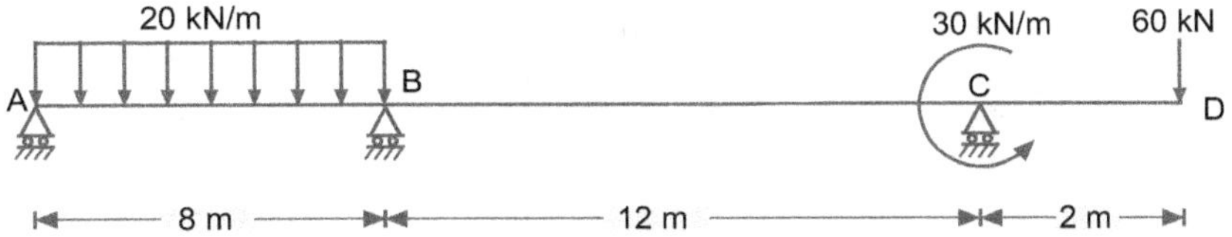

Fig. 4.42

(**Ans.** $M_A = -157$ kNm; $M_B = -5$ kNm; $M_{CD} = 120$ kNm; $M_{CB} = 90$ kNm)

29.

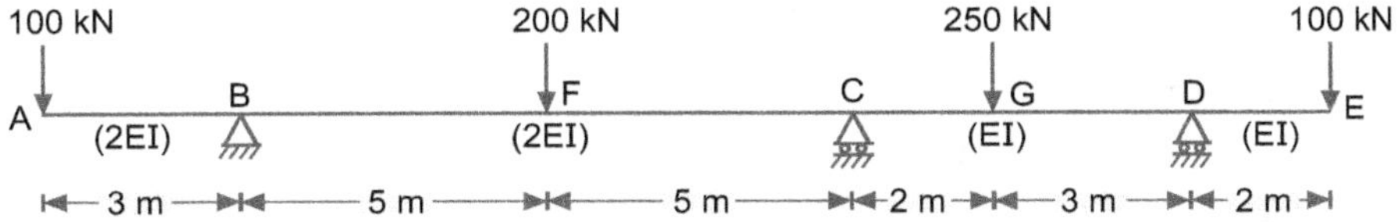

Fig. 4.43

(**Ans.** $M_B = -300$ kNm; $M_C = -182$ kNm; $M_D = -200$ kNm)

30.

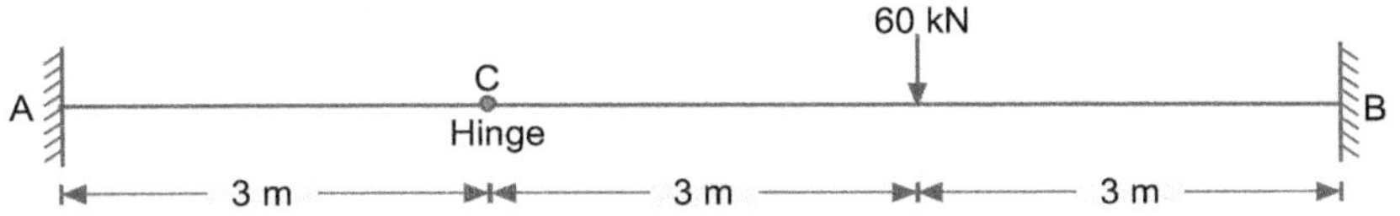

Fig. 4.44

(**Ans.** $M_A = -42.24$ kNm; $M_B = -78.05$ kNm)

31.

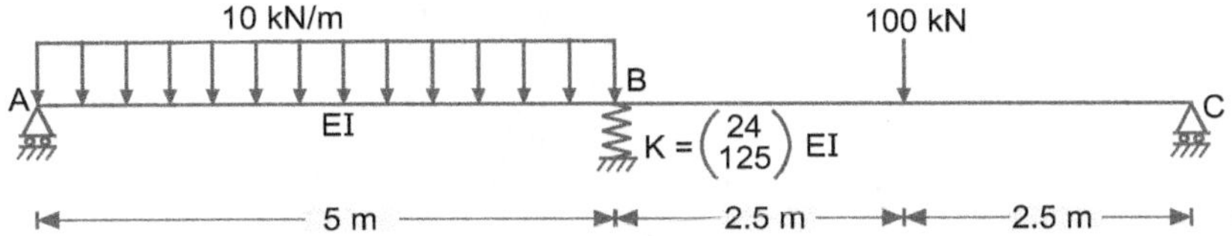

Fig. 4.45

(**Ans.** $M_B = -12.5$ kNm)

32.

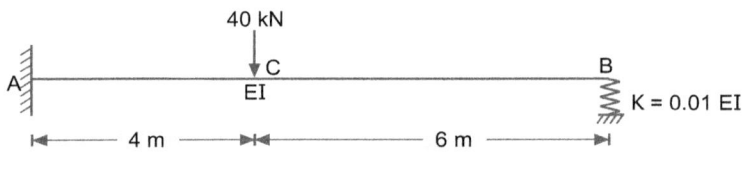

Fig. 4.46

(**Ans.** $M_A = -96$ kNm)

33.

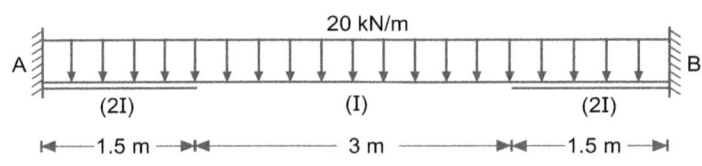

Fig. 4.47

(**Ans.** $M_A = M_B = -67.5$ kNm)

34.

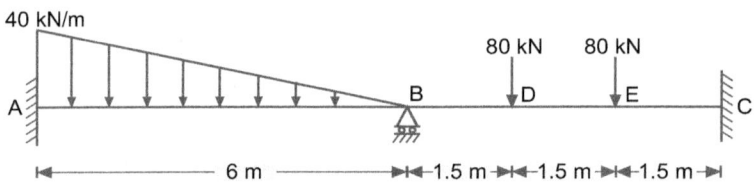

Fig. 4.48

(**Ans.** $M_A = -65.1$ kNm; $M_B = -61.7$ kNm; $M_C = -89.2$ kNm)

35.

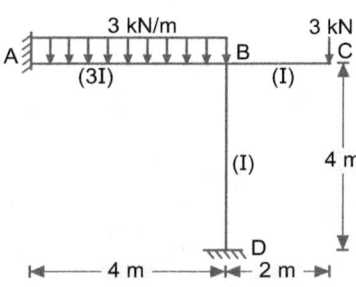

Fig. 4.49

(**Ans.** $M_{AB} = 3.25$ kNm; $M_{BA} = -5.5$ kNm; $M_{CD} = -0.5$ kNm; $M_{DB} = -0.2$ kNm)

36.

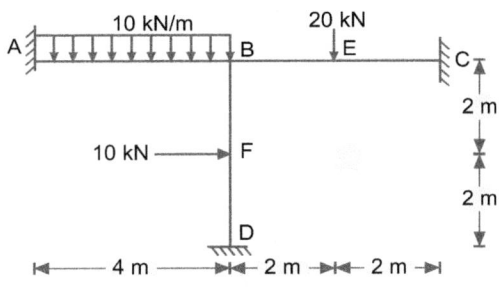

Fig. 4.50

(**Ans.** M_{BC} = 47.5 kNm; M_{CB} = − 8.75 kNm; M_{DB} = 23.75 kNm; M_{BD} = − 32.5 kNm)

37.

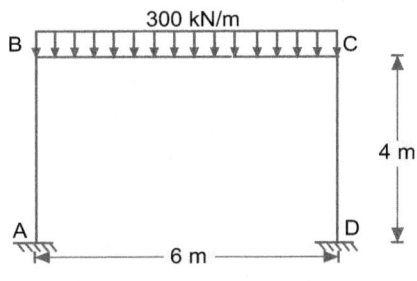

Fig. 4.51

(**Ans.** M_{AB} = − M_{DC} = − 336.9 kNm; M_{BA} = − M_{CD} = − 673.8 kNm;

M_{BC} = − M_{CB} = 673.8 kNm)

38.

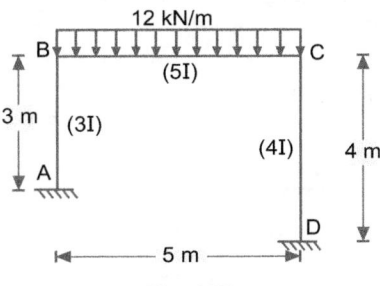

Fig. 4.52

(**Ans.** M_{AB} = − 5.97 kNm; M_{BA} = − 15 kNm; M_{BC} = 15 kNm;

M_{CB} = − 18 kNm; M_{CD} = 18 kNm; M_{DC} = 9.97 kNm)

39.

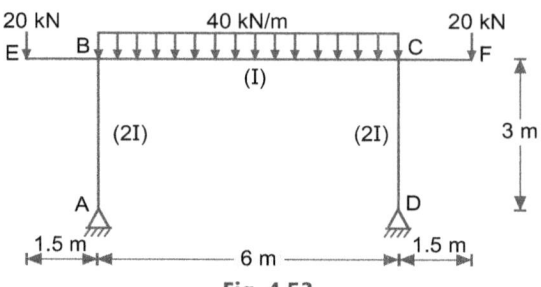

Fig. 4.53

(**Ans.** $M_{AB} = M_{DC} = 0$; $M_{BA} = -M_{CD} = -77$ kNm; $M_{BE} = -M_{CF} = -30$ kNm;
$M_{BC} = -M_{CB} = 107$ kNm)

40.

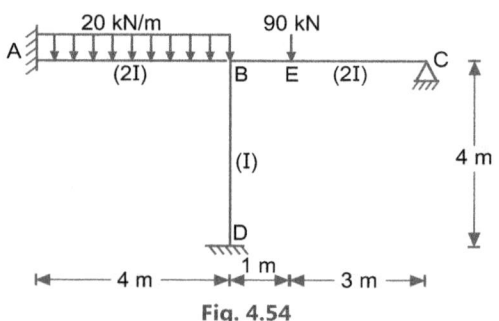

Fig. 4.54

(**Ans.** $M_{AB} = 22$ kNm; $M_{BA} = -36$ kNm; $M_{BD} = -4.67$ kNm;
$M_{BC} = 40.7$ kNm; $M_{CB} = 0$; $M_{DC} = -2.33$ kNm)

41.

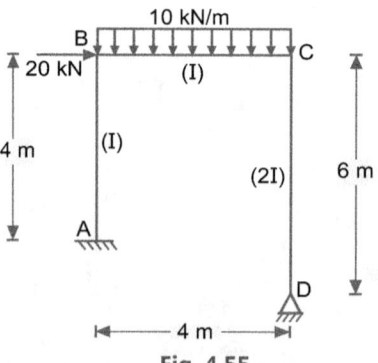

Fig. 4.55

(**Ans.** $M_{AB} = -4.16$ kNm; $M_{BA} = -8.75$ kNm; $M_{BC} = 8.75$ kNm; $M_{CB} = -8.75$ kNm;
$M_{CD} = 8.75$ kNm; $M_{DC} = 0$)

42.

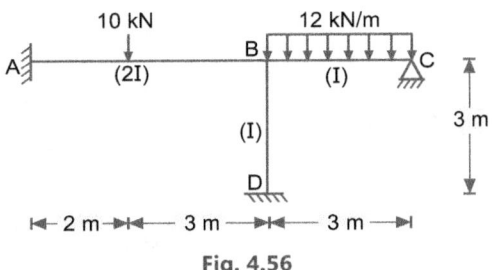

Fig. 4.56

(**Ans.** M_{AB} = 7.72 kNm; M_{BA} = –3.76 kNm; M_{BC} = 2.9 kNm; M_{CB} = 0; M_{BD} = 0.86 kNm;

M_{DB} = 0.48 kNm)

43.

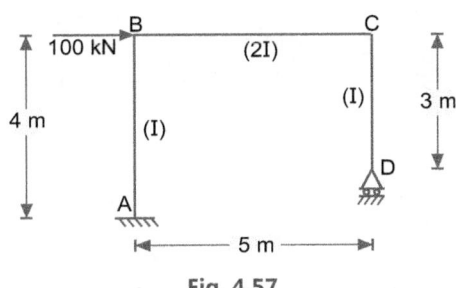

Fig. 4.57

(**Ans.** M_{AB} = 68.4 kNm; M_{BA} = 47.7 kNm; M_{BC} = – 47.7 kNm;

M_{CB} = – 43.7 kNm; M_{CD} = 43.7 kNm; M_{DC} = 0)

44.

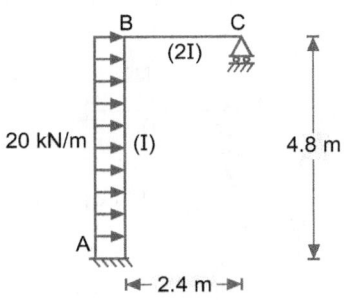

Fig. 4.58

(**Ans.** M_{AB} = 158.5; M_{BA} = – M_{BC} = 70 kNm)

45.

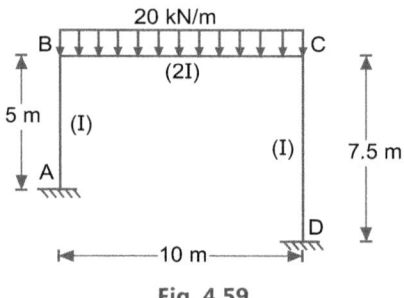

Fig. 4.59

(**Ans.** $M_{AB} = -21$ kNm; $M_{BA} = -M_{BC} = 91$ kNm; $M_{CB} = -M_{CD} = -106$ kN; $M_{DC} = 63.5$ kNm)

46.

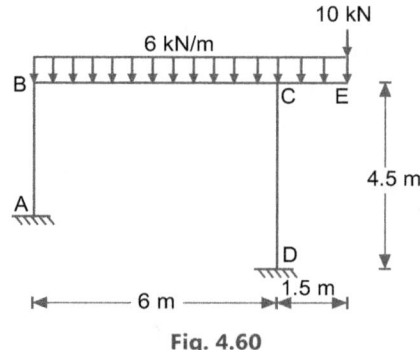

Fig. 4.60

(**Ans.** $M_{AB} = -0.62$ kNm; $M_{BA} = -M_{BC} = -7.14$ kNm; $M_{CB} = -24.94$ kNm;

$M_{CE} = 21.75$ kNm; $M_{CD} = 3.18$ kNm; $M_{DC} = 4.45$ kNm)

47.

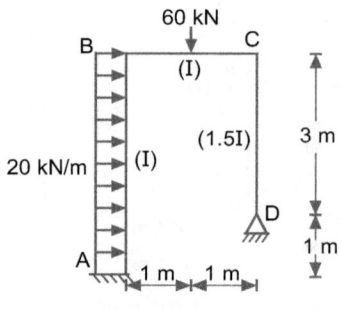

Fig. 4.61

(**Ans.** $M_{AB} = 75.2$ kNm; $M_{BA} = -M_{BC} = 17.1$ kNm; $M_{CB} = -M_{CD} = -50$ kNm; $M_{DC} = 0$)

48.

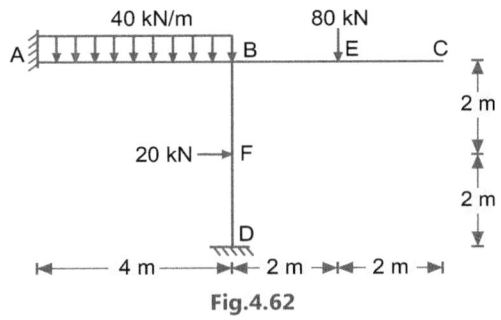

Fig.4.62

(**Ans.** M_{AB} = 55.84 kNm; M_{BA} = –48.52 kNm;

M_{BC} = 63.66 kNm; M_{BD} = 15.12 kNm; M_{DB} = 22.44 kNm)

49.

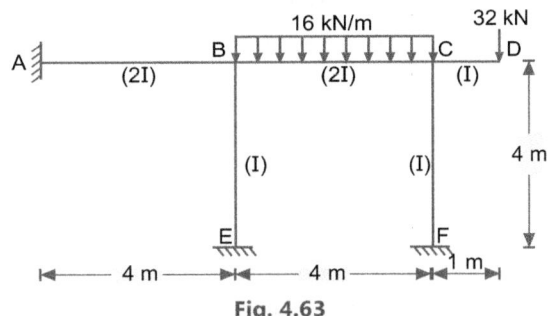

Fig. 4.63

(**Ans.** M_{AB} = – 3.8 kNm; M_{BA} = – 7.6 kNm; M_{BC} = 11.43 kNm; M_{CB} = – 29.72 kNm;

M_{CD} = 42 kNm; M_{BE} = – 3.8 kNm;

M_{EB} = – 1.9 kNm; M_{CF} = – 2.28 kNm; M_{FC} = – 1.14 kNm)

50.

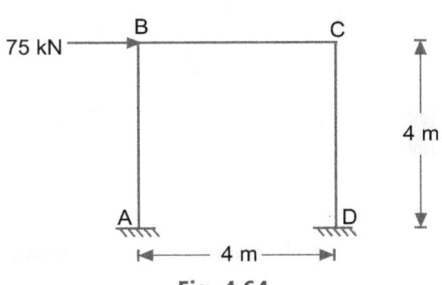

Fig. 4.64

(**Ans.** M_{AB} = 85.71 kNm; M_{BA} = –M_{BC} = 64.29 kNm; M_{CB} = – M_{CD} = – 64.29 kNm;

M_{DC} = 85.71 kNm)

51.

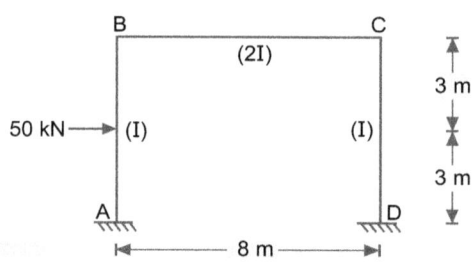

Fig. 4.65

(**Ans.** $M_{AB} = -123.72$ kNm; $B_{BA} = -M_{BC} = -42.527$ kNm; $M_{CB} = -M_{CD} = 58.675$ kNm; $M_{DC} = 75.275$ kNm)

52.

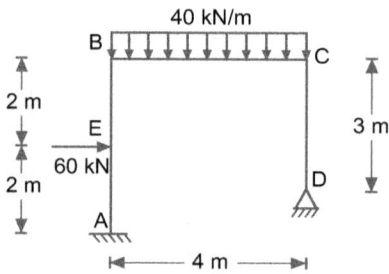

Fig. 4.66

(**Ans.** $M_{AB} = 60.50$ kNm; $M_{BA} = -M_{BC} = -19.70$ kNm; $M_{CB} = -M_{CD} = -59.40$ kNm; $M_{DC} = 0$)

53.

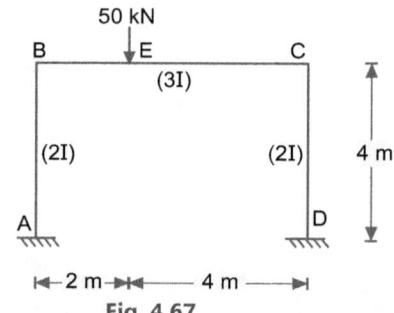

Fig. 4.67

(**Ans.** $M_{AB} = -9.52$ kNm; $M_{BA} = -M_{BC} = -23.82$ kNm; $M_{CB} = -M_{CD} = -20.63$ kNm; $M_{DC} = 12.71$ kNm)

54.

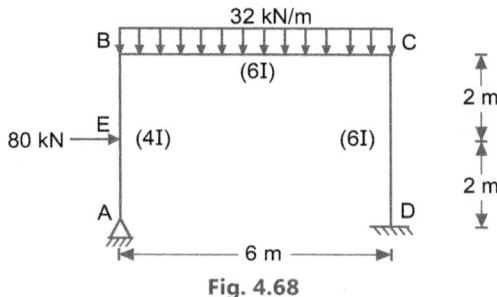

Fig. 4.68

(**Ans.** $M_{AB} = 0$; $M_{BA} = -M_{BC} = -50.92$ kNm; $M_{CB} = -M_{CD} = -108.64$ kNm; $M_{DC} = 102.14$ kNm)

55.

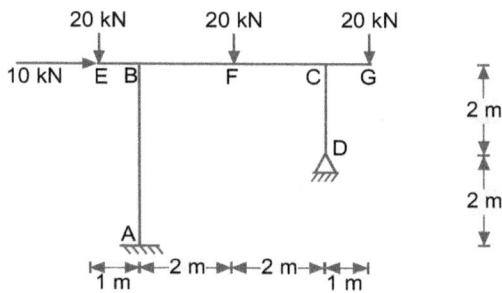

Fig. 4.69

(**Ans.** $M_{AB} = 14.92$ kNm; $M_{BA} = 15.87$ kNm; $M_{BE} = -20$ kNm; $M_{BC} = 4.13$ kNm; $M_{CB} = -24.60$ kNm; $M_{CA} = 20$ kNm; $M_{CD} = 4.60$ kNm)

56.

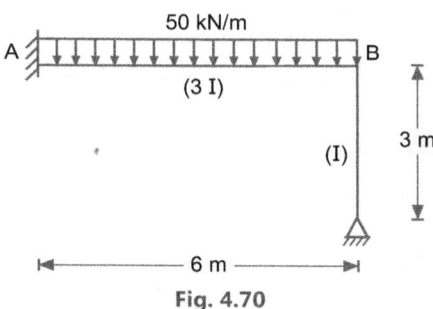

Fig. 4.70

(**Ans.** $M_{AB} = 200$ kNm; $M_{BA} = -50$ kNm; $M_{BC} = 50$ kNm; $M_{CB} = 0$)

57.

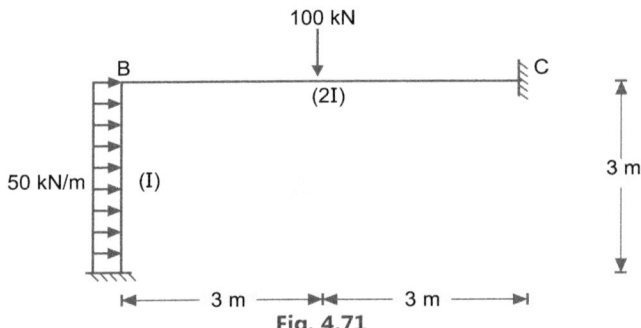

Fig. 4.71

(**Ans.** M_{AB} = 28.125 kNm; M_{BA} = −56.25 kNm; M_{BC} = 56.25 kNm; M_{CB} = −84.375 kNm)

58.

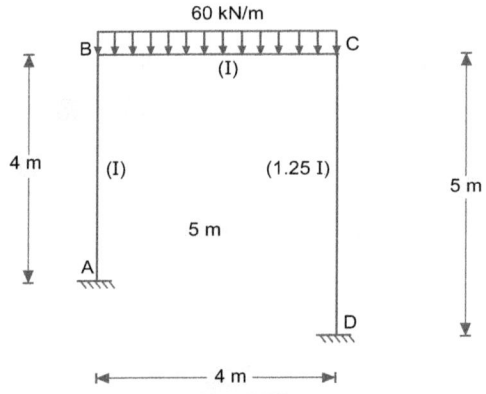

Fig. 4.72

(**Ans.** M_{AB} = 20.92 kNm; M_{BA} = − M_{BC} = − 49.2 kNm; M_{CD} = − M_{CB} = 56.8 kNm; M_{DC} = − 31.2 kNm)

59.

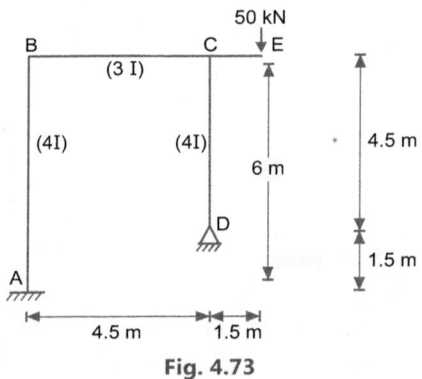

Fig. 4.73

(**Ans.** $M_{AB} = -19.375$ kNm; $M_{BA} = -M_{BC} = 20.625$ kNm; $M_{CB} = -45$ kNm; $M_{CD} = -30$ kNm; $M_{DC} = 0$)

60.

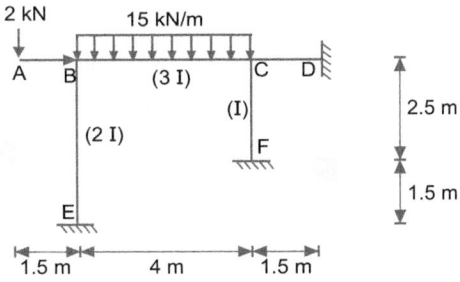

Fig. 4.74

(**Ans.** $M_{BA} = -3$ kNm; $M_{BC} = 11.04$ kNm; $M_{CB} = -19.83$ kNm; $M_{CD} = 16.52$ kNm; $M_{DC} = 8.26$ kNm; $M_{BE} = 8.04$ kNm; $M_{EB} = 4.02$ kNm; $M_{CF} = -3.31$ kNm; $M_{FC} = -1.65$ kNm)

61.

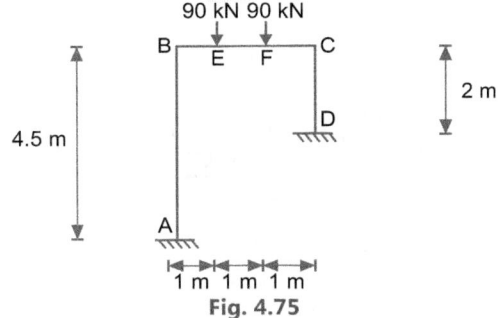

Fig. 4.75

(**Ans.** $M_{AB} = 23.2$ kNm; $M_{BA} = -M_{BC} = 38.5$ kNm; $M_{CB} = -M_{CD} = 34$ kNm; $M_{DC} = 2.8$ kNm)

62.

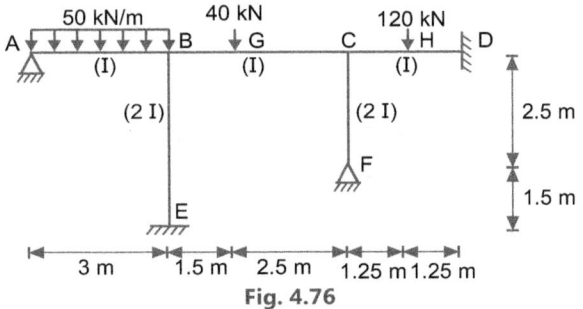

Fig. 4.76

(**Ans.** $M_{AB} = 0$, $M_{BA} = 47.4$ kNm; $M_{BE} = 17.8$ kNm; $M_{BC} = -29.6$ kNm; $M_{CB} = 15.2$ kNm; $M_{CF} = 13.33$ kNm; $M_{CD} = 28.5$ kNm; $M_{DC} = 42$ kNm; $M_{EB} = -8.9$; $M_{FC} = 0$)

63.

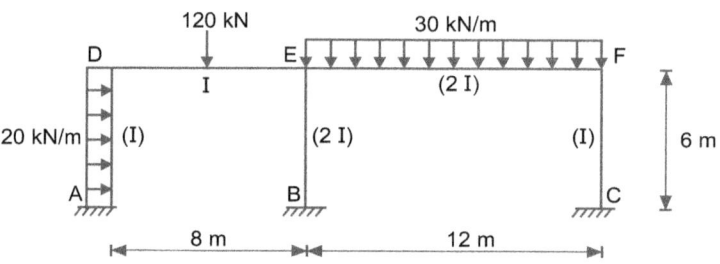

Fig. 4.77

(**Ans.** $M_{AD} = -100$ kNm; $M_{DA} = 42.5$ kNm; $M_{DE} = -42$ kNm; $M_{ED} = 225$ kNm; $M_{EF} = -332.4$ kNm; $M_{EB} = 107.8$ kNm; $M_{FE} = 240$ kNm; $M_{BE} = -9.4$ kNm; $M_{CF} = -152.1$ kNm)

64.

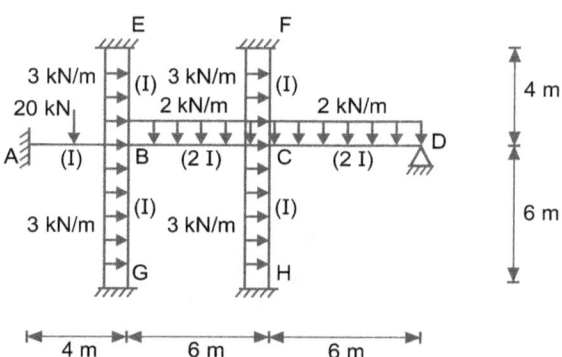

Fig. 4.78

(**Ans.** $M_{AB} = -10.92$ kNm; $M_{BA} = 8.172$ kNm; $M_{EB} = 0$; $M_{BE} = -7.38$ kNm; $M_{BC} = -8.562$ kNm; $M_{BG} = 7.76$ kNm; $M_{GB} = -9.62$ kNm; $M_{CB} = 4.524$ kNm; $M_{CF} = -4.19$ kNm; $M_{CD} = -9.196$ kNm; $M_{CH} = 8.87$ kNm; $M_{FC} = 3.9$ kNm; $M_{HC} = -9.065$ kNm)

65.

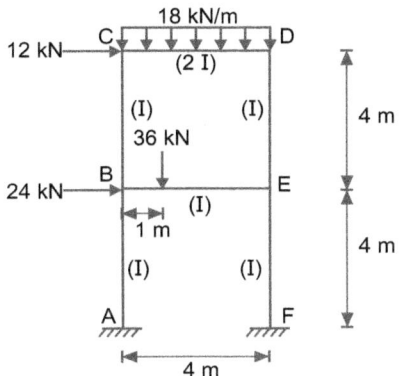

Fig. 4.79

(**Ans.** M_{AB} = 41.34 kNm; M_{BA} = –25.77 kNm; M_{BC} = –2.2 kNm; M_{BE} = –23.565 kNm; M_{CB} = – M_{CD} = 4.935 kNm; M_{DC} = – M_{DE} = –30.39 kNm; M_{ED} = 15.09 kNm; M_{EB} = –47.475 kNm; M_{EF} = 32.35 kNm; M_{FE} = 44.835 kNm)

66.

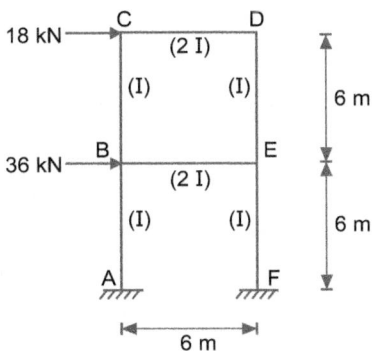

Fig. 4.80

(**Ans.** M_{AB} = M_{FE} = 88.92 kNm; M_{BA} = M_{EF} = 73.08 kNm; M_{BE} = M_{EB} = – 94.86 kNm; M_{BC} = M_{ED} = 21.6 kNm; M_{CD} = M_{DC} = – 32.4 kNm)

67.

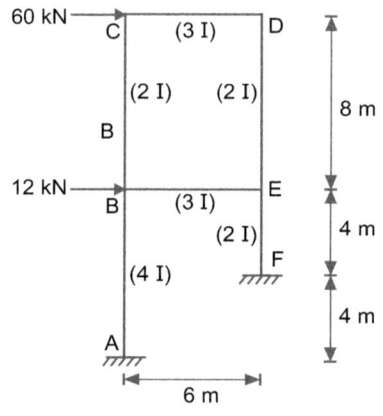

Fig. 4.81

(**Ans.** M_{AB} = 17.4 kNm; M_{BA} = 11.18 kNm; M_{BC} = 13.42 kNm; M_{BE} = –24.6 kNm; M_{CB} = – M_{CD} = 13.9 kNm; M_{DC} = – M_{CD} = – 12.42 kNm; M_{ED} = 8.16 kNm; M_{EB} = – 30.60 kNm; M_{EF} = 22.76 kNm; M_{FE} = 34.9 kNm)

UNIT V

Chapter 5
FINITE DIFFERENCE METHOD AND APPROXIMATE ANALYSIS OF MULTISTORIED FRAMES

(A) FINITE DIFFERENCE METHOD

5.1 INTRODUCTION

In most of the civil engineering problems, ordinary type different equations are required for determination of shear force, bending moments, deflections, etc. Finite difference method is applicable for the problems having complex loading and variable sectional properties.

At each nodal point, differential equation can be applied and a set of simultaneous equations are developed. These equations can be solved by using boundary conditions at nodal points.

5.2 FINITE DIFFERENCES

Suppose that $y = f(x)$ is tabulated for equally spaced values

$$x = x_0, x_0 + h, x_0 + 2h$$

giving $y = y_0, y_1, y_2, \ldots$. To find some intermediate values of $f(x)$ or $f'(x)$ at some value of x, the following three types of differences are as follows :

1. Forward differences : The differences $y_1 - y_0, y_2 - y_1, \ldots, y_n - y_{n-1}$, denoted by $\Delta y_0, \Delta y_1, \Delta y_2, \ldots, \Delta y_{n-1}$ respectively are called the first forward differences and Δ is called forward difference operator.

First forward difference,

$$\Delta y_2 = y_{r+1} - y_r$$

Second forward difference,

$$\Delta y_2^2 = \Delta y_{r+1} - \Delta y_r$$

Ninth forward difference,

$$\Delta y_2^q = \Delta^{q-1} y_{r+1} - \Delta^{q-1} y_r$$

Forward difference table

x	y	First difference	Second difference	Third difference
x_0	y_0	Δy_0		
$x_0 + h$	y_1	Δy_1	$\Delta^2 y_0$	$\Delta^3 y_0$
$x_0 + 2h$	y_2	Δy_2	$\Delta^2 y_1$	
$x_0 + 3h$	y_3			

2. Backward differences : The differences $y_0 - y_0$, $y_2 - y_1$, ..., $y_n - y_{n-1}$, denoted by ∇y_1, ∇y_2, ..., ∇y_n respectively are called first backward differences and ∇ is the backward difference operator.

Backward difference table

x	y	First difference	Second difference	Third difference
x_0	y_0	∇y_1		
$x_0 + h$	y_1	∇y_2	$\nabla^2 y_2$	$\nabla^3 y_3$
$x_0 + 2h$	y_2	∇y_3	$\nabla^2 y_3$	
$x_0 + 3h$	y_3			

3. Central differences : It is most convenient than others. δ is the central difference operator. The differences $y_1 - y_0$, $y_2 - y_1$, $y_n - y_{n-1}$, denoted by $\delta y_{1/2}$, $\delta y_{2/3}$, ..., $\delta_{n-1/2}$ respectively are called first central differences.

Central difference table

x	y	First difference	Second difference	Third difference
x_0	y_0	$\delta y_{1/2}$		
$x_0 + h$	y_1	$\delta y_{3/2}$	$\delta^2 y_1$	$\delta^3 y_{3/2}$
$x_0 + 2h$	y_2	$\delta y_{5/2}$	$\delta^2 y_2$	
$x_0 + 3h$	y_3			

Finite difference method applied to beams, we have

$$\frac{d^2 M}{dx^2} = w$$

$$\frac{d^2 y}{dx^2} = \frac{M}{EI}$$

$$\frac{d^4 y}{dx^4} = \frac{w}{EI}$$

where,

w — Intensity of load

M — Moment at any section

h — Distance interval at any point

STRUCTURAL ANALYSIS – II   FINITE DIFF. METHOD & APPROX. ANALY. OF MULTI. FRAMES

y – Deflection
L – Span of beam
E – Modulus of elasticity
I – Second moment of inertia.

Using central differences the moment and deflection equations for nodal points for the beam shown in Fig. 5.1 are as follows :

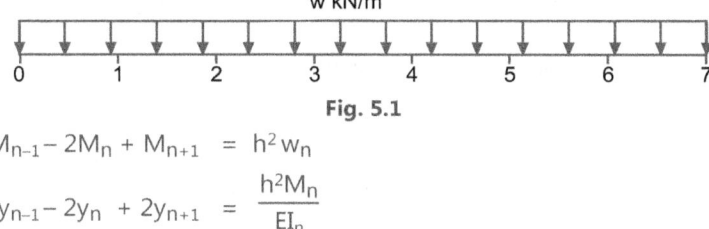

Fig. 5.1

$$M_{n-1} - 2M_n + M_{n+1} = h^2 w_n$$

$$y_{n-1} - 2y_n + 2y_{n+1} = \frac{h^2 M_n}{EI_n}$$

Fourth order central differences equation for deflection is as follows :

$$y_{n+2} - 4y_{n+1} + 6y_n - 4y_{n-1} + y_{n-2} = \left(\frac{w_n h^4}{EI_n}\right).$$

Example 5.1 : A cantilever of length L supports a cantilever load at the free end as shown in Fig. 5.2 (a). Determine the deflection at free end.

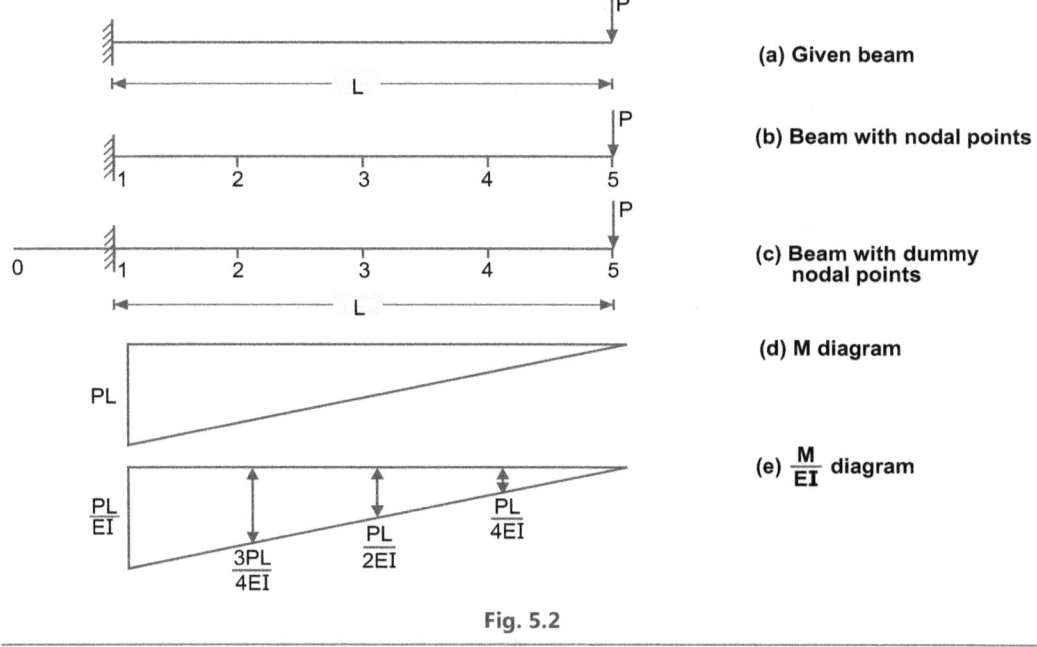

Fig. 5.2

Data : As shown in Fig. 5.2 (a)

Required : Deflection at free end.

Concept : Second order central finite differences equation.

Solution : Step I : Beam is divided into four parts. The nodal points are marked as shown in Fig. 5.2 (b) and (c).

Step II : BMD is plotted for the given load system as shown in Fig. 5.2 (d).

Step III : $\left(\dfrac{M}{EI}\right)$ diagram is plotted for the given loading as shown in Fig. 5.2 (e).

Step IV : As one end 'A' is fixed, so assume a dummy nodal point as '0' on left of A. The deflection at nodal point '0' and nodal point '2' is same due to symmetry with nodal point 1 (fixed support). The deflection at nodal point 1 is zero as it is fixed support.

$$\therefore \quad y_0 = y_2$$
$$y_1 = 0$$

Step V : Applying central finite differences equation to node 1,

$$\therefore \quad y_0 - 2y_1 + y_2 = \dfrac{h^2 M_n}{E I_n}$$

$$M_n = -\dfrac{PL}{EI}$$

$$y_0 - 2y_1 + y_2 = -\left(\dfrac{L}{4}\right)^2 \cdot \left(\dfrac{PL}{EI}\right) \quad \ldots (1)$$

Substituting values of y_0 and y_1 in equation (1),

$$\therefore \quad 2y_2 = -\dfrac{PL^3}{16\,EI}$$

$$\therefore \quad y_2 = -\dfrac{PL^3}{32\,EI} \quad \ldots (2)$$

Step VI : Applying central finite differences equation to node 2,

$$y_1 - 2y_2 + y_3 = -\left(\dfrac{L}{4}\right)^2 \times \left(\dfrac{3\,PL}{4\,EI}\right)$$

Substituting y_1 and y_2 in above equation,

$$-2 \times -\left(\dfrac{PL^3}{32\,EI}\right) + y_3 = -\dfrac{3}{64} \dfrac{PL^3}{EI}$$

∴ $$y_3 = -\frac{3}{64}\frac{PL^3}{EI} - \frac{2\,PL^3}{32\,EI}$$

∴ $$y_3 = -\frac{7\,PL^3}{64\,EI}$$

Step VII : Applying central finite differences equation to node 3,

∴ $$y_2 - 2y_3 + y_4 = -\left(\frac{L}{4}\right)^2 \cdot \left(\frac{PL}{2\,EI}\right)$$

Substituting y_2 and y_3 in above equation,

$$-\frac{PL^3}{32\,EI} - 2\left(-\frac{7\,PL^3}{64\,EI}\right) + y_4 = -\frac{PL^3}{32\,EI}$$

∴ $$y_4 = -\frac{7\,PL^3}{32\,EI}$$

Step VIII : Applying central finite differences equation to node 4,

$$y_3 - 2y_4 + y_5 = -\left(\frac{L}{4}\right)^2 \left(\frac{PL}{4\,EI}\right)$$

Substituting y_3 and y_4 in above equation,

$$-\frac{7\,PL^3}{64\,EI} - 2\left(-\frac{7\,PL^3}{32\,EI}\right) + y_5 = -\frac{PL^3}{64\,EI}$$

$$y_5 = -\frac{PL^3}{64\,EI} + \frac{7\,PL^3}{64\,EI} - \frac{14\,PL^3}{32\,EI}$$

$$y_5 = -\frac{22\,PL^3}{64\,EI}$$

∴ Deflection at free end is $\left(\frac{22\,PL^3}{64\,EI}\right)$ (↓).

Example 5.2 : *A cantilever of length 9 m with varying moment of inertia supports a concentrated load as shown in Fig. 5.3 (a). Determine deflection at cantilever end. Take four nodal points.*

Data : Beam is loaded and supported as shown in Fig. 5.3 (a).

Required : Deflection at free end.

Concept : Second order central finite differences equation.

Solution : Step I : Beam is divided into three parts, 3 m each. The nodal points are marked as shown in Fig. 5.3 (b) and (c).

STRUCTURAL ANALYSIS – II   FINITE DIFF. METHOD & APPROX. ANALY. OF MULTI. FRAMES

Step II : BMD is plotted for the given load system as shown in Fig. 5.3 (d).

Step III : $\left(\dfrac{M}{EI}\right)$ diagram is plotted for the given loading as shown in Fig. 5.3.

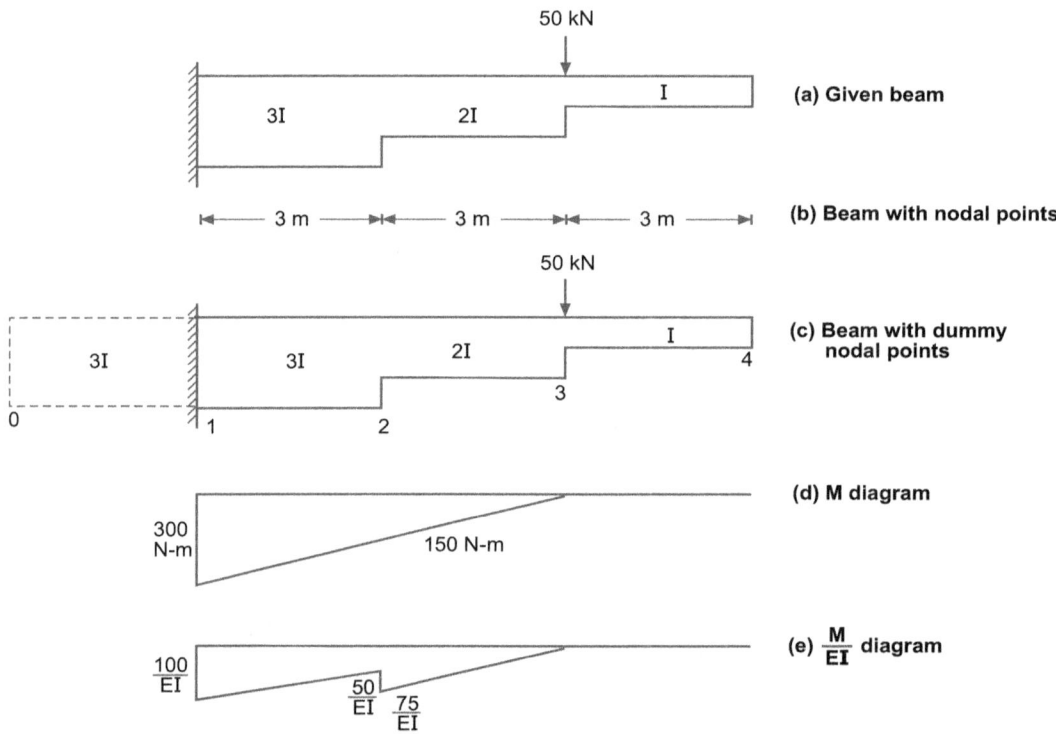

Fig. 5.3

Step IV : As one end 'A' is fixed, so assume a dummy nodal point as '0' on left of 'A'. The deflection at nodal point '0' and nodal point '2' is same due to symmetry with the nodal point 1 (fixed support). The deflection at nodal point 1 is zero as it is fixed support.

∴
$$y_0 = y_2$$
$$y_1 = 0$$
$$h = 3 \text{ m}$$

Step V : Applying central finite difference to node 1,

$$y_0 - 2y_1 + y_2 = \dfrac{h^2 M_n}{E I_n}$$

Ch. 5 | 5.6

$$M_n = -\frac{100}{EI}$$

$$y_0 - 2y_1 + y_2 = -(3)^2 \cdot \left(\frac{100}{EI}\right) \qquad \ldots (1)$$

Substituting values of y_0 and y_1 in equation (1),

$$2y_2 = -\frac{900}{EI}$$

$$\therefore \quad y_2 = -\frac{450}{EI} \qquad \ldots (2)$$

Step VI : Applying central finite difference equation to node 2,

$$y_1 - 2y_2 + y_3 = -(3)^2 \frac{150}{\left(\frac{3EI + 2EI}{2}\right)}$$

$$y_1 - 2y_2 + y_3 = -\frac{540}{EI}$$

Substituting value of y_2 in above equation,

$$-2\left(-\frac{450}{EI}\right) + y_3 = -\frac{540}{EI}$$

$$y_3 = -\frac{540}{EI} - \frac{900}{EI}$$

$$\therefore \quad y_3 = -\frac{1440}{EI} \qquad \ldots (3)$$

Step VII : Applying central finite differences equation to node 3,

$$y_2 - 2y_3 + y_4 = -\frac{(3)^2 \times 0}{EI}$$

Substituting values of y_2 and y_3 in above equation,

$$-\frac{450}{EI} - 2\left(-\frac{1440}{EI}\right) + y_4 = 0$$

$$\therefore \quad y_4 = -\frac{2430}{EI}$$

$\therefore$ Deflection at free end is $\left(\frac{2430}{EI}\right)(\downarrow)$.

Example 5.3 : *A cantilever of length L supports a uniformly distributed load of intensity w kN/m as shown in Fig. 5.4 (a). Determine deflection at free end. Take 5 nodes.*

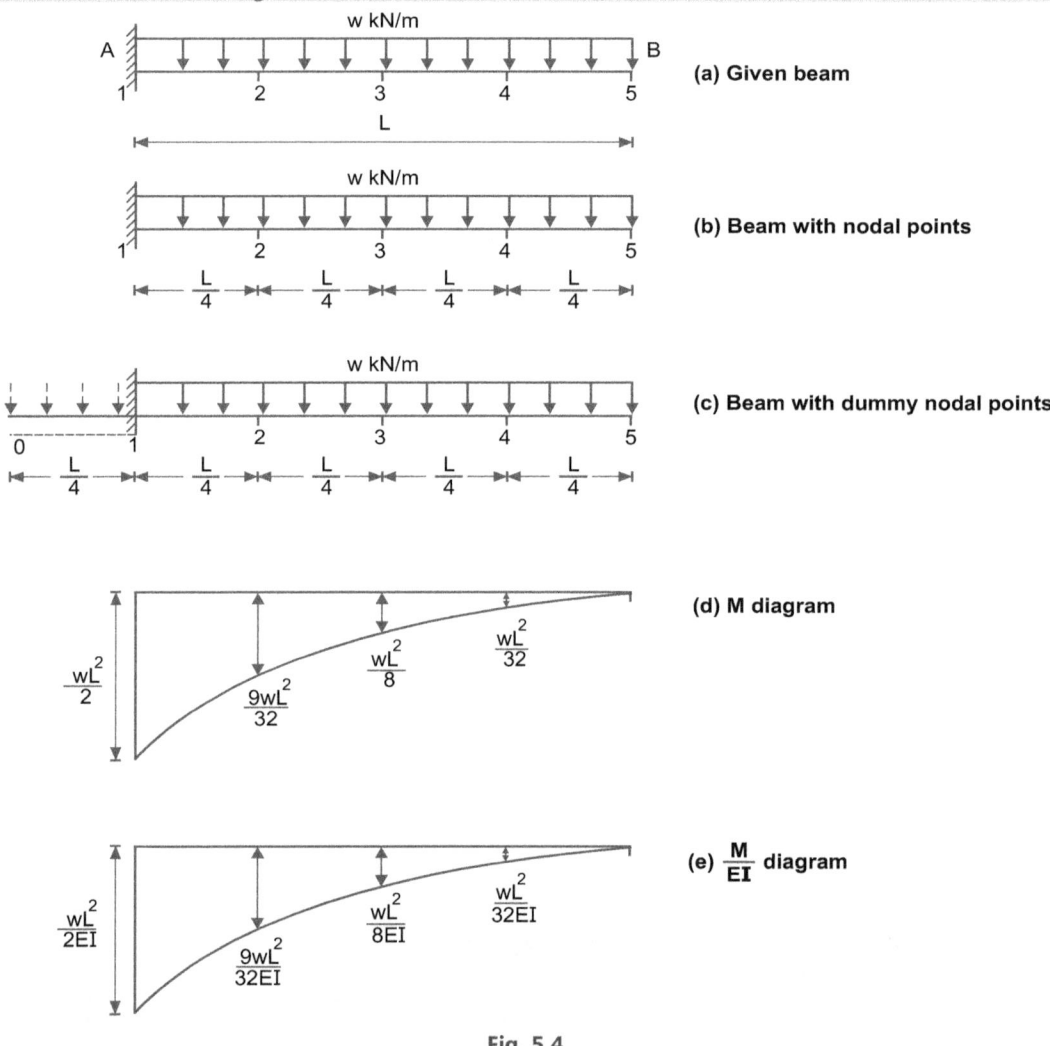

Fig. 5.4

Data : Beam is loaded and supported as shown in Fig. 5.4 (a).

Required : Deflection at free end.

Concept : Second order central differences equation.

Solution : Step I : Beam is divided into four parts, $\frac{L}{4}$ m each. The nodal points are marked as shown in Fig. 5.4 (b) and (c).

Step II : BMD is plotted for the given load system as shown in Fig. 5.4 (d).

Step III : $\left(\frac{M}{EI}\right)$ diagram is plotted for the given loading as shown in Fig. 5.4 (e).

Step IV : As one end 'A' is fixed, so assume a dummy nodal point as '0' on left of A. The deflection at nodal point '0' and nodal point '2' is same due to symmetry with nodal point 1. The deflection at nodal point 1 is zero as it is fixed support.

$$\therefore \quad y_0 = y_2$$
$$y_1 = 0$$

Step V : Applying central finite difference equation to node 1,

$$y_0 - 2y_1 + y_2 = \frac{h^2 M_n}{E I_n}$$

$$M_n = \frac{-WL^2}{2EI}$$

$$y_0 - 2y_1 + y_2 = -\left(\frac{L}{4}\right)^2 \cdot \frac{WL^2}{2 EI} \qquad \ldots (1)$$

Substituting values of y_0 and y_1 in equation (1),

$$\therefore \quad 2y_2 = -\frac{WL^3}{32 EI} \quad \therefore \quad y_2 = -\frac{WL^3}{64 EI} \qquad \ldots (2)$$

Step VI : Applying central finite difference equation to node 2,

$$y_1 - 2y_2 + y_3 = -\left(\frac{L}{4}\right)^2 \cdot \left(\frac{9 WL^2}{32 EI}\right)$$

Substituting value of y_2 in above equation,

$$-2\left(-\frac{WL^3}{64 EI}\right) + y_3 = -\frac{9 WL^4}{512 EI}$$

$$y_3 = -\frac{9}{512} \frac{WL^4}{EI} - \frac{WL^3}{32 EI}$$

$$y_3 = -\frac{25 WL^4}{512 EI} \qquad \ldots (3)$$

Applying central finite difference equation to node 3,

$$y_2 - 2y_3 + y_4 = -\left(\frac{L}{4}\right)^2 \cdot \frac{WL^2}{8 EI}$$

Substituting values of y_2 and y_3 in above equation,

$$\therefore -\frac{WL^4}{64\ EI} - 2\left(-\frac{25\ WL^4}{512\ EI}\right) + y_4 = -\frac{WL^4}{128\ EI}$$

$$y_4 = -\frac{WL^4}{128\ EI} - \frac{25\ WL^4}{256\ EI} + \frac{WL^4}{64\ EI}$$

$$y_4 = -\frac{23\ WL^4}{256\ EI} \qquad \ldots (4)$$

Applying central finite difference equation to node 4,

$$y_3 - 2y_4 + y_5 = -\left(\frac{L}{4}\right)^2 \cdot \frac{WL^2}{32\ EI}$$

$$y_3 - 2y_4 + y_5 = -\frac{WL^4}{128\ EI}$$

Substituting values of y_3 and y_4 in above equation,

$$-\frac{25\ WL^4}{512\ EI} - 2\left(-\frac{23\ WL^4}{256\ EI}\right) + y_5 = -\frac{WL^4}{512\ EI}$$

$$y_5 = -\frac{WL^4}{512\ EI} - \frac{46\ WL^4}{256\ EI} + \frac{25\ WL^4}{512\ EI}$$

$$y_5 = -\frac{68\ WL^4}{512\ EI}$$

$$\therefore \qquad y_5 = -\frac{17\ WL^4}{128\ EI}$$

$\therefore$ Deflection at free end is $\left(\dfrac{17\ WL^4}{128\ EI}\right)(\downarrow)$.

Example 5.4 : *The beam is supported and loaded as shown in Fig. 5.5 (a). Determine deflection at centre.*

Data : Beam is supported and loaded as shown in Fig. 5.5 (a).

Required : Deflection at centre.

Concept : Second order central finite differences equation.

Solution : Step I : Beam is divided into three parts. The nodal points are marked as shown in Fig. 5.5 (b) and (c).

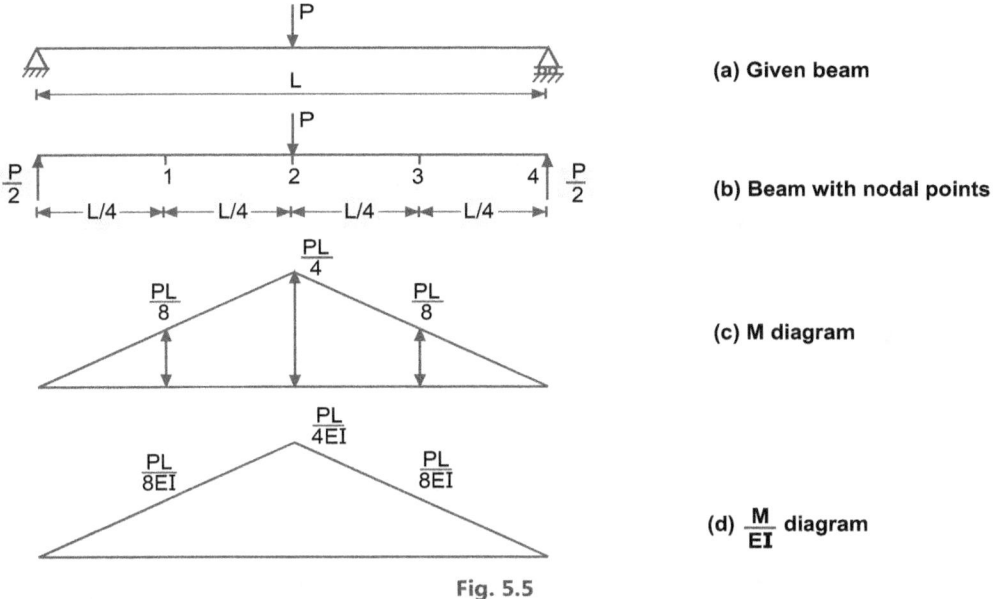

Fig. 5.5

Step II : BMD is plotted for the given load system as shown in Fig. 5.5 (d).

Step III : $\left(\dfrac{M}{EI}\right)$ diagram is plotted for the given loading as shown in Fig. 5.5 (d).

Step IV : Beam is simply supported at nodal points 1 and 5 so that deflection at both nodal points are zero.

$$\therefore \quad y_1 = y_5 = 0$$

Step V : Applying central finite difference equation to nodal point 2,

$$\therefore \quad y_1 - 2y_2 + y_3 = \dfrac{h^2 M_n}{E I_n}$$

$$y_1 - 2y_2 + y_3 = \left(\dfrac{L}{4}\right)^2 \cdot \left(\dfrac{PL}{4\,EI}\right) \qquad \ldots (1)$$

Substituting y_1 in equation (1),

$$\therefore \quad 2y_2 + y_3 = \dfrac{PL^3}{64\,EI} \qquad \ldots (2)$$

Step VI : Applying central finite difference equation to nodal point 3,

$$y_2 - 2y_3 + y_4 = \left(\dfrac{L}{4}\right)^2 \cdot \left(\dfrac{PL}{2\,EI}\right)$$

$$y_2 - 2y_3 + y_4 = \frac{PL^3}{32\,EI} \qquad \ldots (3)$$

Step VII : Applying central finite difference equation to nodal point '4',

$$y_3 - 2y_4 + y_5 = \left(\frac{L}{4}\right)^2 \left(\frac{PL}{4\,EI}\right) \qquad \ldots (4)$$

Substituting y_5 in equation (4),

$$\therefore \quad y_3 - 2y_4 = \frac{PL^3}{64\,EI} \qquad \ldots (5)$$

Step VIII : Solving equations (2), (3) and (5),

$$y_2 = y_4 = -\frac{PL^3}{32\,EI}$$

$$y_3 = -\frac{3\,PL^3}{64\,EI}$$

$\therefore$ Deflection at centre is $\dfrac{3\,PL^3}{64\,EI}$ ($\downarrow$).

Example 5.5 : *The beam is supported and loaded as shown in Fig. 5.6 (a). Find deflection under the load. Take 5 nodes.*

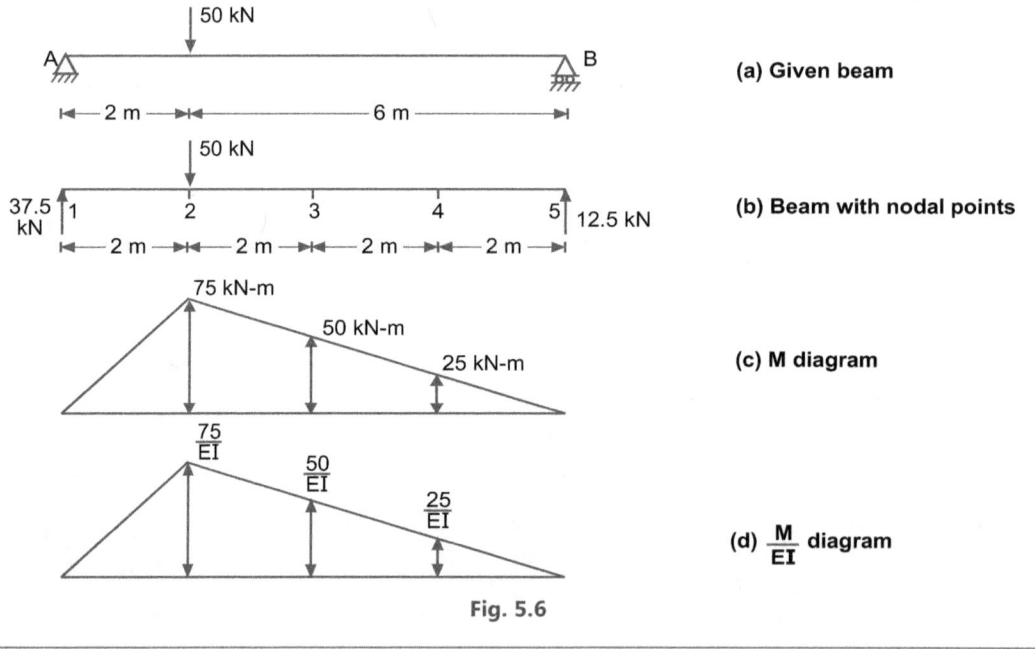

Fig. 5.6

Data : The beam is loaded and supported as shown in Fig. 5.6 (a).

Required : Deflection under the load.

Concept : Second order central finite difference equation.

Solution : Step I : Beam is divided into four parts. The nodal points are marked as shown in Fig. 5.6 (b).

Step II : BMD is plotted for the given beam as shown in Fig. 5.6 (c).

Step III : $\left(\dfrac{M}{EI}\right)$ diagram is plotted for the given beam as shown in Fig. 5.6 (d).

Step IV : Beam is simply supported at nodal points 1 and 5, so that deflections at both nodal points are zero.

$$\therefore \quad y_1 = y_5 = 0$$

Step V : Applying central finite difference equation to nodal point 2,

$$y_1 - 2y_2 + y_3 = \dfrac{h^2 M_n}{E I_n}$$

$$\therefore \quad y_1 - 2y_2 + y_3 = (2)^2 \cdot \left(\dfrac{75}{EI}\right) \qquad \ldots (1)$$

Substituting value of y_1 in equation (1),

$$\therefore \quad -2y_2 + y_3 = \dfrac{300}{EI} \qquad \ldots (2)$$

Step VI : Applying central finite difference equation to nodal point '3',

$$y_2 - 2y_3 + y_4 = (2)^2 \cdot \left(\dfrac{50}{EI}\right)$$

$$y_2 - 2y_3 + y_4 = \dfrac{200}{EI} \qquad \ldots (3)$$

Step VII : Applying central finite difference equation to nodal point 4,

$$y_3 - 2y_4 + y_5 = (2)^2 \cdot \left(\dfrac{25}{EI}\right)$$

$$y_3 - 2y_4 + y_5 = \dfrac{100}{EI} \qquad \ldots (4)$$

Substituting value of y_5 in equation (4),

$$\therefore \quad y_3 - 2y_4 = \dfrac{100}{EI} \qquad \ldots (5)$$

STRUCTURAL ANALYSIS – II   FINITE DIFF. METHOD & APPROX. ANALY. OF MULTI. FRAMES

Step VIII : Solving equations (2), (3) and (5),

$$y_2 = -\frac{350}{EI}$$

$$y_3 = -\frac{400}{EI}$$

$$y_4 = -\frac{250}{EI}$$

∴ Deflection under load is $\frac{350}{EI}$ (↓).

Example 5.6 : The beam is loaded and supported as shown in Fig. 5.7 (a). Determine the deflection at centre of beam.

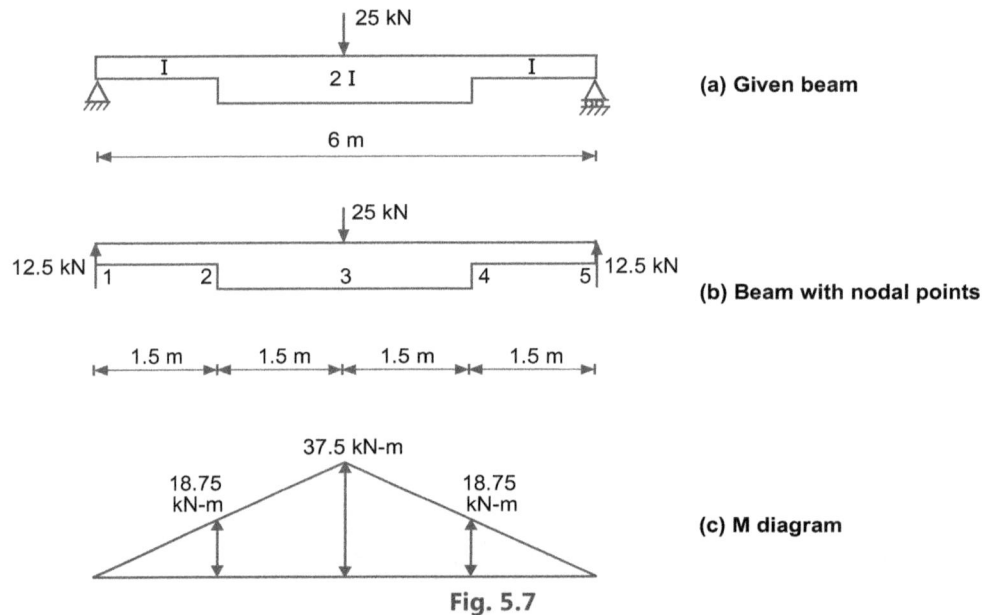

Fig. 5.7

Data : Beam is loaded and supported.

Required : Deflection at centre.

Concept : Second order central finite differences equation.

Solution : Step I : The beam is divided into four parts, 1.5 m each. The nodal points are marked as shown in Fig. 5.7 (b).

Step II : BMD is plotted as shown in Fig. 5.7 (c).

Step III : $\left(\dfrac{M}{EI}\right)$ diagram is plotted as shown in Fig. 5.7.

Step IV : Beam is simply supported at nodal points 1 and 5, so that deflection at both nodal points are zero.

∴ $\quad y_1 = y_5 = 0$

Step V : Applying central finite difference equation to nodal point 2,

$$y_1 - 2y_2 + y_3 = \dfrac{h^2 M_n}{E I_n}$$

$$y_1 - 2y_2 + y_3 = (1.5)^2 \dfrac{18.75}{E} \left(\dfrac{1}{\dfrac{I + 2I}{2}}\right)$$

$$y_1 - 2y_2 + y_3 = \dfrac{28.125}{EI} \quad \ldots (1)$$

Substituting value of y_1 in equation (1),

$$-2y_2 + y_3 = \dfrac{28.125}{EI} \quad \ldots (2)$$

Step VI : Applying central finite difference equation to nodal point 3,

$$y_2 - 2y_3 + y_4 = (1.5)^2 \times \left(\dfrac{18.75}{EI}\right)$$

$$y_2 - 2y_3 + y_4 = \dfrac{42.19}{EI} \quad \ldots (3)$$

Step VII : Applying central finite difference equation to nodal point 4,

$$y_3 - 2y_4 + y_5 = (1.5)^2 \times \dfrac{18.75}{E} \left(\dfrac{1}{\dfrac{I + 2I}{2}}\right)$$

$$y_3 - 2y_4 + y_5 = \dfrac{28.125}{EI} \quad \ldots (4)$$

Substituting y_5 in equation (4),

∴ $\quad y_3 - 2y_4 = \dfrac{28.125}{EI} \quad \ldots (5)$

Step VIII : Solving equations (2), (3) and (5),

$$y_2 = y_4 = -\dfrac{49.22}{EI}$$

STRUCTURAL ANALYSIS – II   FINITE DIFF. METHOD & APPROX. ANALY. OF MULTI. FRAMES

$$y_3 = -\frac{70.32}{EI}$$

∴   Deflection at centre = $\left(\dfrac{70.32}{EI}\right)$ (↓)

Example 5.7 : *The beam is loaded and supported as shown in Fig. 5.8 (a). Determine the deflection under the loads. E = 200 GPa and I = 1.2 × 10⁹ mm⁴.*

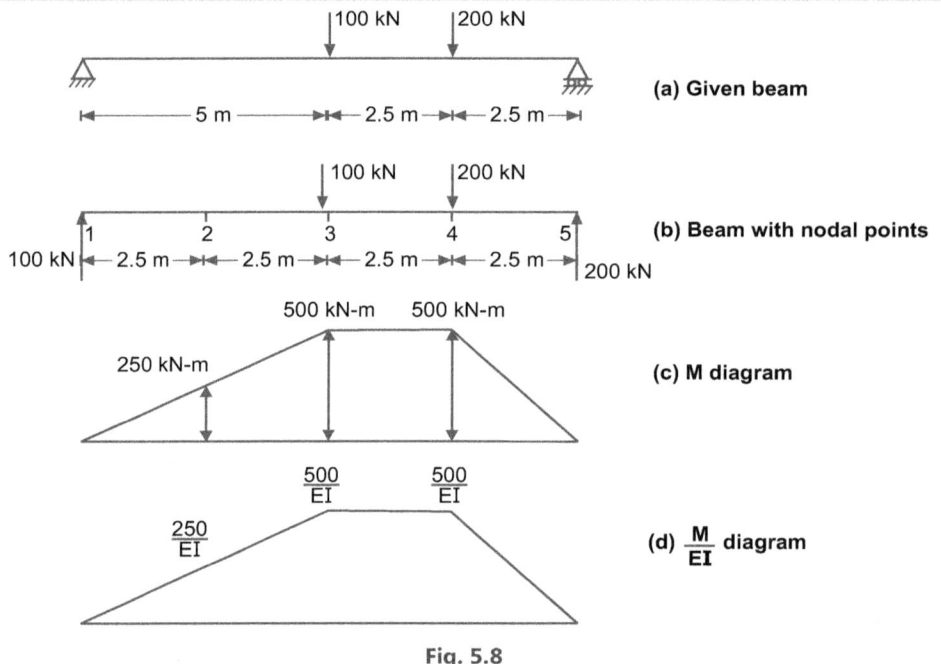

Fig. 5.8

Data : Beam is supported and loaded as shown in Fig. 5.8 (a).

E = 200 GPa and I = 1.2 × 10⁹ mm⁴.

Required : Deflections under concentrated loads.

Concept : Second order central finite differences equation.

Solution : Step I : The beam is divided into four equal parts, 2.5 m each. The nodal points are marked as shown in Fig. 5.8 (b).

Step II : BMD is plotted as shown in Fig. 5.8 (c).

Step III : $\left(\dfrac{M}{EI}\right)$ diagram is plotted as shown in Fig. 5.8 (d).

Step IV : Beam is simply supported at nodal points 1 and 5, so that deflection at both nodal points are zero.

$\therefore \quad y_1 = y_5 = 0$

$EI = 200 \times 10^3 \times 1.2 \times 10^9 = 2.4 \times 10^{14} \text{ Nmm}^2 = 2.4 \times 10^5 \text{ kNm}^2$

Step V : Applying central finite difference equation to nodal point 2,

$$y_1 - 2y_2 + y_3 = \frac{h^2 M_n}{E I_n}$$

$$y_1 - 2y_2 + y_3 = (2.5)^2 \frac{250}{EI}$$

$$y_1 - 2y_2 + y_3 = \frac{1562.5}{EI} \qquad \ldots (1)$$

Substituting the value of y_1 in equation (1),

$$-2y_2 + y_3 = \frac{1562.5}{EI} \qquad \ldots (2)$$

Step VI : Applying central finite difference equation to nodal point 3,

$$y_2 - 2y_3 + y_4 = (2.5)^2 \left(\frac{500}{EI}\right)$$

$$y_2 - 2y_3 + y_4 = \frac{3125}{EI} \qquad \ldots (3)$$

Step VII : Applying central finite difference equation to nodal point 4,

$$y_3 - 2y_4 + y_5 = (2.5)^2 \times \frac{500}{EI}$$

$$y_3 - 2y_4 + y_5 = \frac{3125}{EI} \qquad \ldots (4)$$

Substituting value of y_5 in equation (4),

$\therefore \qquad y_3 - 2y_4 = \frac{3125}{EI} \qquad \ldots (5)$

Step VIII : Solving equations (2), (3) and (5), we get

$$y_2 = -\frac{3515.63}{EI} = -\frac{3515.63}{2.4 \times 10^5} = -0.0146 \text{ m} = -14.65 \text{ mm}$$

$$y_3 = -\frac{5468.75}{EI} = -\frac{5468.75}{2.4 \times 10^5} = -0.0228 \text{ m} = -22.79 \text{ mm}$$

STRUCTURAL ANALYSIS – II   FINITE DIFF. METHOD & APPROX. ANALY. OF MULTI. FRAMES

$$y_4 = -\frac{4296.88}{EI} = -\frac{4296.88}{2.4 \times 10^5} = -0.0179 \text{ m} = -17.90 \text{ mm}$$

∴ Deflection under first 100 kN load is 22.79 mm (↓) and under second load is 17.90 mm (↓).

Example 5.8 : *A simply supported beam of length 8 m is loaded as shown in Fig. 5.9 (a). Determine the maximum deflection.*

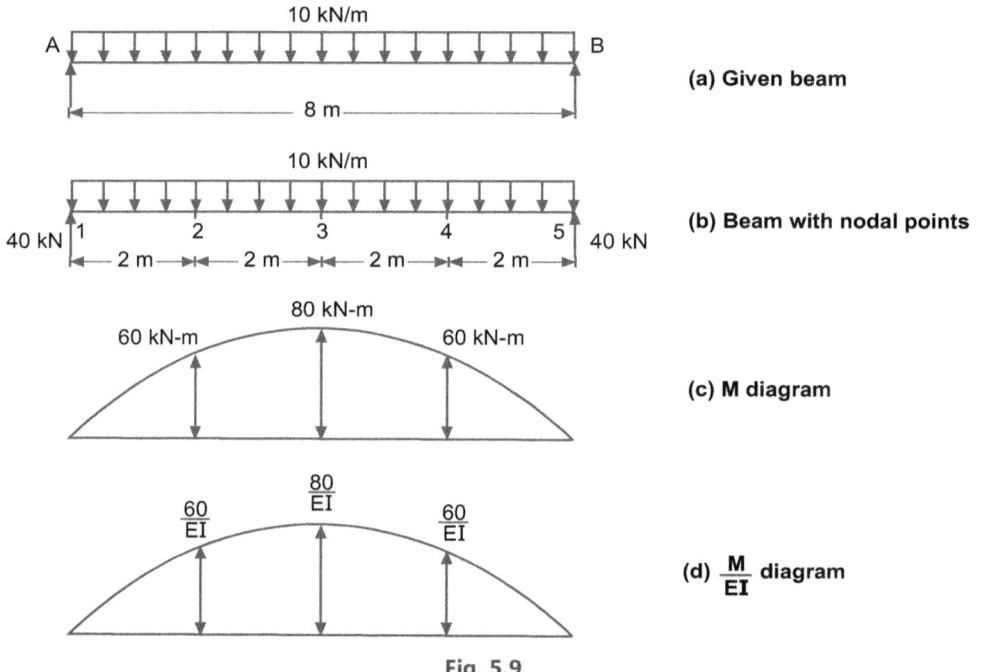

Fig. 5.9

Data : The beam is supported and loaded as shown in Fig. 5.9 (a).

Required : Maximum deflection.

Concept : Second order central finite difference equation.

Solution : Step I : The beam is divided into four equal parts, 2 m each. The nodal points are as shown in Fig. 5.9 (b).

Step II : BMD is plotted as shown in Fig. 5.9 (c) for given loading system.

Step III : $\left(\dfrac{M}{EI}\right)$ diagram is as shown in Fig. 5.9 (d).

Step IV : Beam is simply supported at nodal points 1 and 5, so that deflection at both nodal points are zero.

∴ $y_1 = y_5 = 0$

Beam is symmetrical with centre, so that maximum deflection will be at mid span.

Step V : Applying central finite difference equation to node 2,

$$y_1 - 2y_2 + y_3 = \frac{h^2 M_n}{E I_n}$$

$$y_1 - 2y_2 + y_3 = (2)^2 \left(\frac{60}{EI}\right)$$

$$y_1 - 2y_2 + y_3 = \frac{240}{EI} \qquad \ldots (1)$$

Substituting y_1 in equation (1),

∴ $$-2y_2 + y_3 = \left(\frac{240}{EI}\right) \qquad \ldots (2)$$

Step VI : Applying central finite difference equation to node 3,

$$y_2 - 2y_3 + y_4 = (2)^2 \cdot \left(\frac{80}{EI}\right)$$

∴ $$y_2 - 2y_3 + y_4 = \frac{320}{EI} \qquad \ldots (3)$$

Step VII : Applying central finite difference equation to node 4,

$$y_3 - 2y_4 + y_5 = (2)^2 \times \frac{60}{EI}$$

$$y_3 - 2y_4 + y_5 = \frac{240}{EI} \qquad \ldots (4)$$

Substituting value of y_5 in equation (4),

∴ $$y_3 - 2y_4 = \frac{240}{EI} \qquad \ldots (5)$$

Step VIII : Solving equations (2), (3) and (5), we get

$$y_2 = y_4 = -\frac{400}{EI}$$

$$y_3 = -\frac{560}{EI}$$

∴ Maximum deflection $= \left(\frac{560}{EI}\right) (\downarrow)$

Example 5.9 : *Determine the deflection at nodal points for beam AB loaded and supported as shown in Fig. 5.10 (a). Take five nodes.*

Data : The beam is loaded and supported as shown in Fig. 5.10 (a).

Required : Deflections at nodal points.

Concept : Second order central finite difference equation.

Solution : Step I : The beam is divided into four equal parts, 2 m each. The nodal points are marked as shown in Fig. 5.10 (b)

Step II : BMD is plotted as shown in Fig. 5.10 (c).

Step III : $\left(\dfrac{M}{EI}\right)$ diagram is shown in Fig. 5.10 (d).

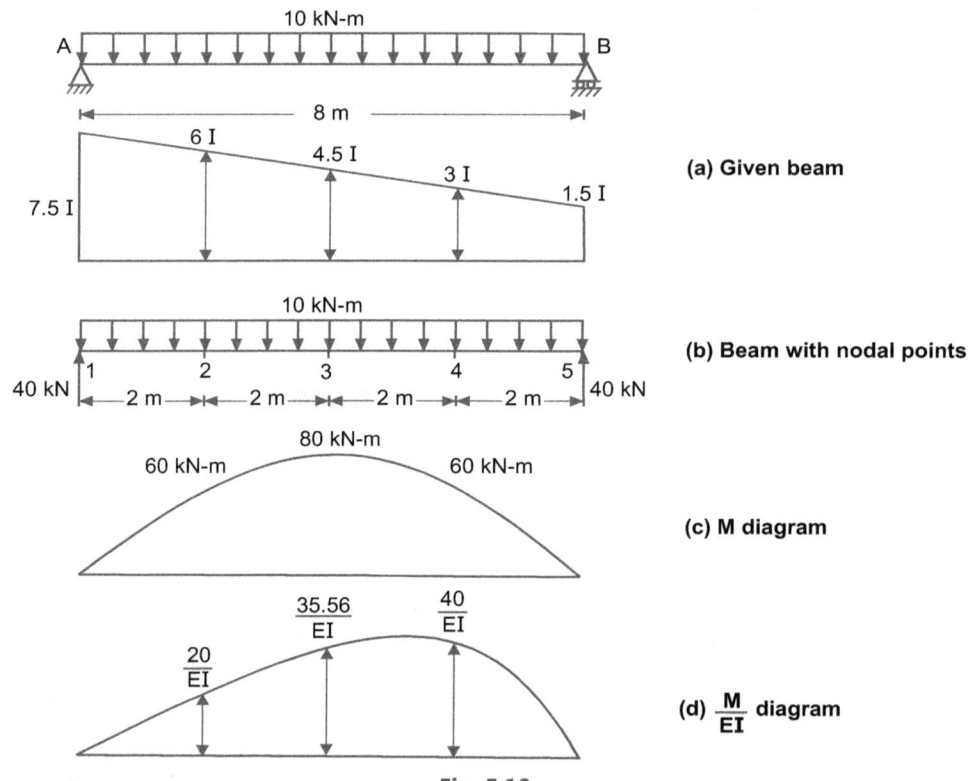

Fig. 5.10

Step IV : Beam is simply supported at nodes 1 and 5, so that deflections at both nodal points are zero.

$$\therefore \quad y_1 = y_5 = 0$$

Step V : Applying central finite difference equation to node 2,

$$y_1 - 2y_2 + y_3 = \frac{h^2 M_n}{E I_n}$$

$$y_1 - 2y_2 + y_3 = (2)^2 \cdot \frac{20}{EI}$$

$$y_1 - 2y_2 + y_3 = \frac{80}{EI} \quad \ldots (1)$$

Substituting y_1 in equation (1),

$$\therefore \quad -2y_2 + y_3 = \frac{80}{EI} \quad \ldots (2)$$

Step VI : Applying central finite difference equation to node 3,

$$y_2 - 2y_3 + y_4 = (2)^2 \times \frac{35.56}{EI}$$

$$\therefore \quad y_2 - 2y_3 + y_4 = \frac{142.24}{EI} \quad \ldots (3)$$

Step VII : Applying central finite difference equation to node 4,

$$\therefore \quad y_3 - 2y_4 + y_5 = (2)^2 \times \frac{40}{EI}$$

$$y_3 - 2y_4 + y_5 = \frac{160}{EI} \quad \ldots (4)$$

Substituting value of y_5 in equation (4),

$$\therefore \quad y_3 - 2y_4 = \frac{160}{EI} \quad \ldots (5)$$

Step VIII : Solving equations (2), (3) and (5), we get

$$y_2 = -\frac{171.12}{EI} \, m$$

$$y_3 = -\frac{262.24}{EI} \, m$$

$$y_4 = -\frac{211.12}{EI} \, m$$

$\therefore$ Deflections at nodal points 2, 3 and 4 are $\frac{171.12}{EI}$ ($\downarrow$), $\frac{262.24}{EI}$ ($\downarrow$) and $\frac{211.12}{EI}$ ($\downarrow$) respectively.

Example 5.10 : The beam is loaded and supported as shown in Fig. 5.11 (a). Determine deflection at nodal points. Take 5 nodes.

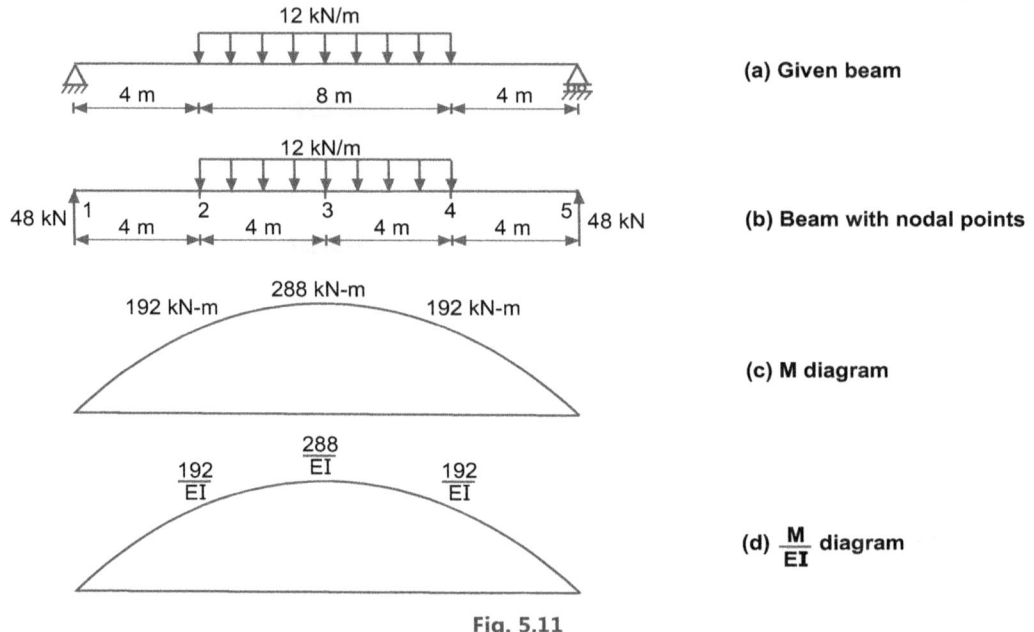

Fig. 5.11

Data : The beam is loaded and supported as shown in Fig. 5.11 (a).

Required : Deflection at nodal points.

Concept : Second order central finite difference equation.

Solution : Step I : The beam is divided into four equal parts, 4 m each. The nodal points are marked as shown in Fig. 5.11 (b).

Step II : BMD is plotted as shown in Fig. 5.11 (c).

Step III : $\left(\dfrac{M}{EI}\right)$ diagram is as shown in Fig. 5.11 (d).

Step IV : Beam is simply supported at nodal points 1 and 5, so that deflections at both nodal points are zero.

∴ $\quad y_1 = y_5 = 0$

Step V : Applying central finite difference equation to node 2,

∴ $\quad y_1 - 2y_2 + y_3 = \dfrac{h^2 M_n}{E I_n}$

$$y_1 - 2y_2 + y_3 = (4)^2 \left(\frac{192}{EI}\right)$$

$$y_1 - 2y_2 + y_3 = \frac{3072}{EI} \quad \ldots (1)$$

Substituting y_1 in equation (1),

$$\therefore \quad -2y_2 + y_3 = \frac{3072}{EI} \quad \ldots (2)$$

Step VI : Applying central finite difference equation to node 3,

$$y_2 - 2y_3 + y_4 = (4)^2 \times \frac{288}{EI}$$

$$\therefore \quad y_2 - 2y_3 + y_4 = \frac{4608}{EI} \quad \ldots (3)$$

Step VII : Applying central finite difference equation to node 4,

$$\therefore \quad y_3 - 2y_4 + y_5 = (4)^2 \times \frac{192}{EI}$$

$$\therefore \quad y_3 - 2y_4 + y_5 = \frac{3072}{EI} \quad \ldots (4)$$

Substituting y_5 in equation (4),

$$\therefore \quad y_3 - 2y_4 = \frac{3072}{EI} \quad \ldots (5)$$

Step VIII : Solving equations (2), (3) and (5), we get

$$y_2 = y_4 = -\frac{5376}{EI}$$

$$y_3 = -\frac{7680}{EI}$$

$\therefore$ Deflection at nodal points 2 and 4 is $\frac{5376}{EI}$ ($\downarrow$) and at nodal point 3 is $\frac{7680}{EI}$ ($\downarrow$).

Example 5.11 : *Determine deflections at nodal points for the beam loaded and supported as shown in Fig. 5.12 (a).*

Data : The beam is loaded and supported as shown in Fig. 5.12 (a).

Required : Deflection at nodal points.

Concept : Second order central finite difference equation.

Solution : Step I : The beam is divided into four equal parts, 1.5 m each. The nodal points are marked as shown in Fig. 5.12 (b).

Step II : BMD is plotted as shown in Fig. 5.12 (c) for given loading system.

Step III : $\left(\dfrac{M}{EI}\right)$ diagram is as shown in Fig. 5.12 (d).

$$\therefore \quad y_1 = y_5 = 0$$

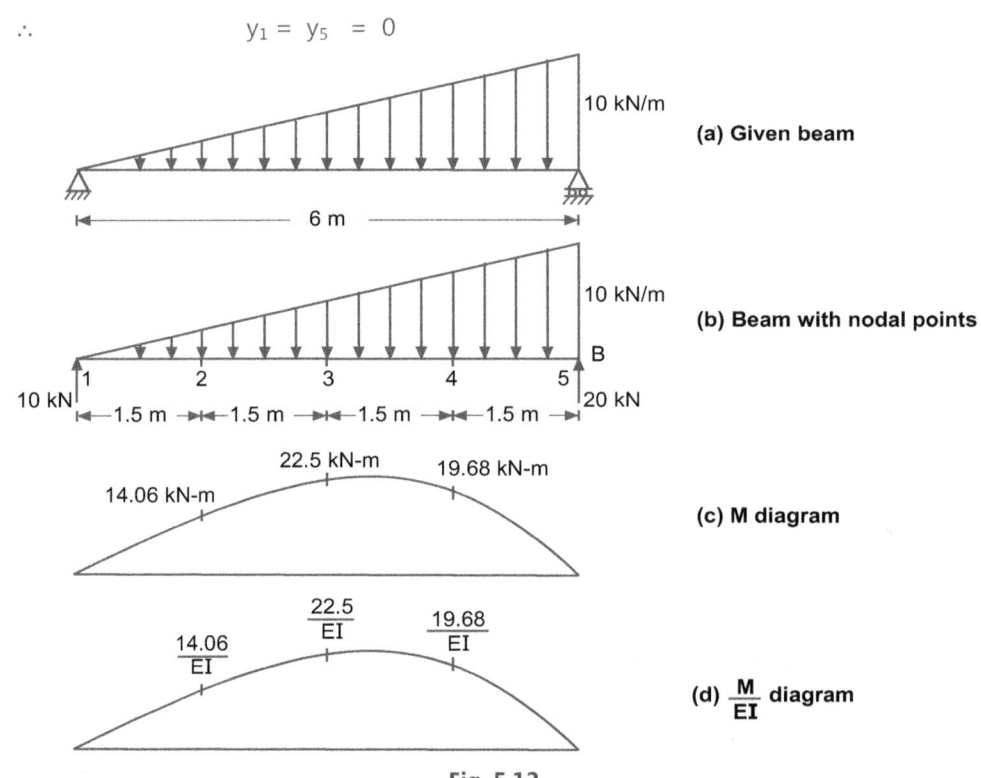

Fig. 5.12

Step IV : Beam is simply supported at nodal points 1 and 5, so that deflection at both nodal points are zero.

Step V : Applying central finite difference equation to node 2,

$$\therefore \quad y_1 - 2y_2 + y_3 = \dfrac{h^2 M_n}{E I_n}$$

$$y_1 - 2y_2 + y_3 = (1.5)^2 \times \dfrac{14.06}{EI}$$

$$y_1 - 2y_2 + y_3 = \dfrac{31.37}{EI} \qquad \ldots (1)$$

Substituting value of y_1 in equation (1),

$$\therefore \quad -2y_2 + y_3 = \frac{31.37}{EI} \quad \ldots (2)$$

Step VI : Applying central finite difference equation to node 3,

$$y_2 - 2y_3 + y_4 = (1.5)^2 \times \frac{22.5}{EI}$$

$$y_2 - 2y_3 + y_4 = \frac{50.63}{EI} \quad \ldots (3)$$

Step VII : Applying central finite difference equation to node 4,

$$y_3 - 2y_4 + y_5 = (1.5)^2 \times \frac{19.68}{EI}$$

$$y_3 - 2y_4 + y_5 = \frac{44.28}{EI} \quad \ldots (4)$$

Substituting value of y_5 in equation (4),

$$\therefore \quad y_3 - 2y_4 = \frac{44.28}{EI} \quad \ldots (5)$$

Step VIII : Solving equations (2), (3) and (5), we get

$$y_2 = -\frac{60.11}{EI}$$

$$y_3 = -\frac{88.58}{EI}$$

$$y_4 = -\frac{66.43}{EI}$$

Deflections at nodal points 2, 3 and 4 are $\frac{60.22}{EI}$ ($\downarrow$), $\frac{88.58}{EI}$ ($\downarrow$) and $\frac{66.43}{EI}$ ($\downarrow$) respectively.

(B) Approximate Analysis Of Multistoreyed Frames

5.3 Introduction

Analysis of multistoreyed structures involves large number of unknowns, also geometric properties of cross-section of members and material properties are pre-requisites of exact analysis. Therefore, it becomes necessary to perform some approximate analysis to arrive at an estimate of member sizes. This type of analysis is also useful in checking the results obtained by computer program which uses more elaborate computations.

In approximate methods of analysis, statically indeterminate structure is converted to statically determinate structure by making appropriate assumptions and then analysed for member forces using laws of statics. This chapter deals with commonly used approximate methods of analysis for rigid jointed multistoreyed, multibay two-dimensional frames.

Following are approximate methods of analysis :

Substitute frame method for vertical loads.

Any one of the following methods for horizontal loads :

    (a) Portal method.

    (b) Cantilever method.

5.4 SUBSTITUTE FRAME METHOD

This method is used for the analysis of multistorey frames subjected to vertical (gravity) loads only. In this method, only a part of the frame is considered for the analysis. The part considered is called a **substitute frame**. Here, it is assumed that moments transferred from one floor to another floor are negligible and hence analysis can be made floor by floor. So, a substitute frame is consisting of floor beams and columns above and below it. Columns are considered as fixed at far ends.

To find moments and shears in the second floor of multistorey frame shown in Fig. 5.13, the substitute frame shown in Fig. 5.14 is considered.

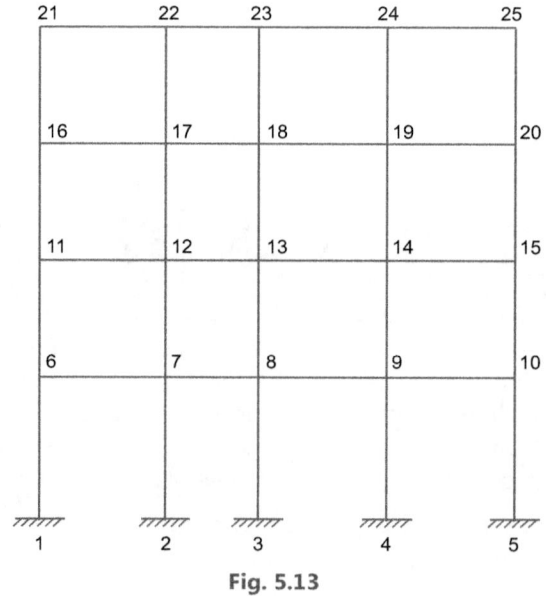

Fig. 5.13

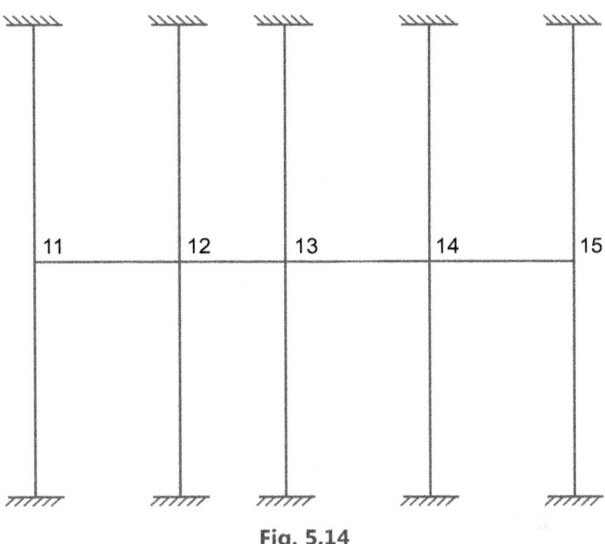

Fig. 5.14

In the multistorey frame, both dead load and live load together constitute the vertical load. Dead load acts throughout the frame and at all times. Live load may act through out the frame or on a part of it at a particular time. Hence, for analysis, various combinations of live loads are to be considered.

Critical live load positions are shown in Fig. 5.15 to Fig. 5.17 to get various design moments in beams.

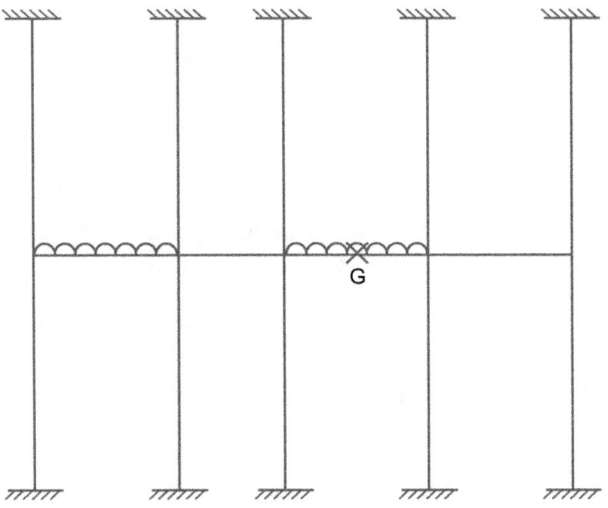

Fig. 5.15 : Live loading for maximum positive moment at G

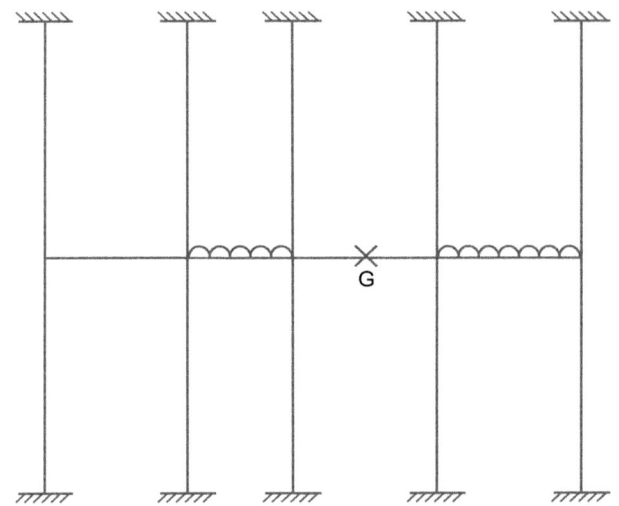

Fig. 5.16 : Live loading for maximum negative moment at G

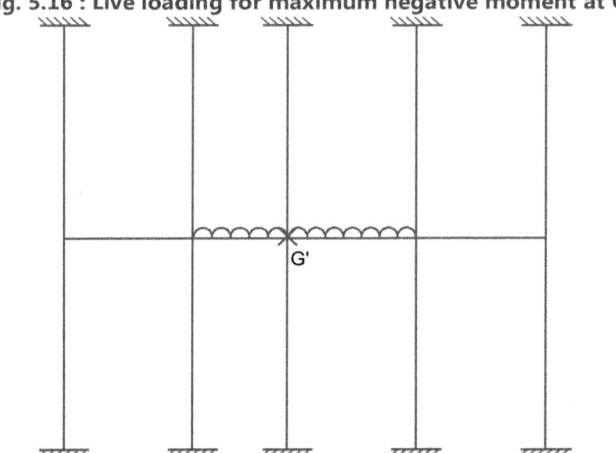

Fig. 5.17 : Live loading for maximum negative moment at G'

The design moment in the column is obtained for any one series of alternate loading of spans.

Moment distribution is done for only two cycles and hence it is called the **two-cycle method**.

At any joint, moment is mainly due to the loadings on the two adjacent spans. Hence, to find the moment at a joint, only two adjacent spans are considered.

Example 5.12 : *Analyse the intermediate frame of a multistoreyed frame shown in Fig. 5.18.*

Given : Spacing of frame   = 4.0 m

D.L. on floors = 4 kN/m²
L.L. on floors = 3 kN/m²
Self weight of beams = 5 kN/m for beams of span 9 m
= 4 kN/m for beams of span 6 m
= 3 kN/m for beams of span 3 m.

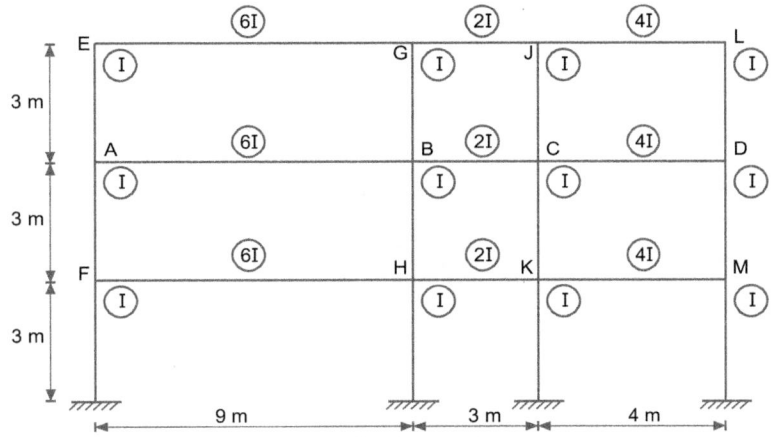

Fig. 5.18

Solution : The analysis for the second floor is given below. Similar analysis may be carried out to all the other floors to get the complete solution.

The substitute frame is as shown in Fig. 5.19.

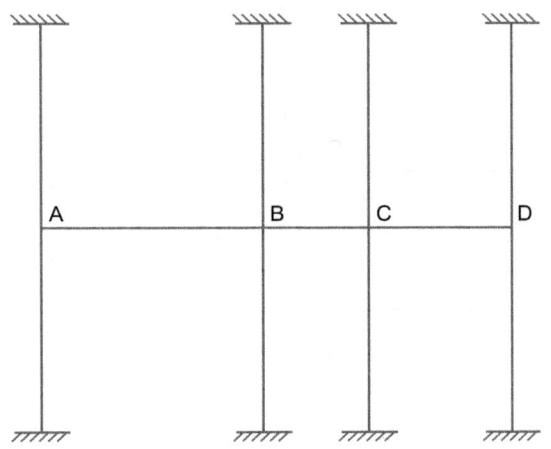

Fig. 5.19

The distribution factors are calculated in Table 5.1.

Table 5.1

Joint	Members	Relative stiffness	Sum	D.F.
	AE	$\dfrac{I}{3}$		$\dfrac{1}{4}$
A	AB	$\dfrac{6I}{9}$	$\dfrac{4I}{3}$	$\dfrac{1}{2}$
	AF	$\dfrac{I}{3}$		$\dfrac{1}{4}$
	BG	$\dfrac{I}{3}$		$\dfrac{1}{6}$
B	BA	$\dfrac{6I}{9}$	$\dfrac{6I}{3}$	$\dfrac{1}{3}$
	BC	$\dfrac{2I}{3}$		$\dfrac{1}{3}$
	BH	$\dfrac{I}{3}$		$\dfrac{1}{6}$
	CJ	$\dfrac{I}{3}$		$\dfrac{1}{6}$
C	CB	$\dfrac{2I}{3}$	$\dfrac{6I}{3}$	$\dfrac{1}{3}$
	CD	$\dfrac{4I}{6}$		$\dfrac{1}{3}$
	CK	$\dfrac{I}{3}$		$\dfrac{1}{6}$
	DL	$\dfrac{I}{3}$		$\dfrac{1}{4}$
D	DC	$\dfrac{4I}{6}$	$\dfrac{4I}{3}$	$\dfrac{1}{2}$
	DM	$\dfrac{I}{3}$		$\dfrac{1}{4}$

Loads :

Live load per meter run of girder = 3×4 = 12 kN/m
Dead load per meter run of girder = 4×4 = 16 kN/m
Dead load on 9 m beam = 16 + 5 = 21 kN/m
Dead load on 3 m beam = 16 + 3 = 19 kN/m
Dead load on 6 m beam = 16 + 4 = 20 kN/m

∴ Fixed-end moments due to dead load and total load are as shown in Table 5.2.

STRUCTURAL ANALYSIS – II   FINITE DIFF. METHOD & APPROX. ANALY. OF MULTI. FRAMES

Table 5.2 : F.E.M. due to dead and total load

Span	F.M.E. due to DL	F.E.M. due to total load (DL + LL)
AB	141.75 kN-m	222.75 kN-m
BC	14.25 kN-m	23.25 kN-m
CD	60.0 kN-m	96.0 kN-m

Design Moments in Beams :

(1) To determine the maximum moments at mid-spans in AB and CD.

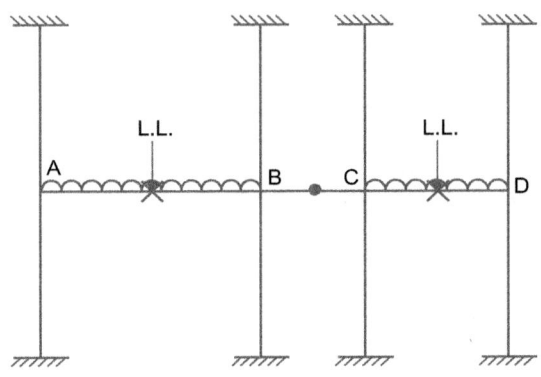

Fig. 5.20

Live load on AB and CD, dead load on ABCD.

	A		B		C		D
D.F.	$\frac{1}{2}$	$\frac{1}{3}$	$\frac{1}{3}$	$\frac{1}{3}$	$\frac{1}{3}$	$\frac{1}{2}$	
F.E.M.	− 222.75	+ 222.75	− 14.25	+ 14.25	− 96.0	+ 96.0	
BAL	+ 111.38	− 69.5	− 69.5	+ 27.25	+ 27.25	− 48.0	
COM	− 34.75	+ 55.69	+ 13.88	− 34.75	− 24.0	+ 13.88	
BAL	+ 17.38	− 23.19	− 23.19	+ 19.58	+ 19.58	− 6.94	
	− 128.74	+ 185.75	− 93.06	+ 26.33	− 73.17	+ 54.94	
Free moment at centre of span = $\frac{wL^2}{8}$		334.12		21.38		144	
Mid-span moment		$334.12 - \frac{128.74 + 185.75}{2}$ $= 176.88$		$21.38 - \frac{93.06 + 26.33}{2}$ $= -38.32$		$144 - \frac{73.17 + 54.94}{2}$ $= 79.95$	

(2) To determine the maximum moment at mid-span in BC.

STRUCTURAL ANALYSIS – II FINITE DIFF. METHOD & APPROX. ANALY. OF MULTI. FRAMES

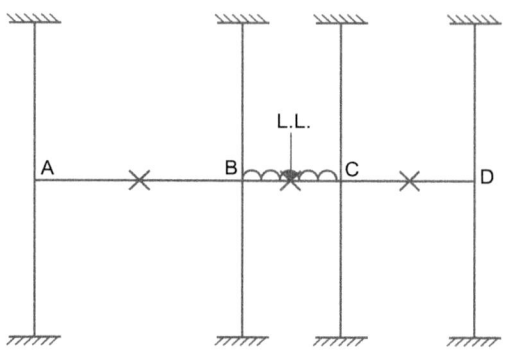

Fig. 5.21

Live load on BC, dead load on ABCD.

	A		B		C		D
D.F.	$\frac{1}{2}$	$\frac{1}{3}$	$\frac{1}{3}$	$\frac{1}{3}$	$\frac{1}{3}$	$\frac{1}{2}$
F.E.M.	– 141.75	+ 141.75	– 23.25	+ 23.25	– 60.0	+ 60.0
BAL	+ 70.88	– 39.5	– 39.5	+ 12.25	+ 12.25	– 30.0
COM	– 19.75	+ 35.44	+ 6.13	– 19.75	– 15.0	+ 6.13
BAL	+ 9.88	– 13.86	– 13.86	+ 11.58	+ 11.58	– 3.06
	–80.74	+ 123.83	– 70.48	+ 27.33	– 51.17	+ 33.07
Free moment at mid-span $\left(=\frac{wl^2}{8}\right)$	212.63		34.88		90	
Final moment at mid-span	$212.63 - \frac{80.74 + 123.83}{2}$ $= 110.35$		$34.88 - \frac{70.48 + 27.33}{2}$ $= -14.02$		$90 - \frac{51.17 + 33.07}{2}$ $= 47.88$	

Design Moments in Columns :

For maximum moments in columns, alternate spans should be loaded with live load. In present case, there are two possibilities.

   (i) Loading conditions are : Live load on AB and CD, while dead load on ABCD.

   (ii) Loading conditions are : Live load on BC, while dead load on ABCD.

Therefore, the possible cases for maximum moment in columns are the same as the two cases considered above. In the above moment distribution table, column moments are not noted down. At each cycle, distribution factor times unbalanced moment should have been noted as column moment. Column moments are not considered for distribution in beams. It can be determined after completing the moment distribution for the beam.

Column moment = Distribution factor of column × (–1) [FEMs + COMs]

STRUCTURAL ANALYSIS – II   FINITE DIFF. METHOD & APPROX. ANALY. OF MULTI. FRAMES

These calculations are shown in tabular form below :

(i) Live load on AB and CD, dead load on ABCD.

	A	B		C		D
FEMs	– 222.75	+ 222.75	– 14.25	+ 14.25	– 96.0	+ 96.0
COMs	– 34.75	+ 55.69	+ 13.88	– 34.75	– 24.0	+ 13.88
FEMs + COMs	– 257.50	278.07		– 140.5		109.88
Column moment						
at top	64.38	– 46.34		+ 23.42		– 27.47
at bottom	64.38	– 46.34		+ 23.42		– 27.47

(ii) Live load on BC only, dead load on ABCD.

	A	B		C		D
FEMs	– 141.75	+ 141.75	– 23.25	+ 23.25	– 60.0	+ 60.0
COMs	– 19.75	+ 35.44	+ 6.13	– 19.75	– 15.0	+ 6.13
FEMs + COMs	– 161.5	160.07		– 71.5		66.13
Column moment						
at top	40.38	– 26.68		+ 11.92		– 16.53
at bottom	40.38	– 26.68		+ 11.92		– 16.53

Design Moments in Columns :

	A	B	C	D
Design moment in columns				
at top	64.38	– 46.34	+ 23.42	– 27.47
at bottom	64.38	– 46.34	+ 23.42	– 27.47

Design Moments at Joints :

Moments at joints are negative (tension at top) moments and their maximum values occur only when adjoining panels are loaded with live loads.

For maximum moment at joint A :

The condition of loading to obtain maximum moment at joint A is as,

Live load on AB only, while dead load on AB and BC.

The effect of dead load on other span is neglected.

STRUCTURAL ANALYSIS – II   FINITE DIFF. METHOD & APPROX. ANAL. OF MULTI. FRAMES

	A		B		C		D
D.F.	$\frac{1}{2}$	$\frac{1}{3}$	$\frac{1}{3}$	$\frac{1}{3}$	$\frac{1}{3}$		$\frac{1}{2}$
F.E.M	− 222.75	+ 222.75	− 14.25	…	…		…
BAL	+ 111.38	− 69.5	− 69.5	…	…		…
COM	− 34.75	…	…	…	…		…
BAL	+ 17.38	…	…	…	…		…
Final	−128.74						

For maximum moment at joint B :

Loading conditions are : Live load on AB and BC, while dead load on ABCD.

	A		B		C		D
D.F.	$\frac{1}{2}$	$\frac{1}{3}$	$\frac{1}{3}$	$\frac{1}{3}$	$\frac{1}{3}$		$\frac{1}{2}$
F.E.M.	− 222.75	+ 222.75	− 23.25	+ 23.25	− 60.0		+ 60.0
BAL	+ 111.38	− 66.50	− 66.50	+ 12.25	+ 12.25		…
COM	…	+ 55.69	+ 6.13	…	…		…
BAL	…	− 20.60	− 20.60	…	…		…
Final		+ 191.34	− 104.22				

For maximum moment at joint C :

Loading conditions are : Live load on BC and CD, while dead load on AB.

	A		B		C		D
D.F.	$\frac{1}{2}$	$\frac{1}{3}$	$\frac{1}{3}$	$\frac{1}{3}$	$\frac{1}{3}$		$\frac{1}{2}$
F.E.M.	− 141.75	+ 141.75	− 23.25	+ 23.25	− 96.0		+ 96.0
BAL	…	− 39.5	− 39.5	+ 24.25	+ 24.25		− 48.0
COM	…	…	…	− 19.75	− 24.0		…
BAL	…	…	…	+ 14.58	+ 14.58		…
Final				+ 42.33	− 81.17		

For maximum moment at joint D :

Loading conditions are : Live load on CD only, while dead load on BC and CD.
The effect of dead load on other spans is neglected.

	A		B		C		D
D.F.	$\frac{1}{2}$	$\frac{1}{3}$	$\frac{1}{3}$	$\frac{1}{3}$	$\frac{1}{3}$		$\frac{1}{2}$
F.E.M.	…	…	…	+ 14.25	− 96.0		+ 96.0
BAL	…	…	…	+ 27.25	+ 27.25		− 48.0
COM	…	…	…	…	…		+ 13.63
BAL	…	…	…	…	…		− 6.81
Final							+ 54.82

5.5 PORTAL METHOD

The Portal method is an approximate analysis used for analysing building frames subjected to lateral loading such as the one shown in Fig. 5.22 (a). This method is more appropriate for low rise (height is less than width) building frames. In the analysis, the following assumptions are made :

An inflection point is located at mid-height of each column,

An inflection point is located at centre of each beam, and

The horizontal shear is divided among all the columns on the basis that each interior column takes twice as much as the exterior columns.

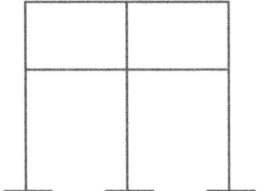
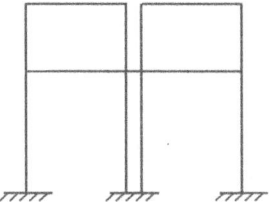

(a) Building frame under lateral loading   (b) Equivalent portals

Fig. 5.22

The basis of third assumption should be clear from Fig. 5.22 which indicates that interior column will resist the shear of two columns of individual portals.

Example 5.13 : *Analyse the frame shown in Fig. 5.23 by portal method.*

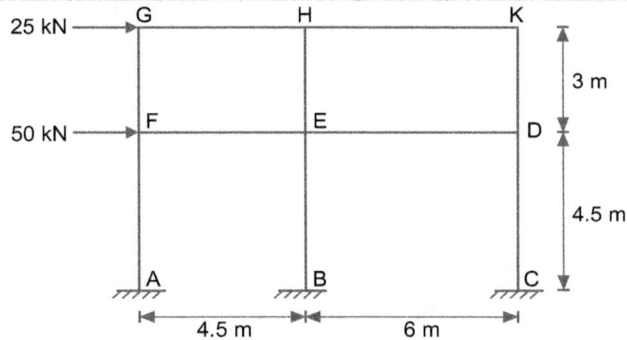

Fig. 5.23 : Given structure

Data : As shown in Fig. 5.23.

Required : BMD

Concept : Portal method.

Solution : Step 1 : Assuming points of contraflexure at mid-height of columns and considering FBD of upper storey as shown in Fig. 5.24 (a).

$\Sigma F_x = 0$, $\quad\quad 25 = H + 2H + H$

$\therefore \quad\quad H = 6.25 H$

Points of contraflexure are also assumed at the centre of each beam and member forces are obtained by equilibrium for each part of the structure as shown in Fig. 5.24 (b).

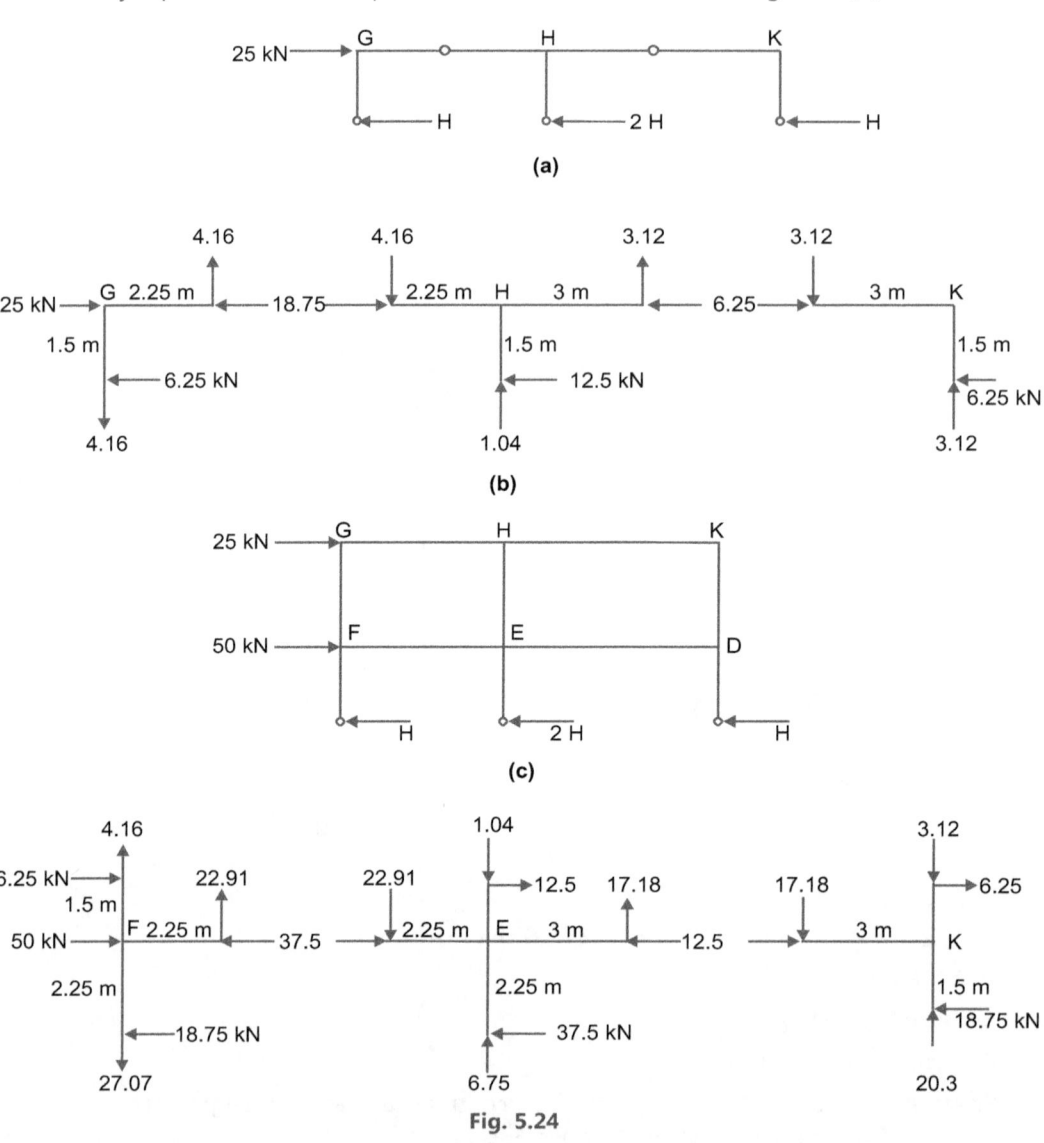

Fig. 5.24

Step II : Points of contraflexure are again assumed at mid-height of lower storey columns.

Thus, for lower storey,

$\sum F_x = 0$, $\qquad 25 + 50 = H + 2H + H$

$\therefore \qquad\qquad\qquad H = 18.75$ kN

The member forces for lower storey are obtained from FBD of part of structure as shown in Fig. 5.24 (d).

Step III : BMD : On tension side as shown in Fig. 5.25.

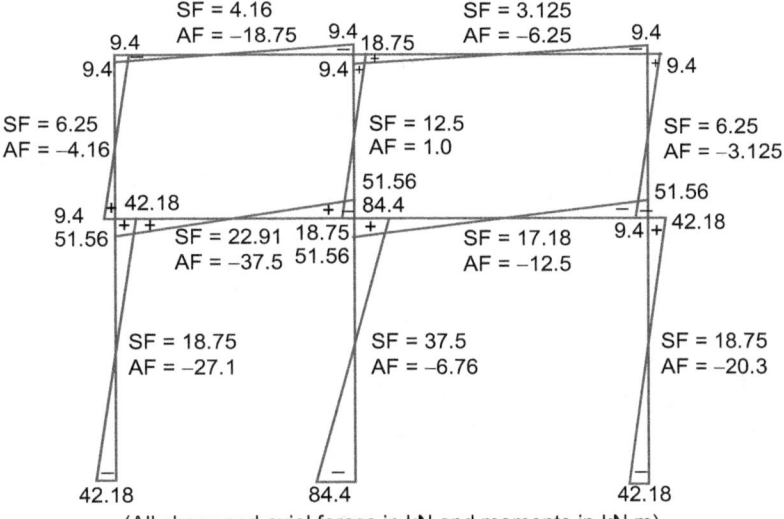

(All shear and axial forces in kN and moments in kN m)

Fig. 5.25

Example 5.14 : *Analyse the frame shown in Fig. 5.26 by portal method and draw BMD.*

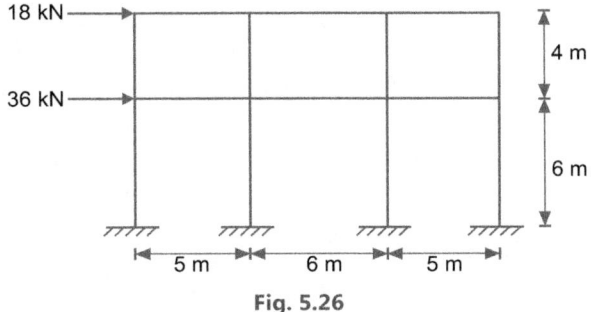

Fig. 5.26

Data : As shown in Fig. 5.27.
Required : BMD.
Concept : Portal method
Solution :

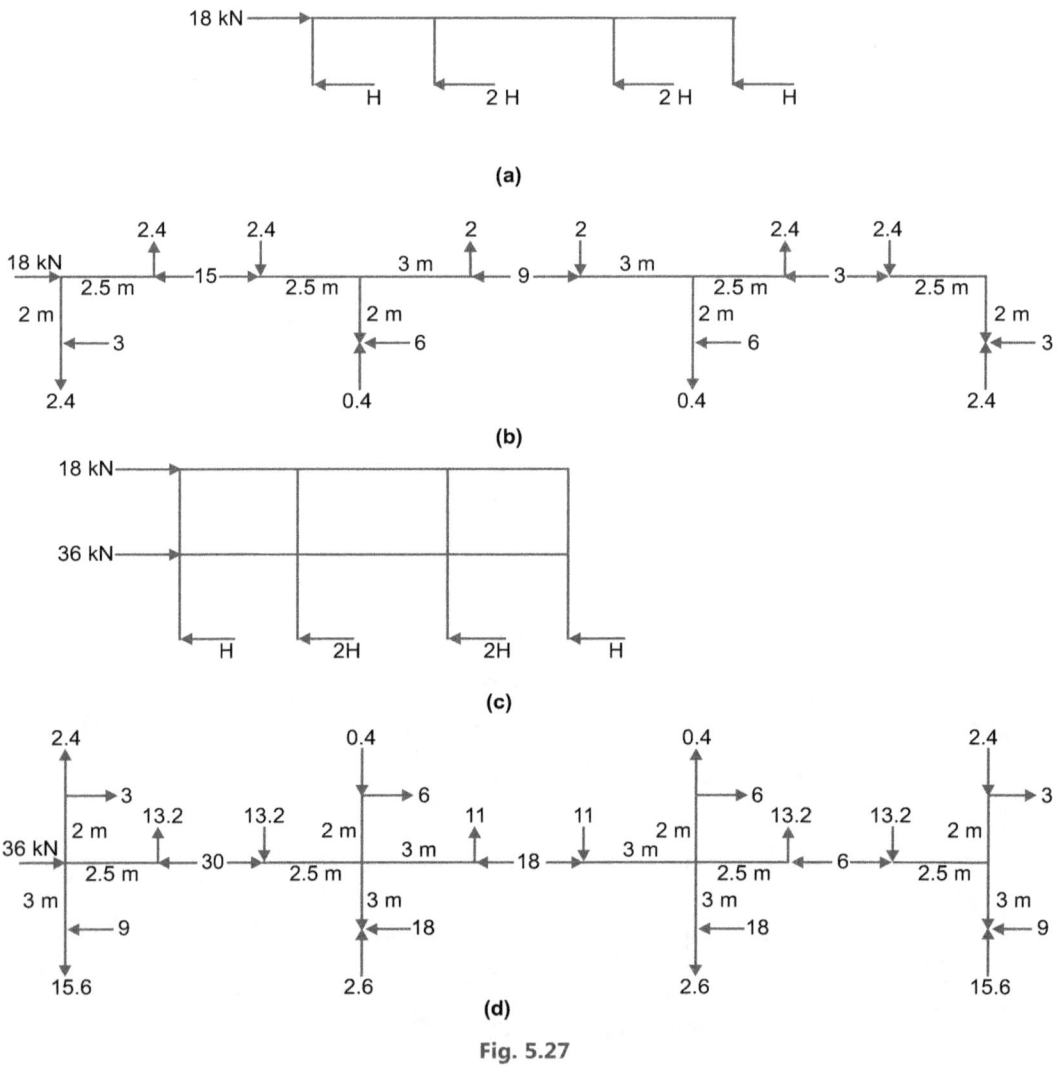

Fig. 5.27

BMD on tension side as shown in Fig. 5.28.

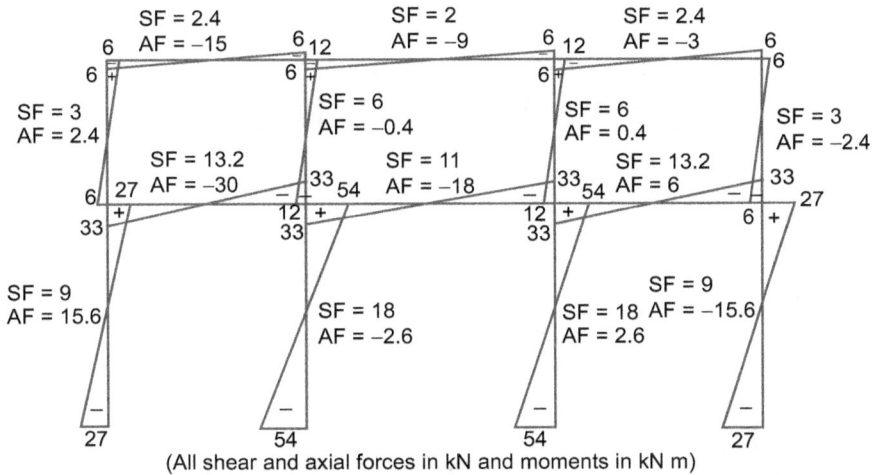

(All shear and axial forces in kN and moments in kN m)

Fig. 5.28

Example 5.15 : Analyse the portal frame shown in Fig. 5.29, under lateral loading by portal method.

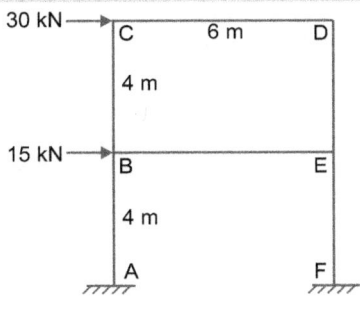

Fig. 5.29

Data : As shown in Fig. 5.29.

Required : BMD.

Concept : Portal method.

Solution : Step I : Assuming points of contraflexure at mid height of columns and considering FBD of upper storey as shown in Fig. 5.30 (a).

$$\sum F_x = 0$$
$$30 = H + H$$
∴ $$H = 15 \text{ kN}$$

STRUCTURAL ANALYSIS – II   FINITE DIFF. METHOD & APPROX. ANALY. OF MULTI. FRAMES

Points of contraflexure are also assumed at the centre of each beam and member forces are obtained by equilibrium for each part of the structure as shown in Fig. 5.30 (b).

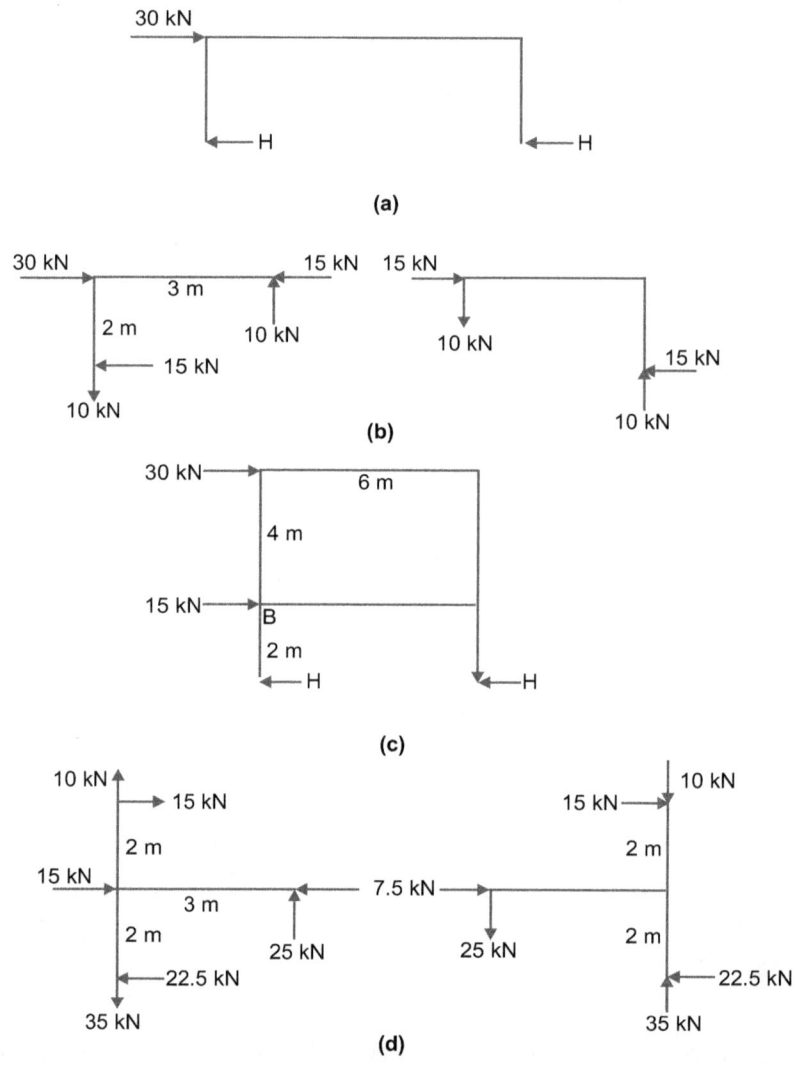

Fig. 5.30

Step II : Points of contraflexure are again assumed at mid-height of lower storey columns.

Thus for lower storey,

$$\Sigma f_x = 0$$
$$30 + 5 = H + H$$
$$\therefore \quad H = 22.5 \text{ kN}$$

The member forces for lower storey are obtained from FBD of part of structure as shown in Fig. 5.30 (a).

Step III : BMD on tension side as shown in Fig. 5.31.

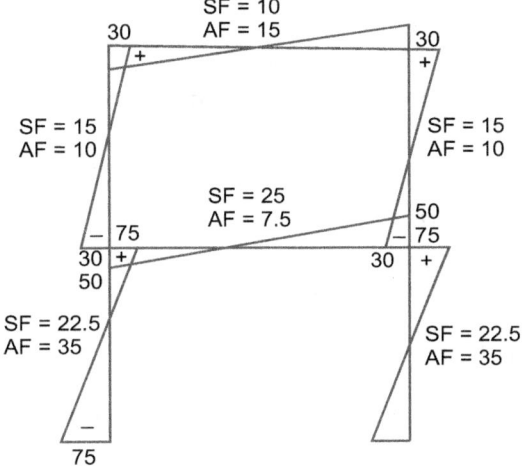

Fig. 5.31

Example 5.16 : Determine the approximate value of moment, shear and axial force in each member of the frame loaded and supported as shown in Fig. 5.32. Use portal method for analysis.

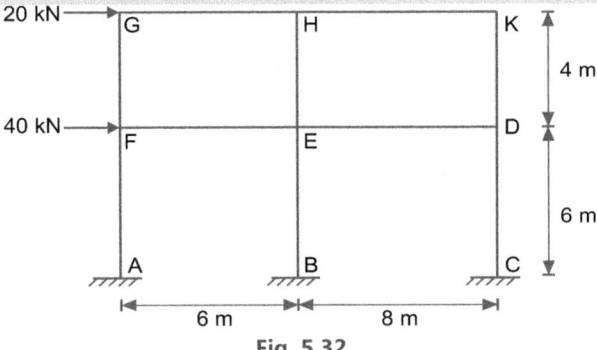

Fig. 5.32

Data : As shown in Fig. 5.32.
Required : BMD.

Concept : Portal method.

Solution : Step I : Assuming points of contraflexure at mid-height of columns and considering FBD of upper storey as shown in Fig. 5.33 (a).

$$\Sigma f_x = 0$$
$$20 = H + 2H + H$$
$$\therefore \quad H = 5 \text{ kN}$$

Points of contraflexure are also assumed at the centre of each beam and member forces are obtained by equilibrium, for each part of the structure as shown in Fig. 5.33 (b).

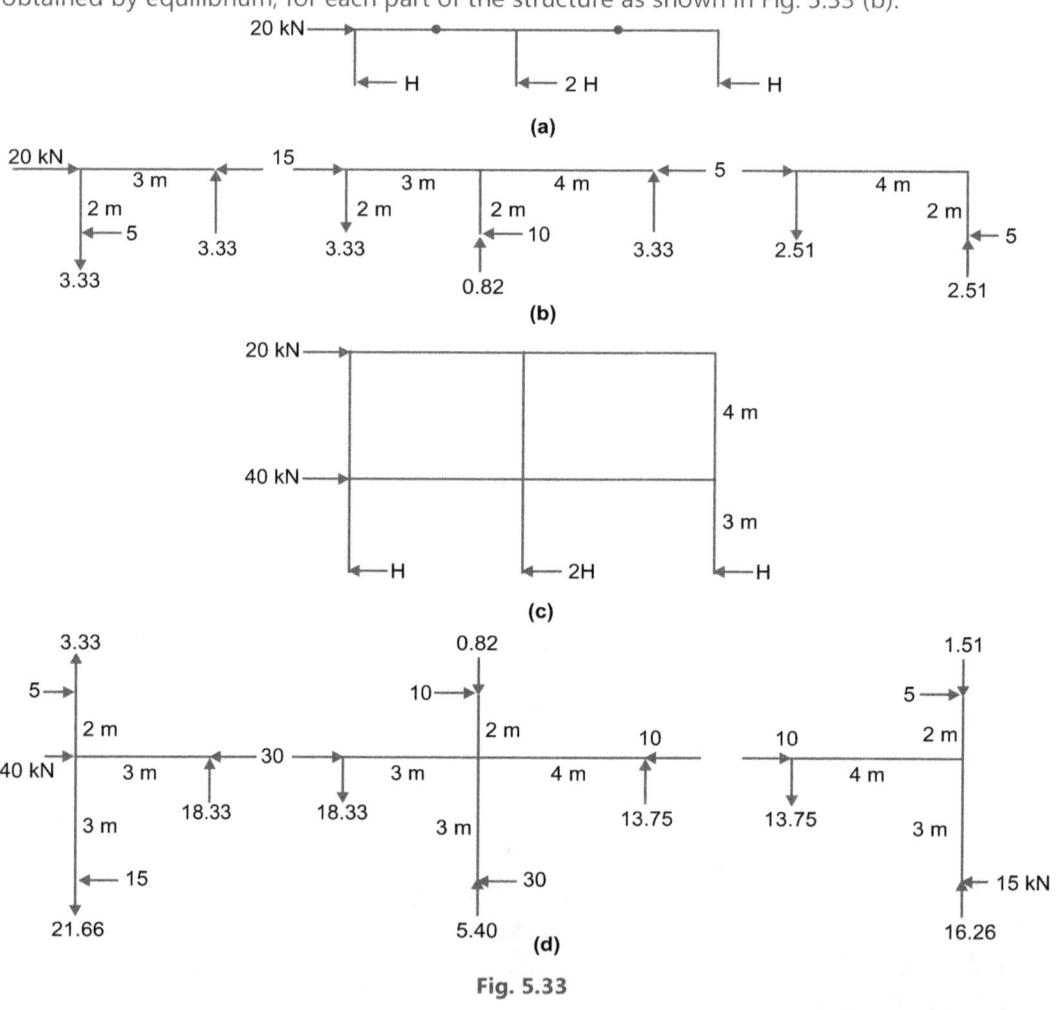

Fig. 5.33

Step II : Points of contraflexure are again assumed at mid-height of lower storey columns.

Thus for lower storey.
$$\sum f_x = 0$$
$$20 + 40 = H + 2H + H$$
$$\therefore \quad H = 15 \text{ kN}$$

The member forces for lower storey are obtained from FBD of part of structure as shown in Fig. 5.33 (d).

Step III : BMD on tension side as shown in Fig. 5.34.

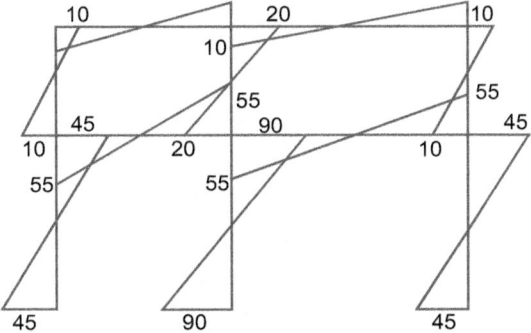

Fig. 5.34 : BMD on tension side

5.6 CANTILEVER METHOD

The cantilever method of analysis is more appropriate for all structures i.e. for a structure that has height greater than its width. This method is based on the assumption that the building frame acts like a cantilever beam with the columns as longitudinal fibres of the beam.

Consider the building frame loaded as shown in Fig. 5.35 (a). For such a tall building, the column strains resulting from the overall bending action are assumed to affect behaviour. We assume that the frame is a laterally loaded cantilever with a cross-section as indicated in Fig. 5.35 (b). The moment at a typical horizontal section AA is resisted by concentrated column forces as shown in Fig. 5.35 (c). The assumptions made in the analysis are :

1. An inflection point is located at the mid-height of the column in each storey;
2. An inflection point is located at the mid-point of each beam; and
3. Direct stresses in each column is proportional to its distance from the centroid of the areas of the column group at that level.

STRUCTURAL ANALYSIS – II   FINITE DIFF. METHOD & APPROX. ANALY. OF MULTI. FRAMES

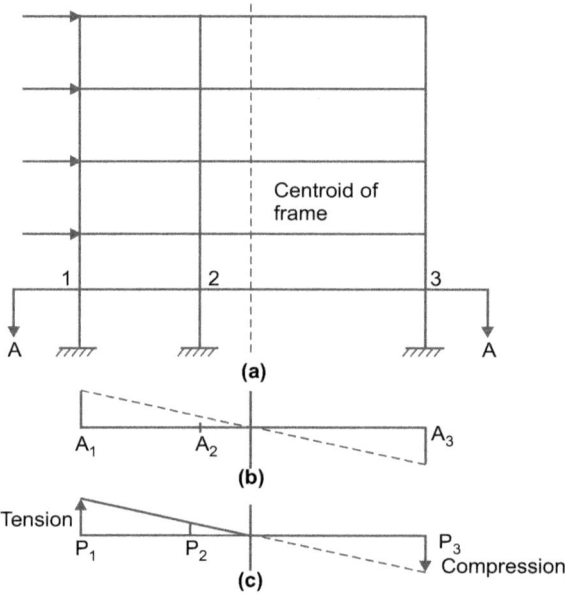

Fig. 5.35 : (a) Building frame, (b) Cross-section of frame, (c) Axial forces in columns

The first two assumptions are the same as in portal method. The third assumption gives the distribution of the axial forces in the columns instead of the distribution of the shear force among the columns as in the portal method. The last assumption enables one to include the effects of column having different cross-sectional areas.

Example 5.17 : *Analyse the frame as shown in Fig. 5.36 by cantilever method. Assume all columns to be of same cross-sectional area.*

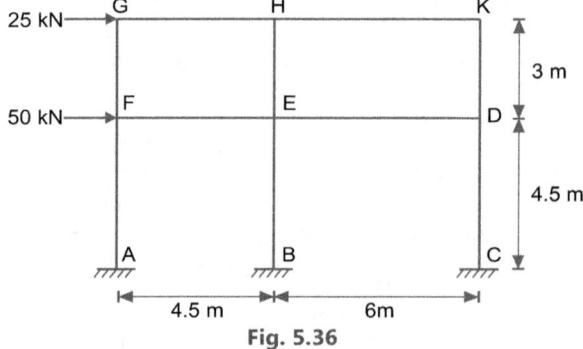

Fig. 5.36

Data : As shown in Fig. 5.36.
Required : BMD.
Concept : Cantilever method.

Solution : Step I : To locate CG of frame.

Taking moments of areas of column about the L.H.S. column,

$$\bar{x} = \frac{4.5 + 10.5}{3} = 5 \text{ m}$$

Considering FBD of frame above the points of contraflexure in columns, as shown in Fig. 5.37 (a).

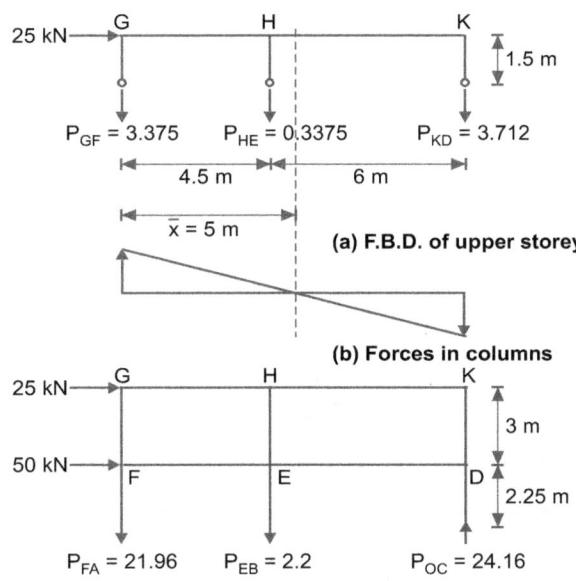

Fig. 5.37

From Fig. 5.37 (b), $\quad \dfrac{P_{GF}}{5} = \dfrac{P_{HE}}{0.5} = \dfrac{P_{KD}}{5.5}$ ... (i)

Taking moments about points of contraflexure of right end column in Fig. 5.37 (a),

$P_{GF} \times 10.5 + P_{HE} \times 6 - 25 \times 1.5 = 0$ ... (ii)

Solving equations (i) and (ii), we get

$P_{GF} = 3.375$ kN   (Tension)
$P_{HE} = 0.3375$ kN   (Tension)
$P_{KD} = 3.712$ kN   (Compression)

Axial forces in columns of lower storey are obtained in similar way and are shown in Fig. 5.37 (c).

Step II : Member forces :

Having determined the axial forces for columns, the member forces are determined from the FBD as shown in Fig. 5.38.

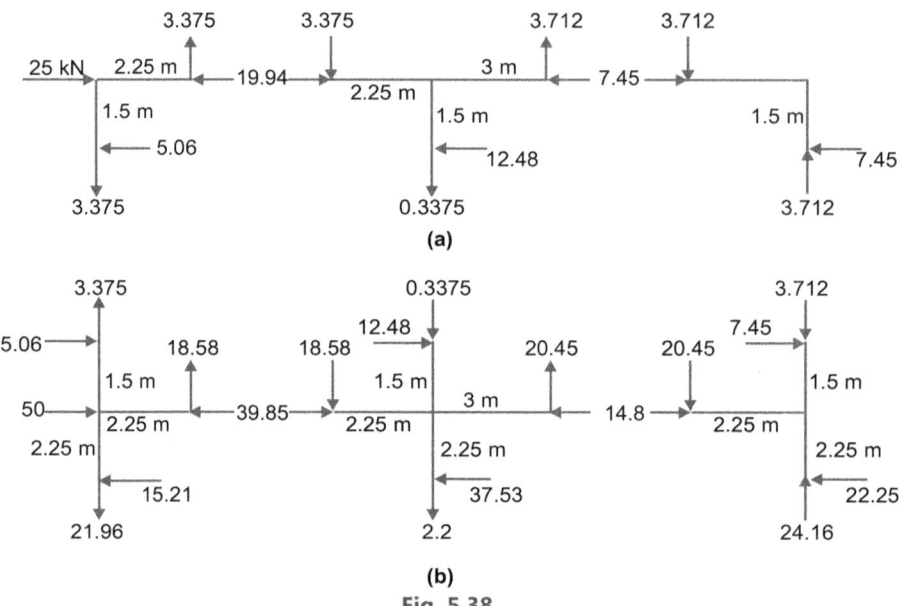

(a)

(b)

Fig. 5.38

Step III : BMD : As shown in Fig. 5.39.

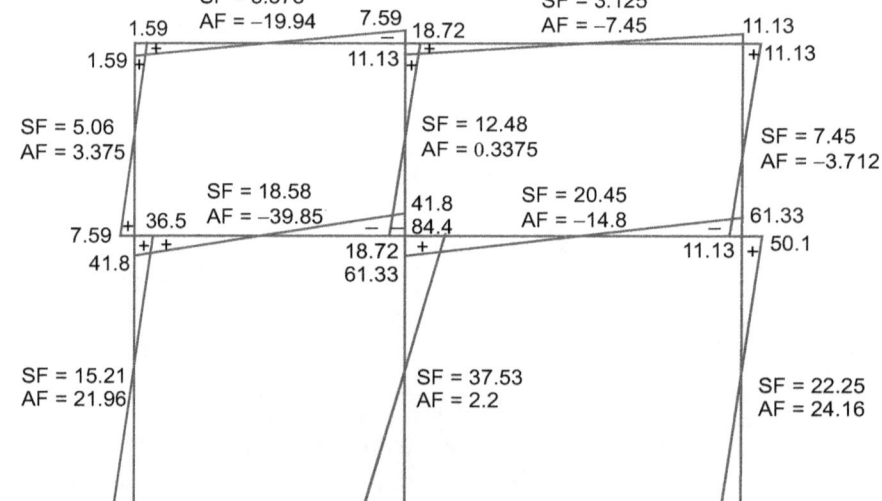

(All shear and axial forces in kN and moments in kN-m)

Fig. 5.39 : Forces in frame members

STRUCTURAL ANALYSIS – II FINITE DIFF. METHOD & APPROX. ANALY. OF MULTI. FRAMES

Example 5.18 : Analyse the frame shown in Fig. 5.40 by cantilever method assuming all columns to be of same cross-sectional area.

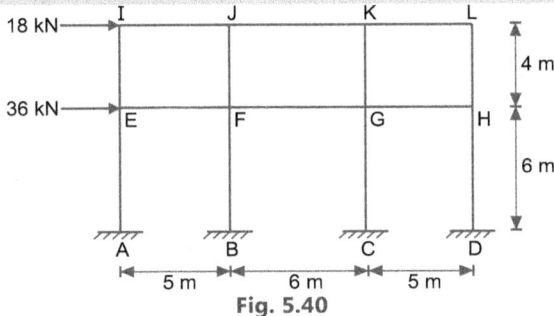

Fig. 5.40

Data : As shown in Fig. 5.40.
Required : BMD.
Concept : Cantilever method.
Solution :

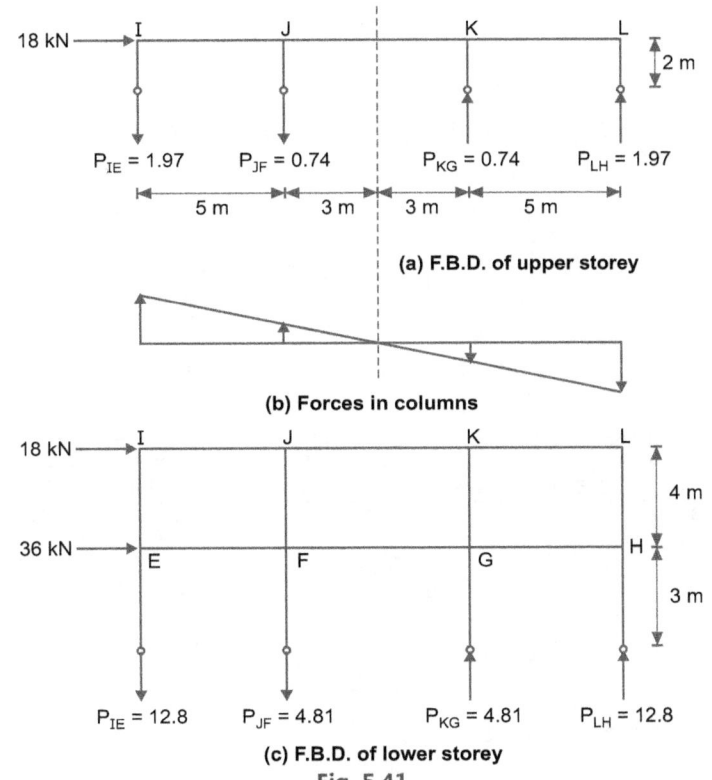

(a) F.B.D. of upper storey

(b) Forces in columns

(c) F.B.D. of lower storey
Fig. 5.41

Step I : By symmetry, CG of frame is as shown in Fig. 5.41.

From Fig. 5.41 (b),

$$P_{JF} = P_{KG} \quad \ldots (i)$$
$$P_{IE} = P_{LH} \quad \ldots (ii)$$
$$\frac{P_{IE}}{8} = \frac{P_{JF}}{3} \quad \ldots (iii)$$

Taking moments about point of contraflexure of right end column in Fig. 6.41 (a),

$$P_{IE}(16) + P_{JF}(11) - P_{KG}(5) - 18 \times 2 = 0$$
$$16\, P_{IE} + 6\, P_{JF} = 36 \quad \ldots (iv)$$

Solving equations (iii) and (i), we get

$$P_{JF} = P_{KG} = 0.74 \text{ kN}$$
$$P_{IE} = P_{LH} = 1.97 \text{ kN}$$

Step II : Member forces :

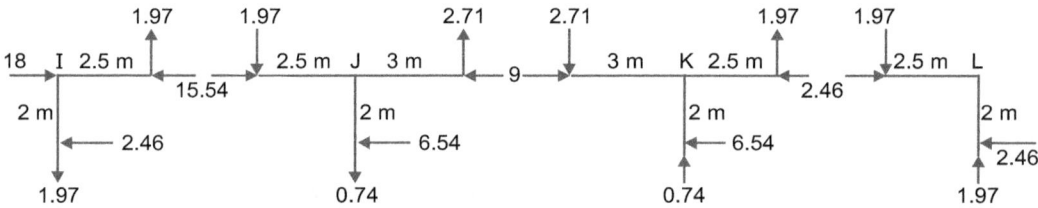

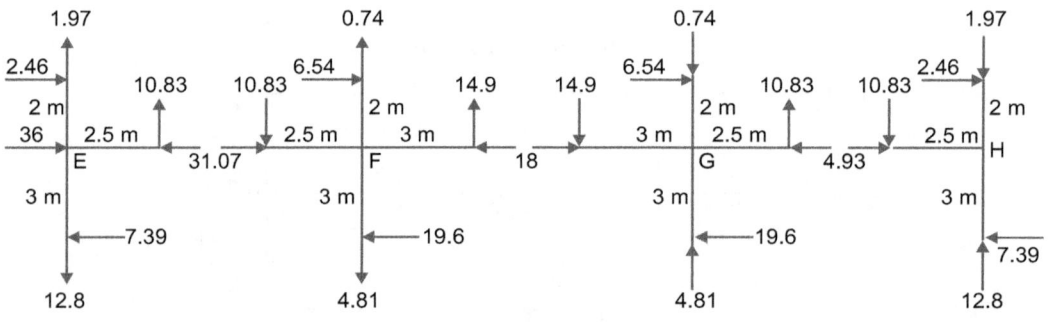

Fig. 5.42

Step III : BMD : As shown in Fig. 5.43.

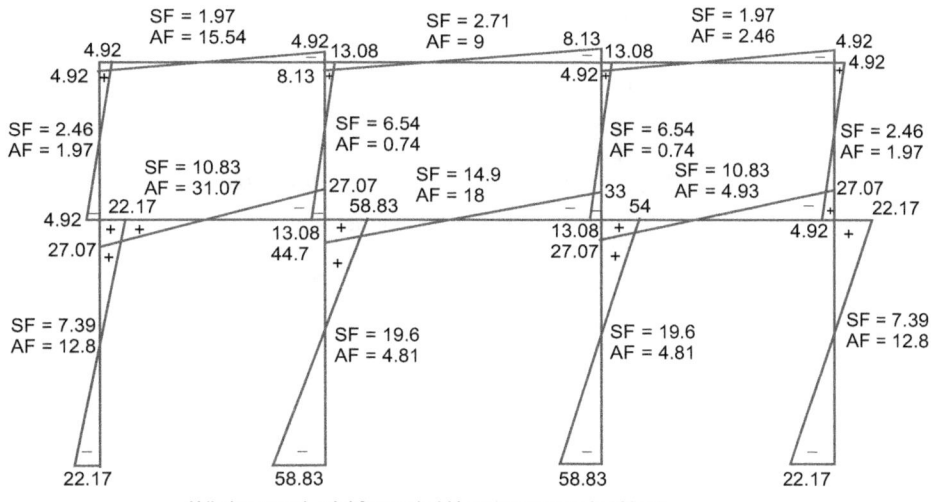

(All shear and axial forces in kN and moments in kN m)

Fig. 5.43 : Forces in frame members

Example 5.19 : *Analyse the portal frame under lateral loading by cantilever method. The columns are assumed to have equal cross-sectional areas.*

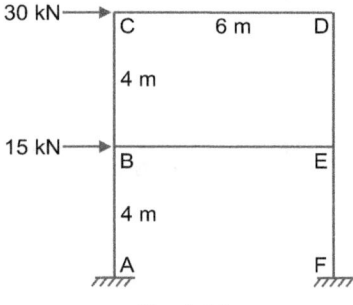

Fig. 5.44

Data : As shown in Fig. 5.44.

Required : BMD.

Concept : Cantilever method.

Solution : Step I : To locate C.G. of frame. Taking moment of areas of column about L.H.S. column.

$$\bar{x} = \frac{6}{2} = 3 \text{ m}$$

Considering F.B.D. of frame above the points of contraflexure in columns as shown in Fig. 5.45 (a).

STRUCTURAL ANALYSIS – II FINITE DIFF. METHOD & APPROX. ANALY. OF MULTI. FRAMES

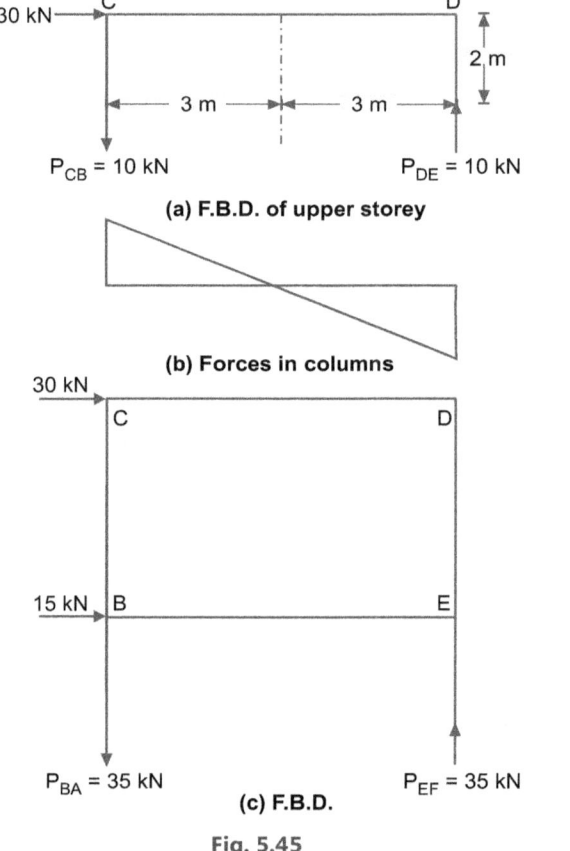

Fig. 5.45

$$\frac{P_{CB}}{3} = \frac{P_{DE}}{3} \qquad \ldots (i)$$

Taking moments about points of contraflexure of right end column in Fig. 5.45 (a).

$$P_{CB} \times 6 - 30 \times 2 = 0 \qquad \ldots (ii)$$

Solving equations (i) and (ii),

$$P_{CB} = 10 \text{ kN (Tension)}$$
$$P_{DE} = 10 \text{ kN (Compression)}$$

Axial forces in columns of lower storey are obtained in similar way and are shown in Fig. 5.45 (c).

Step II : Member forces.

Having determined the axial forces for column the member forces are determined from the FBD as shown in Fig. 5.46.

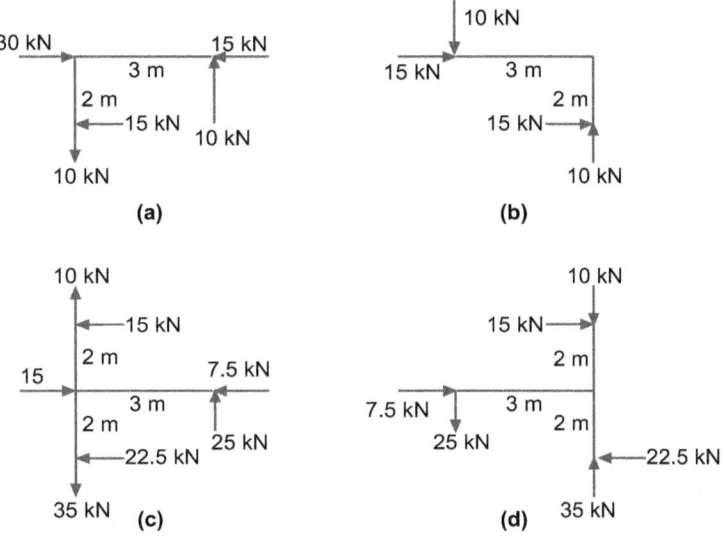

(a) (b)

(c) (d)

Fig. 5.46

Step III : BMD as shown in Fig. 5.47.

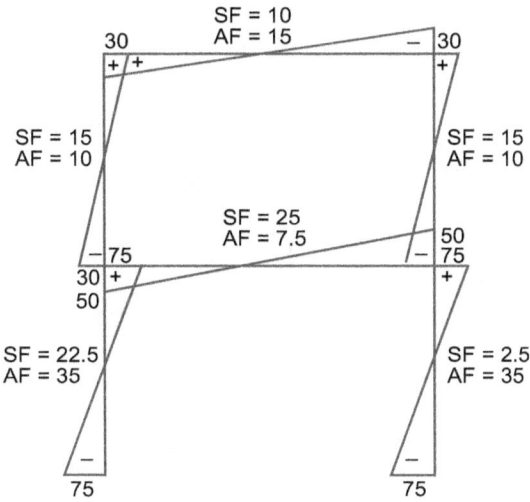

Fig. 5.47 : BMD on tension side

STRUCTURAL ANALYSIS – II FINITE DIFF. METHOD & APPROX. ANALY. OF MULTI. FRAMES

Example 5.20 : *Determine the approximate values of moment, shear and axial force in each member of the frame loaded and supported as shown in Fig. 5.48 using cantilever method of analysis.*

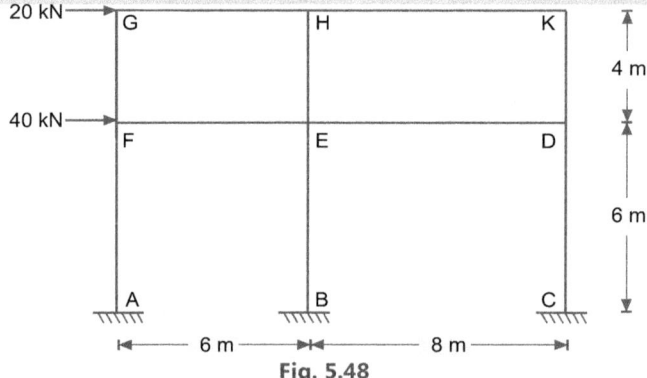

Fig. 5.48

Data : As shown in Fig. 5.48.
Required : BMD.
Concept : Cantilever method.
Solution : Step I : To locate C.G. of frame. Taking moments of areas of column about the L.H.S. column,

$$\bar{x} = \frac{14 + 6}{3} = \frac{20}{3} = 6.67 \text{ m}$$

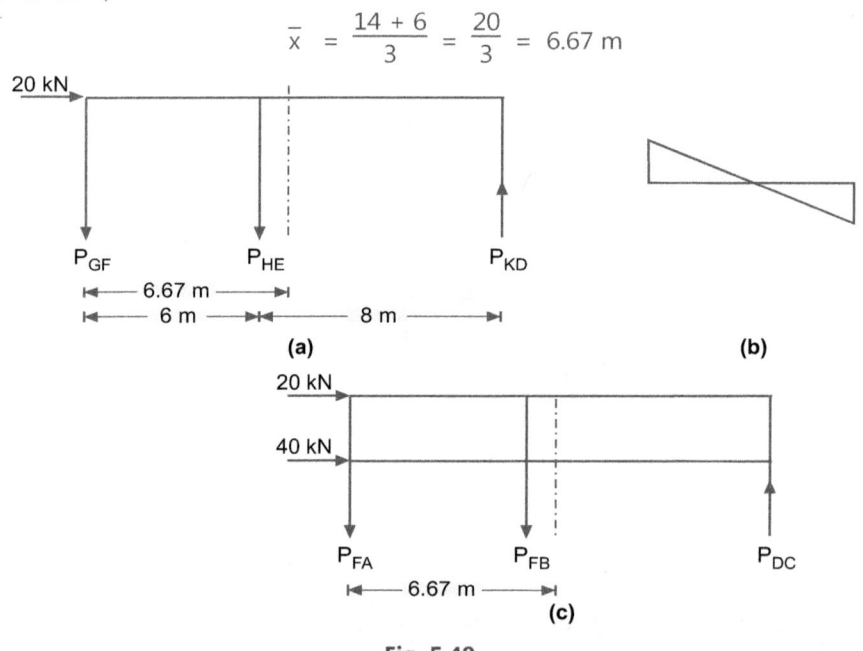

Fig. 5.49

Ch. 5 | 5.52

Considering FBD of frame above the points of contraflexure, as shown in Fig. 5.49 (a).

$$\frac{P_{GF}}{6.67} = \frac{P_{He}}{0.67} = \frac{P_{KD}}{7.33} \qquad \ldots (i)$$

Taking moments about points of contraflexure of right end column in Fig. 5.49 (b).

$$P_{GF} \times 14 + P_{HE} \times 8 - 20 \times 2 = 0$$

$$14 P_{GF} + 8 P_{HE} = 40 \qquad \ldots (ii)$$

Solving equations (i) and (ii), we get,

$$P_{GF} = 2.7 \text{ kN (Tension)}$$

$$P_{HE} = 0.27 \text{ kN (Tension)}$$

$$P_{KD} = 2.97 \text{ kN (Compression)}$$

Axial forces in column of lower storey are obtained in similar way and are shown in Fig. 5.49 (c).

Step II : Member forces : $P_{FA} = 17.57$ kN (Tension)

$$P_{EB} = 1.76 \text{ kN (Tension)}$$

$$P_{DC} = 19.33 \text{ kN (Compression)}$$

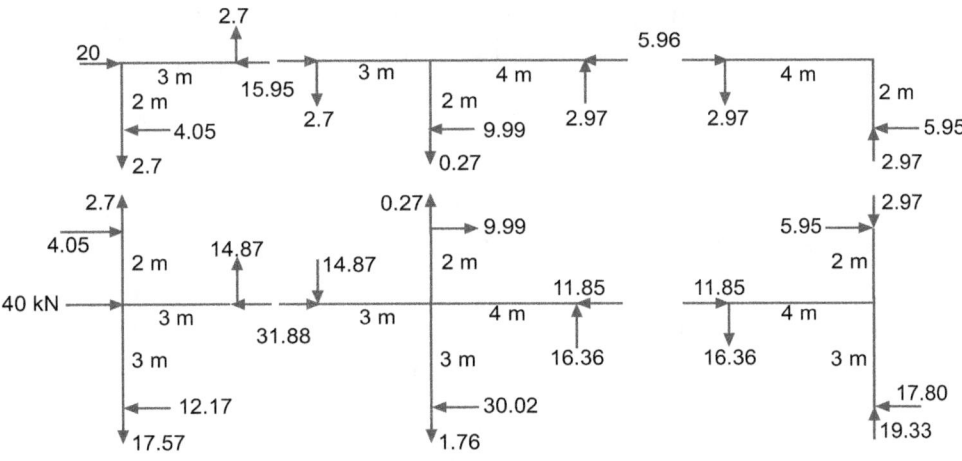

Fig. 5.50

Step III : BMD as shown in Fig. 5.51.

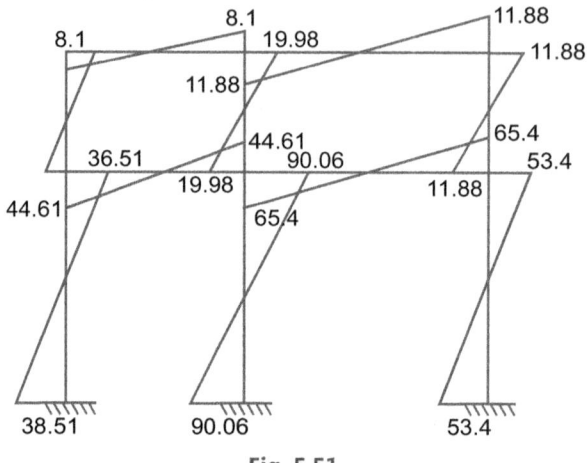

Fig. 5.51

Example 5.21 : *Analyse the frame as shown in Fig. 5.52 by cantilever method. Area of each exterior column is one half of the area of the interior columns.*

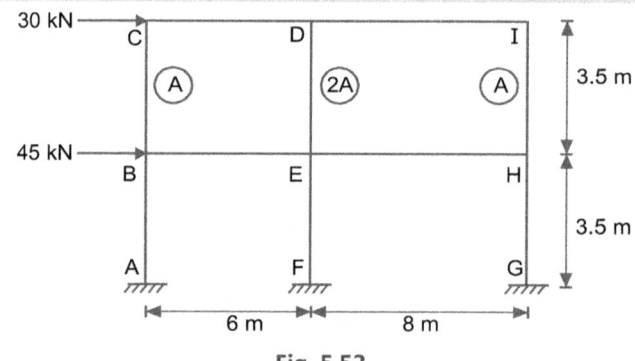

Fig. 5.52

Data : As shown in Fig. 5.52.

Required : BMD.

Concept : Cantilever method.

Solution : Step I : To locate C.G. of frame, taking moments of areas of column about the L.H.S. column.

$$\bar{x} = \frac{A \times 0 + 2A \times 6 + A \times 14}{4A}$$

$$= \frac{12 + 14}{4} = \frac{26}{4} = 6.5 \text{ m}$$

Considering FBD of frame above the points of contraflexure, as shown in Fig. 5.52. Direct stresses in the columns are proportional to the distances from the centroidal vertical axis of the frame. Let σ_{CB}, σ_{DE} and σ_{IH} be the stresses in columns CB, DE and IH respectively.

The stresses in columns BA, EF and HG are σ_{BA}, σ_{EF} and σ_{HG} respectively.

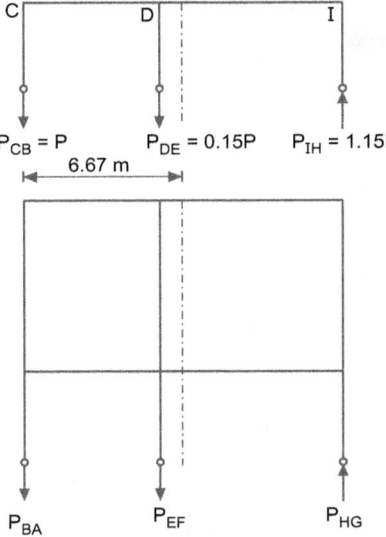

Fig. 5.53

$$\frac{\sigma_{CB}}{6.5} = \frac{\sigma_{DE}}{0.5} = \frac{\sigma_{IH}}{7.5}$$

∴ $\sigma_{DE} = 0.075\, \sigma_{CB}$

$\sigma_{IH} = 1.15\, \sigma_{CB}$

Force in column CB $= \sigma_{CB} \times A$

$$= \frac{P}{A} \times A = P \text{ kN (T)}$$

Force in column DE $= \sigma_{DE} \times 2A$

$$= 0.075 \frac{P}{A} \times 2A = 0.15\, P \text{ kN (T)}$$

Force in column IH $= \sigma_{IH} \times A$

$$= 1.15 \frac{P}{A} \times A = 1.15\, P \text{ kN (T)}$$

Taking moments about the points of contraflexure of the right end column,

$$-30 \times 1.75 + P \times 14 + 0.15\, P \times 8 = 0$$

$$P = 3.45 \text{ kN}$$

∴ Force in column CB (P_{CB}) = 3.45 kN (T)

Force in column DE (P_{DE}) = 0.52 kN (T)

Force in column IH (P_{IH}) = 3.97 kN (C)

Axial forces in column of lower storey are obtained in similar way and are as shown in Fig. 5.54.

Force in column BA (P_{BA}) = 15.54 kN (T)

Force in column EF (P_{EF}) = 2.33 kN (T)

Force in column HG (P_{HG}) = 17.87 kN (C)

Step II : Member forces :

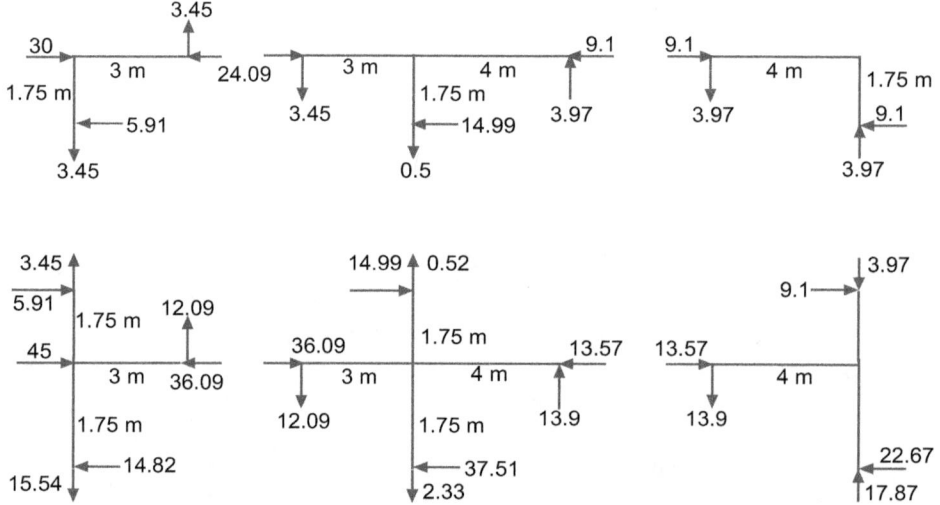

Fig. 5.54

Step III : BMD as shown in Fig. 5.54.

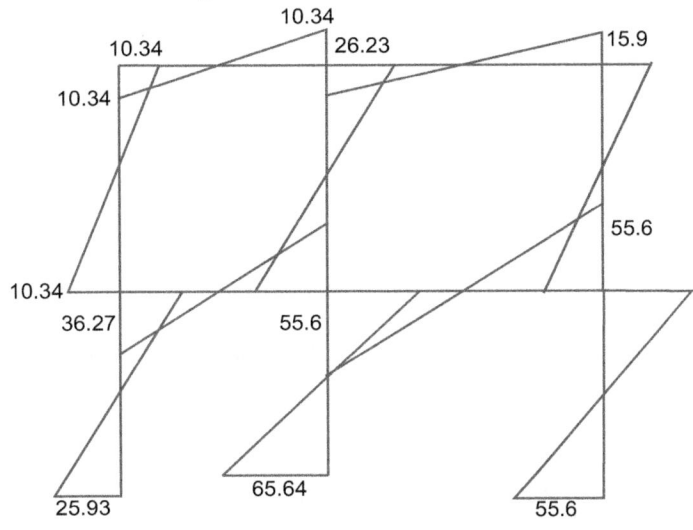

Fig. 5.55

EXERCISE

Solve following examples by Macaulay's method.

1. A 2 m long cantilever made of steel tube 150 mm external diameter and 10 mm thickness is loaded as shown in Fig. 5.56. Determine the maximum deflection. Assume E = 200 GPa. (13.98 mm (↓))

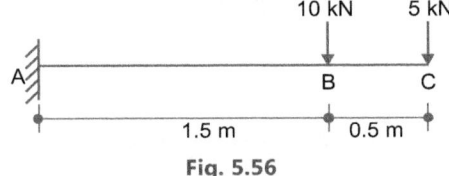

Fig. 5.56

2. A 2 m long cantilever is of rectangular section 100 mm wide and 200 mm deep. It is loaded as shown in Fig. 5.57. Find deflection at free end assuming E = 10 GPa.

(19.39 mm (↓))

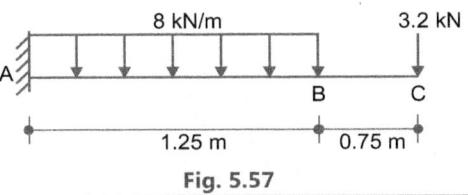

Fig. 5.57

3. A horizontal cantilever of uniform section and span 'L' is loaded as shown in Fig. 5.58. Find the deflection at free end. $\left(\dfrac{26.76}{EI}\ (\uparrow)\right)$

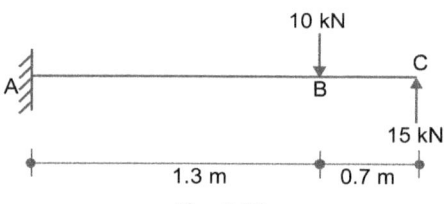

Fig. 5.58

4. A cantilever of uniform section is loaded as shown in Fig. 5.59. Find the deflection at B. If the cantilever is propped at B, find the reaction at prop assuming there is no deflection at B. $\left(y_B = \dfrac{33.75}{EI}\ (\downarrow);\ V_B = 30\ \text{kN}\ (\uparrow)\right)$

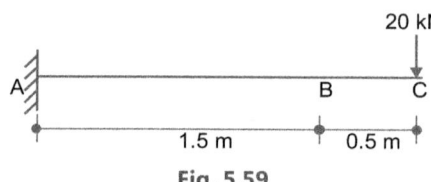

Fig. 5.59

5. A vertical post AB of constant flexural rigidity 4000 kNm² is fixed at the base A and subjected to a horizontal load of 20 kN at C as shown in Fig. 5.60. Determine the necessary force in horizontal tie at B such that the deflection at B is limited to 20 mm to the left. (5.13 kN)

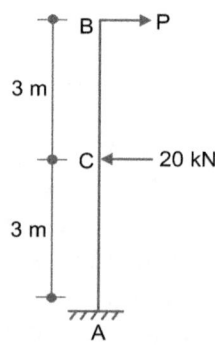

Fig. 5.60

6. The beam is supported and loaded as shown in Fig. 5.61. Find (i) the deflection under the load, (ii) the position and the amount of maximum deflection.

Assume E = 200 GPa and I = 50 × 10⁶ mm⁴

(y_C = 6 mm ($\downarrow$); y_{max} = 6.53 mm ($\downarrow$) at 2.45 m from A)

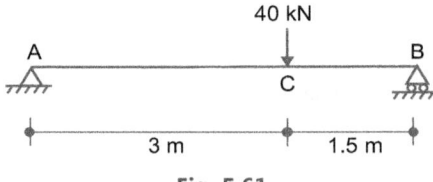

Fig. 5.61

7. The beam is supported and loaded as shown in Fig. 5.62. Find (i) the deflection under loads, (ii) the maximum deflection. Assume E = 200 GPa, I = 70 × 10⁸ mm⁴.

   (y_C = 2.34 mm ($\downarrow$); y_D = 2.98 mm ($\downarrow$); y_{max} = 3.54 mm ($\downarrow$) at 6.87 m from A)

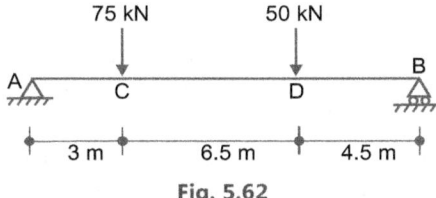

Fig. 5.62

8. The beam is supported and loaded as shown in Fig. 5.63. Determine the position and amount of maximum deflection. EI = 1.39 × 10¹¹ kNmm².

   (y_{max} = 6.82 mm ($\downarrow$) at 4.97 m from A)

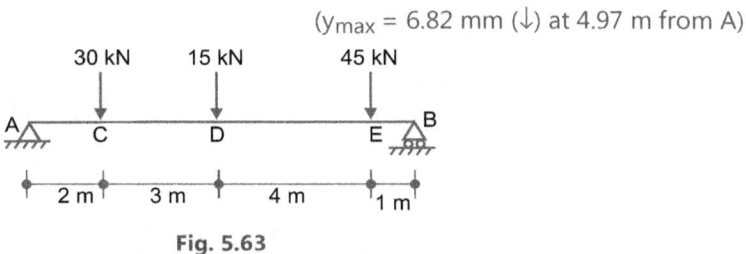

Fig. 5.63

9. The beam is supported and loaded as shown in Fig. 5.64. Find deflection at C.

$$\left(y_C = \frac{3.75}{EI} (\downarrow) \right)$$

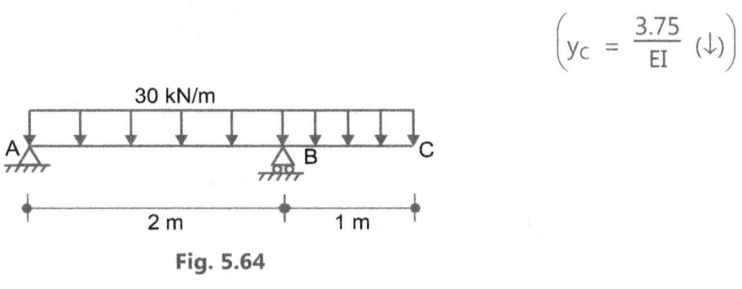

Fig. 5.64

10. The beam is supported and loaded as shown in Fig. 5.65. Assuming E = 200 GPa, I = 40 × 10⁶ mm⁴, find (i) the deflection at C; (ii) the maximum deflection, and (iii) slope at end A.

(y_C = 8.74 mm (↓); y_{max} = 8.75 mm (↓) at 1.958 m from A; θ_A = 0.417° (↻))

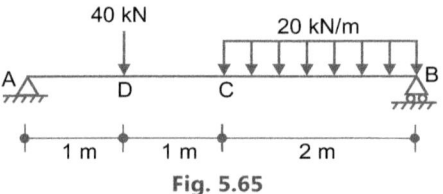

Fig. 5.65

11. Fig. 5.66 shows a rigid-jointed RCC plane frame, subjected to lateral loads, as shown.
    (a) Assuming EI same for all members, analyse the frame using portal method to get bending moments and shear forces in the beam ABC.
    (b) The beam ABC is subjected to ultimate DL of intensity 20 kN/m and ultimate LL of intensity 35 kN/m. Analyse the beam using a proper substitute frame to get maximum span moment in AB and maximum support moment at B.
    (c) Design the beam section for the support moment at 'B' due to combined effect of lateral loads and gravity loads, for flexure only.
    Use M 25 concrete and Fe 415 steel.

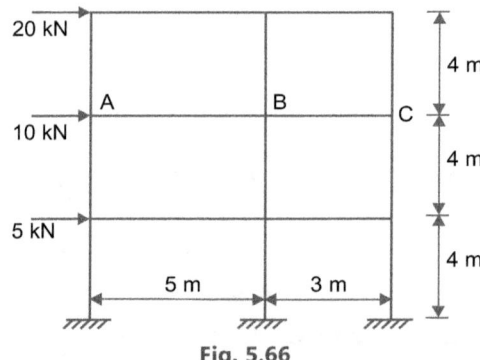

Fig. 5.66

12. In a multistorey RC building, a central frame has the following data :
    Number of bays = 4, Number of storeys = 5.
    Floor to floor height = 4.50 m, Width of bays = 3.5 m.
    Live load = 15 kN/m.
    Dead load including self weight = 10 kN/m.
    Assume, stiffness of column 1.5 times the beam.

Design a beam of lower storey for maximum bending moment at support and mid-span section.

Seismic moments are induced in beam of lower storey of ± 50 kN-m.

Use M 25 and Fe 415.

Show the details of reinforcement.

13. A RC frame has following details.

   Number of bays = 3, Width of bay = 5 m.

   Number of storeys = 4 (total height = 14 m)

   Floor height = 3.5 m.

   $I_{beam} = I_{column}$.

   Horizontal load on each floor level = 30 kN.

   Analyse the frame by portal method and B.M., shear force and axial forces are marked in the free body diagram of the frame.

   Design a section of roof level beam at support if moment and shear force due to gravity load are 30 kN-m and 50 kN respectively.

   Use LSM and Fe 415, M 25.

   Show details of reinforcement.

14. A rigid jointed R.C. plane frame is subjected to lateral loads as shown in Fig. 5.67. Analyse the frame using cantilever method, to get shear force and bending moments in beam ABC. All members have same EI. The beam ABC is subjected to ultimate dead load of intensity 10 kN/m and ultimate live load of intensity 20 kN/m. Analyse the beam ABC, using a proper substitute frame. Find the maximum span moments in AB and BC and the maximum support moment at B. Design the beam section for support moment at B, due to the combined effect of lateral loads and gravity loads for flexure only. Use M 20 concrete and Fe 415 steel.

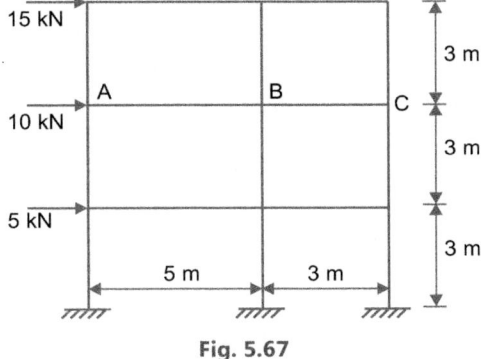

Fig. 5.67

15. A rigid jointed R.C. plane frame is subjected to lateral loads as shown in Fig. 5.68. Analyse the frame using portal method to get bending moments and shear forces in beam ABC. Assume same EI for all members. If the beam ABC is subjected to ultimate dead-load intensity of 12 kN/m and ultimate live load intensity of 22 kN/m, analyse the beam ABC using a proper substitute frame to get maximum span moment in AB and maximum support moment at B. Design the beam section for support moment at B due to combined effect of lateral loads and gravity loads for flexure only. Use M 20 concrete and Fe 415 steel.

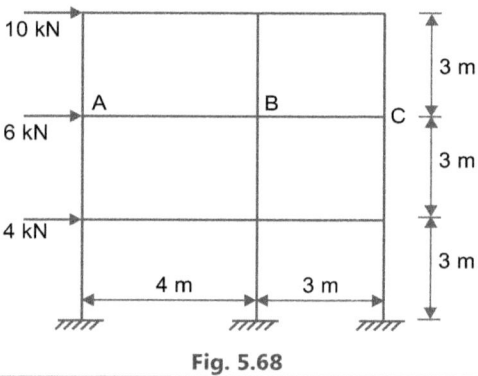

Fig. 5.68

Chapter 6
FINITE ELEMENT METHOD

6.1 INTRODUCTION

Finite element method has become a powerful tool for the numerical solution of engineering problems in all disciplines. The finite element method is the best combination of functional approximation and finite difference method. Due to this method, systematic computer programming can be developed, which gives scope to wide range of analysis of problems.

The basic concept of this method is to descretise the structure into smaller elements of finite dimension. These smaller elements are known as finite elements. These finite elements are connected at a number of joints and these joints are known as Nodes or Nodal points.

The assemblage of the finite elements properties give the solution for that structure. The concept of discretisation is shown in Fig. 6.1.

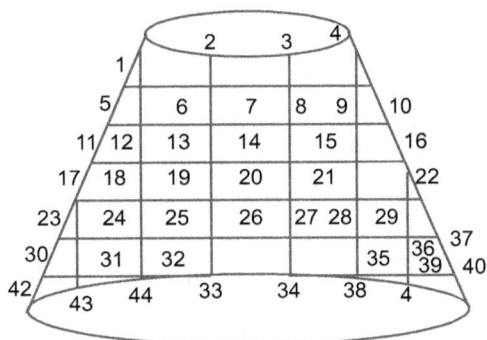

Fig. 6.1

In the finite element method, following steps are used in the analysis of problems :

(1) Selection of suitable field variables and the elements.
(2) Discritization of the domain.
(3) Choice of the approximation function.
(4) Formation of the element properties.

(5) Assembling of the global stiffness matrix.
(6) Apply boundary condition.
(7) Formation of loading matrix.
(8) Analyse the system equations for nodal unknown.
(9) Using nodal unknown calculate the required data.

6.2 DISCRETIZATION

An element also has hypothetical boundaries which defines its shape known as Edges, which are shared b/w adjacent elements. Complete physical arrangement of all elements together defines the system/structure/component geometry completely. This arrangement is called as "Meshing" or "Discretization".

6.3 TRUSS ELEMENT

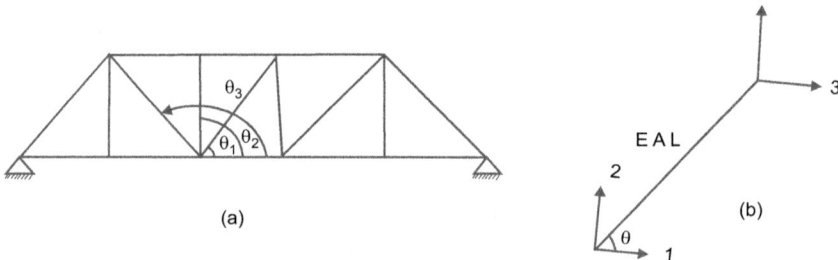

Fig. 6.2

unit displacement in x-direction (direction – 1)

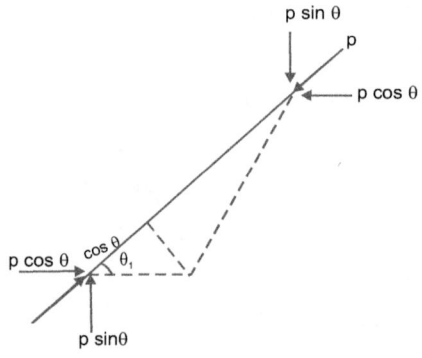

Fig. 6.3

Shortening = cos θ

Strain = $\dfrac{\cos\theta}{L}$

Stress = $\dfrac{E}{L}\cos\theta$

Axial force = $\dfrac{AE}{L}\cos\theta$

Let unit displacement in y – direction (direction-2)

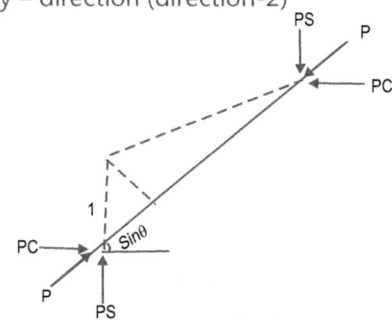

Fig. 6.4

Shortening = sin θ

Strain = $\dfrac{\sin\theta}{L}$

Stress = $\dfrac{E}{L}\sin\theta$

Axial load = $\dfrac{AE}{L}\sin\theta$

Displacement in unit direction 3.

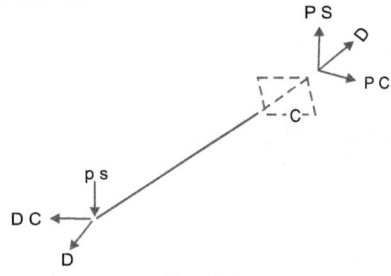

Fig. 6.5

Elongation = cos θ

Strain = $\dfrac{\cos\theta}{L}$

$$\text{Stress} = \frac{E}{L}\cos\theta$$

$$\text{Axial load} = \frac{AE}{L}\cos\theta$$

Displacement in unit direction 4.

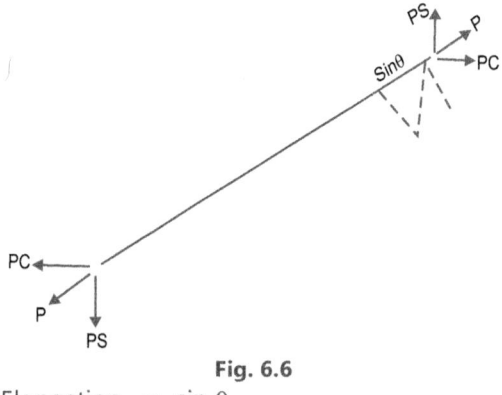

Fig. 6.6

$$\text{Elongation} = \sin\theta$$

$$\text{Strain} = \frac{\sin\theta}{L}$$

$$\text{Stress} = \frac{E}{L}\sin\theta$$

$$\text{Axial load} = \frac{AE}{L}\sin\theta$$

6.3.1 Nodes

Nodes are the selected finite points at which basic unknowns are to be deteremined.

6.3.1.1 External Nodes

Which occur on the edges/surface of the elements and they may be common to two or more elements.

For Example :

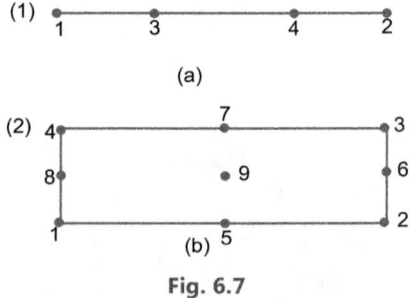

Fig. 6.7

(a) **Primary Nodes :** Occurs at the end of one dimensional elements. At the corner in the two or 3D elements.

(b) **Secondary Nodes :** Occurs along the side of an elements.

6.3.1.2 Internal Nodes

Occurs inside an element. There will not be any other element connecting to this node. Such nodes are selected to satisfy the requirements of geometric isotropy while choosing interpolation functions.

6.4 CO-ORDINATE SYSTEMS

(1) Global Co-ordinates : The co-ordinates system used to define the points in the entire structure is called Global Co-ordinate System.

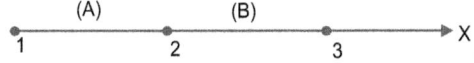

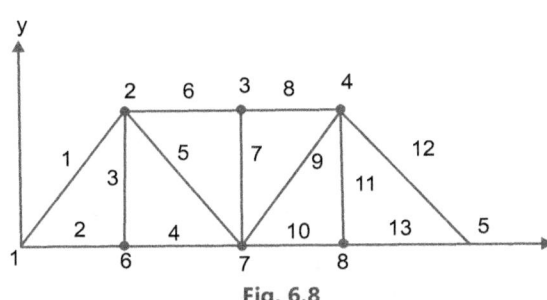

Fig. 6.8

(2) Local Co-ordinates : For the convenient of deriving element properties.

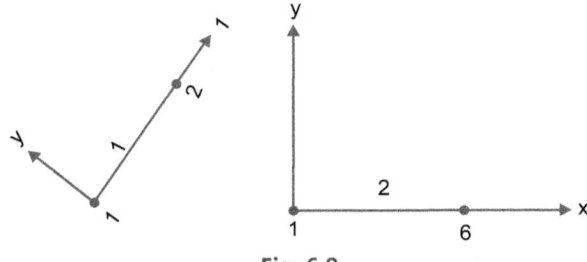

Fig. 6.9

(3) Natural Co-ordinates : Which permits the specification of a point within the element by a set of dimensionless number whose magnitude never exceeds unity. It is obtained by inside assigning weightages to the nodal co-ordinates in defining, the co-ordinates of any point the element.

6.4.1 Natural Co-ordinates in One Dimension

1
P(L1,L2)
2
x
x
x
x–x1
x2-x
L

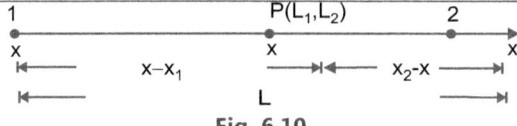

Fig. 6.10

Consider the two noded line elements. Let the natural co-ordinates of point P be (L_1, L_2) and the cartesian co-ordinates be x. Nodes 1 and 2 have the cartesian co-ordinates x_1 and x_2. (Natrual co-ordinates are weightage to the nodal co-ordiantes, total weightage at any point is units).

$$L_1 + L_2 = 1 \qquad \ldots(1)$$

$$L_1 x_1 + L_2 x_2 = x \qquad \ldots(2)$$

$$\begin{bmatrix} 1 & 1 \\ x_1 & x_2 \end{bmatrix} \begin{Bmatrix} L_1 \\ L_2 \end{Bmatrix} = \begin{Bmatrix} 1 \\ x \end{Bmatrix} \begin{bmatrix} 30 & 0 \\ 2.887 & 5 \end{bmatrix}$$

$$\begin{Bmatrix} L_1 \\ L_2 \end{Bmatrix} = \begin{bmatrix} 1 & 1 \\ x_1 & x_2 \end{bmatrix}^{-1} \begin{Bmatrix} 1 \\ x \end{Bmatrix}$$

$$= \frac{1}{x_2 - x_1} \begin{bmatrix} x_2 & -x_1 \\ -1 & 1 \end{bmatrix}^{+} \begin{Bmatrix} 1 \\ x \end{Bmatrix}$$

$$= \frac{1}{x_2 - x_1} \begin{bmatrix} x_2 & -1 \\ -x_1 & 1 \end{bmatrix} \begin{Bmatrix} 1 \\ x \end{Bmatrix}$$

$$= \frac{1}{x_2 - x_1} \begin{bmatrix} x_2 & x \\ -x_1 & x \end{bmatrix}$$

$$\begin{Bmatrix} L_1 \\ L_2 \end{Bmatrix} = \begin{Bmatrix} \dfrac{x_2 - x}{L} \\ \dfrac{x - x_1}{L} \end{Bmatrix}$$

1
2
1
Variation of L1
1
Variation of L2

Fig. 6.11

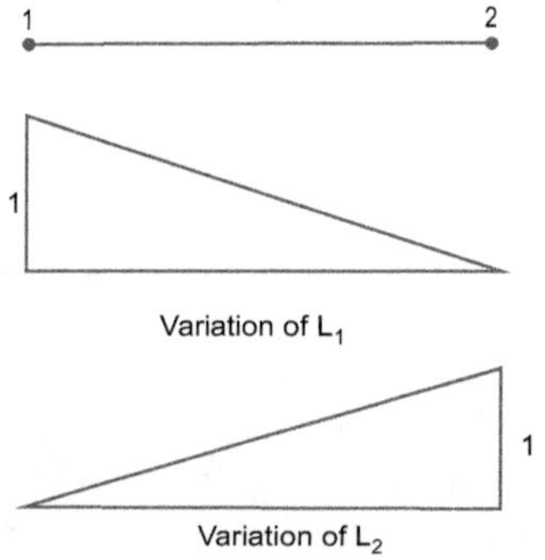

STRUCTURAL ANALYSIS – II   FINITE ELEMENT METHOD

Natural Co-ordinate ε :

$$\xi = \frac{PC}{\left(\frac{x_2 - x_1}{2}\right)}$$

where,   P = Point referred
          C = Centre point of nodes 1 and 2.

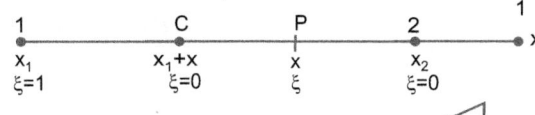

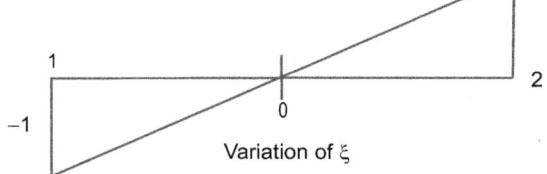

Variation of ξ

Fig. 6.12

$$\xi = \frac{PC}{(L/2)} = \frac{x - x_C}{L/2}$$

$$\xi = \frac{2}{L}\left[x - \left(\frac{x_1 + x_2}{2}\right)\right]$$

$$\xi = \frac{2}{L}\left[x - \left(\frac{x_2 - x_1 + 2x_1}{2}\right)\right]$$

$$\xi = \frac{2}{L}\left[x - \left(\frac{L + 2x_1}{2}\right)\right]$$

$$\xi = \frac{2}{L}\left[x - \frac{L}{2} - \frac{2x_1}{2}\right]$$

$$\xi = \frac{2}{L}\left[x - x_1 - \frac{L}{2}\right]$$

$$\frac{L}{2}\xi = [x - x_1 - L/2]$$

$$\frac{L}{2}(\xi + 1) = (x - x_1) \qquad \qquad ...(i)$$

At node number 1 : $x = x_1$
  From equation (i),

$$\frac{L}{2}(\xi + 1) = 0$$

$$\boxed{\varepsilon = -1}$$

At node number 2 : $x = x_2$

Ch. 6 | 6.7

from equation (ii)

$$\frac{L}{2}(\xi + 1) = x_2 - x_1$$

$$\frac{L}{2}(\xi + 1) = L$$

$$\xi = 1$$

6.4.2 Natural Co-ordinates for Triangular Elements

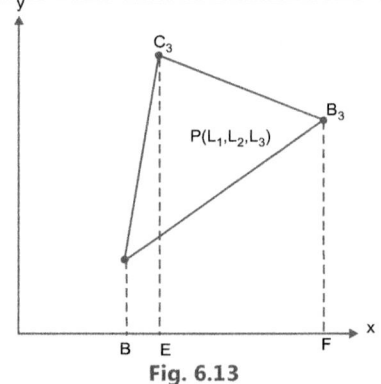

Fig. 6.13

$L_1 + L_2 + L_3 = 1$ ...(i)
$L_1 x_1 + L_2 x_2 + L_3 x_3 = x$ ...(ii)
$L_1 y_1 + L_2 y_2 + L_3 y_3 = y$ ...(iii)

$$\begin{bmatrix} 1 & 1 & 1 \\ x_1 & x_2 & x_3 \\ y_1 & y_2 & y_3 \end{bmatrix} \begin{Bmatrix} L_1 \\ L_2 \\ L_3 \end{Bmatrix} = \begin{Bmatrix} 1 \\ x \\ y \end{Bmatrix}$$

$$\begin{Bmatrix} L_1 \\ L_2 \\ L_3 \end{Bmatrix} = \begin{bmatrix} 1 & 1 & 1 \\ x_1 & x_2 & x_3 \\ y_1 & y_2 & y_3 \end{bmatrix}^{-1} \begin{Bmatrix} 1 \\ x \\ y \end{Bmatrix} \quad \ldots (A)$$

θ et,
$$\begin{vmatrix} 1 & 1 & 1 \\ x_1 & x_2 & x_3 \\ y_1 & y_2 & y_3 \end{vmatrix} = 2A$$

Proof

θ et,
$$\begin{vmatrix} 1 & 1 & 1 \\ x_1 & x_2 & x_3 \\ y_1 & y_2 & y_3 \end{vmatrix} = (x_2 y_3 - x_3 y_2) - (x_1 y_3 - x_3 y_1) + (x_1 y_2 - x_2 y_1)$$

Consider the triangle ABC. Drop perpendicular AD, BE and CF on to x-axis.

Area triangle ABC

$= $ Area of ADEC + Area CEFB − Area ADFB

$= \dfrac{1}{2}$ (AD + CE) DE + $\dfrac{1}{2}$ (CF + BF) EF − $\dfrac{1}{2}$ (AD + BF) DF

$= \dfrac{1}{2} (x_3 - x_1)(y_1 + y_3) + \dfrac{1}{2}[(x_2 - x_3)(y_3 + y_2)] - \dfrac{1}{2}(y_1 + y_2)(x_2 - x_1)$

$= \dfrac{1}{2}[y_1 x_3 - y_1 x_1 + y_3 x_3 - y_3 x_1 + y_3 x_2 - y_3 x_3 + y_2 x_2 - y_2 x_3 - y_1 x_2 - y_2 x_1 + y_1 x_1 + y_2 x_1]$

$= \dfrac{1}{2}[y_1 x_3 - y_3 x_1 + y_3 x_2 - y_2 x_3 - y_1 x_2 + y_2 x_1]$

$= \dfrac{1}{2}[(x_2 y_3 - x_3 y_2) - (x_1 y_3 - x_3 y_1) + (x_1 y_2 - x_2 y_1)]$

$$[A]^{-1} = \dfrac{1}{\det A}\, \text{adj}\, A \quad [\ ]^{-1} = [\text{Transpouse}]^T = \text{co-factor}$$

$$A = \dfrac{1}{2} \text{Det}$$

$$\text{Det} = 2A \qquad \qquad \qquad ...(B)$$

From equation (i)

$$\begin{Bmatrix} L_1 \\ L_2 \\ L_3 \end{Bmatrix} = \dfrac{1}{2A} \begin{bmatrix} (x_2 y_3 - x_3 y_2) & (x_3 y_1 - x_1 y_3) & (x_1 y_2 - x_2 y_1) \\ y_2 - y_3 & y_3 - y_1 & y_1 - y_2 \\ x_3 - x_2 & x_1 - x_3 & x_2 - x_1 \end{bmatrix} \begin{Bmatrix} 1 \\ x \\ y \end{Bmatrix}$$

$$= \dfrac{1}{2A} \begin{bmatrix} (x_2 y_3 - x_3 y_2) & y_2 - y_3 & x_3 - x_2 \\ (x_3 y_1 - x_1 y_3) & y_3 - y_1 & x_1 - x_3 \\ (x_1 y_2 - x_2 y_1) & y_1 - y_2 & x_2 - x_1 \end{bmatrix} \begin{Bmatrix} 1 \\ x \\ y \end{Bmatrix}$$

$$= \dfrac{1}{2A} \begin{bmatrix} a_1 & b_1 & c_1 \\ a_2 & b_2 & c_2 \\ a_3 & b_3 & c_3 \end{bmatrix} \begin{Bmatrix} 1 \\ x \\ y \end{Bmatrix}$$

where,

$a_1 = (x_2 y_2 - x_3 y_2)$ $\qquad b_1 = (y_2 - y_3)$ $\qquad c_1 = (x_3 - x_2)$
$a_2 = (x_3 y_1 - x_{13})$ $\qquad b_2 = (y_3 - y_1)$ $\qquad c_2 = (x_1 - x_3)$
$a_3 = (x_1 y_2 - x_2 y_1)$ $\qquad b_3 = (y_1 - y_2)$ $\qquad c_3 = (x_2 - x_1)$

$$\begin{Bmatrix} L_1 \\ L_2 \\ L_3 \end{Bmatrix} = \dfrac{1}{2A} \begin{bmatrix} a_1 + b_1 x + c_1 y \\ a_2 + b_2 x + c_2 y \\ a_3 + b_3 x + c_3 y \end{bmatrix}$$

6.5 ELEMENT SHAPES

(i) One-dimensional elements.
(ii) Two dimensional elements.
(iii) Axi-symmetric elements.
(iv) 3-D elements.

6.5.1 One-Dimensional Elements

Also called as line elements.

Fig. 6.14

6.5.2 2-D Elements

2D problems – Plane stress, plane strain, constant strain triangles/linear displacement.

6.5.3 Constant Strain/Stress Triangle (CST)

In the CST element, the distribution of displacement is assumed linear and is uniquely defined on the boundary of two adjacent elements by given values at two nodes. Thus, value of x, y along common boundary are the same for the two element hence CST is classified as confirming element.

Fig. 6.15 (a)

Stresses at Nodes :

Stresses calculated as above are the values at the centroid of the elements. If stresses at nodes are deserved then we have to assign these values and then compute the nodal averages at the nodes.

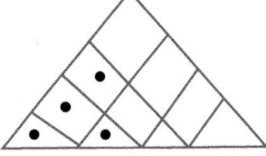

Fig. 6.15 (b)

6.5.4 Linear Strain Triangle (LST)

For a better approximation of variation of strain than in CST, the LST is used. This requires more term in displacement function, more generalised co-ordinate and hence more nodes. This element uses 6 nodes. Also known as quadratic displacement triangle.

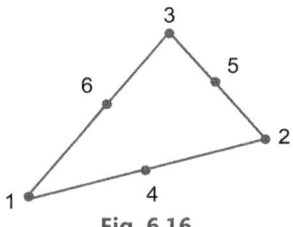

Fig. 6.16

6.5.5 Quadratic Strain Triangle (QST)

Ten nodal triangular elements also known as cubic displacement triangle.

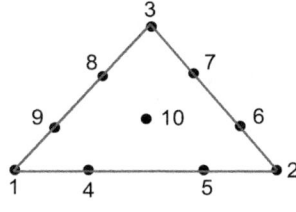

Fig. 6.17

Lagrange Rectangle Elements :

Nodes are in the form of Grid points.

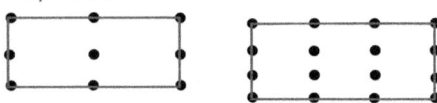

Fig. 6.18

Serendipity Rectangle Elements :

Nodes along the external boundaries.

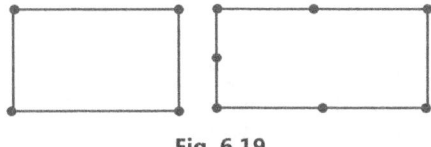

Fig. 6.19

Plane stress and plane strain problems

Stress-strain relation for 2D state :

$$\varepsilon_x = \frac{1}{E}\,[\sigma_x - \nu\,(\sigma_y + \sigma_z)]$$

$$\varepsilon_y = \frac{1}{E}\,[\sigma_y - \nu\,(\sigma_x + \sigma_z)]$$

$$\chi_{xy} = \frac{\tau_{xy}}{G}$$

Strain in Z-direction :

$$\varepsilon_z = \frac{1}{E}[\sigma_z - \nu(\sigma_x + \sigma_y)]$$

where,

E = Modulus of Elasticity
ν = Poissons ratio
G = Modulus of rigidity
E = 2G (1 + ν)

6.5.6 3D Stress-Strain Relation

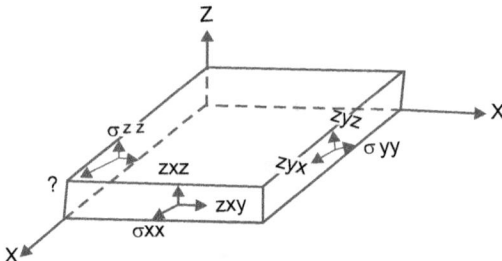

Fig. 6.20

(a) Plane-Stres Condition :

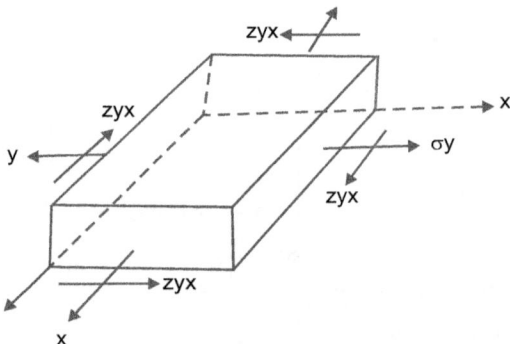

Fig. 6.21

Stresses absent on top and bottom face.

$\sigma_x, \sigma_y, \tau_{xy}$ = present
$\sigma_z, \tau_{yz}, \tau_{zx}$ = 0

STRUCTURAL ANALYSIS – II FINITE ELEMENT METHOD

Stress Strain Relation :

$$\varepsilon_x = \frac{1}{E}[\sigma_x - \nu(\sigma_y + \sigma_z)]$$

$$\varepsilon_y = \frac{1}{E}[\sigma_y - \nu\, \sigma_x]$$

$$\chi_{xy} = \frac{\varepsilon_{xy}}{G}$$

$$\chi_{yz} = \chi_{zx} = 0$$

$$\varepsilon_z = -\frac{\nu}{E}(\sigma_x + \sigma_y)$$

In matrix form :

$$\begin{bmatrix} \varepsilon_x \\ \varepsilon_y \\ \varepsilon_z \end{bmatrix} = \frac{1}{E} \begin{bmatrix} 1 & -\nu & 0 \\ -\nu & 1 & 0 \\ 0 & 0 & 2(1+\nu) \end{bmatrix} \begin{Bmatrix} \sigma_x \\ \sigma_y \\ \sigma_z \end{Bmatrix}$$

Practical Examples :

(1) Beam bending.
(2) Counter fort retaining wall.
(3) Pure torsion of shaft.

(b) Plane Strain Condition :

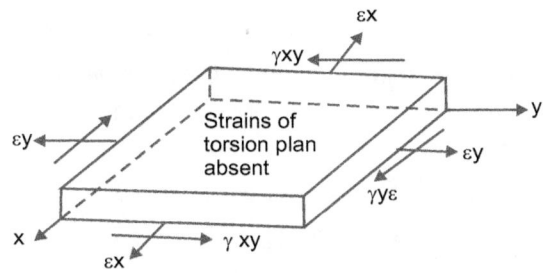

fig. 6.22

$\varepsilon_x = \varepsilon_y = \chi_{xy}$ = present
$\varepsilon_z = \chi_{yz} = \chi_{yz}$ = 0

$$\varepsilon_z = 0 = \frac{1}{E}[\sigma_z - \nu(\sigma_x + \sigma_y)]$$

$$\sigma_z = \nu(\sigma_x + \sigma_y)$$

$$\varepsilon_x = \frac{1}{E}[\sigma_x - \nu(\sigma_y + \sigma_z)]$$

$$\varepsilon_y = \frac{1}{E}[\sigma_y - \nu(\sigma_x + \sigma_z)]$$

$$\chi_{xy} = \frac{\sigma_{xy}}{G}$$

$$\chi_{yz} = 0 \; ; \; \chi_{zx} = 0$$

$$\begin{bmatrix} \varepsilon_x \\ \varepsilon_y \\ \varepsilon_z \end{bmatrix} = \frac{1-\nu^2}{E} \begin{bmatrix} 1 & \frac{-\nu}{1-\nu} & 0 \\ -\frac{\nu}{1-\nu} & 1 & 0 \\ 0 & 0 & \frac{2}{1-\nu} \end{bmatrix} \begin{bmatrix} \sigma_x \\ \sigma_y \\ \sigma_z \end{bmatrix}$$

Practical Examples :
  (i) Dam
  (ii) Retaining wall without counterfort.

6.6 ISOPARAMETRIC ELEMENTS

For the analysis of structural problems of complex shapes involving curved boundaries or surfaces, simple triangular or rectangular elements are no longer sufficient. This has lead to the development of elements of more arbitrary shape and are called isoparametric elements.

The concept of isoparametric element is based on the co-ordinate transformation of the parent element in local or natural co-ordinate system to an arbitrary shape in the cartesian co-ordinate system. The cartesian co-ordinate of a point in an element.

$$x = N_1 x_1 + N_2 x_2 + \ldots + N_n x_4$$
$$y = N_1 y_1 + N_2 y_2 + \ldots + N_n y_n$$
$$z = N_1 z_1 + N_2 z_2 + \ldots + N_n z_n$$

In a matrix form,

$$\{x\} = [N]\{x\}\varepsilon$$

where,
  N = shape functions
  x_e = co-ordinates of nodal points of the element.

The shape functions are to be expressed in natural co-ordinate system.

Example :

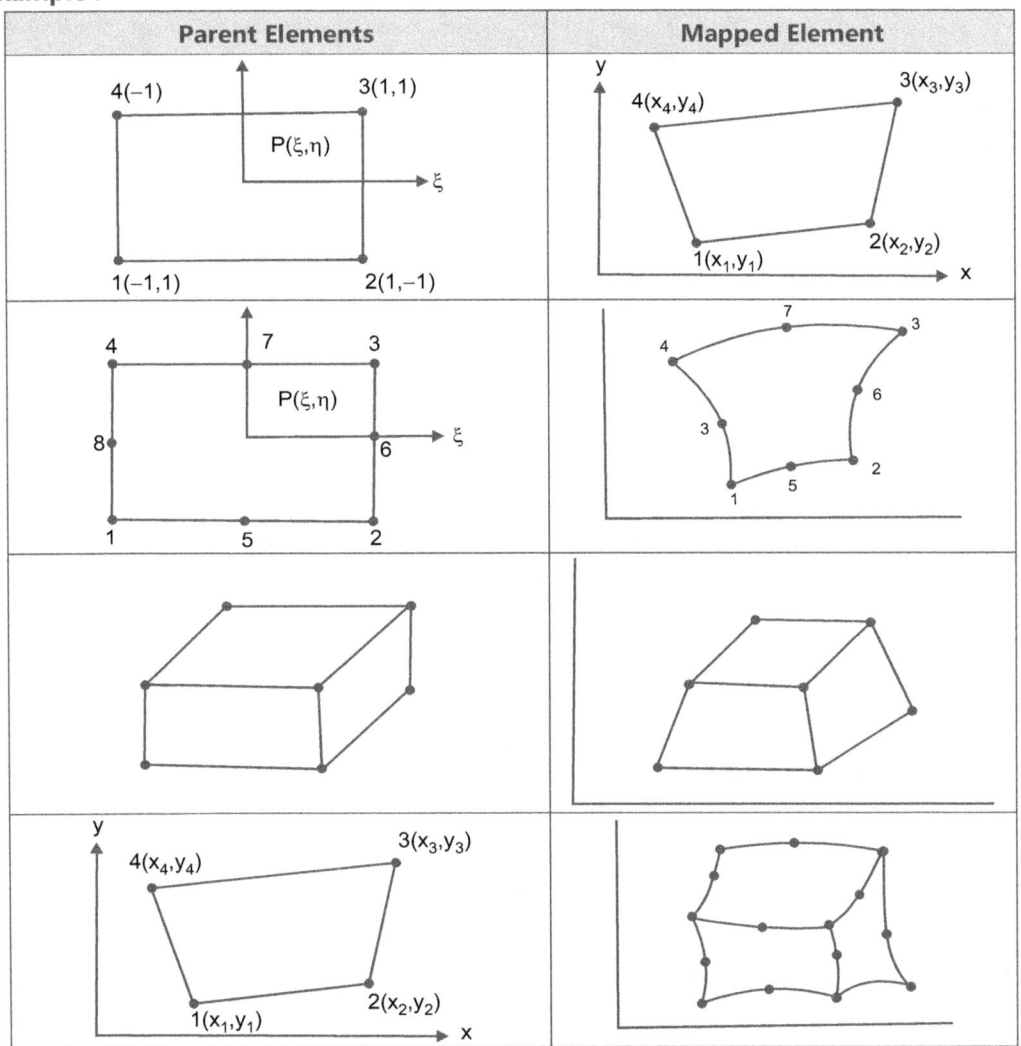

6.7 AXISYMMETRIC STRESS ANALYSIS

When structures and loads acting on it, both are symmetric about an axis of symmetry, the analysis is terms as axisymmetric stress analysis. Due to symmetry at the axis two components of displacement (u – radial and v – axial) defined completely the state of strain and hence state of stress. Thus, the problem any be treated as 2-D radial and axial co-ordinates, z are used for the analysis hence every actual element represents a volume obtained by revolving the element and the axis from volume of revolution or ring elements.

In writing the strain energy however, strains in axial, radial and also circumferential direction are involved. Thus, it is not a plane stress or plane strain case. It is a 3D stress problem. The strains to be considered are ε_z, ε_r, ε_σ and χ_{rz}. Hence $\chi_{r\theta}$ and $\chi_{\theta z} = 0$ d$_o$ to symmetry around the axis.

The loads to have to be axisymmetric if they are not stresses and strains will not be axisymmetric and it will not be an axisymmetric analysis problem. The displacement function similar to those used in plane problem can be used also.

4 Nodel Rectangular Element :

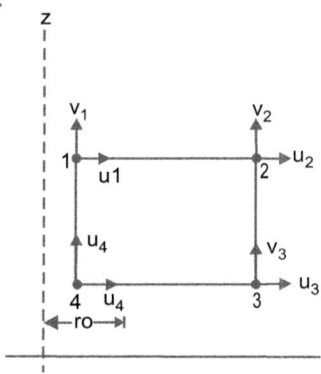

Fig. 6.23

Step I : Displacement Method :

$u = \alpha_1 + \alpha_2 r + \alpha_3 y + \alpha_4 rz$

$v = \alpha_5 + \alpha_6 r + \alpha_7 z + \alpha_8 rz$

$$\begin{Bmatrix} u \\ v \end{Bmatrix} = \begin{bmatrix} 1 & r & z & r & 0 & 0 & 0 & 0 \\ 0 & 0 & 0 & 0 & 1 & r & z & rz \end{bmatrix} \begin{bmatrix} \sigma_1 \\ \sigma_2 \\ ..... \\ \sigma_8 \end{bmatrix}$$

$\{u\} = [p]\{\alpha\}$ ...(1)

By substituting r and z into 4 nodes

$\{\delta_e\}_{1 \times 8} = [A]_{8 \times 8} \{\alpha\}_{1 \times 8}$ ...(2)

$\{\alpha\} = [A]^{-1} \{\delta_e\}$ ...(3)

Substituting equation (3) in equation (1).

$\{u\} = [P][A]^{-1}\{\delta_e\}$ ...(4)

Strains :

$$\{\varepsilon\} = \begin{bmatrix} \varepsilon_z \\ \varepsilon_r \\ \varepsilon_\theta \\ \chi_{rz} \end{bmatrix} = \begin{bmatrix} \partial v/\partial z \\ \partial u/\partial r \\ u/r \\ \dfrac{\partial v}{\partial r} + \dfrac{\partial u}{\partial z} \end{bmatrix}$$

$$\{\varepsilon\} = \begin{bmatrix} 0 & \partial/\partial_z \\ \partial/\partial_r & 0 \\ 1/r & 0 \\ \partial/\partial_z & \partial/\partial_r \end{bmatrix} \begin{Bmatrix} u \\ v \end{Bmatrix}$$

$$\{\varepsilon\} = [\partial]\{u\}$$
$$= [\partial][p][A^{-1}]\{\delta e\}$$
$$\{\varepsilon\} = [B]\{\delta e\}$$

Stress :

$$\sigma = \begin{bmatrix} \sigma_z \\ \sigma_r \\ \sigma_\theta \\ \tau_{rz} \end{bmatrix}$$

$$= \dfrac{E}{(1+v)(1-2v)} \begin{bmatrix} 1-v & v & v & 0 \\ v & 1-v & v & 0 \\ v & v & 1-v & 0 \\ 0 & 0 & 0 & \dfrac{1-2v}{2} \end{bmatrix} \begin{bmatrix} \varepsilon_z \\ \varepsilon_r \\ \varepsilon_\theta \\ \chi_{rz} \end{bmatrix}$$

$$\{\sigma\} = [D][B]\{\delta_e\}$$

Potential of the System :

$$\pi = \dfrac{2\pi}{\pi} \iint \{\varepsilon\}^T \{\sigma\} r \, dr \, dz - \{\delta e\}^T \{F\}$$

By using principal of minimum P.E.

$$\dfrac{\partial \pi}{\partial \delta e} = 0$$

STRUCTURAL ANALYSIS – II FINITE ELEMENT METHOD

$$2\pi \iint [B]^T [D] [B] \, r \, dr \, dz \, \{\delta e\} - (F) = 0$$

$$\boxed{[F] = [K] \{\delta_e\}}$$

where,

$$[k] = 2\pi \iint [B]^T [D] [B] \, r \, dr \, dz$$

Triangular Element :

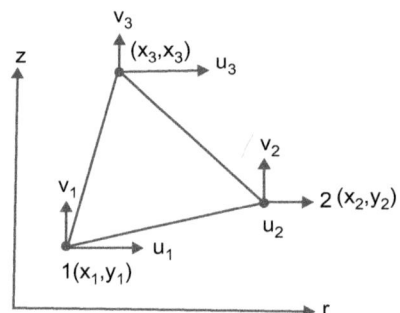

Fig. 6.24

$$u = \alpha_1 + \alpha_2 r + \alpha_3 z$$
$$v = \alpha_4 + \alpha_5 r + \alpha_6 z$$
$$u = [p] \{\alpha\} \qquad \ldots(1)$$

$$\{u\} = \begin{bmatrix} 1 & r & z & 0 & 0 & 0 \\ 0 & 0 & 0 & 1 & r & z \end{bmatrix} \begin{bmatrix} \alpha_1 \\ \alpha_2 \\ \alpha_3 \\ \alpha_4 \\ \alpha_5 \\ \alpha_6 \end{bmatrix}$$

$$\begin{bmatrix} u_1 \\ v_1 \\ u_2 \\ v_2 \\ u_3 \\ v_3 \end{bmatrix} = \begin{bmatrix} 1 & r_1 & z_1 & 0 & 0 & 0 \\ 0 & 0 & 0 & 1 & r_1 & z_1 \\ 1 & r_2 & z_2 & 0 & 0 & 0 \\ 0 & 0 & 0 & 1 & r_2 & z_2 \\ 1 & r_3 & z_3 & 0 & 0 & 0 \\ 0 & 0 & 0 & 1 & r_3 & z_3 \end{bmatrix} \begin{bmatrix} \alpha_1 \\ \alpha_2 \\ \alpha_3 \\ \alpha_4 \\ \alpha_5 \\ \alpha_6 \end{bmatrix}$$

$$\{\delta_e\} = [A] \{\alpha\}$$
$$\{\alpha\} = [A]^{-1} \{\delta e\}$$

In equation (1)

$$\{u\} = [P] [A]^{-1} \{\delta e\}$$

Strains :

$$\{\varepsilon\} = \begin{bmatrix} \varepsilon_r \\ \varepsilon_z \\ \varepsilon_\theta \\ \chi_{rz} \end{bmatrix} = \begin{bmatrix} \partial u/\partial r \\ \partial v/\partial z \\ u/r \\ \dfrac{\partial u}{\partial z} + \dfrac{\partial v}{\partial r} \end{bmatrix}$$

$$= \begin{bmatrix} \partial/\partial r & 0 \\ 0 & \partial/\partial z \\ 1/r & 0 \\ \dfrac{\partial}{\partial z} & \dfrac{\partial}{\partial r} \end{bmatrix} \begin{Bmatrix} u \\ v \end{Bmatrix}$$

$\{\varepsilon\} = [\partial] \{u\}$
$\phantom{\{\varepsilon\}} = [\partial] [P] [A]^{-1} \{\delta\varepsilon\}$
$\{\varepsilon\} = [B] \{\delta e\}$

Stress :

$$\{\sigma\} = \begin{Bmatrix} \sigma r \\ \sigma z \\ \sigma q \\ \sigma rz \end{Bmatrix}$$

$$= \dfrac{E}{(1+v)(1-2v)} \begin{bmatrix} (1-v) & v & v & 0 \\ v & (1-v) & v & 0 \\ v & v & (1-v) & 0 \\ 0 & 0 & 0 & \dfrac{(1-2v)}{2} \end{bmatrix} \{\varepsilon\}$$

$\{\sigma\} = [D] [B] \{\delta e\}$

Potential of the System :

$$\pi = 2\pi \iint (\delta e)^T [B]^T [D] [B] \, r \, dr \, dz \, \{\delta\varepsilon\} - \{\delta e\}^T \{F\}$$

By Minimum P.E. :

$$\dfrac{\partial \pi}{\partial \delta\varepsilon} = 0$$

$$0 = 2\pi \iint [B]^T [D] [B] \, r \, dr \, dz \, (\delta\varepsilon) - [F]$$
$[F] = [K] \{\delta\varepsilon\}$

where,
$$[k] = 2\pi \iint [B]^T [D] [B]\, r\, dr\, dz$$

6.8 STRAIN DISPLACEMENT MATRIX

Strain displacement can be defined as,
$$\{\varepsilon\} = [B]\{\delta\}$$
where,
- $\{\varepsilon\}$ = Strain at any point in the element.
- $\{\delta\}$ = Displacement vector of nodal values of the element.
- $[B]$ = Strain displacement matrix.

6.8.1 Strain Displacement Matrix for Bar Element

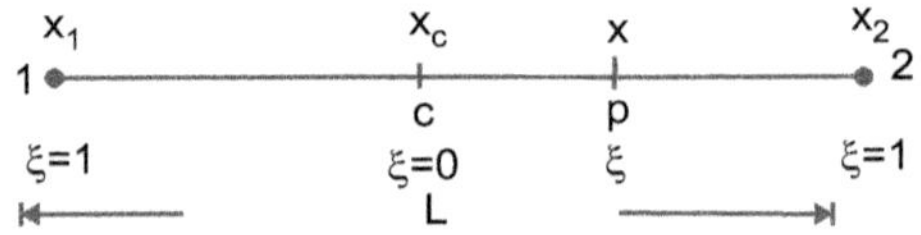

Fig. 6.25

$$u = \alpha_1 + \alpha_2 x$$

$$u = \begin{bmatrix} 1 & x \end{bmatrix} \begin{Bmatrix} \alpha_1 \\ \alpha_2 \end{Bmatrix} \qquad \ldots(1)$$

$$u = [A]\{\alpha\}$$

$$\begin{Bmatrix} u_1 \\ u_2 \end{Bmatrix} = \begin{bmatrix} 1 & x_1 \\ 1 & x_2 \end{bmatrix} \begin{Bmatrix} \alpha_1 \\ \alpha_2 \end{Bmatrix}$$

$$\begin{Bmatrix} \alpha_1 \\ \alpha_2 \end{Bmatrix} = \begin{bmatrix} 1 & x_1 \\ 1 & x_2 \end{bmatrix}^{-1} \begin{Bmatrix} u_1 \\ u_2 \end{Bmatrix}$$

$$\begin{Bmatrix} \alpha_1 \\ \alpha_2 \end{Bmatrix} = \frac{1}{x_2 - x_1} \begin{bmatrix} x_2 & -x_1 \\ -1 & 1 \end{bmatrix} \begin{Bmatrix} u_1 \\ u_2 \end{Bmatrix}$$

From equation (1)

$$u = \begin{bmatrix} 1 & x \end{bmatrix} \frac{1}{L} \begin{bmatrix} x_2 & -x_1 \\ -1 & 1 \end{bmatrix} \begin{Bmatrix} u_1 \\ u_2 \end{Bmatrix}$$

$$= \frac{1}{L} \begin{bmatrix} (x_2 - x) & (x - x_1) \end{bmatrix} \begin{Bmatrix} u_1 \\ u_2 \end{Bmatrix}$$

$$u = \begin{bmatrix} \dfrac{x_2 - x}{L} & \dfrac{x - x_1}{L} \end{bmatrix} \begin{Bmatrix} u_1 \\ u_2 \end{Bmatrix}$$

$$u = \begin{bmatrix} N_1 & N_2 \end{bmatrix} \begin{Bmatrix} u_1 \\ u_2 \end{Bmatrix}$$

Strain :

$$\varepsilon_x = \frac{\partial u}{\partial x} = \frac{\partial}{\partial x}(\alpha_1 + \alpha_2 x) = \alpha_2$$

$$\varepsilon_x = \frac{\partial}{\partial x}[N_1 \ N_2]\begin{Bmatrix} u_1 \\ u_2 \end{Bmatrix}$$

$$\varepsilon_x = \frac{\partial}{\partial x}\begin{bmatrix} \frac{x_2 - x}{L} & \frac{x - x_1}{L} \end{bmatrix}\begin{Bmatrix} u_1 \\ u_2 \end{Bmatrix}$$

$$\varepsilon_x = \begin{bmatrix} \frac{-1}{L} & \frac{1}{L} \end{bmatrix}\begin{Bmatrix} u_1 \\ u_2 \end{Bmatrix}$$

$$\varepsilon_x = [B]\{\delta\}_\varepsilon$$

where,
$$B = \text{strain displacement}$$
$$= \frac{1}{L}[-1 \ 1]$$

In terms of natural co-ordinate (ξ)

$$\{\xi\} = \xi_x = \frac{\partial u}{\partial x} = \frac{\partial \xi}{\partial x}\frac{\partial u}{\partial z}$$

$$= \frac{\partial \xi}{\partial x}\frac{\partial}{\partial \xi}[N_1 \ N_2]\begin{Bmatrix} u_1 \\ u_2 \end{Bmatrix}$$

$$\xi = \frac{2}{L}(x - x_2)$$

$$N_1 = \frac{1-\xi}{2}$$

$$N_2 = \frac{(1+\xi)}{2}$$

$$\frac{\partial \xi}{\partial x} = \frac{Q}{L}, \ \frac{\partial N_1}{\partial \xi} = -\frac{1}{2}, \ \frac{\partial N_2}{\partial \xi} = \frac{1}{2}$$

$$\{\xi_x\} = \frac{2}{L}\begin{bmatrix} \frac{-1}{2} & \frac{1}{2} \end{bmatrix}\begin{Bmatrix} u_1 \\ u_2 \end{Bmatrix}$$

$$\{\xi_x\} = \frac{1}{L}[-1 \ 1]\{\delta_\varepsilon\}$$

$$\{\xi_x\} = [B]\{\delta_\varepsilon\}$$

6.8.2 Strain Displacement Matrix for CST Element

$$b_1 = y_2 - y_3$$
$$b_2 = y_3 - y_1$$
$$b_3 = y_1 - y_2$$
$$c_1 = x_3 - x_2$$

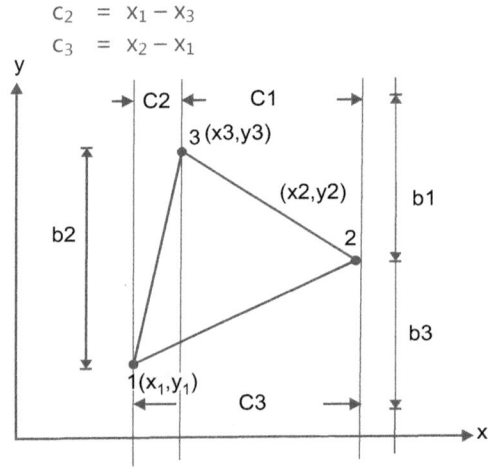

$$c_2 = x_1 - x_3$$
$$c_3 = x_2 - x_1$$

Fig. 6.26

$$\begin{Bmatrix} u \\ v \end{Bmatrix} = \begin{bmatrix} N_1 & N_2 & N_3 & 0 & 0 & 0 \\ 0 & 0 & 0 & N_1 & N_2 & N_3 \end{bmatrix} \begin{Bmatrix} u_1 \\ u_2 \\ u_3 \\ v_1 \\ v_2 \\ v_3 \end{Bmatrix}$$

$$\{\varepsilon\} = \begin{Bmatrix} \dfrac{\partial u}{\partial x} \\ \dfrac{\partial v}{\partial y} \\ \dfrac{\partial v}{\partial b} + \dfrac{\partial v}{\partial x} \end{Bmatrix} = \begin{bmatrix} \dfrac{\partial N_1}{\partial x} & \dfrac{\partial N_2}{2x} & \dfrac{\partial N_3}{\partial x} & 0 & 0 & 0 \\ 0 & 0 & 0 & \dfrac{2N_1}{\partial y} & \dfrac{\partial N_2}{\partial y} & \dfrac{\partial N_3}{\partial y} \\ \dfrac{\partial N_1}{\partial y} & \dfrac{\partial N_2}{\partial y} & \dfrac{\partial N_3}{\partial y} & \dfrac{\partial N_1}{\partial x} & \dfrac{\partial N+\partial}{\partial x} & \dfrac{\partial N_3}{\partial x} \end{bmatrix} \begin{Bmatrix} u_1 \\ u_2 \\ u_3 \\ v_1 \\ v_2 \\ v_3 \end{Bmatrix}$$

where,

$$N_1 = \frac{a_1 + b_1 x + c_1 y}{2A}$$

$$N_2 = \frac{a_2 + b_2 x + c_2 y}{2A}$$

$$N_3 = \frac{a_3 + b_3 x + c_3 y}{2A}$$

STRUCTURAL ANALYSIS – II   FINITE ELEMENT METHOD

$$\{\varepsilon\} = \frac{1}{2A}\begin{bmatrix} b_1 & b_2 & b_3 & 0 & 0 & 0 \\ 0 & 0 & 0 & c_1 & c_2 & c_3 \\ c_1 & c_2 & c_3 & b_1 & b_2 & b_3 \end{bmatrix}\{\delta\}_e$$

$$\{\varepsilon\} = [B]\{\delta\}_e$$

Strain Displacement Matrix for a beam element :

Strain displacement matrix,

$$\{\varepsilon\} = [B]\{\delta_e\} \qquad \ldots(1)$$

Elasticity stress matrix,

$$\{\sigma\} = [D]\{\varepsilon\}$$
$$= [D][B]\{\delta\}_e$$

Strain :

Ignore effect of sharing strain and consider bending action.

$$\frac{M}{I} = \frac{\sigma}{y} = \frac{E}{R}$$

$$\frac{\sigma}{E} = \frac{y}{R}$$

But,

$$R = \frac{\left[1 + \left(\frac{dv}{dx}\right)^2\right]^{3/2}}{\left(\frac{d^2v}{dx^2}\right)}$$

$$R = \frac{1}{\frac{d^2v}{dx^2}}$$

$$\frac{\sigma}{E} = y\frac{d^2v}{dx^2}$$

$$\varepsilon = y\frac{d^2v}{dx^2}$$

But,

$$V = [N]\{\delta\}_e$$

$$= [N_1\ N_2\ N_3\ N_4] = \begin{Bmatrix} v_1 \\ \theta_1 \\ v_2 \\ \theta_2 \end{Bmatrix}$$

$$N_1 = 1 - \frac{3x^2}{L^2} + \frac{2x^3}{L^3}, \frac{-3x^2}{L^2} + \frac{2 \times 3 \times 2x}{L^3}$$

$$N_2 = x - \frac{2x^2}{L} + \frac{x^3}{L^2}, \frac{2 \times 2}{L} + \frac{3 \times 2x}{L^2}$$

Ch. 6 | 6.23

$$N_3 = \frac{2x^2}{L^2} - \frac{2x^3}{L^3}, \frac{2 \times 2}{L^2} - \frac{2 \times 3 \times 2x}{L^3}$$

$$N_4 = -\frac{x^2}{L} + \frac{x^3}{L^2}, -\frac{2 \times 1}{L} + \frac{3 \times 2x}{L^2}$$

$$\varepsilon = \frac{\partial 2v}{\partial x^2}$$

$$\varepsilon = \frac{\partial^2}{\partial x^2} [N_1 \ N_2 \ N_3 \ N_4] \{\delta_\varepsilon\}$$

$$\varepsilon = [B] \{\delta_\varepsilon\}$$

where,

$$[B] = \left[\frac{\partial^2 N_1}{\partial x^2} \ \frac{\partial^2 N_2}{\partial x^2} \ \frac{\partial^2 N_3}{\partial x^3} \ \frac{\partial^2 N_4}{\partial x^4} \right] \{\delta_\varepsilon\}$$

$$= \left[\left(\frac{-6}{L^2} + \frac{12x}{L^3} \right) \left(\frac{-4}{L} + \frac{6x}{L^2} \right) \left(\frac{4}{L^2} - \frac{12x}{L^3} \right) \left(\frac{-2}{L} + \frac{6x}{L^2} \right) \right] \{\delta_\varepsilon\}$$

Strain Displacement Functions for LST Element :

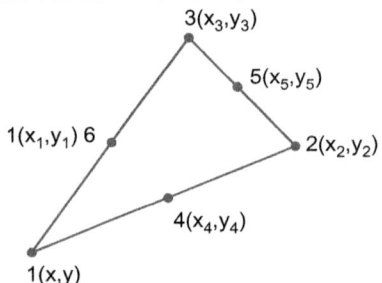

Fig. 6.27

$$u = \alpha_1 + \alpha_2 x + \alpha_3 y + \alpha_4 x^2 + \alpha_5 xy + \alpha_6 y^2$$
$$v = \alpha_7 + \alpha_8 x + \alpha_9 y + \alpha_{10} x^2 + \alpha_{11} xy + \alpha_{12} y^2$$

$$\begin{Bmatrix} u \\ v \end{Bmatrix} = \begin{bmatrix} 1 & x & y & x^2 & xy & y^2 & 0 & 0 & 0 & 0 & 0 & 0 \\ 0 & 0 & 0 & 0 & 0 & 0 & 1 & x & y & x^2 & xy & y^2 \end{bmatrix} \{\alpha\}_\varepsilon$$

$$\{u\} = [A] \{\alpha\} \qquad \qquad ...(A)$$

Strains are given as :

$$\varepsilon_x = \frac{\partial y}{\partial x} = \alpha_2 + 2x\alpha_4 + \alpha_5 y$$

$$\varepsilon_y = \frac{\partial v}{\partial y} = \alpha_9 + \alpha_{11} x + \alpha_{12} y$$

$$\chi_{xy} = \frac{\partial u}{\partial y} + \frac{\partial v}{\partial x} = \alpha_3 + \alpha_5 x + 2y\alpha_6 + \alpha_8 + 2x\alpha_{10} + \alpha_{11} y$$

STRUCTURAL ANALYSIS – II   FINITE ELEMENT METHOD

In Matrix Form :

$$\begin{Bmatrix} \varepsilon_x \\ \varepsilon_y \\ \chi_{xy} \end{Bmatrix} = \begin{bmatrix} 0 & 1 & 0 & 2x & y & 0 & 0 & 0 & 0 & 0 & 0 \\ 0 & 0 & 0 & 0 & 0 & 0 & 0 & 0 & 1 & 0 & x & 2y \\ 0 & 0 & 1 & 0 & x & 2y & 0 & 1 & 0 & 2x & y & 0 \end{bmatrix} \{\alpha\}_\varepsilon$$

$$\{\varepsilon\} = [B]\{\alpha\}$$

Elasticity Matrix in Plane Stress Problem :

$$\begin{Bmatrix} \sigma_x \\ \sigma_y \\ \tau_{xy} \end{Bmatrix} = \frac{E}{1-\nu^2} \begin{bmatrix} 1 & \nu & 0 \\ \nu & 1 & 0 \\ 0 & 0 & \frac{1-\nu}{2} \end{bmatrix} \begin{Bmatrix} \varepsilon_x \\ \varepsilon_y \\ e_z \end{Bmatrix}$$

$$\{\sigma\} = [D]\{\varepsilon\}$$
Elasticity matrix

6.9 PRINCIPLE OF MINIMUM POTENTIAL ENERGY

"All displacement states of body or structure subjected to external loading, that satisfy geometric boundary conditions. That displacement state that also satisfies equilibrium equations is such that total P.E. is minimum for stable equilibrium".

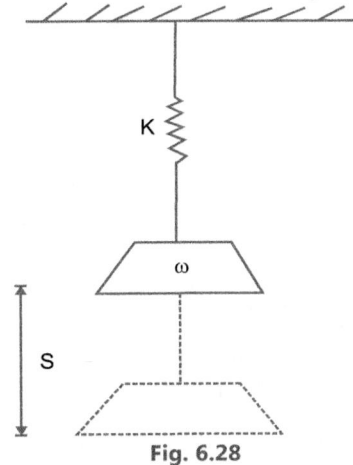

Fig. 6.28

Consider mass spring system as shown in Fig. 6.28.
Total potential energy (π) = Strain energy stored (u) + External load applied (v)

$$\pi = u + v \qquad \qquad ...(1)$$

where,
$$u = \frac{1}{2}\delta^2$$
$$v = -\omega\delta$$

By substituting value of u and v in equation (i)

$$\pi = \frac{1}{2} k\delta^2 - \omega\delta$$

By using minimum P.E.

$$\frac{d\pi}{d\delta} = 0$$

i.e. $\omega = k\delta$

Example 6.1 :
Obtain stiffness matrix co-efficient for given Fig. 6.28 in terms of parameter A, E, L, θ. Where θ is inclination of truss element with x-axis. Use principle of minimum P.E.

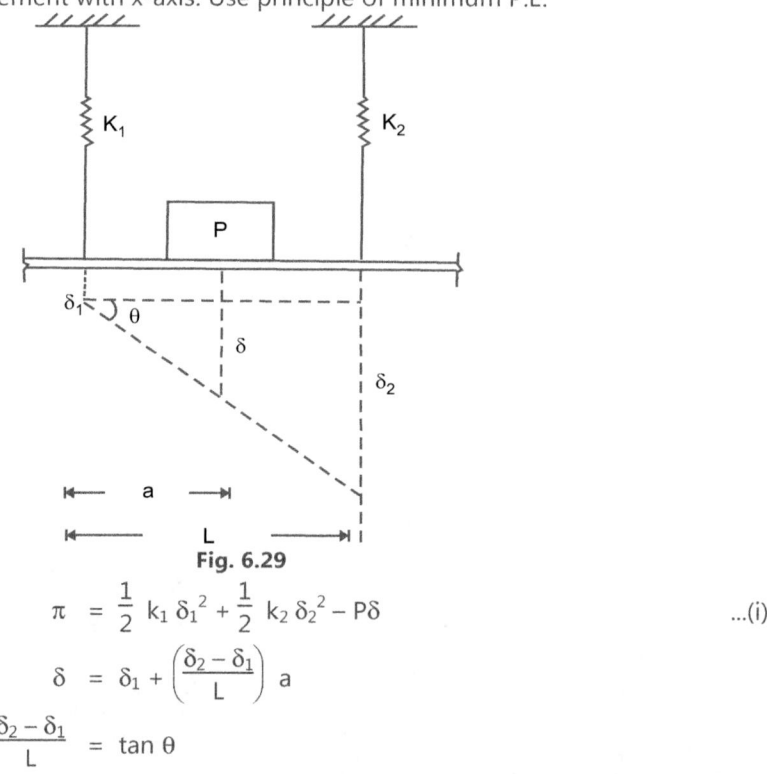

Fig. 6.29

$$\pi = \frac{1}{2} k_1 \delta_1^2 + \frac{1}{2} k_2 \delta_2^2 - P\delta \qquad ...(i)$$

$$\delta = \delta_1 + \left(\frac{\delta_2 - \delta_1}{L}\right) a$$

$$\frac{\delta_2 - \delta_1}{L} = \tan\theta$$

Angle is too small $\tan\theta \approx \theta$

$$\delta = \delta_1 + a\theta$$
$$\delta_2 = \delta_1 + L\theta$$

From equation (i)

$$\pi = \frac{1}{2} K_1\delta_1^2 + \frac{1}{2} k_2 (\delta_1^2 + 2\delta_1 L\theta + L^2\theta^2) - P(\delta_1 - a\theta)$$

By using minimum P.E.

$$\frac{d\pi}{d\delta_1} = 0$$

$$0 = \frac{1}{2} \times 2 k_1\delta_1 + \frac{1}{2}(2\delta_1 + 2L\theta) - P$$

$$P = (k_1 + k_2)\delta_1 + k_2 L\theta \quad \ldots(a)$$

$$\frac{d\pi}{d\theta} = 0$$

$$0 = \frac{1}{2} k_2 [2\delta_1 L + L^2\theta] - pa$$

$$Pa = k_2[\delta_1 L + L^2\theta] \quad \ldots(b)$$

In a matrix form :

$$\begin{Bmatrix} p \\ p_a \end{Bmatrix} = \begin{bmatrix} (k_1 + k_2) & k_2 L \\ k_2 L & k_2 L^2 \end{bmatrix} \begin{Bmatrix} \delta_1 \\ \theta \end{Bmatrix}$$

6.10 Shape Functions

Shape functions are useful to device a displacement model for an element.

Shape functions are polynomial in x, y, z co-ordinate, x, y, z serves to be independent variables. These polynomials are defined over single finite element constant involved in these polynomials like a_0, a_1 …… are obtained by values of co-ordinate of nodes. Number of shape functions and always equal to number of nodes of an element as shape function.

Shape function for an element can be derived with the help of two methods.

(1) Using polynomial defined by pascal triangle or Using Language inter polation function.
(2) By Using Natural co-ordinates.

6.10.1 Properties of Shape Functions

(1) Each shape function and displacement model defined by them are all of same degree shape functions are denoted by N_i and primary field variable (displacement model) is denoted by ϕ (u, v, w) etc.
(2) Each N_i has a value of unity at i^{th} nodes and zero at remaining nodes.
(3) $\sum_{i=1} N_i = 1$

6.10.2 Criteria for Choice of Displacement Model

(1) Convergence to exact solution.

(2) Compatibility.

(3) Geometric invariance.

Every displacement model should satisfy above criteria.

(1) Convergence : Rigid body displacement = a_0 not depends on x.

(a) The choosen displacement function should include all possible rigid body nodes. This affects rate of convergence of FEA solution.

(b) The choosen displacement function must represent constant strain state of the element. This affects the correctness of solution i.e. solution does not converge to exact value solution. This can be ensured by making the element displacement model pass the patch test.

(2) Compatibility : Choosen displacement function should ensure continuity within the element and between adjacent elements. They are called as confirming/compatible elements. The first requirement is satisfied by using polynomial function without missing terms representing the behaviour of element second requirements demands there should not be any gaps or overlaps on common edges of elements. This is achieved by using polynomial function which is inter-polated by values of nodal DOF's only.

This automatically achieves inter element continuity known as **compatible elements.**

(3) Geometrical Invariance : The element should not have preferred directions that is the displacements shape of element will not change with change in local co-ordinate system. This is also known as geometrical isotropy. Invariance can be achieved every by incomplete polynomial. In that case it should be balanced at vertical centre line of a "pascal triangle."

Above all requirement can be satisfied by choosing the polynomial form.

(a) Pascal Triangle.

(b) Using Lagrange/Hermit Polynomial.

6.10.3.1 Pascal Triangle

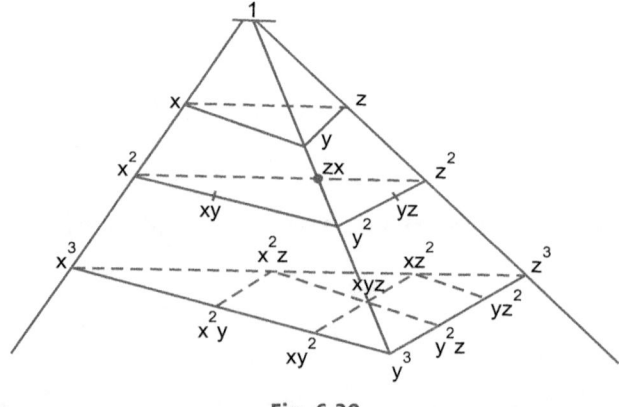

Fig. 6.30

1D : Hypotenous is used.

$$u = a_0 + a_1 x$$

or

$$u = a_0 + a_1 x + a_2 x^2$$

2D : Triangle is used row-wise

$$u = a_0 + a_1 x + a_2 y + a_3 x^2 + a_4 xy + a_5 y^2$$

3D : Pascal tetrahedron is used.

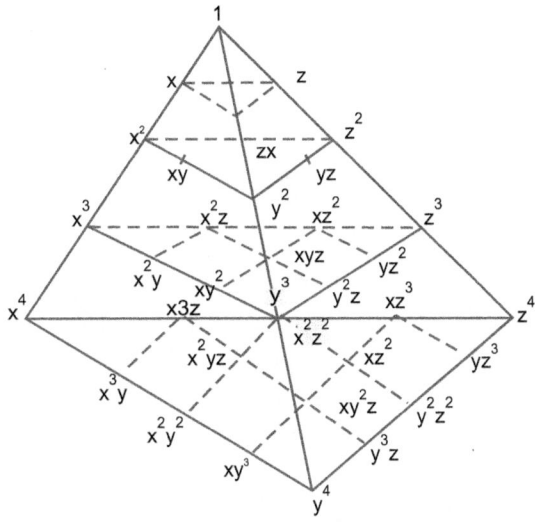

Fig. 6.31

6.10.4 Derivation of Shape Functions Using Polynomials

Polynomial Function in terms of Cartesian Co-ordinates :

- Number of constant = Nodal DOF.
- Care is taken to see that geometrical isotropy is not lost.
- Using nodal values number of equation = Number of constant in the polynomials are formed and then the constant found, then shape function are identified.
- Procedure known as generalized co-ordinates approach, since the constant in the polynomial are called as generalised co-ordinates.
- Using generalised co-ordinate approach find shape functions for two noded element.

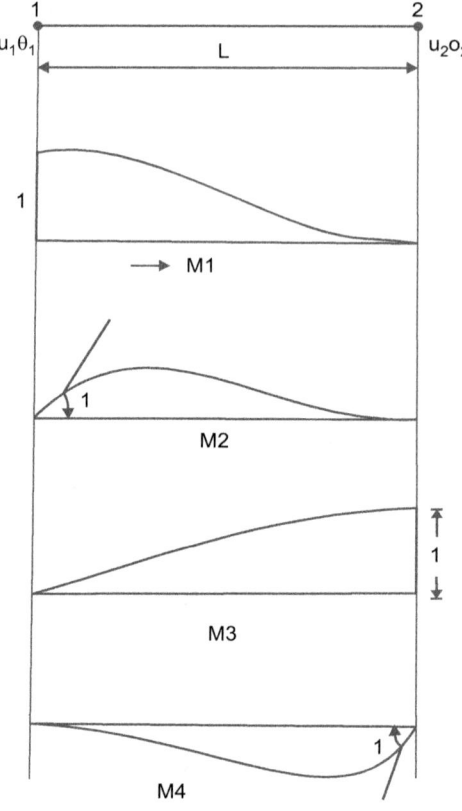

Fig. 6.32

$$\{\delta\} = \begin{Bmatrix} \omega_1 \\ \theta_1 \\ \omega_2 \\ \theta_2 \end{Bmatrix}$$

where,

$$\theta_1 = \frac{\partial \omega_1}{\partial x}$$

$$\theta_2 = \frac{\partial \omega_2}{\partial x}$$

$$\omega = \alpha_1 + \alpha_2 x + \alpha_3 x^2 + \alpha_4 x^3 \qquad \ldots(i)$$

$$\theta = \frac{\partial \omega}{\partial x} = \alpha_2 + 2d_3 x + 3\alpha_4 x^2 \qquad \ldots(ii)$$

STRUCTURAL ANALYSIS – II FINITE ELEMENT METHOD

At $x_1 = 0$ and $x_2 = L$
$\omega_1 = \alpha_1$, $\theta_1 = \alpha_2$
from equations (i) and (ii)

$$\omega_2 = \alpha_1 + \alpha_2 L + \alpha_3 L^2 + \alpha_4 L^3$$
$$\theta_2 = \alpha_2 + 3\alpha_3 L + 3\alpha_4 L^2$$

$$\{\delta\} = \begin{Bmatrix} \omega_1 \\ \theta_1 \\ \omega_2 \\ \theta_2 \end{Bmatrix} \begin{bmatrix} 1 & 0 & 0 & 0 \\ 0 & 1 & 0 & 0 \\ 1 & L & L^2 & L^3 \\ 0 & 1 & 2L & 3L^2 \end{bmatrix} \begin{Bmatrix} \alpha_1 \\ \alpha_2 \\ \alpha_3 \\ \alpha_4 \end{Bmatrix}$$

$$\begin{Bmatrix} \alpha_1 \\ \alpha_2 \\ \alpha_3 \\ \alpha_4 \end{Bmatrix} = \begin{bmatrix} 1 & 0 & 0 & 0 \\ 0 & 1 & 0 & 0 \\ 1 & L & L^2 & L^3 \\ 0 & 1 & 2L & 3L^2 \end{bmatrix}^{-1} \begin{Bmatrix} \omega_1 \\ \theta_1 \\ \omega_2 \\ \theta_2 \end{Bmatrix} \quad \ldots(A)$$

$$|A^{-1}| = \left[\begin{array}{cccc|cccc} 1 & 0 & 0 & 0 & 1 & 0 & 0 & 0 \\ 0 & 1 & 0 & 0 & 0 & 1 & 0 & 0 \\ 1 & L & L^2 & L^3 & 0 & 0 & 1 & 0 \\ 0 & 1 & 2L & 3L^2 & 0 & 0 & 0 & 1 \end{array}\right]$$

$R_3 \rightarrow \dfrac{R_3}{L^2}$

$R_4 \rightarrow \dfrac{R_4}{3L^2}$

$$A^{-1} = \begin{bmatrix} 1 & 0 & 0 & 0 & 1 & 0 & 0 & 0 \\ 0 & 1 & 0 & 0 & 0 & 1 & 0 & 0 \\ \dfrac{1}{L^2} & \dfrac{1}{L} & 1 & L & 0 & 0 & \dfrac{1}{L^2} & 0 \\ 0 & \dfrac{1}{3L^2} & \dfrac{2}{3L} & 1 & 0 & 0 & 0 & \dfrac{1}{3L^2} \end{bmatrix}$$

$R_3 \rightarrow R_3 - \dfrac{R_1}{L^2}$

$R_4 \rightarrow R_4 - \dfrac{R_2}{3L^2}$

$$A^{-1} = \begin{bmatrix} 1 & 0 & 0 & 0 & 1 & 0 & 0 & 0 \\ 0 & 1 & 0 & 0 & 0 & 1 & 0 & 0 \\ 0 & 1/L & 1 & L & -1/L^2 & 0 & 1/L^2 & 0 \\ 0 & 0 & 2/3L & 1 & 0 & -1/3L^2 & 0 & 1/3L^2 \end{bmatrix}$$

$$R_3 \rightarrow R_3 - \frac{R_2}{L}$$

$$A^{-1} = \begin{bmatrix} 1 & 0 & 0 & 0 & 1 & 0 & 0 & 0 \\ 0 & 1 & 0 & 0 & 0 & 1 & 0 & 0 \\ 0 & 0 & 1 & L & -1/L^2 & -1/L & 1/L^2 & 0 \\ 0 & 0 & 2/3L & 1 & 0 & -1/3L^2 & 0 & 1/3L^2 \end{bmatrix}$$

$$R_4 \rightarrow R_4 - \frac{2R_3}{3L}$$

$$A^{-1} = \begin{bmatrix} 1 & 0 & 0 & 0 & 1 & 0 & 0 & 0 \\ 0 & 1 & 0 & 0 & 0 & 1 & 0 & 0 \\ 0 & 0 & 1 & L & -1/L^2 & -1/L & 1/L^2 & 0 \\ 0 & 0 & 0 & 1/3 & 2/3L^3 & 1/3L^2 & -2/3L^3 & 1/3L^2 \end{bmatrix}$$

$$R_4 \rightarrow 3R_4$$

$$A^{-1} = \begin{bmatrix} 1 & 0 & 0 & 0 & 1 & 0 & 0 & 0 \\ 0 & 1 & 0 & 0 & 0 & 1 & 0 & 0 \\ 0 & 0 & 1 & L & -1/L^2 & -1/L & 1/L^2 & 0 \\ 0 & 0 & 0 & 1 & 2/L^3 & 1/L^2 & -2/L^3 & 1/L^2 \end{bmatrix}$$

$$R_3 \rightarrow R_3 - LR_4$$

$$[A^{-1}] = \begin{bmatrix} 1 & 0 & 0 & 0 & 1 & 0 & 0 & 0 \\ 0 & 1 & 0 & 0 & 0 & 1 & 0 & 0 \\ 0 & 0 & 1 & 0 & -3/L^2 & -2/L & 3/L^2 & -1/L \\ 0 & 0 & 0 & 1 & 2/L^3 & 1/L^2 & -2/L^3 & 1/L^2 \end{bmatrix}$$

From equation (A)

$$\begin{Bmatrix} \alpha_1 \\ \alpha_2 \\ \alpha_3 \\ \alpha_4 \end{Bmatrix} = \begin{bmatrix} 1 & 0 & 0 & 0 \\ 0 & 1 & 0 & 0 \\ -3/L^2 & -2/L & 3/L^2 & -1/L \\ 2/L^3 & 1/L^2 & -2/L^3 & 1/L^2 \end{bmatrix} \begin{Bmatrix} \omega_1 \\ \theta_1 \\ \omega_2 \\ \theta_2 \end{Bmatrix}$$

From equation (1),

$$\omega = \alpha_1 + \alpha_2 x + \alpha_3 x^2 + \alpha_4 x^3$$

$$\omega = [1 \ x \ x^2 \ x^3] \begin{Bmatrix} \alpha_1 \\ \alpha_2 \\ \alpha_3 \\ \alpha_4 \end{Bmatrix}$$

$$\omega = [1 \ x \ x^2 \ x^3] \begin{bmatrix} 1 & 0 & 0 & 0 \\ 0 & 1 & 0 & 0 \\ -3/L^2 & -2/L & 3/L^2 & -1/L \\ 2/L^3 & 1/L^2 & -2/L^3 & 1/L^2 \end{bmatrix} \begin{Bmatrix} \omega_1 \\ \theta_1 \\ \omega_2 \\ \theta_2 \end{Bmatrix}$$

$$\omega = \left[1 - \frac{3x^2}{L^2} - \frac{2x^3}{L^3}, \ x - \frac{2x^2}{L} + \frac{x^3}{L^2}, \ \frac{3x^2}{L^2} - \frac{2x^3}{L^3}, \ \frac{-x^2}{L} + \frac{x^3}{L^2} \right] = \begin{Bmatrix} \omega_1 \\ \theta_1 \\ \omega_2 \\ \theta_2 \end{Bmatrix}$$

$$\omega = [N_1 \ N_2 \ N_3 \ N_4]\{\delta\}$$

where,
$$N_1 = 1 - \frac{3x^2}{L^2} + \frac{2x^3}{L^3}$$

$$N_2 = x - \frac{2x^2}{L} + \frac{x^3}{L^2}$$

$$N_3 = \frac{3x^2}{L^2} - \frac{2x^3}{L^3}$$

$$N_4 = -\frac{x^2}{L} + \frac{x^3}{L^2}$$

Variation of these functions :
At node 1 :
$N_1 = 1, \ N_2, \ N_3, \ N_4 = 0$

$$\frac{\partial N_2}{\partial x} = 1$$

$$\frac{\partial N_1}{\partial x} = \frac{\partial N_3}{\partial x} = \frac{\partial N_3}{\partial x} = 0$$

At node 2 :
$N_3 = 1, \ N_1 = N_2 = N_4 = 0$

$$\frac{\partial N_4}{\partial x} = 1$$

$$\frac{\partial N_1}{\partial x} = \frac{\partial N_2}{\partial x} = \frac{\partial N_3}{\partial x} = 0$$

6.11 DETERMINE THE SHAPE FUNCTIONS FOR THE CONSTANT STRAIN TRIANGLE (CST). USE POLYNOMIAL FUNCTIONS

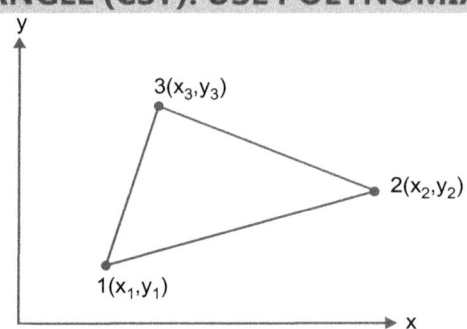

Fig. 6.33

$$\{\delta\}^T = [u_1, u_2, u_3, v_1, v_2, v_3]$$

Displacement model is,

$$u = \alpha_1 + \alpha_2 x + \alpha_3 y \quad \ldots(A)$$
$$v = \alpha_4 + \alpha_5 x + \alpha_6 y \quad \ldots(B)$$

$\therefore$
$$u_1 = \alpha_1 + \alpha_2 x_1 + \alpha_3 y_1 \quad \ldots(i)$$
$$u_2 = \alpha_1 + \alpha_2 x_2 + \alpha_3 y_2 \quad \ldots(ii)$$
$$u_3 = \alpha_1 + \alpha_2 x_3 + \alpha_3 y_3 \quad \ldots(iii)$$

$$\begin{Bmatrix} u_1 \\ u_2 \\ u_3 \end{Bmatrix} = \begin{bmatrix} 1 & x_1 & y_1 \\ 1 & x_2 & y_2 \\ 1 & x_3 & y_3 \end{bmatrix} \begin{Bmatrix} \alpha_1 \\ \alpha_2 \\ \alpha_3 \end{Bmatrix}$$

$$\begin{Bmatrix} \alpha_1 \\ \alpha_2 \\ \alpha_3 \end{Bmatrix} = \begin{bmatrix} 1 & x_1 & y_1 \\ 1 & x_2 & y_2 \\ 1 & x_3 & y_3 \end{bmatrix} \begin{Bmatrix} u_1 \\ u_2 \\ u_3 \end{Bmatrix}$$

But we know that,

$$\begin{vmatrix} 1 & x_1 & y_1 \\ 1 & x_2 & y_2 \\ 1 & x_3 & y_3 \end{vmatrix} = \begin{vmatrix} 1 & 1 & 1 \\ x_1 & x_2 & x_3 \\ y_1 & y_2 & y_3 \end{vmatrix} = 2A$$

$$\begin{Bmatrix} \alpha_1 \\ \alpha_2 \\ \alpha_3 \end{Bmatrix} = \frac{1}{2A} \begin{bmatrix} (x_2 y_3 - x_3 y_2) & (y_2 - y_3) & (x_3 - x_2) \\ (x_3 y_1 - x_1 y_3) & (y_3 - y_1) & (x_1 - x_3) \\ (x_1 y_2 - x_2 y_1) & (y_1 - y_2) & (x_2 - x_1) \end{bmatrix} + \begin{Bmatrix} u_1 \\ u_2 \\ u_3 \end{Bmatrix}$$

$$= \frac{1}{2A} \begin{bmatrix} a_1 & b_1 & c_1 \\ a_2 & b_2 & c_2 \\ a_3 & b_3 & c_3 \end{bmatrix} + \begin{Bmatrix} u_1 \\ u_2 \\ u_3 \end{Bmatrix}$$

$$\begin{Bmatrix} \alpha_1 \\ \alpha_2 \\ \alpha_3 \end{Bmatrix} = \frac{1}{2A} \begin{bmatrix} a_1 & a_2 & a_3 \\ b_1 & b_2 & b_3 \\ c_1 & c_2 & c_3 \end{bmatrix} \begin{Bmatrix} u_1 \\ u_2 \\ u_3 \end{Bmatrix}$$

From equation (A)

$$u = \alpha_1 + \alpha_2 x + \alpha_3 y$$

$$u = [1 \ x \ y] \begin{Bmatrix} \alpha_1 \\ \alpha_2 \\ \alpha_3 \end{Bmatrix}$$

$$u = [1 \ x \ y] \frac{1}{2A} \begin{bmatrix} a_1 & a_2 & a_3 \\ b_1 & b_2 & b_3 \\ c_1 & c_2 & c_3 \end{bmatrix} \begin{Bmatrix} u_1 \\ u_2 \\ u_3 \end{Bmatrix}$$

$$u = \begin{bmatrix} \dfrac{a_1 + b_1 x + c_1 y}{2A} & \dfrac{a_2 + b_2 x + c_2 y}{2A} & \dfrac{a_3 + b_3 x + c_3 y}{2A} \end{bmatrix} \begin{Bmatrix} u_1 \\ u_2 \\ u_3 \end{Bmatrix}$$

$$u = [N_1 \ N_2 \ N_3] \begin{Bmatrix} u_1 \\ u_2 \\ u_3 \end{Bmatrix}$$

$$u = [N]\{\delta\}$$

where,

$$N_1 = \frac{a_1 + b_1 x + c_1 y}{2A}$$

$$N_2 = \frac{a_2 + b_2 x + c_2 y}{2A}$$

$$N_3 = \frac{a_3 + b_3 x + c_3 y}{2A}$$

Parallely,

$$V = [N_1 \ N_2 \ N_3] \begin{Bmatrix} v_1 \\ v_2 \\ v_3 \end{Bmatrix}$$

$$\left\{ \begin{array}{c} u(x,y) \\ v(x,y) \end{array} \right\} = \left[\begin{array}{cccccc} N_1 & N_2 & N_3 & 0 & 0 & 0 \\ 0 & 0 & 0 & N_1 & N_2 & N_3 \end{array} \right] \left\{ \begin{array}{c} u_1 \\ u_2 \\ u_3 \\ v_1 \\ v_2 \\ v_3 \end{array} \right\}$$

6.12 SHAPE FUNCTIONS IN TERMS OF NATURAL CO-ORDINATE SYSTEMS

Derive the expression for shape function for a two noded bar element taking natural co-ordinate (ξ) varying from –1 to 1 :

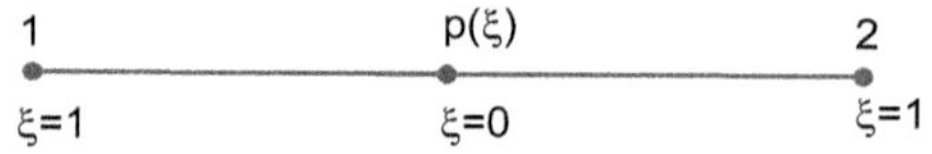

Fig. 6.34

$$u = \alpha_1 + \alpha_2 \xi$$

$$= [1 \; \xi] \left\{ \begin{array}{c} \alpha_1 \\ \alpha_2 \end{array} \right\}$$

$$\left\{ \begin{array}{c} u_1 \\ u_2 \end{array} \right\} = \left[\begin{array}{cc} 1 & -1 \\ 1 & 1 \end{array} \right] \left\{ \begin{array}{c} \alpha_1 \\ \alpha_2 \end{array} \right\}$$

$$\left\{ \begin{array}{c} \alpha_1 \\ \alpha_2 \end{array} \right\} = \left[\begin{array}{cc} 1 & -1 \\ 1 & 1 \end{array} \right]^{-1} \left\{ \begin{array}{c} u_1 \\ u_2 \end{array} \right\}$$

$$= \frac{1}{(1+1)} \left[\begin{array}{cc} 1 & -1 \\ +1 & 1 \end{array} \right] \left\{ \begin{array}{c} u_1 \\ u_2 \end{array} \right\}$$

$$= \frac{1}{2} \left[\begin{array}{cc} 1 & 1 \\ -1 & 1 \end{array} \right] \left\{ \begin{array}{c} u_1 \\ u_2 \end{array} \right\}$$

$$u = [1 \; \xi] \left\{ \begin{array}{c} \alpha_1 \\ \alpha_2 \end{array} \right\}$$

$$u = [1 \; \xi] \frac{1}{2} \left[\begin{array}{cc} 1 & 1 \\ -1 & 1 \end{array} \right] \left\{ \begin{array}{c} u_1 \\ u_2 \end{array} \right\}$$

$$u = \frac{1}{2} [1-\xi \quad 1+\xi] \left\{ \begin{array}{c} u_1 \\ u_2 \end{array} \right\}$$

$$u = \left[\frac{1-\xi}{2} \quad \frac{1+\xi}{2} \right] \left\{ \begin{array}{c} u_1 \\ u_2 \end{array} \right\}$$

STRUCTURAL ANALYSIS – II
FINITE ELEMENT METHOD

$$u = [N_1 \ N_2] \begin{Bmatrix} u_1 \\ u_2 \end{Bmatrix}$$

where, $N_1 = \dfrac{1-\xi}{2}$, $N_2 = \dfrac{1+\xi}{2}$

Determine the shape functions for a three nodded bar element with natural co-ordinate system :

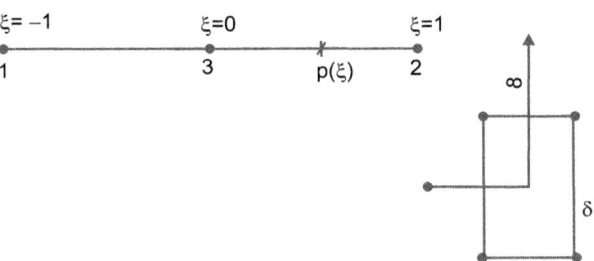

Fig. 6.35

$$u = \alpha_1 + \alpha_2 \xi + \alpha_3 \xi^2$$

$$\{\delta\} = u_1 = \alpha_1 - \alpha_2 + \alpha_3$$
$$= u_2 = \alpha_1 + \alpha_2 + \alpha_3$$
$$= u_3 = \alpha_1 + 0 + 0$$

$$\{\delta\} = \begin{Bmatrix} u_1 \\ u_2 \\ u_3 \end{Bmatrix} = \begin{bmatrix} 1 & -1 & 1 \\ 1 & 1 & 1 \\ 1 & 0 & 0 \end{bmatrix} \begin{Bmatrix} \alpha_1 \\ \alpha_2 \\ \alpha_3 \end{Bmatrix}$$

$$\begin{Bmatrix} \alpha_1 \\ \alpha_2 \\ \alpha_3 \end{Bmatrix} = \begin{bmatrix} 1 & -1 & 1 \\ 1 & 1 & 1 \\ 1 & 0 & 0 \end{bmatrix}^{-1} \begin{Bmatrix} u_1 \\ u_2 \\ u_3 \end{Bmatrix}$$

$$\begin{Bmatrix} \alpha_1 \\ \alpha_2 \\ \alpha_3 \end{Bmatrix} = \dfrac{1}{0 + 1(-1) + 1(-1)} \begin{bmatrix} 0 & -1 & -1 \\ 0 & -1 & -1 \\ -2 & 0 & -2 \end{bmatrix} \begin{Bmatrix} u_1 \\ u_2 \\ u_3 \end{Bmatrix}$$

$$\begin{Bmatrix} \alpha_1 \\ \alpha_2 \\ \alpha_3 \end{Bmatrix} = \dfrac{1}{2} \begin{bmatrix} 0 & -1 & 1 \\ 0 & 1 & 1 \\ 2 & 0 & -2 \end{bmatrix} + \begin{Bmatrix} u_1 \\ u_2 \\ u_3 \end{Bmatrix}$$

$$\begin{Bmatrix} \alpha_1 \\ \alpha_2 \\ \alpha_3 \end{Bmatrix} = \dfrac{1}{2} \begin{bmatrix} 0 & 0 & 2 \\ -1 & 1 & 0 \\ 1 & 1 & -2 \end{bmatrix} \begin{Bmatrix} u_1 \\ u_2 \\ u_3 \end{Bmatrix}$$

$$u = \alpha_1 + \alpha_2 \xi + \alpha_3 \xi^2$$

$$= [1 \; \xi \; \xi^2] \begin{Bmatrix} \alpha_1 \\ \alpha_2 \\ \alpha_3 \end{Bmatrix}$$

$$= [1 \; \xi \; \xi^2] \frac{1}{2} \begin{bmatrix} 0 & 0 & 2 \\ -1 & 1 & 0 \\ 1 & 1 & -2 \end{bmatrix} \begin{Bmatrix} u_1 \\ u_2 \\ u_3 \end{Bmatrix}$$

$$= \frac{1}{2} [(-\xi + \xi^2) \; (\xi + \xi^2) \; (2 - 2\xi^2)] \begin{Bmatrix} u_1 \\ u_2 \\ u_3 \end{Bmatrix}$$

$$u = \left[\frac{-\xi + \xi^2}{2} \; \frac{\xi + \xi^2}{2} \; 1 - \xi^2 \right] \begin{Bmatrix} u_1 \\ u_2 \\ u_3 \end{Bmatrix}$$

$$u = [N_1 \; N_2 \; N_3] \begin{Bmatrix} u_1 \\ u_2 \\ u_3 \end{Bmatrix}$$

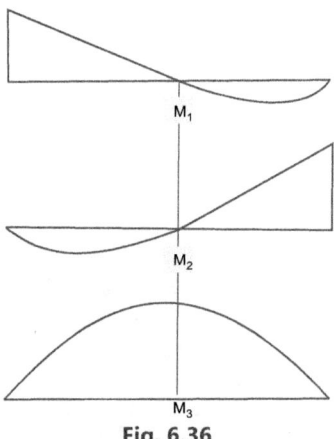

Fig. 6.36

where,
$$N_1 = \frac{-\xi + \xi^2}{2}$$
$$N_2 = \frac{\xi + \xi^2}{2}$$
$$N_3 = 1 - \xi^2$$

Determine the shape functions for a CST element in terms of natural co-ordinates systems :

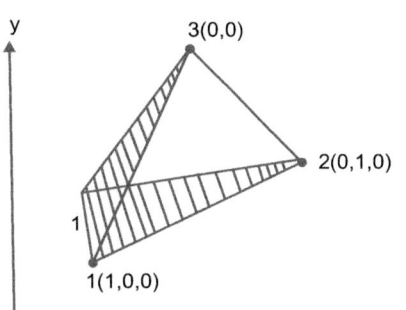

Fig. 6.37

$$u = \alpha_1 L_1 + \alpha_2 L_2 + \alpha_3 L_3$$

$$= [L_1 \ L_2 \ L_3] \begin{Bmatrix} \alpha_1 \\ \alpha_2 \\ \alpha_3 \end{Bmatrix}$$

$$\begin{Bmatrix} u_1 \\ u_2 \\ u_3 \end{Bmatrix} = \begin{bmatrix} 1 & 0 & 0 \\ 0 & 1 & 0 \\ 0 & 0 & 1 \end{bmatrix} \begin{Bmatrix} \alpha_1 \\ \alpha_2 \\ \alpha_3 \end{Bmatrix}$$

$$\begin{Bmatrix} \alpha_1 \\ \alpha_2 \\ \alpha_3 \end{Bmatrix} = \begin{bmatrix} 1 & 0 & 0 \\ 0 & 1 & 0 \\ 0 & 0 & 1 \end{bmatrix} \begin{Bmatrix} u_1 \\ u_2 \\ u_3 \end{Bmatrix}$$

$$= \begin{bmatrix} 1 & 0 & 0 \\ 0 & 1 & 0 \\ 0 & 0 & 1 \end{bmatrix} \begin{Bmatrix} u_1 \\ u_2 \\ u_3 \end{Bmatrix}$$

$$u = [L_1 \ L_2 \ L_3] \begin{bmatrix} 1 & 0 & 0 \\ 0 & 1 & 0 \\ 0 & 0 & 1 \end{bmatrix} \begin{Bmatrix} u_1 \\ u_2 \\ u_3 \end{Bmatrix}$$

$$u = [L_1 \ L_2 \ L_3] \begin{Bmatrix} u_1 \\ u_2 \\ u_3 \end{Bmatrix}$$

$$u = [N_1 \ N_2 \ N_3] \begin{Bmatrix} u_1 \\ u_2 \\ u_3 \end{Bmatrix}$$

Parallely,

$$V = [N_1 \ N_2 \ N_3] \begin{Bmatrix} v_1 \\ v_2 \\ v_3 \end{Bmatrix}$$

$$\begin{Bmatrix} u \\ v \end{Bmatrix} = \begin{bmatrix} L_1 & L_2 & L_3 & 0 & 0 & 0 \\ 0 & 0 & 0 & L_1 & L_2 & L_3 \end{bmatrix} \begin{Bmatrix} u_1 \\ u_2 \\ u_3 \\ v_1 \\ v_2 \\ v_3 \end{Bmatrix}$$

6.13 DETERMINE THE SHAPE FUNCTION FOR LST ELEMENT, USE NATURAL CO-ORDINATE SYSTEM

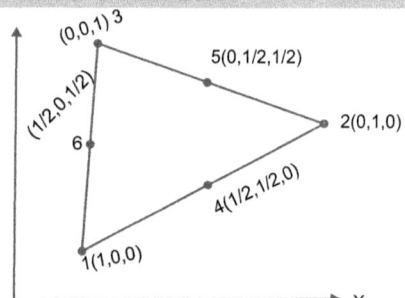

Fig. 6.38

$$u = \alpha_1 L_1^2 + \alpha_2 L_2^2 + \alpha_3 L_3^2 + \alpha_4 L_1 L_2 + \alpha_5 L_2 L_3 + \alpha_6 L_3 L_1 \qquad \ldots(i)$$

$$\begin{Bmatrix} u_1 \\ u_2 \\ u_3 \\ u_4 \\ u_5 \\ u_6 \end{Bmatrix} = \begin{bmatrix} 1 & 0 & 0 & 0 & 0 & 0 \\ 0 & 1 & 0 & 0 & 0 & 0 \\ 0 & 0 & 1 & 0 & 0 & 0 \\ 1/4 & 1/4 & 0 & 1/4 & 0 & 0 \\ 0 & 1/4 & 1/4 & 0 & 1/4 & 0 \\ 1/4 & 0 & 1/4 & 0 & 0 & 1/4 \end{bmatrix} \begin{Bmatrix} \alpha_1 \\ \alpha_2 \\ \alpha_3 \\ \alpha_4 \\ \alpha_5 \\ \alpha_6 \end{Bmatrix}$$

$$\begin{Bmatrix} \alpha_1 \\ \alpha_2 \\ \alpha_3 \\ \alpha_4 \\ \alpha_5 \\ \alpha_6 \end{Bmatrix} = \begin{bmatrix} 1 & 0 & 0 & 0 & 0 & 0 \\ 0 & 1 & 0 & 0 & 0 & 0 \\ 0 & 0 & 1 & 0 & 0 & 0 \\ -1 & -1 & 0 & 4 & 0 & 0 \\ 0 & -1 & -1 & 0 & 4 & 0 \\ -1 & 0 & -1 & 0 & 0 & 4 \end{bmatrix} \begin{Bmatrix} u_1 \\ u_2 \\ u_3 \\ u_4 \\ u_5 \\ u_6 \end{Bmatrix} \quad \ldots(ii)$$

From equations (i) and (ii)

$$[L_1^2 \; L_2^2 \; L_3^2 \; L_1L_2 \; L_2L_3 \; L_3L_1] \begin{Bmatrix} \alpha_1 \\ \alpha_2 \\ \alpha_3 \\ \alpha_4 \\ \alpha_5 \\ \alpha_6 \end{Bmatrix} = u$$

$$u = [L_1^2 \; L_2^2 \; L_3^2 \; L_1L_2 \; L_2L_3 \; L_3L_1] \begin{bmatrix} 1 & 0 & 0 & 0 & 0 & 0 \\ 0 & 1 & 0 & 0 & 0 & 0 \\ 0 & 0 & 1 & 0 & 0 & 0 \\ -1 & -1 & 0 & 4 & 0 & 0 \\ 0 & -1 & -1 & 0 & 4 & 0 \\ -1 & 0 & -1 & 0 & 0 & 4 \end{bmatrix} \begin{Bmatrix} u_1 \\ u_2 \\ u_3 \\ u_4 \\ u_5 \\ u_6 \end{Bmatrix}$$

$$u = [(L_1^2 - L_1L_2 - L_3L_1),\; (L_2^2 - L_1L_2 - L_2L_3),\; (L_3^2 - L_2L_3 - L_3L_1),\; 4L_1L_2,\; 4L_2L_3,\; 4L_3L_1] \begin{Bmatrix} u_1 \\ u_2 \\ u_3 \\ u_4 \\ u_5 \\ u_6 \end{Bmatrix}$$

$$u = [N_1\ N_2\ N_3\ N_4\ N_5\ N_6] \begin{Bmatrix} u_1 \\ u_2 \\ u_3 \\ u_4 \\ u_5 \\ u_6 \end{Bmatrix} \quad \text{Parallely,} \quad V = [N_1\ N_2\ N_3\ N_4\ N_5\ N_6] \begin{Bmatrix} v_1 \\ v_2 \\ v_3 \\ v_4 \\ v_5 \\ v_6 \end{Bmatrix}$$

$$\begin{Bmatrix} u \\ v \end{Bmatrix} = \begin{bmatrix} N_1 & N_2 & N_3 & N_4 & N_5 & N_6 & 0 & 0 & 0 & 0 & 0 & 0 \\ 0 & 0 & 0 & 0 & 0 & 0 & N_1 & N_2 & N_3 & N_4 & N_5 & N_6 \end{bmatrix} = \begin{Bmatrix} u_1 \\ \dots \\ \dots \\ \dots \\ u_6 \\ v_1 \\ \dots \\ \dots \\ \dots \\ v_6 \end{Bmatrix}$$

6.14 DETERMINE THE SHAPE FUNCTIONS FOR FOUR NODED RECTANGULAR ELEMENTS. USE NATURAL CO-ORDINATE SYSTEM

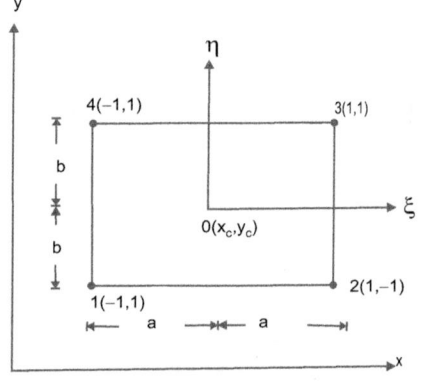

Fig. 6.39

Solution : $\xi = \dfrac{x - x_c}{a}$ and $\eta = \dfrac{y - y_c}{b}$

$$u = \alpha_1 + \alpha_2 \xi + \alpha_3 \eta + \alpha_4 \xi\eta$$

$$u = [1 \; \xi \; \eta \; \xi\eta] \begin{Bmatrix} \alpha_1 \\ \alpha_2 \\ \alpha_3 \\ \alpha_4 \end{Bmatrix} \quad \ldots(A)$$

$$\begin{Bmatrix} u_1 \\ u_2 \\ u_3 \\ u_4 \end{Bmatrix} = \begin{bmatrix} 1 & -1 & -1 & 1 \\ 1 & 1 & -1 & 1 \\ 1 & 1 & 1 & 1 \\ -1 & 1 & -1 & -1 \end{bmatrix} \begin{Bmatrix} \alpha_1 \\ \alpha_2 \\ \alpha_3 \\ \alpha_4 \end{Bmatrix}$$

$$\begin{Bmatrix} \alpha_1 \\ \alpha_2 \\ \alpha_3 \\ \alpha_4 \end{Bmatrix} = \begin{bmatrix} 1 & -1 & -1 & 1 \\ 1 & 1 & -1 & -1 \\ 1 & 1 & 1 & 1 \\ 1 & -1 & 1 & -1 \end{bmatrix} \begin{Bmatrix} u_1 \\ u_2 \\ u_3 \\ u_4 \end{Bmatrix}$$

$$\begin{Bmatrix} \alpha_1 \\ \alpha_2 \\ \alpha_3 \\ \alpha_4 \end{Bmatrix} = \begin{bmatrix} 1/4 & 1/4 & 1/4 & 1/4 \\ -1/4 & 1/4 & 1/4 & -1/4 \\ -1/4 & -1/4 & 1/4 & 1/4 \\ 1/4 & -1/4 & 1/4 & -1/4 \end{bmatrix} \begin{Bmatrix} u_1 \\ u_2 \\ u_3 \\ u_4 \end{Bmatrix}$$

From equation (A)

$$u = [1 \; \xi \; \eta \; \xi\eta] \begin{bmatrix} 1/4 & 1/4 & 1/4 & 1/4 \\ -1/4 & 1/4 & 1/4 & -1/4 \\ -1/4 & -1/4 & 1/4 & 1/4 \\ -1/4 & -1/4 & 1/4 & -1/4 \end{bmatrix} \begin{Bmatrix} u_1 \\ u_2 \\ u_3 \\ u_4 \end{Bmatrix}$$

$\dfrac{1}{4}[1 + \xi + \eta(1 + \xi)] \; \dfrac{1}{4}(1 + \xi)(1 + \eta) \; \dfrac{1}{4} + \dfrac{\xi}{4} + \dfrac{\eta}{4} + \dfrac{\xi\eta}{4}$

$$u = \left[\frac{(1-\xi)(1-\eta)}{4} \quad \frac{(1+\xi)(1-\eta)}{4} \quad \frac{(1+\xi)(1+\eta)}{4} \quad \frac{(1-\xi)(1+\eta)}{4}\right] \begin{Bmatrix} u_1 \\ u_2 \\ u_3 \\ u_4 \end{Bmatrix}$$

$$u = [N_1 \; N_2 \; N_3 \; N_4] \begin{Bmatrix} u_1 \\ u_2 \\ u_3 \\ u_4 \end{Bmatrix}$$

Parallaly, $[N_1 \; N_2 \; N_3 \; N_4] \begin{Bmatrix} v_1 \\ v_2 \\ v_3 \\ v_4 \end{Bmatrix}$

$$\begin{Bmatrix} u \\ v \end{Bmatrix} = \begin{bmatrix} N_1 & N_2 & N_3 & N_4 & 0 & 0 & 0 & 0 \\ 0 & 0 & 0 & 0 & N_1 & N_2 & N_3 & N_4 \end{bmatrix} \{\delta\}_e$$

$N_i = \dfrac{1}{4} (1 + \xi \xi_i)(1 + \eta \eta_i)$ for i = 1, 2, 3, 4

6.15 DETERMINE THE SHAPE FUNCTION FOR QUADRATIC RECTANGULAR ELEMENT

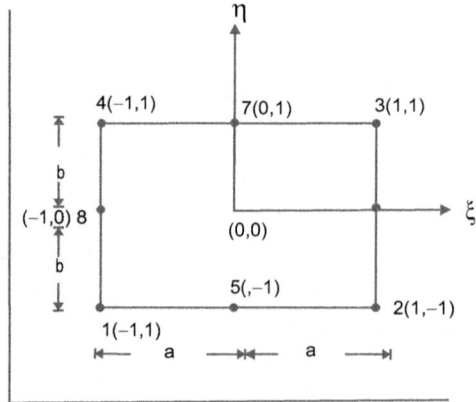

Fig. 6.40

$$u = \alpha_1 + \alpha_2\xi + \alpha_3\eta + \alpha_4\xi^2 + \alpha_5\xi\eta + \alpha_6\eta^2 + \alpha_7\xi^2\eta + \alpha_8\xi\eta^2 \quad \ldots(A)$$

$$\begin{Bmatrix} u_1 \\ u_2 \\ u_3 \\ u_4 \\ u_5 \\ u_6 \\ u_7 \\ u_8 \end{Bmatrix} = \begin{pmatrix} 1 & -1 & -1 & 1 & 1 & 1 & -1 & -1 \\ 1 & 1 & -1 & 1 & -1 & 1 & -1 & 1 \\ 1 & 1 & 1 & 1 & 1 & 1 & 1 & 1 \\ 1 & -1 & 1 & 1 & -1 & 1 & 1 & -1 \\ 1 & 0 & -1 & 0 & 0 & 1 & 0 & 0 \\ 1 & 1 & 0 & 1 & 0 & 0 & 0 & 0 \\ 1 & 0 & 1 & 0 & 0 & 1 & 0 & 0 \\ 1 & -1 & 0 & 1 & 0 & 0 & 0 & 0 \end{pmatrix} \begin{Bmatrix} \alpha_1 \\ \alpha_2 \\ \alpha_3 \\ \alpha_4 \\ \alpha_5 \\ \alpha_6 \\ \alpha_7 \\ \alpha_8 \end{Bmatrix}$$

$$= [A]\{\alpha\}$$

$$\{\alpha\} = [A^{-1}]\{u\}$$

$$= \frac{1}{4}\begin{pmatrix} -1 & -1 & -1 & -1 & 2 & 2 & 2 & 2 \\ 0 & 0 & 0 & 0 & 0 & 2 & 0 & -2 \\ 0 & 0 & 0 & 0 & -2 & 0 & 2 & 0 \\ 1 & 1 & 1 & 1 & -2 & 0 & -2 & 0 \\ 1 & -1 & 1 & -1 & 0 & 0 & 0 & 0 \\ 1 & 1 & 1 & 1 & 0 & -2 & 0 & -2 \\ -1 & -1 & 1 & 1 & 2 & 0 & -2 & 0 \\ -1 & 1 & 1 & -1 & 0 & -2 & 0 & 2 \end{pmatrix}\{u\}$$

From equation (A)

$$\begin{aligned}
u &= [1\ \xi\ \eta\ \xi^2\ \xi\eta\ \eta^2\ \xi^2\eta\ \xi\eta^2]\{\alpha\} \\
&= [1\ \xi\ \eta\ \xi^2\ \xi\eta\ \eta^2\ \xi^2\eta\ \xi\eta^2][A^{-1}]\{u\} \\
&= [1\ \xi\ \eta\ \xi^2\ \xi\eta\ \eta^2\ \xi^2\eta\ \xi\eta^2]
\end{aligned}$$

$$\frac{1}{4}\begin{pmatrix} -1 & -1 & -1 & -1 & 2 & 2 & 2 & 2 \\ 0 & 0 & 0 & 0 & 0 & 2 & 0 & -2 \\ 0 & 0 & 0 & 0 & -2 & 0 & 2 & 0 \\ 1 & 1 & 1 & 1 & -2 & 0 & -2 & 0 \\ 1 & -1 & 1 & -1 & 0 & 0 & 0 & 0 \\ 1 & 1 & 1 & 1 & 0 & -2 & 0 & -2 \\ -1 & -1 & 1 & 1 & 2 & 0 & -2 & 0 \\ -1 & 1 & 1 & -1 & 0 & -2 & 0 & 2 \end{pmatrix}\{u\}$$

$$u = [\frac{1}{4}(1-\xi)(1-\eta)(-\xi-\eta-1), \frac{1}{4}(1+\xi)(1-\eta)(\xi-\eta-1), \frac{1}{4}(1+\xi)(1+\eta)(\xi+\eta-1),$$
$$\frac{1}{4}(1-\xi)(1+\eta)(-\xi+\eta-1), \frac{1}{2}(1+\xi)(1+\xi)(\eta-1), \frac{1}{2}(1+\xi)(1+\eta)(1-\eta), \frac{1}{2}(1+\xi)(1-\xi)(\eta+1), \frac{1}{2}(1-\xi)(1+\eta)(1-\eta)] = \{u\}$$

$$u = [N_1\ N_2\ N_3\ N_4\ N_5\ N_6\ N_7\ N_8]\{u\}$$

$$N_i = \frac{1}{4}(1+\xi\xi_i)(1+\eta\eta_i)(\xi\xi_i+\eta\eta_{i-1})$$

For mid side nodes,

If $\xi_i = 0$, $N_i = \frac{1}{2}(1-\xi^2)(1+\eta\eta_i)$ (for, 5, 7)

$\eta_i = 0$, $N_i = \frac{1}{2}(1-\eta^2)(1+\xi\xi_i)$ (6, 8)

parallely, $V = [N_1\ N_2\ N_3\ N_4\ N_5\ N_6\ N_7\ N_8]\{V\}$

$$\begin{Bmatrix} u \\ v \end{Bmatrix} = \begin{bmatrix} N_{1\times 8} & 0_{1\times 8} \\ 0_{1\times 8} & N_{1\times 8} \end{bmatrix} \begin{Bmatrix} u_e \\ v_e \end{Bmatrix}$$

6.16 SHAPE FUNCTIONS USING LAGRANGE POLYNOMIALS

Lagrange polynomial in one-dimensional is defined by,

$$L_k(x) = \sum_{\substack{m=1 \\ m \neq k}}^{n} \frac{x - x_m}{x_k - x_m}$$

For example, Value equal to zero at all points except at point K. At point K its value is unity.

$$L_3(x) = \frac{(x-x_1)(x-x_2)(x-x_4)(x-x_5)}{(x_3-x_1)(x_3-x_2)(x_3-x_4)(x_3-x_4)}$$

Using Lagrange polynomial find shape functions for :

(i) Two noded bar element :

$$L_k = \frac{(x-x_1)(x-x_2)\ .....\ (x-x_{k-1})(x-x_{k+1})(x-x_n)}{(x_k-x_1)(x_k-x_2)\ ....\ (x_k-x_{k-1})(x_k-x_n)}$$

For n = 2, k = 1

$$L_1 = \frac{(x - x_1)(x - x_2)(x - x_2)}{(x - x_1)(x_1 - x_2)(x_1 - x_2)}$$

$$N_1 = N_2 = \frac{x - x_2}{x_1 - x_2} = \frac{x_2 - x}{x_2 - x_1}$$

k = 2

$$N_2 = L_2 = \frac{x - x_1}{x_2 - x_1}$$

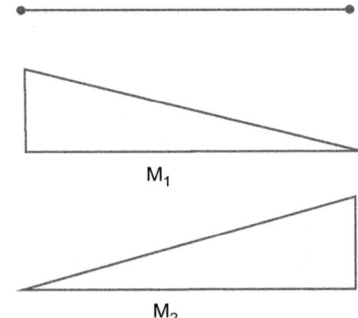

Fig. 6.41

For Five Noded Element :

Fig. 6.42

$$N_1 = L_1 = \frac{(x - x_2)(x - x_3)(x - x_4)(x - x_5)}{(x_1 - x_2)(x_1 - x_3)(x_1 - x_4)(x_1 - x_5)}$$

$$N_2 = L_2 = \frac{(x - x_1)(x - x_3)(x - x_4)(x - x_5)}{(x_2 - x_1)(x_2 - x_3)(x_2 - x_4)(x_2 - x_5)}$$

$$N_3 = L_3 = \frac{(x - x_1)(x - x_2)(x - x_4)(x - x_5)}{(x_3 - x_1)(x_3 - x_2)(x_3 - x_4)(x_3 - x_5)}$$

$$N_4 = L_4 = \frac{(x - x_1)(x - x_2)(x - x_3)(x - x_5)}{(x_4 - x_1)(x_4 - x_2)(x_4 - x_3)(x_4 - x_5)}$$

$$N_5 = L_5 = \frac{(x - x_1)(x - x_2)(x - x_3)(x - x_4)}{(x_5 - x_1)(x_5 - x_2)(x_5 - x_3)(x_5 - x_4)}$$

STRUCTURAL ANALYSIS – II FINITE ELEMENT METHOD

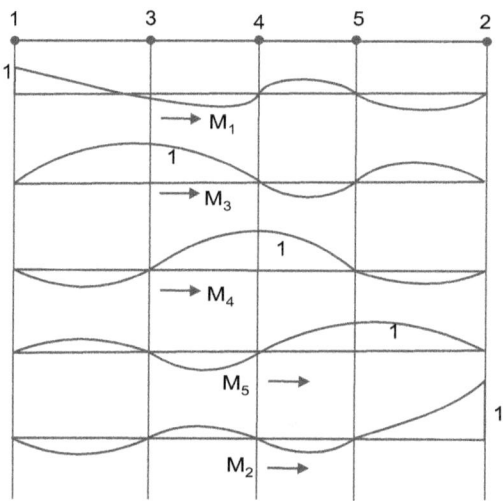

Fig. 6.43

Lagrange Polynomial approach for 2D Element :

Shape function = Product of functions which hold good for the individual 1D co-ordinate directions.

$$N_1 = L_1(\xi) L_1(\eta)$$

Four Noded Rectangular Element

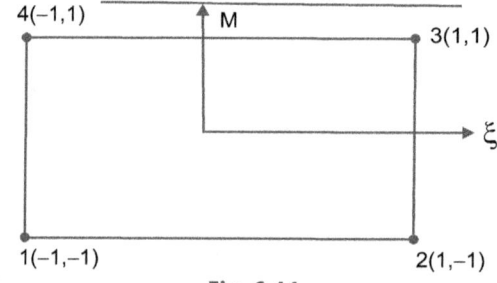

Fig. 6.44

$$N_1 = L_1(\xi) L_1(\eta) = \frac{\xi - \xi_2}{\xi_1 - \xi_2} \cdot \frac{(\eta - \eta_4)}{(\eta - \eta_4)}$$

$$N_1 = \frac{(\xi - 1)(\eta - 1)}{(-1 - 1)(-1 - 1)} = \frac{1}{4}(1 - \xi)(1 - \eta)$$

$$N_2 = L_2(\xi) L_2(\eta) = \frac{(\xi - \xi_1)}{(\xi_2 - \xi_1)} \cdot \frac{(\eta - \eta_3)}{(\eta_2 - \eta_3)}$$

$$N_2 = \frac{(\xi - -1)(\eta - 1)}{(1 - -1)(-1 - 1)} = \frac{1}{4}(\xi + 1)(1 - \eta)$$

$$N_3 = L_3(\xi) L_3(\eta) = \frac{(\xi - \xi_4)}{(\xi_3 - \xi_4)} \frac{(\eta - \eta_2)}{(\eta_3 - \eta_2)}$$

$$N_3 = \frac{(\xi - -1)(\eta - -1)}{(1 - -1)(1 - -1)} = \frac{1}{4}(\xi + 1)(1 + \eta)$$

$$N_4 = L_4(\varepsilon) L_4(\eta) = \left(\frac{\xi - \xi_3}{\xi_4 - \xi_3}\right)\left(\frac{\eta - \eta_1}{\eta_4 - \eta_1}\right)$$

$$= \frac{(\xi - 1)}{(-1 - 1)} \frac{(\eta - -1)}{(1 - -1)}$$

$$= \frac{1}{4}(1 - \xi)(1 + \eta)$$

Using lagrange functions write shape function for the nine noded rectangular element :

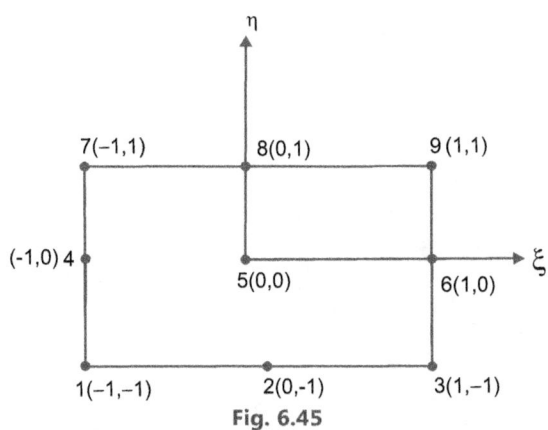

Fig. 6.45

$$N_1 = \frac{(\xi - \xi_2)(\xi - \xi_3)}{(\xi_1 - \xi_2)(\xi_1 - \xi_3)} \frac{(\eta - \eta_4)(\eta - \eta_1)}{(\eta_1 - \eta_4)(\eta_1 - \eta_7)}$$

$$N_1 = \frac{(\xi - 0)(\xi - 1)}{(-1 - 0)(-1 - 1)} \frac{(\eta - 0)(\eta - 1)}{(-1 - 0)(-1 - 1)} = \frac{\xi(\xi - 1)\eta(\eta - 1)}{4}$$

$$N_2 = \frac{(\xi - \xi_1)(\xi - \xi_3)}{(\xi_2 - \xi_1)(\xi_2 - \xi_3)} \frac{(\eta - \eta_5)(\eta - \eta_8)}{(\eta_2 - \eta_5)(\eta_2 - \eta_8)}$$

$$N_2 = \frac{(\xi - -1)(\xi - 1)}{(0 - -1)(0 - 1)} \frac{(\eta - 0)(\eta - 1)}{(-1 - 0)(-1 - 1)} = \frac{(\xi - 1)(\xi - 1)\eta(\eta - 1)}{-2}$$

$$N_3 = \frac{(\xi - \xi_1)(\xi - \xi_2)(\eta - \eta_6)(\eta - \eta_9)}{(\xi_3 - \xi_1)(\xi_3 - \xi_2)(\eta_3 - \eta_6)(\eta_8 - \eta_9)} = \frac{(\xi + 1)(\xi - 0)(\eta - 0)(\eta - 1)}{(1 + 1)(1 - 0)(-1 - 0)(-1 - 1)}$$

$$N_3 = \frac{1}{4}(1 + \xi)\xi\eta(\eta - 1)$$

$$N_4 = \frac{(\xi - \xi_5)(\xi - \xi_6)(\eta - \eta_1)(\eta - \eta_7)}{(\xi_4 - \xi_5)(\xi_4 - \xi_6)(\eta_4 - \eta_1)(\eta_4 - \eta_7)}$$

$$N_4 = \frac{(\xi - 0)(\xi - 1)}{(-1-0)(-1-1)} \cdot \frac{(\eta - 1)(\eta - 1)}{(0--1)(0-1)} = \frac{\xi(\xi-1)(\eta+1)(\eta-1)}{-2}$$

$$N_5 = \frac{(\xi - \xi_4)(\xi - \xi_6)}{(\xi_5 - \xi_6)(\xi_5 - \xi_6)} \cdot \frac{(\eta - \eta_2)(\eta - \eta_8)}{(\eta_5 - \eta_2)(\eta_5 - \eta_8)}$$

$$N_5 = \frac{(\xi--1)(\xi-1)}{(0--1)(0-1)} \cdot \frac{(\eta--1)(\eta-1)}{(0-1-1)(0-1)} = \frac{(\xi+1)(\xi-1)(\eta+1)(\eta-1)}{1}$$

$$N_6 = \frac{(\xi - \xi_4)(\xi - \xi_5)}{(\xi_6 - \xi_4)(\xi_6 - \xi_5)} \cdot \frac{(\eta - \eta_3)(\eta - \eta_9)}{(\eta_6 - \eta_3)(\eta_6 - \eta_9)}$$

$$N_6 = \frac{(\xi+1)(\xi-0)(\eta+1)(\eta-1)}{(1+1)(1-0)(0+1)(0-1)} = \frac{\xi(\xi+1)(\eta+1)(\eta-1)}{-2}$$

$$N_7 = \frac{(\xi - \xi_8)(\xi - \xi_9)(\eta - \eta_1)(\eta - \eta_4)}{(\xi_7 - \xi_8)(\xi_7 - \xi_9)(\eta_7 - \eta_1)(\eta_7 - \eta_4)}$$

$$N_7 = \frac{(\xi-0)(\xi-1)(\eta+0)(\eta-0)}{(-1-0)(-1-1)(1+1)(1-0)} = \frac{\xi(\xi-1)(\eta+1)\eta}{4}$$

$$N_8 = \frac{(\xi - \xi_7)(\xi - \xi_9)(\eta - \eta_2)(\eta - \eta_5)}{(\xi_8 - \xi_7)(\xi_8 - \xi_9)(\eta_8 - \eta_2)(\eta_8 - \eta_5)}$$

$$N_8 = \frac{(\xi+1)(\xi-1)(\eta+1)\eta}{-2}$$

$$N_9 = \frac{(\xi - \xi_7)(\xi - \xi_8)(\eta - \eta_3)(\eta - \eta_6)}{(\xi_9 - \xi_7)(\xi_9 - \xi_8)(\eta_9 - \eta_3)(\eta_9 - \eta_6)}$$

$$N_9 = \frac{(\xi+1)(\xi-0)(\eta+1)(\eta-0)}{(1+1)(1-0)(1+1)(1-0)}$$

$$N_9 = \frac{(\xi+1)\xi(\eta+1)\eta}{4}$$

6.17 STIFFNESS MATRIX FOR A TWO DIMENSIONAL BEAM

(Element with axial deformation).

Consider a beam AB. Both ends of the beam are fixed ends.

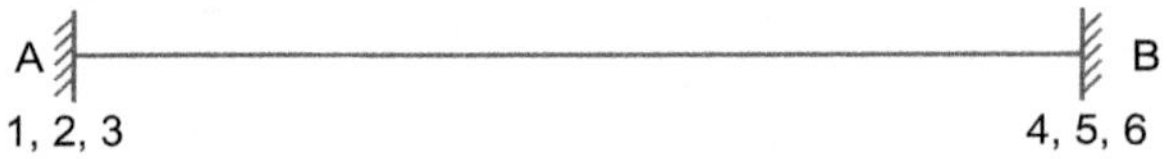

A ⫞————————————⫠ B
1, 2, 3   4, 5, 6

Fig. 6. 46

At each end, consider three displacements as horizontal (i.e. axial) displacement, vertical displacement and rotational displacement. Apply unit displacements at both ends one by one.

(a) Apply unit horizontal displacement at A.

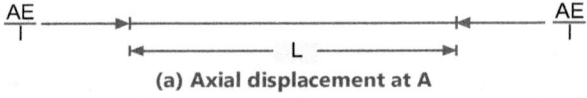

(a) Axial displacement at A

∴ $K_{11} = \dfrac{AE}{l}$

$K_{21} = 0$

$K_{31} = 0$

$K_{41} = -\dfrac{AE}{l}$

$K_{51} = 0$

$K_{61} = 0$

(b) Apply unit vertical displacement at A.

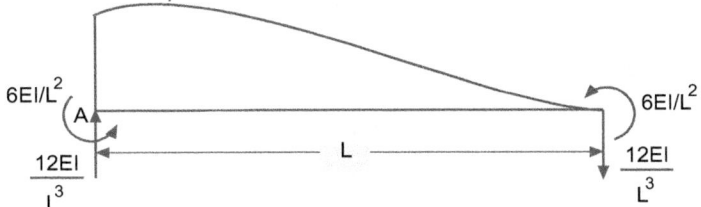

(b) Vertical displacement at A

$K_{12} = 0$ $\qquad K_{22} = \dfrac{12\,EI}{L^3}$

$K_{32} = \dfrac{6\,EI}{L^2}$ $\qquad K_{42} = 0$

$K_{52} = -\dfrac{12\,EI}{L^3}$ $\qquad K_{62} = \dfrac{6\,EI}{L^2}$

(c) Apply unit rotational displacement at A.

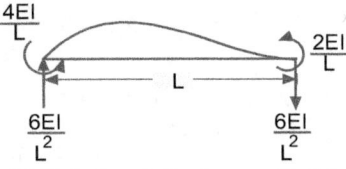

(c) Rotational displacement at A

$K_{13} = 0$ $\qquad K_{23} = \dfrac{6\,EI}{L^2}$

$K_{33} = \dfrac{4\,EI}{L}$ $\qquad K_{43} = 0$

$K_{53} = \dfrac{-6\,EI}{L^2}$ $\qquad K_{63} = \dfrac{2\,EI}{L}$

(d) Apply unit horizontal displacement at B.

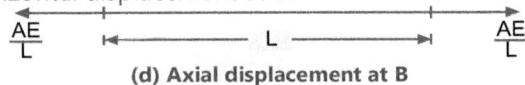

(d) Axial displacement at B

$K_{14} = -\dfrac{AE}{L}$ $K_{24} = 0$

$K_{34} = 0$ $K_{44} = \dfrac{AE}{L}$

$K_{54} = 0$ $K_{64} = 0$

(e) Apply unit vertical displacement at B.

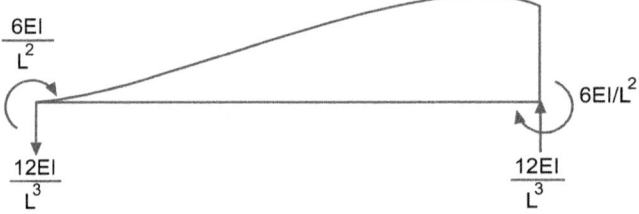

(e) Vertical displacement at B

$K_{15} = 0$ $K_{25} = -\dfrac{12\,EI}{L^3}$

$K_{35} = -\dfrac{6\,EI}{L^2}$ $K_{45} = 0$

$K_{55} = \dfrac{12\,EI}{L^3}$ $K_{65} = -\dfrac{6\,EI}{L^2}$

(f) Apply unit rotational displacement at B.

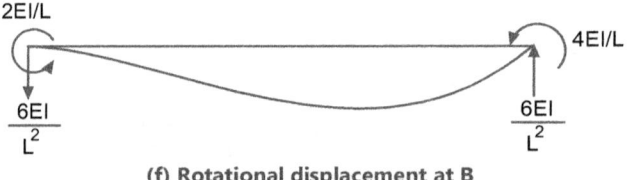

(f) Rotational displacement at B

Fig. 6.47

$K_{16} = 0$ $K_{26} = \dfrac{6\,EI}{L^2}$

$K_{36} = \dfrac{2\,EI}{L}$ $K_{46} = 0$

$K_{56} = \dfrac{-6\,EI}{L^2}$ $K_{66} = \dfrac{4\,EI}{L}$

∴ Stiffness matrix for six degree of freedom is as follows :

$$\begin{bmatrix} \frac{AE}{L} & 0 & 0 & -\frac{AE}{L} & 0 & 0 \\ 0 & \frac{12EI}{L^3} & \frac{6EI}{L^2} & 0 & -\frac{12EI}{L^3} & \frac{6EI}{L^2} \\ 0 & \frac{6EI}{L^2} & \frac{4EI}{L} & 0 & -\frac{6EI}{L^2} & \frac{2EI}{L} \\ -\frac{AE}{L} & 0 & 0 & \frac{AE}{L} & 0 & 0 \\ 0 & -\frac{12EI}{L^3} & -\frac{6EI}{L^2} & 0 & \frac{12EI}{L^3} & -\frac{6EI}{L^2} \\ 0 & \frac{6EI}{L^2} & \frac{2EI}{L} & 0 & -\frac{6EI}{L^2} & \frac{4EI}{L} \end{bmatrix}$$

Stiffness matrix for four degrees of freedom (without axial deformation) is as follows :

$$\begin{bmatrix} \frac{12EI}{L^3} & \frac{6EI}{L^2} & -\frac{12EI}{L^3} & \frac{6EI}{L^2} \\ \frac{6EI}{L^2} & \frac{4EI}{L} & -\frac{6EI}{L^2} & \frac{2EI}{L} \\ -\frac{12EI}{L^3} & -\frac{6EI}{L^2} & \frac{12EI}{L^3} & -\frac{6EI}{L^2} \\ \frac{6EI}{L^2} & \frac{2EI}{L} & -\frac{6EI}{L^2} & \frac{4EI}{L} \end{bmatrix}$$

6.18 ASSEMBLAGE OF STIFFNESS MATRIX

Consider a continuous beam ABC with two degrees of freedom at each node.

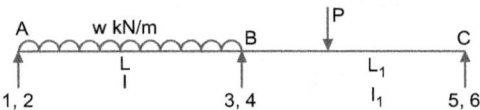

Fig. 6.48

Let 1, 3 and 5 are vertical displacements at A, B and C respectively.
Similarly, 2, 4 and 6 are rotational displacements at A, B, and C respectively.
Member AB :   1   2   3   4

$$[K]_{AB} = \begin{bmatrix} \dfrac{12EI}{L^3} & \dfrac{6EI}{L^2} & -\dfrac{12EI}{L^3} & \dfrac{6EI}{L^2} \\ \dfrac{6EI}{L^2} & \dfrac{4EI}{L} & -\dfrac{6EI}{L^2} & \dfrac{2EI}{L} \\ -\dfrac{12EI}{L^3} & -\dfrac{6EI}{L^2} & \dfrac{12EI}{L^3} & -\dfrac{6EI}{L^2} \\ \dfrac{6EI}{L^2} & \dfrac{2EI}{L} & -\dfrac{6EI}{L^2} & \dfrac{4EI}{L} \end{bmatrix} \begin{matrix} 1 \\ 2 \\ 3 \\ 4 \end{matrix}$$

Member BC:
$$[K]_{BC} = \begin{bmatrix} \dfrac{12EI_1}{L_1^3} & \dfrac{6EI_1}{L_1^2} & -\dfrac{12EI_1}{L_1^3} & \dfrac{6EI_1}{L_1^2} \\ \dfrac{6EI_1}{L_1^2} & \dfrac{4EI_1}{L_1} & -\dfrac{6EI_1}{L_1^2} & \dfrac{2EI_1}{L_1} \\ -\dfrac{12EI_1}{L_1^3} & -\dfrac{6EI_1}{L_1^2} & \dfrac{12EI_1}{L_1^3} & -\dfrac{6EI_1}{L_1^2} \\ \dfrac{6EI_1}{L_1^2} & \dfrac{2EI_1}{L_1} & -\dfrac{6EI_1}{L_1^2} & \dfrac{4EI_1}{L_1} \end{bmatrix} \begin{matrix} 3 \\ 4 \\ 5 \\ 6 \end{matrix}$$

overhead columns: 3, 4, 5, 6

Assemblage of matrix for ABC:

$$[K] = \begin{bmatrix} \dfrac{12EI}{L^3} & \dfrac{6EI}{L^2} & -\dfrac{12EI}{L^3} & \dfrac{6EI}{L^2} & 0 & 0 \\ \dfrac{6EI}{L^2} & \dfrac{4EI}{L} & -\dfrac{6EI}{L^2} & \dfrac{2EI}{L} & 0 & 0 \\ -\dfrac{12EI}{L^3} & -\dfrac{6EI}{L^2} & \left(\dfrac{12EI}{L^3} + \dfrac{12EI_1}{L_1^3}\right) & \left(\dfrac{6EI}{L^2} - \dfrac{6EI_1}{L_1^2}\right) & -\dfrac{12EI_1}{L_1^3} & \dfrac{6EI_1}{L_1^2} \\ \dfrac{6EI}{L^2} & \dfrac{2EI}{L} & \left(\dfrac{6EI}{L^2} + \dfrac{6EI_1}{L_1^2}\right) & \left(\dfrac{4EI}{L} + \dfrac{4EI_1}{L_1}\right) & -\dfrac{6EI_1}{L_1^2} & \dfrac{2EI_1}{L_1} \\ 0 & 0 & -\dfrac{12EI_1}{L_1^3} & -\dfrac{6EI_1}{L_1^2} & \dfrac{12EI_1}{L_1^3} & -\dfrac{6EI_1}{L_1^2} \\ 0 & 0 & \dfrac{6EI_1}{L_1^2} & \dfrac{2EI_1}{L_1} & -\dfrac{6EI_1}{L_1^2} & \dfrac{4EI_1}{L_1} \end{bmatrix} \begin{matrix} 1 \\ 2 \\ 3 \\ 4 \\ 5 \\ 6 \end{matrix}$$

Displacement matrix vector,

STRUCTURAL ANALYSIS – II   FINITE ELEMENT METHOD

$$\delta = \begin{Bmatrix} \delta_A \\ \theta_A \\ \delta_B \\ \theta_B \\ \delta_C \\ \theta_C \end{Bmatrix}$$

Load vector, $Q = \begin{Bmatrix} V_A \\ M_{AB} \\ V_{B1} + V_{B2} \\ M_{BA} + M_{BC} \\ V_{C1} + V_{C2} \\ M_{CB} \end{Bmatrix}$

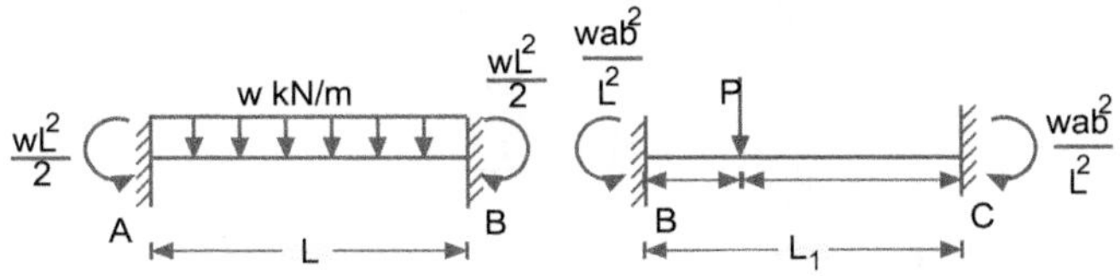

Fig. 6.49

$V_A = \dfrac{wL}{2},$ $\qquad M_{AB} = \dfrac{wL^2}{12}$

$V_{B1} = \dfrac{wL}{2},$ $\qquad M_{BA} = -\dfrac{wL^2}{12}$

$$V_{B2} = \dfrac{Pb}{L} + \dfrac{\left(\dfrac{wab^2}{L^2} - \dfrac{wa^2b}{L^2}\right)}{L}$$

$$M_{BC} = \dfrac{Pab^2}{L^2} \qquad V_C = \dfrac{Pa}{L} - \dfrac{\left(\dfrac{wab^2}{L^2} - \dfrac{wa^2b}{L^2}\right)}{L}$$

$$M_{CB} = -\dfrac{Pa^2b}{L^2}$$

We have, $\qquad \{F\} = [K]\{\delta\}$

Remove the rows and columns of known displacement and reduce the stiffness matrix. In this beam, we know that vertical displacements at A, B and C are zero. So remove the rows and columns related to these displacements i.e. 1, 3 and 5. This gives us the reduced stiffness matrix as

$$\begin{bmatrix} \dfrac{4EI}{L} & \dfrac{2EI}{L} & 0 \\ \dfrac{2EI}{L} & \left(\dfrac{4EI}{L} + \dfrac{4EI_1}{L_1}\right) & \dfrac{2EI_1}{L_1} \\ 0 & \dfrac{2EI_1}{L_1} & \dfrac{4EI_1}{L_1} \end{bmatrix} \begin{Bmatrix} \theta_A \\ \theta_B \\ \theta_C \end{Bmatrix} = \begin{Bmatrix} M_{AB} \\ M_{BA} + M_{BC} \\ M_{CB} \end{Bmatrix}$$

6.18.1 Alternative Method for Assemblage of Matrix

Consider a beam ABC with two degrees of freedom at each node.

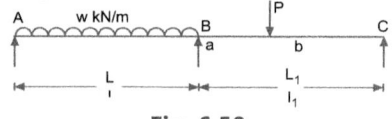

Fig. 6.50

In this we will consider elemental degree of freedom (edof) and global degree of freedom (gdof). In this we know that the vertical displacements at A, B and C are zero.

Member BC:
$$[K]_{BC} = \begin{bmatrix} \dfrac{12EI}{L^3} & \dfrac{6EI}{L^2} & -\dfrac{12EI}{L^3} & \dfrac{6EI}{L^2} \\ \dfrac{6EI}{L^2} & \dfrac{4EI}{L} & -\dfrac{6EI}{L^2} & \dfrac{2EI}{L} \\ -\dfrac{12EI}{L^3} & -\dfrac{6EI}{L^2} & \dfrac{12EI}{L^3} & -\dfrac{6EI}{L^2} \\ \dfrac{6EI}{L^2} & \dfrac{2EI}{L} & -\dfrac{6EI}{L^2} & \dfrac{4EI}{L} \end{bmatrix} \begin{matrix} 1 & 0 \\ 2 & 1 \\ 3 & 0 \\ 4 & 2 \end{matrix}$$

$$K_2 = \begin{vmatrix} \dfrac{12EI_1}{L_1^3} & \dfrac{6EI_1}{L_1^2} & -\dfrac{12EI_1}{L_1^3} & \dfrac{6EI_1}{L_1^2} \\ \dfrac{6EI_1}{L_1^2} & \dfrac{4EI_1}{L_1} & -\dfrac{6EI_1}{L_1^2} & \dfrac{2EI_1}{L_1} \\ -\dfrac{12EI_1}{L_1^3} & -\dfrac{6EI_1}{L_1^2} & \dfrac{12EI_1}{L_1^3} & -\dfrac{6EI_1}{L_1^2} \\ \dfrac{6EI_1}{L_1^2} & \dfrac{2EI_1}{L_1} & -\dfrac{6EI_1}{L_1^2} & \dfrac{4EI_1}{L_1} \end{vmatrix} \begin{matrix} 1 & 0 \\ 2 & 2 \\ 3 & 0 \\ 4 & 4 \end{matrix}$$

STRUCTURAL ANALYSIS – II   FINITE ELEMENT METHOD

∴ Assemblage of matrix :

$$\begin{bmatrix} \dfrac{4EI}{L} & \dfrac{2EI}{L} & 0 \\ \dfrac{2EI}{L} & \left(\dfrac{4EI}{L}+\dfrac{4EI_1}{L_1}\right) & \dfrac{2EI_1}{L_1} \\ 0 & \dfrac{2EI_1}{L_1} & \dfrac{4EI_1}{L_1} \end{bmatrix}$$

Displacement calculations : $\{P\} = [K]\{\delta\}$

$$\begin{bmatrix} \dfrac{4EI}{L} & \dfrac{2EI}{L} & 0 \\ \dfrac{2EI}{L} & \left(\dfrac{4EI}{L}+\dfrac{4EI_1}{L_1}\right) & \dfrac{2EI_1}{L_1} \\ 0 & \dfrac{2EI_1}{L_1} & \dfrac{4EI_1}{L_1} \end{bmatrix} \begin{Bmatrix} \theta_A \\ \theta_B \\ \theta_C \end{Bmatrix} = \begin{Bmatrix} M_{AB} \\ M_{BA}+M_{BC} \\ M_{CB} \end{Bmatrix}$$

Example 6.1 : *Analyse the beam shown in Fig. 6.51 (a). Take EI = constant. Stiffness of spring is EI/2.*

Solution : Data : The beam is loaded and supported as shown in Fig. 6.51 (a).
Object : Structural analysis.
Step I : Degree of kinematic indeterminacy = D_{ki} = 2.
    Unknown displacements : δ_B and θ_B.
    Known displacements : $\delta_A = \theta_A = 0$.
Step II : Stiffness matrix for member I :

$$\begin{bmatrix} \dfrac{12EI}{L^3} & \dfrac{6EI}{L^2} & -\dfrac{12EI}{L^3} & \dfrac{6EI}{L^2} \\ \dfrac{6EI}{L^2} & \dfrac{4EI}{L} & -\dfrac{6EI}{L^2} & \dfrac{2EI}{L} \\ -\dfrac{12EI}{L^3} & -\dfrac{6EI}{L^2} & \dfrac{12EI}{L^3} & -\dfrac{6EI}{L^2} \\ \dfrac{6EI}{L^2} & \dfrac{2EI}{L} & -\dfrac{6EI}{L^2} & \dfrac{4EI}{L} \end{bmatrix}$$

(a) Member AB : L = 3 m.

$\dfrac{12EI}{L^3} = \dfrac{12EI}{3^3} = 0.44\ EI,\ \dfrac{6EI}{L^2} = \dfrac{6EI}{3^2} = 0.667\ EI$

$\dfrac{4EI}{L} = \dfrac{4EI}{3} = 1.33\ EI,\ \dfrac{2EI}{3} = 0.667\ EI$

STRUCTURAL ANALYSIS – II   FINITE ELEMENT METHOD

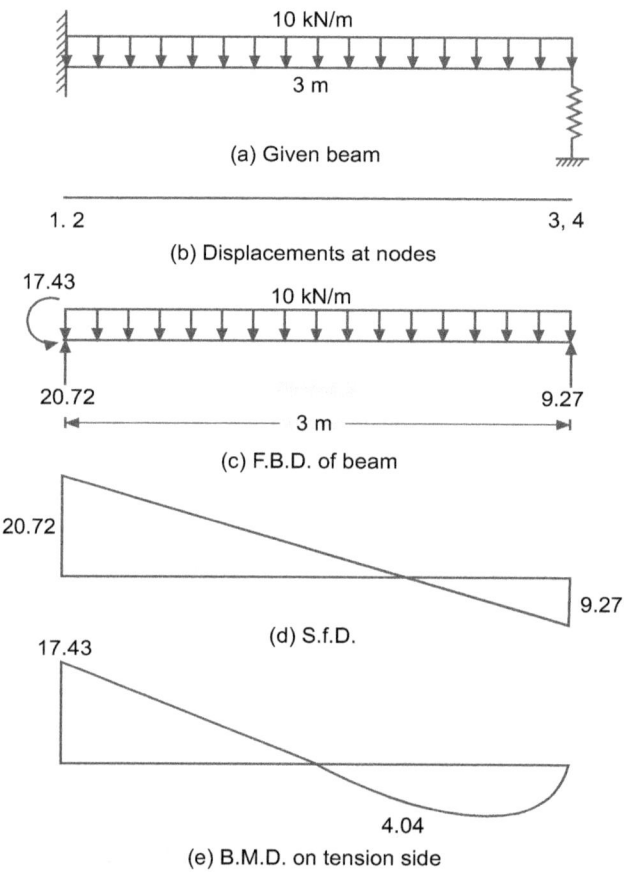

Fig. 6.51

∴ Stiffness matrix of member I :

$$EI \begin{bmatrix} 0.44 & 0.667 & -0.44 & 0.667 \\ 0.667 & 1.33 & -0.667 & 0.667 \\ -0.44 & -0.667 & 0.44 & -0.667 \\ 0.667 & 0.667 & -0.667 & 1.33 \end{bmatrix}$$

The spring has stiffness at supports B = 0.5 EI. This is related with vertical displacement at 3, so added in S_{33} element.

Step III : Elemental nodal load vector :

$$\{Q_1\} = \begin{Bmatrix} \dfrac{wl}{2} \\ \dfrac{wl^2}{12} \\ \dfrac{wl}{2} \\ -\dfrac{wl^2}{12} \end{Bmatrix} = \begin{Bmatrix} 15 \\ 7.5 \\ 15 \\ -7.5 \end{Bmatrix}$$

Step IV : Displacement vector : $\delta = \begin{Bmatrix} \delta_A \\ \theta_A \\ \delta_B \\ \theta_B \end{Bmatrix} = \begin{Bmatrix} 0 \\ 0 \\ \delta_B \\ \theta_B \end{Bmatrix}$

Step V : Formulation of finite element matrix :

$[K]\{\delta\} + \{Q_1\} = 0$

$$EI \begin{bmatrix} 0.44 & 0.667 & -0.44 & 0.667 \\ 0.667 & 1.33 & -0.667 & 0.667 \\ -0.44 & -0.667 & (0.44+0.5) & -0.667 \\ 0.667 & 0.667 & -0.667 & 1.33 \end{bmatrix} \begin{Bmatrix} 0 \\ 0 \\ \delta_B \\ \theta_B \end{Bmatrix} + \begin{Bmatrix} 15 \\ 7.5 \\ 15 \\ -7.5 \end{Bmatrix} = \begin{Bmatrix} 0 \\ 0 \\ 0 \\ 0 \end{Bmatrix}$$

Displacements of Ist row and IInd row are known, so remove Ist and IInd rows and columns.

$\therefore \quad EI \begin{bmatrix} 0.94 & -0.667 \\ -0.667 & 1.33 \end{bmatrix} \begin{Bmatrix} \delta_B \\ \theta_B \end{Bmatrix} + \begin{Bmatrix} 15 \\ -7.5 \end{Bmatrix} = 0$

$\therefore \quad 0.94\,EI\,\delta_B - 0.667\,EI\,\theta_B + 15 = 0$

$\quad\quad -0.667\,EI\,\delta_B + 1.33\,EI\,\theta_B - 7.5 = 0$

Step VI : Solving above equations for unknown displacements, we get

$$\delta_B = \dfrac{-18.55}{EI} \quad\quad\quad \theta_B = \dfrac{-3.656}{EI}$$

Step VII : Other forces :

$$EI \begin{bmatrix} 0.44 & 0.667 & -0.44 & 0.667 \\ 0.667 & 1.33 & -0.667 & 0.667 \\ -0.44 & -0.667 & 0.44 & -0.667 \\ 0.667 & 0.667 & -0.667 & 1.33 \end{bmatrix} \begin{Bmatrix} 0 \\ 0 \\ -\dfrac{18.55}{EI} \\ -\dfrac{3.656}{EI} \end{Bmatrix} + \begin{Bmatrix} 15 \\ 7.5 \\ 15 \\ -7.5 \end{Bmatrix} = \begin{Bmatrix} 20.72 \\ 17.43 \\ 9.27 \\ 0.0 \end{Bmatrix}$$

$V_A = 20.72$ kN

STRUCTURAL ANALYSIS – II   FINITE ELEMENT METHOD

$$M_{AB} = 17.43 \text{ kN-m}$$
$$V_B = 9.27, \quad M_{BA} = 0$$

Example 6.2 : *Analyse the continuous beam shown in Fig. 6.52 (a). Stiffness of spring is 150 N/m. EI = 400 kN-m².*

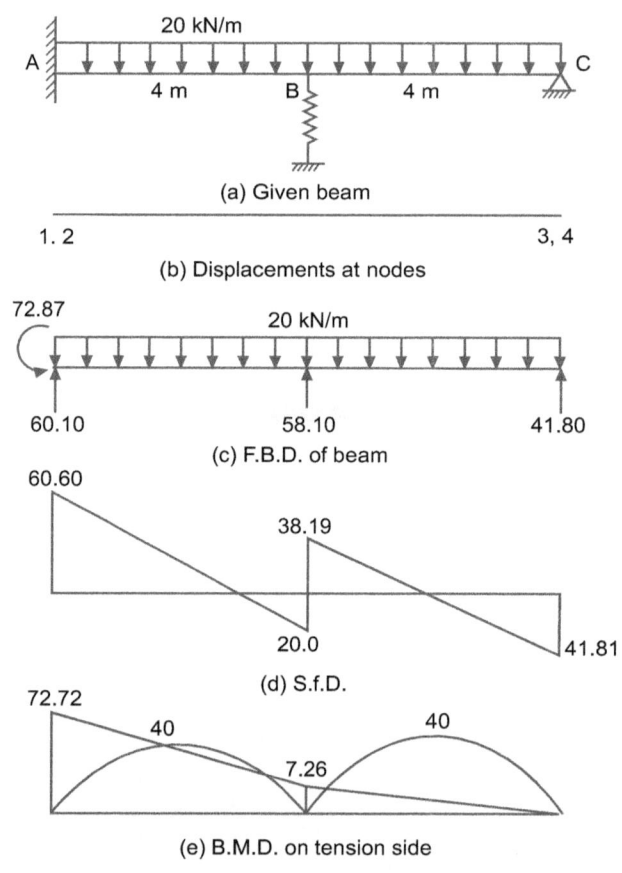

Fig. 6.52

Solution : Data : The beam is loaded and supported as shown in Fig. 6.52 (a).

Object : Structural analysis.

Concept : (i) Stiffness matrix for each element. (ii) Assemblage of matrix for structure.

Step I : Degree of kinematic indeterminacy = D_{ki} = 3.

Unknown displacements : δ_B, θ_B, θ_C. Known displacements : $\delta_A = \theta_A = \delta_C = 0$.

Step II : Stiffness matrix for member I : General stiffness matrix :

$$EI \begin{bmatrix} \dfrac{12}{L^3} & \dfrac{6}{L^2} & -\dfrac{12}{L^3} & \dfrac{6}{L^2} \\ \dfrac{6}{L^2} & \dfrac{4}{L} & -\dfrac{6}{L^2} & \dfrac{2}{L} \\ -\dfrac{12}{L^3} & -\dfrac{6}{L^2} & \dfrac{12}{L^3} & -\dfrac{6}{L^2} \\ \dfrac{6}{L^2} & \dfrac{2}{L} & -\dfrac{6}{L^2} & \dfrac{4}{L} \end{bmatrix}$$

$\dfrac{12\,EI}{L^3} = \dfrac{12 \times 400}{4^3} = 75\,EI, \quad \dfrac{6\,EI}{L^2} = \dfrac{6 \times 400}{16} = 150\,EI$

$\dfrac{4\,EI}{L} = \dfrac{4 \times 400}{4} = 400\,EI, \quad \dfrac{2\,EI}{L} = \dfrac{2 \times 400}{4} = 200\,EI$

(a) Stiffness of matrix of member AB :

	1	2	3	4
1	75	150	–75	150
2	150	400	–150	200
3	–75	–150	75	–150
4	150	200	–150	400

(b) Stiffness matrix for member BC :

	3	4	5	6
3	75	150	–75	150
4	150	400	–150	200
5	–75	–150	75	–150
6	150	200	–150	400

Step III : Assemblage of stiffness matrix :

$$EI \begin{bmatrix} 75 & 150 & -75 & 150 & 0 & 0 \\ 150 & 400 & -150 & 200 & 0 & 0 \\ -75 & -150 & 150 & 0 & -75 & 150 \\ 150 & 200 & 0 & 800 & -150 & 200 \\ 0 & 0 & -75 & -150 & 75 & -150 \\ 0 & 0 & 150 & 200 & -150 & 400 \end{bmatrix}$$

STRUCTURAL ANALYSIS – II   FINITE ELEMENT METHOD

Step IV : : Elemental nodal load vector :

(a) Member AB :
$$\{Q_1\} = \begin{Bmatrix} wl/2 \\ wl^2/12 \\ wl/2 \\ -wl^2/12 \end{Bmatrix} = \begin{Bmatrix} 40 \\ 26.67 \\ 40 \\ -26.67 \end{Bmatrix}$$

(b) Member BC :
$$\{Q_2\} = \begin{Bmatrix} wl/2 \\ wl^2/12 \\ wl/2 \\ -wl^2/12 \end{Bmatrix} = \begin{Bmatrix} 40 \\ 26.67 \\ 40 \\ -26.67 \end{Bmatrix}$$

Step V : Global nodal vector form spring has stiffness at support B = 150. This is related with vertical displacement so added at S_{33} element.

$$\{Q\} = \begin{Bmatrix} 40 \\ 26.67 \\ 40 + 40 \\ -26.67 + 26.67 \\ 40 \\ -26.67 \end{Bmatrix} = \begin{Bmatrix} 40 \\ 26.67 \\ 80 \\ 0 \\ 40 \\ -26.67 \end{Bmatrix}$$

Step VI : Displacement vector :

(a) Member AB :
$$\delta = \begin{Bmatrix} \delta_A \\ \theta_A \\ \delta_B \\ \theta_B \end{Bmatrix} = \begin{Bmatrix} 0 \\ 0 \\ \delta_B \\ \theta_B \end{Bmatrix}$$

(b) Member BC :
$$\delta = \begin{Bmatrix} \delta_B \\ \theta_B \\ \delta_C \\ \theta_C \end{Bmatrix} = \begin{Bmatrix} \delta_B \\ \theta_B \\ 0 \\ \theta_C \end{Bmatrix}$$

Step VII : Global displacement matrix :

$$\delta = \begin{Bmatrix} 0 \\ 0 \\ \delta_B \\ \theta_B \\ 0 \\ \theta_C \end{Bmatrix}$$

Step VIII : $[K]\{\delta\} + \{Q\} = 0$

$$EI \begin{bmatrix} 75 & 150 & -75 & 150 & 0 & 0 \\ 150 & 400 & -150 & 200 & 0 & 0 \\ -75 & -150 & (150+150) & 0 & -75 & 150 \\ 150 & 200 & 0 & 800 & -150 & 200 \\ 0 & 0 & -75 & -150 & 75 & -150 \\ 0 & 0 & 150 & 200 & -150 & 400 \end{bmatrix} \begin{Bmatrix} 0 \\ 0 \\ \delta_B \\ \theta_B \\ 0 \\ \theta_C \end{Bmatrix} + \begin{Bmatrix} 40 \\ 26.67 \\ 80 \\ 0 \\ 40 \\ -26.67 \end{Bmatrix} = \begin{Bmatrix} 0 \\ 0 \\ 0 \\ 0 \\ 0 \\ 0 \end{Bmatrix}$$

Displacements of Ist, IInd and Vth rows are known, so remove the same rows and column from stiffness matrix.

$$\therefore EI \begin{bmatrix} 300 & 0 & 150 \\ 0 & 800 & 200 \\ 150 & 200 & 400 \end{bmatrix} \begin{Bmatrix} \delta_B \\ \theta_B \\ \theta_C \end{Bmatrix} + \begin{Bmatrix} 80 \\ 0 \\ -26.67 \end{Bmatrix} = \begin{Bmatrix} 0 \\ 0 \\ 0 \end{Bmatrix}$$

$300\, EI\, \delta_B + 150\, EI\, \theta_C + 80 = 0$

$800\, EI\, \theta_B + 200\, EI\, \theta_C = 0$

$150\, EI\, \delta_B + 200\, EI\, \theta_B + 400\, EI\, \theta_C - 26.67 = 0$

Step IX : Solving above equations for unknown displacement, we get

$$\delta_B = -\frac{0.3878}{EI}$$

$$\theta_B = -\frac{0.0606}{EI}$$

$$\theta_C = \frac{0.2424}{EI}$$

Step X : Other forces :

Member I :

$$EI \begin{bmatrix} 75 & 150 & -75 & 150 \\ 150 & 400 & -150 & 200 \\ -75 & -150 & 75 & -150 \\ 150 & 200 & -150 & 400 \end{bmatrix} \begin{Bmatrix} 0 \\ 0 \\ -\dfrac{0.3878}{EI} \\ -\dfrac{0.0606}{EI} \end{Bmatrix} + \begin{Bmatrix} 40 \\ 26.67 \\ 40 \\ -26.67 \end{Bmatrix} = \begin{Bmatrix} 60.0 \\ 72.72 \\ 20.0 \\ 7.26 \end{Bmatrix}$$

Member II :

$$EI \begin{bmatrix} 75 & 150 & -75 & 150 \\ 150 & 400 & -150 & 200 \\ -75 & -150 & 75 & -150 \\ 150 & 200 & -150 & 400 \end{bmatrix} \begin{Bmatrix} -\dfrac{0.3878}{EI} \\ -\dfrac{0.0606}{EI} \\ 0 \\ \dfrac{0.2424}{EI} \end{Bmatrix} + \begin{Bmatrix} 40 \\ 26.67 \\ 40 \\ -26.67 \end{Bmatrix} = \begin{Bmatrix} 38.19 \\ 7.26 \\ 41.81 \\ 0 \end{Bmatrix}$$

Step XI : S.F.D. and B.M.D. is as shown in Fig. 6.52 (c) and 6.52 (d).

$$M_{AB} = 60.0 \text{ kN-m}$$
$$V_A = 72.72 \text{ kN}$$
$$M_{BA} = 7.26 \text{ kN-m}$$
$$V_B = 20.0 + 38.19 = 58.19 \text{ kN}$$
$$M_{BC} = -7.26 \text{ kN-m } (\circlearrowleft) = 7.26 \text{ kN-m } (\circlearrowright)$$
$$M_{CB} = 0$$
$$V_C = 41.81 \text{ kN}$$

Example 6.3 : *Analyse the beam shown in Fig. 6.53 (a) by finite element method.*

Solution : Data : The beam is loaded and supported as shown in Fig. 6.53 (a).

Object : Structural analysis.

Procedure : Step I : Degree of kinematic indeterminacy = D_{ki} = 2.

Unknown displacements : θ_B and θ_C.

Known displacements : $\theta_A = \delta_A = \delta_B = \delta_C = 0$.

Step II : Stiffness matrix for members :

STRUCTURAL ANALYSIS – II   FINITE ELEMENT METHOD

$$K = \begin{bmatrix} \dfrac{12EI}{L^3} & \dfrac{6EI}{L^2} & \dfrac{-12EI}{L^3} & \dfrac{6EI}{L^2} \\[6pt] \dfrac{6EI}{L^2} & \dfrac{4EI}{L} & \dfrac{-6EI}{L^2} & \dfrac{2EI}{L} \\[6pt] \dfrac{-12EI}{L^3} & \dfrac{-6EI}{L^2} & \dfrac{12EI}{L^3} & \dfrac{-6EI}{L^2} \\[6pt] \dfrac{6EI}{L^2} & \dfrac{2EI}{L} & \dfrac{-6EI}{L^2} & \dfrac{4EI}{L} \end{bmatrix}$$

(a) Member AB : L = 5 m.

$$[K]_{AB} = EI \begin{bmatrix} 0.096 & 0.24 & -0.096 & 0.24 \\ 0.24 & 0.8 & -0.24 & 0.4 \\ -0.096 & -0.24 & 0.096 & -0.24 \\ 0.24 & 0.4 & -0.24 & 0.8 \end{bmatrix} \begin{matrix} 1 & 0 \\ 2 & 0 \\ 3 & 0 \\ 4 & 1 \end{matrix}$$

with column gdof: 0, 0, 0, 1 and edof: 1, 2, 3, 4.

(b) Member BC : L = 4 m.

$$[K]_{BC} = EI \begin{bmatrix} 0.096 & 0.24 & -0.096 & 0.24 \\ 0.24 & 0.8 & -0.24 & 0.4 \\ -0.096 & -0.24 & 0.096 & -0.24 \\ 0.24 & 0.4 & -0.24 & 0.8 \end{bmatrix} \begin{matrix} 1 & 0 \\ 2 & 1 \\ 3 & 0 \\ 4 & 2 \end{matrix}$$

with column gdof: 0, 1, 0, 2 and edof: 1, 2, 3, 4.

Step III : Assemblage of matrix :

$$[K] = EI \begin{bmatrix} 1.8 & 0.5 \\ 0.5 & 1 \end{bmatrix}$$

Step IV : Elemental nodal load vector :

(a) Member AB :

$$\{Q\}_{AB} = \begin{Bmatrix} \dfrac{wl}{2} \\ \dfrac{wl^2}{12} \\ \dfrac{wl}{2} \\ \dfrac{wl^2}{12} \end{Bmatrix} = \begin{Bmatrix} 15 \\ 12.5 \\ 15 \\ -12.5 \end{Bmatrix}$$

(b) Member BC :

$$\{Q\}_{BC} = \begin{Bmatrix} \dfrac{wl}{2} \\ \dfrac{wl^2}{12} \\ \dfrac{wl}{2} \\ -\dfrac{wl^2}{12} \end{Bmatrix} = \begin{Bmatrix} 20 \\ 13.33 \\ 20 \\ -13.33 \end{Bmatrix}$$

Step V : Assemblage of nodal load vector : $\{Q\} = \begin{Bmatrix} 0.83 \\ -13.33 \end{Bmatrix}$

Step VI : Displacement vector :

$$\{\delta\} = \begin{Bmatrix} \theta_B \\ \theta_C \end{Bmatrix}$$

Step VII : Applied load matrix :

(a) Member AB :

$$\{P\}_{AB} = \begin{Bmatrix} 0 \\ 0 \\ 0 \\ 0 \end{Bmatrix}$$

(b) Member BC :

$$\{P\}_{BC} = \begin{Bmatrix} 0 \\ 0 \\ 20 \\ -20 \end{Bmatrix}$$

Step VIII : Formulation of finite element matrix :

$$EI \begin{bmatrix} 1.8 & 0.5 \\ 0.5 & 1 \end{bmatrix} \begin{Bmatrix} \theta_B \\ \theta_C \end{Bmatrix} + \begin{Bmatrix} 0.83 \\ -13.33 \end{Bmatrix} = \begin{Bmatrix} 0 \\ -20 \end{Bmatrix}$$

i.e. $0.8\ EI\ \theta_B + 0.5\ EI\ \theta_C = -0.83$ ... (A)

$0.5\ EI\ \theta_B + EI\ \theta_C = -6.67$ ... (B)

Step IX : Solution of equations for unknown displacements : Solving equations (A) and (B), we get

$$\theta_B = \frac{1.61}{EI}$$

$$\theta_C = -\frac{7.48}{EI}$$

Step X : Other forces :

(a) Member AB :

$$EI \begin{bmatrix} 0.096 & 0.24 & -0.096 & 0.24 \\ 0.24 & 0.8 & -0.24 & 0.4 \\ -0.096 & -0.24 & 0.096 & -0.24 \\ 0.24 & 0.4 & -0.24 & 0.8 \end{bmatrix} \begin{Bmatrix} 0 \\ 0 \\ 0 \\ \dfrac{1.61}{EI} \end{Bmatrix} + \begin{Bmatrix} 15 \\ 12.5 \\ 15 \\ -12.5 \end{Bmatrix} = \begin{Bmatrix} V_A \\ M_{AB} \\ V_{B1} \\ M_{BA} \end{Bmatrix}$$

$V_A = 15.38$ kN, $M_{AB} = 13.14$ kN-m, $V_{B1} = 14.62$ kN, $M_{BA} = -11.21$ kN-m.

(b) Member BC :

$$EI \begin{bmatrix} 0.1875 & 0.375 & -0.1875 & 0.375 \\ 0.375 & 1 & -0.375 & 0.5 \\ -0.1875 & -0.375 & 0.1875 & -0.375 \\ 0.375 & 0.5 & -0.375 & 1 \end{bmatrix} \begin{Bmatrix} 0 \\ \dfrac{1.61}{EI} \\ 0 \\ \dfrac{-7.48}{EI} \end{Bmatrix} + \begin{Bmatrix} 20 \\ 13.33 \\ 20 \\ -13.33 \end{Bmatrix} = \begin{Bmatrix} V_{B2} \\ M_{BC} \\ V_{C1} \\ M_{CB} \end{Bmatrix}$$

$V_{B2} = 17.80$ kN, $M_{BC} = 11.21$ kN-m, $V_{C1} = 22.2$ kN, $M_{CB} = -20$ kN-m.

(c) Member CD : $V_{C2} = 20$ kN, $M_{CD} = 20$ kN-m.

∴ $V_A = 15.38$ kN

$M_{AB} = 13.14$ kN-m

$M_{BA} = -11.21$ kN-m

$V_B = 32.42$ kN

$M_{BC} = 11.21$ kN-m

$M_{CB} = -20$ kN-m

$V_C = 42.2$ kN-m

$M_{CD} = 20$ kN-m

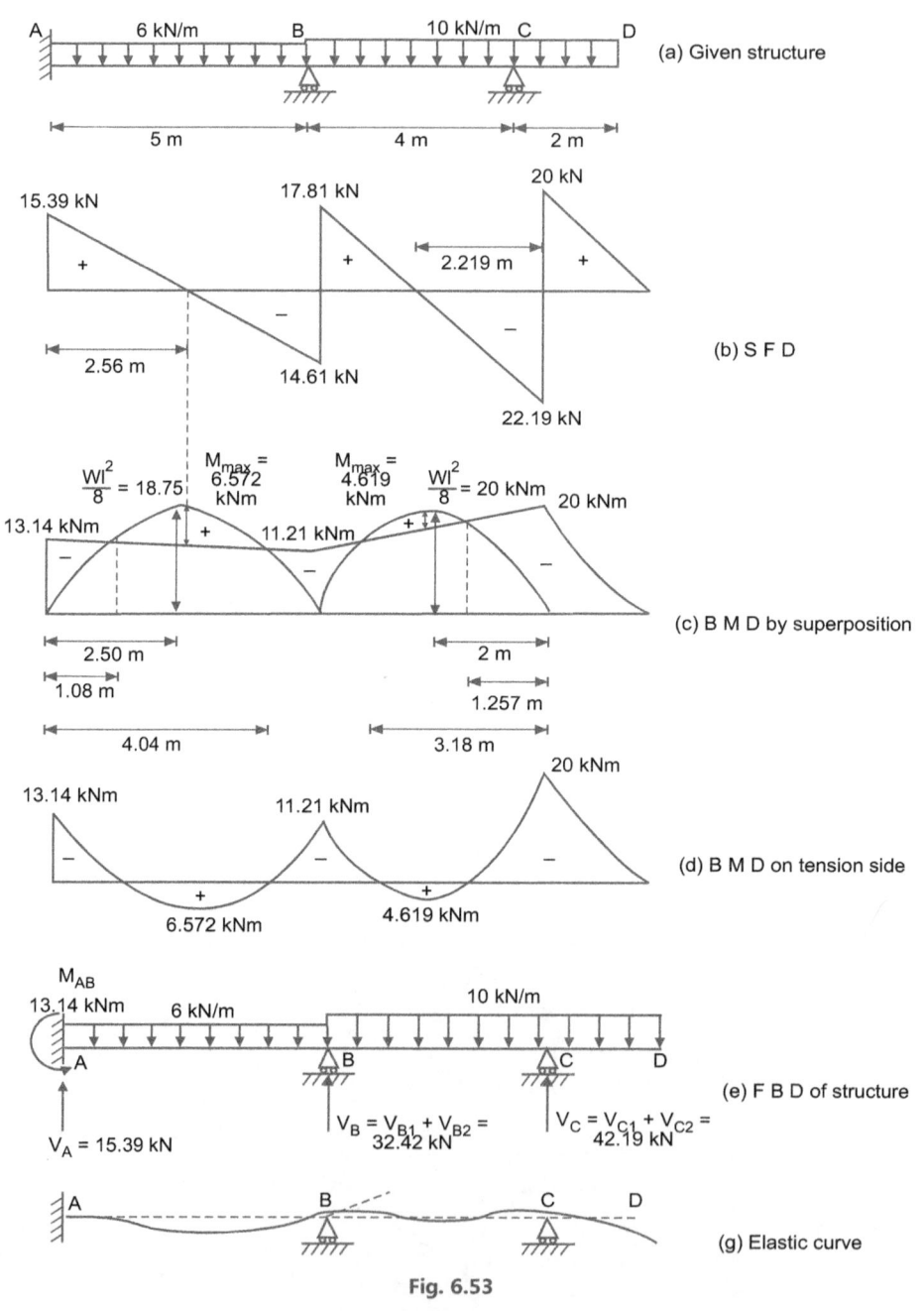

Fig. 6.53

Truss elements : Truss element is also a one dimensional element. The difference between beam and truss element is that the orientation of truss element differs from element to element. Due to change in orientation, local and global systems are introduced in truss element. Truss elements are axial members.

Case I : Horizontal truss element :

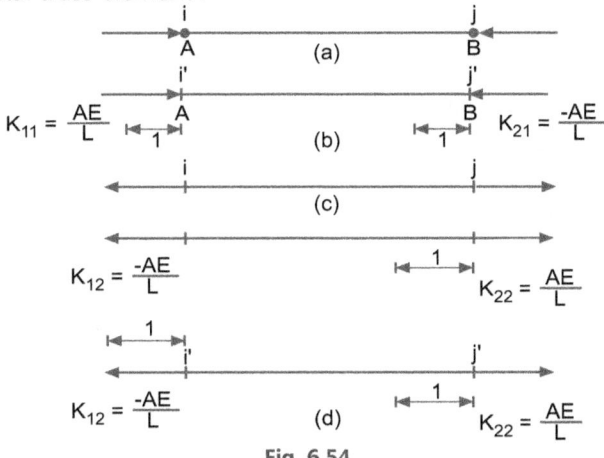

Fig. 6.54

∴ Stiffness matrix for the element is $= \dfrac{AE}{L}\begin{bmatrix} 1 & -1 \\ -1 & 1 \end{bmatrix}$.

Case II : Inclined truss element :

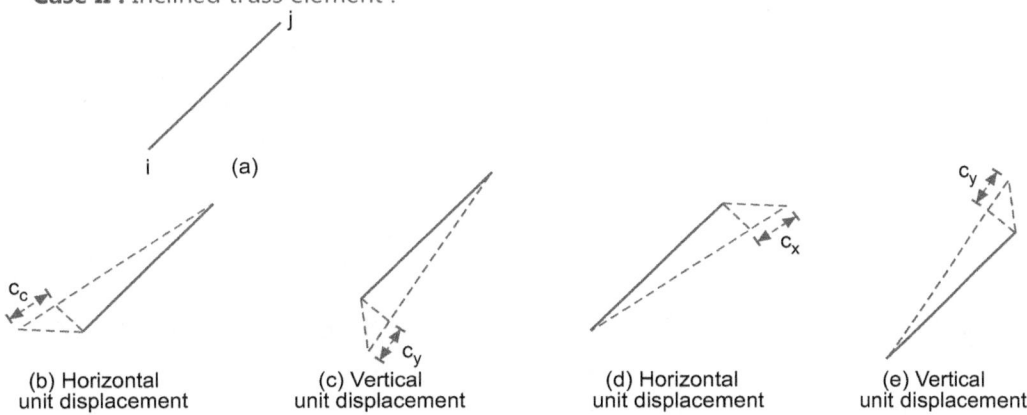

Fig. 6.55

Fig. 6.55 shows a truss element in x-y plane. Apply unit displacement in x and y direction at both nodes. The axial displacements produced are as shown in Fig. 6.55 (b), (c), (d) and (e). The direction cosines c_x and c_y are calculated as follows :

$$\cos\theta_x = c_x = \frac{x_j - x_i}{L}$$

$$\cos\theta_y = c_y = \frac{y_j - y_i}{L}$$

$$L = \sqrt{(x_j - x_i)^2 + (y_j - y_i)^2}$$

These nodal displacements are expressed in terms of global system u_1, u_2, v_1 and v_2.

$\therefore \qquad u_{1r} = c_x u_1 + c_y v_1 = \cos\theta_x\, u_1 + \cos\theta_y\, v_1$

and $\qquad u_{2r} = c_x u_2 + c_y v_2 = \cos\theta_x\, u_2 + \cos\theta_y\, v_2$

$\therefore \qquad$ Strain $= \dfrac{\delta l}{l} = \dfrac{(c_x u_2 + c_y v_2 - c_x u_1 - c_y v_2)}{L}$

$$= \frac{1}{L}(\cos\theta_x\, u_2 + \cos\theta_y\, v_2 - \cos\theta_x\, u_1 - \cos\theta_y\, v_1)$$

$$\varepsilon_r = \frac{1}{L}\{-c_x\ -c_y\ \ c_x\ \ c_y\}\begin{Bmatrix} u_1 \\ v_1 \\ u_2 \\ v_2 \end{Bmatrix}$$

$$= \frac{1}{L}\{-\cos\theta_x\ -\cos\theta_y\ \ \cos\theta_x\ \ \cos\theta_y\}\begin{Bmatrix} u_1 \\ v_1 \\ u_2 \\ v_2 \end{Bmatrix}$$

$\therefore \qquad$ Axial stress $= \varepsilon$

$$\therefore \qquad (\sigma) = E \cdot \frac{1}{L}\{-c_x\ -c_y\ \ c_x\ \ c_y\}\begin{Bmatrix} u_1 \\ v_1 \\ u_2 \\ v_2 \end{Bmatrix}$$

The stiffness matrix in the global system corresponding to the degree of freedom is

$$[K] = \iiint \frac{E}{L^2}\begin{Bmatrix} -c_x \\ -c_y \\ c_x \\ c_y \end{Bmatrix}\{-c_x\ -c_y\ \ c_x\ \ c_y\}\, v$$

STRUCTURAL ANALYSIS – II   FINITE ELEMENT METHOD

$$\therefore \quad [K] = \frac{AE}{L} \begin{bmatrix} c_x^2 & c_x c_y & -c_x^2 & -c_x c_y \\ c_x c_y & c_y^2 & -c_x c_y & -c_y^2 \\ -c_x^2 & -c_x c_y & c_x^2 & c_x c_y \\ -c_x c_y & -c_y^2 & c_x c_y & c_y^2 \end{bmatrix}$$

$$= \frac{AE}{L} \begin{bmatrix} (\cos\theta_x)^2 & (\cos\theta_x \cos\theta_y) & -(\cos\theta_x)^2 & -\cos\theta_x \cos\theta_y \\ \cos\theta_x \cos\theta_y & (\cos\theta_x)^2 & -\cos\theta_x \cos\theta_y & -(\cos\theta_y)^2 \\ -(\cos\theta_x)^2 & -\cos\theta_x \cos\theta_y & (\cos\theta_x)^2 & \cos\theta_x \cos\theta_y \\ -\cos\theta_x \cos\theta_y & -(\cos\theta_y)^2 & \cos\theta_x \cos\theta_y & (\cos\theta_y)^2 \end{bmatrix}$$

Example 6.4 : *Find the vertical and horizontal deflection of joint 'C' for the truss shown in Fig. 6.56. The area of inclined member is 2000 mm^2, while the area of horizontal member is 1600 mm^2. Take E = 200 kN/mm^2.*

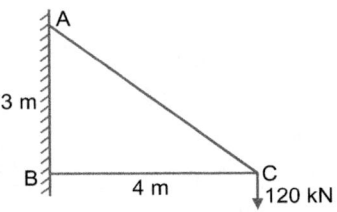

Fig. 6.56

Solution : Data : The truss is loaded and supported as shown in Fig. 6.56.

Object : Structural analysis.

Concept : (i) Stiffness matrix for each element.

(ii) Assemblage of matrix for structure.

Procedure : Step I : Degree of kinematic indeterminacy = D_{ki} = 2.

Unknown displacements : δ_{Ch}, δ_{Cv}.

Known displacements : $\delta_{Ah} = \delta_{Av} = \delta_{Bh} = \delta_{Bv} = 0$.

Step II : Stiffness matrix for elements :

STRUCTURAL ANALYSIS – II   FINITE ELEMENT METHOD

$$[K] = \frac{AE}{L} \begin{bmatrix} c_x^2 & c_x c_y & -c_x^2 & -c_x c_y \\ c_x c_y & c_y^2 & -c_x c_y & -c_y^2 \\ -c_x^2 & -c_x c_y & c_x^2 & c_x c_y \\ -c_x c_y & -c_y^2 & c_x c_y & c_y^2 \end{bmatrix}$$

(a) Member AC : A (0, 3), C (4, 0).

     L = 5000 mm, A = 2000 mm², E = 200 kN/mm²

$$\therefore \quad \frac{AE}{L} = \frac{2000 \times 200}{5000} = 80$$

$$c_x = \frac{C_x - A_x}{AC} = \frac{4-0}{5} = 0.8$$

$$c_y = \frac{C_y - A_y}{AC} = \frac{0-3}{5} = -0.6$$

$$[K]_{AC} = 80 \begin{array}{c} \begin{array}{cccc} 0 & 0 & 1 & 2 \\ 1 & 2 & 3 & 4 \end{array} \\ \begin{bmatrix} 0.64 & -0.48 & -0.64 & 0.48 \\ -0.48 & 0.36 & 0.48 & -0.36 \\ -0.64 & 0.48 & 0.64 & -0.48 \\ 0.48 & -0.36 & -0.48 & 0.36 \end{bmatrix} \begin{array}{cc} 1 & 0 \\ 2 & 0 \\ 3 & 1 \\ 4 & 2 \end{array} \end{array} \begin{array}{c} \text{gdof} \\ \text{edof} \end{array}$$

(b) Member BC : B(0, 0), C(4, 0).

     L = 4000 mm, A = 1600 mm², E = 200 kN/mm²,

$$\frac{AE}{L} = \frac{1600 \times 200}{4000} = 80$$

$$c_x = \frac{C_x - B_x}{BC} = \frac{4-0}{4} = 1$$

$$c_y = \frac{C_y - B_y}{BC} = \frac{0-0}{4} = 0$$

$$[K]_{BC} = 80 \begin{array}{c} \begin{array}{cccc} 0 & 0 & 1 & 2 \\ 1 & 2 & 3 & 4 \end{array} \\ \begin{bmatrix} 1 & 0 & -1 & 0 \\ 0 & 0 & 0 & 0 \\ -1 & 0 & 1 & 0 \\ 0 & 0 & 0 & 0 \end{bmatrix} \begin{array}{cc} 1 & 0 \\ 2 & 0 \\ 3 & 1 \\ 4 & 2 \end{array} \end{array} \begin{array}{c} \text{gdof} \\ \text{edof} \end{array}$$

Step III : Assemblage of matrix : $\begin{bmatrix} -131.2 & 38.4 \\ 38.4 & -28.8 \end{bmatrix}$

Step IV : Nodal load vector :
$$\{P\} = \begin{Bmatrix} 0 \\ -120 \end{Bmatrix}$$

Step V : Displacement vector :
$$\{\delta\} = \begin{Bmatrix} \delta_{Ch} \\ \delta_{Cv} \end{Bmatrix}$$

Step VI : Formation of finite element matrix :
$$[K]\{\delta\} = \{P\}$$
$$\begin{bmatrix} -131.2 & 38.4 \\ 38.4 & -28.8 \end{bmatrix} \begin{Bmatrix} \delta_{Ch} \\ \delta_{Cv} \end{Bmatrix} = \begin{Bmatrix} 0 \\ -120 \end{Bmatrix}$$

i.e. $-131.2\,\delta_{Ch} + 38.4\,\delta_{Cv} = 0$
$38.4\,\delta_{Ch} - 28.8\,\delta_{Cv} = -120$

Step VII : Solution of equations for unknown displacements :
$\delta_{Ch} = 2$ mm
$\delta_{Cv} = 6.83$ mm

Example 6.5 : *Three rods AD, BD and CD having the same cross sectional area and of the same material support a load of W as shown in Fig. 6.57. Find the tension in three rods.*

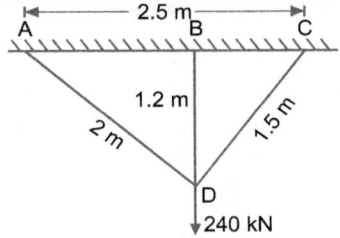

Fig. 6.57

Solution : Data : The truss is loaded and supported as shown in Fig. 6.57.

Object : Structural analysis.

Concept : (i) Stiffness matrix for each element.

(ii) Assemblage of matrix for structure.

Procedure : Step I : Degree of kinematic indeterminacy = D_{ki} = 2.

Unknown displacements = δ_{Dh}, δ_{Dv}.

Known displacements = $\delta_{Ah} = \delta_{Av} = \delta_{Bh} = \delta_{Bv} = \delta_{Ch} = \delta_{Cv} = 0$.

Step II : Stiffness matrix for elements :

$$[K] = \frac{AE}{L}\begin{bmatrix} c_x^2 & c_x c_y & -c_x^2 & -c_x c_y \\ c_x c_y & c_y^2 & -c_x c_y & -c_y^2 \\ -c_x^2 & -c_x c_y & c_x^2 & c_x c_y \\ -c_x c_y & -c_y^2 & c_x c_y & c_y^2 \end{bmatrix}$$

(a) Member AD : A (0, 1.2), D (1.6, 0).

$L = 2$ m, AE = constant

$$\frac{AE}{L} = \frac{AE}{2}$$

$$c_x = \frac{D_x - A_x}{AD} = \frac{1.6 - 0}{2} = 0.8$$

$$c_y = \frac{D_y - D_y}{AD} = \frac{0 - 1.2}{2} = -0.6$$

$$[K]_{AD} = \frac{AE}{2}\begin{bmatrix} 0.64 & -0.48 & -0.64 & 0.48 \\ -0.48 & 0.36 & 0.48 & -0.36 \\ -0.64 & 0.48 & 0.64 & -0.48 \\ 0.48 & -0.36 & -0.48 & 0.36 \end{bmatrix}\begin{matrix} 1 & 0 \\ 2 & 0 \\ 3 & 1 \\ 4 & 2 \end{matrix}$$

with gdof: 0 0 1 2 and edof: 1 2 3 4

(b) Member BD : B (1.6, 1.2), D (1.6, 0)

$L = 1.2$ m, AE = constant

$$\frac{AE}{L} = \frac{AE}{1.2}$$

$$c_x = \frac{D_x - B_x}{BD} = \frac{1.6 - 1.6}{1.2} = 0$$

$$c_y = \frac{D_y - B_y}{BD} = \frac{0 - 1.2}{1.2} = -1$$

gdof: 0 0 1 2
edof: 1 2 3 4

$$[K]_{BD} = \frac{AE}{1.2}\begin{bmatrix} 0 & 0 & 0 & 0 \\ 0 & 1 & 0 & -1 \\ 0 & 0 & 0 & 0 \\ 0 & -1 & 0 & 1 \end{bmatrix} \begin{matrix} 1 & 0 \\ 2 & 0 \\ 3 & 1 \\ 4 & 2 \end{matrix}$$

(c) Member CD : C (2.5, 1.2), D (1.6, 0).

$$L = 1.5 \text{ m, AE = constant}$$

$$\frac{AE}{L} = \frac{AE}{1.5}$$

$$c_x = \frac{D_x - C_x}{DC} = \frac{1.6 - 2.5}{1.5} = -0.6$$

$$c_y = \frac{D_y - C_y}{DC} = \frac{0 - 1.2}{1.5} = -0.8$$

$$\begin{matrix} 0 & 0 & 1 & 2 & \text{gdof} \\ 1 & 2 & 3 & 4 & \text{edof} \end{matrix}$$

$$[K]_{CD} = \frac{AE}{1.5}\begin{bmatrix} 0.36 & 0.48 & -0.36 & -0.48 \\ 0.48 & 0.64 & -0.48 & -0.64 \\ -0.36 & -0.48 & 0.36 & 0.48 \\ -0.48 & -0.64 & 0.48 & 0.64 \end{bmatrix} \begin{matrix} 1 & 0 \\ 2 & 0 \\ 3 & 1 \\ 4 & 2 \end{matrix}$$

Step III : Assemblage of matrix : $\begin{bmatrix} 0.56 & 0.08 \\ 0.08 & 1.44 \end{bmatrix}$.

Step IV : Nodal load vector :

$$\{P\} = \begin{Bmatrix} 0 \\ -240 \end{Bmatrix}$$

Step V : Displacement vector :

$$\{\delta\} = \begin{Bmatrix} \delta_{Dh} \\ \delta_{Dv} \end{Bmatrix}$$

Step VI : Formation of finite element matrix :

$$AE\begin{bmatrix} 0.56 & 0.08 \\ 0.08 & 1.44 \end{bmatrix}\begin{Bmatrix} \delta_{Dh} \\ \delta_{Dv} \end{Bmatrix} = \begin{Bmatrix} 0 \\ -240 \end{Bmatrix}$$

i.e. $\frac{1}{AE}[0.56\,\delta_{Dh} + 0.08\,\delta_{Dv} = 0]$

$$\frac{1}{AE}[0.08\,\delta_{Dh} + 1.44\,\delta_{Dv} = -240]$$

Step VII : Solution of equations for unknown displacements :

$$\delta_{Dh} = \frac{24}{AE}$$

$$\delta_{Dv} = \frac{-168}{AE}$$

Step VIII : Forces in members :

(a) Member AD :

$$[K]\{\delta\} = \{F\}$$

$$\frac{AE}{2} \begin{bmatrix} 0.64 & -0.48 & -0.64 & 0.48 \\ -0.48 & 0.36 & 0.48 & -0.36 \\ -0.64 & 0.48 & 0.64 & -0.48 \\ 0.48 & -0.36 & -0.48 & 0.36 \end{bmatrix} \begin{Bmatrix} 0 \\ 0 \\ \frac{24}{AE} \\ \frac{-168}{AE} \end{Bmatrix} = \begin{Bmatrix} -48 \\ 36 \\ 48 \\ -36 \end{Bmatrix}$$

$$F_{AD} = \sqrt{(48)^2 + (36)^2} = 60 \text{ kN (Tensile)}$$

(b) Member BD : $[K]\{\delta\} = \{F\}$

$$\frac{AE}{1.2} \begin{bmatrix} 0 & 0 & 0 & 0 \\ 0 & 1 & 0 & -1 \\ 0 & 0 & 0 & 0 \\ 0 & -1 & 0 & 1 \end{bmatrix} \begin{Bmatrix} 0 \\ 0 \\ \frac{24}{AE} \\ \frac{-168}{AE} \end{Bmatrix} = \begin{Bmatrix} 0 \\ 160 \\ 0 \\ -160 \end{Bmatrix}$$

$$F_{AE} = 160 \text{ kN (Tensile)}$$

(c) Member CD : $[K]\{\delta\} = \{F\}$

$$\frac{AE}{1.5} \begin{bmatrix} 0.36 & 0.48 & -0.36 & -0.48 \\ 0.48 & 0.64 & -0.48 & -0.64 \\ -0.36 & -0.48 & 0.36 & 0.48 \\ -0.48 & -0.64 & 0.48 & 0.64 \end{bmatrix} \begin{Bmatrix} 0 \\ 0 \\ \frac{24}{AE} \\ \frac{-168}{AE} \end{Bmatrix} = \begin{Bmatrix} 48 \\ 64 \\ -48 \\ -64 \end{Bmatrix}$$

$$F_{CD} = 80 \text{ kN (Tensile)}$$

(1) Axially loaded bar element is S.T. forces as shown in Fig. 6.58. Find nodal displaements and reactive forces at A and B.

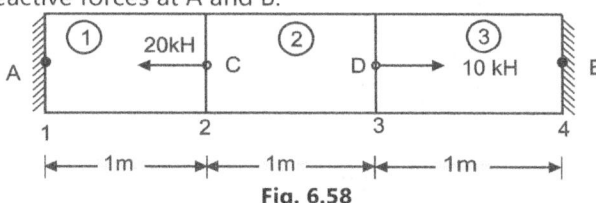

Fig. 6.58

Stiffness matrix :

$$[k] = \frac{AE}{L}\begin{bmatrix} 1 & -1 \\ -1 & 1 \end{bmatrix} = AE \begin{bmatrix} 1 & -1 \\ -1 & 1 \end{bmatrix}$$

Element Matrix :

$$[k]_1 = AE \begin{bmatrix} 1 & -1 \\ -1 & 1 \end{bmatrix}$$

$$[k]_2 = AE \begin{bmatrix} 1 & -1 \\ -1 & 1 \end{bmatrix}$$

$$[k]_3 = AE \begin{bmatrix} 1 & -1 \\ -1 & 1 \end{bmatrix}$$

$$[k] = AE \begin{bmatrix} 1 & -1 & 0 & 0 \\ -1 & 1+1 & -1 & 0 \\ 0 & -1 & +1+1 & -1 \\ 0 & 0 & -1 & 1 \end{bmatrix}$$

$$[k] = AE \begin{bmatrix} 1 & -1 & 0 & 0 \\ -1 & 2 & -1 & 0 \\ 0 & -1 & 2 & -1 \\ 0 & 0 & -1 & 1 \end{bmatrix}$$

$$\{F\} = [K]\{\delta_e\}$$

$$\begin{Bmatrix} H_a \\ -20 \\ 10 \\ H_b \end{Bmatrix} = AE \begin{bmatrix} 1 & -1 & 0 & 0 \\ -1 & 2 & -1 & 0 \\ 0 & -1 & 2 & -1 \\ 0 & 0 & -1 & 1 \end{bmatrix} \begin{Bmatrix} 0 \\ u_2 \\ u_3 \\ 0 \end{Bmatrix}$$

STRUCTURAL ANALYSIS – II   FINITE ELEMENT METHOD

$$\begin{Bmatrix} -20 \\ 10 \end{Bmatrix} = AE \begin{bmatrix} 2 & -1 \\ -1 & 2 \end{bmatrix} \begin{Bmatrix} u_2 \\ u_3 \end{Bmatrix}$$

$$-20 = AE(2u_2 - u_3) \quad \text{...(i)}$$
$$10 = AE(-u_2 + 2u_3) \quad \text{...(ii)}$$

from equations (i) and (ii),

$$u_2 = \frac{-10}{AE}$$

$$u_3 = 0$$

Put values of u_2 and u_3 in overall matrix.

$$HA = -u_2$$
$$HA = \frac{10}{AE}$$
$$HB = -u_3$$
$$HB = 0$$

(2) The figure shows the bar S.T. axial loading using the 2 element discreatization shown in figure write the element stiffness matrix for 2 element and assembled these and apply boundary condition and solve structural stiffness to obtain displacement. Hence obtain the stresses into 2 element. Details of 2 element.

$A_1 = 2400$ mm^2, $A_2 = 600$ mm^2, $E_1 = 70$- GPa, $E_2 = 200$ GPa. Load acting at node 2 = 300 kg

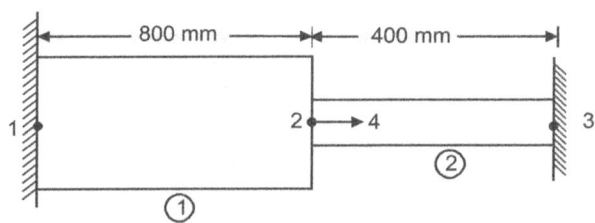

Fig. 6.59

Element Stiffness Matrix :

$$k_1 = \frac{AE}{L} \begin{bmatrix} 1 & -1 \\ -1 & 1 \end{bmatrix} = \frac{2400 \times 70}{300} \begin{bmatrix} 1 & -1 \\ -1 & 1 \end{bmatrix}$$

$$= 560 \begin{bmatrix} 1 & -1 \\ -1 & 1 \end{bmatrix}$$

$$= \begin{bmatrix} 560 & -560 \\ -560 & 560 \end{bmatrix}$$

$$k_2 = \frac{600 \times 200}{400} \begin{bmatrix} 1 & -1 \\ -1 & 1 \end{bmatrix}$$

$$= \begin{bmatrix} 300 & -300 \\ -300 & 300 \end{bmatrix}$$

$$[k] = \begin{bmatrix} 560 & -560 & 0 \\ -560 & 560+300 & -300 \\ 0 & -300 & 300 \end{bmatrix}$$

$$= \begin{bmatrix} 560 & -560 & 0 \\ -560 & 860 & -300 \\ 0 & -300 & 300 \end{bmatrix}$$

$$\{F\} = [K]\{\delta\}$$

$$\begin{Bmatrix} R_1 \\ 300 \\ R_3 \end{Bmatrix} = \begin{bmatrix} 560 & -560 & 0 \\ -560 & 860 & -300 \\ 0 & -300 & 300 \end{bmatrix} \begin{Bmatrix} \delta_1 \\ \delta_2 \\ \delta_3 \end{Bmatrix}$$

$$\delta_2 \times 860 = 300$$

$$\delta_2 = 0.3488 \text{ mm}$$

Stress Matrices :

$$\{\sigma_1\} = \begin{bmatrix} \frac{-E}{L} & \frac{E}{L} \end{bmatrix} \begin{Bmatrix} \delta_1 \\ \delta_2 \end{Bmatrix}$$

$$= \begin{bmatrix} \frac{-70}{300} & \frac{70}{300} \end{bmatrix} \begin{Bmatrix} 0 \\ 0.3488 \end{Bmatrix}$$

$$\sigma_1 = \frac{70}{300} \times 0.3488$$

$$\sigma_1 = 0.081395 \text{ GPA (T)}$$

$$\sigma_2 = \begin{bmatrix} \frac{-200}{400} & \frac{200}{400} \end{bmatrix} \begin{Bmatrix} 0.3488 \\ 0 \end{Bmatrix}$$

$$\sigma_2 = -0.1744 \text{ GPA (c)}$$

(3) Find nodal displacement for truss as shown in fig. E = 200 GPa. Value of A?L is constant for all members having value of 0.1 mm

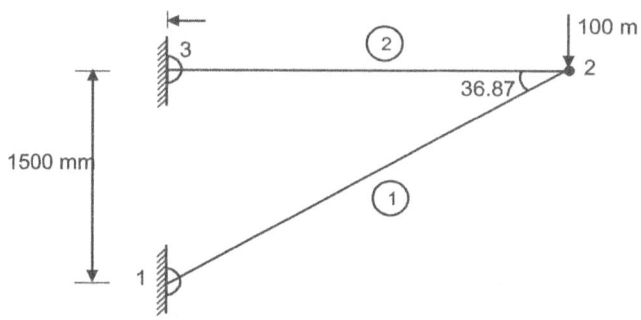

Fig. 6.60

Given : E = 200 GPa = 2300 × 10³ N/mm²

For all members $\dfrac{AE}{L}$ = 0.1 × 200 × 10³ = 20000 N/mm

For member 1 :

$$\cos 36.87 = 0.9 = C$$
$$\sin 36.87 = 0.6 = S$$

$C^2 = 0.64;\ S^2 = 0.36$ and $CS = 0.48$

For element 1 :

$$[k]_1 = \dfrac{AE}{L}\begin{bmatrix} C^2 & CS & -C^2 & -CS \\ CS & S^2 & -CS & -S^2 \\ -C^2 & -CS & C^2 & CS \\ -CS & -S^2 & CS & S^2 \end{bmatrix}$$

$$= 20000 \begin{bmatrix} 0.64 & 0.48 & -0.64 & -0.48 \\ 0.48 & 0.36 & -0.48 & 0.36 \\ -0.64 & -0.48 & 0.64 & 0.48 \\ -0.48 & -0.36 & 0.48 & 0.36 \end{bmatrix}$$

For member 2 :

$\cos 180 = -1 = C$ $\qquad$ $C^2 = 1$
$\sin 180 = 0 = S$ $\qquad$ $S^2 = 0,\ CS = 0$

STRUCTURAL ANALYSIS – II   FINITE ELEMENT METHOD

For element 2 :

$$[k]_2 = 20000 \begin{bmatrix} 1 & 0 & -1 & 0 \\ 0 & 0 & 0 & 0 \\ -1 & 0 & 1 & 0 \\ 0 & 0 & 0 & 0 \end{bmatrix}$$

$$\{F\} = [K]\{\delta\}_c$$

$$\begin{Bmatrix} F_1x \\ F_1y \\ 0 \\ 1000 \\ F_3x \\ F_3y \end{Bmatrix} = 20000 \begin{bmatrix} 0.64 & 0.48 & -0.64 & -0.48 & 0 & 0 \\ 0.48 & 0.36 & -048 & -0.36 & 0 & 0 \\ -0.64 & -0.48 & 0.64 & 0.48 & -1 & 0 \\ -0.48 & -0.36 & 0.48 & 0.36 & 0 & 0 \\ 0 & 0 & -1 & 0 & 1 & 0 \\ 0 & 0 & 0 & 0 & 0 & 0 \end{bmatrix} \begin{Bmatrix} 0 \\ 0 \\ u_2 \\ v_2 \\ 0 \\ 0 \end{Bmatrix}$$

$$\begin{Bmatrix} F_1x \\ F_1y \\ 0 \\ 1000 \\ F_3x \\ F_3y \end{Bmatrix} = 20000 \begin{bmatrix} 0.64 & 0.48 & -0.64 & -0.48 & 0 & 0 \\ 0.48 & 0.36 & -048 & -0.36 & 0 & 0 \\ -0.64 & -0.48 & 0.64 & 0.48 & -1 & 0 \\ -0.48 & -0.36 & 0.48 & 0.36 & 0 & 0 \\ 0 & 0 & -1 & 0 & 1 & 0 \\ 0 & 0 & 0 & 0 & 0 & 0 \end{bmatrix} \begin{Bmatrix} 0 \\ 0 \\ u_2 \\ v_2 \\ 0 \\ 0 \end{Bmatrix}$$

$$\begin{Bmatrix} 0 \\ 100 \end{Bmatrix} = 20000 \begin{bmatrix} 1.64 & 0.48 \\ 0.48 & 0.36 \end{bmatrix} \begin{Bmatrix} u_2 \\ v_2 \end{Bmatrix}$$

$$u_2 = -0.0667 \text{ mm (C)}$$
$$v_2 = 0.228 \text{ mm (T)}$$

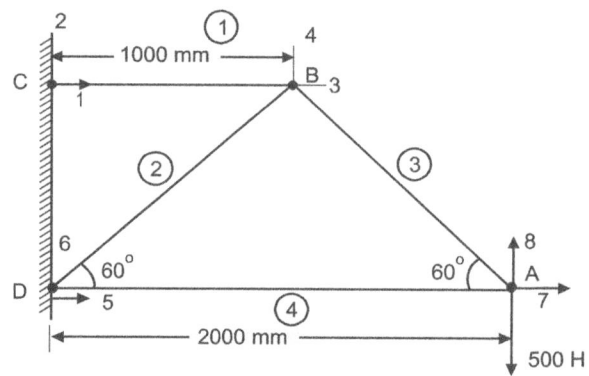

Fig. 6.61

Given : $E = 2 \times 10^5$ MPa; $A = 400$ mm^2

For member 1 :

$\cos 180 = -1 = C \qquad C^2 = 1$
$\sin 180 = 0 = S \qquad S^2 = 0;\ CS = 0$

For element 1 :

$$[K]_1 = \frac{AE}{L}\begin{bmatrix} C^2 & CS & -C^2 & -CS \\ CS & S^2 & -CS & -S^2 \\ -C^2 & -CS & C^2 & CS \\ -CS & -S^2 & CS & S^2 \end{bmatrix}$$

$$= \frac{400 \times 2 \times 10^5}{1000}\begin{bmatrix} 1 & 0 & -1 & 0 \\ 0 & 0 & 0 & 0 \\ -1 & 0 & 1 & 0 \\ 0 & 0 & 0 & 0 \end{bmatrix}$$

$$= 10^3\begin{bmatrix} 80 & 0 & -80 & 0 \\ 0 & 0 & 0 & 0 \\ -80 & 0 & 80 & 0 \\ 0 & 0 & 0 & 0 \end{bmatrix}$$

For member 2 :

$\cos 60° = 0.5 = C \qquad C^2 = 0.25$
$\sin 60 = 0.866 = S \qquad S^2 = 0.749,\ CS = 0.433$

For element 2 :

$$[k]_2 = \frac{400 \times 2 \times 10^5}{2000} \begin{bmatrix} 0.25 & 0.433 & -0.25 & -0.433 \\ 0.433 & 0.75 & -0.433 & -0.75 \\ -0.25 & -0.433 & 0.25 & 0.433 \\ -0.433 & -0.75 & 0.433 & 0.75 \end{bmatrix}$$

$$= 10^3 \begin{bmatrix} 10 & 17.32 & -10 & -17.32 \\ 17.32 & 30 & -17.32 & -30 \\ -10 & -17.32 & 10 & 17.32 \\ -17.32 & -30 & 17.32 & 30 \end{bmatrix}$$

For member 3 :

$\cos 60 = C = 0.5 \qquad C^2 = 0.25$
$\sin 60 = S = 0.86 \qquad S^2 = 0.75, \ CS = 0.433$

$$[k]_3 = 10^3 \begin{bmatrix} 10 & 17.32 & -10 & -17.32 \\ 17.32 & 30 & -17.32 & -30 \\ -10 & -17.32 & 10 & 17.32 \\ -17.32 & -30 & 17.32 & 30 \end{bmatrix}$$

For member 4 :

$\cos 180 = C = -1 \qquad C^2 = 1$
$\sin 180 = S = 0 \qquad S^2 = 0, \ CS = 0$

$$[k]_4 = \frac{400 \times 2 \times 10^5}{2000} \begin{bmatrix} 1 & 0 & -1 & 0 \\ 0 & 0 & 0 & 0 \\ -1 & 0 & 1 & 0 \\ 0 & 0 & 0 & 0 \end{bmatrix}$$

$$[k]_4 = 10^3 \begin{bmatrix} 40 & 0 & -40 & 0 \\ 0 & 0 & 0 & 0 \\ -40 & 0 & 40 & 0 \\ 0 & 0 & 0 & 0 \end{bmatrix}$$

$[k] = 10^3$

EXERCISE

Find the support moments and support reactions for the continuous beam in the examples given below. Draw SF and BM diagrams.

1.

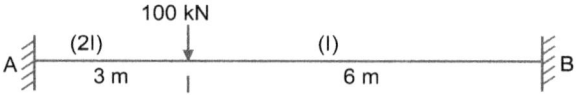

Fig. 6.62

[**Ans.** $M_A = M_C = 0$, $M_B = -\dfrac{wL^2}{8}$, $R_A = R_C = \dfrac{3}{8}wL\ (\overline{\ })$, $R_B = \dfrac{5}{4}wL\ (\uparrow)$]

2.

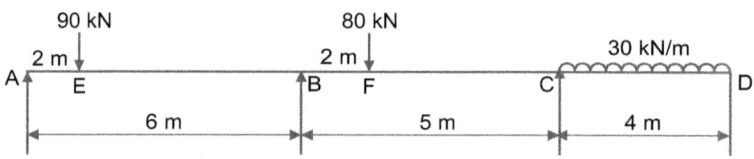

Fig. 6.63

[**Ans.** $M_A = M_D = 0$, $M_B = -68.4$ kN.m, $M_C = -44.8$ kNm, $R_A = 48.6$ kN ($\uparrow$), $R_B = 94.1$ kN ($\uparrow$), $R_C = 98.5$ kN ($\overline{\ }$), $R_D = 48.8$ kN ($\uparrow$)]

3.

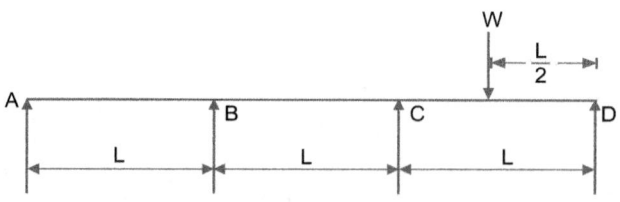

Fig. 6.64

[**Ans.** $M_A = M_D = 0$, $M_B = +\dfrac{WL}{40}$, $M_C = -\dfrac{WL}{10}$, $R_A = \dfrac{W}{40}$ ($\uparrow$),

$R_B = \dfrac{3}{20}W\ (\rightarrow)$, $R_C = \dfrac{29}{40}W$ ($\uparrow$), $R_D = \dfrac{2}{5}W$ ($\uparrow$)]

4.

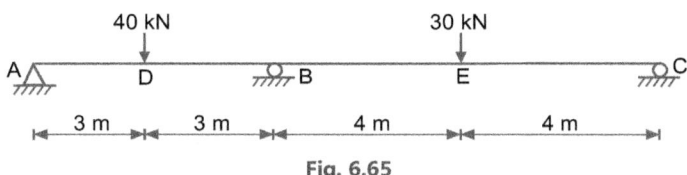

Fig. 6.65

[**Ans.** $M_A = 0$, $M_B = -45$ kNm, $M_C = 0$; $V_A = 12.5$ kN (↑), $V_B = 48.125$ kN (↑), $V_C = 9.375$ kN (↑)]

5.

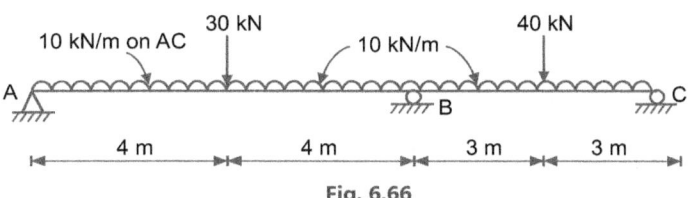

Fig. 6.66

[**Ans.** $M_A = M_C = 0$, $M_B = -110$ kNm, $V_A = 41.25$ kN (↑), $V_B = 137.085$ kN (↑), $V_C = 31.665$ kN (↑)]

6.

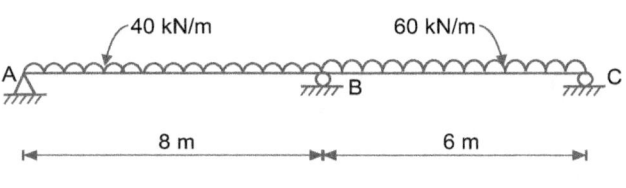

Fig. 6.67

[**Ans.** $M_A = M_C = 0$, $M_B = -298.50$ kN.m, $V_A = 122.68$ kN (↑), $V_B = 427.06$ kN (↑), $V_C = 130.26$ kN (↑)]

7.

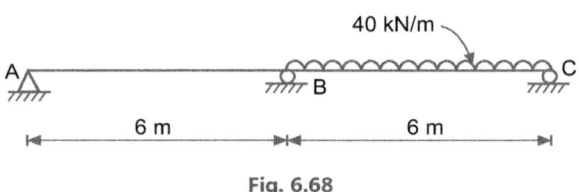

Fig. 6.68

[**Ans.** $M_A = M_C = 0$, $M_B = -90$ kN.m; $V_A = 15$ kN (¬), $V_B = 150$ kN (↑),

$V_C = 105.00$ kN (↑)].

8.

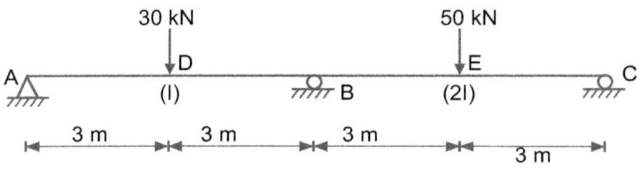

Fig. 6.69

[**Ans.** $M_A = M_C = 0$, $M_B = -41.25$ kN.m; $V_A = 8.125$ kN (↑),

$V_B = 63.75$ kN ($\overline{\ }$), $V_C = 18.125$ kN (↑)]

9. A jib and crane mechanism is shown in Fig. 6.70. The jib, 7.5 m long, has a cross-sectional area of 1500 mm². The horizontal tie, 6 m long, has a cross-sectional area of 1000 mm². Calculate the vertical and horizontal deflection of the crane head C for a load 50 kN suspended from it. Take E = 200 GPa.

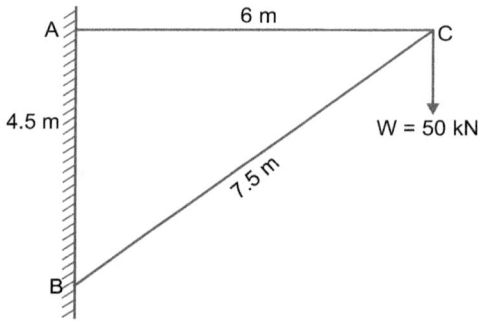

Fig. 6.70

(**Ans.** δC (↓) = 6.385 mm, δC (→) = 2.0 mm)

10. A frame shown in Fig. 6.71 is hinged at A and is supported on rollers at B. It carries a central load of 150 kN. All the members are 1250 mm² in cross-sectional area. Find the horizontal displacement of the roller end B. Take E = 200 GPa.

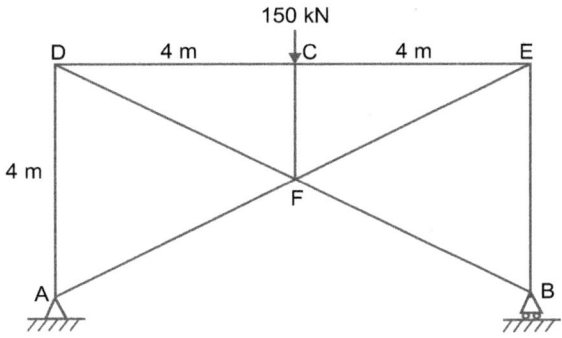

Fig. 6.71

(**Ans.** δ_D = 12.71 mm ($\rightarrow$))

11. A cantilever truss shown in Fig. 6.72 is so loaded at the joints B and C that all struts are stressed to 60 MPa, while all ties are stressed to 100 MPa. If the joint E, supporting the horizontal tie ED yields by 3 mm, calculate the vertical deflection of the joint C.

    Take E = 200 GPa.

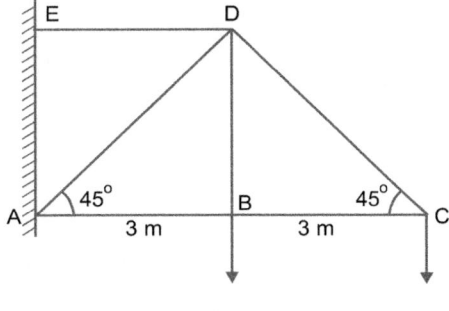

Fig. 6.72

(**Ans.** δ_C = 15.60 mm ($\downarrow$))

12. Determine the vertical and horizontal displacement of the joint C of the frame shown in Fig. 6.73. The cross-sectional area of AB is 500 mm² and that of AC and BC are 750 mm².

    Take E = 200 GPa.

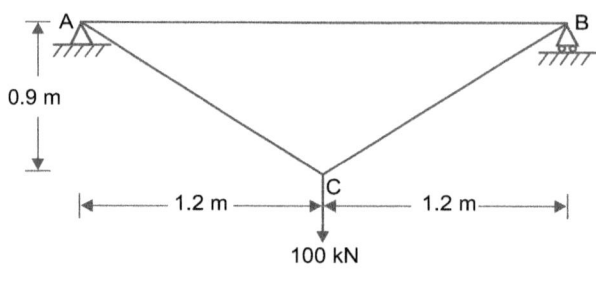

Fig. 6.73

(**Ans.** 2.455 mm, − 0.80 mm)

www.ingramcontent.com/pod-product-compliance
Lightning Source LLC
Chambersburg PA
CBHW080416300426
44113CB00015B/2547